International Law in a

Changing World

Cases, Documents,
and Readings

Consulting Editor

INIS L. CLAUDE, JR.
University of Virginia

International Law in a

Changing World

Cases, Documents, and Readings

Edited, with Introductions, by

Edward Collins, Jr.

University of Maine

 RANDOM HOUSE   NEW YORK

Library of Congress Catalog Card Number: 72-92835

Manufactured in the United States of America.
Printed and bound by Halliday Lithograph Corporation, West Hanover, Mass.

Design by Saul Schnurman
Cover design by Mary Lou Kirby

First Printing

To Marilyn, Karen, Matthew, and Quinn

The dignity and importance [of international law] cannot fail to recommend it to the deep attention of the student; and a thorough knowledge of its principles is necessary to lawyers and statesmen, and highly ornamental to every scholar who wishes to be adorned with the accomplishments of various learning. . . . A comprehensive and scientific knowledge of international law is highly necessary; not only to lawyers practicing in our commercial ports, but to every gentleman who is animated by liberal views, and a generous ambition to assume stations of high public trust. It would be exceedingly to the discredit of any person who should be called to take a share in the councils of the nation, if he should be found deficient in all the great leading principles of this law; and I think I cannot be mistaken in considering the elementary learning of the law of nations, as not only an essential part of the education of an American lawyer, but as proper to be academically taught.—Chancellor James Kent, I *Commentaries on American Law* 19–20 (1826).

In my office and in my Department, we are, first of all, students of international law.—Paul Martin, Canadian Secretary of State for External Affairs, in 16 *External Affairs* 596 (1964).

Foreword

The student of international relations who approaches the subject of international law is all too often embroiled in a contest between the utopians and the cynics—those who conceive law as a kind of magic formula for global peace and justice, needing only to be accepted and put into effect, and those who regard what has passed as international law as no law at all, an ineffectual cover for the essential anarchy that necessarily prevails in a multistate system. The student may choose to dream with the utopians or to scoff with the cynics, but in neither case has he found something to study; between the law that never was and the law that cannot be, the choice is more an expression of temperament than a result of analytical judgment.

There is, however, a substantive ground between the mythical law that will abolish international politics and the fictitious law that vainly attempts to conceal the inexorability of international politics. This is the realm of the international law that has been and is and is becoming, the law that is intertwined with international politics, reflecting political interests, registering political adjustments, and expressing in its stability and its instability the political demands for order and for change. Here is law that neither promises to transform the political system nor serves simply to disguise that system, but provides an instrument whereby states may achieve tentative reconciliations between their simultaneous urges for freedom of action and for predictable patterns of behavior, for individualistic pursuit of national interests and for collective enjoyment of settled relationships. Law, understood in this sense, is not antithetical to politics, dominant over politics, or subservient to politics, but is integral to the political process. Whether in the national or the international setting, such law is a feature of the dynamic interplay of the constituent elements of pluralistic societies; it is an ordering and stabilizing device developed and put to use by human groups that can tolerate neither the termination nor the culmination of their struggles for advantage.

The study of international law, conceived as the exploration of this middle ground between the never-never land of the utopians and the stark landscape described by the cynics, can be a fascinating and rewarding venture into the realm of international relations. The great merit of Professor Collins as editor of this volume is that he provides a guide book for just that sort of exploration. The combination of classical and contemporary materials points up the correlation between political and legal changes. The inclusion of national legal arguments as well as international judicial opinions gives emphasis to the point that law, internationally as domestically, provides a basis for the disputation of interested parties no less than a basis for the decision of impartial tribunals; thus, one is led to recognize that a realistic appraisal of the significance of law must not focus upon judges' decisions to the neglect of lawyers' briefs or give attention to court proceedings to the exclusion of out-of-court negotiations. The varied selection of materials in this book promotes the understanding that law is an instrument of public policy as well as a regulator of private behavior—that is, the functions of law extend beyond the addressing of "thou shalt not's" to members of the society to the formulation and authorization of programs and activities to be conducted by public agencies.

In short, we have here a collection of materials that offers valuable assistance in the important task of promoting a realistic understanding of the place of the legal factor in international relations.

Inis L. Claude, Jr.

Preface

While it is hoped that this book will be of value to law students and general readers, it was prepared primarily to serve the needs of students in political science departments. These students have long been subjected to cases and materials texts that, regardless of their excellence, are expensive and are designed primarily for use in law schools. Many of the cases and documents presented in available texts are highly technical and are particularly significant only to the practicing attorney. And from the perspective of students of international relations, these texts are inadequate in coverage of such politically important matters as the use of law in political crises that do not "go to court," non-Western attitudes toward international law, and the developmental processes of law.

This volume seeks to remedy these deficiencies without departing significantly from the traditional format or omitting the classical opinions. By using this text along with one of the many good treatises now available, it is believed that international law can be made more relevant and exciting to students of international relations. The cases reproduced, both classical and recent, are of a nontechnical nature; most of the documents are recent and of political importance. Essays and statements by government officials are used to introduce the reader to the use of law in political controversies, to non-Western attitudes, and to the role of international organizations in the development of law. The introductory essays seek to interweave legal factors and political complexities. A short guide to Latin terms is included to assist students who come to the study of international law without a year or two of law school behind them.

A number of persons have contributed, in one way or another, to making this a better book than it otherwise would have been. I am especially indebted to Inis L. Claude, Jr., who read the entire manuscript and made numerous helpful suggestions. Anne Dyer Murphy and June Fischbein of Random House also deserve special acknowledgment for their patience and many efforts to help. I am indebted to Robert B. Thomson, Walter S.

Schoenberger, John Helmke, Eugene A. Mawhinney, William M. Reid, and David J. Halperin, colleagues at the University of Maine, who read various parts of the manuscript and gave me the benefit of their criticisms. I wish also to acknowledge my indebtedness to those persons without whose efforts and cooperation a volume like this one is impossible: the authors who wrote the essays and the editors and publishers who granted permission to reproduce them. Finally, the most sincere gratitude must be reserved for my wife, without whose devotion and encouragement this book would never have been completed. If all this assistance did not succeed in sparing the reader from obscurities and errors, the fault lies solely with the author.

E.C.
DECEMBER 1969

Contents

List of Abbreviations

Textbooks

Brierly, *The Law of Nations.* Brierly, J. L., *The Law of Nations*, 6th ed. edited by Sir Humphrey Waldock (New York: Oxford University Press, 1963).

Brownlie, *Principles of Public International Law.* Brownlie, Ian, *Principles of Public International Law* (Oxford: Clarendon Press, 1966).

Fenwick, *International Law.* Fenwick, Charles G., *International Law*, 4th ed. (New York: Appleton-Century-Crofts, 1965).

Gould, *An Introduction to International Law.* Gould, Wesley L., *An Introduction to International Law* (New York: Harper, 1957).

Jacobini, *International Law.* Jacobini, H. B., *International Law: A Text,* rev. ed. (Homewood, Ill.: Dorsey Press, 1968).

Kaplan and Katzenbach, *The Political Foundations of International Law.* Kaplan, Morton A., and Nicholas deB. Katzenbach, *The Political Foundations of International Law* (New York: John Wiley, 1961).

Kelsen, *Principles of International Law.* Kelsen, Hans, *Principles of International Law*, 2nd ed. edited by Robert W. Tucker (New York: Holt, Rinehart and Winston, 1966).

Sørensen, *Manual of Public International Law.* Sørensen, Max (ed.), *Manual of Public International Law* (New York: St. Martin's Press, 1968).

Svarlien, *An Introduction to the Law of Nations.* Svarlien, Oscar, *An Introduction to the Law of Nations* (New York: McGraw-Hill, 1955).

Tung, *International Law in an Organizing World.* Tung, William L., *International Law in an Organizing World* (New York: Crowell, 1968).

von Glahn, *Law Among Nations.* von Glahn, Gerhard, *Law Among Nations* (New York: Macmillan, 1965).

Digests

Hackworth, *Digest of International Law*. Hackworth, Green H., *Digest of International Law*, 8 vols. (Washington, D.C.: U.S. Government Printing Office, 1940–1944).

Moore, *Digest of International Law*. Moore, John Bassett, *Digest of International Law*, 8 vols. (Washington, D.C.: U.S. Government Printing Office, 1906).

Whiteman, *Digest of International Law*. Whiteman, Marjorie M., *Digest of International Law*, 11 vols. (Washington, D.C.: U.S. Government Printing Office, 1963–1969).

Chapter I
The Nature and Uses of International Law

THE NATURE OF INTERNATIONAL LAW

International law is a constantly evolving body of norms that are commonly observed by the members of the international community in their relations with one another. These norms confer rights and impose obligations upon states and, to a lesser extent, upon international organizations and individuals. International law is created and is deemed to be legally binding by authoritative national and international decision-makers because they understand that generally agreed upon rules and principles of action serve the indispensable function of providing a basis for the orderly management of international relations.

Whether or not one wishes to attribute a legal character to the norms of international law depends largely upon the definition of law he chooses to accept. Those who subscribe to the view of Thomas Hobbes and John Austin insist that law "properly so called" is the command of a determinate superior and that, consequently, no law can exist where there is no supreme lawgiver and no coercive enforcement agency. To writers of this persuasion, what is commonly called international law is more properly labeled "positive morality." But the insufficiency of the Austinian concept of law as a legal order backed by threats is now widely recognized. As H. L. A. Hart points out, this concept "plainly approximates closer to a penal statute enacted by the legislature of a modern state than to any other variety of law."[1] J. L. Brierly comments that the Austinian concept of law cannot, "unless we distort the facts so as to fit them into the definition, account for the existence of

[1] H. L. A. Hart, *The Concept of Law* (Oxford: Clarendon Press, 1961), p. 24.

the English Common Law."[2] And he concludes his discussion of the legal character of international law with the following:

. . . If, as Sir Frederick Pollock writes, and as probably most competent jurists would today agree, the only essential conditions for the existence of law are the existence of a political community, and the recognition by its members of settled rules binding upon them in that capacity, international law seems on the whole to satisfy these conditions.[3]

It is important to emphasize that the legal nature and obligatory force of international law norms are clearly recognized by the decision-makers who create and apply them, and that these norms are regularly stated in legal terms and interpreted by legal methods.[4]

The common recognition by authoritative decision-makers of the binding nature of international law distinguishes it from international morality or ethics, which can be defined as standards of "right behavior" that are based on personal moral judgments. Although attitudes about morality, when widely shared, influence the development of international law, there is no recognized legal obligation to obey norms of morality until they are accepted by authoritative decision-makers *as* international law.[5] It is possible for states, like individuals, to act selfishly and inconsiderately without violation of legal norms; and many legal norms, such as those that purport to regulate the demarcation of river boundaries and the "rules of the road" on the high seas, have little or no relation to morality.

The binding nature of international law also distinguishes it from international comity, which consists of practices that are observed between states as a matter of courtesy or convenience. Canada and the United States, for example, allow each other's nationals to enter their territory for short visits without passports, but they do not extend this privilege to other states. Their treatment of each other's diplomatic agents, on the other hand, is covered by international law, and they recognize a legal obligation to observe the norms that govern this interaction.

It is obvious that international law, unlike municipal law, operates in a decentralized political system. It is equally obvious that there are gaps and ambiguities in the law, that its enforcement devices are often inadequate, and that it has not succeeded in eliminating the use of force in international relations. There is no world legislature, no international police force, and no international court with compulsory jurisdiction. Only time will tell whether or not states will create these institutions within the structure of the United Nations. But serious students of international relations readily perceive that a considerable amount of order already exists in the international community and that this order is largely the result of the effectiveness of a body of norms commonly labeled international law. Based on the consent of states, these norms demonstrate an awareness on the part of national decision-makers that, in an increasingly interdependent world, states have an interest in creating and maintaining rules that prescribe acceptable patterns of international behavior and proscribe other forms of conduct, even though these constraints apply to their own states as well as to others. For example, an awareness of the fact that, without standards of official conduct that are normally accepted and followed, even "the movement of people, goods, and capital beyond national borders might be prohibitively

---

[2] Brierly, *The Law of Nations*, p. 70.

[3] *Ibid.*, p. 71.

[4] "States continue to make treaties and expect them to be observed; international courts have held that engagements contained in treaties are of a legal nature and 'not a mere moral obligation' . . . and that the interpretation of a treaty is a legal, not a political, question. . . ." Herbert W. Briggs, *The Law of Nations: Cases, Documents, and Notes*, 2nd ed. (New York: Appleton-Century-Crofts, 1952), pp. 19–20.

[5] "International law . . . has, at times, like the common law within states, a twilight existence during which it is hardly distinguishable from morality or justice, till at length the *imprimatur* of a court attests its jural quality." Justice Cardozo, New Jersey v. Delaware, 291 U.S. 366 (1934).

risky"[6] has led decision-makers to create legal norms that regulate such matters as the jurisdiction of states, the treatment of aliens, and traffic on the high seas. Other norms, including those that relate to the immunities of diplomats and the law of treaties, facilitate contacts and the conclusion of formal agreements between governments.

Most of the business of foreign offices is noncrisis business and is regularly settled by use of the norms and procedures of international law. International communications, trade, travel, diplomacy, and other transnational activities are effectively regulated by international law. This is not to say that foreign policy is invariably determined by legal factors; political, economic, military, and other influences often outweigh the norms of international law in the minds of national decision-makers, particularly when they consider that vital interests are at stake. Then the legal adviser is called in not to give advice as to which course to take but to prepare legal arguments to defend decisions taken on other grounds. This fact may provide ammunition to philosophical critics of international law, but it surely does not undercut the importance of the study of the subject by students of international relations.

The language of the diplomat is largely that of international law, whether his purpose is to observe its norms or to invest his contentions with the respectability of legal principles. And the importance of "law as language" should not be underestimated: by providing "an orderly process for identifying, asserting, and communicating claims to engage in controverted conduct . . . law provides a medium for precise communication between international actors."[7] This is no small contribution to world order. As a generally agreed upon medium of communication, international law "inhibits the tendency of nations to overrespond to perceived crises, and it establishes a matrix and rhetoric that facilitate diplomatic negotiation."[8]

The selections that follow present a variety of perspectives on the nature of international law. The brief excerpts from Green H. Hackworth's *Digest of International Law* and from the Lotus case, decided by the Permanent Court of International Justice in 1927, are classic definitions that, although basically sound, are no longer adequate because they assume that states are the only subjects of international law. As is suggested in the third selection, from Marjorie M. Whiteman's more recent *Digest of International Law*, and as will be illustrated in Chapter II of this book, international organizations and individuals are being increasingly recognized as international legal persons. The fourth selection is a Soviet statement on the nature of international law. A brief excerpt from *The Queen v. Keyn* includes a judicial expression of the Austinian view of international law and is followed by an opposing judicial expression from the Prometheus case. Selections from Hans J. Morgenthau's influential *Politics Among Nations* and an article by Philip C. Jessup, a judge on the International Court of Justice, illustrate the reality of international law. Brief statements by Loftus Becker and William W. Bishop, Jr., are included to point out the relationship of international law to international politics. The role of the legal adviser in the foreign policy process is discussed by H. C. L. Merillat and by Abdullah El-Erian, legal adviser to the United Arab Republic. Finally, the changing nature of international law is discussed by Josef L. Kunz in his article "The Changing Law of Nations."

[6] Oliver J. Lissitzyn, "International Law in a Divided World," *International Conciliation*, No. 542 (March 1963), p. 5.
[7] Richard A. Falk, "Janus Tormented: The International Law of Internal War," in James N. Rosenau (ed.), *International Aspects of Civil Strife* (Princeton, N.J.: Princeton University Press, 1964), p. 211.

[8] *Ibid.*, p. 212.

from *Digest of International Law* (Hackworth) *

International law consists of a body of rules governing the relations between states. It is a system of jurisprudence which, for the most part, has evolved out of the experiences and the necessities of situations that have arisen from time to time. It has developed with the progress of civilization and with the increasing realization by nations that their relations *inter se*, if not their existence, must be governed by and depend upon rules of law fairly certain and generally reasonable. Customary, as distinguished from conventional, international law is based upon the common consent of nations extending over a period of time of sufficient duration to cause it to become crystallized into a rule of conduct. When doubt arises as to the existence or nonexistence of a rule of international law, or as to the application of a rule to a given situation, resort is usually had to such sources as pertinent treaties, pronouncements of foreign offices, statements by writers, and decisions of international tribunals and those of prize courts and other domestic courts purporting to be expressive of the law of nations.

The S. S. "Lotus"†

Permanent Court of International Justice, 1927

International law governs relations between independent States. The rules of law binding upon States therefore emanate from their own free will as expressed in conventions or by usages generally accepted as expressing principles of law and established in order to regulate the relations between these co-existing independent communities or with a view to the achievement of common aims. Restrictions upon the independence of States cannot therefore be presumed.

from *Digest of International Law* (Whiteman) *

International law is the standard of conduct, at a given time, for states and other entities subject thereto. It comprises the rights, privileges, powers, and immunities of states and entities invoking its provisions, as well as the correlative fundamental duties, absence of rights, liabilities, and disabilities. International law is, more or less, in a continual state of change and development. In certain of its aspects the evolution is gradual; in others it is avulsive. International law is based largely on custom, e.g., on practice, and whereas certain customs are recognized as obligatory, others are in retrogression and are recognized as nonobligatory, depending upon the subject matter and its status at a particular time.

Over varying periods of time certain international practices have been found to be reasonable and wise in the conduct of foreign relations, in considerable measure the result of a balancing of interests. Such practices have attained the stature of accepted principles or norms and are recognized as international law or practice. Accordingly, there are in the field of international law, public and private, certain well-recognized principles or norms.

The recognized customs prevailing between states and other subjects of international law are reflected not only in international practice *per se* but also in international treaties and agreements, in the general principles of law recognized by states, in judicial and arbitral decisions, and in the works of qualified scholars. Based largely on custom, thus reflected and recognized, international law is, to a considerable extent, unwritten in form and uncodified.

---

* Reprinted from 1 Hackworth, *Digest of International Law* 1 (Washington, D.C.: U.S. Government Printing Office, 1940).
† Reprinted from [1927] *Permanent Court of International Justice*, Ser. A, No. 10, p. 18.

* Reprinted from 1 Whiteman, *Digest of International Law* 1 (Washington, D.C.: U.S. Government Printing Office, 1963).

A Soviet Definition of International Law*

International Law can be defined as the aggregate of rules governing relations between States in the process of their conflict and co-operation, designed to safeguard their peaceful coexistence, expressing the will of the ruling classes of these States and defended in case of need by coercion applied by States individually or collectively.

This definition notes the class character and significance of International Law, indicates the subjects of international legal relations (States), the nature of the relations between them (conflict and co-operation) and the method of safeguarding and implementing the rules of International Law, i.e., their defence, individually or collectively, by the States themselves.

* * *

The coexistence of States with differing social and economic systems and the transformation of socialism into a world system determine the content and nature of present-day International Law. The purpose of present-day International Law is to regulate relations between all States and in this way strengthen world peace and security.

* * *

Although International Law, like any other branch of law, has a class character and pertains to the superstructure, it cannot express the will of the ruling class of any particular State. It is the expression of the agreed will of a number of States in the form of an international agreement or custom which has grown up over a long period. The purpose of present-day International Law is to promote peaceful coexistence and co-operation between all States regardless of their social systems.

The Queen v. Keyn*

Court for Crown Cases Reserved of Great Britain, 1876

LORD COLERIDGE, C.J. Strictly speaking, international law is an inexact expression, and it is apt to mislead if its inexactness is not kept in mind. Law implies a law-giver, and a tribunal capable of enforcing it and coercing its transgressors. But there is no common law-giver to sovereign states; and no tribunal has the power to bind them by decrees or coerce them if they transgress. The law of nations is that collection of usages which civilized states have agreed to observe in their dealings with one another. What these usages are, whether a particular one has or has not been agreed to, must be a matter of evidence. Treaties and acts of state are but evidence of the agreement of nations, and do not in this country at least per se bind the tribunals. Neither, certainly, does a consensus of jurists; but it is evidence of the agreement of nations on international points; and on such points, when they arise, the English Courts give effect, as part of English law, to such agreement.

The Prometheus †

Supreme Court of Hong Kong, Great Britain, 1906

SIR HENRY BERKELEY, C.J. It was contended on behalf of the owners of the Prometheus that the term "law" as applied to this recognized system of principles and rules known as international law is an inexact expression, that there is, in

---

* Reprinted from F. I. Kozhevnikov (ed.), *International Law: A Textbook for Use in Law Schools* (Moscow: Foreign Languages Publishing House, n.d.), pp. 7, 8, 10, 11.

* Reprinted from 2 Ex. D. 63, 153, 154 (1876).
† Reprinted from 2 *Hong Kong L. Rep.*, 207, 225 (1906).

other words, no such thing as international law; that there can be no such law binding upon all nations inasmuch as there is no sanction for such law, that is to say that there is no means by which obedience to such law can be imposed upon any given nation refusing obedience thereto. I do not concur in that contention. In my opinion a law may be established and become international, that is to say binding upon all nations, by the agreement of such nations to be bound thereby, although it may be impossible to enforce obedience thereto by any given nation party to the agreement. The resistance of a nation to a law to which it has agreed does not derogate from the authority of the law because that resistance cannot, perhaps, be overcome. Such resistance merely makes the resisting nation a breaker of the law to which it has given its adherence, but it leaves the law, to the establishment of which the resisting nation was a party, still subsisting. Could it be successfully contended that because any given person or body of persons possessed for the time being power to resist an established municipal law such law had no existence? The answer to such a contention would be that the law still existed, though it might not for the time being be possible to enforce obedience to it.

* * *

"International Law Has in Most Instances Been Scrupulously Observed"*

Hans J. Morgenthau

* * *

The modern system of international law is the result of the great political transformation that marked the transition from the Middle Ages to the modern period of history. It can be summed up as the transformation of the feudal system into the territorial state. The main characteristic of the latter, distinguishing it from its predecessor, was the assumption by the government of the supreme authority within the territory of the state. The monarch no longer shared authority with the feudal lords within the state territory of which he had been in large measure the nominal rather than the actual head. Nor did he share it with the Church, which throughout the Middle Ages had claimed in certain respects supreme authority within Christendom. When this transformation had been consummated in the sixteenth century, the political world consisted of a number of states that within their respective territories were, legally speaking, completely independent of each other, recognizing no secular authority above themselves. In one word, they were sovereign.

If there was to be at least a certain measure of peace and order in the relations among such entities endowed with supreme authority within their territories and having continuous contact with each other, it was inevitable that certain rules of law should govern these relations. That is to say, there must be certain rules of conduct defined beforehand, whose violation would normally call forth certain sanctions, also defined beforehand as to their nature and the conditions and mode of their application. States must, for instance, know where the frontiers of their territory are on land and on sea. They must know under what conditions they can acquire a valid title to territory either owned by no one at all (as in the case of discovery), or by another state (as in the case of cession or annexation). They must know what authority they have over citizens of other states living on their territory and over their citizens living abroad. When a merchant vessel flying the flag of State A enters a port of State B, what are the rights of

* Reprinted from *Politics Among Nations*, 3rd ed. (New York: Alfred A. Knopf, 1960), pp. 276–277, by permission of the publisher. Copyright, 1948, 1954, © 1960, 1967, by Alfred A. Knopf, Inc.

State B with regard to that vessel? And what if the vessel is a warship? What are the rights of diplomatic representatives accredited to a foreign government, and what are the rights of the head of the state on foreign soil? What is a state allowed and obligated to do in times of war with respect to combatants, civilians, prisoners, neutrals, on sea and on land? Under what conditions is a treaty between two or more states binding, and under what conditions does it lose its binding force? And if a treaty or another rule of international law is claimed to have been violated, who has the right to ascertain the violation and who has the right to take what kind of enforcement measures and under what conditions? These and many other issues of a similar nature rise of necessity from the relations among sovereign states, and if anarchy and violence are not to be the order of the day, legal rules must determine the mutual rights and obligations in such situations.

A core of rules of international law laying down the rights and duties of states in relation to each other developed in the fifteenth and sixteenth centuries. These rules of international law were securely established in 1648, when the Treaty of Westphalia brought the religious wars to an end and made the territorial state the cornerstone of the modern state system. Hugo Grotius's *On the Law of War and Peace*, published in 1628, is the classic codification of that early system of international law. On its foundation, the eighteenth and, more particularly, the nineteenth and twentieth centuries built an imposing edifice, consisting of thousands of treaties, hundreds of decisions of international tribunals, and innumerable decisions of domestic courts. These treaties and decisions regulate, often in minute detail, the relations between nations arising from the multiplicity and variety of international contacts, which are the result of modern communications, international exchange of goods and services, and the great number of international organizations in which most nations have cooperated for the furtherance of their common interests. Such organizations include the International Red Cross, the International Court of Justice, Specialized Agencies of the United Nations, such as the International Labor Organization (ILO), the World Health Organization (WHO), the United Nations Economic, Scientific and Cultural Organization (UNESCO), the Universal Postal Union, the International Monetary Fund, and many others.

It is also worth mentioning, in view of a widespread misconception in this respect, that during the four hundred years of its existence international law has in most instances been scrupulously observed. When one of its rules was violated, it was, however, not always enforced and, when action to enforce it was actually taken, it was not always effective. Yet to deny that international law exists at all as a system of binding legal rules flies in the face of all the evidence. This misconception as to the existence of international law is at least in part the result of the disproportionate attention that public opinion has paid in recent times to a small fraction of international law, while neglecting the main body of it. Public opinion has been concerned mainly with such spectacular instruments of international law as the Briand-Kellogg Pact, the Covenant of the League of Nations, and the Charter of the United Nations. These instruments are indeed of doubtful efficacy (that is, they are frequently violated), and sometimes even of doubtful validity (that is, they are often not enforced in case of violation). They are, however, not typical of the traditional rules of international law concerning, for instance, the limits of territorial jurisdiction, the rights of vessels in foreign waters, and the status of diplomatic representatives.

*   *   *

The Reality of International Law*

Philip C. Jessup

. . . Search the published records of governments and you find them full of questions and answers about problems of international law.

Why do Foreign Ministers and Secretaries of State consult legal advisers about international law?

In the Department of State in Washington there is a Legal Adviser with a staff of some two dozen lawyers to assist him. It would not be an unfair estimate to say that 90 percent of the business of the Department passes over the desk of one of the legal staff. Of that 90 percent, about an equal percentage involves questions of international law; the 10 percent balance is made up of questions of domestic statutory and other branches of private law. The situation is much the same in the Foreign Offices in Downing Street, the Wilhelmstrasse, the Quai d'Orsay, and in the other capitals of the world.

The layman and the common lawyer who find it difficult to fit international law into their concept of "law"—a concept which is generally of the Austinian type—usually are alike in asserting that there isn't any international law. They forget that law has many meanings. There is the law of gravity, the Sherman Anti-Trust law, the law of supply and demand, international law. There is an old Chinese proverb which runs something like this: "One should always have in the background of one's mind a multiplicity of definitions covering the subject at hand, in order to prevent oneself from accepting the most obvious." And Cardozo said: "If the result of a definition is to make . . . [facts] seem to be illusions, so much the worse for the definition; we must enlarge

it till it is broad enough to answer to realities."

In most cases the layman is impressed by the reality of breaches of international law and is not sufficiently aware of the reality of reliance upon it. He does not pause to wonder why foreign offices bother to maintain legal staffs, which are an expense and sometimes a hindrance to the execution of policy. A distinguished student has remarked that in the seventeenth century "state papers are full of allusions and appeals not merely to reasons of policy but to principles of right, of justice and of equity—to the authority of public law and to those principles and rules by which the rights of the weak are protected against the invasion of superior force by the union of all who are interested in the common danger."

Why has this been true for three centuries? Why have the nations been willing for nearly twenty years to subscribe to a budget of over half a million dollars for the maintenance of the Permanent Court of International Justice? Why did the German Government bother to make a legal argument in support of its refusal to accept the demand of the United States that it assume the obligation to pay the bonded obligations of Austria after that country was "absorbed"? Why have the governments of the United States and Mexico filled reams of paper with legal arguments concerning the property rights of American citizens in the latter country? Why does the Constitution of the United States, which, according to Chief Justice Marshall, cannot be presumed to contain any clause which "is intended to be without effect," give Congress the power "to define and punish . . . offenses against the law of nations"? Why has the United States Supreme Court, like the courts of most other countries, asserted that "international law is part of our law"? Why do people commonly emphasize the "lawlessness" of certain nations which have come to be known as "aggressors"? Why was our

* Reprinted by special permission from 18 *Foreign Affairs* 244 (January 1940). Copyright by the Council on Foreign Relations, Inc., New York.

entry into the World War in 1917 justified in part by President Wilson on the ground that Germany had "swept aside" the rules of "international law"?

There must be some reason for this habitual invocation of international law—an invocation which is even more frequent than the assertion of its non-existence. Perhaps a subconscious human urge, a variety of wishful thinking, seeks to give reality to the ancient maxim: *ubi societas, ibi ius*. Perhaps "international law" is merely a slogan of diplomacy, like "manifest destiny," "the white man's burden," or "*Lebensraum*." Surely it is often a convenient weapon for a ministry of propaganda anxious to win the support of world opinion. Yet if international law has no reality, what is the use of convincing peoples in other lands that one's opponent is a violator of that law? Shall we chorus with the Pirate King: "A paradox, a paradox, a most ingenious paradox"? One would scarcely deny that international law is a comparatively weak sister of private law. Yet a great lawyer—John Bassett Moore—bears testimony as the result of wide experience and study that "international law is on the whole as well observed as municipal law."

* * *

It is true, as Professor Goebel has noted, that international adjudication in the twentieth century is in the primitive stage of development which one finds in the law of the Franks in the seventh century. And this is necessary and proper because the international society is still in a primitive stage struggling slowly through the centuries to lift itself from the bog of national superstitions and taboos—the taboo of "absolute sovereignty," for example. It still lacks an effective system of law courts, it lacks sheriffs and police forces, it lacks a legislature. It is often flouted and often the lawbreaker pays no penalty. Sir Austen Chamberlain told the House of Commons

in 1929 that international law is "indeterminate in the first instance, and in the second it is a changing law." It also has loopholes. . . .

* * *

Let it be said at once that it is absurd to assert that governmental policies of any nation are determined solely by reference to legal considerations. Only a doting parent would make a claim so patently oblivious to the infant's obvious defects; and Grotius, who is called the "Father of International Law," is not here to speak.

* * *

Impotent to restrain a great nation which has no decent respect for the opinion of mankind, failing in its severest test of serving as a substitute for war, international law plods on its way, followed automatically in routine affairs, invoked, flouted, codified, flouted again but yet again invoked. The Legal Adviser of the United States Department of State still sits at his desk in the old State, War and Navy Building in Washington and his counterpart sits at Downing Street, the Quai d'Orsay and the Wilhelmstrasse. It is not their task to frame policies. But can one say that the international law with which they deal has no reality?

"International Law and the Political Process"*

Statement by Loftus Becker, Legal Adviser, United States Department of State, in an Address Before the American Society of International Law, April 26, 1958

The topic that you have chosen for discussion at this meeting of the society—"International Law and the Political

* Reprinted from 38 *United States Department of State Bulletin* 832 (1958).

Process"—has a very real meaning for those of us who are charged with legal responsibilities in the Department. One of the first things that we learn is that abstract conceptions of international law, as it should be, must, of necessity, be qualified in application by the realities of the political process.

I know that there are those who assert that international law, in order to be worth its salt, must be based solely upon logic and principle. But international law, notwithstanding the reasoned theses of the commentators, consists, in the last analysis, of those principles upon which sovereign nations can agree. Such agreement is seldom, if ever, reached without regard to the political process.

Please do not imply from my remarks that I would throw logic and principle overboard in favor of pure political pragmatism. There is, however, a mean, a balancing between legal theory and political capabilities, that must be taken into account both in the formulation and in the application of the principles of international law.

"The International Law Focus in International Politics" *

William W. Bishop, Jr.

Usually the international law aspects of international relations are commingled with political, strategic, economic, geographical, social, and other elements, and in consequence it may be difficult to determine the exact part played by international law. Account must be taken of these non-legal factors in analyzing international incidents which have taken place or in predicting what States will do in a given situation; but for the purposes of study and discussion it is desirable to single out

the legal aspects and to focus attention upon them. As a test of what is the international law applicable, most international lawyers trained in the common law tradition would probably ask the question, what would an impartial international court having jurisdiction over the case decide to be the legal rule? The absence in the actual case of such a court having jurisdiction over the dispute would not prevent the international lawyer's attempt to estimate as well as possible what such a court would decide, nor his pronouncing that estimate to be his best judgment as to the international law on the point. This is true, though any realistic international lawyer would, and should, point out the probable results of the nonlegal factors in the situation, which in practice may lead to a consequence very different from that reached by application of the law alone.

Legal Advisers and Foreign Affairs *

H. C. L. Merillat

To help clarify the role of the legal adviser and to provide for an informal exchange of views and experience among some of those responsible for advising their governments on the legal aspects of international dealings, the American Society of International Law sponsored a small conference in September 1963. Officials and scholars from twelve countries, the United Nations Secretariat, and the International Bank for Reconstruction and Development met . . . at Princeton, New Jersey. The participants represented countries varying widely in population, cultural backgrounds, and experience as independent states, in Africa, Asia, Europe, and North and South America.

* * *

* Reprinted from William W. Bishop, Jr., *International Law: Cases and Materials*, 2nd ed. (Boston: Little, Brown and Company, 1962), p. 6, by permission of the author and publisher.

* Reprinted from H. C. L. Merillat, "Varieties of Problems in Law and Policy," in H. C. L. Merillat (ed.), *Legal Advisers and Foreign Affairs* (Dobbs Ferry, N.Y.: Oceana Publications, 1964), pp. v–vi, 16–19, by permission of the American Society of International Law.

Not uncommonly, the legal adviser in a foreign ministry is regarded as primarily concerned with public international law— interpretations of customary law and treaty obligations as they relate to a policy decision. Another office, or other offices, in the government may be primarily responsible for advising on the application of national law, especially constitutional law, and conflicts of private law.

In his application of international law to a particular set of circumstances the legal adviser will first ask himself this question: Is there any "law" on the point? If there is a fairly clear and well-established rule, he will say so. But the law is more often unclear or unsettled, or there may be no recognized rule applicable in such situations. It is here that the lawyer's role as a shaper of policy is most apparent. Like any prudent counsellor in personal or business affairs, he will attempt to outline the consequences for the future of alternative policy decisions. Where customary norms and treaty obligations offer no clear answer, or where norms have been widely challenged by other nations, there is an opportunity to contribute to the establishment of new norms, and in the process the legal adviser may point out that, however much an *ad hoc* decision may seem to satisfy some immediate national interest, it may offer an uncomfortable precedent for the future, taking a longer view of the national interest. And, as was brought out repeatedly in the discussion, national interest may be best served by recognizing the facts of interdependence and the desirability of a consistent ordering of international affairs.

One participant suggested that, apart from the obvious and significant difference of a lack of a central decision-making and decision-enforcing authority in international affairs, the legal adviser on foreign affairs works in much the same way as a lawyer within a national system, at least in the common-law tradition. He marshals

the facts, examines the background of policy statements by responsible ministers and officials in his own and other governments, traces the history of relevant legislation and agreements, analyzes decisions of national and international tribunals, and considers these indicators of law in the context of the conflicting political pressures that have given rise to the problem on which his advice is sought. With this preparation he is ready to advise whether a settlement of a dispute should be negotiated, whether an international commitment should be entered into, whether a claim should be asserted, and the like. In so doing he may have an opportunity to suggest that a proposed course of action be modified, or cast in a different form more consistent with long-term interests, including the interest in a fairly predictable international order.

Several participants suggested that, given the unsettled state of much of international law, it is in the application of legal techniques, in the quality of "lawyership," that the legal adviser makes his most significant contribution. As one trained in analyzing facts, marshalling the variety of legal sources, and encouraging objectivity and long-sightedness that reach beyond the pressures of the moment, the lawyer has a distinctive role. In so acting, he inevitably is concerned with "policy" questions. Whether or not his advice on policy matters is accepted will depend in part on his personal qualities and on the depth of his experience. Through continuously dealing with the problems in a particular geographical or functional area he may have acquired a background of knowledge and competence that gives his advice a weight beyond that of a legal specialist.

It was suggested that what is regarded as a "legal" problem in one country may be highly political in another. For example, the government of a long-established state, itself facing none of the problems of succeeding to the obligations of another state, may regard rules of state succession as largely settled and uncontroversial, and assert the claims of its nationals in legal terms. The rise or fall of its government is probably not at stake. On the other hand, the government of a newly independent state faced with difficult problems of deciding what treaties, concessions, and contracts of a predecessor state (now, typically, a former colonial power) it shall regard as binding upon itself, may find the question deeply affected by political passion and economic and social pressures. Similarly, claims arising from expropriation of the property of foreign nationals may be dealt with as legal problems by the state whose nationals have been expropriated and insist that the law is well settled. In the country where the expropriation took place, on the other hand, the matter may be and often is a highly charged political issue. As Professor Corbett has put it, "the boundary between routine and 'vital' business is fluid. At any moment a minor detail, charged with accidental significance, may become the subject of political dispute that defies settlement by pre-established norm."

It was recognized that not infrequently the legal adviser is asked to rationalize, in legal terms, a policy decision on which he has not been consulted or which, having been consulted, he has advised against. He may be able to win a modification of the decision, or persuade others that it be carried out in ways more consistent with his notions of the applicable norms. He may seek to withhold any public support for a decision he considers unacceptable. The problems of personal conscience are, at least in countries with a pervasive and well-established tradition of law, complicated by the demands of professional integrity and responsibility.

In the discussion of the relationship of law and policy, one participant interjected that a listener might get the impression that legal advisers and their clients spent their time dealing with matters of high policy. His own impression was to the contrary, that officials in foreign ministries including legal advisers were mainly occupied in dealing with an unending series of small crises allowing little time for policy deliberation. Others made a similar point. In private law, and even in public law on the national scene, the urgency of decision-making is seldom as pressing as in rapidly moving international situations. There is a relatively high degree of orderliness on the national scene in the legislative, administrative, and judicial processes. Decisions must be taken quickly in international affairs, in a legal context that provides less certainty and stability in terms of guiding norms.

It was recognized that lawyers are commonly regarded by their non-lawyer colleagues as sticklers for form, and given to raising difficulties and objections that impede decision-making. The lawyer must often say "no" to a proposed course of action but, it was brought out, he is likely to find that his clients simply stop consulting him if he cannot make positive suggestions.

✳ Dr. Riphagen, the Legal Adviser in The Netherlands, remarked in his background paper: "It is submitted that, in the final analysis, the role of the lawyer in the decision-making process in international relations depends on the approach of the policy-makers to 'foreign policy' and on the approach of lawyers to 'law.' If the lawyer does not regard 'law' as the result of a continuous process of creative imagination, and if the policy-maker regards 'policy' as dictated *ad hoc* by the circumstances of the situation and the immediate interests involved, there is not much place for a fruitful collaboration between them. Where, however, the policy-maker has an eye for the general (not necessarily strictly 'legal') aspects of a case, he will be willing to listen to the advice of a lawyer who, on his part, is inclined (to borrow a phrase) 'to find a solution for every difficulty rather than to find a difficulty for every solution.'"

* * *

The Office of Legal Adviser in the United Arab Republic*

Abdullah El-Erian, LEGAL ADVISER,
MINISTRY OF FOREIGN AFFAIRS,
UNITED ARAB REPUBLIC

Organization and Functions of the Office of Legal Adviser in the Ministry of Foreign Affairs of the United Arab Republic

The institutional structure of the Office of Legal Adviser and its functions within the Ministry of Foreign Affairs of the United Arab Republic are at present governed by the Ministerial Decree No. 989 of 1960, dated June 29th, 1960. This decree merged the Office of Legal Adviser and the Department of Treaties in a single department to be called "The Department of Legal Affairs and Treaties."

Article 2 of the said decree sets forth the functions of the new department as follows:

"1. to study international problems with a view to considering the international problems of the United Arab Republic from the point of view of international law.
"2. to participate in the presentation of the position of the United Arab Republic in international conferences.
"3. to prepare the drafts of treaties and agreements to be concluded by the United Arab Republic, and take the necessary measures for their conclusion, promulgation, publication, and registration with international organizations as well as the necessary procedure for the abrogation and termination of these treaties and agreements in accordance with the provisions of the decree of

the Council of Ministers dated September 21st, 1955.
"4. to study, prepare, and draft the subjects and questions referred to it by the Minister for Foreign Affairs."

Article 3 states that the new department shall be considered "the competent legal organ for providing advice to the Ministry on all international legal questions."

Article 4 provides that the new department shall be the "liaison between the Ministry of Foreign Affairs and the division of advisory opinion and legislation in the Council of State in all matters relating to international questions."

* * *

Position of the Office of Legal Adviser in the Ministry of Foreign Affairs; Problems of Recruitment and Continuity

1. *Position.* The department of legal affairs and treaties is an integral part of the Ministry of Foreign Affairs and its foreign service (diplomatic and consular corps). Its officers alternate between the department and the United Arab Republic diplomatic missions abroad.

2. *Recruitment.* The special nature of the work of legal advising on foreign affairs requires in its officers, in addition to training in both national and international law, some diplomatic experience which would enable them to appreciate more fully the political factors which have a bearing on their work and the special character of international relations.

Assignment to the department has therefore been made from among lawyers in the Ministry who have had some postgraduate work in international law at home or abroad or those who have served in our permanent missions to international organizations.

3. *Continuity.* The fact that the officers of the department alternate between it and

---

* Reprinted from Abdullah El-Erian, "The Legal Adviser in the United Arab Republic," in H. C. L. Merillat (ed.), *Legal Advisers and Foreign Affairs* (Dobbs Ferry, N.Y.: Oceana Publications, 1964), pp. 98–100 by, permission of the American Society of International Law.

our diplomatic missions abroad poses the problem of continuity. Plans are at present under consideration and formulation to attract a number of diplomatic officers with legal training to pursue a course of specialization through serving a longer period in the Ministry than abroad.

Continuity would also be assured if upon their return from a diplomatic post abroad, they would be reassigned to the office of legal adviser.

The Changing Law of Nations*

Josef L. Kunz

* * *

The changing character of international law is, first, a consequence of a transformation of general conditions, a transformation the impact of which is equally felt in the municipal legal orders. The "classic" international law presupposed the doctrines of democracy, capitalism, economic liberalism, "laissez faire," the principles of the sanctity of private property, the strict distinction between private enterprise and economic activities by states, the strict distinction between armed forces and the civilian population. All that has fundamentally changed. The coming of total war, of ever expanding economic activities by states, the control by states of the economic life of the nation even in times of peace, and more so in times of war, the appearance of totalitarian regimes, have profoundly influenced old and well-established rules of international law and brought about far-reaching uncertainty. These transformations, while particularly prominent in totalitarian states, are nevertheless more or less universal, to

be seen also in the democracies of the free world. They have shaken the basis of many rules of the laws of war and of the law of neutrality. They have changed and made insecure the rules concerning immunity from jurisdiction of states in their economic activities, of state instrumentalities, of government-owned merchant vessels, government corporations; also with regard to rules concerning state responsibility (political parties, subversive and terrorist activities, hostile propaganda), and finally with regard to rules concerning nationalization, expropriation, confiscation.

There are tendencies to weaken or to question old and well-established rules of international law: there is a tendency against conquest as a title of acquisition of sovereignty; there is uncertainty as to the so-called "doctrine of contiguity"; there is much confusion as to the recognition of states and governments; there are very doubtful areas as far as the law of international treaties is concerned; a weakening of the requirement of effectivity where sovereignty is acquired by occupation of a *terra nullius*; there is a complete lack of agreement as to the acquisition of sovereignty in the Arctic and in the Antarctic.

Technological developments have led to uncertainties in the laws of war, such as aerial war, chemical and bacteriological warfare, magnetic mines and so on; or have led to completely new norms in fields which before had not been of practical importance. The coming of aviation has led in a short time to the new norm of general customary international law according to which the legal status of the airspace is the same as the status of the subjacent space. We are at the threshold of a completely new "international space law." The new interest in making use of the water of streams for purposes of irrigation, hydro-electric power and so on, is transforming the law of international rivers, hitherto dominated by the interests of navigation.

Other changes stem from technological

* Reprinted from Josef L. Kunz, "The Changing Law of Nations," 51 *American Journal of International Law* 77 (1957), by permission of the American Society of International Law.

with another. And in recent years, additional dynamism has resulted from assertions that certain resolutions of international organizations possess the character of legal norms. For example, counsel for Ethiopia and Liberia in the South West Africa cases, decided by the International Court of Justice in 1966, condemned the practice of *apartheid* as illegal under certain law-creating resolutions of the United Nations General Assembly.[5] Their argument illustrates an increasing effort to replace the doctrine of state consent with that of international community consensus as the basis of international law.

It is also important to note that what will be found to be the controlling norm in a given situation will depend largely upon the role of the individual conducting the search through the sources and evidences of international law. International law is used more often by state officials seeking to justify their own policies or to criticize the policies of others than it is by impartial judges. A judge and a foreign office official, or two foreign office officials representing different states, often search through the same body of material, use the same legal techniques, and arrive at radically different conclusions as to the relevant rules. National policies and objectives are obviously in the minds of state officials as they search through the diverse sources and evidences of international law. The task of the student of international law is to attempt to answer the question, what would an impartial judge having jurisdiction over the case decide to be the legal rule?

As was stated above, the first selection in this section is a discussion of Article 38 by Manley O. Hudson. The search through the sources and evidences of international law by judges seeking controlling rules and principles is illustrated in the next three

selections: the Asylum case, the Paquete Habana case, and a dissenting opinion by Judge Chagla, an Indian national, in the "Case Concerning Right of Passage Over Indian Territory." Finally, excerpts from "Remarks on the Juridical Nature of Customary Norms of International Law" by G. I. Tunkin, President of the Soviet Association of International Law and a member of the International Law Commission, provide additional insights into the complicated nature of customary norms of international law and an indication of Soviet reluctance to agree to any digression from the sovereignty-oriented notion of state consent as the underlying basis of international law.

"On Article 38" *

Manley O. Hudson

Sources of Law to Be Applied. Article 38 of the Statute sets out four categories of sources or materials which the Court is directed to apply: (1) international conventions; (2) international custom; (3) general principles of law; (4) judicial decisions and the teachings of publicists. As the text was proposed by the 1920 Committee of Jurists, the application of these categories was to be *in a successive order*; the deletion of this phrase would seem to have had little effect on the meaning of the direction. If an applicable rule has been laid down by the parties in a convention, it will be controlling and the Court may not need to look further; if that is not the case, a sufficient guide may be found in the customary law; if resort to general principles of law is necessary, however, the Court would naturally want to know at the same time how these principles have been applied by courts and how they have been evaluated

[5] See Richard A. Falk and Saul H. Mendlovitz (eds.), *The Strategy of World Order* (New York: World Law Fund, 1966), Vol. III, pp. 75–90, for relevant portions of argument by counsel in the case.

* Reprinted from Manley O. Hudson, *The Permanent Court of International Justice, 1920-1942* (New York: The Macmillan Company, 1943), pp. 606–620, by permission of Manley O. Hudson, Jr.

in juristic writings. Yet Article 38 did not establish a rigid hierarchy. In applying a provision in a convention, the Court may have to take into account the customary law prevailing when the convention was entered into, or general principles of law, as well as judicial precedents. A distinction may also have to be drawn between the categories listed, for they are not on an equal footing; while it is possible to *apply* a conventional or a customary rule of law, it seems more proper to say that general principles of law, judicial precedents, and juristic writings have only the nature of sources from which an applicable rule may be deduced.

* * *

International Conventions. Article 38 of the Statute provides that the Court shall apply "international conventions, whether general or particular, establishing rules expressly recognized by the contesting States." The term *conventions* is used here . . . in a general and inclusive sense. It would seem to apply to any treaty, convention, protocol, or agreement, regardless of its title or form. A convention may be *general* either because of the number of parties to it, or because of the character of its contents; it may be *particular* because of the limited number of parties, or because of the limited character of its subject-matter. A special agreement (*compromis*) or a stipulation between contesting parties may be in this sense a *particular convention*. The phrase *general or particular* seems to add little to the meaning in this connection.

The phrase *establishing rules expressly recognized by the contesting States* seems to place two limitations upon the conventions which the Court is to apply: a limitation based upon the subject-matter of the instrument, and a limitation based upon the identity of the parties to the instrument. Yet it may be doubted whether the phrase creates either of these limitations. No

precise distinction can be drawn between rule-establishing and other conventions. Any instrument which creates obligations for the States which are parties to it, which regulates the conduct of those States in any way, may be said to establish rules (Fr., *règles*) in a broad sense of the term. The rule-form may not be given to the obligation; it may be stated as a principle rather than as a rule, yet no reason exists for a limitation on the Court's application of the instrument for this reason. It was certainly not the purpose to restrict the Court to the application of what are sometimes called law-making treaties or conventions, like the Declaration of Paris of 1856 concerning maritime law. Moreover, a State may have recognized a rule established by a convention though it is not a party to the convention. It has frequently occurred that States have admitted formulations made by other States to be proper statements of the law and as such binding for themselves. In the course of years the classification of diplomatic agents embodied in the Protocol of Vienna of March 9, 1815 was accepted by most States without any formal accession, and the rules thus established may now be said to have been recognized by many States not parties to the Protocol. This result may be reached without saying that the rules have been incorporated into customary law, and it seems to be covered by the phrase in Article 38 (1). To the extent that the rules laid down in an instrument must have been recognized by the contesting States before the Court, that phrase is limitative, but not otherwise.

International Custom. Article 38 of the Statute also directs the Court to apply "international custom, as evidence of a general practice accepted as law." This might have been cast more clearly as a provision for the Court's applying customary international law. It seems to emphasize the general law, as opposed to the special law embodied in conventions accepted by the parties. It is not possible for the Court to apply a custom; instead it can observe the general practice of States, and if it finds that such practice is due to a conception that the law requires it, it may declare that a rule of law exists and proceed to apply it. The elements necessary are the concordant and recurring action of numerous States in the domain of international relations, the conception in each case that such action was enjoined by law, and the failure of other States to challenge that conception at the time. The appreciation of these elements is not a simple matter, and it is a task for persons trained in law.

* * *

General Principles of Law. Article 38 of the Statute also directs the Court to apply "the general principles of law recognized by civilized nations." As all nations are civilized, as "law implies civilization," the reference to "civilized nations" can serve only to exclude from consideration primitive systems of law. Members of the 1920 Committee of Jurists expressed varying views as to the meaning of this provision when it was drafted, and the confusion was not dissipated by the Committee's report. One of its purposes may have been, under the inspiration of the national legislation of some States, to prevent the Court's abstaining from a decision because "no positive applicable rule exists." The provision serves a useful purpose in that it emphasizes the creative role to be played by the Court. It confers such a wide freedom of choice that no fixed and definite content can be assigned to the terms employed. It has been widely hailed as a refutation of the extreme positive conception of international law, and even as revolutionary; on the other hand, it has been deprecated as adding to existing confusion.

Taken out of its context, the phrase "general principles of law recognized by civilized nations" would refer primarily to the general principles of international law, following the provisions in Article 38

relating to international conventions and international custom, however, it must be given a different, perhaps one may say a larger, content. It empowers the Court to go outside the field in which States have expressed their will to accept certain principles of law as governing their relations *inter se*, and to draw upon principles common to various systems of municipal law or generally agreed upon among interpreters of municipal law. It authorizes use to be made of analogies found in the national law of the various States. It makes possible the expansion of international law along lines forged by legal thought and legal philosophy in different parts of the world. It enjoins the Court to consult a *jus gentium* before fixing the limits of the *droit des gens.*

* * *

Judicial Decisions and the Teachings of Publicists. "As subsidiary means (Fr., *moyen auxiliaire*) for the determination of rules of law," the Court is also directed to apply "judicial decisions and the teachings of the most highly qualified publicists of the various nations"; but this direction is expressly made "subject to the provisions of Article 59" that "the decision of the Court has no binding force except between the parties and in respect of that particular case." Judicial decisions and the teachings of publicists are not rules to be applied, but sources to be resorted to for finding applicable rules. What is meant by *subsidiary* is not clear. It may be thought to mean that these sources are to be subordinated to others mentioned in the article, *i.e.*, to be regarded only when sufficient guidance cannot be found in international conventions, international custom and general principles of law; the French term *auxiliaire* seems, however, to indicate that confirmation of rules found to exist may be sought by referring to jurisprudence and doctrine. In view of the reference to Article 59, the term *judicial decisions* must include decisions of the Court itself; it includes also decisions of other international tribunals and of national courts. As to the decisions of national courts, a useful caution was given by Judge Moore in the *Lotus Case* that international tribunals "are not to treat the judgments of the courts of one State on questions of international law as binding on other States, but, while giving to such judgments the weight due to judicial expressions of the view taken in the particular country, are to follow them as authority only so far as they may be found to be in harmony with international law." No standards exist for saying who are "the most highly qualified publicists of the various nations." Judge Weiss said in the *Lotus Case* that "international law is not created by an accumulation of opinions and systems; neither is its source a sum total of judgments, even if they agree with each other." In the *Brazilian Loans Case*, Judge Bustamante emphasized the importance of the time in which a publicist writes, and observed that "writers of legal treatises just as much as any one else, without wanting to and without knowing it, come under the irresistible influence of their surroundings, and the requirements of the national situation are reflected in their thoughts and have a great influence on their teachings."

In its judgments and opinions, the Court has frequently referred to what it had held and what it had said in earlier judgments and opinions, and within limits it has shown itself disposed to build a consistent body of case-law in its jurisprudence. . . .

* * *

The teachings of publicists are treated less favorably at the hands of the Court. No treatise or doctrinal writing has been cited by the Court. In connection with its conclusion in the *Lotus Case* that the existence of a restrictive rule of international law had not been conclusively proved, it referred to "teachings of publicists" without attempting to assess their value, but it failed to find in them any useful indication. Individual judges have not been so restrained in their references to the teachings of publicists; they have not hesitated to cite living authors, and even the published works of members of the Court itself.

* * *

Decisions ex aequo et bono. Article 38 of the Statute also provides that the previous enumeration in the Article "shall not prejudice the power of the Court to decide a case *ex aequo et bono*, if the parties agree thereto." The phrase *ex aequo et bono*, incorporated in the Statute without much explanation, has its roots in Roman law. . . . In a case where the parties are agreed that it may decide *ex aequo et bono*, the provision in the Statute would seem to enable the Court to go outside the realm of law for reaching its decision. It relieves the Court from the necessity of deciding according to law. It makes possible a decision based upon considerations of fair dealing and good faith, which may be independent of or even contrary to the law. Acting *ex aequo et bono*, the Court is not compelled to depart from applicable law, but it is permitted to do so, and it may even call upon a party to give up legal rights. Yet it does not have a complete freedom of action. It cannot act capriciously and arbitrarily. To the extent that it goes outside the applicable law, or acts where no law is applicable, it must proceed upon objective considerations of what is fair and just. Such considerations depend, in large measure, upon the judges' personal appreciation, and yet the Court would not be justified in reaching a result which could not be explained on rational grounds.

No case has arisen to date in which the Court has been called upon to decide *ex aequo et bono*. . . .

The Asylum Case (Colombia v. Peru)*

International Court of Justice, 1950

On October 3rd, 1948, a military rebellion broke out in Peru. It was suppressed on the same day and investigations were at once opened.

On October 4th, the President of the Republic issued a decree in the recitals of which a political party, the American People's Revolutionary Alliance, was charged with having organized and directed the rebellion. The decree consequently enacted that this party had placed itself outside the law, that it would henceforth not be permitted to exercise any kind of activity, and that its leaders would be brought to justice in the national courts as instigators of the rebellion. Simultaneously, the head of the Judicial Department of the Navy issued an order requiring the Examining Magistrate to open at once an enquiry as to the facts constituting the crime of military rebellion.

On October 5th, the Minister of the Interior addressed to the Minister for the Navy a "note of denunciation" against the leader of the American People's Revolutionary Alliance, Victor Raúl Haya de la Torre, and other members of the party as responsible for the rebellion. This denunciation was approved on the same day by the Minister for the Navy and on October 10th by the Public Prosecutor, who stated that the subject-matter of the proceedings was the crime of military rebellion.

On October 11th, the Examining Magistrate issued an order for the opening of judicial proceedings against Haya de la Torre and others "in respect of the crime of military rebellion with which they are charged in the 'denunciation,'" and on October 25th he ordered the arrest of the

* Reprinted from *International Court of Justice Reports* 266 (1950).

persons "denounced" who had not yet been detained.

* * *

On January 3rd, 1949, Haya de la Torre sought asylum in the Colombian Embassy in Lima. On the next day, the Colombian Ambassador sent the following note to the Peruvian Minister for Foreign Affairs and Public Worship:

"I have the honour to inform Your Excellency, in accordance with what is provided in Article 2, paragraph 2, of the Convention on Asylum signed by our two countries in the city of Havana in the year 1928, that Señor Víctor Raúl Haya de la Torre has been given asylum at the seat of this mission as from 9 p.m. yesterday.

In view of the foregoing, and in view of the desire of this Embassy that Señor Haya de la Torre should leave Peru as early as possible, I request Your Excellency to be good enough to give orders for the requisite safe-conduct to be issued, so that Señor Haya de la Torre may leave the country with the usual facilities attaching to the right of diplomatic asylum."

On January 14th, the Ambassador sent to the Minister a further note as follows:

"Pursuant to instructions received from the Chancellery of my country, I have the honour to inform Your Excellency that the Government of Colombia, in accordance with the right conferred upon it by Article 2 of the Convention on Political Asylum signed by our two countries in the city of Montevideo on December 26th, 1933, has qualified Señor Víctor Raúl Haya de la Torre as a political refugee."

A diplomatic correspondence followed, leading up to the Act of Lima of August 31st, 1949, whereby the dispute which had arisen between the two Governments was referred to the Court.

The Colombian Government has presented two submissions, of which the first asks the Court to adjudge and declare

"That the Republic of Colombia, as the country granting asylum, is competent to qualify the offence for the purpose of the said asylum, within the limits of the obligations resulting in particular from the Bolivarian Agreement on Extradition of July 18th, 1911, and the Convention on Asylum of February 20th, 1928, and of American international law in general."

If the Colombian Government by this submission intended to allege that Colombia, as the State granting ayslum, is competent to qualify the offence only provisionally and without binding effect for Peru, the solution would not remain a matter of doubt. It is evident that the diplomatic representative who has to determine whether a refugee is to be granted asylum or not must have the competence to make such a provisional qualification of any offence alleged to have been committed by the refugee. He must in fact examine the question whether the conditions required for granting asylum are fulfilled. The territorial State would not thereby be deprived of its right to contest the qualification. In case of disagreement between the two States, a dispute would arise which might be settled by the methods provided by the Parties for the settlement of their disputes.

This is not, however, the meaning which the Colombian Government has put on its submission. It has not claimed the right of qualification for the sole purpose of determining its own conduct. The written and oral arguments submitted on behalf of that Government show that its claim must be understood in the sense that Colombia, as the State granting asylum, is competent to qualify the nature of the offence by a unilateral and definitive decision binding on Peru. Colombia has based this submission partly on rules resulting from agreement, partly on an alleged custom.

The Colombian Government has referred to the Bolivarian Agreement of 1911, Article 18, which is framed in the following terms:

"Aside from the stipulations of the present Agreement, the signatory States recognize the institution of asylum in conformity with the principles of international law."

In recognizing "the institution of asylum", this article merely refers to the principles of international law. But the principles of international law do not recognize any rule of unilateral and definitive qualification by the State granting diplomatic asylum.

The Colombian Government has also relied on Article 4 of this Agreement concerning extradition of a criminal refugee from the territory of the State in which he has sought refuge. The arguments submitted in this respect reveal a confusion between territorial asylum (extradition), on the one hand, and diplomatic asylum, on the other.

In the case of extradition, the refugee is within the territory of the State of refuge. A decision with regard to extradition implies only the normal exercise of the territorial sovereignty. The refugee is outside the territory of the State where the offence was committed, and a decision to grant him asylum in no way derogates from the sovereignty of that State.

In the case of diplomatic asylum, the refugee is within the territory of the State where the offence was committed. A decision to grant diplomatic asylum involves a derogation from the sovereignty of that State. It withdraws the offender from the jurisdiction of the territorial State and constitutes an intervention in matters which are exclusively within the competence of that State. Such a derogation from territorial sovereignty cannot be recognized unless its legal basis is established in each particular case.

For these reasons, it is not possible to deduce from the provisions of agreements concerning extradition any conclusion which would apply to the question now under consideration.

The Colombian Government further relies on the Havana Convention on Asylum of 1928. This Convention lays down certain rules relating to diplomatic asylum, but does not contain any provision conferring on the State granting asylum a unilateral competence to qualify the offence with definitive and binding force for the territorial State. The Colombian Government contends, however, that such a competence is implied in that Convention and is inherent in the institution of asylum.

A competence of this kind is of an exceptional character. It involves a derogation from the equal rights of qualification which, in the absence of any contrary rule, must be attributed to each of the States concerned; it thus aggravates the derogation from territorial sovereignty constituted by the exercise of asylum. Such a competence is not inherent in the institution of diplomatic asylum. This institution would perhaps be more effective if a rule of unilateral and definitive qualification were applied. But such a rule is not essential to the exercise of asylum.

These considerations show that the alleged right of unilateral and definitive qualification cannot be regarded as recognized by implication in the Havana Convention. Moreover, this Convention, in pursuance of the desire expressed in its preamble of "fixing the rules" which the Governments of the States of America must observe for the granting of asylum, was concluded with the manifest intention of preventing the abuses which had arisen in the previous practice, by limiting the grant of asylum. It did so in a number of ways and in terms which are unusually restrictive and emphatic ("It is not permissible for States. . . ."; "Asylum may not be granted except in urgent cases and for the period of time strictly indispensable. . . .", etc.).

The Colombian Government has invoked Article 2, paragraph 1, of the Havana Convention, which is framed in the following terms:

"Asylum granted to political offenders in legations, warships, military camps or military aircraft, shall be respected to the extent in which allowed as a right or through humanitarian toleration, by the usages, the conventions or the laws of the country in which granted and in accordance with the following provisions:"

This provision has been interpreted by that Government in the sense that the usages, conventions and laws of Colombia relating to the qualification of the offence can be invoked against Peru. This interpretation, which would mean that the extent of the obligation of one of the signatory States would depend upon any modifications which might occur in the law of another, cannot be accepted. The provision must be regarded as a limitation of the extent to which asylum shall be respected. What the provision says in effect is that the State of refuge shall not exercise asylum to a larger extent than is warranted by its own usages, conventions or laws and that the asylum granted must be respected by the territorial State only where such asylum would be permitted according to the usages, conventions or laws of the State of refuge. Nothing therefore can be deduced from this provision in so far as qualification is concerned.

The Colombian Government has further referred to the Montevideo Convention on Political Asylum of 1933. It was in fact this Convention which was invoked in the note of January 14th, 1949, from the Colombian Ambassador to the Peruvian Minister for Foreign Affairs. It is argued that, by Article 2 of that Convention, the Havana Convention of 1928 is interpreted in the sense that the qualification of a political offence appertains to the State granting asylum. Articles 6 and 7 of the Montevideo Convention provide that it shall be ratified and will enter into force as and when the ratifications are deposited. The Montevideo Convention has not been ratified by Peru, and cannot be invoked against that State. The fact that it was considered necessary to incorporate in that Convention an article accepting the right of unilateral qualification, seems to indicate that this solution was regarded as a new rule not recognized by the Havana Convention. Moreover, the preamble of the Montevideo Convention states in its Spanish, French and Portuguese texts that it modifies the Havana Convention. It cannot therefore be considered as representing merely an interpretation of that Convention.

The Colombian Government has finally invoked "American international law in general". In addition to the rules arising from agreements which have already been considered, it has relied on an alleged regional or local custom peculiar to Latin-American States.

The Party which relies on a custom of this kind must prove that this custom is established in such a manner that it has become binding on the other Party. The Colombian Government must prove that the rule invoked by it is in accordance with a constant and uniform usage practised by the States in question, and that this usage is the expression of a right appertaining to the State granting asylum and a duty incumbent on the territorial State. This follows from Article 38 of the Statute of the Court, which refers to international custom "as evidence of a general practice accepted as law".

In support of its contention concerning the existence of such a custom, the Colombian Government has referred to a large number of extradition treaties which, as already explained, can have no bearing on the question now under consideration. It has cited conventions and agreements which do not contain any provision concerning the alleged rule of unilateral and definitive qualification such as the Montevideo Convention of 1889 on international penal law, the Bolivarian Agreement of 1911 and the Havana Convention of 1928. It has invoked conventions which have not been ratified by Peru, such as the Montevideo Conventions of 1933 and 1939. The Convention of 1933 has, in fact, been ratified by not more than eleven States and the Convention of 1939 by two States only.

It is particularly the Montevideo Convention of 1933 which Counsel for the Colombian Government has also relied on in this connexion. It is contended that this Convention has merely codified principles which were already recognized by Latin-American custom, and that it is valid against Peru as a proof of customary law. The limited number of States which have ratified this Convention reveals the weakness of this argument, and furthermore, it is invalidated by the preamble which states that this Convention modifies the Havana Convention.

Finally, the Colombian Government has referred to a large number of particular cases in which diplomatic asylum was in fact granted and respected. But it has not shown that the alleged rule of unilateral and definitive qualification was invoked or —if in some cases it was in fact invoked— that it was, apart from conventional stipulations, exercised by the States granting asylum as a right appertaining to them and respected by the territorial States as a duty incumbent on them and not merely for reasons of political expediency. The facts brought to the knowledge of the Court disclose so much uncertainty and contradiction, so much fluctuation and discrepancy in the exercise of diplomatic asylum and in the official views expressed on various occasions, there has been so much inconsistency in the rapid succession of conventions on asylum, ratified by some States and rejected by others, and the practice has been so much influenced by considerations of political expediency in the various cases, that it is not possible to discern in all this any constant and uniform usage, accepted as law, with regard to the alleged rule of unilateral and definitive qualification of the offence.

The Court cannot therefore find that the

Colombian Government has proved the existence of such a custom. But even if it could be supposed that such a custom existed between certain Latin-American States only, it could not be invoked against Peru which, far from having by its attitude adhered to it, has, on the contrary, repudiated it by refraining from ratifying the Montevideo Conventions of 1933 and 1939, which were the first to include a rule concerning the qualification of the offence in matters of diplomatic asylum.

* * *

The Paquete Habana; The Lola*

Supreme Court of the United States, 1900

MR. JUSTICE GRAY delivered the opinion of the court.

These are two appeals from decrees of the District Court of the United States for the Southern District of Florida, condemning two fishing vessels and their cargoes as prize of war.

Each vessel was a fishing smack, running in and out of Havana, and regularly engaged in fishing on the coast of Cuba; sailed under the Spanish flag; was owned by a Spanish subject of Cuban birth, living in the city of Havana; was commanded by a subject of Spain, also residing in Havana; and her master and crew had no interest in the vessel, but were entitled to shares, amounting in all to two thirds, of her catch, the other third belonging to her owner. Her cargo consisted of fresh fish, caught by her crew from the sea, put on board as they were caught, and kept and sold alive. Until stopped by the blockading squadron, she had no knowledge of the existence of the war, or of any blockade. She had no arms or ammunition on board,

* Reprinted from 175 U.S. 677 (1900).

and made no attempt to run the blockade after she knew of its existence, nor any resistance at the time of the capture.

* * *

Both the fishing vessels were brought by their captors into Key West. A libel for the condemnation of each vessel and her cargo as prize of war was there filed on April 27, 1898; a claim was interposed by her master, on behalf of himself and the other members of the crew, and of her owner; evidence was taken, showing the facts above stated; and on May 30, 1898, a final decree of condemnation and sale was entered, "the court not being satisfied that as a matter of law, without any ordinance, treaty or proclamation, fishing vessels of this class are exempt from seizure."

Each vessel was thereupon sold by auction; the Paquete Habana for the sum of $490; and the Lola for the sum of $800. There was no other evidence in the record of the value of either vessel or of her cargo.

* * *

We are then brought to the consideration of the question whether, upon the facts appearing in these records, the fishing smacks were subject to capture by the armed vessels of the United States during the recent war with Spain.

By an ancient usage among civilized nations, beginning centuries ago, and gradually ripening into a rule of international law, coast fishing vessels, pursuing their vocation of catching and bringing in fresh fish, have been recognized as exempt, with their cargoes and crews, from capture as prize of war.

This doctrine, however, has been earnestly contested at the bar; and no complete collection of the instances illustrating it is to be found, so far as we are aware, in a single published work, although many are referred to and discussed by the writers on international law, notably in 2 Ortolan, Règles Internationales et Diplomatie de la Mer, (4th ed.) lib. 3, c. 2, pp. 51–56; in 4 Calvo, Droit International, (5th ed.) §§ 2367–2373; in De Boeck, Propriété Privée Ennemie sons Pavillon Ennemi, §§ 191–196; and in Hall, International Law, (4th. ed.) § 148. It is therefore worth the while to trace the history of the rule, from the earliest accessible sources, through the increasing recognition of it, with occasional setbacks, to what we may now justly consider as its final establishment in our own country and generally throughout the civilized world.

The earliest acts of any government on the subject, mentioned in the books, either emanated from, or were approved by, a King of England.

In 1403 and 1406, Henry IV issued orders to his admirals and other officers, entitled "Concerning Safety for Fishermen—*De Securitate pro Piscatoribus.*" By an order of October 26, 1403, reciting that it was made pursuant to a treaty between himself and the King of France; and for the greater safety of the fishermen of either country, and so that they could be, and carry on their industry, the more safely on the sea, and deal with each other in peace; and that the French King had consented that English fishermen should be treated likewise; it was ordained that French fishermen might, during the then pending season for the herring fishery, safely fish for herrings and all other fish, from the harbor of Gravelines and the island of Thanet to the mouth of the Seine and the harbor of Hautoune. And by an order of October 5, 1406, he took into his safe conduct, and under his special protection, guardianship and defence, all and singular the fishermen of France, Flanders and Brittany, with their fishing vessels and boats, everywhere on the sea, through and within his dominions, jurisdictions and territories, in regard to their fishery, while sailing, coming and going,

and, at their pleasure, freely and lawfully fishing, delaying or proceeding, and returning homeward with their catch of fish, without any molestation or hindrance whatever; and also their fish, nets, and other property and goods soever; and it was therefore ordered that such fishermen should not be interfered with, provided they should comport themselves well and properly, and should not, by color of these presents, do or attempt, or presume to do or attempt, anything that could prejudice the King, or his kingdom of England, or his subjects. 8 Rymer's Foedera, 336, 451.

The treaty made October 2, 1521, between the Emperor Charles V and Francis I of France, through their ambassadors, recited that a great and fierce war had arisen between them, because of which there had been, both by land and by sea, frequent depredations and incursions on either side, to the grave detriment and intolerable injury of the innocent subjects of each; and that a suitable time for the herring fishery was at hand, and, by reason of the sea being beset by the enemy, the fishermen did not dare to go out, whereby the subject of their industry, bestowed by heaven to allay the hunger of the poor, would wholly fail for the year, unless it were otherwise provided—*quo fit, ut piscaturæ commoditas, ad pauperum levandam famem a cælesti numine concessa, cessare hoc anno omnino debeat, nisi aliter provideatur.* And it was therefore agreed that the subjects of each sovereign, fishing in the sea, or exercising the calling of fishermen, could and might, until the end of the next January, without incurring any attack, depredation, molestation, trouble or hindrance soever, safely and freely, everywhere in the sea, take herrings and every other kind of fish, the existing war by land and sea notwithstanding; and further that, during the time aforesaid, no subject of either sovereign should commit, or attempt or presume to commit, any depredation, force, violence, molestation or vexation, to or upon such fishermen, or their vessels, supplies, equipments, net and fish, or other goods soever truly appertaining to fishing. The treaty was made at Calais, then an English possession. It recites that the ambassadors of the two sovereigns met there at the earnest request of Henry VIII, and with his countenance, and in the presence of Cardinal Wolsey, his chancellor and representative. And towards the end of the treaty it is agreed that the said King and his said representative, "by whose means the treaty stands concluded, shall be conservators of the agreements therein, as if thereto by both parties elected and chosen." 4 Dumont, Corps Diplomatique, pt. 1, pp. 352, 353.

* * *

The doctrine which exempts coast fishermen with their vessels and cargoes from capture as prize of war has been familiar to the United States from the time of the War of Independence.

On June 5, 1779, Louis XVI, our ally in that war, addressed a letter to his admiral, informing him that the wish he had always had of alleviating, as far as he could, the hardships of war, had directed his attention to that class of his subjects which devoted itself to the trade of fishing, and had no other means of livelihood; that he had thought that the example which he should give to his enemies, and which could have no other source than the sentiments of humanity which inspired him, would determine them to allow to fishermen the same facilities which he should consent to grant; and that he had therefore given orders to the commanders of all his ships not to disturb English fishermen, nor to arrest their vessels laden with fresh fish, even if not caught by those vessels; provided they had no offensive arms, and were not proved to have made any signals creating a suspicion of intelligence with the enemy; and the admiral was directed to communicate the King's intentions to all officers under his control. . . .

* * *

In the treaty of 1785 between the United States and Prussia, article 23, (which was proposed by the American Commissioners, John Adams, Benjamin Franklin and Thomas Jefferson, and is said to have been drawn up by Franklin,) provided that, if war should arise between the contracting parties, "all women and children, scholars of every faculty, cultivators of the earth, artisans, manufacturers and fishermen, unarmed and inhabiting unfortified towns, villages or places, and in general all others whose occupations are for the common subsistence and benefit of mankind, shall be allowed to continue their respective employments, and shall not be molested in their persons; . . ."

* * *

Since the United States became a nation, the only serious interruptions, so far as we are informed, of the general recognition of the exemption of coast fishing vessels from hostile capture, arose out of the mutual suspicions and recriminations of England and France during the wars of the French Revolution.

* * *

On January 24, 1798, the English Government, by express order, instructed the commanders of its ships to seize French and Dutch fishermen with their boats. 6 Martens, Recueil des Traités, (2d ed.) 505; 6 Schoell, Histoire des Traités, 119; 2 Ortolan, 53. After the promulgation of that order, Lord Stowell (then Sir William Scott) in the High Court of Admiralty of England condemned small Dutch fishing vessels as prize of war. In one case, the capture was in April, 1798, and the decree was made November 13, 1798. *The Young Jacob and Johanna*, 1 C. Rob. 20. . . .

* * *

Lord Stowell's judgment in *The Young Jacob and Johanna*, 1 C. Rob. 20, above cited, was much relied on by the counsel for the United States, and deserves careful consideration.

The vessel there condemned is described in the report as "a small Dutch fishing vessel taken April, 1798, on her return from the Dogger bank to Holland;" and Lord Stowell, in delivering judgment, said: "In former wars, it has not been usual to make captures of these small fishing vessels; but this rule was a rule of comity only, and not of legal decision; it has prevailed from views of mutual accommodation between neighboring countries, and from tenderness to a poor and industrious order of people. . . ."

* * *

. . . The word "comity" was apparently used by Lord Stowell as synonymous with courtesy or good will. But the period of a hundred years which has since elapsed is amply sufficient to have enabled what originally may have rested in custom or comity, courtesy or concession, to grow, by the general assent of civilized nations, into a settled rule of international law. As well said by Sir James Mackintosh: "In the present century a slow and silent, but very substantial mitigation has taken place in the practice of war; and in proportion as that mitigated practice has received the sanction of time, it is raised from the rank of mere usage, and becomes part of the law of nations." Discourse on the Law of Nations, 38; 1 Miscellaneous Works, 360.

* * *

In the war with Mexico in 1846, the United States recognized the exemption of coast fishing boats from capture. In proof of this, counsel have referred to records of the Navy Department, which this court is clearly authorized to consult upon such a question. *Jones* v. *United States*, 137 U. S. 202; *Underhill* v. *Hernandez*, 168 U. S. 250, 253.

By those records it appears that Commodore Conner, commanding the Home Squadron blockading the east coast of Mexico, on May 14, 1846, wrote a letter from the ship Cumberland, off Brazos Santiago, near the southern point of Texas, to Mr. Bancroft, the Secretary of the Navy, enclosing a copy of the commodore's "instructions to the commanders of the vessels of the Home Squadron, showing the principles to be observed in the blockade of the Mexican ports," one of which was that "Mexican boats engaged in fishing on any part of the coast will be allowed to pursue their labors unmolested;" and that on June 10, 1846, those instructions were approved by the Navy Department, of which Mr. Bancroft was still the head, and continued to be until he was appointed Minister to England in September following. Although Commodore Conner's instructions and the Department's approval thereof do not appear in any contemporary publication of the Government, they evidently became generally known at the time, or soon after; for it is stated in several treatises on international law (beginning with Ortolan's second edition, published in 1853) that the United States in the Mexican War permitted the coast fishermen of the enemy to continue the free exercise of their industry. . . .

* * *

International law is part of our law, and must be ascertained and administered by the courts of justice of appropriate jurisdiction, as often as questions of right depending upon it are duly presented for their determination. For this purpose, where there is no treaty, and no controlling executive or legislative act or judicial decision, resort must be had to the customs and usages of civilized nations; and, as evidence of these, to the works of jurists and commentators, who by years of labor, research and experience, have made themselves peculiarly well acquainted with the subjects of which they treat. Such works are resorted to by judicial tribunals, not for the speculations of their authors concerning what the law ought to be, but for trustworthy evidence of what the law really is. *Hilton* v. *Guyot*, 159 U. S. 113, 163, 164, 214, 215.

Wheaton places, among the principal sources of international law, "Text-writers of authority, showing what is the approved usage of nations, or the general opinion respecting their mutual conduct, with the definitions and modifications introduced by general consent." As to these he forcibly observes: "Without wishing to exaggerate the importance of these writers, or to substitute, in any case, their authority for the principles of reason, it may be affirmed that they are generally impartial in their judgment. They are witnesses of the sentiments and usages of civilized nations, and the weight of their testimony increases every time that their authority is invoked by statesmen, and every year that passes without the rules laid down in their works being impugned by the avowal of contrary principles." Wheaton's International Law, (8th ed.) § 15.

Chancellor Kent says: "In the absence of higher and more authoritative sanctions, the ordinances of foreign States, the opinions of eminent statesmen, and the writings of distinguished jurists, are regarded as of great consideration on questions not settled by conventional law. In cases where the principal jurists agree, the presumption will be very great in favor of the solidity of their maxims; and no civilized nation, that does not arrogantly set all ordinary law and justice at defiance,

will venture to disregard the uniform sense of the established writers on international law." 1 Kent Com. 18.

* * *

Ortolan, in the fourth edition of his *Règles Internationales et Diplomatie de la Mer*, published in 1864, after stating the general rule that the vessels and cargoes of subjects of the enemy are lawful prize, says: "Nevertheless, custom admits an exception in favor of boats engaged in the coast fishery; these boats, as well as their crews, are free from capture and exempt from all hostilities. The coast fishing industry is, in truth, wholly pacific, and of much less importance, in regard to the national wealth that it may produce, than maritime commerce or the great fisheries. Peaceful and wholly inoffensive, those who carry it on, among whom women are often seen, may be called the harvesters of the territorial seas, since they confine themselves to gathering in the products thereof; they are for the most part poor families who seek in this calling hardly more than the means of gaining their livelihood." 2 Ortolan, 51. . . .

* * *

The modern German books on international law, cited by the counsel for the appellants, treat the custom, by which the vessels and implements of coast fishermen are exempt from seizure and capture, as well established by the practice of nations. Heffter, § 137; 2 Kaltenborn, § 237, p. 480; Bluntschli, § 667; Perels, § 37, p. 217.

* * *

Jan Helenus Ferguson, Netherlands Minister to China, and previously in the naval and in the colonial service of his country, in his Manual of International Law for the Use of Navies, Colonies and Consulates, published in 1882, writes: "An exception to the usage of capturing enemy's private vessels at sea is the coast fishery." "This principle of immunity from capture of fishing boats is generally adopted by all maritime powers, and in actual warfare they are universally spared so long as they remain harmless." 2 Ferguson, § 212.

* * *

This review of the precedents and authorities on the subject appears to us abundantly to demonstrate that at the present day, by the general consent of the civilized nations of the world, and independently of any express treaty or other public act, it is an established rule of international law, founded on considerations of humanity to a poor and industrious order of men, and of the mutual convenience of belligerent States, that coast fishing vessels, with their implements and supplies, cargoes and crews, unarmed, and honestly pursuing their peaceful calling of catching and bringing in fresh fish, are exempt from capture as prize of war.

The exemption, of course, does not apply to coast fishermen or their vessels, if employed for a warlike purpose, or in such a way as to give aid or information to the enemy; nor when military or naval operations create a necessity to which all private interests must give way.

Nor has the exemption been extended to ships or vessels employed on the high sea in taking whales or seals, or cod or other fish which are not brought fresh to market, but are salted or otherwise cured and made a regular article of commerce.

This rule of international law is one which prize courts, administering the law of nations, are bound to take judicial notice of, and to give effect to, in the absence of any treaty or other public act of their own government in relation to the matter.

* * *

Upon the facts proved in either case, it is the duty of this court, sitting as the highest prize court of the United States, and administering the law of nations, to declare and adjudge that the capture was unlawful, and without probable cause; and it is therefore, in each case,

Ordered, that the decree of the District Court be reversed, and the proceeds of the sale of the vessel, together with the proceeds of any sale of her cargo, be restored to the claimant, with damages and costs.

Case Concerning Right of Passage Over Indian Territory (Portugal v. India), Preliminary Objections*

International Court of Justice, 1957

Dissenting opinion of JUDGE CHAGLA.

* * *

Now what is the subject-matter of the dispute between Portugal and India? I will not consider the various metamorphoses which Portugal's claim has undergone. But as finally indicated to this Court it is a right of transit between Daman and the Portuguese enclaves of Dadrá and Nagar-Aveli in order to maintain communications between Daman and these two enclaves. . . .

* * *

. . . it is an elementary principle of international law that a State has exclusive competence within its own territory. This principle was emphatically pronounced by Chief Justice Marshall in the *Schooner Exchange* case (1812, 7 Cranch 116): "The jurisdiction of the nation within its

* Reprinted from *International Court of Justice Reports* 175 (1957).

own territory is necessarily exclusive and absolute. It is susceptible of no limitation not imposed by itself. Any restriction upon it, deriving validity from an external source, would imply a diminution of its sovereignty to the extent of the restriction, and an investment of that sovereignty to the same extent in that power which could impose such restriction. All exceptions, therefore, to the full and complete power of a nation within its own territories, must be traced up to the consent of the nation itself. They can flow from no other legitimate source." It is not suggested by Portugal that India has ever given her consent to any limitation upon her territorial sovereignty over the territory in question. Although in her Memorial Portugal relied upon treaties between the Maratha rulers and herself, this contention was given up or at least not pressed at the hearing. As a matter of fact, the only treaty which deals with this subject at all is the Portuguese-Maratha Treaty of 1741, which, surprising as it may seem, provides expressly that soldiers of either power are not to enter the territory of the other without permission. If, therefore, India has not given her consent to any limitation upon her sovereignty, is there any other international obligation undertaken by India independently of any treaty or her consent? I may observe in passing that Portugal concedes that the right of transit claimed by her, even though it may be without any immunity, does constitute a limitation upon India's sovereignty.

An international obligation may arise through local custom. If for a considerable period of time Portugal has been exercising this right, then the right may be upheld by international law. But in order that local custom should be established, it is not sufficient for Portugal merely to state that for a long period she maintained communications between Daman and the enclaves. She must go further and establish that the transit facilities that she had were enjoyed by her as a matter of right and not as a matter of grace or concession on the part of the Indian Government. And if one thing is clear beyond anything else from the record that we have before us, it is that throughout the period in question —from 1818 when the British appeared on the scene onwards—the facilities enjoyed by Portugal with regard to communicating with her enclaves were entirely at the discretion of the Indian Government and they were granted to Portugal as a matter of grace and indulgence. The Indian Government always reserved to itself the right to control the passage or transit facilities and even, if occasion arose, to prohibit it altogether. We have instances where a complete embargo was placed by the Indian Government on the carriage of certain goods. We have instances where no less a person than the Consul-General of Portugal reminded the Governor of Diu that authorization by the British authorities was indispensable before any Portuguese troops could cross British territory. Therefore, India is right when she says that a right of passage subject to be revoked in whole or in part by somebody else is not a right at all. I think that Portugal realizes the weakness of her case under this head and therefore what has been really urged before us by Portugal is that this right which she claims is warranted by general principles of international law. General principles of international law would be applicable if Portugal establishes a general custom in contradistinction to a local custom by which a State has the right to have access to enclaves by transit facilities being given to her in order to maintain communications between herself and her enclaves. Now the only general custom which is comparable to the question we have to consider which international law recognizes is the right of innocent passage in territorial seas and in maritime parts of international rivers, and also immunity given to diplomatic representatives when they are in transit between one

State and another. No general custom has ever been established permitting a State to have access to her enclaves as of right. Portugal has relied on a learned study made by Professor Bauer of other enclaves, but this study only shows that the right of passage either arises out of treaty or out of local custom which is not applicable to the present case.

A principle of international law may also be imported from municipal law where the principle in municipal law is universally recognized and when that principle is not in conflict with any rule of international law itself; and the strongest reliance is placed by Portugal on the principle of municipal law which may be described as an easement of necessity. It is said that when you have an owner of land and his land is surrounded by the lands of other owners, the former has a right of access to a public road. This right of access arises out of necessity because but for this access the owner would be landlocked and would not be able to get out of his land, and therefore, in these circumstances, municipal law presupposes a right of way in the first owner over the lands of other owners. In my opinion, it would be extremely unsafe to draw an analogy between the rights of an owner and the obligations of other owners under municipal law and the rights and obligations of States under international law. There can be no comparison between private property and territorial sovereignty nor can there be any comparison between a citizen and a sovereign State. A sovereign State can pass any legislation affecting private property. It can compel the owner of land to cede any right to neighbouring owners. But that surely cannot be true of territorial sovereigns. Portugal cannot compel India to cede any right to her nor can India be placed under any obligation because Portugal is a under necessity to have access to her enclaves. Further, such a rule would obviously be in contradiction with the one undisputed well-established principle of international law, namely, territorial sovereignty, and therefore there is no scope for importing this principle of municipal law into the domain of international law.

Even in municipal law parties may agree as to the nature and extent of an easement, and if parties agree, then municipal law will not presume an easement of necessity. In this case, the relations between Portugal and the territorial sovereign of India clearly demonstrate that the conditions of Portugal's passage or transit over Indian territory were clearly settled and those conditions were that Portugal had no right to a passage or transit but she could only be afforded such facilities as the Indian Government, in its absolute discretion, thought fit to concede. Therefore, Portugal has failed to make out any case, let alone an arguable case, that India's discretion with regard to this particular subject-matter, which clearly falls within her own domestic jurisdiction, is controlled by any international obligation or that there is any rule of international law which takes this matter out of the reserved domain. Under the circumstances, I think that the Court should uphold this Objection raised by India and should decide that there is no necessity for further investigation of the facts and no useful purpose would be served by joining this Objection to the hearing.

* * *

Remarks on the Juridical Nature of Customary Norms of International Law*

G. I. Tunkin

* * *

Formation of a custom constitutes a definite stage in the process of formation of a customary norm of international law.

* Reprinted from G. I. Tunkin, "Remarks on the Juridical Nature of Customary Norms of International Law," 49 *California Law Review* 421 (1961), by permission of the publisher. Copyright, ©, 1961 California Law Review, Inc.

The consummation of this process is the recognition by the states of the custom as juridically binding, in other words, recognition of a customary rule of conduct as a norm of international law. Only as a result of such recognition is the process of formation of a customary norm of international law completed, and international custom (usage) becomes an international law custom, *i.e.*, a customary norm of international law.

* * *

Such recognition or acceptance represents a tacit proposal to other states to regard this rule as a norm of international law. If such a tacit proposition is accepted by other states, *i.e.*, if other states demonstrate by their actions that they recognize the given customary rule as juridically binding, it may be taken that a customary norm of international law has appeared.

We thus come to the conclusion that the essence of an international custom as a process or means of creating a norm of international law consists in agreement among states.

* * *

One of the basic arguments adduced against the concept that the essence of custom as a specific means of creating norms of international law lies in agreement between states, is the claim that a customary norm of international law binds the states juridically irrespective of the "recognition" or "acceptance" of this norm by the concrete states. Such arguments are advanced both by the proponents and opponents of *opinio juris*.

To begin with, the claim is made that newly emerging states are bound by existing customary norms of international law, irrespective of their attitude toward these norms. "International customary law," says Verdross, "is binding also upon those states which did not exist at the time

of its inception." The same view is taken by Professor Basdevant: "All agree that a new state is bound by international customs formed prior to the emergence of this state."

This question is directly related to the question of the sphere of action of customary norms of international law. Must a customary norm of international law, created by the long practice of "a large number of states," be binding upon all other states, regardless of their attitude to the norm? This is an important question.

The thesis that a customary norm of international law recognized by a large number of states is binding upon all other states is widely supported in the modern international law literature of the West.

An interesting reservation is made by Professor Verdross who says that "although the formation of a general customary norm does not infer its application by all states, no general customary law can appear that contradicts the legal views of any civilized nation." But if recognition of a new customary norm of international law as such is required from an existing state, why must a newly emerging state find itself in an inferior position? Why cannot this new state object to any customary norm of international law if it disagrees with it?

The concept that customary norms of international law accepted as such by a large number of states must be binding upon all other states is actually based upon the presumption that the majority of states is able in international relations to dictate norms of international law to all other states. This concept was brought to its logical conclusion by Professor Quadri. Amplifying his conception of a "collective and social will" (*volontà collettiva è sociale*), Quadri says that the will—the decision of a group of states—can create in international relations juridical norms binding upon all states; in other words, create norms of general international law. According to Quadri, international law is founded upon "the decision of the preponderous force of the international community." In another work Quadri explains what he means by "preponderous force." He writes: "It is enough to have the will, decision, and action common to a definite group capable, if necessary, of imposing its power."

This conception is in crying contradiction with the basic generally recognized principles of modern international law, the principle of equality of states, in particular.

It is beyond dispute that equality of states signifies only juridical equality, which may not accord with the actual inequality of states in international relations. There is a certain contradiction here between the real relations and juridical relations. No doubt the position of the majority of states, the Great Powers in the first place, is of decisive significance in the creation of generally accepted norms of international law. Such is the factual position. Juridically, however, the wills of the different states in the process of creation of norms of international law are equivalent to each other. This juridical equality is of great importance. It means that in international relations no group of states, not even the majority of states, can create norms binding upon other states, or has the right to attempt to impose these norms upon other states.

Customary norms of international law being a result of agreement among states, the sphere of action of such norms is limited to the relations between the states which accepted these norms as norms of international law, *i.e.*, the states participating in this tacit agreement.

The sphere of action of a customary principle or customary norm of international law may gradually expand. This, as a rule, is the way customary norms of international law become generally recognized norms. There are several cases of the declaration of a single state becoming a point of departure. Many principles of international law were proclaimed, for instance, by revolutionary France in the 18th century. Among them were the principles of respect of state sovereignty, non-interference in the internal affairs of another state, equality of states, and the principle that war operations must be directed against military objects only and cannot be directed against the civilian population. The Soviet state has advanced the principle of banning aggressive wars and treating such wars as crimes, the principle of self-determination of nations, the principle of peaceful co-existence, and a number of other principles of international law. In all these cases, the principles originally proclaimed by a single state were gradually recognized by other states and have become, partly by custom and partly by treaty, generally recognized principles of modern international law.

This proposition about the spheres of influence of customary norms is of special significance to modern international law, which regulates the relations between states belonging to two opposed social systems. Only a customary rule which is recognized by the states of both systems can now be regarded as a customary norm of international law.

The will of the states expressed in their recognition of a customary norm of international law is a determinist will. Force of circumstances compels the individual states in most cases to recognize as binding those norms which have already been recognized by the overwhelming majority of states belonging to both systems, including the Great Powers. But such a *de facto* position should not be confused with the *de jure* position.

As for the newly emerging states, they have the juridical right not to recognize this or that customary norm of international law. However, if a new state enters without reservations into official relations with other states, this means that it recognizes a certain body of principles and norms of existing international law, which constitute the basic principles of international relations.

The concept that customary norms of international law recognized as such by a large number of states are binding upon all states not only has no foundation in modern international law but is fraught with grave danger. This concept in essence justifies the attempts made by one group of states to impose upon other states, the socialist states, for instance, or the newly emerging states of Asia and Africa, certain customary norms which, while regarded perhaps by this group of states as customary norms of international law, have never been accepted by the new states and which may prove partly or wholly unacceptable to these new states. Obviously, this tendency to dictate norms of international law to other states is, under present conditions, doomed to failure. But it is no less obvious that such attempts at dictation may lead to grave international complications.

In practically all cases when it is necessary to establish the existence of one or another generally recognized norm of international law, the usual procedure is to investigate if "universal practice" exists; and in case such practice does exist, if it has been recognized as a norm of law, and how many states have recognized such practice as a norm of law.

It may be assumed that recognition of one or another rule as a norm of international law by a large number of states can serve as a basis for the assumption that this norm has won general recognition. However, this is an assumption only, and not a final conclusion.

There is no disputing the fact that it is not always possible, and in most cases even impossible, to determine with mathematical precision that a certain customary norm of international law has been recognized by all states, without exception. But such a situation arises quite frequently in social phenomena, and the difficulties which may come up in the process of such calculation cannot be regarded as undermining the rule itself.

This, it appears to us, was how the International Law Commission acted whenever the question arose of whether this or that customary norm of international law exists. Thus, upon considering the question of the privileges and immunities of the administrative and technical staffs, as well as the service staffs of diplomatic missions, the Commission found that in this sphere "there is no uniformity in the practice of States. . . ." Some of the states (the U.S.A., Great Britain, the Soviet Union, and others) grant diplomatic privileges and immunities to the administrative and technical staffs on the basis of reciprocity, others grant them even to the service staffs of foreign diplomatic missions, although the range of privileges and immunities granted varies considerably. Considering that there is no universal practice in this matter, the Commission easily arrived at the conclusion "that in these circumstances it cannot be claimed that there is a rule of international law on the subject. . . ."

On the question of exemption from customs duties of articles for personal use by diplomats, the Commission noted: "In general, customs duties are . . . not collected on articles intended for the personal use of the diplomatic agent or the members of his family belonging to his household (including articles intended for his establishment)." The Commission thus arrived at the conclusion that in this case the practice of exemption from customs duties is in essence universal. At the same time, the Commission noted that such exemption from customs duties "has been regarded as based on international comity." The Commission thus drew the conclusion that while this is a case of universal practice, this practice has not yet been recognized as a norm of law. On its part, the Commission proposed that "since, however, the practice is so generally current, the Commission considers that it should be accepted as a rule of international law." The Commission embodied this proposal in the draft Convention on diplomatic relations and immunities prepared by it.

The conclusion which we should like to formulate is that agreement between states lies at the basis of the process by which customary norms of international law are created.

This concept of agreement conforms to the law governing social development in our time. Inasmuch as the existence of sovereign states at present is historically conditioned, norms of international law binding upon them in their interrelations can appear only by agreement between them. Agreement between states on the basis of equality is the essence of the norm-formation process in customary international law. It is particularly characteristic of the period of co-existence of states belonging to opposed social systems, since the existence of two opposed systems further accentuates the impossibility of creating norms of law binding upon the states of both systems, except by agreement between them based on equality.

The concept of agreement rules out all attempts to dictate or gamble with votes in international relations. It accords with the interests of preserving and consolidating peace. Sound international law and order can be achieved only by negotiation and agreement between the states of the two social systems, on the basis of respect of their sovereignty and equality and rejection of all attempts to interfere in their internal affairs.

OBLIGATION TO OBEY INTERNATIONAL LAW

It is understandable that legal philosophers influenced by Austinian definitions and laymen in the habit of thinking of law in familiar criminal law terms would question the legal character of international law. It is unfortunate, however, that these doubts have contributed to the popular myth that international law is generally disregarded. The truth is that state officials normally observe the rules and principles of international law and almost always profess to do so. Why do they accord such importance to a body of norms that was not enacted by a supreme lawgiver and is not enforced by centralized agencies?

The possibility of incurring sanctions provides a partial answer. Offended states have resorted to such devices as economic pressures, blockades, and even war to bring a delinquent state to terms. And this self-help system, although riddled with weaknesses, has not been altogether ineffective: diplomatic history is replete with examples of states, upon the demand of other states, making public apologies, paying reparations, ceding territory, and in other ways compensating for illegal acts. But powerful states have been more effective than weak states in pressing their claims and in resisting the claims of others. And even the powerful states, engaged as they are in the politics of conflict and cooperation among themselves, have often found their power to be ineffective when enforcing compliance with the law.

There are considerations other than fear of incurring sanctions that direct state officials toward compliance with the norms of international law. Of particular importance is a general awareness of the need for order and stability in international relations. Reciprocal advantages are also gained from general observance of most of these norms, which, after all, were created by state consent and agreement. Habit and the bureaucratic nature of modern foreign offices also lead to the routine observance of the law. National decision-makers, operating within the complex bureaucratic structure of the modern state, tend naturally to prefer, and, perhaps even to require, a rule-governed environment in which to work.[1] The influence of world opinion, as articulated in the United Nations, should not be omitted from a listing of factors that tend to promote compliance with international law. There is considerable evidence, for example, to support the view that the United States, "in abandoning its abortive intervention against the Castro régime in 1961, was guided in considerable measure by the reluctance to engage in what legally was an act of aggression, in defiance of the Charter and organized world opinion."[2] The observance of international law, like all law, is fostered ultimately by self-interest, convenience, habit, and a sense of moral obligation.

In the following selections, the obligation of states to observe the norms of international law is discussed from three perspectives. J. L. Brierly treats the matter philosophically by discussing the "ultimate explanation of the binding nature of all law." Morton A. Kaplan and Nicholas deB. Katzenbach then discuss the political reasons for norm compliance by stressing their view that national interests are promoted by such behavior. Finally, excerpts from "Perspectives of the Newly Independent States on the Binding Quality of International Law" by S. Prakash Sinha

present the attitude of many of the states of Asia and Africa toward the binding nature of norms that they did not participate in creating.

"Order and Not Chaos"*

J. L. Brierly

There need be no mystery about the source of the obligation to obey international law. The same problem arises in any system of law and it can never be solved by a merely *juridical* explanation. The answer must be sought outside the law, and it is for legal philosophy to provide it. The notion that the validity of international law raises some peculiar problem arises from the confusion which the doctrine of sovereignty has introduced into international legal theory. Even when we do not believe in the absoluteness of state sovereignty we have allowed ourselves to be persuaded that the fact of their sovereignty makes it necessary to look for some specific quality, not to be found in other kinds of law, in the law to which states are subject. We have accepted a false idea of the state as a personality with a life and a will of its own, still living in a 'state of nature', and we contrast this with the 'political' state in which individual men have come to live. But this assumed condition of states is the very negation of law, and no ingenuity can explain how the two can exist together. It is a notion as false analytically as it admittedly is historically. The truth is that states are not persons, however convenient it may often be to personify them; they are merely *institutions*,

---

[1] "A bureaucrat called upon to act on behalf of the state would not normally even consider that the commission of a violation [of international law] to promote national policy was an option open to him. Of course, there exist both a wide range of discretion to interpret rules, and many areas within which rules . . . are not established, but the whole impulse of a bureaucratized response is to find a consistent formula that can deal with recurrent situations and that will be acceptable to as many of the relevant actors as possible." Richard A. Falk, "New Approaches to the Study of International Law," 61 *American Journal of International Law* 480 (1967).
[2] Wolfgang Friedmann, *The Changing Structure of International Law* (New York: Columbia University Press, 1964), p. 87. Professor Friedmann points out that world opinion is more potent in some situations than in others: "When the U.S.S.R. bloodily suppressed the Hungarian Revolution in 1956, it judged, rightly, that the strength of its national interest in the preservation of the existing puppet regime, combined with her overwhelming logistic advantages *vis-à-vis* the forces of the West, whether organized inside or outside the United Nations, made armed intervention and violation of the Charter an acceptable risk." *Ibid.*

* Reprinted from J. L. Brierly, *The Law of Nations*, 6th ed. by Sir Humphrey Waldock (New York and Oxford: Oxford University Press, 1963), pp. 54–56, by permission of the publisher.

that is to say, organizations which men establish among themselves for securing certain objects, of which the most fundamental is a system of order within which the activities of their common life can be carried on. They have no wills except the wills of the individual human beings who direct their affairs; and they exist not in a political vacuum but in continuous political relations with one another. Their subjection to law is as yet imperfect, though it is real as far as it goes; the problem of extending it is one of great practical difficulty, but it is not one of intrinsic impossibility. There are important differences between international law and the law under which individuals live in a state, but those differences do not lie in metaphysics or in any mystical qualities of the entity called state sovereignty.

The international lawyer then is under no special obligation to explain why the law with which he is concerned should be binding upon its subjects. If it were true that the essence of all law is a command, and that what makes the law of the state binding is that for some reason, for which no satisfactory explanation can ever be given, the will of the person issuing a command is superior to that of the person receiving it, then indeed it would be necessary to look for some special explanation of the binding force of international law. But that view of the nature of law has been long discredited. If we are to explain why any kind of law is binding, we cannot avoid some such assumption as that which the Middle Ages made, and which Greece and Rome had made before them, when they spoke of natural law. The ultimate explanation of the binding force of all law is that man, whether he is a single individual or whether he is associated with other men in a state, is constrained, in so far as he is a reasonable being, to believe that order and not chaos is the governing principle of the world in which he has to live.

"States Obey International Law Norms Because They Have an Interest in Doing So"*

Morton A. Kaplan and
Nicholas deB. Katzenbach

Among the cynical reasons for discounting the influence of norms in international politics is the claim that states are interested only in increasing their power, or, more modestly, that unless states strive for power they will fail to survive. The authors think that both formulations are unsound; the first descriptively and the second theoretically. States do observe norms because their leaders want to live in a lawful world and . . . because they have an interest in doing so. The latter conclusion is less obvious in present-day bipolarity than it was during the "balance of power" period, but we believe that this interest is present to some extent even today.

*   *   *

It might . . . be conceded that the values of nations differ and that their international behavior also differs. A more sophisticated version of the cynical position still might contend that in the last analysis nations would implement only national and not international values. We think that this position undervalues the extent to which it is important to strengthen rules that serve to restrain all nations. It is true that almost every norm of international law has been broken at one time or another and that some states are less constrained by a recognition of the importance of normative behavior than others. We do not deny this. We believe, however, that many writers fail to distinguish between frequent

* Reprinted from Morton A. Kaplan and Nicholas deB. Katzenbach, *The Political Foundations of International Law* (New York: John Wiley & Sons, 1961), pp. 341–347, by permission of the publisher.

efforts to change rules and relatively rare rule-less behavior.

In the nineteenth century, for instance, many nations might on specific situations have derived gains from violating the rules concerning the conduct of war or the treatment of property in occupied territory that would have outweighed reprisals possible in the particular case. They would, however, have weakened the general rule and this would have been to their disadvantage. Once a rule is weakened, it is not always easy to renegotiate a new rule. A new bargaining situation develops; there are competing alternatives; and, even if all parties to a dispute prefer some agreement to none, the inability to find some clear rule that naturally secures agreement may result in no agreement. This explains, in part, the durability of recognized "customary" rules and the self-restraint of nations where the potential injured party is helpless to withstand demands made upon him. Even where the norm itself has become undesirable to some of the important actors on the international scene, they may be cautious about violating it, lest the general rule of law be weakened. And, even where they break the old norm because they can no longer abide by it, they may attempt to justify this in terms of other norms or by a reinterpretation of the old norm. This should not be viewed as mere hypocrisy, for it plays an important role in maintaining the rule of law in international affairs. It is one way of "legislating" change; and, precisely because of its irregular nature, may in fact be used more sparingly than legislative change in municipal politics.

Nor should we underestimate the extent to which law-abiding behavior is strongly protective of a nation's interests. A reputation for principled behavior is an asset for nations as well as for individuals despite the factors in international politics that make it somewhat more difficult to remain virtuous than in ordinary civil life.

One obvious instance is that it is important to be dependable. . . .

* * *

. . . Churchill understood better than most . . . the importance of the reputation of virtuous behavior. A splendid instance of this understanding occurred when scarce British forces were removed from the desperate struggle for Egypt to the hopeless defense of Greece. Churchill understood, however, in this dark hour that Great Britain's reputation for honoring its commitments was an important asset that had to be preserved even at great cost under conditions of high risk.

A reputation for principled behavior is highly advantageous for a nation. Its agreements are respected and its offers more acceptable because they can be counted on. . . . These are generalities of course; the heritage of colonialism has done much to create suspicions that principled behavior can do little to diminish. And the United States is still bearing the cross of "dollar diplomacy" with respect to Latin American affairs. We do not deny that contingencies of this sort modify general principles, but we think they still hold. Particularly as we move from the response of the masses to those of professional diplomats do the differences in behavior become important. Whatever reasons some may have had to oppose the American actions in Lebanon— and there were in many cases important political reasons—few professional diplomats thought the United States was attempting to institute colonial rule and therefore that they had to oppose it as urgently as otherwise might have been the case. This is an important consideration for the United States, which is unable or unwilling to use force in the same way as the Soviet Union.

But there is another side to the coin. A principled nation, with a reputation for being principled, is less subject to blackmail and hard bargaining techniques than a nation that continually trims corners to gain some advantage. No one thinks of asking Brooks Brothers to give a cash discount, or of asking Albert Schweitzer to pay graft to get his medicines. No one would have attempted to blackmail Gandhi.

If we move to the international realm, we can think of many cases in which the United States, for instance, is in a weakened bargaining position if it does not stand on principle. Egypt, for instance, can point out that it can hardly pay for the United States to force Egypt into a pro-Soviet position by actively supporting Israel on the Suez Canal issue with respect to the passage of Israeli cargoes. If, however, the United States establishes clear principles governing its policies and demonstrates that it intends to follow those principles, regardless of what that decision costs in any individual instance, the United States becomes a virtual force of nature with respect to its behavior pattern and other nations will be deterred from attempting to exploit the situation to their advantage. If the United States has committed itself to certain principles of action and is willing to lose Egypt rather than to renege on its principles, Egypt might hesitate before backing itself into a corner.

Commitment to principle is not an advantage if it is engaged in mechanically. A nation ought to commit itself only to principles with which it can live—and with which others can also live. Principles that do not give promise of a durable and acceptable international order are likely to stir only rigid opposition rather than acceptance. Moreover, principles cannot be asserted merely as a bluff, for the bluff may be called. To be effective the commitment to principle must be credible in terms of a nation's institutions, its values, and its character. A weak and flabby nation, subject to the political pressures of a satisfied and cowardly public, will not be convincing if it attempts to take a strong international stand. Moreover, even under the best circumstances, the commitment to principle will involve costs, for often other nations will remain unconvinced or, for reasons of their own, will feel that they cannot agree to the solution for which the principles call. We do not assert that commitment to principle always works, but we do feel that we have explained one of the reasons why some nations have committed themselves to principle in the past and why others may do so in the future. And this, in turn, helps, in part, to explain the strength of the normative structure of international law.

In non-zero-sum games like international politics an important part of the play involves influencing the alternatives open to other players, their expectations, and, thus, their future behavior. The expectation that a nation will give way on its principles encourages demands that it give way, and may help to create a situation in which normative behavior breaks down if other nations do not exercise self-restraint. In such a case the international system is either transformed in an undesirable way or the rule of the jungle prevails. The strategy of a nation cannot be divorced from the kind of political order it desires to establish.

Every time the United States compromises its obligations—as in the failure to enforce the Security Council resolution on Israeli passage through the Suez Canal—in order to avoid some immediate undesirable consequence, it demonstrates its susceptibility to blackmail and encourages further blackmail attempts. The moment principles are blurred, without being replaced by new principles, there is no longer a clear standard to guide policy. Most concessions are defended on the basis of the immediate or short-run alternatives, without sufficient consideration being given to the possibility that they may open up a process the costs of which are large and indefinite.

This is not an argument for absolute inflexibility or for refusal to bargain. If each nation stood inflexibly on principle, all negotiations and international intercourse would break down. But there are some principles that are of great importance and that can be made generally effective. To acquiesce in or to condone violations of these principles is to surrender a long-term interest for temporary advantage. On the other hand, the principle need not be enforced in each instance. For example, the United States may not be in a position where it is practicable to enforce the Israeli right under the Convention of 1888 and Security Council resolution to passage through the Suez Canal. To attempt to enforce that right quixotically would impair American prestige, and to enforce the right at great cost to other important political interests might be imprudent.

However, to condone Egyptian violation of the law by, for instance, resuming economic aid or supporting Egypt's bid for a Security Council seat, is to surrender a long-term interest for a temporary advantage. The Egyptians view such actions as evidence of an American surrender to their political strength, lose respect for the United States, and resolve to engage in additional blackmail, thereby serving notice to others that blackmail pays. Patience and moderation undoubtedly are admirable qualities in dealing with the suspicious and rebellious leaders of the new nations. But it is a disservice to them also to lead them to anticipate rewards for their lawless behavior when they do not understand the long-term costs they also will have to pay if the normative standards of international law are weakened. And, when the United States stains its honor by fearing the costs of forthright behavior, it undermines its most important permanent interests and betrays those of the free and democratic world for which it bears responsibility in the present bipolar period.

* * *

Perspectives of the Newly Independent States on the Binding Quality of International Law*

S. Prakash Sinha

The texture of international society has changed in recent years. New States have emerged on the Asian and African continents. The newly independent States aspire to be modernising States. Caught in the revolution of rising expectations, they wish "to transform their political, economic and social institutions so that they may have a greater freedom and a greater opportunity to participate in good life."[1] In this process, they have adopted a revolutionary attitude.[2] They emphasise the emergence of a new international order. They challenge some of the rules of international law as not consistent with their view of the new order and they point to the need for international law to reflect a consensus of the entire world community, including theirs, and promote the widest sharing of values. They criticise the system of international law as being a product of relations among imperialist States and of relations of an imperial character between imperialist States and colonial peoples. They challenge the extent of the universality of some of the doctrines of international law. They challenge some specific principles of international law.

However, they do not deny either the existence or the binding force of international law. They resort to its norms in their disputes with other States. They utter its rules in debates in international organisations. They participate in the work of the Sixth (Legal) Committee of the United Nations General Assembly. They make their influence felt in diplomatic conferences convened for codification of international law. They are active participants in the

* Reprinted from S. Prakash Sinha, "Perspectives of the Newly Independent States on the Binding Quality of International Law," 14 *International and Comparative Law Quarterly* 121 (1965), by permission of the publisher.

proceedings of the International Law Commission, such as in the discussion on the law of State responsibility. They have entered into numerous treaties, thereby extending the scope of the application of international law. They have displayed discontent with the contents of traditional international law. But they do not denigrate the role of law in international affairs. Their discontent arises out of their feeling that some of the norms of international law may be opposed to their interests and their desire that international law should incorporate in it certain principles which are dismissed by the Western States as political rather than legal, for example, the concept of self-determination. They hope that "the progressive development of international law would bring about a greater degree of universality through the contributions and the active participation of the many new nations which had emerged on the international scene."[3]

I. Custom

International law consists of customary norms. These norms were established during a period when, for the evidence of custom, it was "enough to show that the general consensus of opinion within the limits of European civilisation is in favour of the rule."[4] The newly independent States do not lend their unqualified acceptance to norms thus established. With their emphasis on social change rather than on maintenance of *status quo*, these States have shown their tendency not to accept the body of customary international law as a whole. Their attitude toward the three-mile limit of the territorial sea in the United Nations Conferences (Geneva) of 1958 and 1960 illustrates their disregard of custom as an all-important source of international law. The views expressed by the representatives of these States in the United Nations at the time of discussing the Declaration of the Granting of Independence to Colonial Countries and Peoples demonstrate

their rejection of customary rules concerning colonies and protectorates.

These new States cannot be expected to accept the thesis that practice of a norm by a group of States may create rules of international law binding upon all States, that, as one scholar argued, international law is based on the "decision of the overwhelming force in the international community."[5] For not all the rules of customary international law are acceptable to them.

2. Treaties

Treaty formulation of international law is favoured by the newly independent States much more than custom as a source of international law. They find that treaties provide them with an opportunity to participate in the formulation of the rules and they are not bound by these unless they accept them. Treaties appear to be an expedient and effective instrument "to develop not only new norms directly by common agreement, but new power arrangements out of which the norms of a law we do not yet have will come."[6]

As to the binding qualities of general legislative treaties adopted before these States attained independence, their attitude is similar to that concerning customary international law.[7] They would accept only those treaties which are based on universally accepted values, including their own, or those which provide an effective basis of reciprocity.

Under the category of treaties "concluded by the Great Powers on behalf of the international community"[8] come those concluded prior to the creation of the League of Nations or the United Nations. Included in this category are such treaties as the Vienna Treaty of 1815 abolishing the slave trade, the Aix-la-Chapelle Treaty of 1818 classifying diplomatic agents, the Paris Treaty of 1856 prohibiting privateering, the London Treaty of 1871 against unilateral renunciaton of obligations, the Berlin Treaty of 1885 and the Brussels

Treaty of 1890 adopting the Congo Basin arrangements in Africa, the various conventions concerning the régime of the straits, and the Constantinople Agreement of 1888 recognising freedom of passage through the Suez Canal. The newly independent States are not likely to accept the extension of treaties having such an origin. Such acceptance, they fear, would mean an admission of inequality. It might be interpreted as recognition of the quality of law-givers assumed by these Great Powers. It might even mean endorsement of some treaties which are in contradiction with the newly independent States' conception of international law and which run counter to their fundamental interests.

The newly independent States believe that political and economic privileges had been extorted by the colonial powers in the past from the peoples of Asia and Africa. On becoming independent, these States increasingly rely on the argument that "unequal" or "inequitable" treaties thus extracted, and treaties imposed by duress, are invalid *ab initio*. Accordingly, they declare that it is the right of the State which was obliged to enter into such treaties to terminate them by denunciation.

Rebus sic stantibus is frequently resorted to by the newly independent States in order to terminate their inherited burdens. The doctrine is invoked by them not only on the basis of justice but also because a treaty fails to accord with the present position of power in the world.

3. General Principles of Law

Just as the representatives of the new doctrines of natural law see in general principles of law justification of their concept so do the newly independent States see in this source an avenue for their legal and value systems to make a contribution to the development of international law. General principles of law are based on the Common legal consciousness of the peoples and form a source of international law which is distinct from general principles of international law, the latter being contained, for most part, in treaties and custom. The significance of this source of international law is heavily impressed in the context of today's international relations due to the rapid growth of the number and the importance of international organisations and of other trans-national arrangements.

Deriving general principles of law would necessitate consideration of legal systems of all civilised societies. It is here that the newly independent States hope to play a role in the creative development of international law. It would enable them to participate in the creation or development of norms of behaviour which they are supposed to observe. Examples of such participation are found when members of their societies assume their role as judges in the International Court of Justice or as members of the International Law Commission.

* * *

Notes

1. K. S. Carlston, "Universality of International Law Today: Challenge and Response" (1962) 8 *Howard Law Journal* 79, 80.
2. G. M. Abi-Saab, "The Newly Independent States and the Scope of Domestic Jurisdiction" (1960) 54 *Proceedings of the American Society of International Law* 84, 90.
3. R. Pal, "Future Role of the International Law Commission in the Changing World" (1962) 9 *United Nations Review* 31 (September).
4. J. Westlake, *International Law*, Part I, Peace (1904), p. 16.
5. R. Quadri, *Diritto internazionale publico* (1956), p. 89.
6. C. T. Oliver, "Historical Development of International Law: Contemporary Problems of Treaty Law" (1955) 88 *Recueil des Cours* 417, 432.
7. G. M. Abi-Saab, "The Newly Independent State and the Rules of International Law: An Outline" (1962) 8 *Howard Law Journal* 95, 107.
8. C. W. Jenks, *Common Law of Mankind* (1958), p. 96.

THE RELATIONSHIP OF INTERNATIONAL LAW TO MUNICIPAL LAW

International law governs the relations *among* states and other international legal persons; municipal law is the law *of* states. The question whether these two types of law are encompassed within a single, unified system or whether they constitute independent, inherently dissimilar systems has produced considerable controversy among legal philosophers. Writers of the monistic persuasion assert that international law and municipal law are two aspects of one system; dualists regard the two as separate and coordinate systems. Monists differ as to which of the two is to be regarded as supreme, while dualists see their relationship as one of coordination rather than of supremacy or subordination. Arguments to support the various positions are derived from state practice and are colored by doctrinal preferences.

Since no doctrinal position seems to encompass all the facts, it is likely that this controversy will continue indefinitely. Practice suggests that, in fact, a mixture of international law supremacy, municipal law supremacy, and coordination of legal systems exists. When, for example, an international tribunal finds that municipal law conflicts with international law, it will override the municipal law.[1] On the other hand, when national judges find municipal law to be in direct and unavoidable conflict with international law, they will normally give primacy to municipal law.[2] These two practices can be used to support the two sides of the monist coin. And the dualist idea of coordination seems to be most descriptive of the practice of United States courts giving primacy in case of conflict between a treaty and a statute to the one that was adopted more recently.[3] "As matters stand, each situation must be analyzed by itself, including the tribunal before which litigation, if any, is brought, in order to settle the question of which of two conflicting rules of law of different orders prevails in the concrete dispute."[4]

It is in the practice of national courts that the relationship of international law to municipal law is of fundamental importance. Lacking adequate enforcement devices of its own, the international community must rely largely upon the governmental organs of the separate states to give effect to its norms. It is common practice for national judges to enforce the rules and principles of international law under the theory that these norms have been incorporated, either by constitutional prescription or by judicial decision, into the municipal law system. National judges also attempt, whenever possible, to interpret statutes in such a way as to avoid conflict with international law.[5] It is only in the

---

[1] See, for example, the *Greco-Bulgarian "Communities"* advisory opinion of the Permanent Court of International Justice, 1930, Ser. B, No. 17, in which the Court stated:

"In the first place, it is a generally accepted principle of international law that in the relations betwen Powers who are contracting Parties to a treaty, the provisions of the municipal law cannot prevail over the treaty.

"In the second place, according to Article 2, paragraph 1, and Article 15 of the Greco-Bulgarian Convention, the two governments have undertaken not to place any restriction on the right of emigration, notwithstanding any municipal law or regulation to the contrary, and to modify their legislation in so far as may be necessary to secure the execution of the Convention.

"In these circumstances, if a proper application of the Convention were in conflict with some local law, the latter would not prevail over the Convention."

[2] See, for example, *Mortensen v. Peters* and *Shri Krishna Sharma v. The State of West Bengal*, relevant portions of which are reprinted in this section on pp. 46 to 50.
[3] Head Money Cases, 112 U.S. 580 (1884); Whitney v. Robertson, 124 U.S. 190 (1888).
[4] Gould, *An Introduction to International Law*, pp. 161–162.
[5] "The statute should be construed in the light of the purpose of the Government to act within the limitation of the principles of international law, the observance of which is so essential to the peace and harmony of nations, and it should not be assumed that Congress proposed to violate the obligations of this country to other nations, which it was the manifest purpose of the President to scrupulously observe and which were founded upon the principles of international law." MacLeod v. United States, 229 U.S. 434 (1913).

case of an unavoidable conflict, as in *Mortenson v. Peters* (see pp. 46–49), that national judges feel an obligation to give effect to a contravening municipal law. And when this happens, the state is not relieved of its obligations under international law. After the *Mortenson v. Peters* decision, the executive in effect overturned the judgment of the court in order to make Britain's behavior conform with her international obligations.[6]

The first two selections to follow, excerpts from *Mortensen v. Peters* and *Shri Krishna Sharma v. The State of West Bengal*, illustrate the practice of national judges giving primacy to municipal law that is in clear conflict with international law. Articles selected from the constitutions of West Germany and Korea illustrate the constitutional incorporation of international law into municipal law. "The Relation Between International Law and Municipal Law" by Edwin Borchard is included to point out the responsibility of states for their international behavior regardless of the content of their municipal law systems or the decisions of their national judges. Finally, in a brief excerpt from Wallace McClure's *World Legal Order*, an appeal is made to United States courts to give unconditional priority to international law over municipal law.

Mortensen v. Peters*

High Court of Justiciary of Scotland, Great Britain, 1906

[*In the Herring Fishery (Scotland) Act of 1889, the British Parliament forbade trawl fishing "within three miles of low-water mark of any part of the coast of Scotland." Section 7 of the Act provided further that "The Fishery Board may, by bye-law or*

byelaws, direct that the methods of fishing known as beam trawling and otter trawling shall not be used within a line drawn from Duncansby Head in Caithness to Rattray Point in Aberdeenshire, in any area or areas to be defined in such bye-law. . . ." Bye-law No. 10 of the Fishery Board for Scotland prohibited beam trawling and otter trawling in the whole of the area specified, i.e., in the Moray Firth: " . . . no person . . . shall at any time from the date when this bye-law shall come into force use any beam trawl or otter trawl for taking sea fish. . . ."*

Emmanuel Mortensen, a Danish master of a trawler registered in Norway, was arrested and convicted under the provisions of the byelaw for otter fishing in a part of the Moray Firth five miles from shore. He appealed.]

* * *

At the hearing on 29th May 1906 it was argued for the appellant—There was no jurisdiction to try this offence. The expression "any person" in the statute under construction must be confined to any person under the jurisdiction of the Court. British municipal statutes conferred jurisdiction only over (1) British subjects; (2) foreigners when on British territory. The appellant was admittedly a foreign subject, and the locus of this offence was outwith British territory. The statute was to be construed under the presumption that the Legislature did not intend to exceed its jurisdiction or to violate the accepted principles of international law . . .

* * *

LORD JUSTICE-GENERAL: The facts of this case are that the appellant being a foreign subject and master of a vessel registered in a foreign country, exercised the method of fishing known as otter trawling at a point within the Moray Firth more than three miles from the shore, but

---

[6] Brownlie, *Principles of Public International Law*, p. 46.
* Reprinted from 8 Session Cases (5th ser.) 93 (1906).

to the west of a line drawn from Duncansby Head in Caithness to Rattray Point in Aberdeenshire; that being thereafter found within British territory, to wit, at Grimsby, he was summoned to the Sheriff Court at Dornoch to answer to a complaint against him for having contravened the 7th section of the Herring Fishery Act 1889, and the bye-law of the Fishery Board thereunder made, and was convicted.

It is not disputed that if the appellant had been a British subject in a British ship he would have been rightly convicted. Further, in the case of *Peters v. Olsen*, when the person convicted, as here, was a foreigner in a foreign ship, the conviction was held good. The only difference in the facts in that case was that the locus there was, upon a certain view of the evidence, within three miles of a line measured across the mouth of a bay, where the bay was not more than ten miles wide, which cannot be said here. But the conviction proceeded on no such consideration, but simply on the fact that the locus was within the limit expressly defined by the schedule to the 6th section of the Herring Fishery Act; and the three learned Judges in that case did, I think, undoubtedly consider and decide the question whether the 6th section of the Herring Fishery Act (which in this intention is the same as the 7th) was or was not intended to strike at foreigners as well as British subjects. But as this is a full Bench we are at liberty to reconsider that decision.

I apprehend that the question is one of construction and of construction only. In this Court we have nothing to do with the question of whether the Legislature has or has not done what foreign powers may consider a usurpation in a question with them. Neither are we a tribunal sitting to decide whether an Act of the Legislature is *ultra vires* as in contravention of generally acknowledged principles of international law. For us an Act of Parliament duly passed by Lords and Commons and assented to by the King is supreme, and we are bound to give effect to its terms.

The counsel for the appellant advanced the proposition that statutes creating offences must be presumed to apply (1) to British subjects, and (2) to foreign subjects in British territory, but that short of express enactment their application should not be further extended. The appellant is admittedly not a British subject, which excludes (1); and he further argued that the *locus delicti* being in the sea beyond the three-mile limit was not within British territory, and that consequently the appellant was not included in the prohibition of the statute. Viewed as general propositions the two presumptions put forward by the appellant may be taken as correct. This, however, advances the matter but little, for like all presumptions they may be redargued, and the question remains whether they have been redargued on this occasion.

The first thing to be noted is that the prohibition here, a breach of which constitutes the offence, is not an absolute prohibition against doing a certain thing, but a prohibition against doing it in a certain place. Now, when a Legislature— using words of admitted generality, "It shall not be lawful," &c., "Every person who," &c.—conditions an offence by territorial limits, it creates, I think, a very strong inference that it is, for the purposes specified, assuming a right to legislate for that territory against all persons whatsoever. This inference seems to me still further strengthened when it is obvious that the remedy to the mischief sought to be obtained by the prohibition would be either defeated or rendered less effective if all persons whatsoever were not affected by the enactment. It is obvious that the latter consideration applied in the present case. Whatever may be the views of anyone as to the propriety or expediency of stopping trawling, the enactment shows on the face of it that it contemplates such stopping, and it would be most clearly ineffective to debar trawling by the British subject while the subjects of other nations were allowed so to fish.

It is said by the appellant that all this must give way to the consideration that international law has firmly fixed that a locus such as this is beyond the limits of territorial sovereignty, and that consequently it is not to be thought that in such a place the Legislature could seek to affect any but the King's subjects.

It is a trite observation that there is no such thing as a standard of international law extraneous to the domestic law of a kingdom, to which appeal may be made. International law, so far as this Court is concerned, is the body of doctrine regarding the international rights and duties of states which has been adopted and made part of the law of Scotland. Now can it be said to be clear by the law of Scotland that the locus here is beyond what the Legislature may assert right to affect by legislation against all whatsoever for the purpose of regulating methods of fishing?

I do not think I need say anything about what is known as the three-mile limit. It may be assumed that within the three miles the territorial sovereignty would be sufficient to cover any such legislation as the present. It is enough to say that that is not a proof of the counter proposition that outside the three miles no such result could be looked for. The locus although outside the three-mile limit is within the bay known as the Moray Firth, and the Moray Firth, say the respondents, is *intra fauces terræ*. Now, I cannot say that there is any definition of what *fauces terræ* exactly are. But there are at least three points which go far to show that this spot might be considered as lying therein.

1st. The dicta of the Scottish institutional writers seem to show that it would be no usurpation, according to the law of Scotland, so to consider it.

Thus Stair, ii, 1, 5—"The vast ocean is common to all mankind as to navigation and fishing, which are the only uses thereof, because it is not capable of bounds, but when the sea is inclosed in bays, creeks, *or otherwise is capable of any bounds or meiths as within the points of such lands,* or within the view of such shores then it may become proper, but with the reservation of passage for commerce as in the land." And Bell, Prin., 639—"The sovereign . . . is proprietor of the narrow seas within cannon shot of the land, and the *firths*, gulfs, and bays around the kingdom."

2nd. The same statute puts forward claims to what are at least analogous places. If attention is paid to the schedule appended to section 6, many places will be found far beyond the three-mile limit—*e.g.*, the Firth of Clyde near its mouth. I am not ignoring that it may be said that this in one sense is proving *idem per idem*, but none the less I do not think the fact can be ignored.

3rd. There are many instances to be found in decided cases where the right of a nation to legislate for waters more or less landlocked or landembraced although beyond the three-mile limit has been admitted. They will be found collected in the case of the *Direct United States Cable Company v. Anglo-American Telegraph Company*, L.R. 2 App. Cas. 394, the bay there in question being Conception Bay, which has a width at the mouth of rather more than 20 miles.

It seems to me, therefore, without laying down the proposition that the Moray Firth is for every purpose within the territorial sovereignty, it can at least be clearly said that the appellant cannot make out his proposition that it is inconceivable that the British Legislature should attempt for fishery regulation to legislate against all and sundry in such a place. And if that is so, then I revert to the considerations already stated, which, as a matter of construction, make me think that it did so legislate.

An argument was based on the terms of the North Sea Convention, which had been concluded a few years before this Act was passed, and which defines "exclusive fishery limits" in a manner which excludes this part of the Moray Firth. But I do not think any argument can be drawn from that definition, for the simple reason that the Convention as a whole does not deal with the subject-matter here in question, viz., mode of fishing.

If it had been attempted to infer from the terms of the Act a prohibition of which the effect was to give to subjects and deny to foreigners the right to fish, then the Convention might be apt to suggest an argument against such a construction. But that is not so. Subjects and foreigners are *ex hypothesi* in this matter treated alike.

I am therefore of opinion that the conviction was right, that both questions should be answered in the affirmative, and that the appeal should be dismissed.

* * *

Shri Krishna Sharma v. The State of West Bengal*

Calcutta High Court, 1954

* * *

Assuming that according to the Anglo-Tibet Trade Regulations of 1914 free export to Tibet (out of India) of articles not specifically referred to in clause VIII was permitted, it does not appear that so far as Indian citizens are concerned, it received statutory recognition and became a part of the municipal law of India. There is apparent repugnance between the implied provision of the Anglo-Tibet Trade Regulations, 1914, permitting free trade between the two countries on the one hand, and the subsequent Indian statutes, e.g. Essential Supplies Act, 1946, and the numerous orders issued thereunder, the Imports and Exports (Control) Acts of 1945 and 1947 and Notification No. 91—CW(1)/51 dated 7-7-52 putting restrictions on such free trade on the other and it is not easy to reconcile the divergent sets of

* Reprinted from *All India Reporter* 598 (1954).

provisions. In the circumstances the learned Advocate General has contended that in the face of this conflict, the subsequent Indian legislation must prevail.

Mr. Kar [defense counsel], on the other hand, invokes the maxim 'Generalia specialibus non derogant' and contends that the Anglo-Tibet Trade Regulations, 1914, governing the special case of trade and commerce between India and Tibet should prevail over the general Indian law enshrined in the statutes referred to by the learned Advocate General. According to Mr. Kar, the Indian statutes in question including subsidiary legislation under them seek to govern trade and commerce between India and other countries in general. This contention of Mr. Kar would have been more convincing, however, if it was a case of conflict between two Indian statutes only—the prior enactment being special and the subsequent enactment being general. The conflict in the present case goes deeper however in that there is conflict between non-Indian law, assuming for a moment that the implied provisions of Anglo-Tibet Trade Regulations, 1914 constitute law, and subsequent Indian statutes.

The language of the Indian Statutes is clear enough: in the interests of India, they seek to put restrictions in the way of trade between India and other countries. If that language be in conflict with any principle of international law as is said to be deducible from the implied provisions of the Anglo-Tibet Trade Regulations of 1914, municipal Courts of India have got to obey the laws passed by the Legislature of the country to which they owe their allegiance. In interpreting and applying municipal law, these Courts will try to adopt such a construction as will not bring it into conflict with rights and obligations deducible from rules of international law. If such rules, or rights and obligations are inconsistent with the positive regulations of municipal law, municipal Courts cannot override the latter. It is futile in such circumstances to seek to reconcile, by strained construction, what are really irreconcilable.

* * *

The Basic Law of the Federal Republic of Germany, 1949

Article 25

The general rules of public international law form part of the federal law. They take precedence over the laws and directly create rights and duties for the inhabitants of the Federal territory.

The Republic of Korea Constitution, 1948

Article 7

The duly ratified and published treaties and the generally recognized rules of international law shall be valid as a binding constituent part of the law of Korea. The status of aliens shall be guaranteed within the scope of international law and international treaties.

The Relation Between International Law and Municipal Law*

Edwin Borchard

Recent events on this continent make it seem appropriate once more to discuss the much-debated question of the relation between international law and municipal law. For one school, the dualists, municipal law prevails in case of conflict;

* Reprinted from Edwin Borchard, "The Relation Between International Law and Municipal Law," 27 *Virginia Law Review* 137 (1940), by permission of the publisher.

for the other school, the monists, international law prevails.

* * *

The fact is that both these schools are partly right and partly wrong. When it is said that international law cannot "*per se* create or invalidate municipal law nor can municipal law *per se* create or invalidate international law," the fallacy lies in the inference that municipal law can disregard international law and that a country incurs no responsibility under international law when its municipal law violates international law to the injury of a foreign nation or its nationals. As we shall see, international law exerts a definite check upon municipal law and holds the State responsible to the State whose nationals are injured by excesses in conflict with international law. When Article 2 of the Draft Convention of the Harvard Research in International Law provided that a State is internationally responsible for certain types of injuries to aliens, "anything in its national law, in the decisions of its national courts, or in its agreements with aliens to the contrary notwithstanding," it expressed a rule which indicated the control or supremacy of international law over State conduct discriminating against foreigners. . . .

* * *

. . . We have innumerable precedents which have held States liable for their failure to perform international obligations, whether the delinquency arises out of statute or administrative act. Secretary of State Bayard in 1887 made a classic and frequently quoted statement of the rule of law:

"If a government could set up its own municipal law as the final test of its international rights and obligations, then the rules of international law would be but the shadow of a name, and would afford no protection either to states or to individuals. It has been constantly maintained and also admitted by the Government of the United States that a Government can not appeal to its municipal regulations as an answer to demands for the fulfillment of international duties."

* * *

. . . Technically, municipal law cannot authorize what international law prohibits, but in fact it often does, and individuals are bound by the aberrative municipal law. No individual can be punished for observing a municipal law which may be deemed to conflict with international law. On the contrary, his conduct, domestically, is privileged. The explanation of the inconsistency lies in the fact that while individuals are bound by their municipal law, regardless of its conformity with international law, the State may have to repair the wrong done to other States by its internationally unprivileged municipal law or decision.

* * *

. . . Although it is true that international law is addressed to States as entities, it exerts a command upon law-abiding States not to depart from its precepts, subject to international responsibility. The domestic instruments that the State employs to perform its international obligations are a matter of indifference to international law. It may employ statute or administrative official or judicial control. It may directly incorporate international law into the local system, or it may incorporate only treaties and not customary law. Its failure to enact the necessary implementing legislation or law may impose upon it international responsibility, as in the case of the *Alabama* claims. On the other hand, should its local legislation arrogate to itself privileges not permitted by international law, it will be bound either to make restitution or to pay damages throught arbitration or diplomacy.

In the United States the courts are by the Constitution bound to give effect to treaties which even an aggrieved individual may invoke. In England, the rule is different, for there treaties must be adopted or converted into legislation before they become invokable in the courts. But in both cases the treaty is binding on the nation and will be enforced, notwithstanding a conflicting municipal statute, by such instrumentalities as international law possesses. The American courts, like the English, are said to consider international law a part of the law of the land. And this is true, for international law will in principle be enforced directly in the municipal courts provided there is no statute *contra*. Where a reconciliation between international law and municipal law is possible, the courts will make it. Where there is a statute which conflicts with international law, instances of which will presently be noted, the courts must perforce give effect to the statute even as against the treaty, provided the treaty is earlier in time. But this merely indicates that the municipal economy or administration is so arranged that the enforcement of the international obligation is vested not in the courts but in a different department. This phenomenon has led to the inference that the municipal law enforceable in the courts prevails over a contrary rule of international law, which is enforceable by the Executive at the initiative of the aggrieved foreigner or his government. But this merely means that the courts have no local authority to give effect to international law *when it conflicts with municipal statute*, but that such function is vested in his country in the Secretary of State, who is the agent of the American people for the enforcement of international law. The rule that finally prevails on the American people is the rule of international law as evidenced in the taxes they may have to pay to make good the aberrations of the municipal statute.

So in *United States v. La Jeune Eugenie*, the United States felt obliged to pay damages to France for the illegal seizure of a private vessel, although sustained by the Supreme Court. After the Civil War the United States submitted to arbitration twelve prize decisions of the United States Supreme Court during the Civil War. In six of those cases, the arbitral tribunal found the Supreme Court to have been wrong and awarded damages to Great Britain, a phenomenon very common in prize cases, especially where the prize court is bound by municipal order in council regulation and not necessarily by international law. In the nineties, the United States had extended its jurisdiction in the Behring Sea by law beyond the three-mile limit, in order to police the manner of taking seals. The Behring Sea Arbitration held this to have been a legal error and the seizures made under the statute illegal, so that heavy damages had to be paid. Whenever a country by municipal statute or decree authorizes unlawful seizures from or arbitrarily discriminates against foreigners, under the criterion of international law and not merely municipal law, it incurs international responsibility and must repair the wrong in the most practicable manner possible. And when the President disregards the statute or pays damages through congressional appropriation for the municipal delinquency, he is not exercising the pardoning power but acts according to a supervening rule of law. Should he dispute the rule of international law with a foreign government the issue is generally submitted to arbitration or diplomatic negotiation, but in no case would it be consciously asserted that the Foreign Office—except for commanding political reasons which entail responsibility —has knowingly declined to give effect to an admitted or established rule of international law. Even an assertion that the issue involves a domestic question is internationally justiciable, for international law does determine the matters that are within the *domaine reservée*.

But let us hear from the opposition. When Gilchrist says that "each State is independent and interprets for itself how far the principles of international law are to apply," because "there are as yet no international courts to enforce international law, though there are courts to interpret it, and what we find in practice is that States interpret international law for themselves, usually as they find it expedient," he presupposes a condition contrary to fact when States act in accordance with international law and true only when they violate international law. Following the analytical jurists like Austin and Jellinek, he believes that international law, as he views it, is nothing but "international principles of morality." Such duties as it has are self-imposed and hence could hardly be legal.

But when the President or Secretary of State on the demand of foreign nations, invoking a rule of international law, releases an alien from the military service or releases a rumrunner seized outside the three-mile limit and thereby in effect overrules a statute of Congress and a supporting decision of a municipal court, he is acting as a societal agent of the American people and State and is recognizing the binding character of international law as law in the United States and everywhere else. When foreign nations refused to permit Russia and Japan to make foodstuffs contraband or in other respects to violate the rights of neutrals; when foreign nations deny to the countries of Latin-America the privilege of unilaterally defining the term "denial of justice" or by contract with their citizens of exacting a waiver of the privilege of invoking diplomatic protection, they are invoking international law as a rule of law superior to any contrary rule of municipal law. These nations, undertaking to interpret for themselves "how far the principles of international law are to apply" found themselves severely limited in their freedom of action by the foreign States affected by the misinterpretation of their international duties, invoking not their political strength but an established rule of international law from which no State can legally escape. The mere fact that violations of international law occur and occasionally go unredressed is no evidence that the rules violated are not law, any more than the no less frequent violation of municipal law is evidence of its non-legal character. While the sanctions of international law are somewhat different from those operating in municipal law, and while international law is not always certain, any more than is municipal law, the sanctions are none the less effective and the interpretative agencies none the less active. "International courts" do not "enforce international law"; no more do municipal courts "enforce" municipal law. But the declaratory and binding decisions of international courts are observed and carried out with a uniformity equal to that of municipal courts. The agencies for the enforcement of international law are not necessarily courts, but other State constitutional organs, usually the executive. The weakness of the system, which attracts a disproportionate amount of attention, consists in the inability to compel nations to submit their disputes to a court and the physical power of States, exercised on occasion without regard to law, to constitute themselves plaintiff, judge and sheriff in their own cause. The theory that international law is not necessarily binding on States, sustained by so many theorists and jurists, though founded on essential error, can only aggravate this weakness in the system and postpone the maturity of that international legal order for which most of them profess to be working.

"An Appeal"*

Wallace McClure

No proposition would seem more clearly inherent in the concept of law than

---

* Reprinted from Wallace McClure, *World Legal Order* (Chapel Hill: University of North Carolina Press, 1960), pp. vii–ix, by permission of the publisher.

that those rules and principles accepted as regulatory of relations between nation-states should be deemed supranational in the sense that they are superior to and, in case of conflict, overrule legal norms of national origin or merely national applicability. It would seem that the most primitive common sense would exclude any idea of the legal superiority of a part of mankind or of human law to the whole or of the inferiority of the law of a larger group to that of a smaller group within it. Yet in the world of today, a world in which law has been known and has prevailed as long as there is any historical revelation, such conclusion is denied de facto and even de jure, not only in seats of the mighty but in philosophers' sanctums. Seldom has a national court, unless by authorization of nationally created law, accorded clear-cut recognition to the obligation to enforce supranational law over national law—or even to recognize the existence of any law as higher than that of the nation-state under the law of which the court is set up. Thus power, superseated in national government, overrides the logic of human law. Thus the jurist, of all men born for the universe, narrows his mind and to nation gives up what was meant for mankind.

No more ominous fact than this exists in the world as the twentieth Christian century passes its halfway mark. At no point of history has the safety of the people been more inseparable from the prevalence of the common sense of most; nor have the fretful realms been more persistent or more virulent in their disregard of law than now. Never has the vital need for effective universal law been so perilously acute. What contribution can the people of any particular nation make toward the rule of law in the world?

* * *

The simplest contribution by the people of the United States would probably consist of an alteration of the attitude of their courts toward the relative legal position of treaties and national legislative enactments. In their scheme of national law they maintain the usual distinction which gives legal superiority to certain rules and principles designated "fundamental" or "constitutional" as compared with all others, including acts of the national legislature. Their formal constitutional instrument declares that "This Constitution, and the Laws of the United States which shall be made in Pursuance thereof; and all Treaties made, or which shall be made, under the Authority of the United States, shall be the supreme Law of the Land." It does not indicate any difference of level among the three categories of law specified. When litigants' claims have set one against the other, the courts have not hesitated to hold that "Laws" in the sense of congressional statutes are void if found not to have been made in pursuance of the Constitution. Despite the fact that treaties are made in collaboration with other nation-states and on the international level are legally repealable only in accordance with their terms or in collaboration with the co-maker states, when pertinent cases began squarely to confront the United States courts well on in the nineteenth century they took the position that treaties and statutes were on an equal level and hence that the later in date, as the more recent expression of the United States popular will, should prevail in case of conflict. The result was violation of the treaty obligations of the people of the United States— to say nothing of the intellectually devastating nonsunt attitude toward other peoples. As this interpretation can hardly have been based upon any pure theory of law but was rather a reflection of political and social conditions of a century ago and hardly of those today, its supersession in favor of a rule of law maintaining the inviolability of international acts by national legislative acts would seem conceivable: certainly it would be honorable and altogether logical in law.

* * *

. . . It is not enough to determine that, as between treaties and statutes, treaties must in law prevail. What of an entire system of national law vis-à-vis the law in its entirety?

The paragraph of the United States Constitution already quoted goes on to say that "the Judges in every State shall be bound" by the Constitution, laws, and treaties of the Union, "any Thing in the Constitution or Laws of any State to the Contrary notwithstanding," State constitutions, accordingly, are on the same level as state statutes contrasted to national law of any kind. The same relentless legal logic that points to the supremacy of an international act over an act of a national legislature prescribes the supremacy of the law of nations over any national (hence, partially prevailing) law. Supranational law, both enacted (treaty) and customary (including, incidentally, the rule pacta sunt servanda), must be accounted superior to constitutional law no less than to any other in the national category. . . .

INTERNATIONAL POWER TO ADJUDICATE

We have seen that national courts use the rules and principles of international law to decide cases whenever the occasion calls for it. Issues of international law arise indirectly in national courts and not as disputes between states. Thus, an alien ship owner may claim immunity from seizure for his coastal fishing vessels during war or a foreign diplomat may claim immunity from prosecution for a crime committed in the state to which he is accredited. The primary use of international law, however, is by independent states as a means of providing order in international relations, as a technique of foreign policy, and as a way of settling disputes.

This section calls attention to some of the problems and prospects of the use of international law as an assistance to states in adjusting their differences and in settling their disputes. Article 33 of the United Nations Charter calls upon states to settle their disputes peacefully by providing that

The parties to any dispute, the continuance of which is likely to endanger the maintenance of international peace and security, shall, first of all, seek a solution by negotiation, enquiry, mediation, conciliation, arbitration, judicial settlement, resort to regional agencies or arrangements, or other peaceful means of their own choice.

Two of these methods, arbitration and judicial settlement, are based solely on the use of international law, and the others frequently make use of it in adjusting differences.

Direct negotiation between states is the most common means of settling disputes, and since it normally involves a give-and-take process international law may or may not be used. Almost invariably, however, legal norms are put forth by the opposing parties in support of their respective positions and a solution is often based on them; legal norms provide a frame of reference, or at least a point of departure, for the discussions. The use of legal norms is even more apparent when good offices, mediation, or conciliation techniques, which involve "third party" assistance in negotiations, are used because the disputing states tend to appeal to the third party by phrasing their arguments in terms that have universal applicability and appeal. But since third party efforts are directed toward facilitating negotiation, which by definition involves compromise, the solution, if any, may or may not be based on legal norms. The purpose of third party intervention is not to ensure that the law is observed, but that the dispute is settled.

When states desire to use the norms of international law to resolve their differences, they may choose either arbitration or judicial settlement. These two methods are alike in that their use is dependent upon agreement by the parties to the dispute and in that the decision rendered is binding. Arbitration is distinguished from judicial settlement by the *ad hoc* nature of the arbitrator or arbitration tribunal and by the degree to which the parties to the dispute may influence the outcome of the arbitration by their prior agreement on the nature of the issue or issues in contention and by their right even to reach an advance understanding on the interpretation of the rules to be applied. Judicial settlement, on the other hand, is accomplished by a permanent tribunal operating under established rules. The first truly international tribunal established to provide for judicial settlement of disputes was the Permanent Court of International Justice, which began functioning in 1920. The International Court of Justice, which succeeded the Permanent Court in 1945, functions as a principal organ of the United Nations.[1]

The numerical record of successful uses of arbitration and judicial settlement is impressive. Literally thousands of international claims have been disposed of by arbitration, and the two World Courts have rendered more than sixty judgments during their short existence. The record of state compliance with these decisions is also quite good; only a small percentage of the arbitration awards were not given effect, no decision of the Per-

---

[1] The organization and functions of the International Court of Justice are spelled out in its Statute, which is reprinted in the appendix of this book.

manent Court was disregarded, and only one final judgment of the International Court, that of the Corfu Channel case, was not honored. But this record is misleading because it does not indicate that most of the uses of arbitration and judicial settlement have not involved politically important questions. State officials are reluctant to submit issues that they regard as vitally important to impartial tribunals whose decisions are binding; and, in the absence of a specific treaty commitment, they are under no legal compulsion to do so. This fact accounts, in large part, for the good compliance record; if state officials consider that they cannot afford to lose, they simply refuse to submit a dispute to the risks of arbitration or judicial settlement.

The principal difficulty with arbitration and judicial settlement as methods of settling disputes has not been that of enforcement but of jurisdiction. Even the International Court has jurisdiction to consider an issue only when both parties consent to it. Efforts to remedy this situation have logically centered around attempts to get states to consent to increases in the Court's jurisdiction. Numerous bilateral and multilateral treaties contain "compromissary clauses" that confer jurisdiction in advance upon the Court in case of disputes arising over interpretation or application of the treaties. Article 36 of the Statute of the International Court, which is reprinted on page 57, contains an "optional clause" by which states may agree in advance to compulsory jurisdiction over certain types of issues. But by the end of 1966 only twenty-one states had availed themselves of this opportunity without significant reservations, and a large number of states, including the Soviet Union, had not committed themselves at all. The United States, in its advance acceptance of the International Court's jurisdiction, excluded "disputes with regard to matters which are essentially within the domestic

jurisdiction of the United States . . . *as determined by the United States. . . .*" The italicized portion of this reservation, commonly referred to as the Connally amendment, has been widely copied by other states and has had the effect of significantly undermining advance acceptance of the Court's jurisdiction.[2] The principle of reciprocity incorporated into Article 36 of the Statute further reduces the Court's jurisdiction by allowing states that have adhered to the "optional clause" to withhold consent to consideration of any dispute brought by a state that has not similarly agreed in advance to the Court's jurisdiction. The reciprocity principle even allows states to plead each other's reservations when objecting to the authority of the Court to hear a dispute.

The following selections center on the problems and prospects of the use of the International Court as an agency for judicial settlement of disputes. Articles 36 and 37 of the Statute of the Court explain its jurisdiction in general terms. Three varied examples of advance acceptances of jurisdiction are included: the United States' acceptance is replete with nullifying reservations, the French acceptance is a recent and liberalized version of an earlier statement that included a Connally-type reservation, and the Uruguay acceptance contains only a reciprocity reservation. Excerpts from the "Case Concerning the Right of Passage Over Indian Territory," decided by the International Court in 1960, illustrate the authority of the Court to override objections to its jurisdiction in disputes between states that have res-

---

[2] This reservation was proposed by Senator Tom Connally on the floor of the Senate in 1946 and appears still to have considerable support in Congress. Representatives of the executive branch, on the other hand, have on numerous occasions expressed disapproval of this severe restriction on the United States' acceptance of the Court's jurisdiction, as is illustrated by the statement of Secretary of State Dean Rusk on November 14, 1964, that "The United States would like to see more nations submit to the compulsory jurisdiction of the Court. In this connection, I should like to add that the present administration, like its predecessors, would like also to see the Connally amendment repealed." 51 *United States Department of State Bulletin* 803 (1964).

ponded under the "optional clause" of Article 36. The "Case Concerning the Aerial Incident of September 4th, 1954," illustrates the Court's lack of authority to hear a complaint against a state, in this case the Soviet Union, which has neither accepted the Court's jurisdiction in advance nor given its consent in the case at hand. Finally, a thought-provoking article entitled "Step-by-Step Acceptance of the Jurisdiction of the International Court of Justice," by Louis B. Sohn, suggests a number of modest ways of expanding the compulsory jurisdiction of the Court.

Statute of the International Court of Justice (1945), Articles 36 and 37

Article 36

1. The jurisdiction of the Court comprises all cases which the parties refer to it and all matters specially provided for in the Charter of the United Nations or in treaties and conventions in force.

2. The states parties to the present Statute may at any time declare that they recognize as compulsory *ipso facto* and without special agreement, in relation to any other state accepting the same obligation, the jurisdiction of the Court in all legal disputes concerning:
a. the interpretation of a treaty;
b. any question of international law;
c. the existence of any fact which, if established, would constitute a breach of an international obligation;
d. the nature or extent of the reparation to be made for the breach of an international obligation.

3. The declarations referred to above may be made unconditionally or on condition of reciprocity on the part of several or certain states, or for a certain time.

4. Such declarations shall be deposited with the Secretary-General of the United Nations, who shall transmit copies thereof to the parties to the Statute and to the Registrar of the Court.

5. Declarations made under Article 36 of the Statute of the Permanent Court of International Justice and which are still in force shall be deemed, as between the parties to the present Statute, to be acceptances of the compulsory jurisdiction of the International Court of Justice for the period which they still have to run and in accordance with their terms.

6. In the event of a dispute as to whether the Court has jurisdiction, the matter shall be settled by the decision of the Court.

Article 37

Whenever a treaty or convention in force provides for references of a matter to a tribunal to have been instituted by the League of Nations, or to the Permanent Court of International Justice, the matter shall, as between the parties to the present Statute, be referred to the International Court of Justice.

Acceptance of Compulsory Jurisdiction Under Article 36 by the United States, France, and Uruguay*

United States of America

I, Harry S. Truman, President of the United States of America, declare on

* Reprinted from *Yearbook of the International Court of Justice* 225, 240 (1963–1964).

behalf of the United States of America, under Article 36, paragraph 2, of the Statute of the International Court of Justice, and in accordance with the Resolution of August 2, 1946, of the Senate of the United States of America (two-thirds of the Senators present concurring therein), that the United States of America recognizes as compulsory *ipso facto* and without special agreement, in relation to any other State accepting the same obligation, the jurisdiction of the International Court of Justice in all legal disputes hereafter arising concerning

a. The interpretation of a treaty;
b. Any question of international law;
c. The existence of any fact which, if established, would constitute a breach of an international obligation;
d. The nature or extent of the reparation to be made for the breach of an international obligation;

Provided, that this declaration shall not apply to

a. Disputes the solution of which the Parties shall entrust to other tribunals by virtue of agreements already in existence or which may be concluded in the future; or
b. Disputes with regard to matters which are essentially within the domestic jurisdiction of the United States of America as determined by the United States of America; or
c. Disputes arising under a multilateral treaty, unless (1) all Parties to the treaty affected by the decision are also Parties to the case before the Court, or (2) the United States of America specially agrees to jurisdiction; and

Provided further, that this declaration shall remain in force for a period of five years and thereafter until the expiration of six months after notice may be given to terminate this declaration.

DONE at Washington this fourteenth day of August 1946.

(*Signed*) Harry S. TRUMAN.

France

[*Translation from the French*]

On behalf of the Government of the French Republic, I accept as compulsory *ipso facto* and without special agreement, in relation to other Members of the United Nations which accept the same obligation, that is to say, on condition of reciprocity, the jurisdiction of the Court, in conformity with Article 36, paragraph 2, of the Statute, for a period of three years and thereafter until such time as notice may be given of the termination of this acceptance, in all disputes which may arise in respect of facts or situations subsequent to this declaration, with the exception of:

1. disputes with regard to which the Parties may have agreed or may agree to have recourse to another method of peaceful settlement;
2. disputes relating to questions which by international law fall exclusively within the domestic jurisdiction;
3. disputes arising out of any war or international hostilities and disputes arising out of a crisis affecting the national security or out of any measure or action relating thereto;
4. disputes with any State which, at the date of occurrence of the facts or situations giving rise to the dispute, has not accepted the compulsory jurisdiction of the International Court of Justice for a period at least equal to that specified in this declaration.

Paris, 10 July 1959.

(*Signed*) COUVE DE MURVILLE.

Uruguay

[*Translation from the French*]

On behalf of the Government of Uruguay, I recognize in relation to any Member or State accepting the same obligation, that is to say, on the sole condition of reciprocity, the jurisdiction of the Court as compulsory, *ipso facto* and without special convention.

(*Signed*) B. FERNANDEZ Y MEDINA.

Case Concerning the Right of Passage Over Indian Territory (Portugal v. India)*

International Court of Justice, 1960

The present dispute was referred to the Court by an Application filed on 22 December 1955.

In that Application the Government of the Portuguese Republic states that the territory of Portugal in the Indian Peninsula is made up of the three districts of Goa, Daman and Diu. It adds that the district of Daman comprises, in addition to its littoral territory, two parcels of territory completely surrounded by the territory of India which constitute enclaves: Dadra and Nagar-Aveli. It is in respect of the communications between these enclaves and Daman and between each other that the question arises of a right of passage in favour of Portugal through Indian territory, and of a correlative obligation binding upon India. The Application states that in July 1954, contrary to the practice hitherto followed, the Government of India, in pursuance of what the Application calls "the open campaign which it has been carrying on since 1950 for the annexation of Portuguese territories", prevented Portugal from exercising this right of passage. This denial by India having been maintained, it has followed, according to the Application, that the enclaves of Dadra and Nagar-Aveli have been completely cut off from the rest of the Portuguese territory, the Portuguese authorities thus being placed in a position in which it became impossible for them to exercise Portuguese rights of sovereignty there.

It is in that situation, and in order to secure a remedy therefore, that Portugal has referred the matter to the Court.

* * *

* Reprinted from *International Court of Justice Reports* 27 (1960).

Before proceeding to the consideration of the merits, the Court must ascertain whether it has jurisdiction to do so, a jurisdiction which India has expressly contested.

Following upon the Application instituting proceedings by Portugal filed on 22 December 1955, the Court was seised of six preliminary objections raised by the Government of India. By a Judgment given on 26 November 1957 the Court rejected four of them and joined to the merits the two others, by which the Government of India continued to dispute the jurisdiction of the Court to deal with the present case.

The Court has first to adjudicate upon these two objections which, as originally submitted, constituted the Fifth and Sixth Preliminary Objections.

In its Fifth Preliminary Objection the Government of India relied upon the reservation which forms part of its Declaration of 28 February 1940 accepting the jurisdiction of the Court and which excludes from that jurisdiction disputes with regard to questions which by international law fall exclusively within the jurisdiction of India. The Government of India argues that on that score the present dispute is outside the jurisdiction of the Court.

In support of its challenge of the jurisdiction the Government of India contended, in the grounds in support of its Submissions of 21 October 1959, that:

"if its examination of the merits should lead the Court to a finding that Portugal has not established the existence of the titles which she has invoked, and that these titles must accordingly be regarded as non-existent, it must follow that the question of the grant or refusal of the passage claimed over Indian territory falls exclusively within the domestic jurisdiction of India . . .".

That statement admits of no dispute, but it cannot be inferred therefrom, as the Indian Government does, that the Court has no jurisdiction, since the statement proceeds from a finding by the Court that the titles invoked by Portugal are invalid.

The Court can only arrive at that finding after first establishing its competence to examine the validity of these titles.

In the present case Portugal is claiming a right of passage over Indian territory. It asserts the existence of a correlative obligation upon India. It asks for a finding that India has failed to fulfil that obligation. In support of the first two claims it invokes a Treaty of 1779, of which India contests both the existence and the interpretation. Portugal relies upon a practice of which India contests not only the substance, but also the binding character as between the two States which Portugal seeks to attach to it. Portugal further invokes international custom and the principles of international law as it interprets them. To contend that such a right of passage is one which can be relied upon as against India, to claim that such an obligation is binding upon India, to invoke, whether rightly or wrongly, such principles is to place oneself on the plane of international law. Indeed, in the course of the proceedings both Parties took their stand upon that ground and on occasion expressly said so. To decide upon the validity of those principles, upon the existence of such a right of Portugal as against India, upon such obligation of India towards Portugal, and upon the alleged failure to fulfil that obligation, does not fall exclusively within the jurisdiction of India.

The Fifth Objection cannot therefore be upheld.

The Sixth Preliminary Objection by which India has challenged the jurisdiction of the Court likewise relates to a limitation of India's acceptance of the jurisdiction of the Court, as set out in its Declaration of 28 February 1940.

By the terms of that Declaration India accepted the jurisdiction of the Court "over all disputes arising after February 5th, 1930, with regard to situations of facts subsequent to the same date." India contends that the present dispute does not satisfy either of the two conditions stated and that the Court is therefore without jurisdiction.

In order to form a judgment as to the Court's jurisdiction it is necessary to consider what is the subject of the dispute.

A passage in the Application headed "Subject of the Dispute" indicates that subject as being the conflict of views which arose between the two States when, in 1954, India opposed the exercise of Portugal's right of passage. If this were the subject of the dispute referred to the Court, the challenge to the jurisdiction could not be sustained, But it appeared from the Application itself and it was fully confirmed by the subsequent proceedings, the Submissions of the Parties and statements made in the course of the hearings, that the dispute submitted to the Court has a threefold subject:

1. The disputed existence of a right of passage in favour of Portugal;
2. The alleged failure of India in July 1954 to comply with its obligations concerning that right of passage;
3. The redress of the illegal situation flowing from that failure.

The dispute before the Court, having this three-fold subject, could not arise until all its constituent elements had come into existence. Among these are the obstacles which India is alleged to have placed in the way of exercise of passage by Portugal in 1954. The dispute therefore as submitted to the Court could not have originated until 1954. Thus it satisfies the time-condition to which the Declaration of India made its acceptance of the jurisdiction of the Court subject.

* * *

Accordingly there is no justification for saying that the dispute before the Court arose before 5 February 1930. There is not therefore, so far as the date of the birth of the dispute is concerned, any bar to the jurisdiction of the Court.

But India further contends that the

dispute is one with regard to facts and situations prior to that date and that this takes it outside the jurisdiction of the Court.

On the point here under consideration, the Declaration of 28 February 1940, by which India has accepted the jurisdiction of the Court, does not proceed on the principle of excluding from that acceptance any given disputes. It proceeds in a positive manner on the basis of indicating the disputes which are included within that acceptance. By its terms, the jurisdiction of the Court is accepted "over all disputes arising after February 5th, 1930, with regard to situations or facts subsequent to the same date".

In accordance with the terms of the Declaration, the Court must hold that it has jurisdiction if it finds that the dispute submitted to it is a dispute with regard to a situation subsequent to 5 February 1930 or is one with regard to facts subsequent to that date.

* * *

Up to 1954 the situation of those territories may have given rise to a few minor incidents, but passage had been effected without any controversy as to the title under which it was effected. It was only in 1954 that such a controversy arose and the dispute relates both to the existence of a right of passage to go into the enclaved territories and to India's failure to comply with obligations which, according to Portugal, were binding upon it in this connection. It was from all of this that the dispute referred to the Court arose; it is with regard to all of this that the dispute exists. This whole, whatever may have been the earlier origin of one of its parts, came into existence only after 5 February 1930. The time-condition to which acceptance of the jurisdiction of the Court was made subject by the Declaration of India is therefore complied with.

* * *

The Court is therefore of opinion that the Sixth Objection should not be upheld and, consequently, it is of opinion that it has jurisdiction to deal with the present dispute.

Case Concerning the Aerial Incident of September 4th, 1954 (United States of America v. Union of Soviet Socialist Republics)*

International Court of Justice, 1958

Whereas on August 22nd, 1958, the Ambassador of the United States of America to the Netherlands filed in the Registry an Application dated July 25th, 1958, and signed by the Agent for the Government of the United States of America instituting proceedings before the Court against the Government of the Union of Soviet Socialist Republics on account of "certain willful acts committed by military aircraft of the Soviet Government on September 4, 1954, in the international air space over the Sea of Japan against a United States Navy P2-V-type aircraft, commonly known as a Neptune type, and against its crew";

Whereas the Application was duly communicated by the Registry on August 22nd, 1958, to the Ambassador of the Union of Soviet Socialist Republics to the Netherlands;

Whereas the Application was also communicated by the Registry to the Members of the United Nations, through the Secretary-General of the United Nations, and to the other States entitled to appear before the Court;

Whereas the Application contains the following paragraphs:

"The United States Government, in filing this application to the Court, submits to the

---

* Reprinted from *International Court of Justice Reports* 158 (1958).

Court's jurisdiction for the purposes of this case. The Soviet Government appears not to have filed any declaration with the Court thus far, although it was invited to do so by the United States Government in note 176 of August 19, 1957, a copy of which is also annexed hereto. The Soviet Government in a note dated October 10, 1957, which is made an annex to the present application, rejected the United States Government's invitation. The Soviet Government is, however, qualified to submit to the jurisdiction of the Court in this matter and may, upon notification of this application by the Registrar, in accordance with the Rules of the Court, take the necessary steps to enable the Court's jurisdiction over both parties to the dispute to be confirmed.

The United States Government thus founds the jurisdiction of this Court on the foregoing considerations and on Article 36 (1) of the Statute."

Whereas in a letter dated September 26th, 1958, from the Chargé d'affaires *a.i.* of the Union of Soviet Socialist Republics in the Netherlands to the Registrar it was stated that:

"The Government of the USSR in its note of October 10, 1957, as well as in previous notes of September 5 and 8, 1954, and of January 21, 1957, stated that since the American military aircraft of the Neptune-type violated the state frontier of the USSR in the Cape Ostrovnoi region and opened fire on Soviet fighters first, responsibility for the incident taken place on September 4, 1954, and consequences of it fully lie on the American side. In the above-mentioned note of October 10, 1957, the Government of the USSR in response to the proposal of the Government of the USA transmitting this case for hearing in the International Court of Justice communicated that no basis for it can be seen.

I should like to draw your attention to the Article 36 of the Statute of the Court according to which any dispute may be transmitted to the International Court of Justice only by common consent of both sides.

As appears from above-stated the Government of the USSR has already informed the Government of the USA formally that the Soviet Government does not give its consent for hearing this case in the International Court of Justice. Under these conditions the Government of the USA having applied to the Court, acted in disaccord with the Statute of the International Court of Justice.

The Government of the USSR deems that in this case there are no questions which are of need to be considered by the International Court of Justice and as before does not see any basis for turning this question over for examination by the International Court."

Whereas a true copy of the above-mentioned letter was communicated to the Agent for the Government of the USA on September 30th, 1958;

Whereas, in a letter dated November 25th, 1958, and addressed to the Registrar, the Agent for the Government of the United States of America stated:

"The United States has noted that the Soviet Chargé d'Affaires *ad interim* in the Netherlands, upon the instructions of his Government, stated that his Government did not give its consent for the settlement of the dispute described in the United States application by the International Court of Justice.

The United States Government must take this opportunity to express its profound disagreement with the further statement of the Soviet Government that in filing its application for a settlement of the dispute involved by the International Court of Justice the United States Government 'acted in disaccord with the Statute of the International Court of Justice' because the United States Government had not received the prior consent of the Soviet Government to submit the dispute to this Court for decision. The United States Government of course also contests the statement that 'there are no questions which are of need to be considered by the International Court of Justice and . . . does not see any basis for turning this question over for examination by the International Court.' On the contrary, the United States Government believes that international law and order depend on the peaceful settlement of disputes between governments of international questions of fact and law as described in the Statute. It is now well settled that any government qualified to appear before this Court may file its application without prior special agreement."

Whereas, in these circumstances, the Court finds that it has not before it any acceptance by the Government of the Union of Soviet Socialist Republics of the jurisdiction of the Court to deal with the dispute which is the subject of the Application submitted to it by the Government of the United States of America and that therefore it can take no further steps upon this Application;

THE COURT

orders that the case shall be removed from the list.

Step-by-Step Acceptance of the Jurisdiction of the International Court of Justice*

Louis B. Sohn

It is a tragic fact of international life that the International Court of Justice is sidestepped in most international disputes and is, consequently, under-employed. This situation cannot be remedied merely by repetitious insistence that important questions of international law should be immediately sent to the Court, including such questions as Berlin, Vietnam or Formosa. Nor can the fact that only one third of the Members of the United Nations have accepted the jurisdiction of the Court be remedied by an exhortation that the other Members of the United Nations should accept that jurisdiction quickly and without any reservations. Instead, it might be more realistic to follow a wise saying that we should "elevate our sights a little lower," perhaps much lower. Instead of adopting an all-or-nothing attitude, we might explore a step-by-step approach which would gradually increase the Court's permanent

* Reprinted from Louis B. Sohn, "Step-by-Step Acceptance of the Jurisdiction of the International Court of Justice," *Proceedings of the American Society of International Law* 131 (1964), by permission of the American Society of International Law.

jurisdiction. Four lines of approach might be explored in this connection:

1. Acceptance of the jurisdiction of the International Court of Justice over disputes relating to the interpretation and application of treaties.
2. Acceptance of the jurisdiction of the International Court of Justice over specified areas of international law.
3. Acceptance of the jurisdiction of the Court through regional arrangements.
4. Granting to the United Nations the power to make a binding request that parties to a dispute refer the matter to the International Court of Justice.

All these steps can be taken outside the framework of the optional clause in Article 36 of the Statute of the International Court of Justice, and the agreement of states to take these steps might be embodied in a General Act on the Judicial Settlement of International Disputes similar to the Geneva General Act of 1928 on the Pacific Settlement of International Disputes, which was revised by the United Nations in 1949. The proposed Act would permit ratifying states to accept all four obligations mentioned above, or only one or two or three of them, at the discretion of each state. Each of the obligations might, in turn, be subdivided, thus permitting additional options. Such rampant gradualism should permit even the most recalcitrant state to accept something and in this manner to take the first hesitating step toward broader acceptance in the future. Once states find that the first steps did not prove disastrous, they might become more venturesome and start taking several steps in quick succession. Slowly, but surely, the jurisdiction of the Court would expand and, hopefully, the number of cases presented to the Court would increase, and one day we might discover that the problem which seems to be so intractable today has been solved by the process of gradual accretion.

Returning to the four proposals made previously, it might be useful to make some comments on each one in turn.

1. *Disputes relating to the interpretation and application of treaties.* The idea that disputes relating to treaties are especially suitable to international adjudication is not a new one. The First International Conference of American States, meeting in Washington in 1890, was one of the pioneers in proposing that arbitration should be obligatory in all controversies concerning "the validity, construction and enforcement of treaties." In many arbitration treaties states have actually committed themselves to submit such disputes first to arbitration and later to adjudication. In addition, many hundreds of treaties on a large variety of subjects contain so-called compromissary clauses conferring on the International Court of Justice jurisdiction to decide disputes relating to their interpretation or application. There is probably no state in the world which has not accepted at least a few of these treaties and has thus conferred on the Court jurisdiction to interpret them.

It might be possible, therefore, to persuade most of the states of the world to accept the jurisdiction of the Court to interpret all treaties binding upon them. States might be given several options here; for instance, their acceptance might apply: to all treaties or only to treaties registered with the United Nations (of which there were more than 7,000 on January 1, 1964), or to interpretation of treaties only, or to both their interpretation and application. States might also be permitted to exclude a specific number of treaties from their acceptance, but no other reservations should be allowed.

2. *Disputes relating to specified areas of international law.* At the Second Hague Conference in 1907, a joint Anglo-American proposal was discussed in which more than twenty specified subjects were listed, and states were invited to accept the obligation to submit disputes relating to them to arbitration, each state selecting one or more of these subjects. Similar proposals were advocated for many years by Sir Thomas Barclay, but were considered premature. In the Statute of the Permanent Court of International Justice in 1920 the bold step was taken of asking states to accept the jurisdiction of the Court over disputes relating to "any question of international law." It is undoubtedly this provision that scared so many states away from the Court and caused others to make far-reaching reservations. Perhaps we should retrace our steps and return to the more modest proposals of the 1907 vintage. One can easily prepare a list of many subjects of international law, and provide states with an option to accept the jurisdiction of the Court with respect to those areas which they consider least controversial. Such a list might look as on opposite page.

States might again be given several options: for instance, they might agree to accept at the time of ratification at least ten subjects, or they might agree to accept the minimum of ten and at least ten more in each ten-year period thereafter. States would thus have a chance to select at the beginning only subjects which are least likely to involve a danger to their vital interests, and to postpone more difficult areas until later. But once more than one state should accept the Court's jurisdiction over a particular subject, each of these states would be bound with respect to all other states accepting the jurisdiction of the Court over that subject and after a while a network of international commitments would be woven broadening the jurisdiction of the Court over a multitude of subjects.

3. *Acceptance of the jurisdiction of the Court through regional arrangements.* In anticipating "dangerous" international disputes, governments worry not only about the subject-matter of the possible disputes, but also about the parties to them. It is relatively easy to contemplate going to the International Court of Justice in a dispute with a friendly state, and a government does not mind being able to bring to the Court a good case against an adversary.

	AFGHANISTAN	ALBANIA	ALGERIA	ARGENTINA	AUSTRALIA	AUSTRIA	BELGIUM	BOLIVIA	BRAZIL	BULGARIA	BURMA	BURUNDI	ETC.
1. Recognition of states													
2. Recognition of governments													
3. Succession of states													
4. Succession of governments													
5. Acquisition of territory													
6. Boundaries of states													
7. Leased territories													
8. International servitudes													
9. Inviolability of national territory													
10. Ports and inland waters													
11. International rivers and lakes													
12. Territorial waters													
13. Contiguous zones													
14. Continental shelf													
15. International canals and straits													
16. Regime of the high seas													
17. Fisheries													
18. Whaling and sealing													
19. Air navigation													
20. Polar regions													
21. Regime of outer space													
22. Nationality and status of ships													
23. Piracy													
24. Slavery													
25. International traffic in women and children													
26. International traffic in narcotic drugs													
27. Nationality and statelessness													
28. Admission of aliens													
29. Position of aliens													
30. Expulsion of aliens etc.													

It is the other side of the coin that scares governments: the possibility that an unfriendly state would use the Court to harass the government which has accepted the Court's jurisdiction *erga omnes*, without excluding in some way all potential enemies. Some states might prefer, therefore, to limit their commitments to go to the Court to states with which they have long-standing ties of friendship and as to which no bitter disputes should be anticipated. Thus, the members of the Council of Europe could easily agree to submit any legal dispute between them to the International Court of Justice, and the European Convention for the Peaceful Settlement of Disputes in 1957 conferred a large amount of jurisdiction on the Court. Similarly, certain American States (though not the United States) found it possible to accept the jurisdiction of the Court through ratifying the American Treaty on Pacific Settlement (the Pact of Bogotá) of 1948. A regional agreement on pacific settlement is also contemplated by the Charter of the Organization of African Unity (1963).

One might think that when methods are being sought to restore the unity of the

Atlantic community, some attention would be paid to the possibility of strengthening the juridical link by an Atlantic Convention on Pacific Settlement which would, *inter alia*, confer on the Court jurisdiction to deal with legal disputes between the parties to the North Atlantic Pact. If all professions of amity are not mere propaganda, at least these nations should be able to agree that legal disputes between them should be referred to the International Court of Justice.

While the United States might be afraid to have disputes brought to the Court against it by Communist nations (assuming they ever accept the Court's jurisdiction), it cannot in good conscience object to a decision by the Court in a case involving one of its closest allies. The only thing which is necessary here is to forget the old-fashioned notion that it might endanger our relations with our friends if we bring cases against them, or if they bring cases against us, to the Court. In most legal disputes, the points involved do not concern any vital interests of either side, but both sides believe that they have a valid legal point which they do not want to give up in bilateral negotiations. For instance, neither the Congress nor the people of the United States would rise in arms if the United States and the United Kingdom should submit the long-standing dispute about Christmas Island in the Pacific to the Court for final decision; or if the United States and Canada would submit a question of interpretation of an extradition treaty to the Court.

It is amazing, in fact, that despite the close relations between the United States and Canada, and between the United States and the United Kingdom, there is no clear obligation, not hedged with far-reaching reservations, to submit disputes between the United States and those states to the Court for decision. Before tackling the slightly more difficult task of preparing an Atlantic Treaty for pacific settlement of disputes, it might be useful to have bilateral treaties concluded immediately with all the members of the alliance which are willing to do it. Perhaps, more generally, there should be a revival of the bilateral treaties for the pacific (or at least judicial) settlement of international disputes. Despite the great increase in the number of states, only a few such treaties have been concluded in recent years. When Sweden expressed her willingness to conclude bilateral treaties accepting the Court's jurisdiction over legal disputes, only Greece took up this offer in 1956. Perhaps a prize should be made available by the Nobel Peace Institute to the Foreign Minister of the country which concludes the largest number of such treaties in a specified period. There is no excuse for doing nothing in this area for so many years. Some energetic efforts by a few countries could easily change the climate and, thanks to the general tendency to imitate which prevails among the Foreign Offices, a stampede to accept the Court's jurisdiction might quickly follow.

In any case, it might be useful to give states an option to accept the jurisdiction of the Court over all (or some) legal disputes, not with respect to everybody but with respect to selected groups of states (for instance, partners in various alliances or parties to certain treaties) or with respect to specified states only. Each state accepting this obligation might be bound to list at least ten states to which this obligation would apply, and there might be the additional option of agreeing in advance to increase the list by at least ten more states every ten years after the original acceptance. In this way, the circle of states with respect to which the obligation will be binding would extend slowly to most of them. Of course, such an obligation would apply only to states accepting the same obligation and, to confer jurisdiction, it would be necessary that the names of the parties to a particular dispute appear, respectively, on the lists of both parties to that dispute.

4. *Increase in the power of the United Nations to refer disputes to the Court*. Article

36, paragraph 3, of the Charter already provides that in recommending appropriate procedures for the settlement of a dispute referred to it, the Security Council "should also take into consideration that legal disputes should as a general rule be referred by the parties to the International Court of Justice." Such a recommendation was in fact made by the Security Council in the *Corfu Channel* case, and that recommendation seems to have contributed to the acceptance by Albania of the jurisdiction of the Court. There is, however, no general obligation to accept such a recommendation of the Security Council, or a similar recommendation of the General Assembly under Articles 11 and 35.

Some states might be willing to accept in advance an obligation to go to the Court if the Security Council (or the General Assembly) should request them to submit a legal question to the Court. In the Italian Peace Treaty the parties agreed to accept as binding a decision by the General Assembly on the disposition of Italian colonies. It should be even easier to accept as binding a merely procedural decision requiring the parties to solve a particular dispute by recourse to the Court. It need not be feared that the Security Council or the General Assembly would abuse such a power. In each case the Security Council or the General Assembly would, in accordance with Chapter VI of the Charter, have to determine in the first place that the continuance of the dispute is likely to endanger international peace and security; and, secondly, that important issues are involved in the dispute the solution of which would assist in the settlement of the remainder of the dispute. After a while, a line of precedents would be established, indicating in a foreseeable manner which types of cases are likely to be referred to the Court and in what situations such reference is apt to be most fruitful.

As in the previous instances, a state might be given several options. For instance, states could be permitted to choose between accepting as binding the request of the Security Council to go to the Court, or of the General Assembly, or of both of them. Other limitations might also be included.

In conclusion, it might be useful to emphasize that the proposals made here are purely illustrative, and that many other ways of fractionating the obligation to go to the Court can probably be devised. It is the duty of the international legal profession to increase the number of ways in which states should be able to accept the Court's jurisdiction. Once a rich smorgasbord is placed before the states, only the most strong-minded will be able to resist the temptation of nibbling here and there. As is well known, *l'appétit vient en mangeant*, and once they start sampling the available methods, they might be easily carried away.

After the acceptance of the Court's jurisdiction by many more states in many more ways, time would come to try to persuade the states to utilize the new opportunity and to start actually going to the Court. After a few minor cases are decided without disastrous results, more important cases would be submitted, and jurisdiction would be further broadened. If we don't dare to try, we shall never find out whether present obstacles to the Court's jurisdiction can be overcome. As Amelia Earhart Putnam said, "Courage is the price that life exacts for granting peace."

Suggested Readings

Textbooks

Brierly. *The Law of Nations*, pp. 1–93, 346–396.
Brownlie. *Principles of Public International Law*, pp. 1–51, 542–567.
Gould. *An Introduction to International Law*, pp. 1–100, 132–175, 534–575.
Jacobini. *International Law*, pp. 1–44, 235–255.
Kaplan and Katzenbach. *The Political Foundations of International Law*, pp. 1–82, 231–284, 341–354.
Kelsen. *Principles of International Law*, pp. 3–82, 290–301, 437–588.
Sørensen. *Manual of Public International Law*, pp. 1–54, 116–156, 673–738.
Svarlien. *An Introduction to the Law of Nations*, pp. 3–82, 284–332.
Tung. *International Law in an Organizing World*, pp. 1–38, 365–381.
von Glahn. *Law Among Nations*, pp. 3–60, 451–518.

The Nature of International Law

Hart, H. L. A. *The Concept of Law*. Oxford: Clarendon Press, 1961, pp. 208–231.
Henkin, Louis. *How Nations Behave*. New York: Praeger, 1968.
Nussbaum, Arthur. *A Concise History of the Law of Nations*, rev. ed. New York: Macmillan, 1954.

Sources and Evidences of International Law

Finch, George A. *The Sources of Modern International Law*. Washington, D.C.: Carnegie Endowment for International Peace, 1937.
Friedmann, Wolfgang. "The Uses of 'General Principles' in the Development of International Law," 57 *American Journal of International Law* 279 (1963).
Parry, Clive. *Sources and Evidence of International Law*. Dobbs Ferry, N.Y.: Oceana, 1965.

Obligation to Obey International Law

Brierly, J. L. *The Basis of Obligation in International Law and Other Papers,* H. Lauterpacht and C. H. M. Waldoch (eds.). Oxford: Clarendon Press, 1958.
Fitzmaurice, Gerald G. "The Foundations of the Authority of International Law," 19 *Modern Law Review* 1 (1956).

The Relationship of International Law to Municipal Law

Deener, David R. "International Law Provisions in Post-World War II Constitutions," 36 *Cornell Law Quarterly* 505 (1951).
Falk, Richard A. *The Role of Domestic Courts in the International Legal Order*. Syracuse, N.Y.: Syracuse University Press, 1964.
McClure, Wallace. *World Legal Order*. Chapel Hill: University of North Carolina Press, 1960.

International Power to Adjudicate

Anand, R. P. *Compulsory Jurisdiction of the International Court of Justice.* Bombay, London, and New York: Asia Publishing House, 1961.

Jenks, C. Wilfred. *The Prospects of International Adjudication.* Dobbs Ferry, N.Y.: Oceana, 1964.

Jessup, Philip C. *The Uses of International Law.* Ann Arbor: University of Michigan Law School, 1959.

Chapter II
International Legal Persons, Recognition, and Succession

INTERNATIONAL LEGAL PERSONS

The subjects of international law, or international legal persons, are those entities that have the capacity to enjoy rights and assume obligations under international law. Independent nation-states are subjects in the most complete sense of the word; they are universally recognized as having full rights and duties under law. States have the capacity, for example, to enter into treaty relationships, appear as plaintiffs or defendants before international tribunals, join international organizations, and press claims against other states through diplomatic channels. By way of contrast, governmental units within nation-states, such as cities, counties, or "states" within a federal system, are not recognized as subjects. The State of New York, for example, may not become a party to a treaty or appear before an international tribunal; mistreatment under international law standards of an Italian national by New York officials brings responsibility upon the United States itself, not upon New York.

An understanding of international legal personality begins with an awareness that states are the principal subjects of international law. As creators of international law, however, states may, and do, confer international legal personality for certain purposes upon other entities. This practice is not new. Dependent territories have long been permitted to become signatories to certain treaties and have been allowed to join international organizations; groups within a state have been accorded belligerent status and have, consequently, been recognized as having certain rights and duties under international law.

It is now generally agreed that international organizations are subjects of international law. The increasing interdependence of states has led to the creation of numerous universal and regional organizations, and through the treaties creating them and the practice that has grown up around them a certain amount of legal personality has accrued to each of them. Variations in treaty provisions and in practice require that each organization be studied in order to determine the extent of its legal personality. The general trend can be illustrated, however, by reference to the United Nations. Article 104 of the Charter provides that "The Organization shall enjoy in the territory of each of its Members such legal capacity as may be necessary for the exercise of its functions and the fulfillment of its purposes." The capacity of the United Nations to make binding international agreements is illustrated by the trusteeship agreements for dependent territories that were concluded between the organization and such states as Britain and France. The agents of the United Nations are accorded immunities by states,[1] and the organization has successfully brought suit in national courts.[2]

The International Court of Justice has affirmed the capacity of the organization to press claims against states.[3] The practice of maintaining an armed force, under a United Nations command and flag, to which the rules of war apply in so far as the force engages in belligerency, "is a striking example of international personality."[4] And the capacity to exercise jurisdiction over territory was clearly illustrated by the organization's interim administration of Western New Guinea pending the formal transfer of that territory to Indonesia on May 1, 1963.

Individuals are being increasingly recognized as subjects of international law. International law clearly imposes a number of specific obligations upon individuals *qua* individuals, as is illustrated by the rule that prohibits acts of piracy and authorizes any state to capture and to punish anyone guilty of such acts.[5] The owner of a vessel engaged in running a blockade, in the state of which he is not a national, is responsible for his actions, and it is against him as an individual that sanctions are imposed. Individual responsibility for war crimes was clearly demonstrated by the Nuremberg and Tokyo trials following World War II.[6] It must be understood, however, that these illustrations are exceptions rather than the rule. States as entities, rather than their official agents or private individuals, are ordinarily considered to be responsible for international delicts.

International law confers a number of rights upon individuals, but their procedural capacity to enforce the observance of these rights is grossly deficient. If, for example, mistreatment under international law standards befalls an alien,[7] an international claim against the delinquent state can be brought only by the state of which he is a national, and there is no certainty that his home state will be willing to press his claim. Even if it does so, the claim will be based on the fiction that the injury was suffered by the state itself, rather than by

---

[1] See pages 230–231.

[2] See, for example, Balfour, Guthrie and Co. v. United States, 90 F. Supp. 831 (N.D. Cal. 1950) in which it was decided that the United Nations had the capacity to sue the United States as owner of a vessel on which powdered milk was shipped to Europe by the United Nations International Children's Emergency Fund.

[3] See the advisory opinion of the International Court in "Reparations for Injuries Suffered in the Service of the United Nations," reprinted on pages 77–81. Other international organizations have opposed states before arbitration tribunals. See, for example, *Germany v. Reparations Commission* (1923), I *United Nations Reports of International Arbitral Awards* 429.

[4] D. W. Bowett, *The Law of International Institutions* (New York and London: Frederick A. Praeger, 1963), p. 276.

[5] In United States v. Smith, 5 Wheat. 161–162 (1820), Justice Storey stated that "The common law, too, recognizes and punishes piracy as an offence, not against its own municipal code, but as an offence against the law of nations (which is part of the common law), as an offence against the universal law of society, a pirate being deemed an enemy of the human race. . . . The general practice of all nations in punishing all persons, whether natives or foreigners, who have committed this offence against any person whatsoever . . . is a conclusive proof that the offence is supposed to depend, not upon the particular provisions of any municipal code, but upon the law of nations, both for its definition and punishment."

[6] See pages 390, 415–423.

[7] For a discussion of state responsibility for the treatment of aliens, see pages 253–256.

the individual.[8] That the substantive right belongs to the individual, however, is attested to by the fact that the amount of the claim, if monetary damages are sought, is based on the injury suffered by the individual, and the award is normally given to him.

Numerous suggestions that would have the effect of shoring up the procedural capacity of individuals have been put forth, and limited success has been achieved in state practice. Article II of the Convention of December 20, 1907, which established the Central American Court of Justice, provided that the Court

shall also take cognizance of the questions which individuals of one Central American country may raise against any other contracting Governments, because of the violation of treaties or conventions, and in other cases of an international character; no matter whether their own government supports said claim or not. . . .[9]

Other treaties, including the peace treaties following World War I, have given individuals the capacity to press claims before international tribunals. Once again, however, these instances are exceptions rather than the rule. States have been reluctant to expand the procedural capacity of individuals to bring claims against a foreign government as an individual right. Sir Arnold Duncan McNair, former President of the International Court of Justice,

explains the rationale for this reluctance in the following way:

However attractive from the point of view of human rights this proposal may be, it must be remembered that the litigation of a claim between a private individual and a foreign Government before an international tribunal is capable of exciting national feelings between two States, and I submit that an individual uncontrolled by his Government ought not to be allowed to make that possible. I think that is the main reason in favor of the view that, if any machinery is to be created for enabling individuals to bring claims against foreign Governments before international tribunals, their own Government ought to be in a position to give or withhold its *imprimatur*, for one of the main preoccupations of Governments must always be to avoid international friction.[10]

When an individual is injured by his own state, his position under international law is at its lowest point. In the absence of specific treaty provisions conferring rights upon him, the treatment he receives from his own government does not ordinarily involve any question of international law. And even if a treaty right is violated, no other state can press his claim. His international rights against his own government are both meager in content and procedurally unenforcable. This problem has received considerable attention in the United Nations. Article I of the Charter of that organization lists as a purpose of the United Nations the achievement of "international cooperation in solving international problems of an economic, social, cultural, or humanitarian character, and in promoting and encouraging respect for human rights and for fundamental freedoms for all without distinction as to race, sex, language, or religion. . . ." The General Assembly added clarity to the meaning of "human rights" when it adopted, on December 10, 1948, the Universal Declaration of Human Rights.[11] But the Declaration is not a

---

[8] "It is an elementary principle of international law that a State is entitled to protect its subjects, when injured by acts contrary to international law committed by another state, from whom they have been unable to obtain satisfaction through the ordinary channels. By taking up the case of one of its subjects and by resorting to diplomatic action or international judicial proceedings on his behalf, a State is in reality asserting its own rights—its right to ensure, in the person of its subjects, respect for the rules of international law.
. . . Once a state has taken up a case on behalf of one of its subjects before an international tribunal, in the eyes of the latter the State is sole claimant . . ." The Permanent Court of International Justice, *The Mavrommatis Palestine Concessions* (1924), Manley O. Hudson, *World Court Reports* (Washington, D.C.: Carnegie Endowment for International Peace, 1934), Vol. I, pp. 297, 302.
[9] Reprinted in 2 *American Journal of International Law, Supplement* 231 (1908). The Court was terminated in 1917.

[10] Quoted in I Whiteman, *Digest of International Law* 57–58.
[11] Reprinted on pages 82–85.

treaty, and, consequently, it does not impose obligations upon states.[12] It has not been without effect, however, as is illustrated by numerous references to it both in the constitutions of many new states[13] and in national court decisions. And working largely through the Human Rights Commission of ECOSOC, the United Nations has followed up on the Declaration by drafting a number of legally binding conventions covering such matters as forced labor, the rights of women, racial discrimination, and discrimination in education. Some of these conventions are already in force, and others have been submitted for ratification. The major step to date toward the creation of a legally binding international bill of rights was taken, after nineteen years of preparation and debate, on December 16, 1966, when the General Assembly unanimously adopted two far-reaching covenants on human rights. The International Covenant on Civil and Political Rights provides, *inter alia*, for freedom of speech, press, assembly, and religion; freedom from inhuman treatment and arbitrary arrest; and the right to a fair trial. The International Covenant on Economic, Social, and Cultural Rights includes the right to education, employment, medical care, and other social and economic benefits.[14] But without effective sanctions, the enforcement of these covenants, even against ratifying states, will depend chiefly

upon the pressure of world opinion.[15]

The members of the Council of Europe have moved further than the international community in the direction of providing enforceable procedures for the protection of individual rights. Fourteen states are parties to the European Convention for the Protection of Human Rights and Fundamental Freedoms, which went into effect in 1953 and which covers such basic rights as fair criminal and civil procedures and freedom of expression, assembly, and religion.[16] The Convention establishes a European Commission of Human Rights and authorizes it to study and report on alleged violations that may be called to its attention by member states, or by individuals when the state against which the complaint is brought has accepted the competence of the Commission to receive complaints from individuals. Ten of the signatories have accepted the obligation to meet the complaints of their own nationals before the Commission. The Convention also establishes a European Court of Human Rights, before which cases concerning the Convention may be brought by member states of the Commission, if the state complained against has accepted the jurisdiction of the Court.

The first two selections in this section, by L. Oppenheim and Selwyn Lloyd, are brief statements of the traditional view that states are the "proper subjects" of international law. The "Reparations for Injuries Suffered in the Service of the United Nations" advisory opinion of the International Court of Justice is included as an authoritative statement on the legal personality of the United Nations. The position of the individual in international law is discussed in two

---

[12] Mrs. Eleanor Roosevelt, United States Representative on the Human Rights Commission, said on December 9, 1948: "In giving our approval to the Declaration today, it is of primary importance that we keep clearly in mind the basic character of the document. It is not a treaty; it is not an international agreement. It is not and does not purport to be a statement of law or of legal obligation. It is a declaration of basic principles of human rights and freedoms, to be stamped with the approval of the General Assembly by formal vote of its members, and to serve as a common standard of achievement for all peoples of all nations." 19 *United States Department of State Bulletin* 751 (1948).

[13] The Constitution of the Republic of Rwanda, for example, asserts that the "fundamental freedoms as defined by the Universal Declaration of Human Rights are guaranteed to all citizens." Egon Schwelb, *Human Rights and the International Community* (Chicago: Quadrangle Books, 1964), p. 51.

[14] The texts of the two covenants can be found in 61 *American Journal of International Law* 861 (1967).

[15] An Optional Protocol to the International Covenant on Civil and Political Rights, which is open to signature by any state that has signed the Covenant, permits the eighteen-member Human Rights Committee, created by the Covenant, to consider communications from individuals alleging a violation of human rights and to require the state against which the complaint is lodged to explain or clarify the allegation within six months.

[16] See 45 *American Journal of International Law, Supplement* 24 (1954) for the text of the Convention.

United Nations documents, a memorandum prepared by the Secretariat and the Universal Declaration of Human Rights. Finally, an English summary of an article in the *Soviet Yearbook of International Law* states the current Soviet position on the subjects of international law.

States as Subjects of International Law*

L. Oppenheim

Since the Law of Nations is based on the common consent of individual States, and not of individual human beings, States solely and exclusively are the subjects of International Law. This means that the Law of Nations is a law for the international conduct of States, and not of their citizens. Subjects of the rights and duties arising from the Law of Nations are States solely and exclusively. An individual human being, such as a king or an ambassador for example, is never directly a subject of International Law. Therefore, all rights which might necessarily have to be granted to an individual human being according to the Law of Nations are not international rights, but rights granted by Municipal Law in accordance with a duty imposed upon the respective State by International Law. Likewise, all duties which might necessarily have to be imposed upon individual human beings according to the Law of Nations are not international duties, but duties imposed by Municipal Law in accordance with a right granted to or a duty imposed upon the respective State by International Law. Thus the privileges of an ambassador are granted to him by the Municipal Law of the State to which he is accredited, but such State has the duty to grant these

privileges according to International Law. Thus, further, the duties incumbent upon officials and subjects of neutral States in time of war are imposed upon them by the Municipal Law of their home States, but these States have, according to International Law, the duty of imposing the respective duties upon their officials and citizens.

States as Subjects of International Law*

Selwyn Lloyd

[*In his reply to a question about the European Convention on Human Rights, Selwyn Lloyd, British Foreign Secretary, stated that Her Majesty's Government have ratified the Convention but "have not made the optional declaration accepting the competence of the European Commission of Human Rights to receive petitions from individuals, nor that recognizing the compulsory jurisdiction of the proposed European Court of Human Rights." He added:*]

The position which Her Majesty's Government have continuously taken up is that they do not recognise the right of individual petition, because they take the view that States are the proper subject of international law and if individuals are given rights under international treaties effect should be given to those rights through the national law of the States concerned. The reason why we do not accept the idea of the compulsory jurisdiction of a European Court is that it would mean that British codes of common and statute law would be subject to review by an international Court. For many years it has been the position of successive British Governments that we should not accept that status.

---

* Reprinted from L. Oppenheim, *International Law*, 2nd ed. (London and New York: Longmans, Green & Co., 1912), Vol. I, p. 19, by permission of the publisher.

* Reprinted from 574 *Hansard, Parliamentary Debates* cols. 867–868 (Commons, 5th Series, July 29, 1957).

Reparation for Injuries Suffered in the Service of the United Nations*

International Court of Justice, Advisory Opinion of April 11, 1949

[*The United Nations General Assembly requested an advisory opinion concerning the following question: "I. In the event of an agent of the United Nations in the performace of his duties suffering injury in circumstances involving the responsibility of a State, has the United Nations, as an Organization, the capacity to bring an international claim against the responsible de jure or de facto government with a view to obtaining the reparation due in respect of the damage caused (a) to the United Nations, (b) to the victim or to persons entitled through him?"*]

* * *

The questions asked of the Court relate to the "capacity to bring an international claim"; accordingly, we must begin by defining what is meant by that capacity, and consider the characteristics of the Organization, so as to determine whether, in general, these characteristics do, or do not, include for the Organization a right to present an international claim.

Competence to bring an international claim is, for those possessing it, the capacity to resort to the customary methods recognized by international law for the establishment, the presentation and the settlement of claims. Among these methods may be mentioned protest, request for an enquiry, negotiation, and request for submission to an arbitral tribunal or to the Court in so far as this may be authorized by the Statute.

This capacity certainly belongs to the State; a State can bring an international claim against another State. Such a claim

* Reprinted from *International Court of Justice Reports* 174 (1949).

takes the form of a claim between two political entities, equal in law, similar in form, and both the direct subjects of international law. It is dealt with by means of negotiation, and cannot, in the present state of the law as to international jurisdiction, be submitted to a tribunal, except with the consent of the States concerned.

When the Organization brings a claim against one of its Members, this claim will be presented in the same manner, and regulated by the same procedure. It may, when necessary, be supported by the political means at the disposal of the Organization. In these ways the Organization would find a method for securing the observance of its rights by the Member against which it has a claim.

But, in the international sphere, has the Organization such a nature as involves the capacity to bring an international claim? In order to answer this question, the Court must first enquire whether the Charter has given the Organization such a position that it possesses, in regard to its Members, rights which it is entitled to ask them to respect. In other words, does the Organization possess international personality? This is no doubt a doctrinal expression, which has sometimes given rise to controversy. But it will be used here to mean that if the Organization is recognized as having that personality, it is an entity capable of availing itself of obligations incumbent upon its Members.

To answer this question, which is not settled by the actual terms of the Charter, we must consider what characteristics it was intended thereby to give to the Organization.

The subjects of law in any legal system are not necessarily identical in their nature or in the extent of their rights, and their nature depends upon the needs of the community. Throughout its history, the development of international law has been influenced by the requirements of international life, and the progressive increase in the collective activities of States has already given rise to instances of action upon the international plane by certain entities which are not States. This development culminated in the establishment in June 1945 of an international organization whose purposes and principles are specified in the Charter of the United Nations. But to achieve these ends the attribution of international personality is indispensable.

The Charter has not been content to make the Organization created by it merely a centre "for harmonizing the actions of nations in the attainment of these common ends" (Article 1, para. 4). It has equipped that centre with organs, and has given it special tasks. It has defined the position of the Members in relation to the Organization by requiring them to give it every assistance in any action undertaken by it (Article 2, para. 5), and to accept and carry out the decisions of the Security Council; by authorizing the General Assembly to make recommendations to the Members; by giving the Organization legal capacity and privileges and immunities in the territory of each of its Members; and by providing for the conclusion of agreements between the Organization and its Members. Practice— in particular the conclusion of conventions to which the Organization is a party—has confirmed this character of the Organization, which occupies a position in certain respects in detachment from its Members, and which is under a duty to remind them, if need be, of certain obligations. It must be added that the Organization is a political body, charged with political tasks of an important character, and covering a wide field namely, the maintenance of international peace and security, the development of friendly relations among nations, and the achievement of international co-operation in the solution of problems of an economic, social, cultural or humanitarian character (Article 1);

and in dealing with its Members it employs political means. The "Convention on the Privileges and Immunities of the United Nations" of 1946 creates rights and duties between each of the signatories and the Organization (see, in particular, Section 35). It is difficult to see how such a convention could operate except upon the international plane and as between parties possessing international personality.

In the opinion of the Court, the Organization was intended to exercise and enjoy, and is in fact exercising and enjoying, functions and rights which can only be explained on the basis of the possession of a large measure of international personality and the capacity to operate upon an international plane. It is at present the supreme type of international organization, and it could not carry out the intentions of its founders if it was devoid of international personality. It must be acknowledged that its Members, by entrusting certain functions to it, with the attendant duties and responsibilities, have clothed it with the competence required to enable those functions to be effectively discharged.

Accordingly, the Court has come to the conclusion that the Organization is an international person. That is not the same thing as saying that it is a State, which it certainly is not, or that its legal personality and rights and duties are the same as those of a State. Still less is it the same thing as saying that it is "a super-State", whatever that expression may mean. It does not even imply that all its rights and duties must be upon the international plane, any more than all the rights and duties of a State must be upon that plane. What it does mean is that it is a subject of international law and capable of possessing international rights and duties, and that it has capacity to maintain its rights by bringing international claims.

The next question is whether the sum of the international rights of the Organization comprises the right to bring the kind of international claim described in the

Request for this Opinion. That is a claim against a State to obtain reparation in respect of the damage caused by the injury of an agent of the Organization in the course of the performance of his duties. Whereas a State possesses the totality of international rights and duties recognized by international law, the rights and duties of an entity such as the Organization must depend upon its purposes and functions as specified or implied in its constituent documents and developed in practice. The functions of the Organization are of such a character that they could not be effectively discharged if they involved the concurrent action, on the international plane, of fifty-eight or more Foreign Offices, and the Court concludes that the Members have endowed the Organization with capacity to bring international claims when necessitated by the discharge of its functions.

* * *

The traditional rule that diplomatic protection is exercised by the national State does not involve the giving of a negative answer to Question I (*b*).

* * *

The Court is here faced with a new situation. The questions to which it gives rise can only be solved by realizing that the situation is dominated by the provisions of the Charter considered in the light of the principles of international law.

The question lies within the limits already established; that is to say it presupposes that the injury for which the reparation is demanded arises from a breach of an obligation designed to help an agent of the Organization in the performance of his duties. It is not a case in which the wrongful act or omission would merely constitute a breach of the general obligations of a State concerning the position of aliens; claims made under this

head would be within the competence of the national State and not, as a general rule, within that of the Organization.

The Charter does not expressly confer upon the Organization the capacity to include, in its claim for reparations, damage caused to the victim or to persons entitled through him. The Court must therefore begin by enquiring whether the provisions of the Charter concerning the functions of the Organization, and the part played by its agents in the performance of those functions, imply for the Organization power to afford its agents the limited protection that would consist in the bringing of a claim on their behalf for reparation for damage suffered in such circumstances. Under international law, the Organization must be deemed to have those powers which, though not expressly provided in the Charter, are conferred upon it by necessary implication as being essential to the performance of its duties. This principle of law was applied by the Permanent Court of International Justice to the International Labour Organization in its Advisory Opinion No. 13 of July 23rd, 1926 (Series B., No. 13, p. 18), and must be applied to the United Nations.

Having regard to its purposes and functions already referred to, the Organization may find it necessary, and has in fact found it necessary, to entrust its agents with important missions to be performed in disturbed parts of the world. Many missions, from their very nature, involve the agents in unusual dangers to which ordinary persons are not exposed. For the same reason, the injuries suffered by its agents in these circumstances will sometimes have occurred in such a manner that their national State would not be justified in bringing a claim for reparation on the ground of diplomatic protection, or, at any rate, would not feel disposed to do so. Both to ensure the efficient and independent performance of these missions and to afford effective support to its agents, the

Organization must provide them with adequate protection.

* * *

In order that the agent may perform his duties satisfactorily, he must feel that this protection is assured to him by the Organization, and that he may count on it. To ensure the independence of the agent, and, consequently, the independent action of the Organization itself, it is essential that in performing his duties he need not have to rely on any other protection than that of the Organization (save of course for the more direct and immediate protection due from the State in whose territory he may be). In particular, he should not have to rely on the protection of his own State. If he had to rely on that State, his independence might well be compromised, contrary to the principle applied by Article 100 of the Charter. And lastly, it is essential that—whether the agent belongs to a powerful or to a weak State; to one more affected or less affected by the complications of international life; to one in sympathy or not in sympathy with the mission of the agent— he should know that in the performance of his duties he is under the protection of the Organization. This assurance is even more necessary when the agent is stateless.

Upon examination of the character of the functions entrusted to the Organization and of the nature of the missions of its agents, it becomes clear that the capacity of the Organization to exercise a measure of functional protection of its agents arises by necessary intendment out of the Charter.

The obligations entered into by States to enable the agents of the Organization to perform their duties are undertaken not in the interest of the agents, but in that of the Organization. When it claims redress for a breach of these obligations, the Organization is invoking its own right, the right that the obligations due to it should be respected. On this ground, it asks for reparation of the injury suffered, for "it is a principle of international law that the breach of an engagement involves an obligation to make reparation in an adequate form"; as was stated by the Permanent Court in its Judgment No. 8 of July 26th, 1927 (Series A., No. 9, p. 21). In claiming reparation based on the injury suffered by its agent, the Organization does not represent the agent, but is asserting its own right, the right to secure respect for undertakings entered into towards the Organization.

Having regard to the foregoing considerations, and to the undeniable right of the Organization to demand that its Members shall fulfil the obligations entered into by them in the interest of the good working of the Organization, the Court is of the opinion that, in the case of a breach of these obligations, the Organization has the capacity to claim adequate reparation, and that in assessing this reparation it is authorized to include the damage suffered by the victim or by persons entitled through him.

The question remains whether the Organization has "the capacity to bring an international claim against the responsible *de jure* or *de facto* government with a view to obtaining the reparation due in respect of the damage caused (*a*) to the United Nations, (*b*) to the victim or to persons entitled through him" when the defendant State is not a member of the Organization.

. . . On this point, the Court's opinion is that fifty States, representing the vast majority of the members of the international community, had the power, in conformity with international law, to bring into being an entity possessing objective international personality, and not merely personality recognized by them alone, together with capacity to bring international claims.

Accordingly, the Court arrives at the conclusion that an affirmative answer should be given to Question 1 (*a*) and (*b*) whether or not the defendant State is a Member of the United Nations.

Individuals as Subjects of International Law*

Survey of International Law in Relation to the Work of Codification of the International Law Commission, Memorandum Submitted by the Secretary General of the United Nations

The question of the subjects of international law has, in particular in the last twenty-five years, ceased to be one of purely theoretical importance, and it is now probable that in some respects it requires authoritative international regulation. Practice has abandoned the doctrine that States are the exclusive subjects of international rights and duties. Although the Statute of the International Court of Justice adheres to the traditional view that only States can be parties to international proceedings, a number of other international instruments have recognized the procedural capacity of the individual. This was the case not only in the provisions of the Treaty of Versailles relating to the jurisdiction of the Mixed Arbitral Tribunals, but also in other treaties such as the Polish-German Convention of 1922 relating to Upper Silesia in which—as was subsequently held by the Upper Silesian Mixed Tribunal—the independent procedural status of individuals as claimants before an international agency was recognized even as against the State of which they were nationals.

In the sphere of substantive law, the Permanent Court of International Justice recognized, in the advisory opinion relating to the postal service in Danzig, that there is nothing in international law to prevent

individuals from acquiring directly rights under a treaty provided that this is the intention of the contracting parties. A considerable number of decisions of municipal courts rendered subsequently to the advisory opinion of the Permanent Court expressly affirmed that possibility.

In the field of customary international law the enjoyment of benefits of international law by individuals as a matter of right followed from the doctrine, accepted by a growing number of countries, that generally recognized rules of the law of nations form part of the law of the land. In the sphere of duties imposed by international law the principle that the obligations of international law bind individuals directly regardless of the law of their State and of any contrary order received from their superiors was proclaimed in the Charter annexed to the Agreement of 8 August 1945, providing for the setting up of the International Military Tribunal at Nürnberg, as well as in the Charter of the International Military Tribunal at Tokyo of 19 January 1946. That principle was fully affirmed in the judgment of the Nürnberg Tribunal as flowing from the imperative necessity of making international law effective. The Tribunal said: "Crimes against international law are committed by men, not by abstract entities, and only by punishing individuals who commit such crimes can the provisions of international law be enforced." It was reaffirmed in the resolution of the General Assembly of 11 December 1946, expressing adherence to the principles of the Nürnberg Charter and judgment. It has loomed large in the discussions and statements bearing upon the resolution of the General Assembly in the matter of the codification of the law applied in the judgment of the International Military Tribunal. The General Assembly directed the Committee on Codification of International Law "to treat as a matter of primary importance plans for the formulation, in the context of a general codification

* Reprinted from *United Nations Document* A/CN. 4/1/Rev. 1, February 10, 1949, pp. 19–21.

of offences against the peace and security of mankind, or of an International Criminal Code, of the principles recognized in the Charter of the Nürnberg Tribunal and in the judgment of the Tribunal." In a memorandum submitted by the representative of France to the Codification Committee in 1947 it was proposed that the general principle enunciated by the Tribunal and cited above should be confirmed as part of the codification of this aspect of the law: "The individual is subject to international penal law. Without thereby excluding the penal responsibility of the criminal State, international penal law can inflict penalties on the authors of international offences and their accomplices."

On a different plane the Charter of the Nürnberg Tribunal—and the judgment which followed it—proclaimed the criminality of offences against humanity, i.e., of such offences against the fundamental rights of man to life and liberty, even if committed in obedience to the law of the State. To that extent, in a different sphere, positive law has recognized the individual as endowed, under international law, with rights the violation of which is a criminal act. The repeated provisions of the Charter of the United Nations in the matter of human rights and fundamental freedoms are directly relevant in this connexion.

Universal Declaration of Human Rights*

The General Assembly

Proclaims this Universal Declaration of Human Rights as a common standard of achievement for all peoples and all nations, to the end that every individual and every organ of society, keeping this Declaration constantly in mind, shall strive by teaching and education to pro-

* Adopted by the General Assembly of the United Nations, December 10, 1948.

mote respect for these rights and freedoms and by progressive measures, national and international, to secure their universal and effective recognition and observance, both among the peoples of Member States themselves and among the peoples of territories under their jurisdiction.

Article 1

All human beings are born free and equal in dignity and rights. They are endowed with reason and conscience and should act towards one another in a spirit of brotherhood.

Article 2

Everyone is entitled to all the rights and freedoms set forth in this Declaration, without distinction of any kind, such as race, colour, sex, language, religion, political or other opinion, national or social origin, property, birth or other status.

Furthermore, no distinction shall be made on the basis of the political, jurisdictional or international status of the country or territory to which a person belongs, whether it be independent, trust, non-self-governing or under any other limitation of sovereignty.

Article 3

Everyone has the right to life, liberty and the security of person.

Article 4

No one shall be held in slavery or servitude; slavery and the slave trade shall be prohibited in all their forms.

Article 5

No one shall be subjected to torture or to cruel, inhuman or degrading treatment or punishment.

Article 6

Everyone has the right to recognition everywhere as a person before the law.

Article 7

All are equal before the law and are entitled without any discrimination to equal protection of the law. All are entitled to equal protection against any discrimination in violation of this Declaration and against any incitement to such discrimination.

Article 8

Everyone has the right to an effective remedy by the competent national tribunals for acts violating the fundamental rights granted him by the constitution or by law.

Article 9

No one shall be subjected to arbitrary arrest, detention or exile.

Article 10

Everyone is entitled in full equality to a fair and public hearing by an independent and impartial tribunal, in the determination of his rights and obligations and of any criminal charge against him.

Article 11

1. Everyone charged with a penal offence has the right to be presumed innocent until proved guilty according to law in a public trial at which he has had all the guarantees necessary for his defence.

2. No one shall be held guilty of any penal offence on account of any act or omission which did not constitute a penal offence, under national or international law, at the time when it was committed. Nor shall a heavier penalty be imposed than the one that was applicable at the time the penal offence was committed.

Article 12

No one shall be subjected to arbitrary interference with his privacy, family, home or correspondence, nor to attacks upon his honour and reputation. Everyone has the right to the protection of the law against such interference or attacks.

Article 13

1. Everyone has the right to freedom of movement and residence within the borders of each State.

2. Everyone has the right to leave any country, including his own, and to return to his country.

Article 14

1. Everyone has the right to seek and to enjoy in other countries asylum from persecution.

2. This right may not be invoked in the case of prosecutions genuinely arising from non-political crimes or from acts contrary to the purposes and principles of the United Nations.

Article 15

1. Everyone has the right to a nationality.

2. No one shall be arbitrarily deprived of his nationality nor denied the right to change his nationality.

Article 16

1. Men and women of full age, without any limitation due to race, nationality or religion, have the right to marry and to found a family. They are entitled to equal rights as to marriage, during marriage and at its dissolution.

2. Marriage shall be entered into only with the free and full consent of the intending spouses.

3. The family is the natural and fundamental group unit of society and is entitled to protection by society and the State.

Article 17

1. Everyone has the right to own property alone as well as in association with others.

2. No one shall be arbitrarily deprived of his property.

Article 18

Everyone has the right to freedom of thought, conscience and religion; this right includes freedom to change his religion or belief, and freedom, either alone or in community with others and in public or private, to manifest his religion or belief in teaching, practice, worship and observance.

Article 19

Everyone has the right to freedom of opinion and expression; this right includes freedom to hold opinions without interference and to seek, receive and impart information and ideas through any media and regardless of frontiers.

Article 20

1. Everyone has the right to freedom of peaceful assembly and association.

2. No one may be compelled to belong to an association.

Article 21

1. Everyone has the right to take part in the government of his country, directly or through freely chosen representatives.

2. Everyone has the right of equal access to public service in his country.

3. The will of the people shall be the basis of the authority of government; this will shall be expressed in periodic and genuine elections which shall be by universal and equal suffrage and shall be held by secret vote or by equivalent free voting procedures.

Article 22

Everyone, as a member of society, has the right to social security and is entitled to realization, through national effort and international co-operation and in accordance with the organization and resources of each State, of the economic, social and cultural rights indispensable for his dignity and the free development of his personality.

Article 23

1. Everyone has the right to work, to free choice of employment, to just and favourable conditions of work and to protection against unemployment.

2. Everyone, without any discrimination, has the right to equal pay for equal work.

3. Everyone who works has the right to just and favourable remuneration ensuring for himself and his family an existence worthy of human dignity, and supplemented, if necessary, by other means of social protection.

4. Everyone has the right to form and to join trade unions for the protection of his interests.

Article 24

Everyone has the right to rest and leisure, including reasonable limitation of working hours and periodic holidays with pay.

Article 25

1. Everyone has the right to a standard of living adequate for the health and well-being of himself and of his family, including food, clothing, housing and medical care and necessary social services, and the right to security in the event of unemployment, sickness, disability, widowhood, old age or other lack of livelihood in circumstances beyond his control.

2. Motherhood and childhood are entitled to special care and assistance. All children, whether born in or out of wedlock, shall enjoy the same social protection.

Article 26

1. Everyone has the right to education. Education shall be free, at least in the elementary and fundamental stages. Elementary education shall be compulsory. Technical and professional education shall be made generally available and higher education shall be equally accessible to all on the basis of merit.

2. Education shall be directed to the full development of the human personality and to the strengthening of respect for human rights and fundamental freedoms. It shall promote understanding, tolerance and friendship among all nations, racial or religious groups, and shall further the activities of the United Nations for the maintenance of peace.

3. Parents have a prior right to choose the kind of education that shall be given to their children.

Article 27

1. Everyone has the right freely to participate in the cultural life of the community, to enjoy the arts and to share in scientific advancement and its benefits.

2. Everyone has the right to the protection of the moral and material interests resulting from any scientific, literary or artistic production of which he is the author.

Article 28

Everyone is entitled to a social and international order in which the rights and freedoms set forth in this Declaration can be fully realized.

Article 29

1. Everyone has duties to the community in which alone the free and full development of his personality is possible.

2. In the exercise of his rights and freedoms, everyone shall be subject only to such limitations as are determined by law solely for the purpose of securing due recognition and respect for the rights and freedoms of others and of meeting the just requirements of morality, public order and the general welfare in a democratic society.

3. These rights and freedom may in no case be exercised contrary to the purposes and principles of the United Nations.

Article 30

Nothing in this Declaration may be interpreted as implying for any State, group or person any right to engage in any activity or to perform any act aimed at the destruction of any of the rights and freedoms set forth herein.

A Soviet View: Subjects of Contemporary International Law*

N. A. Ushakov

The question of subjects of contemporary international law is to some extent debatable in Soviet literature.

Soviet international law experts are unanimous on the point that states are subjects of international law. They emphasise the indisputable fact that states are the main subjects of international law. Soviet authors are also at one on the point that physical persons, individuals, are not and cannot be subjects of international law. Soviet jurists undoubtedly deserve credit for substantiating the principle that nations which rose up to fight for their liberation are also subjects of contemporary international law.

The difference in views consists in that some Soviet authors regard as subjects of international law only states and peoples and nations fighting for their liberation,

* Reprinted from N. A. Ushakov, "Subjects of Contemporary International Law," *Soviet Yearbook of International Law* 72 (1964-1965), by permission of the Soviet Association of International Law. (English summary)

while others consider that some international (inter-state) organisations are also subjects of international law.

The latter view apparently now prevails among Soviet jurists, but it is often expounded with insufficient clarity.

* * *

Inasmuch as international law has been brought into being by the existence of a system of states and relations between them, which necessitates their regulation by legal rules, there is no need specially to prove that states are subjects of international law. This directly follows from the rules of international law which chiefly determine the nature of behavior of states as subjects of international legal relations. The distinctive feature of states as subjects of international law is their sovereignty.

The quality of sovereignty is inherent solely in states. It determines their main specific features as subjects of international law. By virtue of its sovereignty a state *ipso facto*—by virtue merely of the fact of its existence—is a subject of international law. For this no act or expression of will by other participants in international relations is needed. The mere fact of the formation of a new state makes it a subject of international legal relations, regardless of the will of any other subjects of international law. A state is subject of international law in full scope during the entire period of its existence. It ends only with the termination of the given state, for example, if it becomes part of another state or is divided into two or more independent states.

A state, as distinct from other subjects of international law, is a universal subject of law; this quality is not restricted either as regards the object of international legal regulation or time as long as the state exists.

States, subjects of international legal relations, at the same time are the makers of rules of international law. No authority of any kind which subordinates states exists. The rules of international law are created through agreements between them, are the result of co-ordination of their will.

An important distinction of states, subjects of international law, therefore, is the fact that they can participate only in such legal relations, the very existence of which conforms to their will expressed in a rule of international law recognised by them.

In view of these distinctions and also because rules of international law regulate predominantly relations between states, the latter are the main subjects of international law, possessing specific properties which other subjects of international law do not have.

Contemporary international law recognises and proclaims the right of each people and nation to self-determination up to secession and formation of an independent state. Recognising and proclaiming the principle of national sovereignty, international law does not predetermine the political or legal status of one or another people or nation. It merely demands respect for their free expression of will. Each nation possesses the inalienable right to arrange its life according to its own wishes. It can form an independent state or freely unite with another nation or other nations.

In contemporary international law nations are the subjects of the right to self-determination. They are thus subjects of a definite international legal relation and thereby are subjects of international law. Naturally, we speak of a nation as a subject of international law first of all as regards oppressed nations and peoples in colonial bondage. They have a right to demand political independence and to strive for it by all means at their disposal, up to armed struggle for national liberation.

But it is not only the oppressed nations, but also other nations that are the bearers of the right to self-determining and thereby are subjects of international law.

A nation which has formed a unitary state preserves the right to change the form of its statehood. It can voluntarily unite with other nations in a federal state. In such a case all other states and other participants in international intercourse must respect the freely expressed will and desire of the uniting states and not offer any obstacles.

A nation which has voluntarily become part of a multinational state preserves the right to unhindered secession from that state and the creation of its own independent state. A state in which the given nation is incorporated must not prevent it from forming an independent state.

As in the case of a state being subject of international law, a nation is a subject of law irrespective of any external reasons, for example, its recognition by the participants in international intercourse. A nation is a subject of international law solely by virtue of its existence.

But as distinct from a state, a nation is a special subject of law, inasmuch as it is a subject only of the legal relation which arises on the basis of the international legal principle of self-determination.

The problem of international organisations being subjects of law is relatively new. All Soviet jurists rightly hold that only interstate organisations set up directly by agreement between states can be subjects of law. In the case of the numerous international non-governmental associations and organisations established by individuals or their associations, the question of their being subjects of international law does not arise, inasmuch as their founders cannot invest such international associations with any rights and duties in international intercourse because they do not possess such competence.

International organisations may be set up as a result of a corresponding expression of will by the main, original subjects of international law, by states.

Any such organisation can be legitimately formed only within the bounds of operating international law. For its proclaimed and actual purposes and activities it must conform to the demands of the generally recognised and generally binding principles and rules of international law.

Consequently, the question of international organisations being subjects of law can be raised solely with regard to legally constituted and operating organisations. The rights and duties which founding states may vest international organisations with must strictly conform to the general binding principles and rules of international law.

It may be asserted that any legally formed and operating international (interstate) organisation is a subject of international law because its basic instrument must regulate relations between the organisation and member states at least as regards their membership in this organisation. In most cases the charters of international organisations also contain other rules which define the reciprocal rights and duties of the organisation and its members and also the rights of the given organisation in its possible relations with other organisations.

Thus, every legally existing international organisation is a subject of international law.

In contrast to sovereign states which are *ipso facto* subjects of international law, international organisations are derivative subjects produced by agreement between states which most often is the charter founding the organisation. Such organisations are subject to law only within the bounds of the aims of the given international organisation which must not run counter to the basic principles and rules of international law. It is usually of a temporary nature because it can be terminated by the will of the member states which can dissolve the organisation or change its powers fixed by international agreement.

RECOGNITION

The process by which new political communities acquire the international personality of states and new governments achieve the international status of official representatives of existing states is normally associated with the word "recognition," a term which relates "to the acknowledgement of the existence of a new state or of a new government in an existing foreign state, coupled with an expression of willingness on the part of the recognizing state to enter into relations with the recognized entity or government."[1]

Whether or not a new state, or a new government, has actually commenced existence is a question of fact that can normally be answered by the use of objective tests: when a community acquires the characteristics of statehood, namely a defined territory, an effective government, and freedom from outside control, it is by definition a new state; when a group acquires effective control over the governmental machinery of a state, it is in fact the new government. But factual existence does not necessarily bring recognition to a new state or a new government. Decision-makers in other states feel free to accord or to withhold recognition as national interests dictate, a fact which leads to considerable variation in state practice and confusion in legal theory. As Professor Briggs has said, "Juridical theories of recognition logically deduced from jurisprudential concepts fail to explain the facts of State conduct, and inductions from State conduct have failed to provide a juridically unambiguous theory of recognition."[2]

The writings of Sir Hersch Lauterpacht,

a leading proponent of the "constitutive" theory of recognition, illustrate the gap between the theory and the practice of recognition.[3] According to this school of thought, a state has no standing in international law until it has been recognized by other states; recognition, not factual existence, creates international personality. In the absence of a centralized international institution to confer legal personality upon a community claiming to be a new state, this function is performed by previously existing states acting as "organs" of international law. To avoid the anomalous situation of a new state being bound by international law only in its relations with states that have recognized it, Lauterpacht posits a legal duty on the part of existing states to recognize any community that has in fact acquired the characteristics of statehood. The act of recognition is thereby defined as a clearly legal act, with new states having the legal right to be recognized and established states having the legal duty to recognize them. Similar reasoning is used to posit a legal duty to recognize new governments that in fact come to power in existing states.

Practice indicates, however, that, although established states normally recognize new states and new governments that in fact exist, they have not consented to law norms that obligate them to do so.[4] Numerous considerations in addition to

---

[1] von Glahn, *Law Among Nations*, p. 89. States also "recognize" belligerency, neutrality, and so on.

[2] Herbert W. Briggs, *The Law of Nations: Cases, Documents, and Notes*, 2nd ed. (New York: Appleton-Century-Crofts, 1952), p. 117.

[3] See especially Hersch Lauterpacht, *Recognition in International Law* (Cambridge: University Press, 1947). For a discussion of the "declarative" theory of recognition, see any of the standard textbooks listed at the end of this chapter on page 126.

[4] John Foster Dulles, former United States Secretary of State, said in no uncertain terms that "No government has a right to have recognition. It is a privilege that is accorded, and we accord it when we think it will fit in with our national interests, and if it doesn't we don't accord it." Secretary Dulles' news conference, Canberra, Australia, Department of State press release No. 144, March 14, 1957.

those related to factual existence enter the decision-making process, including such "legally irrelevant" factors as the possibility that recognition might offend an ally or alienate an important segment of voters at home. The international political environment is of particular importance in the determination of state recognition policy, as is illustrated by the obvious influence of the politics of the cold war and anticolonialism on state recognition policy during recent years. Afro-Asian and Communist states, for example, have been quick to recognize entities that claim to be free from Western colonial domination, regardless of the factual situation, while the United States has refused to recognize the government that obviously controls China.

The political nature of the act of recognition is particularly evident in recent state practice regarding new governments that have come to power through revolution or coup d'état. When this occurs, numerous considerations may enter the decision-making process in other states, including judgments as to whether the new regime is in effective control, lacks substantial resistance, and is willing to carry out the obligations of the state under international law. But these "traditional norms" are subject to political interpretations, and additional tests may be added as interests dictate. The most recent semiofficial *Digest of International Law* published by the United States Department of State adds to the traditional criteria of recognition the following:

Other factors increasingly borne in mind, as appropriate, for example, are the existence or nonexistence of evidence of foreign intervention in the establishment of the new regime; the political orientation of the government and its leaders; evidence of intention to observe democratic principles, particularly the holding of elections; the attitude of the new government toward private investment and economic improvement. Importantly, also, the nterest of peoples, as distinguished from gov-

ernments, is of concern. These, and other criteria, depending upon the international situation at the time, have been considered, with varying weight.[5]

Although recognition is essentially a political act, it is important to realize that the consequences of nonrecognition are of both political and legal importance. Recognition can bring, *inter alia*, an opportunity to establish diplomatic and consular relations with recognizing states; an increase in stability at home and prestige abroad; access to foreign aid, loans, and trade; and, in the case of a new government of an established state, access to state funds on deposit in the banks of recognizing states. A decision to withhold recognition can be a powerful or an impotent political weapon, depending upon the relative power of the nonrecognizing and the unrecognized entities. Over the long run, however, it would appear that nonrecognition of new states or new governments that in fact exist is, if not illegal, politically unwise and legally inconvenient. It is largely because decision-makers are aware of this fact that state practice is at least consistent enough to permit references to "traditional norms," or "standard tests," of recognition.

In the first of the following selections, Green H. Hackworth discusses the general nature of recognition and the modes by which it has been accorded in United States practice. A brief statement by President John F. Kennedy emphasizes the importance of intent in the act of recognition. The different uses of the terms "de facto" and "de jure" in matters of recognition are discussed in a brief selection by William W. Bishop, Jr. Several selections from British and United States sources are included to illustrate differences in the recognition policies of those two states toward Communist China. The relationship of recognition to representation in the United Nations is

---

[5] 2 Whiteman, *Digest of International Law* 73.

discussed by Trygve Lie, the first Secretary General of the United Nations. Finally, one of the many consequences of non-recognition is illustrated by the case of *Bank of China v. Wells Fargo and Union Trust Company.*

Nature of Recognition*

Recognition may be of new states, of new governments, or of belligerency. It is evidenced, in the case of a new state or government, by an act officially acknowledging the existence of such state or government and indicating a readiness on the part of the recognizing state to enter into formal relations with it. The existence in fact of a new state or a new government is not dependent upon its recognition by other states. By recognition of belligerency, as here used, is meant the recognition by a state that a revolt within another state has attained such a magnitude as to constitute in fact a state of war, entitling the revolutionists or insurgents to the benefits, and imposing upon them the obligations, of the rules of war.

* * *

Recognition is essentially a matter of intention. It may be express or implied. The mode by which it is accomplished is of no special significance. It is essential, however, that the act constituting recognition shall give a clear indication of an intention (1) to treat with the new state as such, or (2) to accept the new government as having authority to represent the state it purports to govern and to maintain diplomatic relations with it, or (3) to recognize in the case of insurgents that they are entitled to exercise belligerent rights. "Recognition cannot be accomplished by inference merely but by the full

* Reprinted from 1 Hackworth, *Digest of International Law* 161, 166–168 (Washington, D.C.: U.S. Government Printing Office, 1940).

and formal entrance into international relations through the public action of the respective executives of the two countries." Secretary Colby to the Chargé d'Affaires in Mexico (Summerlin), May 25, 1920, MS. Department of State, file 812.00/24071; 1920 For. Rel., vol. III, p. 167. An act which would normally have the effect of recognition—short of one involving formal diplomatic relations with a foreign state or government—may be deprived of that quality by an express declaration of the government performing it that it is not intended to constitute recognition.

Recognition of new states usually carries with it recognition of the government of the state so recognized, since states can speak and act only through their governments. In a majority of the cases referred to below, recognition of new states by the United States was accomplished through a formal note sent by the American diplomatic representative at the capital of the country in question to the Foreign Office, under instructions from the Department of State. This was true in the cases of Bulgaria in 1909; Albania, Estonia, Latvia, Lithuania, and Egypt, all in 1922; and Saudi Arabia in 1931. In certain other instances a formal note was sent by the Department of State to the diplomatic representative in the United States of the state in question. This was the method followed in the cases of Armenia in 1920, and Finland and Yugoslavia in 1919. Poland was recognized in 1919 by means of a telegram from the Secretary of State, then in Paris, to the President of the Polish Provisional Government. Formal reception by the President of an Afghan mission in 1921 was considered to constitute recognition of Afghanistan. Recognition of the Czechoslovak National Council in 1918 as a *de facto* belligerent government was made through a formal public announcement issued by Secretary Lansing, and the recognition of the Government of the Republic in 1918 was made through establishment of relations with it, including the acceptance of its agent in the United States and the negotiation of loans to it. Iraq was recognized in 1931 by accrediting a chargé d'affaires to the King. In the case of Iceland recognition resulted from the conclusion of certain bilateral agreements.

Perhaps the method of recognizing a new government recurring most frequently in the foreign relations of the United States is, as in the case of the recognition of new states, the sending of a note by the representative of the United States at the foreign capital announcing the decision of his Government to establish relations with the new government. It may however assume a variety of forms. Several of the many forms employed are enumerated in the following memorandum:

In the practice of the United States, there are several formulae of recognition.

The first and most usual is, the notification, by the American representative at the foreign capital, that he is instructed to enter into relations with the new government. This is ordinarily supplemented by informing the foreign minister (if there be one) in Washington in a like sense.

The second, and the course very generally followed in other countries, is the acknowledgment, by the President, of a letter addressed to him by the head of the new foreign government announcing his assumption of authority. (It is in this way that King George V is reported to intend to recognize General Huerta as Constitutional *interim* President of the United Mexican States—that being the style and title used by General Huerta in his formal letter of announcement.)

The third, also usual in the intercourse of states, is the reception of an envoy by the President, in audience for the purpose of presenting his letters of credence.

The fourth is the reception, by the President, of the continuing diplomatic agent of the foreign state, for the purpose of making oral announcement of the change of government. In both these two latter cases, the complimentary addresses of the envoy and the President suffice to define and accentuate the scope of the recognition so effected.

A fifth method may be available, namely the formal delivery by the American envoy at the foreign capital, to the head of the new government, of a message of recognition from the President, or of a congratulatory resolution of the American Congress if one have been passed.

The sixth method, which was adopted in the case of Portugal and Spain (and, I think, in the case of the French Republic, 1871) is to supplement the recognition of a provisional or interim government by a formal announcement of recognition, made by the American envoy, upon the adoption of a new form of government by the national assembly of the foreign state.[1]

Note

1. Memorandum of Mar. 28, 1913 of the Second Assistant Secretary of State (Adee) to Secretary Bryan, MS. Department of State, file 893.00/1669; 1913 For. Rel. 100–102.

Recognition and the Nuclear Test Ban Treaty*

President John F. Kennedy

Question. Mr. President, Senator Dirksen and some West German officials have expressed concern that if the nuclear test ban is signed amongst others by this Government, by the Federal Republic of Germany, and by the East German regime, that this will amount to a tacit recognition of East Germany. What is your thinking on this point?

* Statement made at Press Conference No. 59 of the President of the United States.

The President. That is not correct. This matter was discussed and the position of the United States and Britain was made very clear to the Soviet Union, and as a matter of fact, the Soviet Union mentioned a regime which it did not recognize and did not wish to recognize. So that a procedure was developed whereby a regime which is not recognized by one of the other parties to the treaty can file its assent with one of the three parties. This act would not constitute recognition by the remaining signatories. The fact of the matter is that we signed a part of a multilateral treaty on Laos which the Red Chinese also signed, but we do not recognize the Red Chinese regime. This is a matter of intent. Diplomatic procedure, custom, and law provides that recognition is a matter of intent. We do not intend to recognize the East German regime. . . .

"De Facto" and "De Jure" Recognition*

William W. Bishop, Jr.

In recognition matters the terms "de facto" and "de jure" are frequently used, in differing senses. Sometimes the de facto policy of recognition is contrasted with the de jure basis of constitutionality or legitimacy relied upon by some states as the criterion of recognition. At other times there is no recognition at all, but courts or authorities admit the existence of a "de facto" though *unrecognized* government. At yet other times . . . a distinction is drawn between "de facto recognition" and "de jure recognition," or more precisely "recognition as a de facto government" and "recognition as a de jure government." This last distinction appears to be chiefly political rather than legal; though the legal

* Reprinted from William W. Bishop, Jr., *International Law: Cases and Materials,* 2nd ed. (Boston: Little, Brown and Company, 1962), p. 289, by permission of the author and publisher.

results are practically the same, "de facto recognition" frequently precedes "de jure recognition," the former stressing the provisional or temporary or still uncertain status achieved by the regime recognized as the "de facto government."

United States Policy on Nonrecognition of Communist China*

Department of State Memorandum to Missions Abroad, August 11, 1958

* * *

In the effort to block Peiping's attempts to extend Communist rule in Asia the withholding of diplomatic recognition is an important factor. The extension of diplomatic recognition by a great power normally carries with it not only increased access to international councils but enhanced international standing and prestige as well. Denial of recognition on the other hand is a positive handicap to the regime affected and one which makes it that much the more difficult for it to pursue its foreign policies with success. One basic purpose of United States nonrecognition of Communist China is to deny it these advantages and to that extent limit its ability to threaten the security of the area.

In the case of China there are special considerations which influence United States policy with regard to recognition. For one thing, although the Chinese Communists have seized the preponderant bulk of China, they have not completed their conquest of the country. The generally recognized legitimate Government of China continues to exist and in Taiwan is steadily developing its political, economic, and

* Reprinted from 39 *United States Department of State Bulletin* 385 (1958).

military strength. The Government of the Republic of China controls the strategic island of Taiwan and through its possession of a sizable military force—one of the largest on the side of the free world in Asia—presents a significant deterrent to renewed Chinese Communist aggression. Recognition of Communist China by the United States would seriously cripple, if not destroy altogether, that Government. On the other hand, continued United States recognition and support of the Republic of China enables it to challenge the claim of the Chinese Communists to represent the Chinese people and keeps alive the hopes of those Chinese who are determined eventually to free their country of Communist rule.

Recognition of Communist China by the United States would have an adverse effect on the other free governments of Asia which could be disastrous to the cause of the free world in that part of the world. Those nations which are closely allied to the United States and are striving to maintain their independence on the perimeter of Chinese Communist power, especially Korea and Viet-Nam, would be profoundly confused and demoralized. They would interpret such action as abandonment of their cause by the United States. They might reason that their only hope for survival lay in desperate measures, not caring whether these threatened the peace of the area and the world. Governments further removed from the borders of China would see in American recognition of Communist China the first step in the withdrawal of the United States from the Far East. Without the support of the United States they would be unable long to defy the will of Peiping; and some would probably conclude that their wisest course would be speedily to seek the best terms obtainable from Peiping. Needless to say, these developments would place the entire free world position in Asia in the gravest peril.

Another special consideration in the case of China is that large and influential "overseas" Chinese communities exist in most of the countries of Southeast Asia. The efforts of these countries to build healthy free societies and to develop their economies would be seriously retarded if these communities were to fall under the sway of the Chinese Communists; and a grave threat of Communist subversion through these overseas communities would arise. Recognition of Communist China by the United States and the decline in the fortunes of the Republic of China which would inevitably result would have such a profound psychological effect on the overseas Chinese that it would make inevitable the transfer of the loyalties of large numbers to the Communist side. This in turn would undermine the ability of the host countries to resist the pressures tending to promote the expansion of Chinese Communist influence and power.

Still another factor which must be considered in the case of China is the effect which recognition of the Communist regime would have on the United Nations. Recognition of Peiping by the United States would inevitably lead to the seating of Peiping in that body. In the view of the United States this would vitiate, if not destroy, the United Nations as an instrument for the maintenance of international peace. The Korean war was the first and most important effort to halt aggression through collective action in the United Nations. For Communist China, one of the parties against which the effort of the United Nations was directed, to be seated in the United Nations while still unpurged of its aggression and defying the will of the United Nations in Korea would amount to a confession of failure on the part of the United Nations and would greatly reduce the prospects for future successful action by the United Nations against aggression. Moreover, the Republic of China is a charter member in good standing of the United Nations, and its representatives there have contributed importantly to the constructive work of that organization. If the preresentatives of the Chinese Communist regime were to be seated in their place and given China's veto in the Security Council, the ability of that body in the future to discharge the responsibility it has under the charter for the maintaining of international peace and security would be seriously impaired.

Those who advocate recognition of the Chinese Communists often assume that by the standards of international law applied to such cases the Peiping regime is "entitled" to diplomatic recognition. In the view of the United States diplomatic recognition is a privilege and not a right. Moreover, the United States considers that diplomatic recognition is an instrument of national policy which it is both its right and its duty to use in the enlightened self-interest of the nation. However, there is reason to doubt that even by the tests often cited in international law the Chinese Communist regime qualifies for diplomatic recognition. It does not rule all China, and there is a substantial force in being which contests its claim to do so. The Chinese Communist Party, which holds mainland China in its grip, is a tiny minority comprising less than 2 percent of the Chinese people, and the regimentation, brutal repression, and forced sacrifices that have characterized its rule have resulted in extensive popular unrest. To paraphrase Thomas Jefferson's dictum, this regime certainly does not represent "the will of the populace, substantially declared." Finally, it has shown no intention to honor its international obligations. One of its first acts was to abrogate the treaties of the Republic of China, except those it chose to continue. On assuming power it carried out a virtual confiscation without compensation of the properties of foreign nationals, including immense British investments notwithstanding the United Kingdom's prompt recognition of it. It has failed to honor various commitments entered into since, including various provisions of the Korean

armistice and the Geneva accord on Viet-Nam and Laos, as well as the agreed announcement of September 1955 by which it pledged itself to permit all Americans in China to return home "expeditiously."

The United States policy toward recognition of Communist China is then based on a carefully considered judgment of the national interest. Nonrecognition of Peiping coupled with continued recognition and support of the Republic of China facilitates the accomplishment of United States policy objectives in the Far East. Recognition of Peiping would seriously hinder accomplishment of these objectives and would facilitate the advance of Communist power in Asia.

In the process of determining its policy toward China the United States has taken into account the various statements and arguments advanced by proponents of extending diplomatic recognition to Peiping. One of the most commonly advanced reasons for recognition is that reality must be "recognized" and 600 million people cannot be "ignored." While superficially appealing, both statements themselves overlook the realities of the situation. United States policy is, of course, based on full appreciation of the fact that the Chinese Communist regime is currently in control of mainland China. However, it is not necessary to have diplomatic relations with a regime in order to deal with it. Without extending diplomatic recognition the United States has participated in extended negotiations with Chinese Communist reresentatives, in the Korean and Indochina armistice negotiations, and more recently in the ambassadorial talks in Geneva. Similarly, United States policy in no sense "ignores" the existence and the aspirations of the Chinese people. Its attitude toward the people of China remains what it historically has been, one of friendship and sympathetic understanding. It is nonetheless clear that our friendship for the Chinese people must not be permitted to blind us to the threat to our security which the Communist regime in China now presents. Moreover, the United States is convinced that the Chinese Communist regime does not represent the true will or aspirations of the Chinese people and that our policy of withholding recognition from it is in actuality in their ultimate interest.

* * *

An argument often heard is that the Chinese Communists are here "to stay"; that they will have to be recognized sooner or later; and that it would be the course of wisdom to bow to the inevitable now rather than be forced to do so ungracefully at a later date. It is true that there is no reason to believe that the Chinese Communist regime is on the verge of collapse; but there is equally no reason to accept its present rule in mainland China as permanent. In fact, unmistakable signs of dissatisfaction and unrest in Communist China have appeared in the "ideological remodeling" and the mass campaign against "rightists" which have been in progress during the past year. Dictatorships often create an illusion of permanence from the very fact that they suppress and still all opposition, and that of the Chinese Communists is no exception to this rule. The United States holds the view that communism's rule in China is not permanent and that it one day will pass. By withholding diplomatic recognition from Peiping it seeks to hasten that passing.

In public discussions of China policy one of the proposals that has attracted widest attention is that known as the "two Chinas solution." Briefly, advocates of this arrangement propose that the Chinese Communist regime be recognized as the government of mainland China while the Government at Taipei remains as the legal government of Taiwan. They argue that this approach to the Chinese problem has the merit of granting the Communists only what they already control while retaining for the free world the militarily strategic bastion of Taiwan. However, it overlooks or ignores certain facts of basic importance. The Republic of China would not accept any diminution of its sovereignty over China and could be expected to resist such an arrangement with all the means at its disposal. If a "two Chinas solution" were to be forcefully imposed against its will, that Government's effectiveness as a loyal ally to the free-world-cause would be destroyed. Peiping, too, would reject such an arrangement. In fact, over the past year Chinese Communist propaganda has repeatedly and stridently denounced the "two Chinas" concept and, ironically, has been accusing the United States Government of attempting to put it into effect. Peiping attaches great importance to the eventual acquisition of Taiwan and has consistently reserved what it calls its "right" to seize Taiwan by force if other means fail. There is no prospect that it would ever acquiesce in any arrangement which would lead to the permanent detachment of Taiwan from China.

The "two Chinas" concept is bitterly opposed by both Peiping and Taipei. Hence, even if such a solution could be imposed by outside authority, it would not be a stable one. Constant policing would be required to avert its violent overthrow by one side or the other.

It is sometimes said that nonrecognition of Peiping tends to martyrize the Chinese Communists, thereby enabling them to pose, especially before Asian neutralists, as an innocent and injured party. It would be impossible to deny that there is some truth in this. But this disadvantage is far outweighed by the disadvantages that would result from following the opposite course. It is surely better that some neutralists, who are either unable or unwilling to comprehend the threat inherent in Chinese Communist policies, mistakenly consider Peiping unjustly treated than that the allies of the United States in Asia, who are the first line of defense against Chinese Communist expansion, should be confused and demoralized by what to them could only appear to be a betrayal of the common cause.

A British View on Recognition*

Statement by Herbert Morrison, *British Secretary of State for Foreign Affairs*

The question of the recognition of a State or Government should be distinguished from the question of entering into diplomatic relations with it, which is entirely discretionary. On the other hand, it is international law which defines the conditions under which a Government should be recognised *de jure* or *de facto*, and it is a matter of judgment in each particular case whether a régime fulfils the conditions. The conditions under international law for the recognition of a new régime as the *de facto* Government of a State are that the new régime has in fact effective control over most of the State's territory and that this control seems likely to continue. The conditions for the recognition of a new régime as the *de jure* Government of a State are that the new régime should not merely have effective control over most of the State's territory, but that it should, in fact, be firmly established. His Majesty's Government consider that recognition should be accorded when the conditions specified by international law are, in fact, fulfilled and that recognition should not be given when these conditions are not fulfilled. The recognition of a Government *de jure* or *de facto* should not depend on whether the character of the régime is such as to command His Majesty's Government's approval.

* Reprinted from 485 *Hansard, Parliamentary Debates,* cols. 2410–2411 (Commons, 5th Series, March 21, 1951).

British Policy on Recognition of Communist China*

Sir Roger Makins

. . . As you all know, the British Government recognized the Communist Government of China in 1950, in company with a number of other Governments. We continue to recognize it and have no present intention of changing our position. The United States has not recognized the Peking regime, and the administration has recently reaffirmed its refusal to do so.

Now, there are no differences between us in our objectives in the Far East, even if we sometimes differ on the timing, and the method of our approach to them. We are both equally concerned to oppose and to prevent the spread of Communist imperialism. How is it, therefore, that we should be found at variance on this question of recognition? And what is the significance of this divergent position?

The practice of governments in giving diplomatic recognition to each other has fluctuated through the years, and the attitudes of the British and United States governments have sometimes approximated and sometimes diverged. Broadly speaking, there are two main lines of approach to be found in the writings of the authorities, and in the policies of governments. The one treats recognition as an act based solely on the facts, an act which follows upon the fulfillment of certain objective criteria; the other regards it as an act of policy which signifies something more than the recognition of a situation of fact and law. I shall call the former the *de facto* principle, the latter the principle of legitimacy. . . .

The practice of Great Britain has always conformed fairly closely to the *de facto* principle. If a government is in effective

* Reprinted from 2 Whiteman, *Digest of International Law* 110 (Washington, D.C.: U.S. Government Printing Office, 1963). This statement was presented at the Catholic University of America on May 13, 1954, by Sir Roger Makins when he was British Ambassador to the United States.

control of the country in question; if it seems to have a reasonable expectancy of permanence; if it can act for a majority of the country's inhabitants; if it is able (though possibly not willing) to carry out its international obligations; if, in short, it can give a convincing answer to the question, 'Who's in charge here?', then we recognize that government. We are not conferring a favor, we are recognizing a situation of fact. The conduct of foreign affairs (as distinct from the formation of foreign policy) is, after all, not essentially different from the conduct of any other business. You do not have to like a man's face, or manners, or even morals, in doing business with him. And even if you do not want to do business with an ugly customer, shutting your eyes won't make him go away.

* * *

There have been other periods in American history when this realistic, Jeffersonian, *de facto*-type view of recognition has yielded to the belief that what Chief Justice Taft called "legitimacy" was a further requirement. The Union took that view, naturally enough, under Secretary Seward at the time of the Civil War, and later, during President Wilson's first term, there were emphatic reversions to the principle of legitimacy. Britain also applied this principle to some extent during the 19th century. For example, in 1870 Britain refused to recognize the government of the Third Republic in France until it had been elected by a constituent assembly, and again in Portugal in 1910 Britain refused to recognize the revolutionary government until a constitution had been voted and a President elected.

But since 1924 Britain has followed the *de facto* principle closely in a series of cases, the Soviet Union, Chile, Peru, Ecuador, Argentina, and the Nationalist government of Gen. Franco in Spain. So we arrive at the situation today in which Britain and the United States find themselves at opposite points in applying the doctrine of diplomatic recognition in the case of China: we have applied the *de facto* principle, you are applying a contemporary version of the legitimacy principle.

* * *

Recognition and Representation*

Trygve Lie

MEMORANDUM BY THE UNITED NATIONS SECRETARY GENERAL, MARCH 8, 1950

The primary difficulty in the current question of the representation of Member States in the United Nations is that this question of representation has been linked up with the question of recognition by Member Governments.

It will be shown here that this linkage is unfortunate from the practical standpoint, and wrong from the standpoint of legal theory.

From a practical standpoint, the present position is that representation depends entirely on a numerical count of the number of Members in a particular organ which recognize one government or the other. It is quite possible for the majority of the Members in one organ to recognize one government, and for the majority of Members in another organ to recognize the rival government. If the principle of individual recognition is adhered to, then the representatives of different governments could sit in different organs. Moreover in organs like the Security Council, of limited membership, the question of representation may be determined by the purely arbitrary fact of the particular governments which happen to have been elected to serve at a given time.

From the standpoint of legal theory, the

* Reprinted from *United Nations Document* S/1466.

linkage of representation in an international organization and recognition of a government is a confusion of two institutions which have superficial similarities but are essentially different.

The recognition of a new State, or of a new government of an existing State, is a unilateral act which the recognizing government can grant or withhold. It is true that some legal writers have argued forcibly that when a new government, which comes into power through revolutionary means, enjoys, with a reasonable prospect of permanency, the habitual obedience of the bulk of the population, other States are under a legal duty to recognize it. However, while States may regard it as desirable to follow certain legal principles in according or withholding recognition, the practise of States shows that the act of recognition is still regarded as essentially a political decision, which each State decides in accordance with its own free appreciation of the situation.

A recent expression of this doctrine occurred during the consideration of the Palestine question in the Security Council, when the representative of Syria questioned the United States recognition of the Provisional Government of Israel. The representative of the United States (Mr. Austin) replied:

"I should regard it as highly improper for me to admit that any country on earth can question the sovereignty of the United States of America in the exercise of that high political act of recognition of the *de facto* status of a State.

"Moreover, I would not admit here, by implication or by direct answer, that there exists a tribunal of justice or of any other kind, anywhere, that can pass judgment upon the legality or the validity of that act of my country.

"There were certain powers and certain rights of a sovereign State which were not yielded by any of the Members who signed the United Nations Charter and in particular this power to recognize the *de facto* authority of a provisional Government was not yielded. When it was exercised by my Government, it was done as a practical step, in recognition of realities:

the existence of things, and the recognition of a change that had actually taken place. I am certain that no nation on earth has any right to question that, or to lay down a proposition that a certain length of time of the exercise of *de facto* authority must elapse before that authority can be recognized."

Various legal scholars have argued that this rule of individual recognition through the free choice of States should be replaced by collective recognition through an international organization such as the United Nations (e.g. Lauterpacht, *Recognition in International Law*). If this were now the rule then the present impasse would not exist, since there would be no individual recognition of the new Chinese Government, but only action by the appropriate United Nations organ. The fact remains, however, that the States have refused to accept any such rule and the United Nations does not possess any authority to recognize either a new State or a new government of an existing State. To establish the rule of collective recognition by the United Nations would require either an amendment of the Charter or a treaty to which all Members would adhere.

On the other hand *membership* of a State in the United Nations and *representation* of a State in the organs is clearly determined by a collective act of the appropriate organs; in the case of membership, by vote of the General Assembly on recommendation of the Security Council, in the case of representation, by vote of each competent organ on the credentials of the purported representatives. Since, therefore, recognition of either State or government is an individual act, and either admission to membership or acceptance of representation in the Organization are collective acts, it would appear to be legally inadmissible to condition the latter acts by a requirement that they be preceded by individual recognition.

This conclusion is clearly borne out by the practise in the case of admission to membership in both the League of Nations and in the United Nations.

In the practise of the League of Nations, there were a number of cases in which Members of the League stated expressly that the admission of another State to membership did not mean that they recognized such new Member as a State (e.g. Great Britain in the case of Lithuania, Belgium and Switzerland in the case of the Soviet Union; Colombia in the case of Panama).

In the practise of the United Nations there are, of course, several instances of admission to membership of States which had not been recognized by all other Members, and other instances of States for whose admission votes were cast by Members which had not recognized the candidates as States. For example, Yemen and Burma were admitted by a unanimous vote of the General Assembly at a time when they had been recognized by only a minority of Members. A number of the Members who, in the Security Council, voted for the admission of Transjordan [Jordan] and Nepal, had not recognized these candidates as States. Indeed, the declarations made by the delegation of the Soviet Union and its neighbours that they would not vote for the admission of certain States (e.g., Ireland, Portugal and Transjordan [Jordan]), because they were not in diplomatic relations with these applicants, were vigorously disputed by most other Members, and led to the request for an advisory opinion of the International Court of Justice by the General Assembly.

The Court was requested to answer the queston whether a Member, in its vote on the admission to membership of another State, was "juridically entitled to make its consent to the admission dependent on conditions not expressly provided" by paragraph 1 of Article 4 of the Charter. One of the conditions which had been stated by Members had been the lack of diplomatic relations with the applicant State. The Court answered the question in the negative.

At its fourth session the General Assembly recommended that each Member act in accordance with the opinion of the Court.

The practise as regards representation of Member States in the United Nations organs has, until the Chinese question arose, been uniformly to the effect that representation is distinctly separate from the issue of recognition of a government. It is a remarkable fact that, despite the fairly large number of revolutionary changes of government and the larger number of instances of breach of diplomatic relations among Members, *there was not one single instance of a challenge of credentials of a representative* in the many thousands of meetings which were held during four years. On the contrary, whenever the reports of credentials committees were voted on (as in the sessions of the General Assembly), they were always adopted unanimously and without reservation by any Members.

The Members have therefore made clear by an unbroken practise that

1. a Member could properly vote to accept a representative of a government which it did not recognize, or with which it had no diplomatic relations, and

2. that such a vote did not imply recognition or a readiness to assume diplomatic relations.

In two instances involving non-members, the question was explicitly raised—the cases of granting the Republic of Indonesia and Israel the right to participate in the deliberations of the Security Council. In both cases, objections were raised on the grounds that these entities were not States; in both cases the Security Council voted to permit representation after explicit statements were made by members of the Council that the vote did not imply recognition of the State or government concerned.

The practise which has been thus followed in the United Nations is not only legally correct but conforms to the basic character of the Organization. The United Nations is not an association limited to like-minded States and governments of similar ideological persuasion (as is the case in certain regional associations). As an Organization which aspires to universality, it must of necessity include States of varying and even conflicting ideologies.

The Chinese case is unique in the history of the United Nations, not because it involves a revolutionary change of government, but because it is the first in which two rival governments exist. It is quite possible that such a situation will occur again in the future and it is highly desirable to see what principles can be followed in choosing between the rivals. It has been demonstrated that the principle of numerical preponderance of recognition is inappropriate and legally incorrect. Is any other principle possible?

It is submitted that the proper principles can be derived by analogy from Article 4 of the Charter. This Article requires that an applicant for membership must be able and willing to carry out the obligations of membership. The obligations of membership can be carried out only by governments which in fact possess the power to do so. Where a revolutionary government presents itself as representing a State, in rivalry to an existing government, the question at issue should be which of these two governments in fact is in a position to employ the resources and direct the people of the State in fulfilment of the obligations of membership. In essence, this means an inquiry as to whether the new government exercises effective authority within the territory of the State and is habitually obeyed by the bulk of the population.

If so, it would seem to be appropriate for the United Nations organs, through their collective action, to accord it the right to represent the State in the Organization, even though individual Members of the Organization refuse, and may continue to refuse, to accord it recognition as the lawful government for reasons which are valid under their national policies.

Consequences of Nonrecognition: Bank of China v. Wells Fargo Bank and Union Trust Company*

United States District Court, N.D. Cal., 1952

[*"In the case of the* Bank of China v. Wells Fargo Bank & Union Trust Co., *a California bank held deposits of the Bank of China, chartered by the Republic of China in 1912 under the laws of China, two-thirds of the stock being held by the Government of China and the remainder by Chinese nationals. The Bank of China brought an action in 1949 in the United States District Court for the Northern District of California to recover the deposit. On June 27, 1949, Wells Fargo had received a cable from Shanghai informing it that the Bank of China had been taken over on May 28, 1949, by the 'Chinese People's Liberation Army,' and information was subsequently received as to new management. On demand for payment by the Hong Kong office of the Bank of China, Wells Fargo had refused to pay. Thereupon, on December 9, 1949, a motion for summary judgment was filed by attorneys who instituted action on behalf of the Bank of China. Subsequently, on January 26, 1950, a second group of attorneys filed a motion to dismiss the action or to substitute themselves as the attorneys of record, claiming authority to speak for the Bank of China through action taken by the 'Chinese People's Government.' The attorneys for certain émigré directors asserted that the Nationalist Government of China, operating from Formosa, 'is the only government of China recognized by the United States' and that the Court 'cannot recognize any change in the management of the Bank of China resulting from acts of a government unrecognized by the United States.' The Court, in a decision given July 17, 1950, postponed determination of*

* Reprinted from 104 F. Supp. 59 (1952).

the claimants' rights sine die. *In the course of its decision, the Court (District Judge Goodman) stated:*

Controversies regarding property rights rendered uncertain by changing governments have produced a myraid of judicial decisions. These decisions present a confusing picture. No area of that picture is more murky than that depicting the effect of the recognition or non-recognition of a new government by the forum nation. Research reveals no case, with facts sufficiently similar to those of the present controversy, to be accepted as a controlling precedent. But some general principles may be deduced from prior decisions to shape the approach to the present problem. The first guide post is the not too helpful principle that the action of the political department of the government 'in recognizing a foreign government and in receiving its diplomatic representatives is conclusive on all domestic courts, which are bound to accept that determination, although they are free to draw for themselves its legal consequences in litigations pending before them.' Guaranty Trust Co. of New York v. United States, 1938, 304 U.S. 126, 138, 58 S. Ct. 785, 791, 82 L. Ed. 1224. One of the accepted consequences is that a non-recognized government cannot be recognized by the court as a litigant. Guaranty Trust Co. of New York v. United States, supra, 304 U.S. at 137, 58 S. Ct. 785, 82 L. Ed. 1224. But, it does not follow that the existence of a non-recognized government must be completely ignored. The courts of the United States have given effect to the acts of a non-recognized, de facto government done within the territory it controls and affecting its own nationals. This effect has been given when it has appeared that the most realistic and just result will thus be achieved and that the foreign policy of the executive branch of our government will not be thwarted. . . .

The funds here in controversy belong to a Chinese corporation, which has weathered previous governmental upheavals. Although by virtue of majority stock ownership, the Government of China controls this corporation, it is not a public corporation nor are its funds government funds. . . .

The émigré directors of the Bank are now scattered. Some are in New York, others in California, others in Formosa, others in Hong Kong, still others in Shanghai, and Hangchow.

The whereabouts of some is unknown. Some of these directors represent a government which is not now, and may never again be, in a position to speak for the Chinese people in respect to the manner in which the corporation shall function in China. The others, may or may not be the directors whom the private stockholders now desire to speak for them. It is difficult to perceive how the interests of the corporation, its stockholders, and its depositors will be protected by placing the res in dispute at the disposal of a group of these directors.

To deny the émigré directors control of these funds is not to deprive a government, still recognized by the United States, of funds to carry on its fight for survival. For these are corporate funds which should not be dissipated for purposes other than those of the corporation.

On the other hand, the new management in China is not yet so established as to warrant placing these funds in its hands. Who the private stockholders wish to represent them is at present unknown. The new government directors represent a government, which although in control of the Chinese mainland, has not yet put down all organized resistance. Only time will tell whether this government will become a stable government.

Furthermore, recent international developments bar any decision of this Court which would place these funds in the control of the new management of the bank in China. For this Court to recognize the acts of the so-called 'Peoples Government,' in so far as they relate merely to a Chinese corporation which must function under the government, might not necessarily run counter to a merely negative policy of non-recognition on the part of the United States. But, since the announcement of the President on June 27, 1950, that the United States will defend Formosa (the present seat of the de jure Chinese government) the policy of the United States appears to be one of active intervention against the aims of the 'Peoples Government.' Although the Bank of China is a private corporation, the Court must realistically recognize that if the $626,860.07 in controversy were placed in the hands of the new management of the Bank of China, the 'Peoples Government' would be aided and abetted.

The only solution which gives promise of affording protection to the Bank of China, its stockholders, and depositors, and at the same time supporting the foreign policy of the United

States, is to leave these funds where they are for the present. A Court cannot justly rule while a controversy is raging, except to maintain the status quo. A man fording a turbulent stream carrying valuables, cannot be expected then and there to decide the claims of disputing consignees. It is time enough to make decision when solid ground is reached. In the field of international relations, the story must be complete, the facts must be all in, before the judicial function may be properly exercised. Particularly is this so when events are colored by problems of governmental recognition. United States v. Pink, 1942, 315 U.S. 203, 62 S.Ct. 552, 86 L.Ed. 796. Justice Frankfurter concurring 315 U.S. at 236–237, 62 S.Ct. 552, 86 L.Ed. 796, Justice Stone dissenting 315 U.S. at 256, 62 S.Ct. 552, 86 L.Ed. 796.

Therefore, the trial of this case will be continued sine die. The defendant, if it desires to preclude any claim against it for interest for the use of the fund, may either deposit the fund in the registry of the Court, or place the same in a separate trust account in form to be approved by the Court.*

The case having been remanded to the District Court, that Court held that it should recognize the Nationalist Government of China as legally entitled to exercise the controlling corporate authority of the Bank of China in respect to the deposit in suit, and granted the motion for summary judgment in favor of the Bank of China, as controlled by the Nationalist Government." 2 Whiteman, Digest of International Law 620.]

. . . we now reach the question: Which Bank of China is legally entitled to the funds deposited with the defendant Bank?

The controlling corporate authority of the Bank of China is effectively vested in the Government of China by virtue of its majority stock ownership, its dominant voice in the managing directorate, and the

* Bank of China v. Wells Fargo Bank & Union Trust Co., 92 F. Supp. 920, 923–924 (N.D. Cal. 1950). On appeal by the Bank of China, the Circuit Court of Appeals, Per Curiam, dismissed the appeal without prejudice and remanded the cause to the District Court. Bank of China v. Wells Fargo Bank & Union Trust Co., 190 F. 2d 1010 (9th Cir. 1951).

supervisory powers accorded by the Articles of Association to the Minister of Finance. A determination of what government, if any, should be recognized by this court as now entitled to exercise this corporate authority over the deposit in suit, will govern the disposition of these causes.

The issue thus posed focuses attention at the outset on the fact that of the two governments asserting corporate authority, one is recognized by the United States while the other is not. If this fact, per se, is determinative, the issue is resolved. If, whenever this court is called upon to determine whether there is a government justly entitled to act on behalf of a foreign state in respect to a particular matter, the court is bound to say, without regard to the facts before it, that the government recognized by our executive is that government, then nothing more need be said here. To permit this expression of executive policy to usurp entirely the judicial judgment would relieve the court of a burdensome duty, but it is doubtful that the ends of justice would thus be met. It has been argued that such is the accepted practice. But the authorities do not support this view.

There is, of course, the long line of New York decisions arising out of the nationalization of Russian corporations by the Soviet Government at a time when it was unrecognized by the United States. In those decisions, the New York courts stated time and again that no effect would be given to the acts of the unrecognized Soviet Government, in so far as property situated in this country was concerned. But in every instance, the governmental acts, which the courts chose to ignore, were acts of confiscation. Confiscatory acts were held to be repugnant to the public policy of the forum. Public policy, rather than the unrecognized status of the Soviet Government, shaped the decisions in the Russian nationalization cases. . . . Such decisions do not bar the way to giving effect to acts of non-recognized governments even in respect to property within our borders, if justice so requires.

Some more recent decisions of the federal courts, involving Soviet nationalization of corporations of the Baltic states, give great weight to the executive policy of non-recognition. But it cannot be said that these decisions establish an all-embracing rule that no extra-territorial effect may ever be given the acts of an unrecognized government.

Nor, as has been argued, does the decision of the Supreme Court in United States v. Pink, 1942, 315 U.S. 203, 62 S.Ct. 552, 86 L.Ed. 796, impose upon this court a duty to give conclusive effect to every act of a recognized government. Pink requires that full faith and credit be accorded those acts which our executive has expressly sanctioned. But such executive sanction is not expressed by governmental recognition per se.

The decisions just set forth, as well as others in this field, reveal no rule of law obliging the courts to give conclusive effect to the acts of a recognized government to the exclusion of all consideration of the acts of an opposing unrecognized government. Nor does it appear that such a sweeping rule would be a sound one.

Even were the court solely concerned with the implementation of our executive foreign policy, it would be presumptuous to blindly effectuate every act of a recognized government or to treat every act of an unrecognized government as entirely fictional. Early in our national history, our recognition policy was generally based on the executive's view of the stability and effectiveness of the government in question. More recently recognition has been granted and withheld at the diplomatic bargaining table. Our policy has thus become equivocal. Conflicting considerations are balanced in the executive decision. Moreover, an act of recognition does not necessarily mark a sudden reversal in executive policy. It may come as a culmination of a gradual change in attitude. Thus the import of recognition or non-recognition may vary with time and circumstance.

Recognition is not intended to sanctify every act, past and future, of a foreign government. The withholding of recognition may cast a mantle of disfavor over a government. But, it does not necessarily stamp all of its acts with disapproval or brand them unworthy of judicial notice. Our executive, on occasion, has even entered into a treaty with an unrecognized government.

This is not to suggest that the courts should regard executive policy in respect to recognition and non-recognition of foreign governments as meaningless or of little consequence. In any particular situation, executive policy may be crucial, as indeed it appears to be in the present case. But, it is a fact which properly should be considered and weighed along with the other facts before the court.

Turning to the record in this case, it appears that two governments are governments in fact of portions of the territory of the State of China. The "People's" Government has supplanted the "Nationalist" Government in dominion over the entire Chinese Mainland with an area of more than 3,700,000 square miles, and a population of more than 460,000,000. The "Nationalist" Government controls one of the 35 provinces of China, the Island of Formosa, which has an area of 13,885 square miles and a population in excess of 6,000,000. It is obvious that the "People's" Government is now the government in fact of by far the greater part of the territory of the Chinese State. Nevertheless the "Nationalist" Government controls substantial territory, exceeding in area that of either Belgium or the Netherlands, and in population that of Denmark or Switzerland.

Each government, in its respective sphere, functions effectively. Each is recognized by a significant number of the nations of the world. Each maintains normal diplomatic intercourse with those nations which extend recognition. This has been the status quo for more than two years.

Each government is in a position to exercise corporate authority in behalf of the Bank of China. That is, each government is capable of utilizing the corporate structure and certain corporate assets to promote the corporate purposes. The Bank of China was chartered primarily to facilitate Chinese international commercial activities. It was organized as an international exchange bank to deal in domestic and foreign exchange and gold and silver bullion, to discount, purchase, and collect commercial bills and drafts, to issue, service, and redeem government bonds in foreign markets, and to handle public funds deposited abroad. It was also authorized to engage in a general domestic banking business including the acceptance of deposits and valuables for safe keeping, the granting of loans, and the issuance and service of domestic government loans. Each government is in a position to act through the corporate structure of the Bank of China to carry on these international functions in the areas abroad where such Government is recognized and these domestic functions within the territory such Government controls. Each government is in fact doing so. The Bank of China, as controlled by the Nationalist Government, continues to function on the Island of Formosa and through its foreign branches in the United States, Cuba, Australia, Japan, Indo China, and elsewhere where the Nationalist Government is recognized.

The Peoples Government as successor in fact to the Nationalist Government on the Chinese Mainland is exercising the prerogatives of the Government in respect to the Bank of China there. The Peoples Government has not nationalized the Bank of China, nor confiscated its assets, nor denied the rights of private stockholders. It exercises the authority vested in the Government of China as majority stockholder. The Bank of China continues to function in accordance with its Articles of Association under the guidance of the appointees of the Peoples Government and the majority of the directors previously elected by private stockholders on the Chinese Mainland and through branches in London, Hong Kong, Singapore, Penang, Kuala, Lumpar [sic], Batavia, Calcutta, Bombay, Karachi, Chittagong, and Rangoon.

This factual situation is without analogous precedent in any reported case. The resulting legal problem, arising as it does out of sweeping historical changes and the claims of rival governments, cannot be met by the application of technical rules of corporation law.

A year and a half ago, this Court felt that the best course was to withhold judgment. At that time the Nationalist forces had only recently retreated to their last stronghold; their ability to consolidate this position was doubtful. The Peoples Government which had assumed control of the Chinese Mainland had not yet demonstrated its stability. Our executive policy had not assumed definite outlines in the wake of these events. The émigré directors of the Bank who sought control of the deposit in suit could not demonstrate their authority to do so or their ability to apply the funds to corporate purposes. The Bank of China, under new management on the Chinese Mainland, was not yet functioning normally in accordance with its Articles of Association. Whether its assets there would be employed for corporate purposes or diverted to other ends was not known.

Now time has clarified the picture. Both the Nationalist and Peoples Governments have maintained and strengthened their positions. Our national policy toward these governments is now definite. We have taken a stand adverse to the aims and ambitions of the Peoples Government. The armed forces of that Government are now engaged in conflict with our forces in Korea. We recognize only the Nationalist Government as the representative of the

State of China, and are actively assisting in developing its military forces in Formosa. The Bank of China now operates as two corporate entities, each performing within the area of its operations the functions bestowed upon the Bank of China by its Articles of Association. Each Bank of China is in a position to employ the deposit in suit for corporate purposes.

From a practical standpoint, neither of the rival Banks of China is a true embodiment of the corporate entity which made the deposit in the Wells Fargo Bank. The present Nationalist Bank of China is more nearly equivalent in the sense of continuity of management. The Peoples Bank is more representative in ability to deal with the greater number of private stockholders and established depositors and creditors. Were the Court to adopt a strictly pragmatic approach, it might attempt a division of the deposit between these two banks in the degree that each now exercises the functions of the Bank of China. Or the Court might award the entire deposit to the bank it deems to be the closest counterpart of the corporation contemplated by the Articles of Association.

But this, the Court could not do merely by balancing interests of a private nature. Such a course would ultimately entail determining which bank best serves the corporate interests of the State of China.

That determination could not be made, while the State, itself, remains divided, except by an excursion into the realm of political philosophy. Were there only one government, in fact, of the Chinese State, or only one government in a position to act effectively for the State in respect to the matter before the Court, the Court might be justified in accepting such a government as the proper representative of the State, even though our executive declined to deal with it. Here, there co-exist two governments, in fact, each attempting to further, in its own way, the interests of the State of China, in the Bank of China. It is not a proper function of a domestic court of the United States to attempt to judge which government best represents the interests of the Chinese State in the Bank of China. In this situation, the Court should justly accept, as the representative of the Chinese State, that government which our executive deems best able to further the mutual interests of China and the United States.

Since the Court is of the opinion that it should recognize the Nationalist Government of China as legally entitled to exercise the controlling corporate authority of the Bank of China in respect to the deposit in suit, the motion for summary judgment in favor of the Bank of China, as controlled by the Nationalist Government, is granted. . . .

SUCCESSION

A succession of government occurs when the government of a state is replaced with a new one. State succession occurs when a state ceases to exist, or a new state is formed within the territory of an existing state, or territory is transferred from one state to another state. When a succession situation arises, the point of chief legal interest is the effect, if any, on the international rights and obligations of the state or states concerned.

The doctrine of continuity of states has long been accepted as the general principle that regulates succession of governments. According to this doctrine, changes in government do not affect the legal personality of states; the rights acquired and the obligations assumed on behalf of a state by its government pass automatically to successor governments.[1] That the interests of the international community in general, and of the major Western powers in particular, have been well served by this principle is obvious. If, for example, treaty obligations could be disregarded following a change of government, international agreements, particularly with states that are subject to periodic changes of government by force, would have little meaning.[2]

Situations that give rise to matters of state succession, as distinguished from succession of governments, are so numerous, and practice regarding them so varied, that it was not possible even in the nineteenth century to assert that a single controlling principle applied. When a state ceases to exist, as when it is absorbed by one or more other states or when it is broken up into two or more new states, the situation known as universal succession is said to occur. Partial succession occurs when a portion of the territory of a state passes to another state or when a new state emerges within the territory of an existing state. Numerous and complicated legal problems regarding the distribution of the international rights and obligations of the states concerned arise when either type of state succession takes place. Hugo Grotius sought to provide some answers to these problems by introducing into international law the principle of Roman Civil Law under which the heir succeeded

to the assets, rights, and obligations of a deceased person. States have been unwilling, however, to accept a strict application of this principle, particularly as it applies to obligations. When one state absorbs another state, for example, it always "succeeds" to the public property of the extinct state but only occasionally "succeeds" to its public debt and seldom, if ever, "succeeds" to its liabilities for illegal acts committed against other states.

The general nature of the subject of state succession can be illustrated by reference to certain traditional principles regarding succession to rights and obligations created by treaties.[3] It is generally agreed that when a state is totally absorbed by another state, the treaties of the extinct state cease to exist. The same principle applies when a new state is formed by breaking off from an old state; the new state may, if it chooses to do so, start off with a "clean slate" by refusing to be bound by the treaties of the state from which it emerged.[4] An important traditionally accepted exception to this general principle concerns so-called "dispositive" treaties, which, according to J. L. Brierly:

. . . are regarded as impressing a special character on the territory to which they relate, and

---

[1] "Changes in the government or the internal polity of a state do not as a rule affect its position in international law. A monarchy may be transformed into a republic, or a republic into a monarchy; absolute principles may be substituted for constitutional, or the reverse; but, though the government changes, the nation remains, with rights and obligations unimpaired." 1 Moore, *Digest of International Law* 249.

[2] "Money cannot be borrowed or lent, trade cannot thrive unless means of insuring obligations over a period of years can be devised. Thus the state, as a continuing entity, and the capacity of one government to bind its successors are, among other considerations, necessary rules for stable monetary and trade relations. The legal purpose of the distinction between states and governments is precisely to make the obligations of the former independent of, and insulated from, changes in the latter." Kaplan and Katzenbach, *The Political Foundations of International Law*, p. 113.

[3] For a discussion of other aspects of the subject, such as succession to state property, public debts, contractual liabilities, and torts, see one or more of the texts listed in the suggested readings at the end of this chapter on pages 126–127.

[4] Recent practice suggests that new states generally prefer to succeed to at least some of the treaties entered into by their former parent states. According to D. P. O'Connell: "Five possible attitudes toward continuity of treaties might be taken by successor states. They might deny continuity, or succession, altogether with respect to the treaties of their predecessor (an attitude taken by Algeria, Israel, and, with inconsistencies, Upper Volta); they might, in the absence of a devolution agreement, declare their continued application of such treaties (Congo-Brazzaville, Malagasy Republic, Congo-Leopoldville); they might enter into devolution agreements and base positive action upon them (most of the former British countries); they might take a reserved attitude (Tanganyika, Uganda, Zanzibar); or they might, without any commitment to principle, in fact continue to apply treaties (most of the former French countries)." D. P. O'Connell, "Independence and Problems of State Succession," in William V. O'Brien (ed.), *The New Nations in International Law and Diplomacy* (London: Stevens and Sons, 1965), p. 20.

creating something analogous to the servitudes or easements of private law; and there is authority for saying that when a state takes over territory affected by a treaty of this kind it takes over not the mere territory itself, but the territory with rights and obligations attached to it. A treaty of neutralization or one regulating customs zones or the use of a river are examples of such treaties.[5]

The distinction between succession of governments and succession of states, the doctrine of continuity of states, and the complex set of principles regarded by many of the major Western powers as regulatory of problems resulting from state succession were allegedly established during the nineteenth century, at a time when those powers dominated international politics and, consequently, international law. In the twentieth century, which has witnessed the emergence of numerous regimes with interests and ideologies that differ from those of the major Western powers, much of the so-called "law of succession" is being challenged. Newly established Communist governments, in violation of the traditional doctrine of continuity of states, have denounced the public debt, contractual liabilities, and many of the treaties of predecessor regimes. A number of intensely anticolonial regimes in Asia and Africa has expressed an unwillingness to consider themselves bound by dispositive treaties entered into by their former colonial masters. These and other indications of the "loss of consensus" on the relevant norms have thrown the entire subject of succession into a state of confusion. It is clear that, since the Western powers have been unable to convince many of the new regimes of the legal logic of the traditional principles, a reformulation of the norms is needed in order to secure the consensus necessary to make the law effective.

"The Tinoco Arbitration," the first

selection to follow, illustrates the traditional doctrine of continuity of states and sheds further light on the meaning of recognition in international law. The case of *Pema Chibar v. The Union of India* illustrates the effect of state succession on the rights of individuals within territory acquired by conquest. Sections of the Versailles Treaty of 1919 are included to show the use of a treaty to solve problems of state succession, in this case problems related to state property and public debt. The Soviet attitude toward the law of succession is discussed in an English summary of an article by N. V. Zakharova from *The Soviet Yearbook of International Law* (1960). Finally, Gerard V. La Forest discusses the inadequacies of the traditional view of succession and suggests how, in respect to treaty rights and obligations, the law might be reformulated to meet modern needs.

The Tinoco Arbitration: Great Britain-Costa Rica, 1923*

[WILLIAM H. TAFT, ARBITRATOR.]

* * *

In January, 1917, the Government of Costa Rica, under President Alfredo Gonzalez, was overthrown by Frederico Tinoco, the Secretary of War. Gonzalez fled. Tinoco assumed power, called an election, and established a new constitution in June, 1917. His government continued until August, 1919, when Tinoco retired, and left the country. His government fell in September following. After a provisional government under one Barquero, the old constitution was restored and elections held under it. The restored government is a signatory to this treaty of arbitration.

[5] Brierly, *The Law of Nations*, p. 154.

* Reprinted from 1 *United Nations Reports of International Arbitral Awards* 369.

On the 22nd of August, 1922, the Constitutional Congress of the restored Costa Rican Government passed a law known as Law of Nullities No. 41. It invalidated all contracts between the executive power and private persons, made with or without approval of the legislative power between January 27, 1917, and September 2, 1919, covering the period of the Tinoco government. It also nullified the legislative decree No. 12 of the Tinoco government, dated June 28, 1919, authorizing the issue of the fifteen million colones currency notes. The colon is a Costa Rican gold coin or standard nominally equal to forty-six and one-half cents of an American dollar, but it is uncoined and the exchange value of the paper colon actually in circulation is much less. The Nullities Law also invalidated the legislative decree of the Tinoco government of July 8, 1919, authorizing the circulation of notes of the nomination of 1,000 colones, and annulled all transactions with such colones bills between holders and the state, directly or indirectly, by means of negotiation or contract, if thereby the holders received value as if they were ordinary bills of current issue.

The claim of Great Britain is that the Royal Bank of Canada and the Central Costa Rica Petroleum Company are Britain corporations whose shares are owned by British subjects; that the Banco Internacional of Costa Rica and the Government of Costa Rica are both indebted to the Royal Bank in the sum of 998,000 colones, evidenced by 998 one thousand colones bills held by the Bank; that the Central Costa Rica Petroleum Company owns, by due assignment, a grant by the Tinoco government in 1918 of the right to explore for and exploit oil deposits in Costa Rica, and that both the indebtedness and the concession have been annulled without right by the Law of Nullities and should be excepted from its operation. She asks an award that she is entitled on behalf of her subjects to have the claim of the bank paid, and the concession recognized and given effect by the Costa Rican Government.

The Government of Costa Rica denies its liability for the acts or obligations of the Tinoco government and maintains that the Law of Nullities was a legitimate exercise of its legislative governing power. It further denies the validity of such claims on the merits, unaffected by the Law of Nullities.

Coming now to the general issues applicable to both claims, Great Britain contends, first, that the Tinoco government was the only government of Costa Rica de facto and de jure for two years and nine months; that during that time there is no other government disputing its sovereignty, that it was in peaceful administration of the whole country, with the acquiescence of its people.

Second, that the succeeding government could not by legislative decree avoid responsibility for acts of that government affecting British subjects, or appropriate or confiscate rights and property by that government except in violation of international law; that the act of Nullities is as to British interests, therefore itself a nullity, and is to be disregarded, with the consequence that the contracts validly made with the Tinoco government must be performed by the present Costa Rican Government, and that the property which has been invaded or the rights nullified must be restored.

To these contentions the Costa Rican Government answers: First, that the Tinoco government was not a de facto or de jure government according to the rules of international law. This raises an issue of fact.

Second, that the contracts and obligations of the Tinoco government, set up by Great Britain on behalf of its subjects, are void, and do not create a legal obligation, because the government of Tinoco and its acts were in violation of the constitution of Costa Rica of 1871.

Third, that Great Britain is estopped by the fact that it did not recognize the Tinoco government during its incumbency, to claim on behalf of its subjects that Tinoco's was a government which could confer rights binding on its successor.

Fourth, that the subjects of Great Britain, whose claims are here in controversy, were either by contract or the law of Costa Rica bound to pursue their remedies before the courts of Costa Rica and not to seek diplomatic interference on the part of their home government.

Dr. John Bassett Moore, now a member of the Permanent Court of International Justice, in his *Digest of International Law*, Volume I, p. 249, announces the general principle which has had such universal acquiescence as to become well settled international law:

Changes in the government or the internal polity of a state do not as a rule affect its position in international law. A monarchy may be transformed into a republic or a republic into a monarchy; absolute principles may be substituted for constitutional, or the reverse; but, though the government changes, the nation remains, with rights and obligations unimpaired. . . .

The principle of the continuity of states has important results. The state is bound by engagements entered into by governments that have ceased to exist; the restored government is generally liable for the acts of the usurper. The governments of Louis XVIII and Louis Philippe so far as practicable indemnified the citizens of foreign states for losses caused by the government of Napoleon; and the King of the Two Sicilies made compensation to citizens of the United States for the wrongful acts of Murat.

Again Dr. Moore says:

The origin and organization of government are questions generally of internal discussion and decision. Foreign powers deal with the existing *de facto* government, when sufficiently established to give reasonable assurance of its permanence, and of the acquiescence of those who constitute the state in its ability to maintain itself, and discharge its internal duties and its external obligations.

The same principle is announced in Professor Borchard's new work on *The Diplomatic Protection of Citizens Abroad:*

Considering the characteristics and attributes of the *de facto* government, a general government *de facto* having completely taken the place of the regularly constituted authorities in the state binds the nation. So far as its international obligations are concerned, it represents the state. It succeeds to the debts of the regular government it has displaced and transmits its own obligations to succeeding titular governments. Its loans and contracts bind the state and the state is responsible for the governmental acts of the *de facto* authorities. In general its treaties are valid obligations of the state. It may alienate the national territory and the judgments of its courts are admitted to be effective after its authority has ceased. An exception to these rules has occasionally been noted in the practice of some of the states of Latin America, which declare null and void the acts of a usurping *de facto* intermediary government, when the regular government it has displaced succeeds in restoring its control. Nevertheless, acts validly undertaken in the name of the state and having an international character cannot lightly be repudiated and foreign governments generally insist on their binding force. The legality or constitutional legitimacy of a *de facto* government is without importance internationally so far as the matter of representing the state is concerned. . . .

First, what are the facts to be gathered from the documents and evidence submitted by the two parties as to the *de facto* character of the Tinoco government?

In January, 1917, Frederico A. Tinoco was Secretary of War under Alfredo Gonzalez, the then President of Costa Rica. On the ground that Gonzalez was seeking reelection as President in violation of a constitutional limitation, Tinoco used the army and navy to seize the government, assume the provisional headship of the Republic and become Commander-in-Chief of the army. Gonzalez took refuge in the American Legation, thence escaping to the United States. Tinoco constituted a provisional government at once and summoned the people to an election for deputies to a constituent assembly on the first of May, 1917. At the same time he directed an election to take place for the Presidency and himself became a candidate. An election was held. Some 61,000 votes were cast for Tinoco and 259 for another candidate. Tinoco then was inaugurated as the President to administer his powers under the former constitution until the creation of a new one. A new constitution was adopted June 8, 1917, supplanting the constitution of 1871. For a full two years Tinoco and the legislative assembly under him peaceably administered the affairs of the Government of Costa Rica, and there was no disorder of a revolutionary character during that interval. No other government of any kind asserted power in the country. The courts sat, Congress legislated, and the government was duly administered. Its power was fully established and peacefully exercised. The people seemed to have accepted Tinoco's government with great good will when it came in, and to have welcomed the change. Even the committee of the existing government, which formulated and published a report on May 29, 1920, directing the indictment of President Tinoco for the crime of military revolution and declaring the acts of his regime as null and void and without legal value, used this language:

Without having a constitution to establish the office of President and determine his functions, and even to indicate the period for which he was to be elected, the election was held by the sole will of the person who was violently exercising the executive power. And as was natural, the election fell to the same Mr. Tinoco, and, sad to relate, the country applauded! The act, therefore, of decreeing that said election should be held under such conditions is contrary to the most rudimentary principles of political law.

The quotation is only important to show the fact of the then acquiescence of the people in the result. Though Tinoco came in with popular approval, the result of his two years administration of the law was to rouse opposition to him. Con-spiracies outside of the country were projected to organize a force to attack him. But this did not result in any substantial conflict or even a nominal provisional government on the soil until considerably more than two years after the inauguration of his government, and did not result in the establishment of any other real government until September of that year, he having renounced his Presidency in August preceding, on the score of his ill health, and withdrawn to Europe. The truth is that throughout the record as made by the case and counter case, there is no substantial evidence that Tinoco was not in actual and peaceable administration without resistance or conflict or contest by anyone until a few months before the time when he retired and resigned.

Speaking of the resumption of the present government, this passage occurs in the argument on behalf of Costa Rica:

Powerful forces in Costa Rica were opposed to Tinoco from the outset, but his overthrow by ballot or unarmed opposition was impossible and it was equally impossible to organize armed opposition against him in Costa Rican territory.

It is true that action of the supporters of those seeking to restore the former government was somewhat delayed by the influence of the United States with Gonzalez and his friends against armed action, on the ground that military disturbances in Central America during the World War would be prejudicial to the interests of the Allied Powers. It is not important, however, what were the causes that enabled Tinoco to carry on his government effectively and peaceably. The question is, must his government be considered a link in the continuity of the Government of Costa Rica? I must hold that from the evidence that the Tinoco government was an actual sovereign government.

But it is urged that many leading Powers refused to recognize the Tinoco government, and that recognition by other nations is the chief and best evidence of the birth, existence and continuity of succession of a government. Undoubtedly recognition by other Powers is an important evidential factor in establishing proof of the existence of a government in the society of nations. What are the facts as to this? The Tinoco government was recognized by Bolivia on May 17, 1917; by Argentina on May 22, 1917; by Chile on May 22, 1917; by Haiti on May 22, 1917; by Guatemala on May 28, 1917; by Switzerland on June 1, 1917; by Germany on June 10, 1917; by Denmark on June 18, 1917; by Spain on June 18, 1917; by Mexico on July 1, 1917; by Holland on July 11, 1917; by the Vatican on June 9, 1917; by Colombia on August 9, 1917; by Austria on August 10, 1917; by Portugal on August 14, 1917; by El Salvador on September 12, 1917; by Roumania on November 15, 1917; by Brazil on November 28, 1917; by Peru on December 15, 1917; and by Ecuador on April 23, 1917.

What were the circumstances as to the other nations?

The United States, on February 9, 1917, two weeks after Tinoco had assumed power, took this action:

The Government of the United States has viewed the recent overthrow of the established government in Costa Rica with the gravest concern and considers that illegal acts of this character tend to disturb the peace of Central America and to disrupt the unity of the American continent. In view of its policy in regard to the assumption of power through illegal methods, clearly enunciated by it on several occasions during the past four years, the Government of the United States desires to set forth in an emphatic and distinct manner its present position in regard to the actual situation in Costa Rica which is that it will not give recognition or support to any government which may be established unless it is clearly proven that it is elected by legal and constitutional means.

And again on February 24, 1917:

In order that citizens of the United States may have definite information as to the position of this Government in regard to any financial aid which they may give to, or any business transaction which they may have with those persons who overthrew the constitutional Government of Costa Rica by an act of armed rebellion, the Government of the United States desires to advise them that it will not consider any claims which may in the future arise from such dealings, worthy of its diplomatic support.

* * *

Probably because of the leadership of the United States in respect to a matter of this kind, her then Allies in the war, Great Britain, France and Italy, declined to recognize the Tinoco government. Costa Rica was, therefore, not permitted to sign the Treaty of Peace at Versailles, although the Tinoco government had declared war against Germany.

The merits of the policy of the United States in this non-recognition it is not for the arbitrator to discuss, for the reason that in his consideration of this case, he is necessarily controlled by principles of international law, and however justified as a national policy non-recognition on such a ground may be, it certainly has not been acquiesced in by all the nations of the world, which is a condition precedent to considering it as a postulate of international law.

The non-recognition by other nations of a government claiming to be a national personality, is usually appropriate evidence that it has not attained the independence and control entitling it by international law to be classed as such. But when recognition *vel non* of a government is by such nations determined by inquiry, not into its *de facto* sovereignty and complete governmental control, but into its illegitimacy or irregularity of origin, their non-recognition loses something of evidential weight on the issue with which those applying the rules of international law are alone concerned. What is true of the non-recognition of the United States in its bearing upon the existence of a *de facto* government under

Tinoco for thirty months is probably in a measure true of the non-recognition by her Allies in the European War. Such non-recognition for any reason, however, cannot outweigh the evidence disclosed by this record before me as to the *de facto* character of Tinoco's government, according to the standard set by international law.

Second. It is ably and earnestly argued on behalf of Costa Rica that the Tinoco government cannot be considered a *de facto* government, because it was not established and maintained in accord with the constitution of Costa Rica of 1871. To hold that a government which establishes itself and maintains a peaceful administration, with the acquiescence of the people for a substantial period of time, does not become a *de facto* government unless it conforms to a previous constitution would be to hold that within the rules of international law a revolution contrary to the fundamental law of the existing government cannot establish a new government. This cannot be, and is not, true. The change by revolution upsets the rule of the authorities in power under the then existing fundamental law, and sets aside the fundamental law in so far as the change of rule makes it necessary. To speak of a revolution creating a *de facto* government, which conforms to the limitations of the old constitution is to use a contradiction in terms. The same government continues internationally, but not the internal law of its being. The issue is not whether the new government assumes power or conducts its administration under constitutional limitations established by the people during the incumbency of the government it has overthrown. The question is, has it really established itself in such a way that all within its influence recognize its control, and that there is no opposing force assuming to be a government in its place? Is it discharging its functions as a government usually does, respected within its own jurisdiction?

Reference is further made, on behalf of Costa Rica, to the Treaty of Washington, December 20, 1907, entered into by the Republics of Central America, in which it was agreed that

The governments of the contracting parties will not recognize any one who rises to power in any of the five republics in consequence of a coup d'état or by a revolution against a recognized government until the representatives of the people by free elections have reorganized the country in constitutional form.

Such a treaty could not affect the rights of subjects of a government not a signatory thereto, or amend or change the rules of international law in the matter of *de facto* governments. Their action under the treaty could not be of more weight in determining the existence of a *de facto* government under Tinoco than the policy of the United States, already considered. Moreover, it should be noted that all the signatories to the treaty but Nicaragua manifested their conviction that the treaty requirement had been met in the case of the Tinoco government, by recognizing it after the adoption of the constitution of 1917 and the election of Tinoco.

Third. It is further objected by Costa Rica that Great Britain by her failure to recognize the Tinoco government is estopped now to urge claims of her subjects dependent upon the acts and contracts of the Tinoco government. The evidential weight of such non-recognition against the claim of its *de facto* character I have already considered and admitted. The contention here goes further and precludes a government which did not recognize a *de facto* government from appearing in an international tribunal in behalf of its nationals to claim any rights based on the acts of such government.

To sustain this view a great number of decisions in English and American courts are cited to the point that a municipal court cannot, in litigation before it, recognize or assume the *de facto* character of a foreign government which the executive department of foreign affairs of the government of which the court is a branch has not recognized. This is clearly true. It is for the executive to decide questions of foreign policy and not courts. It would be most unseemly to have a conflict of opinion in respect to foreign relations of a nation between its department charged with the conduct of its foreign affairs and its judicial branch. But such cases have no bearing on the point before us. Here the executive of Great Britain takes the position that the Tinoco government which it did not recognize, was nevertheless a *de facto* government that could create rights in British subjects which it now seeks to protect. Of course, as already emphasized, its failure to recognize the *de facto* government can be used against it as evidence to disprove the character it now attributes to that government, but this does not bar it from changing its position. Should a case arise in one of its own courts after it has changed its position, doubtless that court would feel it incumbent upon it to note the change in its further rulings.

Precedents in American arbitrations are cited to show that an estoppel like the one urged does arise. They are Schultz's case (Moore, *International Arbitrations,* Vol. 3, 2973), Janson's case (ibidem, 2902), and Jarvis's case (Ralston, *Venezuela Arbitrations,* 150). In the opinions of these cases delivered by American commissioners, there are expressions sustaining the view that the bar of an estoppel exists, but an examination shows that no authorities are cited and no arguments are made in support of the view. Moreover, the array of facts in the cases was conclusive against the existence of a *de facto* government, and the expressions were unnecessary to the conclusion. . . .

These are, so far as I am advised, the only authorities to be found either in decided cases or in text writers applying the principles of estoppel to bar a nation seeking to protect its nationals in their rights against the successor of a *de facto* government.

I do not understand the arguments on which an equitable estoppel in such case can rest. The failure to recognize the *de facto* government did not lead the succeeding government to change its position in any way upon the faith of it. Non-recognition may have aided the succeeding government to come into power; but subsequent presentation of claims based on the *de facto* existence of the previous government and its dealings does not work an injury to the succeeding government in the nature of a fraud or breach of faith. An equitable estoppel to prove the truth must rest on previous conduct of the person to be estopped, which has led the person claiming the estoppel into a position in which the truth will injure him. There is no such case here.

There are other estoppels recognized in municipal law than those which rest on equitable considerations. They are based on public policy. It may be urged that it would be in the interest of the stability of governments and the orderly adjustment of international relations, and so a proper rule of international law, that a government in recognizing or refusing to recognize a government claiming admission to the society of nations should thereafter be held to an attitude consistent with its deliberate conclusion on this issue Arguments for and against such a rule occur to me; but it suffices to say that I have not been cited to text writers of authority or to decisions of significance indicating a general acquiescence of nations in such a rule. Without this, it cannot be applied here as a principle of international law.

It is urged that the subjects of Great Britain knew of the policy of their home government in refusing to recognize the Tinoco régime and cannot now rely on protection by Great Britain. This is a question solely between the home government and its subjects. That government may take the course which the United

States has done and refuse to use any diplomatic offices to promote such claims and thus to leave its nationals to depend upon the sense of justice of the existing Costa Rican Government, as they were warned in advance would be its policy, or it may change its conclusion as to the *de facto* existence of the Tinoco government and offer its subjects the protection of its diplomatic intervention. It is entirely a question between the claimants and their own government. It should be noted that Great Britain issued no such warning to its subjects as did the United States to its citizens in this matter.

* * *

. . . The courts of the restored government are bound to administer the law of the restored government under its constitution and their decisions are necessarily affected by the limitations of that instrument. This may prevent the courts from giving full effect to international law that may be at variance with the municipal law which under the restored constitution the national courts have to administer. It is obvious that the obligations of a restored government for the acts of the usurping de facto government it succeeds cannot, from the international standpoint, be prejudiced by a constitution which, though restored to life, is for purposes of this discussion, exactly as if it were new legislation which was not in force when the obligations arose. . . .

This is not an exceptional instance of an essential difference between the scope and effect of a decision by the highest tribunal of a country and of an international tribunal. The Constitution of the United States makes the Constitution, laws passed in pursuance thereof, and treaties of the United States the supreme law of the land. Under that provision, a treaty may repeal a statute, and a statute may repeal a treaty. The Supreme Court cannot under the Constitution recognize and enforce rights accruing to aliens under a treaty which Congress has repealed by statute. In an international tribunal, however, the unilateral repeal of a treaty by a statute would not affect the rights arising under it and its judgment would necessarily give effect to the treaty and hold the statute repealing it of no effect. . . .

A consideration of the issues before us, therefore, recurs to the merits of the two claims. The decision of them must be governed by the answer to the question whether the claims would have been good against the Tinoco Government as a government, unaffected by the Law of Nullities, and unaffected by the Costa Rican Constitution of 1871. . . .

My award, therefore, is that the Law of Nullities in its operation upon the validity of the 998 one thousand colones bills and the claim in behalf of the Royal Bank, will work no injury of which Great Britain can complain, if Costa Rica assigns all her interest in the mortgage for $100,000 upon Jose Joaquin Tinoco's estate executed by his widow, together with all interest paid thereon to the Royal Bank, and that, upon Costa Rica's executing this assignment and delivering the mortgage, the Royal Bank should deliver to the Government of Costa Rica the 998 one thousand colones bills held by it.

My award further is that the Law of Nullities in decreeing the invalidity of the Amory concession worked no injury to the Central Costa Rica Petroleum Company, Ltd., its sole stockholder, of which Great Britain can complain, because the concession was in fact invalid under the Constitution of 1917.

Pema Chibar v. The Union of India, 1966*

Wanchoo, J. This writ petition under Art. 32 of the Constitution is by a former Portuguese citizen, who became a citizen

* Reprinted from *All India Reporter*, Supreme Court 442 (1966).

of India after the acquisition of the Portuguese territories in India by the Government of India on December 20, 1961. It may be mentioned that the Portuguese territories were acquired by India after military action. The petitioner was resident in Daman and had obtained 23 licences for import of various goods between October 9 and December 4, 1961. The goods to be imported under these licences were of the value of over one million pounds. The licences were valid for a period of 180 days from the date of issue and could be renewed for a further period. The case for the petitioner is that he had placed firm orders in respect of the goods covered by the said licences with his foreign suppliers prior to December 20, 1961 for the full value of the licences and had made to the said foreign suppliers advance payments either in full or in part of the price of the goods. The total amount said to have been paid by the petitioner was over £3,88,000 and he had to pay a further sum of over £7,62,000 as the balance. The goods covered by these licences had to be shipped in the first quarter of 1962. The petitioner's case further is that as the goods did not arrive within the period of 180 days he had applied on various dates for extension of the licences; but the same was refused. The petitioner then tried to persuade the foreign suppliers to cancel the orders and remit back the money paid to them, but they refused to do so. Consequently, he applied to the Government of India that he might be permitted to import the goods against the said licences, but this was also refused. He therefore filed the present petition in May 1963, and contends that the refusal to permit him to import goods on the basis of the said licences violated his fundamental right[s]. . . .

* * *

We shall assume for purposes of the present petition that the petitioner did hold valid licences before December 20, 1961 from the former Portuguese Government for import of goods worth over a million pounds. The position of law, however, in cases of acquisition of territories by conquest, as in the present case, is undisputed. In such a case the residents of the territories did not carry with them the rights which they possessed as subjects of the ex-sovereign and that as subjects of the new sovereign, they had only such rights as are granted or recognised by him, so far as the relations between the subjects and the sovereign are concerned. In the present case we are not concerned with relations between subject and subject of the former sovereign and their rights inter se when the new sovereign takes over. We are concerned only with relations between subjects of the former sovereign and the new sovereign after the new sovereign has taken over and what we say herein must be confined to that position alone.

In Dalmia Dadri Cement Co. Ltd. v. Commr. of Income-tax, 1959 SCR 729: (AIR 1958 SC 816), this undisputed position of law was laid down by this Court. This position was reiterated by this Court in State of Gujarat v. Vora Fiddali, AIR 1964 SC 1043, where it was held that the rule that cession of territory by one State to another is an act of State and the subjects of the former State may enforce only those rights which the new sovereign recognises is well settled. The same position was again affirmed in Shyamlal's case, AIR 1964 SC 1495, where it was held that as between the new sovereign and the subjects of the former sovereign, who become the subjects of the new sovereign by acquisition of territory, the rights of such subjects against the new sovereign depend upon recognition of liability by the new sovereign. Whether the new sovereign has recognized the rights of the new subjects as against itself and has undertaken the liabilities arising thereunder is a question of fact depending upon the action of the new sovereign after acquisition of the territory concerned. It is on the basis of this well-settled position of law that we have to consider whether the new sovereign, (namely, the Government of India) recognised these rights with which we are concerned in the present petition after December 20, 1961, when the former Portuguese territories in India were acquired. If it did so, the petitioner will be entitled to relief from this Court; but if it did not, the petition must fail on the ground that the new sovereign never recognised the rights arising out of the licences in question.

We therefore turn to the events which happened after December 20, 1961 to decide whether the new sovereign (namely, the Government of India) ever recognised rights of the kind which the petitioner claims on the basis of the licenses which he had from the former Portuguese Government. It appears that after the new territories were acquired, their administration was entrusted to a Military Governor. On December 30, 1961, the Military Governor issued a proclamation with respect to arrangements made for trade in the new territories. By this proclamation, exports were allowed by sea on completion of the necessary formalities in accordance with law that prevailed immediately before the entry of Indian troops into Goa. Further imports of goods already at sea and in regard to which foreign exchange component had already been paid were allowed on the same conditions. This proclamation of the Military Governor clearly shows the extent to which import of goods was allowed i.e. where the goods were already at sea and had been fully paid for. It is not the petitioner's case that his licences were covered by the recognition granted to import of goods by this proclamation. Further it seems to us clear by implication that every other kind of import except the kind permitted by this proclamation

was not recognised. Therefore, as we read this proclamation, it is clear that the new sovereign did not recognise imports on the basis of licences like those granted to the petitioner, unless two conditions were fulfilled, namely, (i) that the goods under the licences were already at sea, and (ii) that the foreign exchange had already been paid with respect to them. If both these conditions were fulfilled, imports were allowed but not otherwise. As it is not the petitioner's case that both these conditions were fulfilled with respect to these licences, it must be held that the imports which he now claims to be allowed were not recognised. . . .

* * *

We have therefore come to the conclusion that merely because the old laws were continued, it cannot necessarily be inferred that the new State recognised and assumed all liabilities of the former State. On the other hand if we refer to the proclamation of the Military Governor of December 30, 1961, we immediately see that only certain types of imports to which we have already referred were recognized by the new State and not others. In the face of that proclamation of December 30, 1961, it would in our opinion be impossible to infer from the mere fact that the old laws were continued that there was recognition of liabilities arising therefrom by the new sovereign. That is one aspect of the matter which in our opinion conclusively shows that the new sovereign did not recognise the rights arising from licences of the kind with which we are dealing at the present petition, and, therefore the petitioner would have no right under these licences for they were never recognised by the new sovereign. In this view of the matter, the petition must fail.

The Treaty of Versailles (1919), Articles 254-257*

Article 254

The Powers to which German territory is ceded shall, subject to the qualifications made in Article 255, undertake to pay:

(1) A portion of the debt of the German Empire as it stood on August 1, 1914, calculated on the basis of the ratio between the average for the three financial years 1911, 1912, 1913, of such revenues of the ceded territory, and the average for the same years of such revenues of the whole German Empire as in the judgment of the Reparation Commission are best calculated to represent the relative ability of the respective territories to make payment;

(2) A portion of the debt as it stood on August 1, 1914, of the German State to which the ceded territory belonged, to be determined in accordance with the principle stated above.

Such portions shall be determined by the Reparation Commission.

The method of discharging the obligation, both in respect of capital and of interest so assumed, shall be fixed by the Reparation Commission. Such method may take the form, *inter alia*, of the assumption by the Power to which the territory is ceded of Germany's liability for the German debt held by her nationals. But in the event of the method adopted involving any payments to the German Government, such payments shall be transferred to the Reparation Commission on account of the sums due for reparation so long as any balance in respect of such sums remains unpaid.

Article 255

(1) As an exception to the above provision and inasmuch as in 1871 Germany

* Reprinted from 13 *American Journal of International Law,* Supplement 151 (1919), by permission of the American Society of International Law.

refused to undertake any portion of the burden of the French debt, France shall be, in respect of Alsace-Lorraine, exempt from any payment under Article 254.

(2) In the case of Poland that portion of the debt which, in the opinion of the Reparation Commission, is attributable to the measures taken by the German and Prussian Governments for the German colonisation of Poland shall be excluded from the apportionment to be made under Article 254.

(3) In the case of all ceded territories other than Alsace-Lorraine, that portion of the debt of the German Empire or German States which, in the opinion of the Reparation Commission, represents expenditure by the Governments of the German Empire or States upon the Government properties referred to in Article 256 shall be excluded from the apportionment to be made under Article 254.

Article 256

Powers to which German territory is ceded shall acquire all property and possessions situated therein belonging to the German Empire or to the German States, and the value of such acquisitions shall be fixed by the Reparation Commission, and paid by the State acquiring the territory to the Reparation Commission for the credit of the German Government on account of the sums due for reparation.

For the purposes of this Article the property and possessions of the German Empire and States shall be deemed to include all the property of the Crown, the Empire or the States, and the private property of the former German Emperor and other Royal personages.

In view of the terms on which Alsace-Lorraine was ceded to Germany in 1871, France shall be exempt in respect thereof from making any payment or credit under this Article for any property or possessions of the German Empire or States situated therein.

Belgium also shall be exempt from making any payment or any credit under this Article for any property or possessions of the German Empire or States situated in German territory ceded to Belgium under the present Treaty.

Article 257

In the case of the former German territories, including colonies, protectorates or dependencies, administered by a Mandatory under Article 22 of Part I (League of Nations) of the present Treaty, neither the territory nor the Mandatory Power shall be charged with any portion of the debt of the German Empire or States.

All property and possessions belonging to the German Empire or to the German States situated in such territories shall be transferred with the territories to the Mandatory Power in its capacity as such and no payments shall be made nor any credit given to those Governments in consideration of this transfer.

For the purposes of this Article the property and possessions of the German Empire and of the German States shall be deemed to include all the property of the Crown, the Empire or the States and the private property of the former German Emperor and other Royal personages.

A Soviet View: Some Problems of Succession*

N. V. Zakharova

It is generally recognized in international law and practice that a state arising as a result of a social revolution is the legal successor to the state on the territory to which it is established. But this indisputable postulate is justified in different ways.

* Reprinted from N. V. Zakharova, "States as Subjects of International Law and Social Revolution (Some Problems of Succession)," *Soviet Yearbook of International Law* 164 (1960), by permission of the Soviet Association of International Law. (English summary)

Some Soviet scholars (M. M. Avakov and others) take the view that a social revolution which radically changes social and state structure causes the destruction of one subject of international law and the emergence of another, new subject. Supporters of this point of view base the right to succession of a state in which a social revolution has taken place on the identity of its territory and population with the territory and population of the former state. Other scholars (F. I. Kozhevnikov, L. A. Madzhoryan) take the view that by creating a state of a new type a social revolution does not bring about the emergence of a new subject of law.

* * *

The problem of the continuity of a state as a subject of international law in the event of a social revolution is a legal problem. A subject of law is the bearer of rights and duties. But the problem cannot be solved by means of the mechanical juxtaposition of the rights and responsibilities of the given state before and after the fundamental change in its social and political system. The rights and obligations of one and the same state change: some treaties cease to exist, others are concluded, etc. A social revolution fundamentally changes the nature of a state as a political organization of a society, but a social revolution does not interrupt the existence of a state as a subject of law.

The recognition of the continuity of subjects in the event of the fundamental alteration of the structure of a state has, however, nothing in common with the bourgeois theory of continuity which asserts that the uninterrupted nature of the existence of a state requires the recognition of all international treaties regardless of internal changes.

The practical conclusions drawn by the adherents of the two theoretical conceptions regarding the question of a state as a subject of law following social revolutions which exist in the Soviet legal science are the same. The adherents of both conceptions acknowledge that a state has after a social revolution the right to repudiate international treaties which do not correspond to the principles of the new system and to its national interests.

Bourgeois scholars also support various points of view regarding a state as a subject of law following social revolution. There are adherents of the point of view that states continue to exist as subjects of international law, and also adherents of the opposite point of view. But the denial of the right of a state to repudiate international treaties following social revolutions is a characteristic feature of bourgeois science. This is a reflection of the hostility of bourgeois scholars to the historical process of the transition of states from capitalism to Socialism.

The right of a state to repudiate treaties because they contradict the principles of the new system fully corresponds to a generally recognized principle of international law. The necessity to observe old treaties would oblige a state to pursue a foreign policy alien to the people and to support principles and aims which the people had repudiated. The right to repudiate international treaties which are incompatible with the principles of the new structure of a state makes it possible for a people to make effective use of the principle of self-determination, upon which the right of a state to repudiate treaties contradicting the new principle of its policy following social revolutions is based. This principle also determines the right of a state to repudiate, following a social revolution, those treaties which do not correspond to the basic principles of the new system of property ownership and the new economy of the country.

The right of a state to repudiate international treaties concluded in the special interests of the overthrown classes or with the aim of suppressing the class which has come to power is also indisputable.

International law gives every state the right to repudiate unequal treaties. International law does not recognize treaties which contradict its basic principles and rules. A state's repudiation of unequal treaties following a social revolution is connected with the revolution only in the sense that its carrying out determines a state's implementation of its right.

The October Revolution played an important part in the consolidation of the democratic principles of international law. One of the first acts of the Soviet state in this direction was the repudiation of the unequal international treaties concluded by tsarist Russia.

Towards a Reformulation of the Law of State Succession*

Gerard V. La Forest

The creation since World War II of a large number of new states has focused attention on the law governing the succession of states to the benefits and burdens incurred by their predecessor states. But for all this attention, attempts at predicting outcomes of claims respecting the continuance of obligations following political changes in the nation-states are probably more hindered than helped by reference to prevalent legal theories. Under these circumstances the need for reformulating the law seems obvious, and important steps have already been taken by such prestigious bodies as the International Law Commission and the International Law Association. Unfortunately, as it seems to me, there is considerable evidence that many approach the work at hand wearing conceptual blinkers. Thus several members of the Sub-Committee on the Succession of States and

* Reprinted from Gerard V. La Forest, "Towards a Reformulation of the Law of State Succession," *Proceedings of the American Society of International Law* 103 (1966), by permission of the American Society of International Law.

Governments of the International Law Commission were prepared to study state succession independently of succession of governments. The primary fallacy here is in treating these two concepts as if they were distinct phenomena rather than labels attached to various happenings to achieve a given result. A second is that they embody policies more or less suitable to the predominant nations during a period when the power structure of the world was radically different from that existing today. Let me elaborate.

The now generally accepted legal division of political changes into changes of state and changes of government is easily explicable in terms of the interests of the dominant Powers during the 19th century, when the doctrine became settled. A change of government under this theory effects no juridical change in the state, and, under the doctrine of the continuity of states, the new government succeeds to the benefits and burdens of the old government. The doctrine of continuity of states, then, provides a concept for maintaining obligations alive in countries that are subject to frequent changes of governmental élites by violent means. On the other hand, the acquisition of new territories by conquest does not fall under this rubric. Though the acquiring state succeeded to the territory and obligations owing to the conquered country, it was not generally subject to its burdens. Where there was partial conquest the state that had lost territory remained subject to pre-existing burdens, and even where there was an extinction of the old state, the acquiring state did not succeed to them. This was generally the situation involving territorial changes outside Europe. However, when a political change involving geographical alterations occurred in Europe, the application of these doctrines was at best uncertain. Frequently reasonable arrangements were made by treaty because the law was otherwise unworkable. In fact, the earlier doctrine of universal succession had been more adapted to political changes

in Europe; owing to the developed and somewhat interdependent economies of European countries, there were advantages to both the state acquiring territory and other states in keeping pre-existing arrangements in being.

Where there is no geographical change it is easy to categorize a political change as a change of government. But in other cases there is no clear-cut factual distinction; the decision whether there has been a change of government or a new state has been created seems to be made *ex post facto* by an emerging government from a consideration of the advantages and disadvantages to it, and the decision is accepted or rejected by other states on similar considerations. Italy's succession to Sardinia and the experience of Katanga may be mentioned here.

From this necessarily impressionistic statement it must be obvious that the traditional dichotomy of change of state and change of government may be of limited value under current world conditions, and should be discarded. Even if these categories were clear, they do not afford adequate tools for considering the variegated factors that should be taken into account. They lay too much stress on purely geographical factors at the expense of others that may have far more cogency. For example, the distinction between a new nation that has achieved independence by violent means and one that has done so by gradual evolution, and that between a revolution marking the emergence of a new ideology and one that merely alters governmental structures may be far more important than geographical changes. Again, the concepts do not allow for discriminating choices. Thus, a decision that a political change has given birth to a new state may afford a satisfactory disposition of some treaty obligations, but perhaps not all, and in any event it may fail to provide for an equitable disposition of the rights of private individuals or corporations.

In attempting to reformulate the law

regarding political change, one should not, I suggest, begin within the confines of the established legal categories. Rather one should examine all aspects of political change, isolate the claims that are likely to be made by or against emerging governmental élites as a result of such change, and propose responses to such claims in the light of policies appropriate to the current world political structure. Assistance can, of course, be derived from past practice but only if one takes into account, and gives due weight to, all the facts involved. In assessing past practice, too, one must steadily keep in mind the general power and economic structure of the world community at the time of a decision and the position of the decision-maker within that structure.

The past, then, deserves examination, and examination taking into account far more factors from broader perspectives than is usually done. But a reformulation of the law should be oriented towards the future. This demands the abandonment of concepts incorporating policies no longer appropriate to our era and the articulation of policies appropriate to our times. In doing this, one must take account of two broad social forces. On the one hand is the common desire for productive stability in the affairs of people and for the employment of peaceful procedure in effecting change. This broad orientation favors the honoring of existing obligations, irrespective of changes of governmental élites and structures or boundaries. Yet account must also be taken of the fact that desire for a change in the *status quo* may be so insistent that violence is resorted to; under these circumstances it is unrealistic to expect the continued honoring of old commitments.

Policies, then, must be devised to provide a reasonable accommodation between the desire for stability, and the need for change. In doing so, I would suggest that one must attempt to satisfy the widest possible measure of conflicting demands by people throughout the globe. To give effect to this broad preference, it is useful to set down specific policy formulations in relation to broad categories of claims. . . . I propose to examine claims made by and against new governmental élites in relation to succession to treaties, and the responses to those claims in the light of a number of tentative policy formulations. I also hope to show that, despite doctrinal rigidity, the decision-makers of the world community, particularly in recent years, have gone a considerable distance in giving effect to these policy preferences, but that established doctrine has sometimes stood in the way of rational decision.

Some of the broad policies I would suggest for consideration in devising appropriate responses to claims relating to the continuance of treaties on a political change are the following. First and foremost, of course, is the goal of minimum world order, that as much as possible action that might lead to armed clashes or threaten the security of states should be avoided. Secondly, the freest possible flow of wealth, skills and people across state lines should be encouraged. This, among other things, assists in maintaining a world economy, the desirability of which should require no demonstration. The same function is served by my third policy suggestion: that a great measure of deference be given to previous arrangements entered into for the benefit of the people or territory in a new political community, whether under existing doctrine the new community would be characterized as a new government or a new state. But the forces of change must often override the benefits of stability. This brings me to a fourth policy: that an emerging élite should have a wide measure of competence to repudiate political arrangements as well as arrangements made by pre-existing élites for their own benefit or for that of people or territory outside that of the new political community or to foster ideologies inimical to that of the emerging élite. This is intended to promote self-determination, to allow the people of the new community a reasonable share of power both at home and abroad. However, others should be given as much opportunity as possible to adjust to change, and this brings me to a fifth policy formulation: that as much as possible expectations be not abruptly terminated but appropriate transitional measures be taken to cushion the shock of change. Last, but by no means least, general or regional prescriptions (except, probably, political arrangements) provided for by multilateral arrangements of a wide cross section of the élites of the world community or region should be respected. The difficulty of reaching decision for the general benefit is too great to allow particular interests to prevail over the general will through the accident of political change.

I will now turn to a review of the law on succession to treaties in the light of these policies.

During the 19th and early 20th centuries, the general rule was that treaties continued to apply to a new governmental élite only where a political change was characterized as a change of government. But even at this early stage, doctrinal rigidity gave way somewhat to overriding policy considerations. "Dispositive" treaties were looked upon as "real" rights that continued uninterrupted despite political change.

These dispositive treaties are of several kinds. Under certain circumstances, particularly in connection with postwar settlements, groups of nations sometimes assume power to create, by multilateral treaty, obligations on some state in the interests of world or regional security; examples are treaties of neutralization and demilitarization. Though authority is not extensive, such obligations appear to be regarded in the nature of "real" rights and to extend beyond the actual contracting parties to all interested parties. The underlying rationale is that there is an expectation among interested parties that a regime established for the maintenance of minimum world order should be honored.

Restrictions may also be imposed on the territory of a state for the benefit of international commerce. The importance of commerce to the world community is such that an attempt to interfere with long-acquired rights of this kind is likely to lead to a breach of the peace, as the Suez incident shows.

In addition to these "universal servitudes" there are also "particular servitudes," a term covering such rights by one or several states over the territory of another as waterways, railway passages and rights of fisheries. These are often primarily aimed at the promotion of commerce but, as the leased-bases agreements attest, they may also be intended to assure the national security of the contracting states. In any event there is considerable state practice to support the view that states succeeding to territory burdened by such "dispositive" treaties continue to be subject to them and succeed to their benefits.

In general I am strongly in favor of the continuance of "dispositive" treaties, particularly general arrangements for the maintenance of international peace and security or of the world economy. I am also generally favorable to the continuance of "particular servitudes" because an interruption of such rights may seriously disrupt the economy or endanger the security of the beneficiary state. For example, many economic patterns of the Great Lakes region are based on the expectation that the St. Lawrence River will continue to be free and open to the citizens of Canada and the United States.

There has been a tendency by some nations, however, to regard dispositive treaties as a vestige of colonialism, and therefore out of place in the modern world. This is certainly true of some treaty rights ordinarily classified as dispositive, for example, capitulations. But a reasonable doctrine of servitudes is of inestimable value to the world economy and sometimes to the maintenance of minimum world order; an absolutist doctrine of sovereignty in an age of interdependence is simply anachronistic.

During this century there has been an increasing tendency to continue to apply treaties in many situations where there has been a "change of state." This has caused difficulty with theorists because of an anthropomorphic attitude towards states and the tendency to equate treaties with contracts under private law. In truth, of course, treaties are arrangements between governmental élites for the benefit of persons and territory within their jurisdiction. Except where such treaties are intimately connected with the orientation of a particular élite or were intended specifically for its benefit rather than that of the people or territory within its control, there seems no reason not to continue treaty arrangements merely because the élite has been replaced.

The earliest situations where all treaties, or at least all treaties other than political treaties, have been recognized by the international community as continuing following a political change characterized as giving birth to a new state occurred where the local governmental élite of the territory in the new state had a considerable measure of independence in the conduct of its affairs, both internal and external, before the territory became recognized as a separate state. The classic examples of this are the older Commonwealth countries. But these are not the only instances of this phenomenon, though variations in practice occurred because of differing conditions. Thus, on the dissolution of the union between Norway and Sweden in 1905, the proposals of these states for the continuance of pre-existing treaties were accepted by other states. In all these cases the local élites of the new states had had a say in the formation of policy before severance and there was no reason to interfere with the stability of expectations.

Even where the local élites of a pre-existing political entity had less control over its affairs than in the foregoing situations, there may be considerable advantages to a new state in maintaining treaty obligations that were applicable to such entity. Consequently claims that such treaties continue to apply have frequently been made by the newly emerging nations, and there appears to have been unanimous acceptance of such claims by other states. These claims are usually made where there are circumstances creating expectations of continuity. Thus they often relate to treaties which either by their terms or by special extension were made applicable to, or entered into on behalf of, the territory of the new state as a special entity. The claim is all the stronger if the treaty was applied on the initiative of local élites. For example, Great Britain often provided for adherence by the Dominions to extradition and commercial treaties. Sometimes the expectation of continuity is created by the manner in which a new nation is established. Examples are the various British Independence Acts and agreements made by predecessor states, notably Great Britain and France, and local élites providing for the continuance of treaties on the accession of a new state to independence.

Some writers view these arrangements for continuity as at best creating mere bilateral obligations, but this loses sight of the realities of the situation. The original treaties were entered into in the expectation by all parties that they would apply to territory which, though not recognized as a state, was nonetheless considered for many reasons as a separate entity. Then when, with the acquiescence of the governmental élite of the emerging state, provision is made for the continuance of the treaties, there seems no rational ground for not giving effect to the expectations of all the parties. Contrary expectations may arise in connection with political treaties where the political orientation of the governing élites may be of paramount importance, but these are seldom if ever made subject to Independence Acts or succession agreements.

Continuity of treaties has been encouraged by procedures of international organizations despite a change of state. For example, where a new state has been established by the United Nations, it is often made subject to treaties prescribed by that organization. There has been a considerable degree of conformity with these arrangements, no doubt because the newly emerging nations find little advantage in starting off with a "clean slate."

Again claims that new states succeed to multilateral conventions have increasing chances of acceptance. This applies in varying degrees to different types of treaties, but the tendency to continue to apply multilateral conventions to the territory of newly emerging nations is perhaps more marked where the convention is of a technical character such as postal agreements. But the trend is not limited to these; for example a technique has been devised for continuing GATT in force in respect of new states pending their formal accession.

The desire for continuity is by no means limited to the older states. In fact the more recent devices for securing continuity have been initiated by the newly emerging nations. Not unnaturally, however, they have shown a disposition to be selective. Thus, claims that a new state may choose which treaties of its predecessor shall apply to it have expressly or implicitly been made by several of the newly emerging nations, and there has been a considerable acquiescence by other states.

A more recent development, and one that offers a reasonable accommodation between the necessity for change resulting from altered conditions and the advantages of continuity both to new and older states, is claims by new states that treaties made by predecessor states apply to new states for a determinate period unless earlier modified or abrogated by mutual consent. Uganda and Kenya have adopted this course, and the United States, at least, has accepted these claims.

In the absence of automatic continuity for indefinite periods, there is much to commend the new devices for continuing treaties for a temporary period to allow negotiations for more permanent arrangements. It is undesirable that the new states, especially, should be left to operate without the benefit of arrangements for accommodating their necessary relations with other states. The last consideration also favors the tendency of allowing newly emerging nations to decide if pre-existing treaties shall apply to them. These treaties are of greater importance to the new nations, since other states have established patterns with most of the world community, and the new state is in a better position to judge whether pre-existing arrangements are suitable to the new conditions. This does not make the older states subject to the whims of the new nations. If continuity is not automatic, older states should probably be given the choice of accepting or rejecting the proposals of the new nations. In any event, most treaties provide for termination on relatively short notice, so no great harm would result from a policy of continuity.

The purpose of this brief and necessarily incomplete review has been to show that in determining the extent of applicability of treaties, other than political treaties, international decision-makers, despite doctrinal rigidities, have wisely examined the facts of political changes to determine if pre-existing arrangements were still relevant. Nonetheless, the influence of past doctrines may have played a retarding influence. The slow pace at which the continuity of multilateral treaties has been accepted where there has been a "change of state" is an instance in point.

Generally I suggest that multilateral conventions of all kinds, except political arrangements, should continue. These conventions have been worked out for the common benefit by a large cross section of the world's decision-makers and not to serve the particular needs of any one group. In the absence of an international legislature such conventions are among the most promising methods for the development of international law. The need for continuance is all the greater in relation to technical treaties, and particularly those relating to communications. In an interdependent world it is necessary to keep open the lines of communication if only to be able to make an intelligent appraisal of the nature of disagreements. I have excepted political multilateral treaties (not, however, including general servitudes) because these were based on the orientation and power of the governmental élite that formerly had control over the territory of a new state; the new élite should be free to determine its future political orientation.

Even more than in the case of multilateral treaties, continuity or determination of bilateral treaties has been largely governed by whether a political change is characterized as a change of government or a change of state, whether the treaty in question is "political," "economic," "judicial," "administrative" or "technical." One can understand that political treaties (for example, treaties of alliance) should not survive a change of state. Such treaties are obviously entered into with certain expectations on the part of the parties relating to the power of the signatories, their territory and the orientation of the governing élites, and it would normally not conform to their expectations that such treaties should continue to apply after a political change considered so fundamental as to give birth to a new state. The same applies to economic treaties (for example, of commerce). Here the difference in wealth and territory between the new state and its predecessor will usually remove the underlying basis on which the parties entered into the treaty. Similar considerations may also apply to judicial treaties (for example, treaties of extradition or enforcement of judgments). Thus, an extradition treaty imposes a peremptory obligation to surrender a fugitive to the demanding state. Compliance presupposes trust by the sur-

rendering state in the adequacy and fairness of the judicial institutions of the demanding state. This is surely a matter closely linked with the effective élite. But such reasoning is not so cogent in relation to administrative treaties (for example, treaties for the control of drugs) and technical treaties (for example, treaties relating to telegraph and the post). I am aware, of course, that classification of treaties in this way gives rise to numerous preliminary problems (for example, when may treaties be categorized as "political," "economic," etc.?; what is to be the fate of treaties having provisions falling within several of these categories?); but these are not insuperable problems.

By contrast when a political change is categorized as a mere change of government (and there is often no empirical way of determining this ahead of time), treaties are held to continue, though the conditions underlying their formation may have drastically changed. Here again the facts should be closely examined in the light of rational policy. While there is no question that in many situations characterized as a change of government continuity of treaties should be the rule, this is not always so. Thus, where there has been a violent revolution accompanied by a radical change in ideology, it seems absurd to hold the new government, or for that matter other states, subject to arrangements entered into on the basis of a fundamentally different political background. In these circumstances political treaties at least should not be continued and this is probably true of bilateral economic and judicial treaties as well.

There may well be disagreement regarding some of the specific proposals I have suggested. This is to be expected, but the main burden . . . has been to show that the rigid dichotomy between changes of government and changes of state should no longer be retained as a framework for the law of political change. Though the examples chosen have been limited to treaties, the same is true of other aspects of the subject. Instead of proceeding from the traditional dichotomy, an attempt should be made to devise appropriate policy based on detailed examination of the various claims that may arise out of a political change, taking into account the multiplicity of factors that may reasonably be expected to affect decision, such as the degree of change, the types of obligations and benefits claimed, the methods by which change was effected, the types of claimants and the consequences for all concerned in honoring or dishonoring the expectation of claimants in the particular context.

Suggested Readings

Textbooks

Brierly. *The Law of Nations,* pp. 126–161.
Brownlie. *Principles of Public International Law,* pp. 52–97, 445–486.
Fenwick. *International Law,* pp. 121–203.
Gould. *An Introduction to International Law,* pp. 176–258, 411–437.
Jacobini. *International Law,* pp. 45–67.
Kaplan and Katzenbach. *The Political Foundations of International Law,* pp. 83–134.
Kelsen. *Principles of International Law,* pp. 177–289, 381–433.
Sørenson. *Manual of Public International Law,* pp. 247–310.
Svarlien. *An Introduction to the Law of Nations,* pp. 83–121, 419–445.
Tung. *International Law in an Organizing World,* pp. 39–63, 233–299.
von Glahn. *Law Among Nations,* pp. 61–122.

International Legal Persons

Friedman, Wolfgang. *The Changing Structure of International Law.* New York: Columbia University Press, 1964, pp. 231–252.
Norgaard, Carl Aage. *The Position of the Individual in International Law.* Copenhagen: Ejnor Munksgaard, 1962.
Robertson, A. H. *Human Rights and the International Community.* Chicago: Quadrangle Books, 1964.
Weissberg, Guenter. *The International Status of the United Nations.* Dobbs Ferry, N.Y.: Oceana, 1961.

Recognition

Briggs, Herbert W. "Non-Recognition in the Courts: The Ships of the Baltic Republics," 37 *American Journal of International Law* 585 (1943).
Chen, Ti-Chiang. *The International Law of Recognition.* London: Stevens, 1951.
Lauterpacht, Hersch. *Recognition in International Law.* Cambridge: University Press, 1947.
Newman, Robert P. *Recognition of Communist China?* New York: Macmillan, 1961.

Succession

Committee on State Succession to Treaties and Other Governmental Obligations. *The Effect of Independence on Treaties.* London: Stevens, 1965.

Marek, Krystyna. *Identity and Continuity of States in Public International Law.* Geneva: Droz, 1954.

O'Connell, D. P. *The Law of State Succession.* Cambridge: University Press, 1956.

Chapter III
State
Territory

ACQUISITION OF TERRITORY

The earth's surface can be viewed as consisting of three types of territory: that which belongs to some state, that which belongs to no state (*terra nullius*), and that which belongs to all states (*terra communis*). New York City is part of the territory of the United States; an undiscovered island belongs to no one; the high seas belong to everyone. International law is concerned with delimiting these respective areas, with regulating the change of territory from one category to another and the change of title in territory from one state to another. It is particularly concerned with conflicting state claims to territory and with disputes over the boundary lines that separate the territory of states.

There is a tendency of states to expand by acquiring additional territory, because new territory can bring added resources, markets, strategic bases, and the like. But it can also bring problems, for states often come into conflict in their struggle for territory. The norms that international law provides to regulate this process are extremely important; without rules, the struggle for territory would be even more productive of international discord than it is.

Territorial changes occur at a fairly rapid rate. Traditional international law regulated these changes by recognizing five principal modes of territorial acquisition: occupation, prescription, accretion, cession, and conquest. Each of these, except conquest, was derived from the Roman law of property by European jurists during the "age of discovery" (1450–1750). They satisfied an urgent need by providing norms to guide states in establishing title and in adjusting conflicting claims. They are still useful at a time when little of the earth's surface is unappropriated: many of today's territorial disputes center around the validity of yesterday's acquisitions, territory still changes hands, and space exploration poses the problem of future struggles to acquire control over celestial bodies.

Occupation is a means of acquiring unappropriated territory. To constitute a valid claim, the occupation must satisfy two conditions. First, the territory must be *terra nullius*. Second, the occupation must be "effective," which denotes the actual, continuous, and peaceful display of state authority over the territory. Mere discovery of territory gives the discoverer an "inchoate title" only, that is to say, a temporary right to make an effective occupation. If, within a reasonable time, the area is not occupied, it is subject to appropriation by another state.

Prescription is similar to occupation in that it is based on actual, continuous, and undisturbed display of state authority. It differs from occupation, however, for it applies not to territory that was previously *terra nullius* but to territory that was lawfully claimed by another state. The effectiveness of title by prescription depends largely upon whether the prior claimant has acquiesced in the usurper's display of state authority. Acquiescence is implied when the prior possessor fails to manifest its opposition in a sufficiently positive manner, for example, by reference to an international tribunal or by strong diplomatic protest. The length of time necessary to establish title by prescription and the strength of the protest necessary to prevent it are matters that can best be settled by bringing the matter before a tribunal for adjudication or arbitration.

A state acquires territory by accretion when new land is formed within its existing territorial limits: the sea recedes, a river dries up, an island appears within the territorial sea. These acquisitions seldom result in either significant additions of territory or in controversy.

Cession, which refers to the transfer of territory from one state to another by treaty, often results in significant territorial change and frequently produces controversy. Cession may be either voluntary or forced. The purchase of Alaska from Russia by the United States in 1867 was a voluntary cession; the cession in 1870 to Germany by France of Alsace-Lorraine was forced. In either case, the cession gives valid title. It is obvious, though, that a forced cession is not as likely to be permanent, as the forced return by cession of Alsace-Lorraine to France following World War I illustrates.

Conquest is similar to forced cession in that it too involves the forcible seizure of another state's territory; it differs because it is not accompanied by a treaty acknowledging the transfer. Recent illustrations of conquest are the Italian annexation of Ethiopia in 1936 and the Indian annexation of Goa in 1961.

Current principles of international law regarding the permissible uses of force, particularly those included in the League of Nations Covenant and the United Nations Charter, lead some writers to conclude that both forced cession and conquest no longer give valid title to territory. The Stimson Doctrine of non-recognition and the refusal of the United States to recognize the annexation of Lithuania, Latvia, and Estonia by the Soviet Union are based on this view. The ultimate success or failure of this position will depend upon whether states continue to acquiesce in such forcible seizures; continued possession by victorious states will, in time, surely result in valid title.

Although it is important for the student of international law to be familiar with the traditionally recognized modes of territorial acquisition, it is even more important that he realize that the labels "occupation," "prescription," "accretion," "cession," and "conquest" are not a substitute for analysis. The issue of title to territory is often complex and involves the application of various principles of law to the facts at hand. As Ian Brownlie points out:

> ... The result of this process cannot always be ascribed to any single dominant rule or "mode of acquisition." The orthodox analysis does not prepare the student for the interaction of principles of acquiescence and recognition with the other rules. Furthermore, a category like "cession" or "prescription" might bring quite distinct situations into unhappy fellowship. .... the importance of showing a better right to possess in contentious cases, i.e. of relative title, is obscured if too much credit is given to the five "modes."[1]

It is also important to note that a number of widely recognized principles relating to title to territory supplements the traditionally accepted norms. For example, the Latin American states have agreed through practice to give significant weight in territorial disputes to the principle of *uti possidetis*, that is to say, they have agreed to regard their titles to territory as coextensive with those of the period of the Spanish empire. After both World War I and World War II, the major victor states assumed a power of disposition over certain territories of the defeated states. And, although the defeated states often renounced title in a peace treaty, "the dispositions were assumed to be valid irrespective of such renunciation and the recipients were usually in possession prior to the coming into force of a peace treaty."[2]

Finally, the student of international law should be aware that the traditionally accepted modes of territorial acquisition did not attach any legal significance to the principle of self-determination. Sovereignty over nonself-governing territories, no matter how acquired, is now challenged, particularly by the new states of Asia and Africa.[3] If international law is to be used with maximum utility in resolving the territorial disputes of our time, the norms must be reformulated to meet modern needs and expectations.

Acquisition of territory in the polar regions presents special problems because of the difficulty of occupation. Here, most state claims are based on the less widely accepted methods of discovery, exploration, and contiguity. Although there has been no common agreement on the Arctic, the "sector theory," a variation of the doctrine of contiguity, is used by Canada and the Soviet Union to claim "all the area between a base line connecting the meridians of longitude marking the limits of [their] easterly and westerly frontiers and extending as far north as the final intersection of those meridians at the North Pole."[4] Norway, however, seems to be opposed to the sector theory solution; and Denmark, Iceland, and the United States, other states that front on the Arctic, do not appear to have become committed.[5] Within the sector claimed by the Soviet Union lie Nansen Island, claimed by Norway, and Wrangel Island, claimed by the United States. Uncertainty and overlapping claims portend future conflict in the area. Claims to Antarctic areas, also based largely on discovery, exploration, and contiguity, are even more numerous and more volatile. Argentina, Australia, Britain, Chile, France, New Zealand, and Norway have made formal claims, some of them overlapping. The Soviet Union and the United States refuse to recognize the validity of any of these claims. The Antarctic Treaty of 1959, reprinted below on pages 139–142, although it does not reconcile conflicting claims, goes a long way toward establishing an ordered regime in Antarctica. It prohibits all military measures, including the

---

[1] Brownlie, *Principles of Public International Law*, pp. 122-123.
[2] *Ibid.*, p. 126.
[3] See the debate in the Security Council of the United Nations on the Indian conquest of Goa, reprinted below on pages 349–352.

[4] Charles Cheney Hyde, *International Law Chiefly as Interpreted and Applied by the United States*, 2nd ed. (Boston: Little, Brown and Company, 1945), Vol. I, p. 346.
[5] *Ibid.*, pp. 349–350.

testing of any kind of weapon, and it calls for the continuation of, and cooperation in, scientific investigation. Each of the twelve signatories is given the right to appoint observers to conduct inspections of all installations, equipment, ships, aircraft, and personnel in all parts of Antarctica. The treaty is an important attempt to remove a section of the world from international rivalries. A similar effort is now being made to keep the cold war from spreading into outer space.[6]

The decision of Max Huber in The Island of Palmas case, the first selection in this section, is a classic statement of the traditional rules of international law that regulate territorial acquisitions. Then follows The Antarctic Treaty of 1959, which went into force in June 1961.

The Island of Palmas Case *

United States - The Netherlands, Tribunal of the Permanent Court of Arbitration, 1928

[Palmas, an island about two miles long and three-fourths of a mile wide, with a population of about 750, is situated within the boundaries of the Philippines as ceded by Spain to the United States in 1898. When United States authorities visited the island in 1906, they were surprised to learn that The Netherlands claimed sovereignty over it. Thus began a diplomatic controversy over the island that lasted until 1925, when the United States and The Netherlands agreed to arbitration. The decision by Max Huber, a Swiss jurist acting for the Permanent Court of Arbitration, follows:]

* * *

[6] See the Outer Space Treaty of 1966, reprinted on pages 180–184.
* Reprinted from 2 *United Nations Reports of International Arbital Awards* 829.

Sovereignty in the relations between States signifies independence. Independence in regard to a portion of the globe is the right to exercise therein, to the exclusion of any other State, the functions of a State. The development of the national organisation of States during the last few centuries and, as a corollary, the development of international law, have established this principle of the exclusive competence of the State in regard to its own territory in such a way as to make it the point of departure in settling most questions that concern international relations. The special cases of the composite State, of collective sovereignty, etc., do not fall to be considered here and do not, for that matter, throw any doubt upon the principle which has just been enunciated. Under this reservation it may be stated that territorial sovereignty belongs always to one, or in exceptional circumstances to several States, to the exclusion of all others. The fact that the functions of a State can be performed by any State within a given zone is, on the other hand, precisely the characteristic feature of the legal situation pertaining in those parts of the globe which, like the high seas or lands without a master, cannot or do not yet form the territory of a State.

Territorial sovereignty is, in general, a situation recognized and delimited in space, either by so-called natural frontiers as recognized by international law or by outward signs of delimitation that are undisputed, or else by legal engagements entered into between interested neighbours, such as frontier conventions, or by acts of recognition of States within fixed boundaries. If a dispute arises as to the sovereignty over a portion of territory, it is customary to examine which of the States claiming sovereignty possesses a title— cession, conquest, occupation, etc.— superior to that which the other State might possibly bring forward against it. However, if the contestation is based on the fact that the other Party has actually displayed sovereignty, it cannot be sufficient to establish the title by which territorial sovereignty was validly acquired at a certain moment; it must also be shown that the territorial sovereignty has continued to exist and did exist at the moment which for the decision of the dispute must be considered as critical. This demonstration consists in the actual display of State activities, such as belongs only to the territorial sovereign.

Titles of acquisition of territorial sovereignty in present-day international law are either based on an act of effective apprehension, such as occupation or conquest, or, like cession, presuppose that the ceding and the cessionary Powers or at least one of them, have the faculty of effectively disposing of the ceded territory. In the same way natural accretion can only be conceived of as an accretion to a portion of territory where there exists an actual sovereignty capable of extending to a spot which falls within its sphere of activity. It seems therefore natural that an element which is essential for the constitution of sovereignty should not be lacking in its continuation. So true is this, that practice, as well as doctrine, recognizes—though under different legal formulae and with certain differences as to the conditions required—that the continuous and peaceful display of territorial sovereignty (peaceful in relation to other States) is as good as a title. The growing insistence with which international law, ever since the middle of the 18th century, has demanded that the occupation shall be effective would be inconceivable, if effectiveness were required only for the act of acquisition and not equally for the maintenance of the right. If the effectiveness has above all been insisted on in regard to occupation, this is because the question rarely arises in connection with territories in which there is already an established order of things. Just as before the rise of international law, boundaries of lands were necessarily determined by the fact that the power of a State was

exercised within them, so too, under the reign of international law, the fact of peaceful and continuous display is still one of the most important considerations in establishing boundaries between States.

Territorial sovereignty, as has already been said, involves the exclusive right to display the activities of a State. This right has as corollary a duty: the obligation to protect within the territory the rights of other States, in particular their right to integrity and inviolability in peace and in war, together with the rights which each State may claim for its nationals in foreign territory. Without manifesting its territorial sovereignty in a manner corresponding to circumstances, the State cannot fulfil this duty. Territorial sovereignty cannot limit itself to its negative side, i.e. to excluding the activities of other States; for it serves to divide between nations the space upon which human activities are employed, in order to assure them at all points the minimum of protection of which international law is the guardian.

Although municipal law, thanks to its complete judicial system, is able to recognize abstract rights of property as existing apart from any material display of them, it has none the less limited their effect by the principles of prescription and the protection of possession. International law, the structure of which is not based on any super-State organisation, cannot be presumed to reduce a right such as territorial sovereignty, with which almost all international relations are bound up, to the category of an abstract right, without concrete manifestations.

The principle that continuous and peaceful display of the functions of State within a given region is a constituent element of territorial sovereignty is not only based on the conditions of the formation of independent States and their boundaries (as shown by the experience of political history) as well as on an international jurisprudence and doctrine widely accepted; this principle has further been recognized in more than one federal State, where a jurisdiction is established in order to apply, as need arises, rules of international law to the interstate relations of the States members. This is the more significant, in that it might well be conceived that in a federal State possessing a complete judicial system for interstate matters—far more than in the domain of international relations properly so-called—there should be applied to territorial questions the principle that, failing any specific provision of law to the contrary, a *jus in re* once lawfully acquired shall prevail over *de facto* possession however well established.

It may suffice to quote among several non dissimilar decisions of the Supreme Court of the United States of America that in the case of the State of Indiana *v.* State of Kentucky (136 U.S. 479) 1890, where the precedent of the case of Rhode Island *v.* Massachusetts (4 How. 591, 639) is supported by quotations from Vattel and Wheaton, who both admit prescription founded on length of time as a valid and incontestable title.

Manifestations of territorial sovereignty assume, it is true, different forms, according to conditions of time and place. Although continuous in principle, sovereignty cannot be exercised in fact at every moment on every point of a territory. The intermittence and discontinuity compatible with the maintenance of the right necessarily differ according as inhabited or uninhabited regions are involved, or regions enclosed within territories in which sovereignty is incontestably displayed or again regions accessible from, for instance, the high seas. It is true that neighbouring States may by convention fix limits to their own sovereignty, even in regions such as the interior of scarcely explored continents where such sovereignty is scarcely manifested, and in this way each may prevent the other from any penetration of its territory. The delimitation of Hinter-

land may also be mentioned in this connection.

If, however, no conventional line of sufficient topographical precision exists or if there are gaps in the frontiers otherwise established, or if a conventional line leaves room for doubt, or if, as e.g. in the case of an island situated in the high seas, the question arises whether a title is valid *erga omnes*, the actual continuous and peaceful display of State functions is in case of dispute the sound and natural criterium of territorial sovereignty.

* * *

The *title alleged by the United States of America* as constituting the immediate foundation of its claim is that of *cession*, brought about by the Treaty of Paris, which cession transferred all rights of sovereignty which Spain may have possessed in the region indicated in Article III of the said Treaty and therefore also those concerning the Island of Palmas (or Miangas).

It is evident that Spain could not transfer more rights than she herself possessed. This principle of law is expressly recognized in a letter dated April 7th, 1900, from the Secretary of State of the United States to the Spanish Minister at Washington concerning a divergence of opinion which arose about the question whether two islands claimed by Spain as Spanish territory and lying just outside the limits traced by the Treaty of Paris were to be considered as included in, or excluded from the cession. This letter, reproduced in the Explanations of the United States Government, contains the following passage:

The metes and bounds defined in the treaty were not understood by either party to limit or extend Spain's right of cession. Were any island within those described bounds ascertained to belong in fact to Japan, China, Great Britain or Holland, the United States could derive no valid title from its ostensible inclusion in the

Spanish cession. The compact upon which the United States negotiators insisted was that all Spanish title to the archipelago known as the Philippine Islands should pass to the United States—no less or no more than Spain's actual holdings therein, but all. This Government must consequently hold that the only competent and equitable test of fact by which the title to a disputed cession in that quarter may be determined is simply this: "Was it Spain's to give? If valid title belonged to Spain, it passed; if Spain had no valid title, she could convey none."

Whilst there existed a divergence of views as to the extension of the cession to certain Spanish islands outside the treaty limits, it would seem that the cessionary Power never envisaged that the cession, in spite of the sweeping terms of Article III, should comprise territories on which Spain had not a valid title, though falling within the limits traced by the Treaty. It is evident that whatever may be the right construction of a treaty, it cannot be interpreted as disposing of the rights of independent third Powers.

* * *

It is recognized that the United States communicated, on February 3rd, 1899, the Treaty of Paris to the Netherlands, and that no reservations were made by the latter in respect to the delimitation of the Philippines in Article III. The question whether the silence of a third Party, in regard to a treaty notified to it, can exercise any influence on the rights of this Power, or on those of the Powers signatories of the treaty, is a question the answer to which may depend on the nature of such rights. Whilst it is conceivable that a conventional delimitation duly notified to third Powers and left without contestation on their part may have some bearing on an inchoate title not supported by any actual display of sovereignty, it would be entirely contrary to the principles laid down above as to territorial sovereignty to suppose

that such sovereignty could be affected by the mere silence of the territorial sovereign as regards a treaty which has been notified to him and which seems to dispose of a part of his territory.

The essential point is therefore whether the Island of Palmas (or Miangas) at the moment of the conclusion and coming into force of the Treaty of Paris formed a part of the Spanish or Netherlands territory. . . .

* * *

It is admitted by both sides that international law underwent profound modifications between the end of the Middle-Ages and the end of the 19th century, as regards the rights of discovery and acquisition of uninhabited regions or regions inhabited by savages or semi-civilised peoples. Both Parties are also agreed that a juridical fact must be appreciated in the light of the law contemporary with it, and not of the law in force at the time when a dispute in regard to it arises or falls to be settled. The effects of discovery by Spain is therefore to be determined by the rules of international law in force in the first half of the 16th century—or (to take the earliest date) in the first quarter of it, i.e. at the time when the Portuguese or Spaniards made their appearance in the Sea of Celebes.

If the view most favourable to the American arguments is adopted—with every reservation as to the soundness of such view—that is to say, if we consider as positive law at the period in question the rule that discovery as such, i.e. the mere fact of seeing land, without any act, even symbolical, of taking possession, involved *ipso jure* territorial sovereignty and not merely an "inchoate title", a *jus ad rem*, to be completed eventually by an actual and durable taking of possession within a reasonable time, the question arises whether sovereignty yet existed at the critical date, i.e. the moment of conclusion and coming into force of the Treaty of Paris.

As regards the question which of different legal systems prevailing at successive periods is to be applied in a particular case (the so-called intertemporal law), a distinction must be made between the creation of rights and the existence of rights. The same principle which subjets [sic] the act creative of a right to the law in force at the time the right arises, demands that the existence of the right, in other words its continued manifestation, shall follow the conditions required by the evolution of law. International law in the 19th century, having regard to the fact that most parts of the globe were under the sovereignty of States members of the community of nations, and that territories without a master had become relatively few, took account of a tendency already existing and especially developed since the middle of the 18th century, and laid down the principle that occupation, to constitute a claim to territorial sovereignty, must be effective, that is, offer certain guarantees to other States and their nationals. It seems therefore incompatible with this rule of positive law that there should be regions which are neither under the effective sovereignty of a State, nor without a master, but which are reserved for the exclusive influence of one State, in virtue solely of a title of acquisition which is no longer recognized by existing law, even if such a title ever conferred territorial sovereignty. For these reasons, discovery alone, without any subsequent act, cannot at the present time suffice to prove sovereignty over the Island of Palmas (or Miangas); and in so far as there is no sovereignty, the question of an abandonment properly speaking of sovereignty by one State in order that the sovereignty of another may take its place does not arise.

If on the other hand the view is adopted that discovery does not create a definitive title of sovereignty, but only an "inchoate"

title, such a title exists, it is true, without external manifestation. However, according to the view that has prevailed at any rate since the 19th century, an inchoate title of discovery must be completed within a reasonable period by the effective occupation of the region claimed to be discovered. This principle must be applied in the present case, for the reasons given above in regard to the rules determining which of successive legal systems is to be applied (the so-called intertemporal law). Now, no act of occupation nor, except as to a recent period, any exercise of sovereignty at Palmas by Spain has been alleged. But even admitting that the Spanish title still existed as inchoate in 1898 and must be considered as included in the cession under Article III of the Treaty of Paris, an inchoate title could not prevail over the continuous and peaceful display of authority by another State; for such display may prevail even over a prior, definitive title put forward by another State. . . .

* * *

In the last place there remains to be considered *title arising out of contiguity*. Although States have in certain circumstances maintained that islands relatively close to their shores belonged to them in virtue of their geographical situation, it is impossible to show the existence of a rule of positive international law to the effect that islands situated outside territorial waters should belong to a State from the mere fact that its territory forms the *terra firma* (nearest continent or island of considerable size). Not only would it seem that there are no precedents sufficiently frequent and sufficiently precise in their bearing to establish such a rule of international law, but the alleged principle itself is by its very nature so uncertain and contested that even Governments of the same State have on different occasions maintained contradictory opinions as to its soundness. The principle of contiguity, in regard to islands, may not be out of place when it is a question of allotting them to one State rather than another, either by agreement between the Parties, or by a decision not necessarily based on law; but as a rule establishing *ipso jure* the presumption of sovereignty in favour of a particular State, this principle would be in conflict with what has been said as to territorial sovereignty and as to the necessary relation between the right to exclude other States from a region and the duty to display therein the activities of a State. Nor is this principle of contiguity admissible as a legal method of deciding questions of territorial sovereignty; for it is wholly lacking in precision and would in its application lead to arbitrary results. This would be especially true in a case such as that of the island in question, which is not relatively close to one single continent, but forms part of a large archipelago in which strict delimitations between the different parts are not naturally obvious.

* * *

The conclusions to be derived from the above examination of the arguments of the Parties are the following:

The claim of the United States to sovereignty over the Island of Palmas (or Miangas) is derived from Spain by way of cession under the Treaty of Paris. The latter Treaty, though it comprises the island in dispute within the limits of cession, and in spite of the absence of any reserves or protest by the Netherlands as to these limits, has not created in favour of the United States any title of sovereignty such as was not already vested in Spain. The essential point is therefore to decide whether Spain had sovereignty over Palmas (or Miangas) at the time of the coming into force of the Treaty of Paris.

The United States base their claim on the titles of discovery, of recognition by treaty and of contiguity, i.e. titles relating to acts or circumstances leading to the acquisitions of sovereignty; they have however not established the fact that sovereignty so acquired was effectively displayed at any time.

The Netherlands on the contrary found their claim to sovereignty essentially on the title of peaceful and continuous display of State authority over the island. Since this title would in international law prevail over a title of acquisition of sovereignty not followed by actual display of State authority, it is necessary to ascertain in the first place, whether the contention of the Netherlands is sufficiently established by evidence, and, if so, for what period of time.

In the opinion of the Arbitrator the Netherlands have succeeded in establishing the following facts:

a. The Island of Palmas (or Miangas) is identical with an island designated by this or a similar name, which has formed, at least since 1700, successively a part of two of the native States of the Island of Sangi (Talautse Isles).

b. These native States were from 1677 onwards connected with the East India Company, and thereby with the Netherlands, by contracts of suzerainty, which conferred upon the suzerain such power as would justify his considering the vassal State as a part of his territory.

c. Acts characteristic of State authority exercised either by the vassal State or by the suzerain Power in regard precisely to the Island of Palmas (or Miangus) have been established as occurring at different epochs between 1700 and 1898, as well as in the period between 1898 and 1906.

The acts of indirect or direct display of Netherlands sovereignty at Palmas (or Miangas), especially in the 18th and early 19th centuries are not numerous, and there are considerable gaps in the evidence of continuous display. But apart from the consideration that the manifestations of sovereignty over a small and distant island, inhabited only by natives, cannot be expected to be frequent, it is not necessary that the display of sovereignty should go back to a very far distant period. It may suffice that such display existed in 1898, and had already existed as continuous and peaceful before that date long enough to enable any Power who might have considered herself as possessing sovereignty over the island, or having a claim to sovereignty, to have, according to local conditions, a reasonable possibility for ascertaining the existence of a state of things contrary to her real or alleged rights.

* * *

Since the moment when the Spaniards, in withdrawing from the Moluccas in 1666, made express reservations as to the maintenance of their sovereign rights, up to the contestation made by the United States in 1906, no contestation or other action whatever or protest against the exercise of territorial rights by the Netherlands over the Talautse (Sangi) Isles and their dependencies (Miangas included) has been recorded. The peaceful character of the display of Netherlands sovereignty for the entire period to which the evidence concerning acts of display relates (1700–1906) must be admitted.

There is moreover no evidence which would establish any act of display of sovereignty over the island by Spain or another Power, such as might counterbalance or annihilate the manifestations of Netherlands sovereignty. As to third Powers, the evidence submitted to the Tribunal does not disclose any trace of such action, at least from the middle of the 17th century onwards. These circumstances, together with the absence of any evidence of a conflict between Spanish and Netherlands authorities during more than two centuries as regards Palmas (or Miangas), are an indirect proof of the ex-

clusive display of Netherlands sovereignty.

* * *

As to the conditions of acquisition of sovereignty by way of continuous and peaceful display of State authority (so-called prescription), some of which have been discussed in the United States Counter-Memorandum, the following must be said:

The display has been open and public, that is to say that it was in conformity with usages as to exercise of sovereignty over colonial States. A clandestine exercise of State authority over an inhabited territory during a considerable length of time would seem to be impossible. An obligation for the Netherlands to notify to other Powers the establishment of suzerainty over the Sangi States or of the display of sovereignty in these territories did not exist.

* * *

The Netherlands title of sovereignty, acquired by continuous and peaceful display of State authority during a long period of time going probably back beyond the year 1700, therefore holds good.

* * *

For these reasons the Arbitrator, in conformity with Article I of the Special Agreement of January 23rd, 1925, decides that: The Island of Palmas (or Miangas) forms in its entirety a part of Netherlands territory.

The Antarctic Treaty, 1959*

The Governments of Argentina, Australia, Belgium, Chile, the French Republic, Japan, New Zealand, Norway, the Union of South Africa, the Union of Soviet

* Reprinted from 41 *United States Department of State Bulletin* 914 (1959).

Socialist Republics, the United Kingdom of Great Britain and Northern Ireland, and the United States of America,

Recognizing that it is in the interest of all mankind that Antarctica shall continue forever to be used exclusively for peaceful purposes and shall not become the scene or object of international discord;

Acknowledging the substantial contributions to scientific knowledge resulting from international cooperation in scientific investigation in Antarctica;

Convinced that the establishment of a firm foundation for the continuation and development of such cooperation on the basis of freedom of scientific investigation in Antarctica as applied during the International Geophysical Year accords with the interests of science and the progress of all mankind;

Convinced also that a treaty ensuring the use of Antarctica for peaceful purposes only and the continuance of international harmony in Antarctica will further the purposes and principles embodied in the Charter of the United Nations;

Have agreed as follows:

Article I

1. Antarctica shall be used for peaceful purposes only. There shall be prohibited, *inter alia*, any measures of a military nature, such as the establishment of military bases and fortifications, the carrying out of military maneuvers, as well as the testing of any type of weapons.

2. The present Treaty shall not prevent the use of military personnel or equipment for scientific research or for any other peaceful purpose.

Article II

Freedom of scientific investigation in Antarctica and cooperation toward that end, as applied during the International Geophysical Year, shall continue, subject to the provisions of the present Treaty.

Article III

1. In order to promote international cooperation in scientific investigation in Antarctica, as provided for in Article II of the present Treaty, the Contracting Parties agree that, to the greatest extent feasible and practicable:

a. information regarding plans for scientific programs in Antarctica shall be exchanged to permit maximum economy and efficiency of operations;

b. scientific personnel shall be exchanged in Antarctica between expeditions and stations;

c. scientific observations and results from Antarctica shall be exchanged and made freely available.

2. In implementing this Article, every encouragement shall be given to the establishment of cooperative working relations with those Specialized Agencies of the United Nations and other international organizations having a scientific or technical interest in Antarctica.

Article IV

1. Nothing contained in the present Treaty shall be interpreted as:

a. a renunciation by any Contracting Party of previously asserted rights of or claims to territorial sovereignty in Antarctica;

b. a renunciation or diminution by any Contracting Party of any basis of claim to territorial sovereignty in Antarctica which it may have whether as a result of its activities or those of its nationals in Antarctica, or otherwise;

c. prejudicing the position of any Contracting Party as regards its recognition or non-recognition of any other State's right of or claim or basis of claim to territorial sovereignty in Antarctica.

2. No acts or activities taking place while the present Treaty is in force shall constitute a basis for asserting, supporting or denying a claim to territorial sovereignty in Antarctica or create any rights of

sovereignty in Antarctica. No new claim, or enlargement of an existing claim, to territorial sovereignty in Antarctica shall be asserted while the present Treaty is in force.

Article V

1. Any nuclear explosions in Antarctica and the disposal there of radioactive waste material shall be prohibited.

2. In the event of the conclusion of international agreements concerning the use of nuclear energy, including nuclear explosions and the disposal of radioactive waste material, to which all of the Contracting Parties whose representatives are entitled to participate in the meetings provided for under Article IX are parties, the rules established under such agreements shall apply in Antarctica.

Article VI

The provisions of the present Treaty shall apply to the area south of 60° South Latitude, including all ice shelves, but nothing in the present Treaty shall prejudice or in any way affect the rights, or the exercise of the rights, of any State under international law with regard to the high seas within that area.

Article VII

1. In order to promote the objectives and ensure the observance of the provisions of the present Treaty, each Contracting Party whose representatives are entitled to participate in the meetings referred to in Article IX of the Treaty shall have the right to designate observers to carry out any inspection provided for by the present Article. Observers shall be nationals of the Contracting Parties which designate them. The names of observers shall be communicated to every other Contracting Party having the right to designate observers, and like notice shall be given of the termination of their appointment.

2. Each observer designated in accordance with the provisions of paragraph 1 of this Article shall have complete freedom of access at any time to any or all areas of Antarctica.

3. All areas of Antarctica, including all stations, installations and equipment within those areas, and all ships and aircraft at points of discharging or embarking cargoes or personnel in Antarctica, shall be open at all times to inspection by any observers designated in accordance with paragraph 1 of this Article.

4. Aerial observation may be carried out at any time over any or all areas of Antarctica by any of the Contracting Parties having the right to designate observers.

5. Each Contracting Party shall, at the time when the present Treaty enters into force for it, inform the other Contracting Parties, and thereafter shall give them notice in advance, of

a. all expeditions to and within Antarctica, on the part of its ships or nationals, and all expeditions to Antarctica organized in or proceeding from its territory;

b. all stations in Antarctica occupied by its nationals; and

c. any military personnel or equipment intended to be introduced by it into Antarctica subject to the conditions prescribed in paragraph 2 of Article I of the present Treaty.

Article VIII

1. In order to facilitate the exercise of their functions under the present Treaty, and without prejudice to the respective positions of the Contracting Parties relating to jurisdiction over all other persons in Antarctica, observers designated under paragraph 1 of Article VII and scientific personnel exchanged under subparagraph 1(b) of Article III of the Treaty, and members of the staffs accompanying any such persons, shall be subject only to the jurisdiction of the Contracting Party of which they are nationals in respect of all acts or

omissions occurring while they are in Antarctica for the purpose of exercising their functions.

2. Without prejudice to the provisions of paragraph 1 of this Article, and pending the adoption of measures in pursuance of subparagaph 1(e) of Article IX, the Contracting Parties concerned in any case of dispute with regard to the exercise of jurisdiction in Antarctica shall immediately consult together with a view to reaching a mutually acceptable solution.

Article IX

1. Representatives of the Contracting Parties named in the preamble to the present Treaty shall meet at the City of Canberra within two months after the date of entry into force of the Treaty, and thereafter at suitable intervals and places, for the purpose of exchanging information, consulting together on matters of common interest pertaining to Antarctica, and formulating and considering, and recommending to their Governments, measures in furtherance of the principles and objectives of the Treaty, including measures regarding:

a. use of Antarctica for peaceful purposes only;
b. facilitation of scientific research in Antarctica;
c. facilitation of international scientific cooperation in Antarctica;
d. facilitation of the exercise of the rights of inspection provided for in Article VII of the Treaty;

e. questions relating to the exercise of jurisdiction in Antarctica;
f. preservation and conservation of living resources in Antarctica.

2. Each Contracting Party which has become a party to the present Treaty by accession under Article XIII shall be entitled to appoint representatives to participate in the meetings referred to in paragraph 1 of the present Article, during such time as that Contracting Party demonstrates its interest in Antarctica by conducting substantial scientific research activity there, such as the establishment of a scientific station or the despatch of a scientific expedition.

3. Reports from the observers referred to in Article VII of the present Treaty shall be transmitted to the representatives of the Contracting Parties participating in the meetings referred to in paragraph 1 of the present Article.

* * *

Article XIII

1. The present Treaty shall be subject to ratification by the signatory States. It shall be open for accession by any State which is a Member of the United Nations, or by any other State which may be invited to accede to the Treaty with the consent of all the Contracting Parties whose representatives are entitled to participate in the meetings provided for under Article IX of the Treaty.

* * *

LAND BOUNDARIES

Boundaries demarcating the territory of one state from that of another are commonly drawn by agreement. The basic rule is that the boundary is located wherever the parties agree that it should be located. This is simple enough when an agreement exists, and its terms are clear. But such is not always the case. Consequently, there are numerous rules of international law designed to fill the void. If, for example, there is no specific document certifying a particular line of demarcation between two states, prescription may serve as a valid determination. If a treaty designates a mountain as the boundary but does not specify where on the mountain the line is to be, the rule is that it runs along the water divide. Unless otherwise fixed, a boundary drawn through a lake usually runs equidistant from both shores. A river boundary is divided along the center of the main channel (doctrine of the *Thalweg*) if the river is navigable; if it is not, the boundary runs along the middle of the river.

Numerous controversies have arisen over disputed boundaries; some have been resolved by agreement, some by arbitration or judicial settlement, some by force and subsequent acquiescence, and some are still simmering. The Republic of Somalia questions its border with Ethiopia, and Morocco with Mauritania; Communist China has challenged the colonial boundaries of India and Burma; in Kashmir and along the Arab-Israeli borders, instability is the order of the day. It is significant that most of the boundaries of states that have come into existence since World War II were demarcated by colonial powers and were inherited by the new states. What R. J. Harrison Church has written about African boundaries applies, to a considerable extent, to Asian boundaries as well:

Boundaries drawn on maps by European politicians bore little relation to the physical and even less to the social, economic, or political fabric of indigenous societies. . . . the rapid and intensive partition of Africa took place when little or no detailed knowledge was available of the terrain, peoples, and economy of the interior. Nevertheless, even if that knowledge had been available, the mood of the statesmen who partitioned Africa was not such as to suggest that they would have been willing to use it in their boundary deliberations.[1]

It is indeed remarkable that the boundaries of the new states, where the fires of

[1] W. Gordon East and A. E. Moodie (eds.), *The Changing World* (Yonkers-on-Hudson, N.Y.: World Book Company, 1956), p. 745.

nationalism are raging, have remained as stable as they have.

International law norms are of importance in any boundary dispute. If the controversy is of low intensity, which is usually the case when the territory involved is of minor importance and the relations of the parties to the dispute are generally good, a legal settlement through arbitration or judicial settlement is possible. Otherwise, the party whose legal arguments are weak will normally prefer to seek a solution through political means, possibly including the use of force. When this occurs, the norms of international law serve not as a means of solution but as a focal point for the arguments of state officials. When a settlement is sought through negotiation, legal norms are used to bolster the positions of the two sides in the bargaining process. All this is not to say that international law is the only normative force in international boundary disputes; arguments based on such "nonlegal factors" as the strategic importance of the territory, the wishes of the inhabitants, and the needs and expectations of third states usually enter the political debate and the bargaining process. International law is the single controlling force only when the dispute is submitted to arbitrators or judges for a legal settlement.

The selections that follow illustrate the use of international law principles and processes in settling boundary disputes. In the *Case Concerning the Temple of Preah Vihear,* the International Court of Justice made use of a treaty, maps, and "subsequent practice of the parties" to resolve a recent boundary dispute between Cambodia and Thailand. The decision by Justice Cardozo in *New Jersey v. Delaware* is a classic statement of the doctrine of the *Thalweg,* an international law principle that is often used to settle boundary disputes between "states" in a federal system. Finally, the complex Chamizal Tract Dispute between Mexico and the United

States is considered in two documents, an arbitration award of 1911, which was rejected by the United States, and a treaty of 1963, which finally resolved the dispute along the lines of the earlier award.

Case Concerning the Temple of Preah Vihear (Cambodia v. Thailand) *

International Court of Justice, 1962

* * *

In its Judgment of 26 May 1961, by which it upheld its jurisdiction to adjudicate upon the dispute submitted to it by the Application filed by the Government of Cambodia on 6 October 1959, the Court described in the following terms the subject of the dispute:

"In the present case, Cambodia alleges a violation on the part of Thailand of Cambodia's territorial sovereignty over the region of the Temple of Preah Vihear and its precincts. Thailand replies by affirming that the area in question lies on the Thai side of the common frontier between the two countries, and is under the sovereignty of Thailand. This is a dispute about territorial sovereignty."

Accordingly, the subject of the dispute submitted to the Court is confined to a difference of view about sovereignty over the region of the Temple of Preah Vihear. To decide this question of territorial sovereignty, the Court must have regard to the frontier line between the two States in this sector. Maps haven [sic] been submitted to it and various considerations have been advanced in this connection. The Court will have regard to each of these only to such extent as it may find in them reasons for the decision it has to give in order to settle the sole dispute submitted

* Reprinted from *International Court of Justice Reports* 6 (1962).

to it, the subject of which has just been stated.

The Temple of Preah Vihear is an ancient sanctuary and shrine situated on the borders of Thailand and Cambodia. Although now partially in ruins, this Temple has considerable artistic and archaeological interest, and is still used as a place of pilgrimage. It stands on a promontory of the same name, belonging to the eastern sector of the Dangrek range of mountains which, in a general way, constitutes the boundary between the two countries in this region—Cambodia to the south and Thailand to the north. Considerable portions of this range consist of a high cliff-like escarpment rising abruptly above the Cambodian plain. This is the situation at Preah Vihear itself, where the main Temple buildings stand in the apex of a triangular piece of high ground jutting out into the plain. From the edge of the escarpment, the general inclination of the ground in the northerly direction is downwards to the Nam Moun river, which is in Thailand.

It will be apparent from the description just given that a frontier line which ran along the edge of the escarpment, or which at any rate ran to the south and east of the Temple area, would leave this area in Thailand; whereas a line running to the north, or to the north and west, would place it in Cambodia.

Thailand has urged that the edge of this escarpment constitutes the natural and obvious line for a frontier in this region. In support of this view Thailand has referred to the documentary evidence indicative of the desire of the Parties to establish frontiers which would not only be "natural", but visible and unmistakable —such as rivers, mountain ranges, and hence escarpments, where they exist.

The desire of the Parties for a natural and visible frontier could have been met by almost any line which followed a recognizable course along the main chain of the Dangrek range. It could have been a crest line, a watershed line or an escarpment line (where an escarpment existed, which was far from always being the case). As will be seen presently, the Parties provided for a watershed line. In so doing, they must be presumed to have realized that such a line would not necessarily, in any particular locality, be the same line as the line of the crest or escarpment. They cannot therefore be presumed to have intended that, wherever an escarpment existed, the frontier must lie along it, irrespective of all other considerations.

The Parties have also relied on other arguments of a physical, historical, religious and archaeological character, but the Court is unable to regard them as legally decisive.

* * *

Until Cambodia attained her independence in 1953 she was part of French Indo-China, and her foreign relations—like those of the rest of French Indo-China— were conducted by France as the protecting Power. It is common ground between the Parties that the present dispute has its *fons et origo* in the boundary settlements made in the period 1904–1908, between France and Siam (as Thailand was then called) and, in particular, that the sovereignty over Preah Vihear depends upon a boundary treaty dated 13 February 1904, and upon events subsequent to that date. The Court is therefore not called upon to go into the situation that existed between the Parties prior to the Treaty of 1904.

The relevant provisions of the Treaty of 13 February 1904, which regulated *inter alia* the frontier in the eastern Dangrek region were as follows (translation by the Registry):

"Article 1
The frontier between Siam and Cambodia starts, on the left shore of the Great Lake, from the mouth of the river Stung Roluos, it follows the parallel from that point in an easterly

direction until it meets the river Prek Kompong Tiam, then, turning northwards, it merges with the meridian from that meeting-point as far as the Pnom Dang Rek mountain chain. From there it follows the watershed between the basins of the Nam Sen and the Mekong, on the one hand, and the Nam Moun, on the other hand, and joins the Pnom Padang chain the crest of which it follows eastwards as far as the Mekong. Upstream from that point, the Mekong remains the frontier of the Kingdom of Siam, in accordance with Article 1 of the Treaty of 3 October 1893."

"Article 3
There shall be a delimitation of the frontiers between the Kingdom of Siam and the territories making up French Indo-China. This delimitation will be carried out by Mixed Commissions composed of officers appointed by the two contracting countries. The work will relate to the frontier determined by Articles 1 and 2, and the region lying between the Great Lake and the sea."

* * *

The final stage of the operation of delimitation was the preparation and publication of maps. For the execution of this technical work, the Siamese Government, which at that time did not dispose of adequate means, had officially requested that French topographical officers should map the frontier region. . . .

* * *

The eleven maps were in due course communicated to the Siamese Government, as being the maps requested by the latter, and the Court will consider later the circumstances of that communication and the deductions to be drawn from it. Three of the maps had been overtaken by events, inasmuch as the former frontier areas they showed had, by virtue of the Treaty of March 1907, now become situated wholly in Cambodia. Siam was not therefore called upon either to accept or reject them. Her interest in the other maps remained. Amongst these was one of that part of the Dangrek range in which the Temple is situated, and on it was traced a frontier line purporting to be the outcome of the work of delimitation and showing the whole Preah Vihear promontory, with the Temple area, as being on the Cambodian side. If therefore the delimitation carried out in respect of the Eastern Dangrek sector established or was intended to establish a watershed line, this map purported to show such a line. This map was filed by Cambodia as Annex I to its Memorial, and has become known in the case (and will be referred to herein) as the Annex I map.

It is on this map that Cambodia principally relies in support of her claim to sovereignty over the Temple. Thailand, on the other hand, contests any claim based on this map, on the following grounds: first, that the map was not the work of the Mixed Commission, and had therefore no binding character; secondly, that at Preah Vihear the map embodied a material error, not explicable on the basis of any exercise of discretionary powers of adaptation which the Commission may have possessed. This error, according to Thailand's contention, was that the frontier line indicated on the map was not the true watershed line in this vicinity, and that a line drawn in accordance with the true watershed line would have placed, and would now place, the Temple area in Thailand. It is further contended by Thailand that she never accepted this map or the frontier line indicated on it, at any rate so far as Preah Vihear is concerned, in such a way as to become bound thereby; or, alternatively that, if she did accept the map, she did so only under, and because of, a mistaken belief (upon which she relied) that the map line was correctly drawn to correspond with the watershed line.

The Court will, for the moment, confine itself to the first of these contentions, based on an argument which the Court considers to be correct, namely that the map was never formally approved by the first Mixed Commission as such, since that Commission had ceased to function some months before the production of the map. The record does not show whether the map and the line were based on any decisions or instructions given by the Commission to the surveying officers while it was still functioning. What is certain is that the map must have had a basis of some sort, and the Court thinks there can be no reasonable doubt that it was based on the work of the surveying officers in the Dangrek sector. Being one of the series of maps of the frontier areas produced by French Government topographical experts in response to a request made by the Siamese authorities, printed and published by a Paris firm of repute, all of which was clear from the map itself, it was thus invested with an official standing; it had its own inherent technical authority; and its provenance was open and obvious. The Court must nevertheless conclude that, in its inception, and at the moment of its production, it had no binding character.

* * *

Thailand has argued that in the absence of any delimitation approved and adopted by the Mixed Commission, or based on its instructions, the line of the frontier must necessarily—by virtue of Article 1 of the Treaty of 1904—follow strictly the line of the true watershed, and that this line, at Preah Vihear, would place the Temple in Thailand. While admitting that the Mixed Commission had a certain discretion to depart from the watershed line in order to avoid anomalies, and to take account of certain purely local considerations, Thailand contends that any departure such as to place Preah Vihear in Cambodia would have far exceeded the scope of any discretionary powers the Mixed Commission could have had authority to exercise without specific reference to the Governments.

Whatever substance these contentions may have, taken by themselves, the Court considers that they do not meet the real issues here involved. Even if there was no delimitation of the frontier in the eastern sector of the Dangrek approved and adopted by the Mixed Commission, it was obviously open to the Governments themselves to adopt a delimitation for that region, making use of the work of the technical members of the Mixed Commission. As regards any departures from the watershed line which any such delimitation embodied—since, according to Thailand's own contention, the delimitation indicated on the Annex I map was not the Mixed Commission's—there is no point in discussing whether such departures as may have occurred at Preah Vihear fell within the Commission's discretionary powers or not. The point is that it was certainly within the power of the Governments to adopt such departures.

The real question, therefore, which is the essential one in this case, is whether the Parties did adopt the Annex I map, and the line indicated on it, as representing the outcome of the work of delimitation of the frontier in the region of Preah Vihear, thereby conferring on it a binding character.

Thailand denies this so far as she is concerned, representing herself as having adopted a merely passive attitude in what ensued. She maintains also that a course of conduct, involving at most a failure to object, cannot suffice to render her a consenting party to a departure at Preah Vihear from the watershed line specified by Article I of the Treaty of 1904, so great as to affect the sovereignty over the Temple area.

The Court sees the matter differently. It is clear from the record that the publication and communication of the eleven maps referred to earlier, including the Annex I map, was something of an occasion. This was no mere interchange between the French and Siamese Governments, though, even if it had been, it could have sufficed in law. On the contrary, the maps were given wide publicity in all technically interested quarters by being also communicated to the leading geographical societies in important countries, and to other circles regionally interested; to the Siamese legations accredited to the British, German, Russian and United States Governments; and to all the members of the Mixed Commission, French and Siamese. The full original distribution consisted of about one hundred and sixty sets of eleven maps each. Fifty sets of this distribution were allocated to the Siamese Government. That the Annex I map was communicated as purporting to represent the outcome of the work of delimitation is clear from the letter from the Siamese Minister in Paris to the Minister of Foreign Affairs in Bangkok, dated 20 August 1908, in which he said that "regarding the Mixed Commission of Delimitation of the frontiers and the Siamese Commissioners' request that the French Commissioners prepare maps of various frontiers, the French Commissioners have now finished their work". He added that a series of maps had been brought to him in order that he might forward them to the Siamese Minister of Foreign Affairs. He went on to give a list of the eleven maps, including the map of the Dangrek region—fifty sheets of each. He ended by saying that he was keeping two sheets of each map for his Legation and was sending one sheet of each to the Legations in London, Berlin, Russia and the United States of America.

It has been contended on behalf of Thailand that this communication of the maps by the French authorities was, so to speak, *ex parte*, and that no formal acknowledgment of it was either requested of, or given by, Thailand. In fact . . . an acknowledgment by conduct was undoubtedly made in a very definite way;

but even if it were otherwise, it is clear that the circumstances were such as called for some reaction, within a reasonable period, on the part of the Siamese authorities, if they wished to disagree with the map or had any serious question to raise in regard to it. They did not do so, either then or for many years, and thereby must be held to have acquiesced. *Qui tacet consentire videtur si loqui debuisset ac potuisset.*

* * *

It follows from the preceding findings that the Siamese authorities in due course received the Annex I map and that they accepted it. Now, however, it is contended on behalf of Thailand, so far as the disputed area of Preah Vihear is concerned, that an error was committed, an error of which the Siamese authorities were unaware at the time when they accepted the map.

It is an established rule of law that the plea of error cannot be allowed as an element vitiating consent if the party advancing it contributed by its own conduct to the error, or could have avoided it, or if the circumstances were such as to put that party on notice of a possible error. The Court considers that the character and qualifications of the persons who saw the Annex I map on the Siamese side would alone make it difficult for Thailand to plead error in law. These persons included the members of the very Commission of Delimitation within whose competence this sector of the frontier had lain. But even apart from this, the Court thinks that there were other circumstances relating to the Annex I map which make the plea of error difficult to receive.

An inspection indicates that the map itself drew such pointed attention to the Preah Vihear region that no interested person, nor anyone charged with the duty of scrutinizing it, could have failed to see what the map was purporting to do in respect of that region. If, as Thailand has argued, the geographical configuration of the place is such as to make it obvious to anyone who has been there that the watershed must lie along the line of the escarpment (a fact which, if true, must have been no less evident in 1908), then the map made it quite plain that the Annex I line did not follow the escarpment in this region since it was plainly drawn appreciably to the north of the whole Preah Vihear promontory. Nobody looking at the map could be under any misapprehension about that.

Next, the map marked Preah Vihear itself quite clearly as lying on the Cambodian side of the line, using for the Temple a symbol which seems to indicate a rough plan of the building and its stairways.

It would thus seem that, to anyone who considered that the line of the watershed at Preah Vihear ought to follow the line of the escarpment, or whose duty it was to scrutinize the map, there was everything in the Annex I map to put him upon enquiry. Furthermore, as has already been pointed out, the Siamese Government knew or must be presumed to have known, through the Siamese members of the Mixed Commission, that the Annex I map had never been formally adopted by the Commission. The Siamese authorities knew it was the work of French topographical officers to whom they had themselves entrusted the work of producing the maps. They accepted it without any independent investigation, and cannot therefore now plead any error vitiating the reality of their consent. The Court concludes therefore that the plea of error has not been made out.

* * *

Thailand having temporarily come into possession of certain parts of Cambodia, including Preah Vihear, in 1941, the Ministry of Information of Thailand published a work entitled "Thailand during national reconstruction" in which it was stated in relation to Preah Vihear that it had now been "retaken" for Thailand. This has been represented by Thailand as being an error on the part of a minor official. Nevertheless, similar language, suggesting that Thailand had been in possession of Preah Vihear only since about 1940, was used by representatives of Thailand in the territorial negotiations that took place between Thailand and Cambodia at Bangkok in 1958.

After the war, by a Settlement Agreement of November 1946 with France, Thailand accepted a reversion to the *status quo ante* 1941. It is Thailand's contention that this reversion to the *status quo* did not affect Preah Vihear because Thailand already had sovereignty over it before the war. The Court need not discuss this contention, for whether Thailand did have such sovereignty is precisely what is in issue in these proceedings. The important point is that, in consequence of the war events, France agreed to set up a Franco-Siamese Conciliation Commission consisting of the two representatives of the Parties and three neutral Commissioners, whose terms of reference were specifically to go into, and make recommendations on an equitable basis in regard to, any complaints or proposals for revision which Thailand might wish to make as to, *inter alia*, the frontier settlements of 1904 and 1907. The Commission met in 1947 in Washington, and here therefore was an outstanding opportunity for Thailand to claim a rectification of the frontier at Preah Vihear on the ground that the delimitation embodied a serious error which would have caused Thailand to reject it had she known of the error in 1908–1909. In fact, although Thailand made complaints about the frontier line in a considerable number of regions, she made none about Preah Vihear. She even (12 May 1947) filed with the Commission a map showing Preah Vihear as lying in

Cambodia. Thailand contends that this involved no adverse implications as regards her claim to the Temple, because the Temple area was not in issue before the Commission, that it was other regions that were under discussion, and that it was in relation to these that the map was used. But it is precisely the fact that Thailand had raised these other questions, but not that of Preah Vihear, which requires explanation; for, everything else apart, Thailand was by this time well aware, from certain local happenings in relation to the Temple, to be mentioned presently, that France regarded Preah Vihear as being in Cambodian territory—even if this had not already and long since been obvious from the frontier line itself, as mapped by the French authorities and communicated to the Siamese Government in 1908. The natural inference from Thailand's failure to mention Preah Vihear on this occasion is, again, that she did not do so because she accepted the frontier at this point as it was drawn on the map, irrespective of its correspondence with the watershed line.

As regards the use of a map showing Preah Vihear as lying in Cambodia, Thailand maintains that this was for purely cartographical reasons, that there were no other maps, or none that were so convenient, or none of the right scale for the occasion. The Court does not find this explanation convincing. Thailand could have used the map but could also have entered some kind of reservation with France as to its correctness. This she did not do.

* * *

In general, when two countries establish a frontier between them, one of the primary objects is to achieve stability and finality. This is impossible if the line so established can, at any moment, and on the basis of a continuously available process, be called in question, and its rectification claimed, whenever any inaccuracy by reference to a clause in the parent treaty is discovered. Such a process could continue indefinitely, and finality would never be reached so long as possible errors still remained to be discovered. Such a frontier, so far from being stable, would be completely precarious. It must be asked why the Parties in this case provided for a delimitation, instead of relying on the Treaty clause indicating that the frontier line in this region would be the watershed. There are boundary treaties which do no more than refer to a watershed line, or to a crest line, and which make no provision for any delimitation in addition. The Parties in the present case must have had a reason for taking this further step. This could only have been because they regarded a watershed indication as insufficient by itself to achieve certainty and finality. It is precisely to achieve this that delimitations and map lines are resorted to.

Various factors support the view that the primary object of the Parties in the frontier settlements of 1904–1908 was to achieve certainty and finality. From the evidence furnished to the Court, and from the statements of the Parties themselves, it is clear that the whole question of Siam's very long frontiers with French Indo-China had, in the period prior to 1904, been a cause of uncertainty, trouble and friction, engendering what was described in one contemporary document placed before the Court as a state of "growing tension" in the relations between Siam and France. The Court thinks it legitimate to conclude that an important, not to say a paramount object of the settlements of the 1904–1908 period (which brought about a comprehensive regulation of all outstanding frontier questions between the two countries), was to put an end to this state of tension and to achieve frontier stability on a basis of certainty and finality.

* * *

The indication of the line of the watershed in Article 1 of the 1904 Treaty was itself no more than an obvious and convenient way of describing a frontier line objectively, though in general terms. There is, however, no reason to think that the Parties attached any special importance to the line of the watershed as such, as compared with the overriding importance, in the interests of finality, of adhering to the map line as eventually delimited and as accepted by them. The Court, therefore, feels bound, as a matter of treaty interpretation, to pronounce in favour of the line as mapped in the disputed area.

* * *

THE COURT,
by nine votes to three,
finds that the Temple of Preah Vihear is situated in territory under the sovereignty of Cambodia;
finds in consequence,
by nine votes to three,
that Thailand is under an obligation to withdraw any military or police forces, or other guards or keepers, stationed by her at the Temple, or in its vicinity on Cambodian territory;
by seven votes to five,
that Thailand is under an obligation to restore to Cambodia any objects of the kind specified in Cambodia's fifth Submission which may, since the date of the occupation of the Temple by Thailand in 1954, have been removed from the Temple or the Temple area by the Thai authorities.

New Jersey v. Delaware*

Supreme Court of the United States, 1934

Mr. Justice Cardozo delivered the opinion of the court.

Invoking our original jurisdiction, New Jersey brings Delaware into this court and

* Reprinted from 291 U.S. 361 (1934).

prays for a determination of the boundary in Delaware Bay and River.

* * *

International law today divides the river boundaries between states by the middle of the main channel, when there is one, and not by the geographical centre, half way between the banks. *Iowa* v. *Illinois,* 147 U.S. 1, 7, 8, 9; *Keokuk & Hamilton Bridge Co.* v. *Illinois,* 175 U.S. 626, 631; *Louisiana* v. *Mississippi,* 202 U.S. 1, 49; *Arkansas* v. *Tennessee,* 246 U.S. 158, 169, 170; *Arkansas* v. *Mississippi,* 250 U.S. 39; *Minnesota* v. *Wisconsin,* 252 U.S. 273, 282. It applies the same doctrine, now known as the doctrine of the *Thalweg,* to estuaries and bays in which the dominant sailing channel can be followed to the sea. *Louisiana* v. *Mississippi, supra*; and compare 1 Halleck, International Law, 4th ed., p. 182; Moore, Digest International Law, vol. 1, p. 617; . . . The *Thalweg,* or downway, is the track taken by boats in their course down the stream, which is that of the strongest current. . . . Delaware makes no denial that this is the decisive test whenever the physical conditions define the track of navigation. Her position comes to this, that the bay is equally navigable in all directions, or at all events was so navigable in 1783, and that in the absence of a track of navigation the geographical centre becomes the boundary, not of choice, but of necessity. As to the section of the river between the bay and the circle, the same boundary is to be accepted, we are told, as a matter of convenience.

The findings of the Special Master, well supported by the evidence, overcome the argument thus drawn from physical conditions. He finds that "as early as Fisher's Chart of Delaware Bay (1756) there has been a well-defined channel of navigation up and down the Bay and River," in which the current of water attains its maximum velocity; that "Delaware River

and Bay, on account of shoals, are not equally navigable in all directions, but the main ship channel must be adhered to for safety in navigation"; that the Bay, according to the testimony, "is only an expansion of the lower part of the Delaware River," and that the fresh water of the river does not spread out uniformly when it drains into the bay, but maintains a continuing identity through its course into the ocean. "The record shows the existence of a well-defined deep water sailing channel in Delaware River and Bay constituting a necessary track of navigation, and the boundary between the States of Delaware and New Jersey in said bay is the middle of said channel."

The underlying rationale of the doctrine of the *Thalweg* is one of equality and justice. "A river," in the words of Holmes, J. (*New Jersey* v. *New York,* 283 U.S. 336, 342), "is more than an amenity, it is a treasure." If the dividing line were to be placed in the centre of the stream rather than in the centre of the channel, the whole track of navigation might be thrown within the territory of one state to the exclusion of the other. Considerations such as these have less importance for commonwealths or states united under a general government than for states wholly independent. Per Field, J., in *Iowa* v. *Illinois, supra,* p. 10. None the less, the same test will be applied in the absence of usage or convention pointing to another. *Iowa* v. *Illinois, supra.* Indeed, in 1783, the equal opportunity for use that was derived from equal ownership may have had a practical importance for the newly liberated colonies, still loosely knit together, such as it would not have today. They were not taking any chances in affairs of vital moment. Bays and rivers are more than geometrical divisions. They are the arteries of trade and travel.

The commentators tell us of times when the doctrine of the *Thalweg* was still unknown or undeveloped. Anciently, we are informed, there was a principle of co-dominion by which boundary streams to their entire width were held in common ownership by the proprietors on either side. 1 Hyde, International Law, p. 243, § 137. Then, with Grotius and Vattel, came the notion of equality of division (Nys, Droit International, vol. 1, pp. 425, 426; Hyde, *supra*, p. 244, citing Grotius, De Jure Belli ac Pacis, and Vattel, Law of Nations), though how this was to be attained was still indefinite and uncertain, as the citations from Grotius and Vattel show. Finally, about the end of the eighteenth century, the formula acquired precision, the middle of the "stream" becoming the middle of the "channel." There are statements by the commentators that the term *Thalweg* is to be traced to the Congress of Rastadt in 1797 (Engelhardt, Du Régime Conventionnel des Fleuves Internationaux, p. 72; Koch, Histoire des Traités de Paix, vol. 5, p. 156), and the Treaty of Lunéville in 1801. Hyde, *supra*, pp. 245, 246; Kaeckenbeck, International Rivers, p. 176; Adami, National Frontiers, translated by Behrens, p. 17. If the term was then new, the notion of equality was not. There are treaties before the Peace of Lunéville in which the boundary is described as the middle of the channel, though, it seems, without thought that in this there was an innovation, or that the meaning would have been different if the boundary had been declared to follow the middle of the stream. Hyde, *supra*, p. 246. Thus, in the Treaty of October 27, 1795, between the United States and Spain (Article IV), it is "agreed that the western boundary of the United States which separates them from the Spanish colony of Louisiana is in the middle of the channel or bed of the River Mississippi." Miller, Treaties and other International Acts of the United States of America, vol. 2, p. 321. There are other treaties of the same period in which the boundary is described as the middle of the river without further definition, yet this court has held that the phrase was

intended to be equivalent to the middle of the channel. *Iowa* v. *Illinois; Arkansas* v. *Tennessee; Arkansas* v. *Mississippi, supra.* See, e.g., the Treaty of 1763 between Great Britain, France and Spain, which calls for "a line drawn along the middle of the River Mississippi." The truth plainly is that a rule was in the making which was to give fixity and precision to what had been indefinite and fluid. There was still a margin of uncertainty within which conflicting methods of division were contending for the mastery. Conceivably that is true today in unusual situations of avulsion or erosion. Hyde, *supra*, pp. 246, 247. Even so, there has emerged out of the flux of an era of transition a working principle of division adapted to the needs of the international community. Through varying modes of speech the law has been groping for a formula that will achieve equality in substance, and not equality in name only. Unless prescription or convention has intrenched another rule (1 Westlake, International Law, p. 146), we are to utilize the formula that will make equality prevail.

In 1783, when the Revolutionary War was over, Delaware and New Jersey began with a clean slate. There was no treaty or convention fixing the boundary between them. There was no possessory act nor other act of dominion to give to the boundary in bay and river below the circle a practical location, or to establish a prescriptive right. In these circumstances, the capacity of the law to develop and apply a formula consonant with justice and with the political and social needs of the international legal system is not lessened by the fact that at the creation of the boundary the formula of the *Thalweg* had only a germinal existence. The gap is not so great that adjudication may not fill it. Lauterpacht, The Function of Law in the International Community, pp. 52, 60, 70, 85, 100, 110, 111, 255, 404, 432. Treaties almost contemporaneous, which were to be followed by a host of others, were declaratory of a principle that was making its way into the legal order. Hall, International Law, 8th ed., p. 7. International law, or the law that governs between states, has at times, like the common law within states, a twilight existence during which it is hardly distinguishable from morality or justice, till at length the *imprimatur* of a court attests its jural quality. Lauterpacht, *supra*, pp. 110, 255; Hall, *supra*, pp. 7, 12, 15, 16; Jenks, The New Jurisprudence, pp. 11, 12. "The gradual consolidation of opinions and habits" (Vinogradoff, Custom and Right, p. 21) has been doing its quiet work.

It is thus with the formula of the *Thalweg* in its application to the division between Delaware and New Jersey. We apply it to that boundary, which goes back to the Peace of Paris, just as we applied it to the boundary between Illinois and Iowa, which derives from a treaty of 1763 (*Iowa* v. *Illinois . . . supra*), or to that between Louisiana and Mississippi (202 U.S. 1, 16), which goes back to 1812, or between Minnesota and Wisconsin (252 U.S. 273), going back to 1846. Indeed, counsel for Delaware make no point that the result is to be affected by difference of time. In requests submitted to the Master they have asked for a finding that "there was in 1783 no well defined channel in the Delaware Bay constituting a necessary track of navigation and the boundary line between the States of Delaware and New Jersey in said bay is the geographical center thereof." The second branch of the request is dependent on the first. This is clear enough upon its face, but is made doubly clear by the exceptions to the report and by the written and oral arguments. The line of division is to be the centre of the main channel unless the physical conditions are of such a nature that a channel is unknown.

We have seen that even in the bay the physical conditions are consistent with a track of navigation, which is also the course of safety. Counsel do not argue that such a track is unknown in the five miles of river between the bay and the circle. The argument is, however, that the geographical centre is to be made the boundary in the river as a matter of convenience, since otherwise there will be need for a sharp and sudden turn when the river meets the bay. Inconvenient such a boundary would unquestionably be, but the inconvenience is a reason for following the *Thalweg* consistently through the river and the bay alike instead of abandoning it along a course where it can be followed without trouble. If the boundary be taken to be the geographical centre, the result will be a crooked line, conforming to the indentations and windings of the coast, but without relation to the needs of shipping. *Minnesota* v. *Wisconsin, supra*. If the boundary be taken to be the *Thalweg*, it will follow the course furrowed by the vessels of the world.

* * *

The Chamizal Arbitration (United States-Mexico)*

International Boundary Commission, June 10, 1911

[*El Chamizal, the area in dispute, is a 600-acre tract of land that was left north of the Rio Grande in the El Paso-Juarez region as a result of the southward movement of that boundary river during the latter half of the nineteenth century. The arbitration award of 1911, which the United States and Mexico had agreed was to be "final and conclusive," gave a large part of the tract to Mexico. After more than half a century of embittered relations over the refusal of the United States to accept the award, the settlement of 1963 gave back to Mexico some 437 acres. At a cost of about $30*

* Reprinted from 5 *American Journal of International Law* 785 (1911) by permission of the American Society of International Law.

million, the United States has reimbursed and relocated 3,700 of its citizens who lived in the transferred area. The two states agreed to share the costs of rerouting the Rio Grande to conform with the transfer and of lining its new channel with concrete to prevent future waywardness.]

By the Commission: Lafleur, Mills, and Beltram y Puga.

* * *

The Chamizal tract consists of about six hundred acres, and lies between the old bed of the Rio Grande, as it was surveyed in 1852, and the present bed of the river, as more particularly described in Article 1 of the Convention of 1910. It is the result of changes which have taken place through the action of the water upon the banks of the river causing the river to move southward into Mexican territory.

With the progressive movement of the river to the south, the American city of El Paso has been extending on the accretions formed by the action of the river on its north bank, while the Mexican city of Juarez to the south has suffered a correspondingly loss of territory.

By the Treaties of 1848 and 1853 the Rio Grande, from a point a little higher than the present City of El Paso to its mouth in the Gulf of Mexico, was constituted the boundary line between the United States and Mexico.

The contention on behalf of the United States of Mexico is that this dividing line was fixed, under those treaties, in a permanent and invariable manner, and consequently that the changes which have taken place in the river have not affected the boundary line which was established and marked in 1852.

On behalf of the United States of America it is contended that according to the true intent and meaning of the Treaties of 1848 and 1853, if the channel of the river changes by gradual accretion the boundary follows the channel, and that it

is only in case of a sudden change of bed that the river ceases to be the boundary, which then remains in the abandoned bed of the river.

It is further contended on behalf of the United States of America that by the terms of a subsequent boundary convention in 1884, rules of interpretation were adopted which became applicable to all changes in the Rio Grande, which have occurred since the river became the international boundary, and that the changes which determined the formation of the Chamizal tract are changes resulting from slow and gradual erosion and deposit of alluvion within the meaning of that convention, and consequently changes which left the channel of the river as the international boundary line.

The Mexican Government, on the other hand, contends that the Chamizal tract having been formed before the coming in force of the Convention of 1884, that convention was not retroactive and could not affect the title to the tract, and further contends that even assuming the case to be governed by the Convention of 1884 the changes in the channel have not been the result of slow and gradual erosion and deposit of alluvion.

Finally the United States of America have set up a claim to the Chamizal tract by prescription, alleged to result from the undisturbed, uninterrupted, and unchallenged possession of the territory since the Treaty of 1848.

In 1889 the Governments of the United States and of Mexico by a convention, created the International Boundary Commission for the purpose of carrying out the principles contained in the Convention of 1884 and to avoid the difficulties occasioned by the changes which take place in the bed of the Rio Grande where it serves as the boundary between the two republics, and for other purposes enumerated in Article I of the Convention of 1889.

At a session of the Boundary Commissioners, held on the 28th September,

1894, the Mexican Commissioner presented the papers in a case known as "El Chamizal No. 4." These included a complaint made by Pedro Ignacio Garcia, who alleged, in substance, that he had acquired certain property formerly lying on the south side of the Rio Grande, known as El Chamizal, which, in consequence of the abrupt and sudden change of current of the Rio Grande, was now on the north side of the river, and within the limits of El Paso, Texas. This claim was examined by the International Boundary Commissioners, who heard witnesses upon the facts, and who, after consideration, were unable to come to any agreement, and so reported to their respective governments.

As a result of this disagreement the Convention of 24th June, 1910, was signed, and the decision of the question was submitted to the present Commission.

* * *

The Treaty of Guadalupe Hidalgo, signed on the 2nd February, 1848, provides that the boundary line between the two republics from the Gulf of Mexico shall be the middle of the Rio Grande, following the deepest channel where it has more than one, to the point where it strikes the southern boundary of New Mexico. It is conceded, on both sides, that if this provision stood alone it would undoubtedly constitute a natural, or arcifinious, boundary between the two nations and that according to well-known principles of international law, this fluvial boundary would continue, notwithstanding modifications of the course of the river caused by gradual accretion on the one bank or degradation of the other bank; whereas if the river deserted its original bed and forced for itself a new channel in another direction the boundary would remain in the middle of the deserted river bed. It is contended, however, on behalf of Mexico, that the provisions in the treaty providing for a designation of the boundary line with due precision, upon authoritative maps, and for establishing upon the grounds landmarks showing the limits of both republics, and the direction to commissioners and surveyors to run and mark the boundary in its full course to the mouth of the Rio Grande, coupled with the final stipulation that the boundary line thus established should be religiously respected by the two republics, and no change should ever be made therein, except by the express and free consent of both nations, takes this case out of the ordinary rules of international law, and by a conventional agreement converts a natural, or arcifinious, boundary into an artificial and invariable one. . . . The difficulty in this case does not arise from the fact that the territories in question are established by any measurement, but because the boundary is ordered to be run and marked along the fluvial portion as well as on the land, and on account of the further stipulation that no change shall ever be made therein. Do these provisions and expression, in so far as they refer to the fluvial portion of the boundary, convert it into an artificial boundary which will persist notwithstanding all changes in the course of the river? In one sense it may be said that the adoption of a fixed and invariable line, so far as the river is concerned, would not be a perpetual retaining of the river boundary provided for by the treaty, and would be at variance with the agreement of the parties that the boundary should forever run in the middle of the river. The direction as to marking the course of the river as it existed at the time of the Treaty of 1848 is not inconsistent with a fluvial line varying only in accordance with the general rules of international law, by erosion on one bank and alluvial deposits on the other bank, for this marking of the boundary may serve the purpose of preserving a record of the old river bed to serve as a boundary in cases in which it cuts a new channel.

Numerous treaties containing provisions as to river boundaries have been referred to by the two parties, showing that in some cases conventional arrangements are made that the river *simpliciter* shall be the boundary, or that the boundary shall run along the middle of the river, or along the *thalweg* or center or thread of the channel, while a small number of treaties contain elaborate dispositions for a fixed line boundary, notwithstanding the alterations which may take place in the river, with provision, however, for periodical re-adjustments in certain specified cases. The difficulty with these instances is that no cases appear to have arisen upon the treaties in question and their provisions throw little, if any, light upon the present controversy. In one case only among those cited there appears to have been a decision by the Court of Cassation in France (Dalloz, 1858, Part I, page 401) holding that when a river separates two departments or two districts, the boundary is fixed in an irrevocable manner along the middle of the bed of the river as it existed at the time of the establishment of the boundary and that it is not subject to any subsequent variation, notwithstanding the changes in the river. Whatever authority this decision may have in the delimitation of departmental boundaries in France, it does not seem to be in accordance with recognized principles of international law, if, as appears from the report, it holds that the mere designation of a river as a boundary establishes a fixed and invariable line.

The above observations as to the Treaty of 1848 would seem to apply to the Gadsden Treaty of 1853, taken by itself, for it provides, in similar language, that the boundary shall follow the middle of the Rio Grande, that the boundary line shall be established and marked, and that the dividing line shall in all time be faithfully respected by the two governments without any variation therein.

While, however, the Treaty of 1848

standing alone, or the Treaty of 1853, standing alone, might seem to be more consistent with the idea of a fixed boundary than one which would vary by reason of alluvial processes, the language of the Treaty of 1853, taken in conjunction with the existing circumstances, renders it difficult to accept the idea of a fixed and invariable boundary. During the five years which elapsed between the two treaties, notable variations of the course of the Rio Grande took place, to such an extent that surveys made in the early part of 1853, at intervals of six months, revealed discrepancies which are accounted for only by reason of the changes which the river had undergone in the meantime. Notwithstanding the existence of such changes, the Treaty of 1853 reiterates the provision that the boundary line runs up the middle of the river, which could not have been an accurate statement upon the fixed line theory.

* * *

It is in consequence of this legitimate doubt as to the true construction of the boundary treaties of 1848 and 1853 that the subsequent course of conduct of the parties, and their formal conventions, may be resorted to as aids to construction. In the opinion of the majority of this Commission the language of the subsequent conventions, and the consistent course of conduct of the high contracting parties, is wholly incompatible with the existence of a fixed line boundary.

* * *

The Presiding Commissioner and the American Commissioner therefore hold that the Treaties of 1848 and 1853, as interpreted by subsequent conventions between the parties and by their course of conduct, created an arcifinious boundary, and that the Convention of 1884 was intended to be and was made retroactive by the high contracting parties.

* * *

In the countercase of the United States, the contention is advanced that the United States has acquired a good title by prescription to the tract in dispute, in addition to its title under treaty provisions.

In the argument it is contended that the Republic of Mexico is estopped from asserting the national title over the territory known as "El Chamizal" by reason of the undisturbed, uninterrupted, and unchallenged possession of said territory by the United States of America since the Treaty of Guadalupe Hidalgo.

Without thinking it necessary to discuss the very controversial question as to whether the right of prescription invoked by the United States is an accepted principle of the law of nations, in the absence of any convention establishing a term of prescription, the commissioners are unanimous in coming to the conclusion that the possession of the United States in the present case was not of such a character as to found a prescriptive title. Upon the evidence adduced it is impossible to hold that the possession of El Chamizal by the United States was undisturbed, uninterrupted and unchallenged from the date of the Treaty of Guadalupe Hidalgo in 1848 until the year 1895, when, in consequence of the creation of a competent tribunal to decide the question, the Chamizal case was first presented. On the contrary it may be said that the physical possession taken by citizens of the United States and the political control exercised by the local and federal governments, have been constantly challenged and questioned by the Republic of Mexico, through its accredited diplomatic agents.

* * *

It is quite clear . . . that however much the Mexicans may have desired to take physical possession of the district, the result of any attempt to do so would have provoked scenes of violence and the Republic of Mexico can not be blamed for resorting to the milder forms of protest contained in its diplomatic correspondence.

In private law, the interruption of prescription is effected by a suit, but in dealings between nations this is of course impossible, unless and until an international tribunal is established for such purpose. In the present case, the Mexican claim was asserted before the International Boundary Commission within a reasonable time after it commenced to exercise its functions, and prior to that date the Mexican Government had done all that could be reasonably required of it by way of protest against the alleged encroachment.

Under these circumstances the Commissioners have no difficulty in coming to the conclusion that the plea of prescription should be dismissed.

* * *

The Presiding Commissioner and the Mexican Commissioner are of the opinion that the evidence establishes that from 1852 to 1864 the changes in the river, which during that interval formed a portion of the Chamizal tract, were caused by slow and gradual erosion and deposit of alluvium within the meaning of Article I of the Convention of 1884.

They are further of opinion that all the changes which have taken place in the Chamizal district from 1852 up to the present date have not resulted from any change of bed of the river. It is sufficiently shown that the Mexican bank opposite the Chamizal tract was at all times high and that it was never overflowed, and there is no evidence tending to show that the Rio Grande in that vicinity ever abandoned its existing bed and opened a new one. The changes, such as they were, resulted from the degradation of the Mexican bank, and the alluvial deposits formed on the American bank, and as has been said, up to 1864 this erosion and deposit appears to come within Article I of the Convention of 1884.

With respect to the nature of the changes which occurred in 1864, and during the four succeeding years, the Presiding Commissioner and the Mexican Commissioner are of opinion that the phenomena described by the witnesses as having occurred during that period can not properly be described as alterations in the river effected through the slow and gradual erosion and deposit of alluvium.

The following extracts from the evidence are quoted by the Presiding Commissioner and the Mexican Commissioner in support of their views:

Jesus Serna.—Q. When the change took place was it slow or violent?

A. The change was violent, and destroyed the trees, crops and houses.

Ynocente Ochoa—Q. When the change took place was it slow or violent?

A. As I said before, it was sometimes slow and sometimes violent, and with such force that the noise of the banks falling seemed like the boom of cannon, and it was frightful.

E. Provincio—Q. Explain how you know what you have stated.

A. Because the violent changes of the river in 1864 caused considerable alarm to the city, and the people went to the banks of the river and pulled down trees and tried to check the advance of the waters. I was there sometimes to help and sometimes simply to observe. I helped to take out furniture from houses in danger and to remove beams of houses, etc.

Q. When the change took place was it slow or violent?

A. I cannot appreciate what is meant by slow or violent, but sometimes as much as fifty yards would be washed away at certain points in a day.

Q. Please describe the destruction of the bank on the Mexican side that you spoke of in your former testimony. Describe the size of the pieces of earth that you saw fall into the river.

A. When the river made the alarming change it carried away pieces of earth one yard, two yards, etc., constantly, in intervals of a few minutes. At the time of these changes the people would be standing on the banks watching a piece going down, and somebody would call "look out, there is more going to fall" and they would have to jump back to keep from falling into the river.

* * *

The Presiding Commissioner and the Mexican Commissioner consider that the changes referred to in this testimony can not by any stretch of the imagination, or elasticity of language, be characterized as slow and gradual erosion.

* * *

It has been suggested, and the American Commissioner is of opinion, that the bed of the Rio Grande as it existed in 1864, before the flood, can not be located, and moreover that the present Commissioners are not authorized by the Convention of the 5th December, 1910, to divide the Chamizal tract and attribute a portion thereof to the United States and another portion to Mexico. The Presiding Commissioner and the Mexican Commissioner can not assent to this view and conceive that in dividing the tract in question between the parties, according to the evidence as they appreciate it, they are following the precedent laid down by the Supreme Court of the United States in *Nebraska* v. *Iowa* [143 U.S. 359]. In that case the court found that up to the year 1877 the changes in the Missouri River were due to accretion, and that, in that year, the river made for itself a new channel. Upon these findings it was held that the boundary between Iowa and Nebraska was a varying line in so far as affected by accretion, but that from and after 1877 the boundary was not changed, and remained as it was before the cutting of a new channel. Applying this principle, *mutatis mutandis*, to the present case, the Presiding Commissioner and

Mexican Commissioner are of opinion that the accretions which occurred in the Chamizal tract up to the time of the great flood in 1864 should be awarded to the United States of America, and that inasmuch as the changes which occurred in that year did not constitute slow and gradual erosion within the meaning of the Convention of 1884, the balance of the tract should be awarded to Mexico.

* * *

Wherefore the Presiding Commissioner and the Mexican Commissioner, constituting a majority of the said Commission, hereby award and declare that the international title to the portion of the Chamizal tract lying between the middle of the bed of the Rio Grande, as surveyed by Emory and Salazar in 1852, and the middle of the bed of the said river as it existed before the flood of 1864, is in the United States of America, and the international title to the balance of the said Chamizal tract is in the United States of Mexico.

The American Commissioner dissents from the above award.

Chamizal Treaty of 1963*

[*"A Convention between the United States of America and the United Mexican States for the Solution of the Problem of the Chamizal was concluded at Mexico City on August 29 [1963]. Ambassador Thomas C. Mann signed for the United States, and the Foreign Minister of Mexico, Manuel Tello, signed for Mexico. . . . [In] accordance with the convention, the United States Section of the International Boundary and Water Commission would proceed to acquire the lands and structures to be transferred to Mexico, and when the lands have been evacuated, and the structures passing intact to Mexico have been paid for by a Mexican banking institu-*

* Reprinted from 49 *United States Department of State Bulletin* 480 (1963).

tion, these lands and structures would be transferred to Mexico. The Mexican Government would at the same time transfer to the United States approximately one-half of Cordova Island, a Mexican enclave north of the present channel of the Rio Grande. The International Commission would then relocate the Rio Grande at El Paso so that all Mexican territory in that area would be south of the new river channel.

. . . The Department of State looks upon the Chamizal convention as a notable achievement in inter-American relations and as a major contribution in the peaceful settlement of boundary disputes." 49 United States Department of State Bulletin 480 (*1963*).]

The United States of America and the United Mexican States: . . .

Desiring to give effect to the 1911 arbitration award. . . .

have agreed as follows:

Article 1

In the El Paso-Ciudad Juarez sector, the Rio Grande shall be relocated into a new channel. . . .

Article 2

The river channel shall be relocated so as to transfer from the north to the south of the Rio Grande a tract of 823.50 acres composed of 366.00 acres in the Chamizal tract, 193.16 acres in the southern part of Cordova Island, and 264.34 acres to the east of Cordova Island. A tract of 193.16 acres in the northern part of Cordova Island will remain to the north of the river.

Article 3

The center line of the new river channel shall be the international boundary. The lands that, as a result of the relocation of the river channel, shall be to the north of the center line of the new channel shall be the territory of the United States of America and the lands that shall be to the south of the center line of the new channel shall be the territory of the United Mexican States.

Article 4

No payments will be made, as between the two Governments, for the value of the lands that pass from one country to the other as a result of the relocation of the international boundary. The lands that, upon relocation of the international boundary, pass from one country to the other shall pass to the respective Governments in absolute ownership, free of any private titles or encumbrances of any kind.

* * *

Article 6

After this Convention has entered into force and the necessary legislation has been enacted for carrying it out, the two Governments shall, on the basis of a recommendation by the International Boundary and Water Commission, determine the period of time appropriate for the Government of the United States to complete the following:

a. The acquisition, in conformity with its laws, of the lands to be transferred to Mexico and for the rights of way for that portion of the new river channel in the territory of the United States;
b. The orderly evacuation of the occupants of the lands referred to in paragraph (a).

* * *

Article 8

The costs of constructing the new river channel shall be borne in equal parts by the two Governments. However, each Government shall bear the costs of compensation for the value of the structures or improvements which must be destroyed, within the territory under its jurisdiction prior to the relocation of the international boundary, in the process of constructing the new channel.

Article 9

The International Boundary and Water Commission is charged with the relocation of the river channel, the construction of the bridges herein provided for, and the maintenance, preservation and improvement of the new channel. The Commission's jurisdiction and responsibilities, set forth in Article XI of the 1933 Convention for the maintenance and preservation of the Rio Grande Rectification Project, are extended upstream from that part of the river included in the Project to the point where the Rio Grande meets the land boundary between the two countries.

Article 10

The six existing bridges shall, as a part of the relocation of the river channel, be replaced by new bridges. The cost of constructing the new bridges shall be borne in equal parts by the two Governments. . . .

Article 11

The relocation of the international boundary and the transfer of portions of territory resulting therefrom shall not affect in any way:

a. The legal status, with respect to citizenship laws, of those persons who are present or former residents of the portions of territory transferred;
b. The jurisdiction over legal proceedings of either a civil or criminal character which are pending at the time of, or which were decided prior to, such relocation;
c. The jurisdiction over acts or omissions occurring within or with respect to the said portions of territory prior to their transfer;
d. The law or laws applicable to the acts or omissions referred to in paragraph (c).

* * *

MARITIME TERRITORY

The domain of a coastal state includes certain areas of the sea, the delimitation of which has been a continuing source of controversy. In the late middle ages and early modern times, states claimed vast areas of the sea. Spain, for example, claimed the Pacific Ocean and Portugal claimed the Indian Ocean. By the beginning of the twentieth century, however, a territorial sea extending out only three miles was almost universally accepted. This significant development is attributable to several factors. Doctrinally, the principle of freedom of the seas—the idea that the oceans are open to all (*terra communis*)—had much to commend it, particularly to the major maritime states, which wanted free navigation for their merchant ships, fishing fleets, and navies. Precision was given to the idea of a narrow territorial sea by the Dutch jurist Cornelius Bynkershoek, who proposed, in 1702, that a state's territorial sea should extend out only as far as a cannon shot would reach, which in the eighteenth century was considered to be one league or three nautical miles. Other writers followed Bynkershoek's lead, as did state practice. In 1793, the United States proposed, and warring Britain and France accepted, a three-mile area as her territorial, and hence neutral, waters. Nineteenth-century fisheries treaties, beginning with the Treaty of Ghent of 1818, generally defined the territorial sea as three miles in breadth. Weaker maritime states sought for a while to keep control over extensive areas of the sea off their coasts, but most of these claims vanished before superior sea power. The powerful states would accept for others only what they claimed for themselves.

While the beginning of the twentieth century witnessed the nearly complete victory of the three-mile principle, the middle of the century brought the origins of its demise. From a table of relevant laws and regulations in force in the 86 states that were represented at the 1958 Geneva Conference on the Law of the Sea, it was evident that only 21 states claimed a three-mile territorial sea, while the others claimed anywhere from four miles to two hundred miles.[1] Economic and security interests and, more particularly, the desire of coastal states to maintain exclusive fishing rights in adjacent waters for their own nationals and to protect their coasts and coastal waters against foreign warships seem to have been the primary reasons for the claims to wider territorial seas.

No agreement was reached on the breadth of the territorial sea at the 1958 Geneva Conference. The states claiming three miles, led by Britain and the United States, showed some willingness to compromise, but the Soviet and Arab blocs steadfastly insisted on the right of coastal states to establish twelve-mile limits. Toward the end of the conference, the United States proposed a six-mile territorial sea, with an additional six-mile contiguous zone in which the coastal state would have exclusive fishing rights, subject only to "historic rights" for states whose nationals had fished in the area for the previous five years. Although the proposal failed to achieve the necessary two-thirds vote, it fared well enough for it to be considered worthwhile to convene a second conference in 1960 to try to resolve the issue. At the 1960 Geneva Conference, a joint United States-Canadian proposal included the United States proposal of 1958, and added that after ten years the coastal state would have exclusive fishing rights over the six-mile contiguous zone. The proposal failed by a single vote. After this failure, some states claiming three miles reverted to their

[1] *United Nations Document* A/Conf. 13/C.1/L.11.

preconference positions and declined to recognize any larger limit as valid against them without their agreement, while others joined in the movement toward a greater territorial sea by claiming wider zones.[2]

Although it is readily apparent that there is no longer any general agreement on a uniform breadth for the territorial sea, this does not mean that each state is free, without limit, to determine the extent of its territorial waters; state practice suggests that any claim to more than twelve miles is invalid. It is significant in this regard that the Convention on the Territorial Sea and the Contiguous Zone, one of the four conventions adopted at the 1958 Geneva Conference, rejected the idea of a territorial sea greater than twelve miles in breadth by declaring that the contiguous zone may not extend beyond twelve miles from the baseline from which the territorial sea is measured. If the outer limit of the contiguous zone—which is a zone of the high seas contiguous to the territorial sea over which the coastal state may exercise that

control necessary to prevent infringements of its customs, fiscal, sanitation, and immigration regulations—is only twelve miles from shore, surely the territorial sea over which the coastal state may exercise complete authority, cannot extend farther.[3]

It is clear that the present trend is toward the twelve-mile limit. Even those states that still claim three miles are, in increasing number, establishing twelve-mile fishery zones; the United Kingdom made this move in 1964 and was followed in 1965 by New Zealand. As of June 1966, 49 of 91 coastal states claimed a twelve-mile fishery jurisdiction; 10 claimed more than three but less than twelve miles; 17 claimed more than twelve miles; and only 15 still claimed three miles.[4] On October 14, 1966, the United States joined the movement by adopting a twelve-mile fishery zone.[5] And, as Guenter Weissberg points out, "thirty-nine States have moved to a twelve-mile fishery zone, either as part of their territorial sea or by extending their zone independently, since the 1958 Conference."[6]

[2] "The present tally, drawn from various sources and based on the actual practice, legislation, or official declarations of states, is as follows: 23 states claim 3 miles: Argentina (1959), Australia (1878), Belgium (1832, 1891), Brazil (1914), Canada (1906), Denmark (1812), Dominican Rep. (1952), Federal German Rep., France (1862), Ireland (1959), Japan (1870), Jordan (1943), Liberia (1914), Malaysia, Morocco, Netherlands (1889), New Zealand (1908), Nicaragua, Pakistan (1878), Poland (1932), United Kingdom, United States, Vietnam (South). 4 states claim 4 miles: Finland (1920), Iceland (1952), Norway (1812), Sweden (1779). 5 miles: Cambodia (1957). 17 states claim 6 miles: Cameroon, Ceylon (1957), Colombia (1930), Greece (1936), Haiti (1950), India (1956), Israel (1955), Italy (1942), Portugal (1885, 1927), Senegal (1961), South Africa (1963), Spain (1760), Thailand (1958), Tunisia (1963), Turkey (1964), Uruguay (1925), Yugoslavia (1948). 9 miles: Mexico (1935). 10 miles: Albania (1952). 29 states claim 12 miles: Algeria (1963), Bulgaria (1951), China, People's Republic (1958), Nationalist China (1956) (China counts as one above), Cuba (1955), Cyprus (1964), Ecuador (1950), Egypt (1958), El Salvador (1955), Ethiopia (1953), Ghana (1963), Guatemala (1939, 1941), Indonesia (1957), Iran (1959), Iraq (1958), Ivory Coast, Libya (1959), Malagasy (1963), Panama (1958), Rumania (1952), Saudi Arabia (1958), Sierra Leone (1965), Sudan (1960), Syria (1963), Tanzania (1963), Togo (1964), U.S.S.R. (1921), Venezuela (1956), Vietnam (North), Yemen. Honduras claims 12 km.; Chile 50 km.; East Germany has variable limits of 3, 5, 6, 8, and 9½ miles (1958); Guinea claims 130 miles (1964). India and Turkey have favoured 12 miles in principle. . . . Claims of 200 miles, e.g. by Chile and Peru, or over the continental shelf and the waters above, e.g. by Honduras (1950), may in fact be fishery conservation zones. . . ." Brownlie, *Principles of Public International Law*, p. 178, n. 1.

[3] If a coastal state claims a twelve-mile territorial sea, as in the case of the Soviet Union, there is no contiguous zone seaward of its territorial waters.
[4] See the table prepared by the United States Department of State and provided to the United States Senate Committee on Commerce in 60 *American Journal of International Law* 832 (1966).
[5] Public Law 89–658:
Be it enacted by the Senate and House of Representatives of the United States of America in Congress assembled, That there is established a fisheries zone contiguous to the territorial sea of the United States. The United States will exercise the same exclusive rights in respect to fisheries in the zone as it has in its territorial sea, subject to the continuation of traditional fishing by foreign states within this zone as may be recognized by the United States.

Sec. 2. The fisheries zone has as its inner boundary the outer limits of the territorial sea and as its seaward boundary a line drawn so that each point on the line is nine nautical miles from the nearest point in the inner boundary.

Sec. 3. Whenever the President determines that a portion of the fisheries zone conflicts with the territorial waters or fisheries zone of another country, he may establish a seaward boundary for such portion of the zone in substitution for the seaward boundary described in section 2.

Sec. 4. Nothing in this Act shall be construed as extending the jurisdiction of the States to the natural resources beneath and in the waters within the fisheries zone established by this Act or as diminishing their jurisdiction to such resources beneath and in the waters of the territorial seas of the United States.
[6] Guenter Weissberg, "Fisheries, Foreign Assistance, Custom and Conventions," 16 *International and Comparative Law Quarterly* 718 (1967).

Further evidence of the trend toward the twelve-mile limit was provided by the initial reaction of the United States to the seizure by North Korea of its spy ship, the *Pueblo*, in January 1968. The complaint of the United States was not based on the contention that North Korea, a twelve-mile state, could not under international law claim more than three miles, but instead on the ground that the ship was outside the twelve-mile limit claimed by North Korea and, consequently, in "international waters."

Although the Geneva conferences of 1958 and 1960 failed to delimit the breadth of the territorial sea, the Convention on the Territorial Sea and the Contiguous Zone resolved several technical difficulties in measuring the territorial sea, a problem that exists regardless of whatever breadth is eventually accepted. For example, the width of the territorial sea should be measured from the "low-water line along the coast." And where the coast is heavily indented or island-fringed, "the method of straight baselines joining appropriate points may be employed in drawing the baseline from which the breadth of the territorial sea is measured," but the lines must follow the "general direction of the coast."

The Convention on the Continental Shelf, which was also adopted at the 1958 conference, is declaratory of the general acceptance of a principle stated thirteen years earlier by President Harry S. Truman. On September 28, 1945, President Truman proclaimed that the United States regarded the natural resources of the subsoil and seabed of the continental shelf beneath the high seas but contiguous to its coast as subject to its "jurisdiction and control." He added that "the character as high seas of the waters above the continental shelf and the right to their free and unimpeded navigation are in no way thus affected."[7] This claim, which was based on the desire

to acquire undisputed legal control over the oil resources off the coasts of the United States without undermining the traditional rights of free navigation and fishing off the coasts of other states, was quickly followed by similar declarations by numerous other governments.

The Convention, like Truman's proclamation, draws a clear distinction between the "sovereignty" a coastal state has over its territorial sea and the limited rights it has over its continental shelf. Only a few states, mostly in Latin America, do not accept this distinction. Argentina, El Salvador, Cambodia, and Cuba, for example, claim not only the resources of the subsoil and the seabed of their continental shelves but also the resources of the high seas over such areas. Some Latin American states with virtually no shallow submarine areas off their coasts claim sovereignty over the resources of all adjacent seas at whatever depth to a distance of two hundred miles. It would seem that these unilateral extensions of coastal state control over fishing are incompatible with the principle of freedom of the high seas.

The first of the four selections that follow, the Elida case, illustrates several practices of national courts during the heyday of the three-mile period, including the unwillingness of three-mile states to accept a greater territorial sea for other states. Also reprinted are provisions from the Convention on the Territorial Sea and the Contiguous Zone and the Convention on the Continental Shelf, both of which are now in force; the remainder of the Convention on the Territorial Sea and the Contiguous Zone, which deals with matters of jurisdiction, is reprinted in the following chapter on pages 198 to 200. Finally, the official position of the United States on the seizure of the *U.S.S. Pueblo* is discussed by Leonard C. Meeker, Legal Adviser to the Department of State.

[7] 10 *Federal Register* 12303 (1945).

The Elida*

Imperial Supreme Prize Court of Germany, 1915

* * *

On October 13, 1914, the Swedish S.S. *Elida*, with a cargo of wood (rafters), bound from Kago to Hull, was captured by a German torpedo boat near Trelleborg and taken into Swinemünde. The bill of lading read "to order"; the wood is said to have been sold by V. Svensson & Co. A. G. of Stockholm to Roberts, Cooper & Co. in Hull. The owner of the steamer, J. Ingmarssen of Stensnäs, avers that the seizure of the ship and cargo was illegal and claims damages. The Prize Court at Kiel decided that the steamer and cargo should be released, but that sufficient reasons existed to justify the seizure and that the claim for compensation should be dismissed.

The appeal from this decision is sustained.

The illegality of the seizure is first of all based on the fact that it took place within the zone of neutrality claimed by Sweden, *i.e.*, within four miles of the Swedish coast. Whether this was really the case is disputed, whilst it is certain that the seizure took place outside the three mile limit. In any event this is of no importance, since this objection was properly dismissed by the judge.

It is true that a considerable number of states have extended by national law their territorial jurisdiction beyond the three mile limit, either generally or with regard to certain legal rights. This particularly applies to Sweden and Norway, which extended their national waters to a distance of four miles. A number of other states even went much further in this respect. But a special international title, valid in

* Reprinted from 10 *American Journal of International Law* 916 (1916) by permission of the American Society of International Law.

relation to the German Empire, and therefore to be taken into account by the prize court, does not exist, for up to the present time the Swedish claim has been recognized only by the Norwegian Government. According to official information from the German Foreign Office, Germany especially in the course of the discussion concerning this matter which took place in 1874, did not accept Sweden's point of view but treated the question of national waters as an open one, while England insisted upon the three mile limit. Similarly in 1897, when the Swedish Government addressed a communication to the German Legation at Stockholm concerning the fishery jurisdiction, the German Government restricted itself to raising no objection against Sweden's claim to a four mile boundary for the fishery and the question of the neutralization of this marine area in case of war was not thereby affected.

Therefore, under these circumstances, the decision must rest upon the basis of the German Prize Regulations, which in No. 3a forbids the application of prize law within a zone of only three nautical miles from the low water mark of neutral coasts. The Prize Regulations contain the principles laid down by the Kaiser as Commander in Chief within his Imperial jurisdiction for the practice of prize law pertaining to naval warfare, and are, therefore, primarily law not only for the Navy, but also for the inland authorities, particularly the prize courts, in so far as they have to pass upon the legality of the actions of commanders at sea falling within the prize law. International law only lays down rights and duties as between different states. The prize courts, when judging of the legality of prize actions, can take general international principles only into account when the Prize Regulations contain no instructions and, therefore, tacitly refer to the principles of international law. Therefore, the question whether an instruction of the Prize Regulations agrees with general international law is not for the prize court to decide. If a contradiction in this connection is asserted, the point in controversy is to be settled in another manner. Thus far this conception also agrees with the legal opinion of Professor Dr. von Liszt, produced by the claimants.

Contrary to this opinion, however, the Supreme Prize Court further is of the opinion that the instruction in question of the German Prize Regulations in no way violates the general principles of international law. Heretofore, the maritime boundary of states has been generally recognized in theory and practice as being three nautical miles distant from the coast. Originally, it was based on the carrying distance, corresponding to the gunnery technique of those times, of ships' and coast guns. It is true that now-a-days this reason is no longer applicable. Here however the axiom *cessante ratione non cessat lex ipsa* applies, and although numerous proposals and opinions have been put forward with regard to a different delimitation of the national waters, it cannot be asserted that any other method has in practice met with the general concurrence of the maritime states. This is also true of the view put forward in the above mentioned opinion, according to which each individual state is entitled to extend, by means of independent regulations, the boundary of its national waters beyond the three mile zone as far as gun range, the former limit nevertheless to be regarded as a subsidiary international boundary. With the range of present day guns this would lead to quite intolerable conditions, and give to single states the possibility of including within their national territory extensive tracts of the open sea the freedom of which is in the interest of all maritime states. To a certain extent this is also acknowledged by Liszt in his opinion, for according thereto the regulation of the individual state is not alone sufficient; the absence of objection on the part of other states is also required. Thereby in reality the permissibility of an extension

of the territorial waters is founded not so much upon the independent regulation by the single state, as upon the supposition of a tacit acknowledgment of such an extension by the other states. A mere failure to object, however, is not identical with a positive concurrence of the nations. Furthermore, it must be remembered that even if the exercise by a maritime nation of certain official functions, such as those of the health and customs authorities, is tolerated beyond the three mile zone, this by no means represents a concession to the effect that in all other respects the waters in question are included within the territorial jurisdiction. Accordingly, in more recent international agreements to which a number of maritime states were parties, as, for instance, in the agreement of May 6, 1882, for the police regulation of the North Sea fisheries, and in the convention of October 29, 1888, for the neutralization of the Suez Canal, the three mile boundary was recognized as the standard. Likewise, according to official information from the Foreign Office, in the second session of the International Congress for the Protection of Submarine Cables, held at Paris on October 18, 1882, Germany's representative explicitly declared, without meeting with opposition, that by the term "coastal waters" a zone of three miles was to be understood. Furthermore, according to the same official information, the British Government during the negotiations in the year 1911 with regard to the holding of an international congress for the regulation of the question of coastal waters, decidedly adhered to the three mile zone; and, accordingly, even in the present war, it had Admiral Craddock inform the Government of Uruguay that it would not recognize the claims of Uruguay and Argentina to an extension of the territorial waters beyond the three mile zone. It can, therefore, be still less assumed that this boundary has been supplanted by another generally acknowledged international regulation.

In the case under consideration, however,

the legality of the seizure should have been denied for another reason.

In agreement with the court of first instance, it is to be taken that the wood,—which after the release of the ship and cargo was sold in Luebeck—was not contraband. . . .

* * *

Wherefore, the petitioner's claim, in so far as he, in his capacity of owner of the *Elida*, has suffered loss, appears fundamentally justified. . . .

Convention on the Territorial Sea and the Contiguous Zone, 1958*

Part I: Territorial Sea

SECTION I. GENERAL

Article 1

1. The sovereignty of a State extends, beyond its land territory and its internal waters, to a belt of sea adjacent to its coast, described as the territorial sea.

2. This sovereignty is exercised subject to the provisions of these articles and to other rules of international law.

Article 2

The sovereignty of a coastal State extends to the air space over the territorial sea as well as to its bed and subsoil.

SECTION II. LIMITS OF THE TERRITORIAL SEA

Article 3

Except where otherwise provided in these articles, the normal baseline for measuring the breadth of the territorial sea is the low-water line along the coast as marked on large-scale charts officially recognized by the coastal State.

* Reprinted from *United Nations Document* A/Conf. 13/L.52.

Article 4

1. In localities where the coastline is deeply indented and cut into, or if there is a fringe of islands along the coast in its immediate vicinity, the method of straight baselines joining appropriate points may be employed in drawing the baseline from which the breadth of the territorial sea is measured.

2. The drawing of such baselines must not depart to any appreciable extent from the general direction of the coast, and the sea areas lying within the lines must be sufficiently closely linked to the land domain to be subject to the régime of internal waters.

3. Baselines shall not be drawn to and from low-tide elevations, unless lighthouses or similar installations which are permanently above sea level have been built on them.

4. Where the method of straight baselines is applicable under the provisions of paragraph 1, account may be taken, in determining particular baselines, of economic interests peculiar to the region concerned, the reality and the importance of which are clearly evidenced by a long usage.

5. The system of straight baselines may not be applied by a State in such a manner as to cut off from the high seas the territorial sea of another State.

6. The coastal State must clearly indicate straight baselines on charts, to which due publicity must be given.

Article 5

1. Waters on the landward side of the baseline of the territorial sea form part of the internal waters of the State.

2. Where the establishment of a straight baseline in accordance with article 4 has the effect of enclosing as internal waters areas which previously had been considered as part of the territorial sea or of the high seas, a right of innocent passage . . . shall exist in those waters.

Article 6

The outer limit of the territorial sea is the line every point of which is at a distance from the nearest point of the baseline equal to the breadth of the territorial sea.

Article 7

1. This article relates only to bays the coasts of which belong to a single state.

2. For the purposes of these articles, a bay is a well-marked indentation whose penetration is in such proportion to the width of its mouth as to contain landlocked waters and constitute more than a mere curvature of the coast. An indentation shall not, however, be regarded as a bay unless its area is as large as, or larger than, that of the semi-circle whose diameter is a line drawn across the mouth of that indentation.

3. For the purpose of measurement, the area of an indentation is that lying between the low-water mark around the shore of the indentation and a line joining the low-water mark of its natural entrance points. Where, because of the presence of islands, an indentation has more than one mouth, the semi-circle shall be drawn on a line as long as the sum total of the lengths of the lines across the different mouths. Islands within an indentation shall be included as if they were part of the water area of the indentation.

4. If the distance between the low-water marks of the natural entrance points of a bay does not exceed twenty-four miles, a closing line may be drawn between these two low-water marks, and the waters enclosed thereby shall be considered as internal waters.

5. Where the distance between the low-water marks of the natural entrance points of a bay exceeds twenty-four miles, a straight baseline of twenty-four miles shall be drawn from within the bay in such a manner as to enclose the maximum area of water that is possible with a line of that length.

6. The foregoing provisions shall not apply to so-called "historic" bays, or in any case where the straight baseline system provided for in article 4 is applied.

Article 8

For the purpose of delimiting the territorial sea, the outermost permanent harbour works which form an integral part of the harbour system shall be regarded as forming part of the coast.

Article 9

Roadsteads which are normally used for the loading, unloading and anchoring of ships, and which would otherwise be situated wholly or partly outside the outer limit of the territorial sea, are included in the territorial sea. The coastal State must clearly demarcate such roadsteads and indicate them on charts together with their boundaries, to which due publicity must be given.

Article 10

1. An island is a naturally formed area of land, surrounded by water, which is above water at high tide.

2. The territorial sea of an island is measured in accordance with the provisions of these articles.

Article 11

1. A low-tide elevation is a naturally formed area of land which is surrounded by and above water at low-tide but submerged at high tide. Where a low-tide elevation is situated wholly or partly at a distance not exceeding the breadth of the territorial sea from the mainland or an island, the low-water line on that elevation may be used as the baseline for measuring the breadth of the territorial sea.

2. Where a low-tide elevation is wholly situated at a distance exceeding the breadth of the territorial sea from the mainland or an island, it has no territorial sea of its own.

Article 12

1. Where the coasts of two States are opposite or adjacent to each other, neither of the two States is entitled, failing agreement between them to the contrary, to extend its territorial sea beyond the median line every point of which is equidistant from the nearest points on the baselines from which the breadth of the territorial seas of each of the two States is measured. The provisions of this paragraph shall not apply, however, where it is necessary by reason of historic title or other special circumstances to delimit the territorial seas of the two States in a way which is at variance with this provision.

2. The line of delimitation between the territorial seas of two States lying opposite to each other or adjacent to each other shall be marked on large-scale charts officially recognized by the coastal States.

Article 13

If a river flows directly into the sea, the baseline shall be a straight line across the mouth of the river between points on the low-tide line of its banks.

* * *

Part II: Contiguous Zone

Article 24

1. In a zone of the high seas contiguous to its territorial sea, the coastal State may exercise the control necessary to:
a. Prevent infringement of its customs, fiscal, immigration or sanitary regulations within its territory or territorial sea;
b. Punish infringements of the above regulations committed within its territory or territorial sea.

2. The contiguous zone may not extend beyond twelve miles from the baseline from which the breadth of the territorial sea is measured.

3. Where the coasts of two States are opposite or adjacent to each other, neither of the two States is entitled, failing agreement between them to the contrary, to extend its contiguous zone beyond the median line every point of which is equidistant from the nearest points on the baselines from which the breadth of the territorial seas of the two States is measured.

* * *

Convention on the Continental Shelf, 1958*

Article 1

For the purpose of these articles, the term "continental shelf" is used as referring (a) to the seabed and subsoil of the submarine areas adjacent to the coast but outside the area of the territorial sea, to a depth of 200 metres or, beyond that limit to where the depth of the superjacent water admits of the exploitation of the natural resources of the said areas; (b) to the seabed and subsoil of similar submarine areas adjacent to the coasts of islands.

Article 2

1. The coastal State exercises over the continental shelf sovereign rights for the purpose of exploring it and exploiting its natural resources.

2. The rights referred to in paragraph 1 of this article are exclusive in the sense that if the coastal State does not explore the continental shelf or exploit its natural resources, no one may undertake these activities, or make a claim to the continental shelf, without the express consent of the coastal State.

* Reprinted from *United Nations Document* A/Conf. 13/L.55.

3. The rights of the coastal State over the continental shelf do not depend on occupation, effective or notional, or on any express proclamation.

4. The natural resources referred to in these articles consist of the mineral and other non-living resources of the seabed and subsoil together with living organisms belonging to sedentary species, that is to say, organisms which, at the harvestable stage, either are immobile on or under the seabed or are unable to move except in constant physical contact with the seabed or the subsoil.

Article 3

The rights of the coastal State over the continental shelf do not affect the legal status of the superjacent waters as high seas, or that of the air space above those waters.

Article 4

Subject to its right to take reasonable measures for the exploration of the continental shelf and the exploitation of its natural resources, the coastal State may not impede the laying or maintenance of submarine cables or pipelines on the continental shelf.

Article 5

1. The exploration of the continental shelf and the exploitation of its natural resources must not result in any unjustifiable interference with navigation, fishing or the conservation of the living resources of the sea, nor result in any interference with fundamental oceanographic or other scientific research carried out with the intention of open publication.

2. Subject to the provisions of paragraphs 1 and 6 of this article, the coastal State is entitled to construct and maintain or operate on the continental shelf installations and other devices necessary for its exploration and the exploitation of its natural resources, and to establish safety zones around such installations and devices and to take in those zones measures necessary for their protection.

3. The safety zones referred to in paragraph 2 of this article may extend to a distance of 500 metres around the installations and other devices which have been erected, measured from each point of their outer edge. Ships of all nationalities must respect these safety zones.

4. Such installations and devices, though under the jurisdiction of the coastal State, do not possess the status of islands. They have no territorial sea of their own, and their presence does not affect the delimitation of the territorial sea of the coastal State.

5. Due notice must be given of the construction of any such installations, and permanent means for giving warning of their presence must be maintained. Any installations which are abandoned or disused must be entirely removed.

6. Neither the installations or devices, nor the safety zones around them, may be established where interference may be caused to the use of recognized sea lanes essential to international navigation.

7. The coastal State is obliged to undertake, in the safety zones, all appropriate measures for the protection of the living resources of the sea from harmful agents.

8. The consent of the coastal State shall be obtained in respect of any research concerning the continental shelf and undertaken there. Nevertheless, the coastal State shall not normally withhold its consent if the request is submitted by a qualified institution with a view to purely scientific research into the physical or biological characteristics of the continental shelf, subject to the proviso that the coastal State shall have the right, if it so desires, to participate or to be represented in the

research, and that in any event the results shall be published.

Article 6

1. Where the same continental shelf is adjacent to the territories of two or more States whose coasts are opposite each other, the boundary of the continental shelf appertaining to such States shall be determined by agreement between them. In the absence of agreement, and unless another boundary line is justified by special circumstances, the boundary is the median line, every point of which is equidistant from the nearest points of the baselines from which the breadth of the territorial sea of each State is measured.

2. Where the same continental shelf is adjacent to the territories of two adjacent States, the boundary of the continental shelf shall be determined by agreement between them. In the absence of agreement, and unless another boundary line is justified by special circumstances, the boundary shall be determined by application of the principle of equidistance from the nearest points of the baselines from which the breadth of the territorial sea of each State is measured.

3. In delimiting the boundaries of the continental shelf, any lines which are drawn in accordance with the principles set out in paragraphs 1 and 2 of this article should be defined with reference to charts and geographical features as they exist at a particular date, and reference should be made to fixed permanent identifiable points on the land.

Article 7

The provisions of these articles shall not prejudice the right of the coastal State to exploit the subsoil by means of tunnelling irrespective of the depth of water above the subsoil.

*　*　*

Seizure of the U.S.S. Pueblo*

Leonard C. Meeker, LEGAL ADVISER OF THE UNITED STATES DEPARTMENT OF STATE

I turn now to the case of the U.S.S. *Pueblo*, which was seized by North Korea on January 23 of this year. This case presents a number of questions of international law. There is first the question of the breadth of the territorial sea.

Then there is the question of where the *Pueblo* was when it was seized by North Korean naval units. The *Pueblo* was under firm instructions to remain at least 13 miles from the North Korean coast. At the time of seizure the *Pueblo* itself radioed that its position was at a point more than 15 miles from the nearest North Korean island. This location was confirmed by another report sent at the same time by a North Korean submarine chaser and monitored so that we have been able to know what it was that this latter vessel reported to its own headquarters. North Korea, however, has asserted that the *Pueblo*, at the time of seizure, was only 7.6 miles from the nearest North Korean territory. It supports this assertion with three kinds of alleged evidence: first, purported confessions by members of the *Pueblo*'s crew; second, purported navigational plots made on the *Pueblo*; and third, purported entries in the *Pueblo*'s log. It is, of course, not possible to reach any conclusions about these asserted items of evidence without being able to examine the originals and to have the freely given testimony of the *Pueblo*'s crew. On the basis of experience, we have a very plain and realistic understanding of the incommunicado conditions under which any alleged confessions must have been obtained.

There are still further legal issues. No matter where the *Pueblo* was, North Korea was not entitled to make a forcible seizure.

* Reprinted from 58 *United States Department of State Bulletin* 468 (1968).

Article 8 of the 1958 Geneva Convention on the High Seas states categorically that "Warships on the high seas have complete immunity from the jurisdiction of any State other than the flag State." Even if the *Pueblo* were within North Korea's territorial sea, there was still no right to seize the *Pueblo*.

The international law rules for the treatment of vessels within the territorial sea are set forth quite clearly in the 1958 Geneva Convention on this subject. After a series of articles limiting the right of the coastal state to exercise jurisdiction over merchant ships and government ships other than warships within the territorial sea, the convention contains the following single article on the treatment to be accorded by the coastal state to a warship in the territorial sea:

If any warship does not comply with the regulations of the coastal State concerning passage through the territorial sea and disregards any request for compliance which is made to it, the coastal State may require the warship to leave the territorial sea.

This is article 23. No right is provided, as in the case of merchant ships or certain government ships other than warships, to stop or forcibly board a vessel of war, to arrest any persons on it, or to take any legal action against the vessel itself. The rule of article 23 concerning warships is a wise rule designed to protect the legitimate interests of the coastal state and the state of the vessel's registry and to avoid armed conflict—a possibility that would obviously exist in the case of war vessels.

Other legal issues are also conceivable in the case of the *Pueblo*, although most of them would not bear on the question of lawfulness of the seizure: for example, claims to historic waters, assertions possibly based on the doctrine of hot pursuit, and charges that the mission of the *Pueblo* was illegal or constituted a hostile act. On the score of this last point, it is worth recalling that the Soviet Union operates a sub-

stantial number of intelligence-collection vessels all around the world. On occasion, these have approached within less than 3 miles of the coast of the United States. In each instance where this occurred, the United States authorities acted in strict accordance with international law and required the vessel in question to leave the territorial sea, without taking any action against it.

Again, in the case of the *Pueblo* there has been a United Nations phase. The United States took the matter to the Security Council and invoked the processes of that body. We presented our case to public scrutiny in the forum of the Council.

The Council has taken no action. This outcome is obviously connected with the fact that North Korea is not a member of the United Nations, rejected its jurisdiction, and instead proposed bilateral discussion in the Military Armistice Commission under the Korean Armistice Agreement.

More than a month has now gone by since the seizure of the *Pueblo*. The United States Government has with great forbearance continued a series of discussions on the *Pueblo* with North Korean representatives. We are continuing to press for release of the crew and the vessel. In a better ordered world, the various legal issues could all be placed before an international tribunal for decision.

[*The crew of the* Pueblo *was released on December 22, 1968, after the following document was signed "on behalf of the Government of the United States" by Major General Gilbert H. Woodward:**]

To the Government of the Democratic People's Republic of Korea,

The Government of the United States of America,

Acknowledging the validity of the confessions of the crew of the USS Pueblo and of the documents of evidence

* Reprinted from 7 *International Legal Materials: Current Documents* 199 (1969).

produced by the Representative of the Government of the Democratic People's Republic of Korea to the effect that the ship, which was seized by the self-defense measures of the naval vessels of the Korean People's Army in the territorial waters of the Democratic People's Republic of Korea on January 23, 1968, had illegally intruded into the territorial waters of the Democratic People's Republic of Korea,

Shoulders full responsibility and solemnly apologizes for the grave acts of espionage committed by the U.S. ship against the Democratic People's Republic of Korea after having intruded into the territorial waters of the Democratic People's Republic of Korea,

And gives firm assurance that no U.S. ships will intrude again in the future into the territorial waters of the Democratic People's Republic of Korea.

Meanwhile, the Government of the United States of America earnestly requests the Government of the Democratic People's Republic of Korea to deal leniently with the former crew members of the USS Pueblo confiscated by the Democratic People's Republic of Korea side, taking into consideration the fact that these crew members have confessed honestly to their crimes and petitioned the Government of the Democratic People's Republic of Korea for leniency.

Simultaneously with the signing of this document, the undersigned acknowledges receipt of 82 former crew members of the Pueblo and one corpse.

On behalf of the Government
of the United States of America
GILBERT H. WOODWARD, *Major General, USA*

[*On the same day, United States Secretary of State Dean Rusk made the following statement:**]

President Johnson and I are pleased to report that the United States representative

* 7 *International Legal Materials: Current Documents* 198 (1969).

at Panmunjom has just obtained the release of the 82 officers and men of the U.S.S. *Pueblo* who last January were illegally seized with their ship on the high seas.

* * *

The men were released after long and difficult negotiations. The North Korean negotiator insisted from the beginning that the men would not be released unless the United States falsely confessed to espionage and to violations of North Korean territory and apologized for such alleged actions.

We necessarily refused these demands. We repeatedly offered to express our regrets if shown valid evidence of a transgression. But this Government had—and has now—no reliable evidence that the *Pueblo* in any way violated her sailing orders and intruded into waters claimed by North Korea.

After 10 months of negotiations during which we made every sort of reasonable offer, all of which were harshly rejected, we had come squarely up against a most painful problem: how to obtain the release of the crew without having this Government seem to attest to statements which simply are not true. Then within the past week, a way which does just that was found, and a strange procedure was accepted by the North Koreans. Apparently the North Koreans believe there is propaganda value even in a worthless document which General Woodward publicly labeled false before he signed it.

General Woodward said:

The position of the United States Government with regard to the *Pueblo*, as consistently expressed in the negotiations at Panmunjom and in public, has been that the ship was not engaged in illegal activity, that there is no convincing evidence that the ship at any time intruded into the territorial waters claimed by North Korea, and that we could not apologize for actions which we did not believe took place. The document which I am going to sign was prepared by the North Koreans and is at variance with the above position, but my signature will not and cannot alter the facts. I will sign the document to free the crew and only to free the crew.

If you ask me why these two contradictory statements proved to be the key to effect the release of our men, the North Koreans would have to explain it. I know of no precedent in my 19 years of public service. The simple fact is that the men are free and our position on the facts of the case is unchanged.

We regret that the ship itself, U.S.S. *Pueblo*, has not yet been returned; that will have to be pursued further.

AIR SPACE AND OUTER SPACE

States have complete legal control over the air space above their territory; other states have only such rights in it as are acquired by treaty. There is no customary right of innocent passage through territorial air space; and, until recently, states refused even to admit the right of foreign planes in distress to enter their air space.

Efforts to open territorial air space to freer international traffic have been less than moderately successful. The International Civil Aviation Conference, held in Chicago in 1944, produced several liberalizing conventions, but the most far-reaching of these proved to be abortive. The International Air Services Transit Agreement, or the "Two Freedoms" Agreement, has been widely accepted: it grants to the scheduled aircraft of contracting parties the right to fly without landing over the territory of other contracting parties and the right to land within their territory for nontraffic purposes, e.g., to refuel. The International Transport Agreement, or the "Five Freedoms" Agreement, on the other hand, has had so few adherents that its effect is minimal at best. It would have added to the two freedoms

"the privilege to put down passengers, mail and cargo taken on in the territory of the State whose nationality the aircraft possesses; the privilege to take on passengers, mail and cargo destined for the territory of the State whose nationality the aircraft possesses; [and] the privilege to take on passengers, mail and cargo destined for the territory of any other contacting State and the privilege to put down passengers, mail and cargo coming from any such territory."[1]

In the absence of thorough and effective multilateral conventions, regular airline services are made possible only by a complicated network of bilateral agreements.[2]

Prior to the space age, it was assumed that a state's territorial air space extended indefinitely in height. This view was made obsolete by the orbiting of satellites around the earth without prior approval and without significant protest. Proposals to define the limits of territorial air space range from a few to several thousand miles, but it is unlikely that agreement will be reached within a short time.

On the other hand, the groundwork of a legal regime for outer space has already been laid. In December 1966, agreement was reached on the first international treaty governing the activities of states in the exploration and use of outer space. This historic document, which is reprinted on pages 180–184, provides, *inter alia*, that outer space, like the high seas, is to be kept free for exploration, research, and use by all states without discrimination;

[1] *United States Executive Agreement Series* 488.
[2] See, for example, the Civil Air Transport Agreement signed by the Soviet Union and the United States in November 1966, in 55 *United States Department of State Bulletin* 792 (1966).

that sovereignty over celestial bodies cannot be claimed by any state "by means of occupation or by any other means"; and that "nuclear weapons or any other kinds of weapons of mass destruction" may not be placed in orbit around the earth or installed on celestial bodies.

The first two documents that follow are brief excerpts from the Chicago Convention on International Civil Aviation and the Chicago International Air Services Transit Agreement. The next selection, "Some Legal Implications of the U-2 and RB-47 Incidents" by Oliver J. Lissitzyn, is an analysis of United States and Soviet attitudes toward national sovereignty over air space and outer space. The final document in this section is the Outer Space Treaty of 1966, which went into force on October 10, 1967.

Chicago Convention on International Civil Aviation, 1944*

Article 1

The contracting States recognize that every State has complete and exclusive sovereignty over the airspace above its territory.

Article 2

For the purposes of this Convention the territory of a State shall be deemed to be the land areas and territorial waters adjacent thereto under the sovereignty, suzerainty, protection or mandate of such State.

Article 3

a. This Convention shall be applicable only

* Reprinted from *Treaties and Other International Acts Series* 1591.

to civil aircraft, and shall not be applicable to state aircraft.

b. Aircraft used in military, customs and police services shall be deemed to be state aircraft.

c. No state aircraft of a contracting State shall fly over the territory of another State or land thereon without authorization by special agreement or otherwise, and in accordance with the terms thereof.

* * *

Article 5

Each contracting State agrees that all aircraft of the other contracting States, being aircraft not engaged in scheduled international air services shall have the right, subject to the observance of the terms of this Convention, to make flights into or in transit non-stop across its territory and to make stops for non-traffic purposes without the necessity of obtaining prior permission, and subject to the right of the State flown over to require landing. Each contracting State nevertheless reserves the right, for reasons of safety of flight, to require aircraft desiring to proceed over regions which are inaccessible or without adequate air navigation facilities to follow prescribed routes, or to obtain special permission for such flights.

* * *

Article 6

No scheduled international air service may be operated over or into the territory of a contracting State, except with the special permission or other authorization of that State, and in accordance with the terms of such permission or authorization.

Chicago International Air Services Transit Agreement, 1944*

Article I

Section 1.—Each contracting State grants to the other contracting States the following freedoms of the air in respect of scheduled international air services:

1. The privilege to fly across its territory without landing;
2. The privilege to land for non-traffic purposes.

* * *

Some Legal Implications of the U-2 and RB-47 Incidents†

Oliver J. Lissitzyn

. . . Among the questions of international law on which these incidents have a bearing are the following: What is the legal basis of national sovereignty in airspace? How far up does such sovereignty extend? What action may a state lawfully take against a foreign aircraft which intrudes into its national airspace? Is deliberate intrusion of aircraft into foreign airspace for military reconnaissance purposes an act of aggression? Is a state entitled to interfere with flights of foreign aircraft over the high seas in close proximity to its territorial sea ("contiguous zone")? By analogy, is a state entitled to control the passage of foreign space vehicles in a zone immediately above its national airspace?

On May 1, 1960, Francis Gary Powers, a citizen of the United States, was arrested

on Soviet territory near Sverdlovsk after he had descended by parachute from a United States aircraft. According to public Soviet statements, this aircraft, a high-altitude plane of the Lockheed U-2 type, had been shot down by a Soviet rocket, apparently without warning, while flying over the Soviet Union at an altitude of approximately 60,000 to 68,000 feet. Powers was subsequently convicted of espionage by the Military Division of the Supreme Court of the Soviet Union and sentenced to ten years of confinement.

The United States Government did not protest against the shooting down of the U-2 plane flown by Powers or against the imprisonment, trial and conviction of Powers. It eventually admitted that the U-2 flight had been deliberately undertaken for military intelligence purposes pursuant to a policy approved by the President, and that similar flights over Soviet territory had been conducted for approximately four years. Shortly thereafter, President Eisenhower ordered the suspension of further U-2 flights over the U.S.S.R. and President Kennedy subsequently ordered that they not be resumed.

The absence of protest by the United States against the actions of the Soviet authorities toward Powers and his plane is in sharp contrast with the strong remonstrances invariably made by the United States against the shooting down by the Soviets of American military aircraft over the high seas and the imprisonment of crew members of the aircraft so shot down. Such remonstrances were made, for example, in the case of the United States Air Force RB-47 plane shot down by Soviet aircraft on July 1, 1960, in which the United States denied that the aircraft had been flying above Soviet territory.

There are two differences which might account for the contrast—differences in the nature of the missions of the aircraft and in the location of the incidents. The admitted purpose of the U-2 flight was

* Reprinted from *United States Executive Agreement Series* 487.
† Reprinted from Oliver J. Lissitzyn, "Some Legal Implications of the U-2 and RB-47 Incidents," 56 *American Journal of International Law* 135 (1962), by permission of the American Society of International Law.

military reconnaissance of Soviet territory. The United States, however, has never admitted that an American aircraft over the high seas could be lawfully attacked and shot down by Soviet forces, and its crew tried in Soviet courts for espionage, merely because it was observing Soviet territory. Furthermore, the Soviet Union itself does not appear to have ever protested on legal grounds against the observation of its territory by foreign aircraft flying over the high seas. In both the U-2 and the RB-47 incidents, its complaints were based on the real or alleged "violation" of its "frontiers" or airspace by American aircraft. As President Kennedy has said, the significant differences between the U-2 and the RB-47 flights was that "one was an overflight and the other was a flight of a different nature." The difference then, that accounts for the contrast in the American attitudes toward the two incidents is the difference in the location of the incidents.

The Soviet Union is not a party to the Chicago Convention of 1944 or to any other general treaty which expressly recognizes national sovereignty in airspace. Nevertheless, the validity of the Soviet Union's claim of sovereignty over the airspace above its territory does not appear to have been ever challenged by any state. Conversely, the Soviet Union has not challenged the sovereignty of other states over the airspace above their respective territories. Soviet spokesmen, in fact, often dwell on the respect accorded by the Soviet Union to the airspace sovereignty of other states. The Soviet claim of sovereignty and jurisdiction in airspace, asserted diplomatically on numberless occasions, is explicitly made in the Soviet Air Code of 1935 in the following terms:

1. To the Union of S.S.R. belongs the full and exclusive sovereignty over the airspace of the Union of S.S.R. The airspace of the Union of S.S.R. means the airspace above the land and water territory of the Union of S.S.R. and over the coastal maritime zone established by the laws of the Union of S.S.R.

66. The laws and regulations in force in the Union of S.S.R. extend to foreign civil aircraft, their crews and passengers in flight in the airspace of the Union of S.S.R.

The failure of the United States to protest against the action of the Soviet authorities toward Powers and the plane he was flying provides additional evidence that national sovereignty in airspace is a rule of customary international law and that it applies to the Soviet Union.

But how far up does such sovereignty extend? Soviet law, like the legislation of other countries and the Chicago Convention, contains no definition of "airspace" or of the upward limit, if any, of national sovereignty. Many space vehicles launched by the United States Government have passed directly above Soviet territory at heights of more than 100 miles both during and after the International Geophysical Year without objection on the part of the Soviet Government; similarly, space vehicles launched by the Soviet Union have passed over the United States and many other nations, also without protest. Since the launching of Sputnik I in October, 1957, Soviet writers have been virtually unanimous in expressing the view that state sovereignty has or should have an upward limit and should not extend infinitely into space, but have not suggested any specific boundary between airspace which is under national sovereignty and outer space which is not. In these circumstances, Powers, as an individual on trial before a Soviet court, might well have pleaded ignorance of the upward extent of Soviet sovereignty in extenuation of his guilt; but the failure of the United States to rely on altitude in justification of the flight and to protest against the Soviet action in the U-2 incident suggests recognition that Soviet sovereignty extends upward to at least the altitude of the U-2 flights. Such recognition is implicit in President Kennedy's language in announcing his order against the resumption of U-2 flights: "Flights of American aircraft penetrating the air space of the Soviet Union have been suspended since May, 1960. I have ordered that they not be resumed." It is also apparent, explicitly or by implication, in the remarks of representatives of five states other than the U.S.S.R. in the U.N. Security Council debates concerning the two incidents. These states include Ceylon, Ecuador, Poland, Tunisia and, somewhat less clearly, Argentina.[1] The representatives of only three states (China, France and Italy) sought to minimize the importance of sovereignty in airspace by pointing to the launchings of space vehicles which pass over the territories of other states.[2] Thus, if the United States and the U.S.S.R. are included, not less than seven out of the eleven members of the Security Council appear to have recognized that Soviet sovereignty extends upward at least to the altitude of the U-2 flights.

The U-2 incident—and particularly the absence of a United States protest against the shooting down of the plane—further suggests that in some circumstances no previous warning or order to land is required by international law before an intruding foreign aircraft is shot down, even if the intruder does not itself attack or is likely to attack. On most occasions of real or alleged intrusion, including the RB-47 incident, the Soviet Union has asserted that the intruder was ordered to land or to turn away before it was shot down, or that the intruder opened fire first. The ostensible Soviet practice— whether or not actually followed—in previous instances of "intrusion" was described by Soviet Foreign Minister Gromyko as follows: "Soviet fighter planes never opened fire on invading United States aircraft first, and only when such aircraft themselves opened fire were our airmen compelled to return their fire."[3] Following the U-2 and RB-47 incidents, however, this alleged policy of "restraint" on the part of the Soviet Union—if it ever existed in fact—was apparently given up. During the debate on the RB-47 incident, the Soviet representative stated:

The Soviet Government is known to have given the order to its armed forces to shoot down American military aircraft, and any other aircraft, forthwith in the event of their violation of the airspace of the Soviet Union . . .[4]

It thus appears that the Soviet Union does not recognize any duty, at least under the conditions of a "cold war," to give warning or an order to land or turn away to an aerial intruder before shooting him down.

In its complaint to the Security Council, the Soviet Union alleged that the U-2 flights were "aggressive acts" by the United States and offered a draft resolution to that effect.[5] This draft resolution was rejected by a vote of 7 to 2 (Poland and U.S.S.R.), with 2 abstentions (Ceylon and Tunisia).[6] Instead, the Security Council, on May 27, 1960, adopted by 9 votes to 0, with 2 abstentions (Poland and U.S.S.R.),[7] a resolution[8] in which, *inter alia*, it expressed conviction "of the necessity to make every effort to restore and strengthen international good will and confidence, based on the established principles of international law," and appealed to all Member Governments "to respect each other's sovereignty, territorial integrity and political independence." In the course of the debate,[9] many representatives pointed out that the Security Council had to take into account the political aspects of the situation and not merely the legal merits of the dispute. In rebutting the Soviet charge of aggression, the United States cited Soviet secrecy, the danger of surprise attack, and the need to protect the non-Communist world against such attack. It also pointed to the numerous acts of espionage committed by Soviet agents in the United States and elsewhere. Nevertheless, it refrained from claiming a legal right to overfly the Soviet Union for reconnaissance purposes, and some representatives attached importance to the announcement of the United States that the U-2 flights over the U.S.S.R. had been discontinued. In these circumstances, the rejection by the Security Council of the Soviet charge against the United States does not warrant the drawing of any general legal conclusions, but it does suggest that deliberate intrusions of single unarmed aircraft for reconnaissance purposes need not be regarded in all cases as aggressive acts.

In the RB-47 incident, unlike the U-2 affair, the dispute between the United States and the Soviet Union was primarily about the facts. The Soviet Union alleged that the American plane, a United States Air Force patrol aircraft similar in type to a bomber, was shot down over Soviet territorial waters off the northern coast of the U.S.S.R. after it had deliberately intruded into Soviet airspace and disobeyed an order to land. The two surviving members of the crew were imprisoned in Soviet jails, apparently with a view to being brought to trial before a Soviet court, until January, 1961, when they were released and returned to the United States. The United States denied that the plane had at any time been closer than thirty miles to the Soviet coast, denounced the attack on it by Soviet forces as illegal, and demanded the release of the two survivors. It asserted that the plane had been engaged in electromagnetic observations over the Barents Sea, and that a Soviet fighter had tried to force it to enter Soviet airspace before shooting it down over the high seas.[10]

As in the U-2 affair, the Soviet Union complained to the Security Council of "aggressive acts" by the United States and offered a draft resolution condemning such acts.[11] This draft resolution failed of adoption by 2 votes (Poland and U.S.S.R.) to 9. A resolution proposed by the United States, recommending that the Soviet Union and the United States submit their differences arising out of the incident either to a fact-finding commission or to

the International Court of Justice,[12] obtained 9 favorable votes, but the negative vote of the U.S.S.R., operating as a veto, prevented its adoption.[13]

From the legal point of view, the most striking feature of the RB-47 incident is that none of the nations involved—the U.S.S.R., the United States, and the members of the U.N. Security Council which discussed the incident—either claimed or admitted the right of a state to shoot down a foreign aircraft over the high seas, even if it flies within close proximity of the state's territory and even if it is a military aircraft which may be engaged in military reconnaissance. In the course of the debates,[14] the representatives of several states, including the U.S.S.R., Argentina, Tunisia and Ceylon, suggested that flights close to the territorial sea of another country may be undesirable as possibly leading to incidents, but none asserted that this is a sufficient justification for shooting down the aircraft engaged in such flights. The representative of the United Kingdom expressly upheld the right to conduct such flights for reconnaissance purposes, and said that Soviet aircraft had engaged in such flights without being shot down. Most of the other representatives upheld the freedom of flight over the high seas without express reference to reconnaissance.

The 1960 debate was in many respects similar to another debate which took place in the Security Council in September, 1954, after an American patrol plane had been apparently shot down by the Soviets over the Sea of Japan. On that occasion, too, no participant in the debate asserted or admitted the right to shoot down foreign reconnaissance aircraft over the high seas, no matter how closely it approached to the territorial sea. Vyshinsky, the Soviet representative, stated:

Mr. Lodge said that the Soviet Union representative was apparently defending the right of the Soviet Union to shoot aircraft down over the high seas. If he had not made his speech in haste then I am sure Mr. Lodge would not have said that, for my whole argument on this question was concentrated on proving that the incident involving the Soviet and United States aircraft occurred over Soviet territory and not over the high seas. It is therefore absurd to suggest that I could be defending the right of any State to shoot aircraft down over the high seas.

It is others who wish to defend this right. We are opposed to it. . . .[15]

Occasional non-compliance in fact by the Soviet Union or other states with the principle of freedom of flight over the high seas does not weaken the legal force of the principle unless such non-compliance is claimed to be lawful.

Significantly, the existence or nonexistence of publicly proclaimed Air Defense Identification Zones (ADIZ), such as have been established over the high seas off the United States and Canada, does not appear to have been regarded as affecting the rights of a coastal state with respect to the freedom of flight over the high seas. In the debate on the RB-47 incident, only the Polish representative alluded to the existence of such zones off the United States, but even he refrained from suggesting that within such zones foreign aircraft could be lawfully shot down. The United States presented maps plainly showing that on several occasions in 1959 and 1960 Soviet military aircraft penetrated the Alaskan Coastal ADIZ and flew considerable distances within the zone. According to the uncontradicted statement of the American representative, no attempt was made by the United States forces to shoot down these aircraft. The Soviet Union does not appear to have ever publicly proclaimed any ADIZ's over the high seas.

That the Soviet Union purports to uphold the freedom of flight over the high seas was further made evident in February, 1961, after a Soviet transport plane carrying the Chairman of the Presidium of the Supreme Soviet and

other Soviet officials to Morocco had been intercepted by a French fighter over the Mediterranean Sea some eighty miles off the coast of Algeria, within what the French apparently call "the French zone of responsibility" or "zone of identification." The French fighter fired some warning shots, apparently in the belief that the Soviet plane had deviated from its flight plan and was flying too close to Algeria. The French also alleged that the plane had failed to reply to the fighter's request for identification. The Soviet Government sharply protested against the French action. It asserted that the plane had established radio contact with Algiers and was on course, but added:

But first of all it is permissible to ask: Who gave the French authorities the right to engage in "identification" of other states' aircraft flying in airspace over the high seas? It should be well known to the French Government that the generally accepted norms of international law provide for the freedom of flight in the airspace over the high seas, and no state, if it does not wish to be a violator of international laws, has the right to limit this freedom and to dictate arbitrarily for the aircraft of other states any routes over international waters.[16]

The French Government expressed regret over the incident.

The seemingly wide consensus, shared by the United States, the United Kingdom and the Soviet Union, as well as by smaller Powers, that a nation is not entitled to interfere with the movements of foreign aircraft (except, of course, in self-defense against an armed attack) over the high seas, even in a "contiguous zone" adjacent to its territorial sea, has interesting implications for the nascent law of outer space. If, as some have suggested, space beyond the airspace subject to national sovereignty should be regarded as analogous to the high seas, it would seem that subjacent states would not be entitled to interfere with the movements of foreign space vehicles in the space immediately above their national airspace on any theory of "contiguous zones." . . .

Notes

1. U.N. Security Council, 15th Year, Official Records, 858th, 859th, 861st, 863rd and 883rd Meetings (May 24–27 and July 26, 1960), Docs. S/P.V. 858, 859, 861, 863, 883.
2. *Ibid.,* 858th Meeting (May 24, 1960), Doc. S/P.V. 858.
3. *Ibid.,* 857th Meeting (May 23, 1960), Doc. S/P.V.857.
4. *Ibid.,* 880th Meeting (July 22, 1960), Doc. S/P.V.880.
5. U.N. Docs. S/4314 and S/4315; U.N. Security Council, 15th Year, Official Records, 857th Meeting (May 23, 1960), Doc. S/P.V.857.
6. *Ibid.,* 860th Meeting (May 26, 1960), Doc. S/P.V.860.
7. *Ibid.,* 863rd Meeting (May 27, 1960), Doc. S/P.V.863.
8. U.N. Doc. S/4328.
9. U.N. Security Council, 15th Year, Official Records, 857th to 863rd Meetings (May 23–27, 1960), Docs. S/P.V.857–863.
10. New York Times, July 13, 1960, Jan. 26, and March 4, 1961; 43 Dept. of State Bulletin 163–165, 209–212, 274–276 (1960); U.N. Security Council, 15th Year, Official Records, 880th to 883rd Meetings (July 22–26, 1960), Docs. S/P.V.880–883.
11. U.N. Docs. S/4384, S/4385 and S/4406.
12. U.N. Doc. S/4409/Rev. 1.
13. U.N. Security Council, 15th Year, Official Records, 883rd Meeting (July 26, 1960), Doc. S/P.V.883. Poland also voted against the U. S. draft resolution. The Soviet Union also vetoed a resolution proposed by Italy which would have expressed the hope that the International Committee of the Red Cross would be permitted to fulfill its tasks with respect to the members of the RB-47 crew.
14. U.N. Security Council, 15th Year, Official Records, *loc. cit.* note 10 above.
15. U.N. Security Council, 9th Year, Official Records, 679th and 680th Meetings (Sept. 10, 1954), Docs. S/P.V.679, 680. Freedom of flight over the high seas is affirmed in Art. 2 of the 1958 Geneva Convention on the High Seas, 52 A.J.I.L. 842 (1958); 38 Dept. of State Bulletin 1115 (1958).
16. Pravda (Moscow), Feb. 12, 1961. Translation.

Outer Space Treaty of 1966 *

The States Parties to this Treaty,

Inspired by the great prospects opening up before mankind as a result of man's entry into outer space,

Recognizing the common interest of all mankind in the progress of the exploration and use of outer space for peaceful purposes,

Believing that the exploration and use of outer space should be carried on for the benefit of all peoples irrespective of the degree of their economic or scientific development,

Desiring to contribute to broad international co-operation in the scientific as well as the legal aspects of the exploration and use of outer space for peaceful purposes,

Believing that such co-operation will contribute to the development of mutual understanding and to the strengthening of friendly relations between States and peoples,

Recalling resolution 1962 (XVIII), entitled "Declaration of Legal Principles Governing the Activities of States in the Exploration and Use of Outer Space", which was adopted unanimously by the United Nations General Assembly on 13 December 1963,

Recalling resolution 1884 (XVIII), calling upon States to refrain from placing in orbit around the earth any objects carrying nuclear weapons or any other kinds of weapons of mass destruction or from installing such weapons on celestial bodies, which was adopted unanimously by the United Nations General Assembly on 17 October 1963,

Taking account of United Nations General Assembly resolution 110 (II) of

* Reprinted from 55 *United States Department of State Bulletin* 953 (1966).

3 November 1947, which condemned propaganda designed or likely to provoke or encourage any threat to the peace, breach of the peace or act of aggression, and considering that the aforementioned resolution is applicable to outer space,

Convinced that a Treaty on Principles Governing the Activities of States in the Exploration and Use of Outer Space, including the Moon and Other Celestial Bodies, will further the Purposes and Principles of the Charter of the United Nations,

Have agreed on the following:

Article I

The exploration and use of outer space, including the moon and other celestial bodies, shall be carried out for the benefit and in the interests of all countries, irrespective of their degree of economic or scientific development, and shall be the province of all mankind.

Outer space, including the moon and other celestial bodies, shall be free for exploration and use by all States without discrimination of any kind, on a basis of equality and in accordance with international law, and there shall be free access to all areas of celestial bodies.

There shall be freedom of scientific investigation in outer space, including the moon and other celestial bodies, and States shall facilitate and encourage international co-operation in such investigation.

Article II

Outer space, including the moon and other celestial bodies, is not subject to national appropriation by claim of sovereignty, by means of use or occupation, or by any other means.

Article III

States Parties to the Treaty shall carry on activities in the exploration and use of outer space, including the moon and other celestial bodies, in accordance with international law, including the Charter of the United Nations, in the interest of maintaining international peace and security and promoting international co-operation and understanding.

Article IV

States Parties to the Treaty undertake not to place in orbit around the earth any objects carrying nuclear weapons or any other kinds of weapons of mass destruction, install such weapons on celestial bodies, or station such weapons in outer space in any other manner.

The moon and other celestial bodies shall be used by all States Parties to the Treaty exclusively for peaceful purposes. The establishment of military bases, installations and fortifications, the testing of any type of weapons and the conduct of military manoeuvres on celestial bodies shall be forbidden. The use of military personnel for scientific research or for any other peaceful purposes shall not be prohibited. The use of any equipment or facility necessary for peaceful exploration of the moon and other celestial bodies shall also not be prohibited.

Article V

States Parties to the Treaty shall regard astronauts as envoys of mankind in outer space and shall render to them all possible assistance in the event of accident, distress, or emergency landing on the territory of another State Party or on the high seas. When astronauts make such a landing, they shall be safely and promptly returned to the State of registry of their space vehicle.

In carrying on activities in outer space and on celestial bodies, the astronauts of one State Party shall render all possible assistance to the astronauts of other States Parties.

States Parties to the Treaty shall immediately inform the other States Parties to the Treaty or the Secretary-General of the United Nations of any phenomena they discover in outer space, including the moon and other celestial bodies, which could constitute a danger to the life or health of astronauts.

Article VI

States Parties to the Treaty shall bear international responsibility for national activities in outer space, including the moon and other celestial bodies, whether such activities are carried on by governmental agencies or by non-governmental entities, and for assuring that national activities are carried out in conformity with the provisions set forth in the present Treaty. The activities of non-governmental entities in outer space, including the moon and other celestial bodies, shall require authorization and continuing supervision by the State concerned. When activities are carried on in outer space, including the moon and other celestial bodies, by an international organization, responsibility for compliance with this Treaty shall be borne both by the international organization and by the States Parties to the Treaty participating in such organization.

Article VII

Each State Party to the Treaty that launches or procures the launching of an object into outer space, including the moon and other celestial bodies, and each State Party from whose territory or facility an object is launched, is internationally liable for damage to another State Party to the Treaty or to its natural or juridical persons by such object or its component parts on the Earth, in air space or in outer space, including the moon and other celestial bodies.

Article VIII

A State Party to the Treaty on whose registry an object launched into outer space is carried shall retain jurisdiction and control over such object, and over any personnel thereof, while in outer space or on a celestial body. Ownership of objects launched into outer space, including objects landed or constructed on a celestial body, and of their component parts, is not affected by their presence in outer space or on a celestial body or by their return to the Earth. Such objects or component parts found beyond the limits of the State Party to the Treaty on whose registry they are carried shall be returned to that State, which shall, upon request, furnish identifying data prior to their return.

Article IX

In the exploration and use of outer space, including the moon and other celestial bodies, States Parties to the Treaty shall be guided by the principle of co-operation and mutual assistance and shall conduct all their activities in outer space, including the moon and other celestial bodies, with due regard to the corresponding interests of all other States Parties to the Treaty. States Parties to the Treaty shall pursue studies of outer space, including the moon and other celestial bodies, and conduct exploration of them so as to avoid their harmful contamination and also adverse changes in the environment of the Earth resulting from the introduction of extraterrestrial matter and, where necessary, shall adopt appropriate measures for this purpose. If a State Party to the Treaty has reason to believe that an activity or experiment planned by it or its nationals in outer space, including the moon and other celestial bodies, would cause potentially harmful interference with activities of other States Parties in the peaceful exploration and use of outer space, including the moon and other celestial bodies, it shall undertake appropriate international consultations before proceeding with any such activity or experiment. A State Party to the Treaty which has reason to believe that an activity or experiment planned by another State Party in outer space, including the moon and other celestial bodies, would cause potentially harmful interference with activities in the peaceful exploration and use of outer space, including the moon and other celestial bodies, may request consultation concerning the activity or experiment.

Article X

In order to promote international co-operation in the exploration and use of outer space, including the moon and other celestial bodies, in conformity with the purposes of this Treaty, the States Parties to the Treaty shall consider on a basis of equality any requests by other States Parties to the Treaty to be afforded an opportunity to observe the flight of space objects launched by those States.

The nature of such an opportunity for observation and the conditions under which it could be afforded shall be determined by agreement between the States concerned.

Article XI

In order to promote international co-operation in the peaceful exploration and use of outer space, States Parties to the Treaty conducting activities in outer space, including the moon and other celestial bodies, agree to inform the Secretary-General of the United Nations as well as the public and the international scientific community, to the greatest extent feasible and practicable, of the nature, conduct, locations and results of such activities. On receiving the said information, the

Secretary-General of the United Nations should be prepared to disseminate it immediately and effectively.

Article XII

All stations, installations, equipment and space vehicles on the moon and other celestial bodies shall be open to representatives of other States Parties to the Treaty on a basis of reciprocity. Such representatives shall give reasonable advance notice of a projected visit, in order that appropriate consultations may be held and that maximum precautions may be taken to assure safety and to avoid interference with normal operations in the facility to be visited.

Article XIII

The provisions of this Treaty shall apply to the activities of States Parties to the Treaty in the exploration and use of outer space, including the moon and other celestial bodies, whether such activities are carried on by a single State Party to the Treaty or jointly with other States, including cases where they are carried on within the framework of international inter-governmental organizations.

Any practical questions arising in connexion with activities carried on by international inter-governmental organizations in the exploration and use of outer space, including the moon and other celestial bodies, shall be resolved by the States Parties to the Treaty either with the appropriate international organization or with one or more States members of that international organization, which are Parties to this Treaty.

Article XIV

1. This Treaty shall be open to all States for signature. Any State which does not sign this Treaty before its entry into force

in accordance with paragraph 3 of this article may accede to it at any time.

2. This Treaty shall be subject to ratification by signatory States. Instruments of ratification and instruments of accession shall be deposited with the Governments of the Union of Soviet Socialist Republics, the United Kingdom of Great Britain and Northern Ireland and the United States of America, which are hereby designated the Depositary Governments.

3. This Treaty shall enter into force upon the deposit of instruments of ratification by five Governments including the Governments designated as Depositary Governments under this Treaty.

4. For States whose instruments of ratification or accession are deposited subsequent to the entry into force of this Treaty, it shall enter into force on the date of the deposit of their instruments of ratification or accession.

5. The Depositary Governments shall promptly inform all signatory and acceding States of the date of each signature, the date of deposit of each instrument of ratification of and accession to this Treaty, the date of its entry into force and other notices.

6. This Treaty shall be registered by the Depositary Governments pursuant to Article 102 of the Charter of the United Nations.

Article XV

Any State Party to the Treaty may propose amendments to this Treaty. Amendments shall enter into force for each State Party to the Treaty accepting the amendments upon their acceptance by a majority of the States Parties to the Treaty and thereafter for each remaining State Party to the Treaty on the date of acceptance by it.

Article XVI

Any State Party to the Treaty may give notice of its withdrawal from the Treaty one year after its entry into force by written notification to the Depositary Governments. Such withdrawal shall take effect one year from the date of receipt of this notification.

* * *

Suggested Readings

Textbooks

Brierly. *The Law of Nations*, pp. 162–221.
Brownlie. *Principles of Public International Law*, pp. 98–225.
Fenwick. *International Law*, pp. 402–495.
Gould. *An Introduction to International Law*, pp. 347–370.
Jacobini. *International Law*, pp. 90–116.
Kaplan and Katzenbach. *The Political Foundations of International Law*, pp. 135–172.
Kelsen. *Principles of International Law*, pp. 307–343.
Sørensen. *Manual of Public International Law*, pp. 311–380.
Svarlien. *An Introduction to the Law of Nations*, pp. 155–228.
Tung. *International Law in an Organizing World*, pp. 144–189.
von Glahn. *Law Among Nations*, pp. 253–332.

Acquisition of Territory

Hill, Norman D. *Claims to Territory in International Law and Relations.* New York: Oxford University Press, 1945.

Jennings, R. Y. *The Acquisition of Territory in International Law.* Dobbs Ferry, N.Y.: Oceana, 1963.

Simsarian, James. "Inspection Experience Under the Antarctic Treaty and the International Atomic Energy Agency," 60 *American Journal of International Law* 502 (1966).

Taubenfeld, Howard J. "A Treaty for Antarctica," *International Conciliation* (January 1961).

Land Boundaries

Boggs, S. W. *International Boundaries.* New York: Columbia University Press, 1940.

Bouchez, L. C. "Fixing of Boundaries in International Boundary Rivers," 12 *International and Comparative Law Quarterly* 789 (1963).

Jones, Stephen B. *Boundary-Making.* Washington, D.C.: Carnegie Endowment for International Peace, 1945.

O'Connell, D. P. "International Law and Boundary Disputes," *Proceedings of the American Society of International Law* 77 (1960).

Maritime Territory

Dean, Arthur H. "The Geneva Conference on the Law of the Sea: What Was Accomplished," 52 *American Journal of International Law* 607 (1958).

Higgins, A. P., and C. J. Colombos. *The International Law of the Sea,* 4th ed. by C. J. Colombos. New York: Longmans, Green and Co., 1959.

McDougal, Myres S., and William T. Burke. *The Public Order of the Oceans: A Contemporary International Law of the Sea.* New Haven, Conn.: Yale University Press, 1962.

Mouton, M. W. *The Continental Shelf.* The Hague: Martinus Nijhoff, 1952.

Potter, Pitman B. *The Freedom of the Seas in History, Law and Politics.* New York: Longmans, Green and Co., 1924.

Whiteman, Marjorie M. "Conference on the Law of the Sea: Convention on the Continental Shelf," 52 *American Journal of International Law* 629 (1958).

Air Space and Outer Space

Crane, Robert D. "Soviet Attitude Toward International Space Law," 56 *American Journal of International Law* 685 (1962).

Jessup, Philip C., and Howard J. Taubenfeld. *Controls for Outer Space and the Antarctic Analogy.* New York: Columbia University Press, 1959.

Johnson, David. *Rights in Air Space.* Dobbs Ferry, N.Y.: Oceana, 1965.

McNair, Lord. *The Law of the Air,* 3rd ed. by M. R. E. Kerr and A. H. M. Evens. London: Stevens, 1964.

Wright, Quincy. "Legal Aspects of the U-2 Incident," 54 *American Journal of International Law* 836 (1960).

Chapter IV
Jurisdiction

TERRITORIAL JURISDICTION

The term "jurisdiction" refers to the legal competence of state officials to prescribe and enforce rules with regard to persons, things, and events. By distinguishing between those situations in which a state may exercise its jurisdiction and those situations in which it may not, international law serves to clarify the authority of officials and to minimize friction among states. The essence of the distinction is contained in the concept of state sovereignty, the principal corollaries of which are an exclusive jurisdiction over the territory of the state and a correlative duty of nonintervention in the area of exclusive jurisdiction of other states. With few exceptions, imposed by international law, a state has the legal authority to do whatever it wants inside its territory; persons and things situated within its borders are subject to the application of its laws and the judgments of its courts. The law was stated by Judge John Bassett Moore as follows:

It is an admitted principle of international law that a nation possesses and exercises within its own territory an absolute and exclusive jurisdiction, and that any exception to this right must be traced to the consent of the nation, either express or implied. . . . The benefit of this principle equally enures to all independent and sovereign States, and is attended with a corresponding responsibility for what takes place within the national territory. . . .

The principle of absolute and exclusive jurisdiction within the national territory applies to foreigners as well as to citizens or inhabitants of the country, and the foreigner can claim no exemption from the exercise of such jurisdiction, except so far as he may be able to show either: (1) that he is, by reason of some special immunity, not subject to the operation of the local law, or (2) that the local law is not in conformity with international law. No presumption of immunity arises from the fact that the person accused is a foreigner. . . .[1]

The principle of territorial supremacy is based largely on effective state power. but it is also supported by logic. It is generally agreed that states are primarily interested in conduct that affects persons and things situated within their borders, that jurisdiction should be linked to capacity to enforce judgments, and that the best possibilities for investigation are usually at the locale of the event being adjudicated. It is mainly for these reasons that governments enter into extradition agreements to provide for the return of persons who violate the laws of a state and then flee its territory.[2]

The territory over which a state may exercise its jurisdiction encompasses not only its land mass but also its national waters[3] and the air space above its land and water territory. In general, a state has the same legal authority over its national waters and air space that it has over its land territory. But there is an important limitation that international law places upon the authority of coastal states to control their national waters: foreign ships have a right to pass through the territorial sea of any state so long as such passage is innocent, that is to say, so long as "it is not prejudicial to the peace, good order, or security of the coastal state."[4] And, although a coastal state may, for security reasons, temporarily suspend the right of innocent passage in specified areas of its territorial sea, the 1958 Convention on the Territorial Sea and the Contiguous Zone unequivocally states that there "shall be no suspension of the innocent passage of foreign ships through straits which are used for international navigation between one part of the high seas and an-

other part of the high seas or the territorial sea of a foreign state."[5]

The high seas, which are all parts of the sea that are not included in the national waters of a state, and the air space above them are open to use by all states. This does not mean, however, that these areas, by being outside state territory, are outside the law. By an extension of the territorial principle, each state has jurisdiction over its own vessels upon, and its aircraft above, the high seas. The basic principle, as applied to ships, was stated by the Permanent Court of International Justice in the Lotus case:

. . . vessels on the high seas are subject to no authority except that of the State whose flag they fly. In virtue of the principle of the freedom of the seas, that is to say, the absence of any territorial sovereignty upon the high seas, no State may exercise any jurisdiction over foreign vessels upon them.[6]

The 1958 Convention on the High Seas codifies this basic principle and then goes on to recognize three customary exceptions to the exclusive jurisdiction of the flag state: piracy, "hot pursuit," and the slave trade.[7] Since pirates are offenders against the law of nations, they may be arrested by the warships of any state and brought into port for trial and punishment. Regarding "hot pursuit," the Convention permits a coastal state, with some specified limitations, to pursue a foreign ship on to the high seas when there is good reason to believe that

---

[1] Dissenting opinion in the Lotus case, *Permanent Court of International Justice,* Series A, No. 10 (1927), 68,88.
[2] For a discussion of extradition, see pp. 216–217.
[3] National waters include internal waters—rivers, lakes, bays, estuaries, and other enclosed sea areas—and the territorial sea.
[4] Convention on the Territorial Sea and the Contiguous Zone, Article 14, is reprinted in this section on pp. 198–200.

[5] *Ibid.,* Article 16. Authorites are divided over the question whether or not these provisions apply to the right of passage of warships in peacetime. The position of the Soviet Union was stated in a reserva.ion to the Convention: "To Article 23: (Subsection D. The Rule Applying to Warships) The Government of the USSR considers that a coastal state has the right to establish an authorization procedure for the passage of foreign warships through its territorial waters." Quoted in William E. Butler, "The Legal Regime of Russian Territorial Waters," 62 *American Journal of International Law* 65 (1968). The support of the Soviet view by many other states at the Geneva Conference suggests that "no international consensus has been reached on the passage of warships, notwithstanding a strict reading of the Convention." *Ibid.,* p. 69.
[6] Series A, No. 10.
[7] See the Convention on the High Seas, Articles 13–23, reprinted in this section on pp. 207–212.

the ship has broken its laws.[8] Finally, warships may stop and board foreign ships that are suspected of engaging in the slave trade.

Although a state may *take action to exercise its authority* only within its own territory, or in areas not forming part of the territory of any other state, it must be recognized that there are certain additional bases for the exercise of state jurisdiction. It is widely accepted, for example, that a state may determine the legal character of acts committed by its nationals outside the state's territorial limits. As Hall put it, the laws of a state

travel with them [its nationals] wherever they go, both within and without the jurisdiction of other powers. A state cannot enforce its laws within the territory of another state, but its subjects remain under an obligation not to disregard them . . . and it preserves the power of compelling observance by punishment if a person who has broken them returns within its jurisdiction.[9]

The first selection that follows, the 1965 Viet-Nam Decree on Sea Surveillance, illustrates the use by a coastal state of its jurisdictional authority to police the waters off its coast. Much of the wording of the decree is copied verbatim from the Convention on the Territorial Sea and the Contiguous Zone and the Convention on the High Seas. Two United Nations documents relating to the Cuban-United States fishing dispute of February 1964 are reprinted as an example of the many disputes that arise over charges that foreign vessels are fishing within the

territorial sea of a state. The controversial and highly volatile right of innocent passage is considered in : (1) excerpts from the Corfu Channel case, which is the leading judicial statement on the subject; (2) relevant sections of the Convention on the Territorial Sea and the Contiguous Zone; and (3) documents stating the positions of Israel and the United Arab Republic on the right of Israeli ships and other ships bound for Israel to use the Strait of Tiran, which is situated within the territorial sea of the United Arab Republic and serves as the only navigable connection between the Red Sea and the Gulf of Aqaba. Finally, the 1958 Geneva Convention on the High Seas and the 1958 Geneva Convention on Fishing and the Living Resources of the High Seas, which are now in force, are reprinted.

Viet-Nam Decree on Sea Surveillance*

Communique of the Ministry of Foreign Affairs, Republic of Viet-Nam, April 27, 1965

Due to the fact of a constant and increasing infiltration by sea into the Republic of Viet Nam of Viet Cong personnel, arms, ammunition and various war supplies,

the Prime Minister has signed Decree No 81 /NG of the 27th of April 1965, by which the following measures have been decided upon to ensure the security and the defence of the territorial waters of Viet-Nam:

I. The territorial waters up to the three mile limit is declared a defensive sea area. The passage of vessels through the territorial sea of the Republic of Viet Nam which is prejudicial to the peace, good

---

[8] On March 22, 1967, a Soviet shrimp trawler was spotted fishing, in violation of United States law, 5.5 miles east of Seal Cape in the Shumagins. After ten miles of "hot pursuit," a Coast Guard cutter boarded the trawler. The Russian captain was subsequently fined $10,000 by a United States District Court. *The New York Times*, March 27, 1967, p. 14; *ibid.*, March 26, 1967, p. 4.

[9] W. E. Hall, *A Treatise on International Law*, 8th ed. by A. P. Higgins (Oxford: Clarendon Press, 1924), pp. 56–57. Other principles used to justify jurisdiction, including the widely used objective territorial principle and the security principle, are discussed in the standard textbooks listed at the end of this chapter.

* Reprinted from 4 *International Legal Materials: Current Documents* 461 (1965) by permission of the American Society of International Law.

order or security of the Republic of Viet Nam is not considered as innocent passage and is forbidden by the law of the Republic of Viet Nam. Ships of any country operating within the territorial sea of the Republic of Viet Nam which are not clearly engaged in innocent passage are subject to visit and search, and may be subject to arrest and disposition, as provided by the law of the Republic of Viet Nam in conformity with accepted principles of international law.

Cargoes will be considered suspect unless it can be clearly established that they are destined for a port outside the Republic of Viet Nam or a legitimate recipient in the Republic of Viet Nam. Cargoes will be considered particularly suspect if containing any of the items listed below.

1. Weapons, ammunition, electrical and communications equipment.
2. Primer, mine, gunpowder and other explosives.
3. Chemical products which can serve military purposes. . . .
4. Medical supplies of Communist North Vietnam, Communist China or Soviet Bloc origin.
5. Foodstuffs of Communist North Vietnam, Communist China or Soviet Bloc origin.

II. The passage of vessels through the water contiguous to the territorial sea of the Republic of Vietnam up to twelve nautical miles from the baseline from which the breadth of the territorial sea is measured are subject to the control of the Republic of Viet Nam to the extent necessary to prevent or punish infringements of the customs, fiscal, immigration and sanitary regulations effective within the territory or territorial sea of the Republic of Viet Nam. Entry of materials and merchandises into the Republic of Viet Nam other than through recognized routes or ports of entry is forbidden by customs regulations of the Republic of Viet Nam.

Entry into the Republic of Vietnam of persons other than through recognized routes or ports of entry is forbidden by immigration regulations of the Republic of Vietnam. The Government of the Republic of Vietnam intends to enforce strictly these customs, fiscal and immigration regulations.

Accordingly, vessels within the contiguous zone suspected of preparing to aid in infringements of the customs, fiscal or immigration regulations of the Republic of Vietnam are subject to visit and search, and may be subject to arrest and disposition, as provided by the law of the Republic of Vietnam in conformity with accepted principles of international law.

III. It is the intention of the Republic of Vietnam to act beyond the 12 mile contiguous zone to prevent or punish any infringement of the laws of the Republic of Vietnam by vessels flying the flag of the Republic of Vietnam or reasonably believed to be South Vietnamese, though flying a foreign flag or refusing to show a flag; the action taken against such ships may include stopping, visiting, and searching. If the reasonable suspicions as to Vietnamese nationality prove unfounded and the vessel has not committed any act justifying these suspicions, the vessel will be permitted to continue with prompt and reasonable compensation paid by the Government of Vietnam for any loss or damage which may have been sustained.

IV. Vessels which are within the territory, the territorial sea or the contiguous zone of the Republic of Vietnam and which are suspected of infringing the above regulations within the territory or territorial sea of the Republic of Vietnam are subject to hot pursuit on the high seas as provided for in international law.

V. The Government of the Republic of Vietnam has requested and obtained the assistance of the Government of the U.S.A. for the full cooperation of the U.S. Navy with the Naval Forces of the Republic of Vietnam to enforce the new security and defense measures as ordered by the Prime Minister of the Republic of Vietnam.

Cuba-United States Fishing Dispute, February 1964*

[*On February 4, 1964, the Cuban Delegation to the United Nations transmitted to the President of the Security Council a note from Dr. Raul Róa, Cuban Minister for Foreign Affairs:*]

The Revolutionary Government of Cuba hereby denounces an act of intolerable aggression committed on the morning of 2 February by the Government of the United States of America, in that its naval forces boarded and seized four small Cuban fishing-vessels carrying out their operations peaceably in the fishing ground off the Dry Tortugas, in international waters, in strict compliance with the international regulations on the subject. The United States Government was notified in advance of this fishing operation, in an area which has always been used by Cuban fishermen, through the Swiss Embassy in Havana on 9 December 1963, in order to avoid any friction with the United States authorities likely to increase tensions in the Caribbean area. . . .

This demonstration of good intentions by our Government . . . was received by the United States Government in a manner inspired by its colonialist pride, which made it seek to restrict the area where Cuba had a right to obtain food from the sea . . . as if international law was not in our favour. The United States Government, in a most irregular communication, stated that it would feel concern at any Cuban fishing operation outside Cuban waters. The dispatch of our vessels to those waters, which are not the exclusive property of anybody, as you will be aware, is not only an act in exercise of our sovereignty in accordance with the juridical principles governing operations of this nature, but is also in obedience to the imperative of subsistence, to enable us to provide our people with the food they need and to develop our econ-

omy. To this attitude, the United States Government has responded by a typical act of piracy, which is a violation of the Charter of the United Nations, as it helps to aggravate the Caribbean crisis and constitutes a threat to international peace and security.

* * *

At 11 a.m. on 2 February this act of violence, whose end is not yet known, began. At that time a Coast Guard cutter of the United States Navy to the south east of Dry Tortuga threatened the fishing vessels *Lambda 33*, *Lambda 8*, *Cardenas 14* and *Cardenas 19* with its guns ordering them to go in closer to the shore and not to move for six hours, when they would receive further instructions. The fishing fleet was outside territorial waters; five miles off the coast of the Dry Tortugas in a fishing-ground always used by Cuban vessels for catching the fish known as sawfish.

At 6 p.m. on the same day another, larger vessel of the United States Navy appeared and lowered a boat containing many sailors and officers, who boarded the *Lambda 33*, asked for the ship's papers and took the crew list. Almost immediately afterwards other naval surface units and aircraft began to arrive and an officer again boarded the *Lambda 33* and stated that it was not to leave the area. At 8 p.m. another two gunboats appeared, increasing the pressure on our unarmed vessels, and while one of them kept our vessels illuminated and trained its calibre-30 machine-guns on them, the crew of the other boarded the fishing vessels and made a thorough search with detector apparatus, photographing not only the fishing tackle but also, as a measure of harassment, all the crew of the four vessels, one by one. This operation lasted the whole night, until 6 a.m. of 3 February, when another gunboat came up with eleven members of the United States Navy, who boarded the *Lambda 33*, ordering the crew to start up the engines and sail

*Reprinted from *United Nations Document* S/5530.

for a place that they would indicate. In these circumstances, then, surrounded by many warships, aircraft and helicopters, they made the whole fleet set off for Key West. Just as they had prevented any use of the radio on the *Lambda 33*, they placed a Coast Guard cutter behind the *Lambda 8* to jam its radio and prevent any communication with Cuba. . . .

We wish to draw the attention of the President of the Security Council to the fact that, in contrast to this crude act of piracy and display of force, the four Cuban vessels were manned almost entirely by young fishing-school students with their instructors, completely unarmed, who were on a training voyage to prepare technicians for our growing fleet.

At the present time the four vessels and the thirty-eight members of their crew are held at Key West naval base, in utter disregard of the principles of peace and tolerance on which the aims of the United Nations are based and with no respect for its purposes and principles, especially those relating to the equality of nations and self-determination of peoples.

The course of action adopted by the United States Government, first in threatening to use force and then in actually using it, its contempt for the international fishing agreements and its deliberate disregard for international law have created an extremely serious situation, which may appropriately be brought to the attention of the Security Council. . . .

[*On February 7, 1964, Ambassador Adlai E. Stevenson, United States Representative to the United Nations, responded to the Cuban charge in a letter to the President of the Security Council:**]

I refer to the letter sent to you by the Permanent Delegation of Cuba on February 4, 1964 (Document S/5530) protesting the alleged illegal seizure by the Government of the United States of four Cuban

* Reprinted from *United Nations Document* S/5532.

fishing boats in the area of the Dry Tortuga Island. In order that members of the Security Council will be properly informed on this matter, I am addressing this note to you to set forth the facts of the situation.

The facts of the case were communicated by my Government to the Government of Cuba in a note delivered on February 4, 1964, protesting the violation of the territorial sea of the United States by the Cuban fishing boats. The facts communicated and subsequent developments are as follows:

1. On February 2, 1964, four Cuban fishing vessels were observed by units of the United States Coast Guard to be fishing within the territorial sea (i.e., inside the three mile limit) of the United States off East Key in the Dry Tortugas.

2. The United States Coast Guard patrol craft ordered the Cuban vessels to anchor and stand by for boarding and search which they did. When they anchored, the various vessels were between 1.5 and 1.9 miles off East Key. Two of the masters of the fishing boats—Jose Manuel Ventura of the Cardenas No. 14 and Manuel Gomez Barrios of the Lambda No. 8 admitted to United States Coast Guard officials that they were knowingly fishing in United States waters.

3. On the morning of February 3, 1964, following a preliminary search of the vessels and questioning of their masters, the United States Coast Guard vessels brought the Cuban fishing boats to Key West for further investigation and interrogation in connection with violation of Federal law. The boarding, inspection and escort of the boats from East Key to Key West by personnel of the United States Coast Guard was conducted in the normal manner with due regard for the welfare of crews.

4. During this entire procedure and until such time as the four boats were within the naval base at Key West, they had unrestricted use of their radio communications. Clear evidence of this is to be found in the fact that conversations between the boats and Habana were monitored by commercial

monitoring services in the Florida area. Once the Cuban vessels had docked at Key West, they were at liberty to communicate with the Czechoslovakian Embassy in Washington, D. C., which is representing Cuban interests in the United States, had they chosen to do so.

5. Federal authorities completed their investigation and interrogation of the crews on February 5, 1964. The authorities concluded that the Cuban vessels were fishing in the territorial waters of the United States contrary to Section 251 of Title 46 of the United States Code. However, as this statute contains no sanctions, prosecution by Federal authorities was not undertaken.* At the same time, the Cuban fishing boats were also in probable violation of laws of the State of Florida and thus subject to prosecution by state authorities. State officials formally requested the United States Coast Guard to turn the boats and crews over to the jurisdiction of the state. In accordance with United States law, this was done on February 5, 1964. Legal proceedings before the state courts are pending.

6. Two crews' members have on their own initiative requested political asylum in the United States. This has been granted.

In summary, Mr. President, this is a case involving the unauthorized intrusion into the territorial sea of the United States in violation of international law and the laws of the United States. Those charged with the violation stand before the appropriate court where they will receive a fair trial surrounded by the full guarantees offered by the Constitution and laws of this country. I reject the political motives ascribed by the Cuban Government to the action which has been taken.

As the facts of the case demonstrate, there is absolutely no basis for the intemperate and distorted language in the Cuban

letter. I can only conclude that the purpose of the letter was to obscure the fact of the clear violation of international laws and of the laws of the United States.

[*On February 16, United States authorities returned crew members who were minors to Cuba. Two days later, the other crew members were arraigned before a Florida court, where the captains were fined $500 each. The fines were paid through the Embassy of Czechoslovakia, and the crews and boats were returned to Cuba on February 21.*]

The Corfu Channel Case (United Kingdom-Albania)*

International Court of Justice, 1949

[*Upon recommendation of the Security Council of the United Nations, this case was submitted to the International Court of Justice by a special agreement between Albania and Britain. The part of the decision reprinted here concerns the right of innocent passage through territorial water. See Chapter VI for additional excerpts from the decision.*]

* * *

In the second part of the Special Agreement, the following question is submitted to the Court:

"(2) Has the United Kingdom under international law violated the sovereignty of the Albanian People's Republic by reason of the acts of the Royal Navy in Albanian waters on the 22nd October . . .?"

On May 15th, 1946, the British cruisers *Orion* and *Superb*, while passing southward through the North Corfu Channel, were

---

* On May 20, 1964, the United States adopted an Act to Prohibit Fishing by Foreign Vessels in the Territorial Waters of the United States and in Certain Other Areas. The law provides that violators "shall be fined not more than $10,000 or imprisoned not more than one year, or both." Public Law 88–308, 78 Stat. 194.

* Reprinted from *International Court of Justice Reports* 4 (1949).

fired at by an Albanian battery in the vicinity of Saranda. It appears from the report of the commanding naval officer dated May 29th, 1946, that the firing started when the ships had already passed the battery and were moving away from it; that from 12 to 20 rounds were fired; that the firing lasted 12 minutes and ceased only when the ships were out of range; but that the ships were not hit although there were a number of "shorts" and of "overs". An Albanian note of May 21st states that the Coastal Commander ordered a few shots to be fired in the direction of the ships "in accordance with a General Order founded on international law".

The United Kingdom Government at once protested to the Albanian Government, stating that innocent passage through straits is a right recognized by international law. There ensued a diplomatic correspondence in which the Albanian Government asserted that foreign warships and merchant vessels had no right to pass through Albanian territorial waters without prior notification to, and the permission of, the Albanian authorities. This view was put into effect by a communication of the Albanian Chief of Staff, dated May 17th, 1946, which purported to subject the passage of foreign warships and merchant vessels in Albanian territorial waters to previous notification to and authorization by the Albanian Government. The diplomatic correspondence continued, and culminated in a United Kingdom note of August 2nd, 1946, in which the United Kingdom Government maintained its view with regard to the right of innocent passage through straits forming routes for international maritime traffic between two parts of the high seas. The note ended with the warning that if Albanian coastal batteries in the future opened fire on any British warship passing through the Corfu Channel, the fire would be returned.

The contents of this note were, on August

1st, communicated by the British Admiralty to the Commander-in-Chief, Mediterranean, with the instruction that he should refrain from using the Channel until the note had been presented to the Albanian Government. On August 10th, he received from the Admiralty the following telegram: "The Albanians have now received the note. North Corfu Strait may now be used by ships of your fleet, but only when essential and with armament in fore and aft position. If coastal guns fire at ships passing through the Strait, ships should fire back." On September 21st, the following telegram was sent by the Admiralty to the Commander-in-Chief, Mediterranean: "Establishment of diplomatic relations with Albania is again under consideration by His Majesty's Government who wish to know whether the Albanian Government have learnt to behave themselves. Information is requested whether any ships under your command have passed through the North Corfu Strait since August and, if not, whether you intend them to do so shortly." The Commander-in-Chief answered the next day that his ships had not done so yet, but that it was his intention that *Mauritius* and *Leander* and two destroyers should do so when they departed from Corfu on October 22nd.

It was in such circumstances that these two cruisers together with the destroyers *Saumarez* and *Volage* were sent through the North Corfu Strait on that date.

The Court will now consider the Albanian contention that the United Kingdom Government violated Albanian sovereignty by sending the warships through this Strait without the previous authorization of the Albanian Government.

It is, in the opinion of the Court, generally recognized and in accordance with international custom that States in time of peace have a right to send their warships through straits used for international navigation between two parts of the high seas without the previous authorization of a coastal State, provided that the passage is *innocent*. Unless otherwise prescribed in an international convention, there is no right for a coastal State to prohibit such passage through straits in time of peace.

The Albanian Government does not dispute that the North Corfu Channel is a strait in the geographical sense; but it denies that this Channel belongs to the class of international highways through which a right of passage exists, on the grounds that it is only of secondary importance and not even a necessary route between two parts of the high seas, and that it is used almost exclusively for local traffic to and from the ports of Corfu and Saranda.

It may be asked whether the test is to be found in the volume of traffic passing through the Strait or in its greater or lesser importance for international navigation. But in the opinion of the Court the decisive criterion is rather its geographical situation as connecting two parts of the high seas and the fact of its being used for international navigation. Nor can it be decisive that this Strait is not a necessary route between two parts of the high seas, but only an alternative passage between the Ægean and the Adriatic Seas. It has nevertheless been a useful route for international maritime traffic. In this respect, the Agent of the United Kingdom Government gave the Court the following information relating to the period from April 1st, 1936, to December 31st, 1937: "The following is the total number of ships putting in at the Port of Corfu after passing through or just before passing through the Channel. During the period of one year nine months, the total number of ships was 2,884. The flags of the ships are Greek, Italian, Roumanian, Yugoslav, French, Albanian and British. Clearly, very small vessels are included, as the entries for Albanian vessels are high, and of course one vessel may make several journeys, but 2,884 ships for a period of one year nine months is quite a large figure. These figures relate to vessels visited by the Customs at Corfu and so do not include the large number of vessels which went through the Strait without calling at Corfu at all." There were also regular sailings through the Strait by Greek vessels three times weekly, by a British ship fortnightly, and by two Yugoslav vessels weekly and by two others fortnightly. The Court is further informed that the British Navy has regularly used this Channel for eighty years or more, and that it has also been used by the navies of other States.

One fact of particular importance is that the North Corfu Channel constitutes a frontier between Albania and Greece, that a part of it is wholly within the territorial waters of these States, and that the Strait is of special importance to Greece by reason of the traffic to and from the port of Corfu.

Having regard to these various considerations, the Court has arrived at the conclusion that the North Corfu Channel should be considered as belonging to the class of international highways through which passage cannot be prohibited by a coastal State in time of peace.

On the other hand, it is a fact that the two coastal States did not maintain normal relations, that Greece had made territorial claims precisely with regard to a part of Albanian territory bordering on the Channel, that Greece had declared that she considered herself technically in a state of war with Albania, and that Albania, invoking the danger of Greek incursions, had considered it necessary to take certain measures of vigilance in this region. The Court is of opinion that Albania, in view of these exceptional circumstances, would have been justified in issuing regulations in respect of the passage of warships through the Strait, but not in prohibiting such passage or in subjecting it to the requirement of special authorization.

For these reasons the Court is unable to accept the Albanian contention that the Government of the United Kingdom has violated Albanian sovereignty by sending the warships through the Strait without having obtained the previous authorization of the Albanian Government.

In these circumstances, it is unnecessary to consider the more general question, much debated by the Parties, whether States under international law have a right to send warships in time of peace through territorial waters not included in a strait.

The Albanian Government has further contended that the sovereignty of Albania was violated because the passage of the British warships on October 22nd, 1946, was not an *innocent passage*. The reasons advanced in support of this contention may be summed up as follows: The passage was not an ordinary passage, but a political mission; the ships were manoeuvring and sailing in diamond combat formation with soldiers on board; the position of the guns was not consistent with innocent passage; the vessels passed with crews at action stations; the number of the ships and their armament surpassed what was necessary in order to attain their object and showed an intention to intimidate and not merely to pass; the ships had received orders to observe and report upon the coastal defences and this order was carried out.

It is shown by the Admiralty telegram of September 21st, cited above, and admitted by the United Kingdom Agent, that the object of sending the warships through the Strait was not only to carry out a passage for purposes of navigation, but also to test Albania's attitude. As mentioned above, the Albanian Government, on May 15th, 1946, tried to impose by means of gunfire its view with regard to the passage. As the exchange of diplomatic notes did not lead to any clarification, the Government of the United Kingdom wanted to ascertain by other means whether the Albanian Government would maintain its illegal attitude and again impose its view by firing at passing ships. The legality of this measure taken by the Government of the United Kingdom cannot be disputed, provided that it was carried out in a manner consistent with the requirements of international law. The "mission" was designed to affirm a right which had been unjustly denied. The Government of the United Kingdom was not bound to abstain from exercising its right of passage, which the Albanian Government had illegally denied.

It remains, therefore, to consider whether the *manner* in which the passage was carried out was consistent with the principle of innocent passage and to examine the various contentions of the Albanian Government in so far as they appear to be relevant.

When the Albanian coastguards at St. George's Monastery reported that the British warships were sailing in combat formation and were manoeuvring, they must have been under a misapprehension. It is shown by the evidence that the ships were not proceeding in combat formation, but in line, one after the other, and that they were not manoeuvring until after the first explosion. Their movements thereafter were due to the explosions and were made necessary in order to save human life and the mined ships. It is shown by the evidence of witnesses that the contention that soldiers were on board must be due to a misunderstanding probably arising from the fact that the two cruisers carried their usual detachment of marines.

It is known from the above-mentioned order issued by the British Admiralty on August 10th, 1946, that ships, when using the North Corfu Strait, must pass with armament in fore and aft position. That this order was carried out during the passage on October 22nd is stated by the Commander-in-Chief, Mediterranean, in a telegram of October 26th to the Admiralty. The guns were, he reported, "trained fore and aft, which is their normal position at sea in peace time, and were not loaded". It is confirmed by the commanders of *Saumarez* and *Volage* that the guns were in this position before the explosions. The navigating officer on board *Mauritius* explained that all guns on that cruiser were in their normal stowage position. The main guns were in the line of the ship, and the anti-aircraft guns were pointing outwards and up into the air, which is the normal position of these guns on a cruiser both in harbour and at sea. In the light of this evidence, the Court cannot accept the Albanian contention that the position of the guns was inconsistent with the rules of innocent passage.

In the above-mentioned telegram of October 26th, the Commander-in-Chief reported that the passage "was made with ships at action stations in order that they might be able to retaliate quickly if fired upon again". In view of the firing from the Albanian battery on May 15th, this measure of precaution cannot, in itself, be regarded as unreasonable. But four warships—two cruisers and two destroyers—passed in this manner, with crews at action stations, ready to retaliate quickly if fired upon. They passed one after another through this narrow channel, close to the Albanian coast, at a time of political tension in this region. The intention must have been, not only to test Albania's attitude, but at the same time to demonstrate such force that she would abstain from firing again on passing ships. Having regard, however, to all the circumstances of the case, as described above, the Court is unable to characterize these measures taken by the United Kingdom authorities as a violation of Albania's sovereignty.

* * *

Having thus examined the various contentions of the Albanian Government in so far as they appear to be relevant, the Court has arrived at the conclusion that the United Kingdom did not violate the sovereignty of Albania by reason of the acts of the British Navy in Albanian waters on October 22nd, 1946.

Convention on the Territorial Sea and the Contiguous Zones, 1958*

* * *

Section III. Right of Innocent Passage

SUB-SECTION A. RULES APPLICABLE TO
ALL SHIPS

Article 14

1. Subject to the provisions of these articles, ships of all States, whether coastal or not, shall enjoy the right of innocent passage through the territorial sea.

2. Passage means navigation through the territorial sea for the purpose either of traversing that sea without entering internal waters, or of proceeding to internal waters, or of making for the high seas from internal waters.

3. Passage includes stopping and anchoring, but only in so far as the same are incidental to ordinary navigation or are rendered necessary by *force majeure* or by distress.

4. Passage is innocent so long as it is not prejudicial to the peace, good order or security of the coastal State. Such passage shall take place in conformity with these articles and with other rules of international law.

5. Passage of foreign fishing vessels shall not be considered innocent if they do not observe such laws and regulations as the coastal State may make and publish in order to prevent these vessels from fishing in the territorial sea.

6. Submarines are required to navigate on the surface and to show their flag.

Article 15

1. The coastal State must not hamper innocent passage through the territorial sea.

* Reprinted from *United Nations Document* A/Conf. 13/L.52.

2. The coastal State is required to give appropriate publicity to any dangers to navigation, of which it has knowledge, within its territorial sea.

Article 16

1. The coastal State may take the necessary steps in its territorial sea to prevent passage which is not innocent.

2. In the case of ships proceeding to internal waters, the coastal State shall also have the right to take the necessary steps to prevent any breach of the conditions to which admission of those ships to those waters is subject.

3. Subject to the provisions of paragraph 4, the coastal State may, without discrimination amongst foreign ships, suspend temporarily in specified areas of its territorial sea the innocent passage of foreign ships if such suspension is essential for the protection of its security. Such suspension shall take effect only after having been duly published.

4. There shall be no suspension of the innocent passage of foreign ships through straits which are used for international navigation between one part of the high seas and another part of the high seas or the territorial sea of a foreign State.

Article 17

Foreign ships exercising the right of innocent passage shall comply with the laws and regulations enacted by the coastal State in conformity with these articles and other rules of international law and, in particular, with such laws and regulations relating to transport and navigation.

SUB-SECTION B. RULES APPLICABLE TO MERCHANT SHIPS

Article 18

1. No charge may be levied upon foreign ships by reason only of their passage through the territorial sea.

2. Charges may be levied upon a foreign ship passing through the territorial sea as payment only for specific services rendered to the ship. These charges shall be levied without discrimination.

Article 19

1. The criminal jurisdiction of the coastal State should not be exercised on board a foreign ship passing through the territorial sea to arrest any person or to conduct any investigation in connexion with any crime committed on board the ship during its passage, save only in the following cases:

a. If the consequences of the crime extend to the coastal State; or

b. If the crime is of a kind to disturb the peace of the country or the good order of the territorial sea; or

c. If the assistance of the local authorities has been requested by the captain of the ship or by the consul of the country whose flag the ship flies; or

d. If it is necessary for the suppression of illicit traffic in narcotic drugs.

2. The above provisions do not affect the right of the coastal State to take any steps authorized by its laws for the purpose of an arrest or investigation on board a foreign ship passing through the territorial sea after leaving internal waters.

3. In the cases provided for in paragraphs 1 and 2 of this article, the coastal State shall, if the captain so requests, advise the consular authority of the flag State before taking any steps, and shall facilitate contact between such authority and the ship's crew. In cases of emergency this notification may be communicated while the measures are being taken.

4. In considering whether or how an arrest should be made, the local authorities shall pay due regard to the interests of navigation.

5. The coastal State may not take any steps on board a foreign ship passing through the territorial sea to arrest any

person or to conduct any investigation in connexion with any crime committed before the ship entered the territorial sea, if the ship, proceeding from a foreign port, is only passing through the territorial sea without entering internal waters.

Article 20

1. The coastal State should not stop or divert a foreign ship passing through the territorial sea for the purpose of exercising civil jurisdiction in relation to a person on board the ship.

2. The coastal State may not levy execution against or arrest the ship for the purpose of any civil proceedings, save only in respect of obligations or liabilities assumed or incurred by the ship itself in the course or for the purpose of its voyage through the waters of the coastal State.

3. The provisions of the previous paragraph are without prejudice to the right of the coastal State, in accordance with its laws, to levy execution against or to arrest, for the purpose of any civil proceedings, a foreign ship lying in the territorial sea, or passing through the territorial sea after leaving internal waters.

SUB-SECTION C. RULES APPLICABLE TO GOVERNMENT SHIPS OTHER THAN WARSHIPS

Article 21

The rules contained in sub-sections A and B shall also apply to government ships operated for commercial purposes.

Article 22

1. The rules contained in sub-section A and in article 18 shall apply to government ships operated for non-commercial purposes.

2. With such exceptions as are contained in the provisions referred to in the preceding paragraph, nothing in these articles affects the immunities which such ships enjoy under these articles or other rules of international law.

SUB-SECTION D. RULES APPLICABLE TO WARSHIPS

Article 23

If any warship does not comply with the regulations of the coastal State concerning passage through the territorial sea and disregards any request for compliance which is made to it, the coastal State may require the warship to leave the territorial sea.

The Gulf of Aqaba Crisis, 1967

[*The Gulf of Aqaba, which is ninety-six miles long and about fifteen miles in breadth at its widest point, extends south from Israel to the Red Sea. Saudi Arabia controls the east coast of the gulf and the United Arab Republic controls the west coast, but Israel has a six-mile, and Jordan a four-mile, frontage at the northern end. The Strait of Tiran, a three-mile-wide waterway between Sharm el Sheikh in the Sinai Peninsula and the Island of Tiran, is the only navigable channel between the gulf and the Red Sea, and it is situated within the territorial waters of the United Arab Republic. The*

importance to Israel of its small strip of land on the gulf is difficult to exaggerate, particularly in light of the Egyptian closure of the Suez Canal to ships flying the Israeli flag and to ships of other states with cargoes bound for Israel. The Israeli port of Eilat, situated on the gulf, can serve international trade between Israel and East Africa, Southeast Asia, and East Asia. Eilat is joined to the Mediterranean Sea by a major system of highways, and the bulk of Israel's oil imports can reach her heavily populated areas by being sent through the pipeline that stretches from Eilat to Haifa. But for Eilat to serve

Israel, the Strait of Tiran must be open for her use.

From 1950 until 1956, the United Arab Republic kept the strait closed to Israeli shipping. Following the Israeli military successes during the Suez hostilities of 1956, however, Israeli troops were at Sharm el Sheikh and the strait was open for her use; and from 1957 until May 1967, units of the United Nations Emergency Force were deployed at Sharm el Sheikh and Israeli shipping freely entered and left the Gulf of Aqaba. Then, on May 23, 1967, after UNEF units were withdrawn at his request, President Nasser announced that the United Arab Republic had once again closed the strait to Israeli shipping. But United Arab Republic control of the strait was this time short-lived. Following the third Arab-Israeli war, Israel's forces were once again at Sharm el Sheikh and her ships were free to use the strait.

If this seesaw sequence of events illustrates anything, it is surely that military power, not international law, has controlled events in the intensely hostile relations of Arabs and Israelis. Nevertheless, the claims and counterclaims of the disputing states have been couched throughout in the terminology of international law, and it appears that any lasting settlement must eventually be based on the principles of international law. Such a settlement must await either the establishment of more amicable relations between Arabs and Israelis or a willingness on the part of the major powers to enforce legal rights in the Gulf of Aqaba. But which side does the law favor? The Israeli case is based on the customary right of innocent passage, as confirmed in the Corfu Channel case and codified in the Convention on the Territorial Sea and the Contiguous Zone; it also has the support of many other states, particularly the major maritime powers. On the other hand, the United Arab Republic is not without a legal leg to stand on, as is illustrated by the statement of Ambassador El Kony reprinted below.]

Position of Israel

Information Division, Ministry of Foreign Affairs, Jerusalem

* * *

On 1 March 1957, in the General Assembly, the Foreign Minister of Israel, Mrs. Golda Meir, responding to a call from the United Nations that it withdraw from the occupied area, declared the readiness of her Government to quit Sharm-el-Sheikh, the point on the mainland opposite Tiran Island, in the confidence that there would be continued freedom of navigation for international and Israeli shipping in the Gulf and through the Straits.

"We have repeatedly stated that Israel has no interest in the strip of land overlooking the western coast of the Gulf of Aqaba. Our sole purpose has been to ensure that, on the withdrawal of Israel forces, continued freedom of navigation will exist for Israel and international shipping in the Gulf of Aqaba and the Straits of Tiran. Such freedom of navigation is a vital national interest for Israel, but it is also of importance and legitimate concern to the maritime Powers and to many States whose economies depend upon trade and navigation between the Red Sea and the Mediterranean Sea.

* * *

The Government of Israel believes that the Gulf of Aqaba comprehends international waters and that no nation has the right to prevent free and innocent passage in the Gulf through the Straits giving access thereto, in accordance with the generally accepted definition of those terms in the law of the sea.

In its capacity as a littoral State, Israel will gladly offer port facilities to the ships of all nations and all flags exercising free passage in the Gulf of Aqaba. We have received with gratification the assurances of leading maritime Powers that they foresee a normal and regular flow of traffic of all cargoes in the Gulf of Aqaba.

Israel will do nothing to impede free and innocent passage by ships of Arab countries bound to Arab ports or to any other destination.

Israel is resolved on behalf of vessels of Israel registry to exercise the right of free and innocent passage and is prepared to join with others to secure universal respect of this right.

Israel will protect ships of its own flag exercising the right of free and innocent passage on the high seas and in international waters.

Interference, by armed force, with ships of Israel flag exercising free and innocent passage in the Gulf of Aqaba and through the Straits of Tiran, will be regarded by Israel as an attack entitling it to exercise its inherent right of self-defence under Article 51 of the Charter and to take all such measures as are necessary to ensure the free and innocent passage of its ships in the Gulf and in the Straits.

We make this announcement in accordance with the accepted principles of international law under which all States have an inherent right to use their forces to protect their ships and their rights against interference by armed force. My Government naturally hopes that this contingency will not occur.

In a public address on 20 February, President Eisenhower stated:

'We should not assume that, if Israel withdraws, Egypt will prevent Israeli shipping from using the Suez Canal, or the Gulf of Aqaba.'

This declaration has weighed heavily with my Government in determining its action today.

Israel is now prepared to withdraw its forces from the Gulf of Aqaba and the Straits of Tiran in the confidence that there will be continued freedom of navigation for international and Israeli shipping in the Gulf of Aqaba and through the Straits of Tiran."

* * *

Appendix

The attitude of the world's maritime States concerning the principle and practice of free navigation through the Straits of Tiran and in the Gulf of Aqaba was publicly expressed both before and after Israel's announcement on 1 March 1957. In a State Department memorandum dated 11 February 1957; at a press conference given by Secretary of State Dulles on 19 February; and in an address to the American people by President Eisenhower, the next day, the United States Government went on record as recognizing the international character of these waters and as being prepared to exercise the right of free passage therein. The position of fourteen other nations—including Great Britain, France, Holland, Italy, Norway and other important maritime Powers—was clarified from the rostrum of the General Assembly on 1 March, 4 March and 8 March 1957.

GOVERNMENTAL STATEMENTS

United States of America. "The United States believes that the Gulf comprehends international waters and that no nation has the right to prevent free and innocent passage in the Gulf and through the Straits giving access thereto. We have in mind not only commercial usage, but the passage of pilgrims on religious missions, which should be fully respected. The United States recalls that, on 28 January 1950, the Egyptian Ministry of Foreign Affairs informed the United States that the Egyptian occupation of the two islands of Tiran and Sanafir at the entrance of the Gulf of Aqaba was only to protect the islands themselves against possible damage or violation and that 'this occupation being in no way conceived in a spirit of obstructing in any way innocent passage through the stretch of water separating these two islands from the Egyptian coast of Sinai, it follows that this passage, the only practicable one, will remain free as in the past, in conformity with international practice and recognized principles of the law of nations.' In the absence of some overriding decision to the contrary, as by the International Court of Justice, the United States, on behalf of vessels of United States registry, is prepared to exercise the right of free and innocent passage and to join with others to secure general recognition of this right."

(From State Department memorandum of 11 February 1957)

* * *

France. "The French Government considers that the Gulf of Aqaba, on the one hand because of its width and on the other hand because of the fact that its coast belongs to four different States, constitutes international waters. Therefore, we consider that, in accordance with international law, freedom of navigation must be ensured in this Gulf and through the straits which lead into it. Under these circumstances, no country has the right to prevent free and innocent passage of ships of whatever nationality or type. The French Government, for its part, has the intention of making effective use of its right of free navigation in the Gulf of Aqaba and the Straits of Tiran. It considers that any obstruction put forth to free passage would be in contradiction to international law and would, in consequence, open the possibility of resort to measures which are authorized under Article 51 of the Charter of the United Nations. In this connection, it would specify that none of the littoral States of the Gulf of Aqaba, in its view, is in a state of belligerency with any other State, and that in this connection the position of

Israel is in perfect conformity with international law. . . ."

(From a statement by Mr. Georges-Picot of France at the General Assembly, 1 March 1957)

* * *

United Kingdom. "I listened the other day with great attention when the representative of India, Mr. Krishna Menon, argued that the Straits of Tiran was not an international waterway. Although I admired the ingenuity of his reasoning and the wealth of his examples, I fear that I could not follow him to his conclusions. For he overlooked one fact simple enough in itself but, as I see it, essential to consideration of this problem: the fact that—unlike the fjords of Norway or the Hudson Bay in Canada, or the Hudson River here in New York, or any of the other instances which Mr. Menon quoted—the Gulf of Aqaba is not only bounded at its narrow point of entry, that is, the Straits of Tiran, by two different countries, Egypt and Saudi Arabia, but contains at its head the ports of two further countries: Jordan and Israel. This simple, undeniable fact is in itself enough to put it in a different category from any of the inland waters mentioned by Mr. Krishna Menon. It is the view of Her Majesty's Government in the United Kingdom that the Straits of Tiran must be regarded as an international waterway, through which the vessels of all nations have a right of passage. Her Majesty's Government will assert this right on behalf of all British shipping. They are prepared to join with others to secure general recognition of this right. Now we all, of course, assume that when Israel's forces are withdrawn from the Sharm-el-Sheikh area, units of the United Nations Emergency Force will be stationed there, and there is no reason to think that any attempt will be made to interfere with free and innocent passage through the Straits. . . ."

(From a statement by Commander Noble of the United Kingdom, at the General Assembly, 4 March 1957)

Netherlands. "The Netherlands Government is in full agreement with the statements made by Isreal [sic], the United States, France and a number of other countries to the effect that passage through the Straits of Tiran should be free, open and unhindered for the ships of all nations. My Government bases its opinion on the following reasons: First, the Gulf of Aqaba, inasmuch as it is bordered by four different States and has a width in excess of the three-mile strip of territorial waters of the four littoral States on either side, is under the rules of international law to be regarded as part of the open seas. Second, the Straits of Tiran consequently are, in the legal sense, straits connecting two open seas, normally used for international navigation. Third, in regard to such straits, there is a right of free passage even if the straits are so narrow that they fall entirely within the territorial waters of one or more States. This rule was acknowledged by the International Court of Justice in the case of the Corfu Channel and also by the International Law Commission in its report of 1956. Fourth, if a strait falls entirely within the territorial waters of one or more of the littoral States, there is still a right of innocent passage, but then the littoral States have the right, if necessary, to verify the innocent character of the passage. Fifth, this right of verification, however, does not exist in those cases where the Strait connects two parts of the open sea. It must, therefore, be concluded that all States have the right of free and unhampered passage for their vessels through the Strait of Tiran."

(From a statement by Dr. Schurmann of the Netherlands, at the General Assembly, 4 March 1957)

* * *

Position of the United Arab Republic*

Statement Delivered by Ambassador Mohamed Awad El Kony Before the Security Council of the United Nations on May 29, 1967

* * *

As the members of the Council are well aware the Gulf of Aqaba is a long narrow gulf on the eastern side of the Sinai Peninsula. The length of the Gulf is about ninety-six miles and the widest breadth less than fifteen miles. The entrance to the Gulf is situated in the joint territorial waters of Saudi Arabia and the United Arab Republic. Due to navigational hazards the only navigable route to the Gulf runs less than one mile from the Sinai Peninsula. Hence, it crosses our undisputed territorial waters.

The Israelis claim that they have the right to navigate in the Gulf. This we proclaim is without foundation. A cogent reply which refutes the allegation of the Israelis rests on the following facts:

Historically, the Gulf has been under continued and uninterrupted Arab domination for over one thousand years. It always has been a national inland waterway subject to absolute Arab sovereignty. Its geographical location is conclusive proof of its national character. By its configuration it has a nature of a *mare clausum* which does not belong to the class of international waterways. An accepted norm of international law is that some bays with more than one littoral State are not considered open sea due to geographical and historical conditions. An international tribunal adjudicating a similar gulf case in Central America reached that conclusion—a conclusion which was recognized by several countries, including the United States. In 1917, the International Court of the Central American Republics ruled that the Gulf of

* Reprinted from a press release, United Arab Republic Mission to the United Nations.

Fonseca, which is surrounded by three countries—Honduras, El Salvador and Nicaragua—"is a historic bay possessed of the characteristics of a closed sea" and that it therefore was "part of the territories of El Salvador, Honduras, and Nicaragua."

Hence, it was decided that the three littoral countries are entitled to exclude the vessels of other countries when at war. Therefore, as I have already said, since the Gulf of Aqaba has only three legitimate littoral States, namely, Saudi Arabia, Jordan and the United Arab Republic, all of which are in a state of war with Israel the three legitimate littoral States on the Gulf of Aqaba have a right recognized by public international law to ban the vessels of an enemy.

It certainly will be argued that the Israelis have a port on the Gulf. But even that presence lacks legitimate foundation.

The Israeli armed forces on 10 March 1949 usurped and occupied the village of Om Rashrash, along with a stretch of about five miles overlooking the Gulf of Aqaba. This . . . occurred four months after the Security Council decision calling on all parties concerned to desist from further military actions and territorial accruement. This illegal act was perpetrated two weeks after the signing of the Egyptian-Israeli General Armistice Agreement on 24 February 1949. This action completely and drastically violated the letter and spirit of the Agreement, Article IV, paragraph 1 of which stipulates explicitly that:

"The principle that no military or political advantage should be gained under the truce ordered by the Security Council is recognized."

It is also relevant to read out paragraph 2 of Article IV of the Armistice Agreement:

"It is also recognized that the basic purposes and spirit of the Armistice would not be served by the restoration of previously held military positions, changes from those now held other than as specifically provided for in this Agreement, or by the advance of the military forces of either side beyond positions held at the time this Armistice Agreement is signed."

Furthermore, this illegal occupation of that port in Palestine and the advance of the Israeli armed forces was put before the Egyptian-Israeli Mixed Armistice Commission, whose Special Committee decided on the matter on 20 March 1950. This was further examined by the Security Council which in its resolution of 17 November 1950 stated that the Council:

"Takes note of the statement of the Government of Israel that Israel armed forces will evacuate Bir Qattar pursuant to the 20 March 1950 decision of the Special Committee provided for in Article X, paragraph 4, of the Egyptian-Israel General Armistice Agreement, and that the Israel armed forces will withdraw to positions authorized by the Armistice Agreement." (*Security Council Resolution 89 (1950)*)

In this respect, I would like to clarify that the reference to Bir Qattar includes the vicinity of Om Rashrash which the Israelis called "Elath" after their illegal occupation of the territory. This Israeli occupation violated also the Security Council resolution of 15 July 1948, ordering the parties "pursuant to Article 40 of the Charter, to desist from further military action" (*Security Council Resolution 54 (1948)*). It also violated the resolution adopted by the Council on 19 August 1948, in which it was stated that "No party is entitled to gain military or political advantage through violation of the truce" (*Security Council Resolution 56 (1948)*).

In fact, this Israeli action violated decisions of the Security Council, including that of 15 July 1948, which invoked Article 40 and therefore, according to the Charter, should have entailed the application against Israel of the enforcement action provided for in Chapter VII.

In view of these specific orders, Israel's possession of the coastal strip does not entitle it to any legal claim to sovereignty. This is in conformity with the well-established doctrine in international law that belligerent occupation cannot legally be converted into sovereignty over the occupied territory. An occupant, according to international law, and I quote Oppenheim, Volume II, page 433, "in no wise acquires sovereignty over such territory through the mere fact of having occupied it." Annexing a territory occupied by military force can have legal effects only if the state of war ends by the conclusion of a peace treaty. This view was held by the United States, as portrayed in 1932 by the United States Secretary of State Henry Stimson, who declared that the United States "cannot admit the legality of any situation *de facto*." Therefore it would be natural for the United States Government to abide by this doctrine in its international relations. This doctrine was also incorporated in several international multilateral treaties such as the treaty signed in Rio de Janeiro on 10 October 1933 and at the seventh Pan American Conference in December 1933.

Thus the Arabs' consistent refusal to accept Israel's claim to authority over the coastal strip is in strict conformity with the Stimson doctrine of non-recognition. It is ironic that the United States position in the matter under consideration is contrary to that doctrine.

In the light of these facts, it is quite obvious that the Israeli authorities have no legitimate right to be present on the shores of Aqaba since no legal right or claim, in either municipal or international law, could be based on illegal actions. Moreover, I wish to state that, according to international law, a state of war confers certain rights upon the belligerents. Also, it is a general incontestable law that the conclusion of a partial or general armistice agreement does not end the state of war. It only terminates the hostilities.

Oppenheim states that armistices and truces are

"all agreements between belligerent forces for a temporary cessation of hostilities. They are in no wise . . . to be called temporary peace, because the condition of war remains between the belligerents themselves and between the belligerents and neutrals, on all points beyond the mere cessation of the hostilities. In spite of such cessation, the right of visit and search over neutral merchantmen therefore remains intact, as does likewise the right to capture neutral vessels attempting to break a blockade, and the right to seize contraband of war." (*Oppenheim International Law, Seventh Edition, Vol. II, p. 746*)

Basing ourselves on either legal facts, as we shall read them from the provisions of the General Armistice Agreement, or the facts of life in our part of the world, as we have been witnessing them through the years, there is no shade of a doubt as to the continued existence of the state of war between the Israelis and both the Arabs of Palestine and their brethren in the Arab countries.

* * *

The continued violations and the numerous premeditated acts of aggression in all dimensions, against the Arabs, which culminated in the cowardly attack on Sinai in 1956, clearly mean that a state of overt war has been existing. Hence my Government has the legitimate right, in accordance with international law, to impose restrictions on navigation in the Strait of Tiran with respect to shipping to an enemy.

After this rather lengthy elaboration, it is quite evident and unequivocal that according to international law a state of belligerency exists between the Arab States whose territories circumscribe the entirety of the Gulf of Aqaba, and Israel. The Armistice Agreement does not vitiate our rights to impose restrictions on the navigation in the Gulf of Aqaba.

The 1956 aggression did not change the legal status of the Gulf of Aqaba and consequently did not affect the United Arab Republic's rights over its territorial waters. . . .

* * *

The attitude of the United Arab Republic Government regarding navigation in the Gulf of Aqaba is not new. In 1950 the Egyptian and Saudi Arabian Governments decided that since the entrance to the Gulf was in their joint territorial waters, it was incumbent upon both Governments to preclude enemy vessels from ingress into and egress from the Gulf. Egyptian troops established military installations to exclude all Israeli naval traffic and bar strategic material from reinforcing its war effort.

This practice has been scrupulously maintained since 1950. The Egyptian Government sent two memoranda to the United States and United Kingdom Embassies in Cairo, on 30 January and 28 February 1950 respectively, informing them of the decision to occupy the islands of Tiran and Sinafir and to protect the two islands and the entrance of the Gulf.

Furthermore, the Government of Egypt declared its intention to guarantee "free and innocent passage according to International Law." This obviously could never be construed to guarantee "free and innocent passage" to an enemy during a state of war. . . .

* * *

Geneva Convention on the High Seas, 1958*

Article 1

The term "high seas" means all parts of the sea that are not included in the territorial sea or in the internal waters of a State.

Article 2

The high seas being open to all nations, no State may validly purport to subject any part of them to its sovereignty. Freedom of the high seas is exercised under the conditions laid down by these articles and by the

* Reprinted from *United Nations Document* A/Conf. 13/L.53.

other rules of international law. It comprises, *inter alia,* both for coastal and non-coastal States:

1. Freedom of navigation;
2. Freedom of fishing;
3. Freedom to lay submarine cables and pipelines;
4. Freedom to fly over the high seas.

These freedoms, and others which are recognized by the general principles of international law, shall be exercised by all States with reasonable regard to the interests of other States in their exercise of the freedom of the high seas.

Article 3

1. In order to enjoy the freedom of the seas on equal terms with coastal States, States having no sea-coast should have free access to the sea. To this end States situated between the sea and a State having no sea-coast shall by common agreement with the latter and in conformity with existing international conventions accord:

a. To the State having no sea-coast, on a basis of reciprocity, free transit through their territory; and
b. To ships flying the flag of that State treatment equal to that accorded to their own ships, or to the ships of any other States, as regards access to seaports and the use of such ports.

2. States situated between the sea and a State having no sea-coast shall settle, by mutual agreement with the latter, and taking into account the rights of the coastal State or State of transit and the special conditions of the State having no sea-coast, all matters relating to freedom of transit and equal treatment in ports, in case such States are not already parties to existing international conventions.

Article 4

Every State, whether coastal or not, has the right to sail ships under its flag on the high seas.

Article 5

1. Each State shall fix the conditions for the grant of its nationality to ships, for the registration of ships in its territory, and for the right to fly its flag. Ships have the nationality of the State whose flag they are entitled to fly. There must exist a genuine link between the State and the ship; in particular, the State must effectively exercise its jurisdiction and control in administrative, technical and social matters over ships flying its flag.

2. Each State shall issue to ships to which it has granted the right to fly its flag documents to that effect.

Article 6

1. Ships shall sail under the flag of one State only and, save in exceptional cases expressly provided for in international treaties or in these articles, shall be subject to its exclusive jurisdiction on the high seas. A ship may not change its flag during a voyage or while in a port of call, save in the case of a real transfer of ownership or change of registry.

2. A ship which sails under the flags of two or more States, using them according to convenience, may not claim any of the nationalities in question with respect to any other State, and may be assimilated to a ship without nationality.

Article 7

The provisions of the preceding articles do not prejudice the question of ships employed on the official service of an intergovernmental organization flying the flag of the organization.

Article 8

1. Warships on the high seas have complete immunity from the jurisdiction of any State other than the flag State.

2. For the purposes of these articles, the term "warship" means a ship belonging to the naval forces of a State and bearing the external marks distinguishing warships of its nationality, under the command of an officer duly commissioned by the government and whose name appears in the Navy List, and manned by a crew who are under regular naval discipline.

Article 9

Ships owned or operated by a State and used only on government non-commercial service shall, on the high seas, have complete immunity from the jurisdiction of any State other than the flag State.

Article 10

1. Every State shall take such measures for ships under its flag as are necessary to ensure safety at sea with regard *inter alia* to:
a. The use of signals, the maintenance of communications and the prevention of collisions;
b. The manning of ships and labour conditions for crews taking into account the applicable international labour instruments;
c. The construction, equipment and seaworthiness of ships.

2. In taking such measures each State is required to conform to generally accepted international standards and to take any steps which may be necessary to ensure their observance.

Article 11

1. In the event of a collision or of any other incident of navigation concerning a ship on the high seas, involving the penal or disciplinary responsibility of the master or of any other person in the service of the ship, no penal or disciplinary proceedings may be instituted against such persons except before the judicial or administrative

authorities either of the flag State or of the State of which such person is a national.

2. In disciplinary matters, the State which has issued a master's certificate or a certificate of competence or licence shall alone be competent, after due legal process, to pronounce the withdrawal of such certificates, even if the holder is not a national of the State which issued them.

3. No arrest or detention of the ship, even as a measure of investigation, shall be ordered by any authorities other than those of the flag State.

Article 12

1. Every State shall require the master of a ship sailing under its flag, in so far as he can do so without serious danger to the ship, the crew or the passengers:
a. To render assistance to any person found at sea in danger of being lost;
b. To proceed with all possible speed to the rescue of persons in distress if informed of their need of assistance, in so far as such action may reasonably be expected of him;
c. After a collision, to render assistance to the other ship, her crew and her passengers and, where possible, to inform the other ship of the name of his own ship, her port of registry and the nearest port at which she will call.

2. Every coastal State shall promote the establishment and maintenance of an adequate and effective search and rescue service regarding safety on and over the sea and—where circumstances so require—by way of mutual regional arrangements co-operate with neighbouring States for this purpose.

Article 13

Every State shall adopt effective measures to prevent and punish the transport of slaves in ships authorized to fly its flag, and to prevent the unlawful use of its flag for that purpose. Any slave taking refuge on board any ship, whatever its flag, shall, *ipso facto*, be free.

Article 14

All States shall co-operate to the fullest possible extent in the repression of piracy on the high seas or in any other place outside the jurisdiction of any State.

Article 15

Piracy consists of any of the following acts:

1. Any illegal acts of violence, detention or any act of depredation, committed for private ends by the crew or the passengers of a private ship or a private aircraft, and directed:
a. On the high seas, against another ship or aircraft, or against persons or property on board such ship or aircraft;
b. Against a ship, aircraft, persons or property in a place outside the jurisdiction of any State;

2. Any act of voluntary participation in the operation of a ship or of an aircraft with knowledge of facts making it a pirate ship or aircraft;

3. Any act of inciting or of intentionally facilitating an act described in sub-paragraph 1 or sub-paragraph 2 of this article.

Article 16

The acts of piracy, as defined in article 15, committed by a warship, government ship or government aircraft whose crew has mutinied and taken control of the ship or aircraft are assimilated to acts committed by a private ship.

Article 17

A ship or aircraft is considered a pirate ship or aircraft if it is intended by the persons in dominant control to be used for the purpose of committing one of the acts referred to in article 15. The same applies if the ship or aircraft has been used to commit any such act, so long as it remains under the control of the persons guilty of that act.

Article 18

A ship or aircraft may retain its nationality although it has become a pirate ship or aircraft. The retention or loss of nationality is determined by the law of the State from which such nationality was derived.

Article 19

On the high seas, or in any other place outside the jurisdiction of any State, every State may seize a pirate ship or aircraft, or a ship taken by piracy and under the control of pirates, and arrest the persons and seize the property on board. The courts of the State which carried out the seizure may decide upon the penalties to be imposed, and may also determine the action to be taken with regard to the ships, aircraft or property, subject to the rights of third parties acting in good faith.

Article 20

Where the seizure of a ship or aircraft on suspicion of piracy has been effected without adequate grounds, the State making the seizure shall be liable to the State the nationality of which is possessed by the ship or aircraft, for any loss or damage caused by the seizure.

Article 21

A seizure on account of piracy may only be carried out by warships or military aircraft, or other ships or aircraft on government service authorized to that effect.

Article 22

1. Except where acts of interference derive from powers conferred by treaty, a warship which encounters a foreign merchant ship on the high seas is not justified in boarding her unless there is reasonable ground for suspecting:
a. That the ship is engaged in piracy; or
b. That the ship is engaged in the slave trade; or
c. That, though flying a foreign flag or refusing to show its flag, the ship is, in reality, of the same nationality as the warship.

2. In the cases provided for in subparagraphs a, b and c above, the warship may proceed to verify the ship's right to fly its flag. To this end, it may send a boat under the command of an officer to the suspected ship. If suspicion remains after the documents have been checked, it may proceed to a further examination on board the ship, which must be carried out with all possible consideration.

3. If the suspicions prove to be unfounded, and provided that the ship boarded has not committed any act justifying them, it shall be compensated for any loss or damage that may have been sustained.

Article 23

1. The hot pursuit of a foreign ship may be undertaken when the competent authorities of the coastal State have good reason to believe that the ship has violated the laws and regulations of that State. Such pursuit must be commenced when the foreign ship or one of its boats is within the internal waters or the territorial sea or the contiguous zone of the pursuing State, and may only be continued outside the territorial sea or the contiguous zone if the pursuit has not been interrupted. It is not necessary that, at the time when the foreign ship within the territorial sea or the contiguous zone receives the order to stop, the ship giving the order should likewise be within

the territorial sea or the contiguous zone. If the foreign ship is within a contiguous zone, as defined in article 24 of the Convention on the Territorial Sea and the Contiguous Zone, the pursuit may only be undertaken if there has been a violation of the rights for the protection of which the zone was established.

2. The right of hot pursuit ceases as soon as the ship pursued enters the territorial sea of its own country or of a third State.

3. Hot pursuit is not deemed to have begun unless the pursuing ship has satisfied itself by such practicable means as may be available that the ship pursued or one of its boats or other craft working as a team and using the ship pursued as a mother ship are within the limits of the territorial sea, or as the case may be within the contiguous zone. The pursuit may only be commenced after a visual or auditory signal to stop has been given at a distance which enables it to be seen or heard by the foreign ship.

4. The right of hot pursuit may be exercised only by warships or military aircraft, or other ships or aircraft on government service specially authorized to that effect.

5. Where hot pursuit is effected by an aircraft:

a. The provisions of paragraphs 1 to 3 of this article shall apply *mutatis mutandis*;
b. The aircraft giving the order to stop must itself actively pursue the ship until a ship or aircraft of the coastal State, summoned by the aircraft, arrives to take over the pursuit, unless the aircraft is itself able to arrest the ship. It does not suffice to justify an arrest on the high seas that the ship was merely sighted by the aircraft as an offender or suspected offender, if it was not both ordered to stop and pursued by the aircraft itself or other aircraft or ships which continue the pursuit without interruption.

6. The release of a ship arrested within the jurisdiction of a State and escorted to a port of that State for the purposes of an inquiry before the competent authorities may not be claimed solely on the ground that the ship, in the course of its voyage, was escorted across a portion of the high seas, if the circumstances rendered this necessary.

7. Where a ship has been stopped or arrested on the high seas in circumstances which do not justify the exercise of the rights of hot pursuit, it shall be compensated for any loss or damage that may have been thereby sustained.

Article 24

Every State shall draw up regulations to prevent pollution of the seas by the discharge of oil from ships or pipelines or resulting from the exploitation and exploration of the seabed and its subsoil, taking account of existing treaty provisions on the subject.

Article 25

1. Every State shall take measures to prevent pollution of the seas from the dumping of radio-active waste, taking into account any standards and regulations which may be formulated by the competent international organizations.

2. All States shall co-operate with the competent international organizations in taking measures for the prevention of pollution of the seas or air space above, resulting from any activities with radio-active materials or other harmful agents.

Article 26

1. All States shall be entitled to lay submarine cables and pipelines on the bed of the high seas.

2. Subject to its right to take reasonable measures for the exploration of the continental shelf and the exploitation of its natural resources, the coastal State may not impede the laying or maintenance of such cables or pipelines.

3. When laying such cables or pipelines the State in question shall pay due regard to

cables or pipelines already in position on the seabed. In particular, possibilities of repairing existing cables or pipelines shall not be prejudiced.

Article 27

Every State shall take the necessary legislative measures to provide that the breaking or injury by a ship flying its flag or by a person subject to its jurisdiction of a submarine cable beneath the high seas done wilfully or through culpable negligence, in such a manner as to be liable to interrupt or obstruct telegraphic or telephonic communications, and similarly the breaking or injury of a submarine pipeline or high-voltage power cable shall be a punishable offence. This provision shall not apply to any break or injury caused by persons who acted merely with the legitimate object of saving their lives or their ships, after having taken all necessary precautions to avoid such break or injury.

Article 28

Every State shall take the necessary legislative measures to provide that, if persons subject to its jurisdiction who are the owners of a cable or pipeline beneath the high seas, in laying or repairing that cable or pipeline, cause a break in or injury to another cable or pipeline, they shall bear the cost of the repairs.

Article 29

Every State shall take the necessary legislative measures to ensure that the owners of ships who can prove that they have sacrificed an anchor, a net or any other fishing gear, in order to avoid injuring a submarine cable or pipeline, shall be indemnified by the owner of the cable or pipeline, provided that the owner of the ship has taken all reasonable precautionary measures beforehand.

* * *

Geneva Convention on Fishing and Conservation of the Living Resources of the High Seas, 1958*

Article 1

1. All States have the right for their nationals to engage in fishing on the high seas subject (a) to their treaty obligations, (b) to the interests and rights of coastal States as provided for in this Convention, and (c) to the provisions contained in the following articles concerning conservation of the living resources of the high seas.

2. All States have the duty to adopt, or to co-operate with other States in adopting, such measures for their respective nationals as may be necessary for the conservation of the living resources of the high seas.

Article 2

As employed in this Convention, the expression "conservation of the living resources of the high seas" means the aggregate of the measures rendering possible the optimum sustainable yield from those resources so as to secure a maximum supply of food and other marine products. Conservation programmes should be formulated with a view to securing in the first place a supply of food for human consumption.

Article 3

A State whose nationals are engaged in fishing any stock or stocks of fish or other living marine resources in any area of the high seas where the nationals of other States are not thus engaged shall adopt, for its own nationals, measures in that area when necessary for the purpose of the conservation of the living resources affected.

* Reprinted from *United Nations Document* A/Conf. 13/L.54.

Article 4

1. If the nationals of two or more States are engaged in fishing the same stock or stocks of fish or other living marine resources in any area or areas of the high seas, these States shall, at the request of any of them, enter into negotiations with a view to prescribing by agreement for their nationals the necessary measures for the conservation of the living resources affected.

2. If the States concerned do not reach agreement within twelve months, any of the parties may initiate the procedure contemplated by article 9.

Article 5

1. If, subsequent to the adoption of the measures referred to in articles 3 and 4, nationals of other States engage in fishing the same stock or stocks of fish or other living marine resources in any area or areas of the high seas, the other States shall apply the measures, which shall not be discriminatory in form or in fact, to their own nationals not later than seven months after the date on which the measures shall have been notified to the Director-General of the Food and Agriculture Organization of the United Nations. The Director-General shall notify such measures to any State which so requests and, in any case, to any State specified by the State initiating the measure.

2. If these other States do not accept the measures so adopted and if no agreement can be reached within twelve months, any of the interested parties may initiate the procedure contemplated by article 9. Subject to paragraph 2 of article 10, the measures adopted shall remain obligatory pending the decision of the special commission.

Article 6

1. A coastal State has a special interest in the maintenance of the productivity of the living resources in any area of the high seas adjacent to its territorial sea.

2. A coastal State is entitled to take part on an equal footing in any system of research and regulation for purposes of conservation of the living resources of the high seas in that area, even though its nationals do not carry on fishing there.

3. A State whose nationals are engaged in fishing in any area of the high seas adjacent to the territorial sea of a State shall, at the request of that coastal State, enter into negotiations with a view to prescribing by agreement the measures necessary for the conservation of the living resources of the high seas in that area.

4. A State whose nationals are engaged in fishing in any area of the high seas adjacent to the territorial sea of a coastal State shall not enforce conservation measures in that area which are opposed to those which have been adopted by the coastal State, but may enter into negotiations with the coastal State with a view to prescribing by agreement the measures necessary for the conservation of the living resources of the high seas in that area.

5. If the States concerned do not reach agreement with respect to conservation measures within twelve months, any of the parties may initiate the procedure contemplated by article 9.

Article 7

1. Having regard to the provisions of paragraph 1 of article 6, any coastal State may, with a view to the maintenance of the productivity of the living resources of the sea, adopt unilateral measures of conservation appropriate to any stock of fish or other marine resources in any area of the high seas adjacent to its territorial sea, provided that negotiations to that effect with the other States concerned have not led to an agreement within six months.

2. The measures which the coastal State

adopts under the previous paragraph shall be valid as to other States only if the following requirements are fulfilled:

a. That there is a need for urgent application of conservation measures in the light of the existing knowledge of the fishery;
b. That the measures adopted are based on appropriate scientific findings;
c. That such measures do not discriminate in form or in fact against foreign fishermen.

3. These measures shall remain in force pending the settlement, in accordance with the relevant provisions of this Convention, of any disagreement as to their validity.

4. If the measures are not accepted by the other States concerned, any of the parties may initiate the procedure contemplated by article 9. Subject to paragraph 2 of article 10, the measures adopted shall remain obligatory pending the decision of the special commission.

5. The principles of geographical demarcation as defined in article 12 of the Convention on the Territorial Sea and the Contiguous Zone shall be adopted when coasts of different States are involved.

Article 8

1. Any State which, even if its nationals are not engaged in fishing in an area of the high seas not adjacent to its coast, has a special interest in the conservation of the living resources of the high seas in that area, may request the State or States whose nationals are engaged in fishing there to take the necessary measures of conservation under articles 3 and 4 respectively, at the same time mentioning the scientific reasons which in its opinion make such measures necessary, and indicating its special interest.

2. If no agreement is reached within twelve months, such State may initiate the procedure contemplated by article 9.

Article 9

1. Any dispute which may arise between States under articles 4, 5, 6, 7 and 8 shall, at the request of any of the parties, be submitted for settlement to a special commission of five members, unless the parties agree to seek a solution by another method of peaceful settlement, as provided for in Article 33 of the Charter of the United Nations.

2. The members of the commission, one of whom shall be designated as chairman, shall be named by agreement between the States in dispute within three months of the request for settlement in accordance with the provisions of this article. Failing agreement they shall, upon the request of any State party, be named by the Secretary-General of the United Nations, within a further three-month period, in consultation with the States in dispute and with the President of the International Court of Justice and the Director-General of the Food and Agriculture Organization of the United Nations, from amongst well-qualified persons being nationals of States not involved in the dispute and specializing in legal, administrative or scientific questions relating to fisheries, depending upon the nature of the dispute to be settled. Any vacancy arising after the original appointment shall be filled in the same manner as provided for the initial selection.

3. Any State party to proceedings under these articles shall have the right to name one of its nationals to the special commission, with the right to participate fully in the proceedings on the same footing as a member of the commission, but without the right to vote or to take part in the writing of the commission's decision.

4. The commission shall determine its own procedure, assuring each party to the proceedings a full opportunity to be heard and to present its case. It shall also determine how the costs and expenses shall be divided between the parties to the dispute,

failing agreement by the parties on this matter.

5. The special commission shall render its decision within a period of five months from the time it is appointed unless it decides, in case of necessity, to extend the time limit for a period not exceeding three months.

6. The special commission shall, in reaching its decisions, adhere to these articles and to any special agreements between the disputing parties regarding settlement of the dispute.

7. Decisions of the commission shall be by majority vote.

Article 10

1. The special commission shall, in disputes arising under article 7, apply the criteria listed in paragraph 2 of that article. In disputes under articles 4, 5, 6 and 8, the commission shall apply the following criteria, according to the issues involved in the dispute:

(a) Common to the determination of disputes arising under articles 4, 5 and 6 are the requirements:

i. That scientific findings demonstrate the necessity of conservation measures;

ii. That the specific measures are based on scientific findings and are practicable; and

iii. That the measures do not discriminate, in form or in fact, against fishermen of other States;

(b) Applicable to the determination of disputes arising under article 8 is the requirement that scientific findings demonstrate the necessity for conservation measures, or that the conservation programme is adequate, as the case may be.

2. The special commission may decide that pending its award the measures in dispute shall not be applied, provided that, in the case of disputes under article 7, the measures shall only be suspended when it is apparent to the commission on the basis of *prima facie* evidence that the need for the urgent application of such measures does not exist.

Article 11

The decisions of the special commission shall be binding on the States concerned and the provisions of paragraph 2 of Article 94 of the Charter of the United Nations shall be applicable to those decisions. If the decisions are accompanied by any recommendations, they shall receive the greatest possible consideration.

Article 12

1. If the factual basis of the award of the special commission is altered by substantial changes in the conditions of the stock or stocks of fish or other living marine resources or in methods of fishing, any of the States concerned may request the other States to enter into negotiations with a view to prescribing by agreement the necessary modifications in the measures of conservation.

2. If no agreement is reached within a reasonable period of time, any of the States concerned may again resort to the procedure contemplated by article 9 provided that at least two years have elapsed from the original award.

Article 13

1. The regulation of fisheries conducted by means of equipment embedded in the floor of the sea in areas of the high seas adjacent to the territorial sea of a State may be undertaken by that State where such fisheries have long been maintained and conducted by its nationals, provided that non-nationals are permitted to participate in such activities on an equal footing with nationals except in areas where such fisheries have by long usage been exclusively enjoyed by such nationals. Such regulations will not, however, affect the general status of the areas as high seas.

2. In this article, the expression "fisheries conducted by means of equipment embedded in the floor of the sea" means those fisheries using gear with supporting members embedded in the sea floor, constructed on a site and left there to operate permanently or, if removed, restored each season on the same site.

Article 14

In articles 1, 3, 4, 5, 6 and 8, the term "nationals" means fishing boats or craft of any size having the nationality of the State concerned, according to the law of that State, irrespective of the nationality of the members of their crews.

* * *

EXTRADITION

The inability of a state to exercise its jurisdiction within the territory of another state would seriously undermine the maintenance of law and order if there were no international cooperation in the administration of justice. The awareness among national decision-makers of the social necessity of jurisdictional cooperation is illustrated by the widespread practice of returning a person who is accused or who has been convicted of a crime to the state in which the crime was committed.[1] This surrender, known as "extradition," is not required by customary international law, but by numerous bilateral treaties; the return of a fugitive from justice in the absence of a specific treaty obligation is an act of comity, not of law.[2]

Lack of uniformity in the hundreds of bilateral extradition treaties now in force makes it impossible to state any general rule of international law on the subject. It is possible only to suggest some of the more common practices. Extradition treaties usually list as "extradatable offenses" only those offenses that are considered by both parties to be of such importance as to bring at least one year imprisonment upon conviction, and they normally specify that the fugitive may be tried only for the offense, or offenses, for which he was surrendered. Most states refuse to commit themselves to extradite their own nationals or any person charged with "political crimes," that is to say, crimes committed for political purposes or crimes that are politically motivated. The difficulty of applying the political crimes exception is obviously a problem that regularly plagues the courts.[3]

The extradition procedure is initiated by

[1] States cooperate in other jurisdictional matters, for example, by compelling testimony from persons within their territory for use in foreign courts. Requests for these depositions are so regularly honored that Charles Fenwick can write, with considerable justification, that the practice "may be said to approximate closely to a rule of customary international law." Fenwick, *International Law*, p. 399.

[2] "The principles of international law recognize no right to extradition apart from treaty. While a government may, if agreeable to its own constitution and laws, voluntarily exercise the power to surrender a fugitive from justice to the country from which he fled . . . the legal right to demand his extradition and the correlative duty to surrender him to the demanding state exist only when created by treaty." Factor v. Laubenheimer 290 U.S. 276 (1933).

[3] On July 2, 1968, a London court decided that James Earl Ray should be returned to the United States to stand trial as the accused assassin of Dr. Martin Luther King, Jr. The principal argument of Ray's attorney was that, since Dr. King was "a political figure," his murder was a political crime and, consequently, not an extraditable offense. This defense was based on the provision of the British-United States Extradition Treaty of 1931 which states that "a fugitive criminal shall not be surrendered if the crime or the offense in respect of which his surrender is demanded is one of a political character." But the argument of David Calcutt, the barrister who represented the United States, was decisive: "A lone murder of a politician, still less of a mere public figure, cannot satisfy the definition of an offense of a political character. . . . There is not one shred of evidence here to show that the killing took place to further a larger enterprise. There is no evidence of a conspiracy. . . . It is no doubt said that there is an undertone in this case of a conspiracy, but all the evidence is of a lone assassin." Mr. Frank Milton, the chief metropolitan magistrate, agreed with Mr. Calcutt's view of the evidence and what it meant for the political crime argument. The decision was not appealed. *The New York Times*, July 3, 1968, pp. 1 and 16.

a diplomatic request, followed usually by a judicial hearing to determine whether or not a *prima facie* evidence of guilt exists. Whether or not there is occasion for a judicial hearing, however, it is common practice to leave the final determination of whether to extradite to the political officials responsible for the conduct of foreign policy.

The first two documents that follow, the United States-Venezuela Extradition Treaty and the case of *Jimenez v. Aristeguieta*, provide a case study on extradition that includes an effort to resist return on the grounds of the political crimes exception. The final document, the case of *Coumas v. The Superior Court of San Joaquin County*, illustrates the importance of the nationality of the fugitive from justice in the extradition process.

United States-Venezuela Extradition Treaty, 1922*

* * *

The United States of America and the United States of Venezuela, desiring to strengthen their reciprocal relations, to facilitate the course of punitive justice and to limit the crimes which may be committed in their respective territories; to prevent the impunity which would result from the escape of guilty persons and of their asylum in the territory of one or the other nation, have resolved to conclude a Treaty for the extradition of the accused as well as of those who have been sentenced, . . .

Article I

The Government of the United States of America and the Government of the

* Reprinted from 43 *United States Statutes at Large* 1698.

United States of Venezuela agree to deliver up to justice, by means of requisition duly made as herein provided, any person who may be charged with or may have been convicted of any of the crimes committed within the jurisdiction of one of the Contracting Parties and specified in Article II of this Convention, while said person was actually within such jurisdiction when the crime was committed, and who shall seek an asylum or who shall be found within the territories of the other. Such surrender shall take place only upon such evidence of guilt as, according to the laws of the country in which the fugitive or accused shall be found, would justify his detention and commitment for trial if the crime or offense had been committed there.

Article II

In accordance with the provisions of this Convention, the persons shall be delivered who shall have been charged with or convicted of any of the following crimes:

1. Murder, comprehending the crimes designated by the terms of parricide, assassination, manslaughter, when voluntary; poisoning or infanticide.

2. The attempt to commit murder.

3. Rape, abortion, carnal knowledge of children under the age of twelve years.

4. Bigamy.

5. Arson.

6. Willful and unlawful destruction or obstruction of railroads, which endangers human life.

7. Crimes committed at sea:

a. Piracy, as commonly known and defined by the law of nations, or by statute;

b. Wrongfully sinking or destroying a vessel at sea, or attempting to do so.

c. Mutiny or conspiracy by two or more members of the crew or other persons on board of a vessel on the high seas, for the purpose of rebelling against the authority of the captain or commander of such vessel or by fraud or violence taking possession of such vessel;

d. Assault on board ships upon the high seas with intent to do bodily harm.

8. Burglary, defined to be the act of breaking into and entering the house of another in the night time with intent to commit a felony therein.

9. The act of breaking into and entering into the offices of the Government and public authorities, or the offices of banks, banking houses, saving banks, trust companies, insurance companies, or other buildings not dwellings with intent to commit a felony therein.

10. Robbery, defined to be the act of feloniously and forcibly taking from the person of another, goods or money by violence or by putting him in fear.

11. Forgery or the utterance of forged papers, or illegal sale of documents belonging to the national archives.

12. The forgery or falsification of the official acts of the Government or public authority, including courts of justice, or the uttering or fraudulent use of the same.

13. The fabrication of counterfeit money, whether coin or paper, counterfeit titles or coupons of public debt, created by national, state, provincial, territorial, local or municipal governments, banknotes or other instruments of public credit, counterfeit seals, stamps, dies and marks of state or public administrations, and the utterance, circulation, or fraudulent use of the above mentioned objects.

14. Embezzlement or criminal malversation committed within the jurisdiction of one of the parties by public officers or depositaries, where the amount embezzled exceeds 200 dollars in the United States of America or B. 1.000 in the United States of Venezuela.

15. Embezzlement by any person or persons hired, salaried or employed, to the detriment of their employers or principals, when the crime or offense is punishable by imprisonment or other corporal punishment by the laws of both countries, and where the amount embezzled exceeds 200 dollars in the United States of America or B. 1.000 in the United States of Venezuela.

16. Kidnapping of minors or adults, defined to be the abduction or detention of a person or persons, in order to exact money from them or their families, or for any other unlawful end.

17. Larceny, defined to be the theft of effects, personal property, or money, of the value of 50 dollars or B. 250 or more, accordingly.

18. Obtaining money, valuable securities or other property by false pretenses or receiving any money, valuable securities or other property knowing the same to have been unlawfully obtained, where the amount of money or the value of the property so obtained or received exceeds 200 dollars in the United States of America or B 1.000 in the United States of Venezuela.

19. Perjury or subornation of perjury.

20. Fraud or breach of trust by a bailee, banker, agent, factor, trustee, executor, administrator, guardian, director, or officer of any company or corporation, or by any one in any fiduciary position, where the amount of money or the value of the property misappropriated exceeds 200 dollars in the United States of America or B. 1.000 in the United States of Venezuela.

21. The extradition is also to take place for participation in any of the aforesaid crimes as an accessory before or after the fact, provided such participation be punishable by imprisonment by the laws of both Contracting Parties.

Article III

The provisions of this Convention shall not import claim of extradition for any crime or offense of a political character, nor for acts connected with such crimes or offenses; and no person surrendered by or to either of the Contracting Parties in virtue of this Convention shall be tried or punished for a political crime or offense. When the offense charged comprises the act either of murder or assassination or of poisoning, either consummated or attempted, the fact that the offense was committed or attempted against the life of the sovereign or head of a foreign state or against the life of any member of his family, shall not be deemed sufficient to sustain that such a crime or offense was of a political character, or was an act connected with crimes or offenses of a political character.

Article IV

In view of the abolition of capital punishment and of imprisonment for life by Constitutional provision in Venezuela, the Contracting Parties reserve the right to decline to grant extradition for crimes punishable by death and life imprisonment. Nevertheless, the Executive Authority of each of the Contracting Parties shall have the power to grant extradition for such crimes upon the receipt of satisfactory assurances that in case of conviction the death penalty or imprisonment for life will not be inflicted.

Article V

A fugitive criminal shall not be surrendered under the provisions hereof, when, from lapse of time or other lawful cause, according to the laws of the country within the jurisdiction of which the crime was committed, the criminal is exempt from prosecution or punishment for the offense for which the surrender is asked.

* * *

Article VIII

Under the stipulations of this Convention, neither of the Contracting Parties shall be bound to deliver up its own citizens.

* * *

Article XI

The stipulations of this Convention shall be applicable to all territories wherever situated, belonging to either of the Contracting Parties or under the jurisdiction or control of either of them.

Applications for the surrender of fugitives shall be made by the respective diplomatic agents of the Contracting Parties. In case of the absence of such agents from the country or its seat of government, or where extradition is sought from territory included in the preceding paragraph other than the United States, application may be made by superior consular officers.

It shall be competent for such diplomatic or superior Consular officers to ask and obtain the preliminary arrest of the person whose surrender is requested, before the Government of whom such request is made. The judicial functionaries shall prescribe the method of complying with the legal formalities of the country of which the extradition is requested.

If the fugitive criminal shall have been convicted of the crime for which his surrender is asked, a copy of the sentence of the court before which such conviction took place, duly authenticated, shall be produced. If, however, the fugitive is merely charged with crime, a duly authenticated copy of the warrant of arrest in the country where the crime was committed, and of the depositions upon which such warrant may have been issued, shall be produced, with such other evidence or proof as may be deemed competent in the case.

* * *

Article XIV

No person shall be tried for any crime or offense other than that for which he was surrendered.

Jimenez v. Aristeguieta*

*United States Court of Appeals,
Fifth Circuit, 1962*

* * *

Venezuela's Second Amended Complaint, upon which the extradition proceeding and orders under attack were based, charged appellant, chief executive of Venezuela (first as a member of a three-man junta, then as provisional President, and later as President), having legal responsibility for the administration of the funds and contracting authority of Venezuela, with two distinct groups of crimes committed in Venezuela during the years 1948–1958, the first group composed of four charges of murder and participation in murder as an accessory before the fact, the second group comprised financial crimes for his own private personal gain. The financial crimes are separately and independently charged in the complaint and are based on certain alleged transactions briefly summarized as follows:

1. The appellant secured commissions or kickbacks in ten specific instances on Venezuelan Government contracts, some of which the appellant himself had executed.

2. Through a "front" or alter ego the appellant secured a portion of the compensation paid by the Venezuelan Government for two tracts of land expropriated by decrees promulgated by him.

3. By his twenty per cent ownership of EVICSA, a construction company, the appellant secured a portion of the compensation paid by the Venezuelan Government on construction contracts with the appellant's Ministry of Development, with the connivance of two of his ministers, one of whom was head of that ministry.

4. The appellant secured improvements on and maintenance of his private, personal

estate at public expense at specified times.

The charges of financial crimes allege that the transactions numbered 1 through 4 above make appellant guilty of embezzlement or criminal malversation by a public officer as provided in paragraph 14 of Article II of the Treaty [of Extradition], guilty of fraud or breach of trust as provided in paragraph 20 of Article II of the Treaty, and that the transactions numbered 1 through 3 above make him guilty of receiving money or valuable securities knowing the same to have been unlawfully obtained as provided in paragraph 18 of Article II of the Treaty.

The same charges are pending in the Supreme Court of Justice (formerly the Federal Court), the highest court of Venezuela, upon petition of the Attorney General of Venezuela with a substantial quantity of supporting evidence. The Supreme Court of Justice determined that if the charges are proved they would constitute violations of the penal code of Venezuela and that such charges are crimes specified in the Treaty of Extradition Article II, paragraphs 14, 18 and 20; found that good cause had been shown for prosecution and issued its warrant of arrest. The proceedings before the Supreme Court of Justice, with a substantial amount of evidence from its record—all documentary— were transmitted to the United States through appropriate diplomatic channels. Venezuela invokes these Treaty provisions in its complaint and requisition for surrender of appellant.

Appellant contends that Judge McRae [United States District Court for the Southern District of Florida] erred in not discharging appellant from custody on the grounds that: . . . (3) the acts for which appellant's extradition is sought are acts in the exercise of sovereign authority or acts of state the legality of which the judicial authorities of the United States have no authority to determine, (4) failure of the extradition magistrate to determine whether

* Reprinted from 311 F. 2d 547 (1962).

the claim for extradition was for any crime or offense of a political character or for acts connected with such crimes or offenses, (5) the decision of Judge Whitehurst was not based on legal, competent and adequate evidence, (6) the alleged financial crimes were not within the Treaty of Extradition, ...

* * *

Appellant contends that the acts with which he is charged are "acts done in the exercise of or in color of his sovereign authority and by virtue of the law of nations as stated in Underhill v. Hernandez, 168 U.S. 250, 18 S.Ct. 83, 42 L.Ed. 456, was entitled to be discharged from custody inasmuch as the judicial authorities cannot review the acts done by a sovereign in his own territory to determine illegality".

Seizing upon Venezuela's characterization of appellant as a "dictator" he argues that as a "dictator" he himself would be the sovereign—the government of Venezuela—and that all his acts constituting the financial crimes with which he is charged and as to which probable cause of guilt has been found are acts of state or sovereign acts, the legality of which the Act of State Doctrine precludes an extradition judge or magistrate from adjudicating.

Essentially the Act of State Doctrine is "the principle that the conduct of one independent government cannot be successfully questioned in the courts of another * * *." Oetjen v. Central Leather Co., 246 U.S. 297, 303, 38 S.Ct. 309, 311, 62 L.Ed. 726 (1918).

Even though characterized as a dictator, appellant was not himself the sovereign—government—of Venezuela within the Act of State Doctrine. He was chief executive, a public officer, of the sovereign nation of Venezuela. It is only when officials having sovereign authority act in an official capacity that the Act of State Doctrine applies. ...

Appellant's acts constituting the financial crimes of embezzlement or malversation,

fraud or breach of trust, and receiving money or valuable securities knowing them to have been unlawfully obtained as to which probable cause of guilt had been shown were not acts of Venezuela sovereignty. . . . each of these acts was "for the private financial benefit" of the appellant. They constituted common crimes committed by the Chief of State done in violation of his position and not in pursuance of it. They are as far from being an act of state as rape which appellant concedes would not be an "Act of State".

* * *

In this extradition case the executive branch, through its representation of the appellee United States Marshal, has manifested its desire that the judiciary act and decide this case on its merits.

* * *

The very reason for this extradition case is that the United States has agreed with Venezuela for the extradition of persons charged with crimes enumerated in the Treaty. This Treaty deals expressly in paragraph 14 of Article II with embezzlement or criminal malversation by public officers. Appellant notes that a public officer is one who exercises "in part sovereign power". The two governments intended the tribunals to act when the accused is a public officer charged with crimes enumerated in the Treaty. The acts constituting crimes charged for which the extradition of appellant is sought are not "acts of Venezuela" . . . , and the Act of State Doctrine is no bar to this extradition proceeding or justification for the discharge from custody of appellant.

Even though Judge Whitehurst [Chief Judge of the United States District Court for the Southern District of Florida] found that the evidence failed to connect appellant with the murders and that it was unnecessary to determine whether or not these crimes were of a political character, appellant contends that Judge Whitehurst also should have made a finding as to whether the murders were political crimes and found that the murders were political and that the financial crimes were "acts connected with such (political) crimes or offenses" within the meaning of Article III of the Treaty because they were joined in the same complaint with the murders. He argues that the word "claim" in Article III (that "the provisions of this convention shall not import claim of extradition" for political offenses) refers to the extradition complaint and that if any crime or offense contained in the complaint is of a political character or is an act connected with a political crime or offense, the entire "claim" must be denied, notwithstanding the absence of any relationship of the several crimes or offenses with each other. Article III speaks of "*acts* connected with" political crimes and not of "charges" in a legal document. The necessary connection is between such acts or events and other acts or events. It is not the connection effected by charges being in the same legal paper.

Since appellant had no connection with the murders charged in the complaint, those acts could not be political acts or crimes attributable to appellant and whether or not the homicides were political crimes by those who committed them can have no bearing on the appellant.

The murders are no longer in the case.

Judge Whitehurst's decision that the financial crimes were not political was based upon the evidence and is not reviewable here. . . .

* * *

There is no evidence that the financial crimes charged were committed in the course of and incidentally to a revolutionary uprising or other violent political disturbance.

Venezuela seeks the surrender of appellant by the executive officers of the United States (who must ultimately determine whether fugitives shall be surrendered) for trial of appellant on the financial crimes only. The claim of extradition for appellant, within the meaning of the Treaty, is not based on any crime or offense of a political character or on acts connected with such crimes or offenses. Judge McRae did not err in failing to remand the extradition proceedings for further findings.

Judge Whitehurst's finding that the evidence was sufficient to sustain the charges specified, as certified to the Secretary of State, was based upon legal, competent and adequate evidence under 18 U.S.C. § 3190. A *prima facie* case was established by the filing of the charges by the Attorney General of Venezuela, the findings of the highest court of that country that the charges and evidence established cause for prosecution and arrest, the warrant of arrest, and a substantial quantity of evidence submitted to the Supreme Court of Justice of Venezuela. First National City Bank of New York v. Aristeguieta, 287 F.2d 219, 227 (2 Cir., 1960), cert. granted 365 U.S. 840, 81 S.Ct. 803, 5 L.Ed.2d 807.

The record shows that appellant, in November, 1948, was a young lieutenant colonel in the Venezuelan army, of very modest means. By a coup d'etat, appellant and two other lieutenant colonels established a three-man military junta, which was to rule in accordance with the Constitution and laws of Venezuela. As a member of the Junta, the appellant was required by law to file a statement of his assets upon taking office. His sworn statement, filed on March 14, 1949, showed that he and his wife then possessed total net assets equivalent to $31,343.28.

In the succeeding nine years the record discloses that appellant was enriched by more than $13,000,000 in excess of his opening net worth and his legitimate compensation. All during this period the laws of Venezuela prohibited anyone in appellant's position from engaging in commercial transactions with the nation, directly or indirectly. Evidence of Appellant's financial dealings was found in a suitcase which he left behind when he hastily fled Venezuela, on January 23, 1958. . . .

* * *

It has been held by the Supreme Court and the lower federal courts that "competent evidence to establish reasonable ground is not necessarily evidence sufficient to convict, nor only such as can pass technical rules governing the admissibility of evidence in criminal trials." U. S. ex rel. Klein v. Mulligan, 50 F.2d 687, 688 (2 Cir. 1931), cert. den., 284 U.S. 665, 52 S.Ct. 41, 76 L.Ed. 563 (1931), and the cases cited therein.

With respect to the evidence upon which the extradition magistrate acted, it must be remembered that the extradition magistrate merely determines probable cause, making an inquiry like that of a committing magistrate and no more. . . .

* * *

The crimes charged to appellant as to which probable cause has been found are offenses extraditable by Article II of the Treaty of Extradition. The record is clear that these charges are, if proved; crimes in the demanding nation, that question having been determined by the highest court of Venezuela. . . .

* * *

The record contains no reversible error and the judgment of the District Court dismissing the appellant's petition for habeas corpus and discharging the orders to show cause issued thereon is hereby Affirmed.

[*On August 12, 1963, United States Secretary of State Dean Rusk sent the following note to Dr. Enrique Tejera-Paris, Venezuelan Ambassador to the United States:**]

---

* 49 *United States Department of State Bulletin* 365 (1963).

". . . I have taken note of your Government's assurances, contained in your note No. 1396, dated July 22, 1963, that careful security arrangements have been made by your Government to eliminate any risk of physical harm to Marcos Perez Jimenez should he be extradited, that he would be tried only for those offenses for which his extradition is granted, that he would be given all the rights accorded an accused under the laws of your country, including the right to full and effective defense, and that he would have the right to adequate legal counsel of his own choice.

Accordingly, there is enclosed my warrant directing the United States Marshal for the Southern District of Florida or any other public officer or person having charge or custody of Marcos Perez Jimenez to surrender and deliver him up to such person or persons as may be duly authorized by your Government to receive him in order that he may be returned to Venezuela for trial for the crimes of embezzlement or criminal malversation, receiving money or valuable securities knowing the same to have been unlawfully obtained, and fraud or breach of trust. . . .

Inasmuch as the extradition magistrate found sufficient evidence of criminality of Marcos Perez Jimenez only with respect to these crimes, his extradition is granted on the condition, specified in Article XIV of the Extradition Treaty of 1922, that he shall be tried only for those crimes. . . ."

Coumas v. The Superior Court of San Joaquin County*

United States, Supreme Court of California, 1948

Petitioner seeks a writ of prohibition to restrain the respondent court from proceeding with his scheduled trial under an amended indictment returned on March 14,

---

* Reprinted from 192 P. 2d 449 (1948).

1934, and charging him in two counts with connected offenses perpetrated on April 20, 1932, in the city of Manteca, county of San Joaquin: (1) "murder [of] one Olive Taylor"; and (2) "assault upon the person of William Duval with a deadly weapon with the intent * * * to commit murder." He was arrested in Manteca on September 26, 1947, and imprisoned in the county jail awaiting trial. Upon arraignment, he pleaded the defenses of "prior conviction" and "former jeopardy" by reason of a judgment entered after criminal prosecution of the same charges in the Felony Court of Corinth, Greece.

Section 793 of the Penal Code provides as follows: "When an act charged as a public offense is within the jurisdiction of another state or country, as well as of this state, a conviction or acquittal thereof in the former is a bar to the prosecution or indictment therefor in this state." Petitioner's pleas come precisely within the contemplated scope of this penal statute, and "prohibition is an appropriate remedy to prevent [his] retrial" on the offenses in question. . . .

There is no dispute as to the facts. Petitioner, a native of Greece, emigrated on January 4, 1907, to the United States. He was then seventeen years of age. On February 25, 1914, he became a naturalized citizen of this country, at which time he took the required oath in renouncement of "allegiance * * * to any * * * state, or sovereignty of * * * which [he] was before a subject or citizen" and in pledge of "true faith and allegiance" to the United States. . . . The Greek Government never at any time consented to his foreign naturalization.

Petitioner resided in this country continuously from his entry until shortly after April 20, 1932, the date on which he allegedly committed the two above-mentioned crimes of "murder" and "assault * * * with a deadly weapon" in the city of Manteca. To avoid arrest petitioner immediately fled from this state and ultimately reached

Greece. On May 12, 1932, he was indicted for the two criminal offenses by the Grand Jury of San Joaquin County. An amended indictment was filed on March 14, 1934, and thereupon the United States Government instituted proceedings with the Greek Government for the extradition of petitioner as a fugitive from justice. Petitioner successfully resisted these proceedings upon the decision of the Council of the Court of Appeals at Nauplia, Greece, on August 26, 1934, that "he [had] never divested himself of [his] Greek citizenship," and that Greek law therefore absolutely forbade his extradition but required his prosecution and punishment in Greece in accordance with its criminal law. Thereafter petitioner stood trial in the Felony Court of Corinth, Greece, on precisely the same two alleged criminal acts and on October 16, 1935, judgment was entered against him pursuant to a jury verdict (1) finding him "guilty of manslaughter" on the alleged murder charge and (2) acquitting him on the assault charge but finding him "guilty of the unlawful carrying of a firearm." He was sentenced to serve consecutive terms of imprisonment for the respective crimes as so determined: (1) four years and (2) four months. He served those terms, with credit for thirteen months' preliminary imprisonment. Subsequently petitioner returned to the United States, and since his arrest on September 26, 1947, in the city of Manteca, he has been confined in the county jail of San Joaquin County awaiting trial on the criminal charges contained in the amended indictment of March 14, 1934, as above mentioned.

Section 3 of the Greek Code of Penal Procedure provided, at all times here pertinent, as follows: "Hellenes are never extradited to Foreign Authorities not even for the acts committed by them abroad. They are subjected to trial, however, in this country, even for the felonies and misdemeanors committed by them abroad and they are punished in accordance with the laws of this country as if they had committed these acts within the boundary lines of the state, subject, however, to the provisions of existing Government treaties." By Article VIII of the Treaty of Extradition as then in force between the Governments of Greece and the United States, it was provided: "Under the stipulations of this Treaty, neither of the High Contracting Parties shall be bound to deliver up its own citizens, except in cases where such citizenship has been obtained after the perpetration of the crime for which extradition is sought. The State appealed to shall decide whether the person claimed is its own citizen." (47 Stats. 2185, 2191.) Accordingly, petitioner properly maintains that Greece had jurisdiction over his person because it had never consented to this expatriation, and over the offenses because of its penal law.

While the United States has long supported the doctrine of expatriation in the fullest sense—as involving a "natural and inherent right" of a person to depart from his country of origin and absolve himself from his original allegiance, upon identifying himself with another political community, through naturalization . . . —such principle of election as a matter primarily for the individual's determination is contrary to the common-law concept of "perpetual allegiance" to one's native land, which still prevails in many countries today, particularly on the continent of Europe, and precludes the voluntary severance of national ties unless the consent of the government is obtained. (Wilson on International Law, sec. 50, p. 217.) So it is with Greece as its pertinent law is recited in the "true copy" of the extradition proceedings had against petitioner—"according to which naturalization in a foreign country is not itself sufficient for the loss of Greek citizenship, but there is also required on the one hand the permission of the Greek Government, obtained through the Ministry for Foreign Affairs, and, on the other, the performance of the military duty of the person concerned, nonperformance of which excludes anyone from the right to obtain the aforesaid permission of the Greek Government." Admittedly, petitioner never obtained the consent of the Greek Government for his foreign naturalization—in fact, he never made such request —though compliance with such formality was necessary to bring about his loss of Greek citizenship. The taking of the oath of allegiance to the United States and the accompanying renunciation of national ties to any foreign state upon petitioner's naturalization in this country would not automatically divest him of his Greek citizenship, for the matter of denationalization is one for domestic regulation by the government concerned under its particular laws of expatriation. (Wilson on International Law, supra, sec. 50, p. 217; 2 Am.Jur., sec. 182, p. 559.) The so-called American doctrine of "voluntary expatriation" as a matter of absolute right cannot postulate loss of original nationality on naturalization in this country as a principle of international law, for that would be tantamount to interference with the exclusive jurisdiction of a nation within its own domain. . . .

The matter of extradition is a proper subject for treaty negotiations between sovereign nations, and any point of controversy with regard thereto will be governed by the prevailing stipulations of the contracting powers. . . .

In the present case, the Treaty of Extradition with Greece expressly provided that "the State appealed to shall decide whether the person claimed is its own citizen," an explicit stipulation according full recognition to any variance in the laws of expatriation existing between the two signatory powers and indicating their mutual intent that the citizenship status of the person seeking refuge in either's territorial limits should be determined in a manner consistent with its standards. . . .

So here, according to Greek law, petitioner on April 20, 1932, the date of his alleged commission of the crimes in Manteca, was still a citizen of Greece by reason of his failure to procure the necessary consent to his foreign naturalization and, upon return to its territorial jurisdiction, he was amenable to prosecution under its penal statutes. . . .

* * *

. . . There is no evidence in the record indicating any fraud, collusion, trickery or subterfuge on the part of petitioner in procuring, according to Greek law, the determination of his guilt on the criminal charges in question. Rather, it appears that petitioner's trial in the Felony Court of Corinth, Greece, was fair and impartial; that depositions of witnesses before the Grand Jury of San Joaquin County were duly submitted along with the oral testimony of petitioner for the consideration of the jury in reaching its verdict; and that substantial terms of imprisonment were imposed on petitioner—four years and four months—

and served by him, with appropriate credit for preliminary imprisonment, in accord with the judgment entered on the findings of guilt on the alleged crimes as above mentioned. In other words, petitioner's trial in the Greek court was not a mere farce, resulting in a sentence of imprisonment of inconsequential degree as related to the import of the criminal charges against him, but, on the contrary, its "bona fide" character in every respect is clearly shown by the record. The jurisdiction of the Greek court was established in pursuance of the Treaty of Extradition with Greece as then existing; such treaty, like others, is a part of "the supreme law" of our land and binding upon the courts. (U.S. Const. art. VI, cl. 2; 52 Am.Jur., sec. 17, p. 815.)

It is ordered that a peremptory writ of prohibition issue as prayed, restraining the respondent court from proceeding further with petitioner's trial.

IMMUNITIES FROM JURISDICTION

"In general, every state has exclusive jurisdiction within its own territory, but this jurisdiction is not absolute, because it is subject to certain limitations imposed by international law."[1] Among the more important of these limitations are the immunities from the exercise of local jurisdiction accorded to foreign states, their agents, their armed forces, and to international organizations. State practice indicates that general agreement exists on the nature of these immunities, but differences in interpretation and application occur. And in some cases it is not clear whether a particular rule is one of international law or of municipal law only, which raises the question of whether or not

[1] Brierly, *The Law of Nations*, p. 222.

it may be unilaterally modified or abrogated. Nevertheless, an awareness among national decision-makers of reciprocal advantages lends strong support to the general principles and to most of the specific rules.

The doctrine of state immunity, which bars the exercise of jurisdiction by domestic courts over a foreign state, its instrumentalities, and its properties has its genesis in the medieval rule that rendered feudal magnates answerable only to superiors, not to equals. This rule, buttressed by the ancient practice of according personal immunity to sovereigns, served as the basis for the assertion by classical writers in international law that any exercise of jurisdiction by one territorial sovereign over another was forbidden. By the early nineteenth century, national courts had developed a doctrine of state immunity that was virtually unlimited. When, for example, in *Vavasseur v. Krupp*, the plaintiff sought to stop delivery of certain shells bought by the Japanese government on the grounds that they were manufactured in infringement of his patent rights, a British court ruled that, even if his patent were infringed, the court had no jurisdiction "to interfere with the property of a foreign sovereign, more especially with what we call the public property of the state of which he is sovereign. . . ."[2]

In the period when the doctrine of state immunity was being fashioned into a rule of international law, governments concerned themselves more or less exclusively with the governing of their own territories and the protection of the interests of their states; activities of a commercial and economic nature were usually conducted by private persons. As governments increasingly entered the economic and commercial domain, particularly in the twentieth century, they continued to claim total immunity for their activities, even in suits arising out of their competitive activities, and individuals doing business with them were placed at an unfair disadvantage. Stateowned agencies for international trade, shipping, commerce, and finance claimed the immunities possessed by the more traditional government agencies, such as the foreign office and the defense ministry. The response to this development has been a growing emphasis on exceptions to, and modifications of, the rule of state immunity. Two competing theories now exist: that of absolute immunity, which grants almost unlimited immunity to all activities of foreign states, and that of restrictive immunity, which grants immunity with regard to public, or traditional, acts (*jure imperii*), but not with regard to private, or commercial and economic, acts (*jure gestionis*).

The choice of theories by national de-cision-makers has clearly been influenced by appreciations of national interests. Communist states, which have moved most completely into the economic and commercial domain, continue to adhere to the traditional theory of absolute immunity, while numerous non-Communist states, led by Greece and Italy, have adopted the restrictive theory. The United States, once a leading proponent of the absolute theory, is currently altering its position. As late as 1926, the Supreme Court of the United States held that a merchant vessel owned and operated by the Italian government and engaged in commerce was entitled to the same immunity as warships. "We know," the Court said, "of no international usage which regards the maintenance and advancement of the economic welfare of a people in time of peace as any less a public purpose than the maintenance and training of a naval force."[3] In 1952, the State Department indicated to the Justice Department that in the future its policy would be to follow the restrictive theory in advising upon requests by foreign governments for a grant of immunity.[4] Although this shift in policy does not bind United States courts, there are clear indications that they are moving in the direction suggested. In 1964, for example, a United States Court of Appeals affirmed a District Court refusal to grant immunity to the Spanish Ministry of Commerce in a suit involving the chartering of a private ship for the transport of wheat from the United States to Spain. The Court of Appeals held that the chartering of a ship for transporting wheat is by its nature a private commercial act: "The Comisaria General's chartering of the appellee's ship to transport wheat is not a strictly public or political act. Indeed, it partakes far more of the character of a private commercial act than a public or political act."[5]

---

[2] 9 Ch. Div. 351 (1878).

[3] Berizzi Bros. Co. v. S.S. Pesaro, 271 U.S. 574 (1926).
[4] See the so-called "Tate Letter," reprinted in this section on pp. 235–236.
[5] Victory Transport, Inc. v. Comisaria General de Abastecimientos y Transportes, 336 F. 2d 354 (1964).

In view of the variations in state practice, coupled with the absence of authoritative international conventions or judicial decisions on the scope of immunities to be accorded foreign states, it must be concluded that, while international law prescribes full immunities for acts *jure imperii*, it does not require conformity to the absolute immunity theory. The most pervasive current difficulty is that of devising workable standards for distinguishing between acts *jure imperii* and acts *jure gestionis*. At present, international law leaves it to the forum state to draw the dividing line. The national courts of some states inquire into the "final purpose" of the activity to see if it is directly connected with a public function, such as defense, while other national courts look into the "nature" of the transaction in question to see if it could have been undertaken by private individuals. For example, states using the "nature" test may refuse to grant immunity in a suit concerning a contract for the supply of leather for a foreign army on the ground that the purpose of the transaction does not alter the fact that the act of entering into a contract is essentially private. On the other hand, states using the "final purpose" test may grant immunity in such a case on the ground that supplying an army is an obvious exercise of a traditional state function.

The wide-ranging immunities from the exercise of local jurisdiction that states accord foreign heads of state and their representatives are among the most ancient and universally recognized rules of international law. A head of state, when visiting or passing through another state, is wholly immune from the exercise of local jurisdiction, both criminal and civil.[6] With few exceptions, a foreign diplomat and the members of his family are also immune from all criminal and civil processes in the state to which the diplomat is accredited; unless the immunity is waived by the head of the mission or the home government, they may be neither arrested nor sued. If a foreign diplomat violates the laws of the receiving state, the only recourse is to register a diplomatic complaint to his government or, in an extreme case, to demand his withdrawal as *persona non grata*. The premises of a diplomatic mission and the residences of diplomatic officers are inviolable and are exempt from taxes.

National decision-makers have long realized that there is a greater advantage to be gained by considering the agents of foreign states to be immune from the exercise of local jurisdiction than by punishing them for their acts. The reciprocal nature of the immunities obviously lends support to compliance with the rules. Also, the arrest of an ambassador or the invasion of an embassy disrupts diplomatic intercourse and inflames opinion in the sending state; reprisals are likely to follow norm violations. These rules are not taken lightly by foreign offices that are seeking to facilitate diplomatic intercourse and to maintain friendly relations with other states. Consequently, states incorporate the generally accepted rules into their domestic law systems.[7]

This is not to say that there are no inconsistencies in the application of the rules. The courts of some states—for example, the common law countries, France, and Germany—interpret the scope of immunities broadly and normally refuse to exercise jurisdiction whenever a plea for immunity is made; others, especially Belgium and Italy, tend to grant immunity only when the exercise of jurisdiction would interfere with diplomatic functions. There are also inconsistencies in state practice regarding the categories of personnel entitled to diplo-

---

[6] When, for example, the Sultan of Johore was sued in a British court for breach of promise of marriage, the promise having been made to the plaintiff under an assumed name, the court dismissed the suit for want of jurisdiction after the true identity of the defendant was disclosed. Mighell v. Sultan of Johore, I Q.B. Div. 149 (1894).

[7] United States statutory law, for example, imposes penalties for assaulting a foreign diplomat (18 U.S.C. sect. 112) or for attempting to serve process on him (22 U.S.C. secs. 252–255). Picketing of foreign missions is also prohibited (22 U.S.C. secs. 255a, 255b).

matic immunities. Most states extend immunities to all the diplomatic personnel[8] of a mission and to members of their immediate families, as long as the diplomat is not a national of the receiving state. But practice regarding the grant of immunities to "nondiplomatic" personnel, such as administrative and technical staff and "service personnel" (cooks, chauffeurs, guards, and the like), has been varied.

In 1961, at a United Nations sponsored conference held in Vienna, much of the customary law of diplomatic immunities was codified and several of the inconsistencies in state practice, including those relating to the scope of immunities and the persons to whom they apply, were resolved. The Vienna Convention on Diplomatic Relations,[9] which went into force on April 24, 1964, had been ratified, by June 30, 1968, by more than sixty states. This Convention, most of which is binding as customary law even upon states that have not ratified it, is the authoritative statement of the law of diplomatic immunities.

The immunities of consular officers, whose main function is to take care of the commercial interests of their home states and its nationals in the territory of a foreign state, are much more restricted than those of diplomatic agents. Indeed, it seems that customary international law establishes only two general consular immunities: the inviolability of consular archives and correspondence and the personal immunity of consular officers from both civil and criminal proceedings in respect to acts performed in their official capacity.[10] Greater immunities are regularly accorded in bilateral conventions, however, as is illustrated by Article 19 of the United States-Soviet Union Consular Convention, which confers on consular officers unconditional immunity from criminal juris-

diction.[11] In the absence of such treaty-based immunities, international law requires only that consular officers be accorded the customary immunities.

A significant effort to strengthen the position of career consular officers was made in 1963, when a United Nations sponsored conference adopted the Vienna Convention on Consular Relations.[12] The Convention was signed by 51 of the 92 participating states; it entered into force following the twenty-second ratification on March 19, 1967. While the Convention does not attempt to place the consul on an equal footing with the diplomat, it clearly seeks to move him in that direction. Article 41, for example, provides that career consular officers are not liable to arrest pending trial, except in case of a "grave crime," and that they cannot be imprisoned prior to a judicial decision of final effect. And, according to Article 36, the receiving state must protect the freedom of all official consular communication, including the freedom to communicate with and visit nationals who are in jail or prison.

Customary international law regarding the immunities of armed forces on foreign territory is uncertain. Consequently, with the post-World War II practice of stationing large bodies of troops in foreign countries for an indefinite period of time, sending and receiving states have spelled out the applicable rules in multilateral and bilateral treaties. Following the pattern established in the N.A.T.O. Status of Forces Agreement,[13] these treaties recognize the dual system of the territorial jurisdiction of the receiving state and the disciplinary jurisdiction of the sending state. In the inevitably large area of concurrent jurisdiction, "primary rights" to exercise authority are spelled out, and provision is made for waiver of jurisdiction by either the sending

---

[8] "Diplomatic personnel" includes the chief of the mission, whether ambassador, minister, or chargé d'affaires, and such diplomatic officers as counsellors, secretaries of legation, and attachés.
[9] See the text of the Convention, reprinted in this section on pp. 238–244.
[10] Brierly, *The Law of Nations*, p. 265.

[11] For the text of the Convention, see 50 *United States Department of State Bulletin* 979 (1964). It entered into force on July 13, 1968.
[12] Reprinted in 57 *American Journal of International Law* 995 (1963).
[13] Reprinted in 48 *American Journal of International Law*, Supplement 83 (1954).

or the receiving state. The N.A.T.O. Agreement, for example, permits the sending state to exercise jurisdiction over the members of its armed forces when the offense is committed against the security or the property of the sending state or against the person or property of another national attached to the military establishment, or if the offense arises out of an act or omission done in performance of an official duty. Members of the armed forces are obliged to respect the law of the receiving state and are usually subject to trial and punishment for crimes committed off duty.

In recent decades, governments have consented to a new body of rules that further limit the jurisdiction of states over their own territory. These rules take the form of immunities granted to representatives of states accredited to international organizations, to officials of international organizations, and to the international organizations themselves. The history of these immunities can be traced back to the instruments establishing international river commissions and administrative unions in the second half of the nineteenth century, but their present content derives from the experience of the League of Nations. Article 7, paragraphs 4 and 5 of the League Covenant provided that:

> Representatives of the Members of the League and Officials of the League when engaged on the business of the League shall enjoy diplomatic privileges and immunities. The buildings and other property occupied by the League or its officials or by representatives attending its meetings shall be inviolable.

Detailed arrangements concerning these provisions were worked out in agreements between the Secretary-General of the League and the government of Switzerland.

Similarly, Article 105 of the United Nations Charter provides that:

> The Organization shall enjoy in the territory of each of its Members such privileges and immunities as are necessary for the fulfillment of its purposes.

> Representatives of the Members of the United Nations and officials of the Organization shall similarly enjoy such privileges and immunities as are necessary for the independent exercise of their functions in connection with the Organization.

The Charter then authorizes the General Assembly to make recommendations concerning the details of these immunities and to propose conventions to the members for this purpose. In 1946, the General Assembly approved the General Convention on the Privileges and Immunities of the United Nations,[14] which has been acceded to by more than eighty states but not by the United States. The General Assembly also adopted, in 1947, a Convention on the Privileges and Immunities of Specialized Agencies of the United Nations,[15] which has also been widely accepted but not by the United States. The constitutional instruments of regional organizations also contain provisions on privileges and immunities, and these provisions have been implemented by general conventions. "Headquarters agreements" between the organizations and the states in which they maintain headquarters or other offices further supplement the constitutional provisions. Finally, municipal legislation, such as the United States International Organization Immunities Act of 1945,[16] safeguards the immunities and exemptions accorded to international organizations, their officials, and representatives of member states.

Representatives of member states accredited to international organizations are accorded immunities similar to those possessed by diplomats. These include, *inter alia*, immunity from arrest and detention, immunity from legal process of every kind, and inviolability of all papers and documents. The representatives who possess these immunities include delegates, deputy delegates, advisers, technical experts, and secretaries of delegations. The head of the

[14] I *United Nations Treaty Series* 15.
[15] 33 *United Nations Treaty Series* 261.
[16] 59 Stat. 669, 22 U.S.C.A. secs. 228 ff.

delegation notifies the secretariat of the organization of the arrival and departure of representatives, and the secretariat in turn notifies the government of the host state.

The immunities accorded to officials of international organizations vary according to their rank. The general practice is to accord full diplomatic immunities only to the Secretary General and Assistant Secretaries General; other officials are granted immunities only in respect of words spoken or written and acts performed by them in their official capacity. Immunities for subordinate officials may normally be waived by the Secretary General.

The immunities of the international organizations themselves normally fall into four categories: (a) immunity from every form of legal process; (b) inviolability of premises and archives; (c) currency privileges; and (d) freedom of communication. Section 2 of the General Convention on the Privileges and Immunities of the United Nations, for example, provides that "the United Nations, its property and assets, wherever located and by whomsoever held, shall enjoy immunity from every form of legal process, except insofar as in any particular case it has expressly waived its immunity. . . ." The extent of the inviolability of the premises and archives of the United Nations is equally comprehensive; authorities of the host state may not enter the premises even to arrest a person without the consent of the Secretary General. International organizations may normally hold and move funds, gold, or any other form of currency without being restricted by financial controls or regulations of any kind; their assets, income, and property are exempt from all forms of direct taxation. They may use codes, bags, and couriers, and their communications may not be censored.

The first selection to follow, Chief Justice John Marshall's opinion in *The Schooner Exchange v. McFaddon*, is the *locus classicus*

in the law of jurisdictional immunity. The second selection, the so-called "Tate Letter," is a statement of the ostensible rationale behind the shift in United States policy from the absolute theory of state immunity to the restrictive theory. This is followed by a Soviet statement in support of the more traditional view. The specifics of diplomatic privileges and immunities are outlined in the next selection, the Vienna Convention on Diplomatic Relations. The case of *Carrera v. Carrera* is presented to illustrate the case law on diplomatic immunities in general and the liberal practice of the United States in according such immunities in particular. The nature of the privileges and immunities accorded to international organizations is illustrated by the United Nations-United States Headquarters Agreement, by the case of *United States v. Egorov*, and by a statement made by Ambassador Sidney R. Yates, Representative of the United States to the United Nations, before the Fourth Committee of the General Assembly.

The Schooner Exchange v. McFaddon*

Supreme Court of the United States, 1812

[*Two American citizens filed a libel in the United States District Court for Pennsylvania claiming that they were entitled to possession of* The Schooner Exchange. *They stated that their ship had been illegally seized on the high seas in 1810 by persons acting on behalf of the Emperor Napoleon of France. The United States Attorney for the District of Pennsylvania filed a statement in which he said that the ship was a public vessel of France that had come into port in distress; he asked that the libel be dismissed. The District Court dismissed the libel but the Circuit Court reversed. The Supreme Court*

* Reprinted from 7 Cranch 116 (1812).

took the case on appeal by the United States Attorney.]

MARSHALL, CH. J., delivered the opinion of the court as follows:

This case involves the very delicate and important inquiry, whether an American citizen can assert, in an American court, a title to an armed national vessel, found within the waters of the United States.

* * *

The jurisdiction of the nation within its own territory is necessarily exclusive and absolute. It is susceptible of no limitation not imposed by itself. Any restriction upon it, deriving validity from an external source, would imply a diminution of its sovereignty to the extent of the restriction, and an investment of that sovereignty to the same extent in that power which could impose such restriction.

All exceptions, therefore, to the full and complete power of a nation within its own territories, must be traced up to the consent of the nation itself. They can flow from no other legitimate source.

This consent may be either express or implied. In the latter case, it is less determinate, exposed more to the uncertainties of construction; but, if understood, not less obligatory.

The world being composed of distinct sovereignties, possessing equal rights and equal independence, whose mutual benefit is promoted by intercourse with each other, and by an interchange of those good offices which humanity dictates and its wants require, all sovereigns have consented to a relaxation in practice, in cases under certain peculiar circumstances, of that absolute and complete jurisdiction within their respective territories which sovereignty confers.

This consent may, in some instances, be tested by common usage, and by common opinion, growing out of that usage.

A nation would justly be considered as violating its faith, although that faith might not be expressly plighted, which should suddenly and without previous notice, exercise its territorial powers in a manner not consonant to the usages and received obligations of the civilized world.

This full and absolute territorial jurisdiction being alike the attribute of every sovereign, and being incapable of conferring extraterritorial power, would not seem to contemplate foreign sovereigns nor their sovereign rights as its objects. One sovereign being in no respect amenable to another, and being bound by obligations of the highest character not to degrade the dignity of his nation, by placing himself or its sovereign rights within the jurisdiction of another, can be supposed to enter a foreign territory only under an express license, or in the confidence that the immunities belonging to his independent sovereign station, though not expressly stipulated, are reserved by implication, and will be extended to him.

This perfect equality and absolute independence of sovereigns, and this common interest impelling them to mutual intercourse, and an interchange of good offices with each other, have given rise to a class of cases in which every sovereign is understood to waive the exercise of a part of that complete exclusive territorial jurisdiction, which has been stated to be the attribute of every nation.

1st. One of these is admitted to be the exemption of the person of the sovereign from arrest or detention within a foreign territory.

* * *

2d. A second case, standing on the same principles with the first, is the immunity which all civilized nations allow to foreign ministers.

* * *

3d. A third case in which a sovereign is understood to cede a portion of his territorial jurisdiction is, where he allows the troops of a foreign prince to pass through his dominions.

* * *

. . . The grant of free passage therefore implies a waiver of all jurisdiction over the troops during their passage, and permits the foreign general to use that discipline, and to inflict those punishments which the government of his army may require.

But if, without such express permit, an army should be led through the territories of a foreign prince, might the jurisdiction of the territory be rightfully exercised over the individuals composing this army?

Without doubt, a military force can never gain immunities of any other description than those which war gives, by entering a foreign territory against the will of its sovereign. But if his consent, instead of being expressed by a particular license, be expressed by a general declaration that foreign troops may pass through a specified tract of country, a distinction between such general permit and a particular license is not perceived. It would seem reasonable that every immunity which would be conferred by a special license, would be in like manner conferred by such general permit.

* * *

But the rule which is applicable to armies, does not appear to be equally applicable to ships of war entering the ports of a friendly power. The injury inseparable from the march of an army through an inhabited country, and the dangers often, indeed generally, attending it, do not ensue from admitting a ship of war, without special license, into a friendly port. A different rule therefore with respect to this species of military force has been generally adopted. If, for reasons of state, the ports of a nation generally, or any particular ports be closed

against vessels of war generally, or the vessels of any particular nation, notice is usually given of such determination. If there be no prohibition, the ports of a friendly nation are considered as open to the public ships of all powers with whom it is at peace, and they are supposed to enter such ports and to remain in them while allowed to remain, under the protection of the government of the place.

In almost every instance, the treaties between civilized nations contain a stipulation to this effect in favor of vessels driven in by stress of weather or other urgent necessity. In such cases the sovereign is bound by compact to authorize foreign vessels to enter his ports. The treaty binds him to allow vessels in distress to find refuge and asylum in his ports, and this is a license which he is not at liberty to retract. It would be difficult to assign a reason for withholding from a license thus granted, any immunity from local jurisdiction which would be implied in a special license.

If there be no treaty applicable to the case, and the sovereign, from motives deemed adequate by himself, permits his ports to remain open to the public ships of foreign friendly powers, the conclusion seems irresistible, that they enter by his assent. And if they enter by his assent necessarily implied, no just reason is perceived by the court for distinguishing their case from that of vessels which enter by express assent.

* * *

To the court, it appears, that where, without treaty, the ports of the nation are open to the private and public ships of a friendly power, whose subjects have also liberty without special license, to enter the country for business or amusement, a clear distinction is to be drawn between the rights accorded to private individuals or private trading vessels, and those accorded to public armed ships which constitute a part of the military force of the nation.

The preceding reasoning has maintained the propositions that all exemptions from territorial jurisdiction must be derived from the consent of the sovereign of the territory; that this consent may be implied or expressed; and that when implied, its extent must be regulated by the nature of the case, and the views under which the parties requiring and conceding it must be supposed to act.

When private individuals of one nation spread themselves through another as business or caprice may direct, mingling indiscriminately with the inhabitants of that other, or when merchant vessels enter for the purposes of trade, it would be obviously inconvenient and dangerous to society, and would subject the laws to continual infraction, and the government to degradation, if such individuals or merchants did not owe temporary and local allegiance, and were not amenable to the jurisdiction of the country. Nor can the foreign sovereign have any motive for wishing such exemption. His subjects thus passing into foreign countries, are not employed by him, nor are they engaged in national pursuits. Consequently there are powerful motives for not exempting persons of this description from the jurisdiction of the country in which they are found, and no one motive for requiring it. The implied license, therefore, under which they enter can never be construed to grant such exemption.

But in all respects different is the situation of a public armed ship. She constitutes a part of the military force of her nation; acts under the immediate and direct command of the sovereign; is employed by him in national objects. He has many and powerful motives for preventing those objects from being defeated by the interference of a foreign state. Such interference cannot take place without affecting his power and his dignity. The implied license, therefore, under which such vessel enters a friendly port, may reasonably be construed, and it seems to the court, ought to be construed, as containing an exemption from the jurisdiction of the sovereign, within whose territory she claims the rights of hospitality.

Upon these principles, by the unanimous consent of nations, a foreigner is amenable to the laws of the place; but certainly in practice, nations have not yet asserted their jurisdiction over the public armed ships of a sovereign entering a port open for their reception.

* * *

It seems, then, to the court, to be a principle of public law, that national ships of war, entering the port of a friendly power open for their reception, are to be considered as exempted by the consent of that power from its jurisdiction.

Without doubt, the sovereign of the place is capable of destroying this implication. He may claim and exercise jurisdiction either by employing force, or by subjecting such vessels to the ordinary tribunals. But until such power be exerted in a manner not to be misunderstood, the sovereign cannot be considered as having imparted to the ordinary tribunals a jurisdiction which it would be a breach of faith to exercise. Those general statutory provisions, therefore, which are descriptive of the ordinary jurisdiction of the judicial tribunals, which give an individual, whose property has been wrested from him, a right to claim that property in the courts of the country in which it is found, ought not, in the opinion of this court, to be so construed as to give them jurisdiction in a case in which the sovereign power has impliedly consented to waive its jurisdiction.

* * *

If the preceding reasoning be correct, the Exchange, being a public armed ship, in the service of a foreign sovereign, with whom the government of the United States is at peace, and having entered an American port open for her reception, on the terms on which ships of war are generally permitted to enter the ports of a friendly power, must be considered as having come into the American territory under an implied promise, that while necessarily within it, and demeaning herself in a friendly manner, she should be exempt from the jurisdiction of the country.

* * *

Letter of the Acting Legal Adviser of the United States Department of State, Jack B. Tate, to the Department of Justice, May 19, 1952*

The Department of State has, for some time had under consideration the question whether the practice of the Government in granting immunity from suit to foreign governments made parties defendant in the courts of the United States without their consent should not be changed. The Department has now reached the conclusion that such immunity should no longer be granted in certain types of cases. In view of the obvious interest of your Department in this matter I should like to point out briefly some of the facts which influenced the Department's decision.

A study of the law of sovereign immunity reveals the existence of two conflicting concepts of sovereign immunity, each widely held and firmly established. According to the classical or absolute theory of sovereign immunity, a sovereign cannot, without his consent, be made a respondent in the courts of another sovereign. According to the newer or restrictive theory of sovereign immunity, the immunity of the sovereign is recognized with regard to sovereign or public acts (*jure imperii*) of a state, but not

---

* Reprinted from 26 *United States Department of State Bulletin* 984 (1952).

with respect to private acts (*jure gestionis*). There is agreement by proponents of both theories, supported by practice, that sovereign immunity should not be claimed or granted in actions with respect to real property (diplomatic and perhaps consular property excepted) or with respect to the disposition of the property of a deceased person even though a foreign sovereign is the beneficiary.

The classical or virtually absolute theory of sovereign immunity has generally been followed by the courts of the United States, the British Commonwealth, Czechoslovakia, Estonia, and probably Poland.

The decisions of the courts of Brazil, Chile, China, Hungary, Japan, Luxembourg, Norway, and Portugal may be deemed to support the classical theory of immunity if one or at most two old decisions anterior to the development of the restrictive theory may be considered sufficient on which to base a conclusion.

The position of the Netherlands, Sweden, and Argentina is less clear since although immunity has been granted in recent cases coming before the courts of those countries, the facts were such that immunity would have been granted under either the absolute or restrictive theory. However, constant references by the courts of these three countries to the distinction between public and private acts of the state, even though the distinction was not involved in the result of the case, may indicate an intention to leave the way open for a possible application of the restrictive theory of immunity if and when the occasion presents itself.

A trend to the restrictive theory is already evident in the Netherlands where the lower courts have started to apply that theory following a Supreme Court decision to the effect that immunity would have been applicable in the case under consideration under either theory.

The German courts, after a period of hesitation at the end of the nineteenth century have held to the classical theory, but it should be noted that the refusal of the

Supreme Court in 1921 to yield to pressure by the lower courts for the newer theory was based on the view that that theory had not yet developed sufficiently to justify a change. In view of the growth of the restrictive theory since that time the German courts might take a different view today.

The newer or restrictive theory of sovereign immunity has always been supported by the courts of Belgium and Italy. It was adopted in turn by the courts of Egypt and of Switzerland. In addition, the courts of France, Austria, and Greece, which were traditionally supporters of the classical theory, reversed their position in the 20's to embrace the restrictive theory. Rumania, Peru, and possibly Denmark also appear to follow this theory.

Furthermore, it should be observed that in most of the countries still following the classical theory there is a school of influential writers favoring the restrictive theory and the views of writers, at least in civil law countries, are a major factor in the development of the law. Moreover, the leanings of the lower courts in civil law countries are more significant in shaping the law than they are in common law countries where the rule of precedent prevails and the trend in these lower courts is to the restrictive theory.

Of related interest to this question is the fact that ten of the thirteen countries which have been classified above as supporters of the classical theory have ratified the Brussels Convention of 1926 under which immunity for government owned merchant vessels is waived. In addition the United States, which is not a party to the Convention, some years ago announced and has since followed, a policy of not claiming immunity for its public owned or operated merchant vessels. Keeping in mind the importance played by cases involving public vessels in the field of sovereign immunity, it is thus noteworthy that these ten countries (Brazil, Chile, Estonia, Germany, Hungary, Netherlands, Norway, Poland, Portugal, Sweden) and the United States have already relinquished by treaty or in practice an important part of the immunity which they claim under the classical theory.

It is thus evident that with the possible exception of the United Kingdom little support has been found except on the part of the Soviet Union and its satellites for continued full acceptance of the absolute theory of sovereign immunity. There are evidences that British authorities are aware of its deficiencies and ready for a change. The reasons which obviously motivate state trading countries in adhering to the theory with perhaps increasing rigidity are most persuasive that the United States should change its policy. Furthermore, the granting of sovereign immunity to foreign governments in the courts of the United States is most inconsistent with the action of the Government of the United States in subjecting itself to suit in these same courts in both contract and tort and with its long established policy of not claiming immunity in foreign jurisdictions for its merchant vessels. Finally, the Department feels that the widespread and increasing practice on the part of governments of engaging in commercial activities makes necessary a practice which will enable persons doing business with them to have their rights determined in the courts. For these reasons it will hereafter be the Department's policy to follow the restrictive theory of sovereign immunity in the consideration of requests of foreign governments for a grant of sovereign immunity.

It is realized that a shift in policy by the executive cannot control the courts but it is felt that the courts are less likely to allow a plea of sovereign immunity where the executive has declined to do so. There have been indications that at least some Justices of the Supreme Court feel that in this matter courts should follow the branch of the Government charged with responsibility for the conduct of foreign relations.

* * *

Present Day Bourgeois Practice Regarding the Immunity of States from Foreign Jurisdiction*

S. N. Lebedev

The centuries-old axiom governing the practice of international intercourse reads *paz in parem non habet imperium*, or, in contemporary language, sovereignty does not permit the subordination of one state to another, including to the jurisdiction of its courts.

The international legal principle of the jurisdictional or legal immunity of a state or its property means that a foreign court is not competent in law to examine suits directly or indirectly taken against a state if the latter has not given its express consent.

This principle is now so well established that it is rarely challenged even by bourgeois jurists who are most opposed to it.

The campaign which began in bourgeois doctrine (in the main following the appearance in the world arena of the first Socialist state) for the limitation of this principle which, it is alleged, no longer corresponds to the "requirements of economic relations" (read "interests of the major monopolies", which are most frequently the partners of states in foreign trade) has not produced any arguments of a political, economic, historical, legal or other nature substantiating a real need to revise this principle of international law. The "theory" of "functional immunity" was advanced, in accordance with which a state acting in the field of "commercial activity" (engaging in foreign trade, international traffic, etc.), and carrying out *actus iure gestionia* as opposed to *acta iure imperii* allegedly loses its sovereign quality and, together

* Reprinted from S. N. Lebedev, "Present Day Bourgeois Practice Regarding the Immunity of States from Foreign Jurisdiction," *Soviet Yearbook of International Law* 306 (1960), by permission of the Soviet Association of International Law (English summary).

with it, the right of immunity from foreign jurisdiction. The contrived and contradictory nature of the theory of the duality of a state, which has been subjected to strong criticism not only in Socialist but also in bourgeois literature, is so obvious that it is now difficult to find a work by a bourgeois author dealing with the question of immunity which does not reflect dissatisfaction with this conception. While continuing to argue in favour of the restriction by every means of the immunity of states from foreign jurisdictions, bourgeois doctrine is attempting, however, to find new "grounds", to formulate new "theories" (Lauterpacht, Niboyet etc.), which on examination prove to be no less untenable than the theory of functional immunity.

Such "theories" which have been noted by the press of a certain political tendency, together with certain deviations of bourgeois legal practice from the generally-recognized principle of international law regarding absolute immunity clearly illustrate Lenin's postulate regarding the intermittent endeavours of the contemporary bourgeoisie to evade legality which it itself established and which has now become intolerable to it, in this case it is a question of a fundamental principle of the international rule of law—the principle of state sovereignty, which now constitutes an essential obstacle to the expansionist aspirations of the imperialist bourgeoisie.

An examination of the legal practice of the majority of capitalist countries shows that bourgeois courts are as a rule extremely cautious and restrained in their application of the "theory" of functional immunity, bearing in mind the undesirable consequences which a decision violating international law might have for international relations. With the exception of an extremely small number of countries in which the unjustified restriction of the principle of immunity in accordance with functional criteria is permitted (Italy, Belgium), in the overwhelming majority of countries legal practice during the post-war period has based itself upon the recognition of the principles of immunity. Deviations from this principle have been much more infrequent and less important than is claimed by some bourgeois scholars, who attach undue importance to these illegal deviations while unscrupulously hushing up or distorting the overwhelming majority of judgements in which the immunity of foreign states is recognized in full.

A study of international practice regarding the immunity of states and their property from foreign jurisdiction leads to the following conclusion. This rule is recognized by many present-day bourgeois international lawyers and—which is particularly important—bourgeois courts (although not without certain vacillations and contradictions). This rule is constantly cited by a state (regardless of the practice of its own courts) when its own interests are affected abroad. This rule continues to retain its force today.

The conclusion of a number of international agreements (bilateral and multilateral) providing for certain exceptions to the principle of immunity, contrary to the assertions of some bourgeois laywers, is a limitation by convention of a principle of international law applying only in the relations between the states which are parties to the agreement concerned. It in no way affects the rights of states which have not agreed to such limitations (*res interalies acta alteri accere non debet*).

Therefore the subjection of a state to foreign jurisdiction against its will constitutes an arbitrary illegal act incompatible with the consolidation of normal inter-state relations. Extensive international co-operation, above all in the economic field, can develop successfully only on condition that the generally-recognized rules of international law, of which one is that of the immunity of states from foreign jurisdiction flowing from the principle of sovereignty set down in the U.N. Charter, are unconditionally respected by all states.

Vienna Convention on Diplomatic Relations, 1961 *

The States Parties to the present Convention,

Recalling that peoples of all nations from ancient times have recognized the status of diplomatic agents,

Having in mind the purposes and principles of the Charter of the United Nations concerning the sovereign equality of states, the maintenance of international peace and security, and the promotion of friendly relations among nations,

Believing that an international convention on diplomatic intercourse, privileges and immunities would contribute to the development of friendly relations among nations, irrespective of their differing constitutional and social systems,

Realizing that the purpose of such privileges and immunities is not to benefit individuals but to ensure the efficient performance of the functions of diplomatic missions as representing states,

Affirming that the rules of customary international law should continue to govern questions not expressly regulated by the provisions of the present Convention,

Have agreed as follows:

Article I

For the purpose of the present Convention, the following expressions shall have the meanings hereunder assigned to them:
a. the "head of the mission" is the person charged by the sending state with the duty of acting in that capacity;
b. the "members of the mission" are the head of the mission and the members of the staff of the mission;
c. the "members of the staff of the mission" are the members of the diplomatic staff, of the administrative and technical staff and of the service staff of the mission;

* Reprinted from *United Nations Document* A/Conf. 20/13.

d. the "members of the diplomatic staff" are the members of the staff of the mission having diplomatic rank;

e. a "diplomatic agent" is the head of the mission or a member of the diplomatic staff of the mission;

f. the "members of the administrative and technical staff" are the members of the staff of the mission employed in the administrative and technical service of the mission;

g. the "members of the service staff" are the members of the staff of the mission in the domestic service of the mission;

h. a "private servant" is a person who is in the domestic service of a member of the mission and who is not an employee of the sending state;

i. the "premises of the mission" are the buildings or parts of buildings and the land ancillary thereto, irrespective of ownership, used for the purposes of the mission including the residence of the head of the mission.

Article 2

The establishment of diplomatic relations between states, and of permanent diplomatic missions, takes place by mutual consent.

Article 3

1. The functions of a diplomatic mission consist *inter alia* in:

a. representing the sending state in the receiving state;

b. protecting in the receiving state the interests of the sending state and of its nationals, within the limits permitted by international law;

c. negotiating with the government of the receiving state;

d. ascertaining by all lawful means conditions and developments in the receiving state; and reporting thereon to the government of the sending state;

e. promoting friendly relations between the sending state and the receiving state, and developing their economic, cultural and scientific relations.

2. Nothing in the present Convention shall be construed as preventing the performance of consular functions by a diplomatic mission.

* * *

Article 9

1. The receiving state may at any time and without having to explain its decision, notify the sending state that the head of the mission or any member of the diplomatic staff of the mission is *persona non grata* or that any other member of the staff of the mission is not acceptable. In any such case, the sending state shall, as appropriate, either recall the person concerned or terminate his functions with the mission. A person may be declared *non grata* or not acceptable before arriving in the territory of the receiving state.

2. If the sending state refuses or fails within a reasonable period to carry out its obligations under paragraph 1 of this article, the receiving state may refuse to recognize the person concerned as a member of the mission.

* * *

Article 22

1. The premises of the mission shall be inviolable. The agents of the receiving state may not enter them, except with the consent of the head of the mission.

2. The receiving state is under a special duty to take all appropriate steps to protect the premises of the mission against any intrusion or damage and to prevent any disturbance of the peace of the mission or impairment of its dignity.

3. The premises of the mission, their furnishings and other property thereon and

the means of transport of the mission shall be immune from search, requisition, attachment or execution.

Article 23

1. The sending state and the head of the mission shall be exempt from all national, regional or municipal dues and taxes in respect of the premises of the mission, whether owned or leased, other than such as represent payment for specific services rendered.

2. The exemption from taxation referred to in this article shall not apply to such dues and taxes payable under the law of the receiving state by persons contracting with the sending state or the head of the mission.

Article 24

The archives and documents of the mission shall be inviolable at any time and wherever they may be.

Article 25

The receiving state shall accord full facilities for the performance of the functions of the mission.

Article 26

Subject to its laws and regulations concerning zones entry into which is prohibited or regulated for reasons of national security, the receiving state shall ensure to all members of the mission freedom of movement and travel in its territory.

Article 27

1. The receiving state shall permit and protect free communication on the part of the mission for all official purposes. In communicating with the government and the other missions and consulates of the sending state, wherever situated, the mission may employ all appropriate means, including diplomatic couriers and messages in code or cipher. However, the mission may install and use a wireless transmitter only with the consent of the receiving state.

2. The official correspondence of the mission shall be inviolable. Official correspondence means all correspondence relating to the mission and its functions.

3. The diplomatic bag shall not be opened or detained.

4. The packages constituting the diplomatic bag must bear visible external marks of their character and may contain only diplomatic documents or articles intended for official use.

5. The diplomatic courier, who shall be provided with an official document indicating his status and the number of packages constituting the diplomatic bag, shall be protected by the receiving state in the performance of his functions. He shall enjoy personal inviolability and shall not be liable to any form of arrest or detention.

6. The sending state or the mission may designate diplomatic couriers *ad hoc*. In such cases the provisions of paragraph 5 of this article shall also apply, except that the immunities therein mentioned shall cease to apply when such a courier has delivered to the consignee the diplomatic bag in his charge.

7. A diplomatic bag may be entrusted to the captain of a commercial aircraft scheduled to land at an authorized port of entry. He shall be provided with an official document indicating the number of packages constituting the bag but he shall not be considered to be a diplomatic courier. The mission may send one of its members to take possession of the diplomatic bag directly and freely from the captain of the aircraft.

Article 28

The fees and charges levied by the mission in the course of its official duties shall be exempt from all dues and taxes.

Article 29

The person of a diplomatic agent shall be inviolable. He shall not be liable to any form of arrest or detention. The receiving state shall treat him with due respect and shall take all appropriate steps to prevent any attack on his person, freedom or dignity.

Article 30

1. The private residence of a diplomatic agent shall enjoy the same inviolability and protection as the premises of the mission.

2. His papers, correspondence and, except as provided in paragraph 3 of Article 31, his property, shall likewise enjoy inviolability.

Article 31

1. A diplomatic agent shall enjoy immunity from the criminal jurisdiction of the receiving state. He shall also enjoy immunity from its civil and administrative jurisdiction, except in the case of:

a. a real action relating to private immovable property situated in the territory of the receiving state, unless he holds it on behalf of the sending state for the purposes of the mission;

b. an action relating to succession in which the diplomatic agent is involved as executor, administrator, heir or legatee as a private person and not on behalf of the sending state;

c. an action relating to any professional or commercial activity exercised by the diplomatic agent in the receiving state outside his official functions.

2. A diplomatic agent is not obliged to give evidence as a witness.

3. No measures of execution may be taken in respect of a diplomatic agent except in the cases coming under subparagraphs a, b and c of paragraph 1 of this article, and provided that the measures concerned can be taken without infringing the inviolability of his person or of his residence.

4. The immunity of a diplomatic agent from the jurisdiction of the receiving state does not exempt him from the jurisdiction of the sending state.

Article 32

1. The immunity from jurisdiction of diplomatic agents and of persons enjoying immunity under Article 37 may be waived by the sending state.

2. Waiver must always be express.

3. The initiation of proceedings by a diplomatic agent or by a person enjoying immunity from jurisdiction under Article 37 shall preclude him from invoking immunity from jurisdiction in respect of any counter-claim directly connected with the principal claim.

4. Waiver of immunity from jurisdiction in respect of civil or administrative proceedings shall not be held to imply waiver of immunity in respect of the execution of the judgment, for which a separate waiver shall be necessary.

* * *

Article 34

A diplomatic agent shall be exempt from all dues and taxes, personal or real, national, regional or municipal, except:

a. indirect taxes of a kind which are normally incorporated in the price of goods or services;

b. dues and taxes on private immovable property situated in the territory of the receiving state, unless he holds it on behalf of the sending state for the purposes of the mission;

c. estate, succession or inheritance duties levied by the receiving state, subject to the provisions of paragraph 4 of Article 39;

d. dues and taxes on private income having its source in the receiving state and capital taxes on investments made in commercial undertakings in the receiving state;

e. charges levied for specific services rendered;

f. registration, court or record fees, mortgage dues and stamp duty, with respect to immovable property, subject to the provisions of Article 23.

Article 35

The receiving state shall exempt diplomatic agents from all personal services, from all public service of any kind whatsoever, and from military obligations such as those connected with requisitioning, military contributions and billeting.

Article 36

1. The receiving state shall, in accordance with such laws and regulations as it may adopt, permit entry of and grant exemption from all customs duties, taxes, and related charges other than charges for storage, cartage and similar services, on:

a. articles for the official use of the mission;

b. articles for the personal use of a diplomatic agent or members of his family forming part of his household, including articles intended for his establishment.

2. The personal baggage of a diplomatic agent shall be exempt from inspection, unless there are serious grounds for presuming that it contains articles not covered by the exemptions mentioned in paragraph 1 of this article, or articles the import or export of which is prohibited by the law or controlled by the quarantine regulations of the receiving state. Such inspection shall be conducted only in the presence of the diplomatic agent or of his authorized representative.

Article 37

1. The members of the family of a diplomatic agent forming part of his household shall, if they are not nationals of the receiving state, enjoy the privileges and immunities specified in Articles 29 to 36.

2. Members of the administrative and technical staff of the mission, together with members of their families forming part of their respective households, shall, if they are not nationals of or permanently resident in the receiving state, enjoy the privileges and immunities specified in Articles 29 to 35, except that the immunity from civil and administrative jurisdiction of the receiving state specified in paragraph 1 of Article 31 shall not extend to acts performed outside the course of their duties. They shall also enjoy the privileges specified in Article 36, paragraph 1, in respect of articles imported at the time of first installation.

3. Members of the service staff of the mission who are not nationals of or permanently resident in the receiving state shall enjoy immunity in respect of acts performed in the course of their duties, exemption from dues and taxes on the emoluments they receive by reason of their employment and the exemption contained in Article 33.

4. Private servants of members of the mission shall, if they are not nationals of or permanently resident in the receiving state, be exempt from dues and taxes on the emoluments they receive by reason of their employment. In other respects, they may enjoy privileges and immunities only to the extent admitted by the receiving state. However, the receiving state must exercise its jurisdiction over those persons in such a manner as not to interfere unduly with the performance of the functions of the mission.

Article 38

1. Except insofar as additional privileges and immunities may be granted by the receiving state, a diplomatic agent who is a national of or permanently resident in that state shall enjoy only immunity from jurisdiction, and inviolability, in respect of

official acts performed in the exercise of his functions.

2. Other members of the staff of the mission and private servants who are nationals of or permanently resident in the receiving state shall enjoy privileges and immunities only to the extent admitted by the receiving state. However, the receiving state must exercise its jurisdiction over those persons in such a manner as not to interfere unduly with the performance of the functions of the mission.

Article 39

1. Every person entitled to privileges and immunities shall enjoy them from the moment he enters the territory of the receiving state on proceeding to take up his post or, if already in its territory, from the moment when his appointment is notified to the Ministry for Foreign Affairs or such other ministry as may be agreed.

2. When the functions of a person enjoying privileges and immunities have come to an end, such privileges and immunities shall normally cease at the moment when he leaves the country, or on expiry of a reasonable period in which to do so, but shall subsist until that time, even in case of armed conflict. However, with respect to acts performed by such a person in the exercise of his functions as a member of the mission, immunity shall continue to subsist.

3. In case of the death of a member of the mission, the members of his family shall continue to enjoy the privileges and immunities to which they are entitled until the expiry of a reasonable period in which to leave the country.

Article 40

1. If a diplomatic agent passes through or is in the territory of a third state, which has granted him a passport visa if such visa was necessary, while proceeding to take up or to return to his post, or when returning to his own country, the third state shall accord him inviolability and such other immunities as may be required to ensure his transit or return. The same shall apply in the case of any members of his family enjoying privileges or immunities who are accompanying the diplomatic agent, or travelling separately to join him or to return to their country.

2. In circumstances similar to those specified in paragraph 1 of this article, third states shall not hinder the passage of members of the administrative and technical or service staff of a mission, and of members of their families, through their territories.

3. Third states shall accord to official correspondence and other official communications in transit, including messages in code or cipher, the same freedom and protection as is accorded by the receiving state. They shall accord to diplomatic couriers, who have been granted a passport visa if such visa was necessary, and diplomatic bags in transit the same inviolability and protection as the receiving state is bound to accord.

4. The obligations of third states under paragraphs 1, 2 and 3 of this article shall also apply to the persons mentioned respectively in those paragraphs, and to official communications and diplomatic bags, whose presence in the territory of the third state is due to *force majeure*.

Article 41

1. Without prejudice to their privileges and immunities, it is the duty of all persons enjoying such privileges and immunities to respect the laws and regulations of the receiving state. They also have a duty not to interfere in the internal affairs of that state.

2. All official business with the receiving state entrusted to the mission by the sending state shall be conducted with or through the Ministry for Foreign Affairs of the receiving state or such other ministry as may be agreed.

3. The premises of the mission must not be used in any manner incompatible with

the functions of the mission as laid down in the present Convention or by other rules of general international law or by any special agreements in force between the sending and the receiving state.

Article 42

A diplomatic agent shall not in the receiving state practise for personal profit any professional or commercial activity.

Article 43

The function of a diplomatic agent comes to an end, *inter alia:*
a. on notification by the sending state to the receiving state that the function of the diplomatic agent has come to an end;
b. on notification by the receiving state to the sending state that, in accordance with paragraph 2 of Article 9, it refuses to recognize the diplomatic agent as a member of the mission.

Article 44

The receiving state must, even in case of armed conflict, grant facilities in order to enable persons enjoying privileges and immunities, other than nationals of the receiving state, and members of the families of such persons irrespective of their nationality, to leave at the earliest possible moment. It must, in particular, in case of need, place at their disposal the necessary means of transport for themselves and their property.

Article 45

If the diplomatic relations are broken off between two states, or if a mission is permanently or temporarily recalled:
a. the receiving state must, even in case of armed conflict, respect and protect the premises of the mission, together with its property and archives;
b. the sending state may entrust the custody of the premises of the mission, together with its property and archives,

to a third state acceptable to the receiving state;
c. the sending state may entrust the protection of its interests and those of its nationals to a third state acceptable to the receiving state.

Article 46

A sending state may, with the prior consent of a receiving state, and at the request of a third state not represented in the receiving state, undertake the temporary protection of the interests of the third state and of its nationals.

Article 47

1. In the application of the provisions of the present Convention, the receiving state shall not discriminate as between states.
2. However, discrimination shall not be regarded as taking place:
a. where the receiving state applies any of the provisions of the present Convention restrictively because of a restrictive application of that provision to its mission in the sending state;
b. where by custom or agreement states extend to each other more favourable treatment than is required by the provisions of the present Convention.

* * *

Carrera v. Carrera*

United States Court of Appeals, District of Columbia Circuit, 1949

Rosa H. Carrera sued her husband, Amable H. Carrera, in the United States District Court for the District of Columbia for separate maintenance for herself, and for the custody of and support for their fifteen-year old son. The Carreras are nationals of Ecuador, permanently resident

* Reprinted from 174 F. 2d 496 (1949).

in the United States. When the action was instituted, both were domestic servants in the Czechoslovakian Embassy.

Amable moved to quash the return showing service of process upon him and also moved to dismiss the complaint, claiming diplomatic immunity from the action. Such immunity was requested for him by the Czechoslovakian Ambassador in a communication to the Secretary of State. A copy of the Ambassador's note was transmitted to the district judge by the legal adviser to the Secretary of State with the following letter:

"There is enclosed for the information of the District Court of the United States for the District of Columbia a copy of a note received by the Department of State from the Czechoslovak Ambassador in which diplomatic immunity is requested on behalf of Amable Hidalgo Carrera, an Ecuadoran national, employed by the Czechoslovak Ambassador as a butler and chauffeur.

"The name of Mr. Carrera has been previously registered in the Department of State in accordance with Section 254 of Title 22 of the United States Code and has been included in the 'List of Employees in the Embassies and Legations in Washington not Printed in the Diplomatic List', commonly known as the 'White List', which has been transmitted by the Secretary of State to the Marshal of the District of Columbia.

"It would be appreciated if the Court would take into consideration the request of the Czechoslovak Ambassador and take such action as the Court deems to be appropriate in the circumstances."[1]

The District Court dismissed the complaint on the ground that Amable was diplomatically immune from the action. Rosa appeals.

Her first ground for reversal is that the right of the appellee to diplomatic immunity was not properly presented to the District Court. . . . It is enough that an ambassador has requested immunity, that the State Department has recognized that the person for whom it was requested is

entitled to it, and that the Department's recognition has been communicated to the court. "The courts are disposed to accept as conclusive of the fact of the diplomatic status of an individual claiming an exemption, the views thereon of the political department of their government."[2]

The next contention of the appellant is that the inclusion of Amable's name on the so-called "White List" was not sufficient to bring him within the second clause of § 254 which would extend to him the protection of §§ 252 and 253. In support of this proposition the appellant cites Trost v. Tompkins, D.C.Mun.App.1945, 44 A.2d 226. But in the Trost case the court held no more than that, certification of the Secretary of State being absent, a court otherwise having jurisdiction should determine whether the person claiming immunity was properly placed on the "White List." But here, the Secretary having certified Carrera's name as included in the list, judicial inquiry into the propriety of its listing was not appropriate.

It is further suggested by the appellant that this action is not within the purview of § 252 since it is not one in which the defendant's goods or chattels were distrained, seized or attached. The rule of immunity is not confined to those actions which have as a direct objective the distraint, seizure or attachment of goods or chattels. "It has long been a settled rule of law that foreign diplomatic representatives are exempt from all local processes in the country to which they are accredited.   1 Kent's Commentaries 15, 38. The same immunity is not only given to an ambassador himself, but to his subordinates, family and servants as well." 27 Harv.L. Rev. 489 (1914). See also 27 Yale L.J. 392 (1917).

The appellant also invokes the first portion of § 254, which is

"Sections 252 and 253 of this title shall not apply to any case where the person against whom the process is issued is a citizen or inhabitant of the United States, in the service of an ambassador or a public minister, and the process if founded upon a debt contracted before he entered upon such service; * * *"

The suggestion is that Amable is an inhabitant of the United States in the service of an ambassador and that the process against him in this case was founded upon a debt contracted before he entered upon such service, in that the child for whom support was sought was born before he began to serve the Ambassador. A parent's moral or legal obligation to support his infant child is not usually considered as a debt within the ordinary significance of the word. We are here concerned with the word "debt" as it is used in § 254; and we do not regard Amable's moral or legal obligation to support his child, which this action sought to enforce, as a "debt contracted before he entered upon" the Ambassador's service.

The final contention of the appellant is that the rule of diplomatic immunity does not apply in the field of domestic relations, in support of which she cites State of Ohio ex rel. Popovici v. Agler, 1930, 280 U.S. 379, 50 S.Ct. 154, 74 L.Ed. 489. But the question of diplomatic immunity was not raised in that case, as Popovici was a vice consul of Rumania, and it is universally recognized as a principle of international law that, in the absence of express agreement therefor, immunity does not extend to consuls, who are merely commercial representatives of foreign states. 16 Am.Jur. 964. Cf. The Sao Vicente, 1922, 260 U.S. 151, 155, 43 S.Ct. 15, 67 L.Ed. 179.

We have no doubt that the case was properly decided by the District Court.

Affirmed.

Notes

1. Sections 252, 253 and 254 of Title 22 of the United States Code, Annotated, which have to do with the diplomatic immunity of ambassadors and public ministers, are as follows:

" § 252. Suits against ministers and their domestics prohibited. Whenever any writ or process is sued out or prosecuted by any person in any court of the United States, or of a State, or by any judge or justice, whereby the person of any ambassador or public minister of any foreign prince or State, authorized and received as such by the President, or any domestic or domestic servant of any such minister, is arrested or imprisoned, or his goods or chattels are distrained, seized, or attached, such writ or process shall be deemed void.

" § 253. Penalty for wrongful suit. Whenever any writ or process is sued out in violation of section 252 of this title, every person by whom the same is obtained or prosecuted, whether as party or as attorney or solicitor, and every officer concerned in executing it, shall be deemed a violator of the laws of nations and a disturber of the public repose, and shall be imprisoned for not more than three years, and fined at the discretion of the court.

" § 254. Exceptions as to suits against servants, etc., of minister; listing servants. Sections 252 and 253 of this title shall not apply to any case where the person against whom the process is issued is a citizen or inhabitant of the United States, in the service of an ambassador or a public minister, and the process is founded upon a debt contracted before he entered upon such service; nor shall section 253 of this title apply to any case where the person against whom the process is issued is a domestic servant of an ambassador or a public minister, unless the name of the servant has, before the issuing thereof, been registered in the Department of State, and transmitted by the Secretary of State to the marshal of the District of Columbia, who shall upon receipt thereof post the same in some public place in his office. All persons shall have resort to the list of names so posted in the marshal's office, and may take copies without fee."

2. II Hyde, International Law, 1268.

United Nations-United States Agreement Regarding the Headquarters of the United Nations, 1947*

The United Nations and the United States of America:

* Reprinted from 17 *United States Department of State Bulletin* 27 (1947).

Desiring to conclude an agreement for the purpose of carrying out the Resolution adopted by the General Assembly on 14 December 1946 to establish the seat of the United Nations in The City of New York and to regulate questions arising as a result thereof;

Have appointed as their representatives for this purpose:

The United Nations:

Trygve Lie, Secretary-General, and

The United States of America:

George C. Marshall, Secretary of State, Who have agreed as follows:

* * *

Article III: Law and Authority in the Headquarters District

SECTION 7

a. The headquarters district shall be under the control and authority of the United Nations as provided in this agreement.

b. Except as otherwise provided in this agreement or in the General Convention,† the federal, state and local law of the United States shall apply within the headquarters district.

c. Except as otherwise provided in this agreement or in the General Convention, the federal, state and local courts of the United States shall have jurisdiction over acts done and transactions taking place in the headquarters district as provided in applicable federal, state and local laws.

d. The federal, state and local courts of the United States, when dealing with cases arising out of or relating to acts done or transactions taking place in the headquarters district, shall take into account the regulations enacted by the United Nations under Section 8.

† Convention on Privileges and Immunities of the United Nations, approved by the General Assembly of the United Nations on February 13, 1946. 1 *United Nations Treaty Series* 15.

SECTION 8

The United Nations shall have the power to make regulations, operative within the headquarters district, for the purpose of establishing therein conditions in all respects necessary for the full execution of its functions. No federal, state or local law or regulation of the United States which is inconsistent with a regulation of the United Nations authorized by this section shall, to the extent of such inconsistency, be applicable within the headquarters district. Any dispute, between the United Nations and the United States, as to whether a regulation of the United Nations is authorized by this section or as to whether a federal, state or local law or regulation is inconsistent with any regulation of the United Nations authorized by this section, shall be promptly settled as provided in Section 21. Pending such settlement, the regulation of the United Nations shall apply, and the federal, state or local law or regulation shall be inapplicable in the headquarters district to the extent that the United Nations claims it to be inconsistent with the regulation of the United Nations. This section shall not prevent the reasonable application of fire protection regulations of the appropriate American authorities.

SECTION 9

a. The headquarters district shall be inviolable. Federal, state or local officers or officials of the United States, whether administrative, judicial, military or police, shall not enter the headquarters district to perform any official duties therein except with the consent of and under conditions agreed to by the Secretary-General. The service of legal process, including the seizure of private property, may take place within the headquarters district only with the consent of and under conditions approved by the Secretary-General.

b. Without prejudice to the provisions of the General Convention or Article IV of this agreement, the United Nations shall prevent the headquarters district from becoming a refuge either for persons who are avoiding arrest under the federal, state, or local law of the United States or are required by the Government of the United States for extradition to another country, or for persons who are endeavoring to avoid service of legal process.

SECTION 10

The United Nations may expel or exclude persons from the headquarters district for violation of its regulations adopted under Section 8 or for other cause. Persons who violate such regulations shall be subject to other penalties or to detention under arrest only in accordance with the provisions of such laws or regulations as may be adopted by the appropriate American authorities.

Article IV: Communications and Transit

SECTION 11

The federal, state or local authorities of the United States shall not impose any impediments to transit to or from the headquarters district of (1) representatives of Members or officials of the United Nations, or of specialized agencies as defined in Article 57, paragraph 2, of the Charter, or the families of such representatives or officials, (2) experts performing missions for the United Nations or for such specialized agencies, (3) representatives of the press, or of radio, film or other information agencies, who have been accredited by the United Nations (or by such a specialized agency) in its discretion after consultation with the United States, (4) representatives of non-governmental organizations recognized by the United Nations for the purpose of consultation under Article 71 of the Charter, or (5) other persons invited to the headquarters district by the United Nations or by such specialized agency on official business. The appropriate American authorities shall afford any neces-

sary protection to such persons while in transit to or from the headquarters district. . . .

SECTION 12

The provisions of Section 11 shall be applicable irrespective of the relations existing between the Governments of the persons referred to in that section and the Government of the United States.

SECTION 13

a. Laws and regulations in force in the United States regarding the entry of aliens shall not be applied in such manner as to interfere with the privileges referred to in Section 11. When visas are required for persons referred to in that Section, they shall be granted without charge and as promptly as possible.

* * *

Article V: Resident Representative to the United Nations

SECTION 15

1. Every person designated by a Member as the principal resident representative to the United Nations of such Member or as a resident representative with the rank of ambassador or minister plenipotentiary,

2. such resident members of their staffs as may be agreed upon between the Secretary-General, the Government of the United States and the Government of the Member concerned,

3. every person designated by a Member of a specialized agency, as defined in Article 57, paragraph 2, of the Charter, as its principal resident representative, with the rank of ambassador or minister plenipotentiary, at the headquarters of such agency in the United States, and

4. such other principal resident representatives of members to a specialized agency and such resident members of the staffs of representatives to a specialized agency as may be agreed upon between the

principal executive officer of the specialized agency, the Government of the United States and the Government of the Member concerned,

shall, whether residing inside or outside the headquarters district, be entitled in the territory of the United States to the same privileges and immunities, subject to corresponding conditions and obligations, as it accords to diplomatic envoys accredited to it. In the case of Members whose governments are not recognized by the United States, such privileges and immunities need be extended to such representatives, or persons on the staffs of such representatives, only within the headquarters district, at their residences and offices outside the district, in transit between the district and such residences and offices, and in transit on official business to or from foreign countries.

Article VI: Police Protection of the Headquarters District

SECTION 16

a. The appropriate American authorities shall exercise due diligence to ensure that the tranquility of the headquarters district is not disturbed by the unauthorized entry of groups of persons from outside or by disturbances in its immediate vicinity and shall cause to be provided on the boundaries of the headquarters district such police protection as is required for these purposes.

b. If so requested by the Secretary-General, the appropriate American authorities shall provide a sufficient number of police for the preservation of law and order in the headquarters district, and for the removal therefrom of persons as requested under the authority of the United Nations. The United Nations shall, if requested, enter into arrangements with the appropriate American authorities to reimburse them for the reasonable cost of such services.

* * *

Article VIII: Matters Relating to the Operation of this Agreement

* * *

SECTION 21

a. Any dispute between the United Nations and the United States concerning the interpretation or application of this agreement or of any supplemental agreement, which is not settled by negotiation or other agreed mode of settlement, shall be referred for final decision to a tribunal of three arbitrators, one to be named by the Secretary-General, one to be named by the Secretary of State of the United States, and the third to be chosen by the two, or, if they should fail to agree upon a third, then by the President of the International Court of Justice.

b. The Secretary-General or the United States may ask the General Assembly to request of the International Court of Justice an advisory opinion on any legal question arising in the course of such proceedings. Pending the receipt of the opinion of the Court, an interim decision of the arbitral tribunal shall be observed by both parties. Thereafter, the arbitral tribunal shall render a final decision, having regard to the opinion of the Court.

* * *

United States v. Egorov*

United States District Court, E. D. N. Y., 1963

On July 15, 1963 a two-count indictment was filed herein. Count 1 thereof charges that from in or about March, 1957, and continuously thereafter up to and including the date of the filing thereof, the defendants, in violation of Section 794(c) of Title 18 United States Code, unlawfully,

* * *

* Reprinted from 222 F. Supp. 106 (1963).

knowingly and wilfully conspired and agreed with certain named and unnamed officials of the Soviet Military Intelligence, all co-conspirators, but none named as a defendant therein, and with divers other persons, to violate Section 794(a) of said Title, by agreeing to communicate, deliver and transmit to a foreign government, the Union of Soviet Socialist Republics, or to representatives or agents thereof, information relating to the national defense of the United States, with intent or reason to believe that it would be used to the advantage of said foreign government.

Count 2 thereof charges that in or about and between the same dates, in Moscow, in the District of Columbia and Maryland, and elsewhere, the defendants, not being diplomatic or consular officers or attachés of a foreign government, in violation of Section 371 of said Title, conspired with various named and unnamed officials of the Soviet Military Intelligence, all co-conspirators, but none named as a defendant therein, to violate the provisions of Section 951 of said Title.

The defendants Ivan Dmitrievich Egorov, also known as Ivan D. Yegorov (Egorov), and Aleksandra Ivanovna Egorova, also known as Alexandra I. Egorova (Egorova), have moved for an order dismissing the indictment against them (1) on the ground that the defendant Ivan Egorov is a diplomat of a foreign government, the Union of Soviet Socialist Republics (U.S.S.R.), and, hence, that he and Aleksandra Egorova, who is his wife, are immune from arrest and prosecution under the Law of Nations and (2) the further ground that, pursuant to Article III, Section 2, Clause 2 of the Constitution of the United States, the Supreme Court of the United States has original and exclusive jurisdiction of all cases involving persons with diplomatic status, and, accordingly, this Court is without jurisdiction in the matter.

Point 1

[1] The defendants base their claim on the fact that the U.S.S.R., exercising its right as a sovereign power, invested Egorov with immunity by issuing to him a diplomatic passport (Exhibit No. 3) wherein he was designated as First Secretary of the Ministry of Foreign Affairs; that subsequently he presented the same at the United States Embassy at Moscow, where he made application for a visa in order to obtain entry into the United States, stating his aforementioned diplomatic rank, and expressing his intention to enter the United States to accept a post in the Personnel Office of the United Nations; and that on September 23, 1960 the said Embassy issued to the defendants and their son, Michael, non-immigrant visas to secure their entry into the United States. They contend that this, without more, clothes them with the diplomatic immunity which precludes their arrest and prosecution. I disagree. The visa issued to Egorov was not a diplomatic visa but a G–4 visa, which is issued to officers and employees of international organizations, and bore the notation "Employee of U.N. Secretariat." A diplomatic visa is defined by Section 1101(a) (11) of Title 8 U.S. Code, as a "nonimmigrant visa *bearing that title and issued to a nonimmigrant in accordance with such regulations as the Secretary of State may prescribe.*"

The issuance to Egorov of a diplomatic passport is not controlling of his status. The title of "First Secretary of the Ministry of Foreign Affairs" would entitle him to diplomatic immunity provided that he had been accepted and recognized as such by the United States. Section 252 of Title 22 U.S. Code, grants immunity from arrest only to those ambassadors or public ministers of foreign states who have been "*authorized and received as such by the President.*"

Hon. Angier Biddle Duke, Chief of Protocol, United States Department of State, is responsible for registering and maintaining his Department's records respecting the official status of all officers and employees of foreign governments in this country who are entitled to diplomatic immunity pursuant to Section 252, supra, or to the agreement between the United States and the United Nations concerning the Headquarters of the United Nations. He is responsible also for registering and maintaining his Department's records concerning representatives in or to international organizations and officers and employees thereof who are entitled to the privileges, exemptions and immunities granted by Sections 288–288f of Title 22 of said Code. Hon. Dean Rusk, Secretary of State, has certified (Exhibit No. 2) that Mr. Duke's acts as Chief of Protocol are entitled to full faith and credit. As appears from said Exhibit No. 2 Mr. Duke has certified that a diligent search of his records has disclosed "no record which would indicate that Ivan Dmitrievich Egorov * * * is or ever has been notified to and recognized by the Department of State in any capacity which would entitle him to diplomatic immunity pursuant to the above-mentioned Sections 252–254 of Title 22 of the United States Code."

He further certified that his records do not reflect that Egorov "is, or ever has been, the principal resident representative of a Member of the United Nations under Section 15(1) of the Headquarters Agreement, or that his name was ever notified to or accepted by the Department of State as a member of the staff of such a representative under Section 15(2) of that agreement," and that "the only records ever received in the Department of State regarding the said Mr. Egorov list him as an *employee* of the United Nations Secretariat, entitled to the privileges and immunities granted by Sections 288–288(f) of Title 22 of the United States Code," (Emphasis mine.)

The said series of sections constitute the "International Organizations Immunity Act." Section 288d (b) thereof provides that "Representatives of foreign governments in or to international organizations (the United Nations became one by Executive Order of the President) and officers and employees of such organizations shall be immune from suit and legal process *relating to acts performed by them in their official*

capacity and falling within their functions as such representatives, officers, or employees * * *." The limitation created by the underscored provisions of the said Section precludes Egorov from claiming general immunity. United States v. Melekh, D.C., 190 F. Supp. 67. Article 105 of the United Nations Charter, 59 Stat. 1053, urged by Egorov as a further basis for his claim of immunity, provides that representatives of the members of the organization and officials thereof shall enjoy such privileges and immunities *as are necessary to the independent exercise of their function in the Organization.* Egorov, as hereinabove stated, was an employee of the United Nations, from which he received his compensation for services rendered. His duties and functions were entirely non-diplomatic in character. *Employees* of the United Nations are separate and distinct from persons designated by foreign governments to serve *as their foreign representatives* in or to the United Nations, United States v. Melekh, supra. His duties and functions in the Personnel Section of the United Nations did not, of course, contemplate or include such acts as those charged in the indictment herein.

To argue that despite the absence of acceptance and recognition of his claimed diplomatic status Egorov is entitled to diplomatic immunity is to deny this government its sovereign right to pass upon the acceptability to it of diplomatic representatives of foreign governments.

The well established principles respecting diplomatic immunity enunciated in the case and textbook authorities cited in support of the defendants' motion are wholly inapplicable to the instant case.

As to Point 2

[2] Inasmuch as Egorov, for the reasons hereinabove stated, does not have diplomatic status, he does not come within the purview of Article 3, Section 2, Clause 2 of the Constitution of the United States, which gives the Supreme Court original and exclusive jurisdiction in all cases affecting

Ambassadors, other public Ministers and Consuls.

Accordingly, the defendants' motion is in all respects denied.

Statement by Ambassador Sidney R. Yates, Representative of the United States to the United Nations, Concerning the Request of Captain Galvao to Appear Before the Fourth Committee of the General Assembly*

[*"In November, 1963, Captain Enrique Galvão, a Portuguese national and former Governor General of Angola and an opponent of the administration of President Salazar of Portugal, requested that the Fourth Committee (Trusteeship) of the United Nations General Assembly grant him a hearing so that he could testify on conditions in Portuguese overseas territories. Mr. Galvão, a leading participant in the seizure of the Portuguese passenger liner* S.S. Santa Maria *in 1961, had been granted asylum in Brazil following that incident, and was residing in Brazil at the time of his request. On November 11, 1963, Ambassador Sidney R. Yates, United States representative, made the following statement in the Fourth Committee with regard to Mr. Galvão's request:"* 58 American Journal of International Law 457 (1964).]

I have asked for the floor briefly at this point to bring to the Committee's attention certain factors in connection with the request for a hearing we are now considering. Let me say first, we do not object to Mr. Galvao's appearance. We desire only to point out possible consequences of Mr. Galvao's appearance before this Committee. . . .

I would point out, Mr. Chairman, that the United States has extradition agree-

* Reprinted from 58 *American Journal of International Law* 457 (1964) by permission of the American Society of International Law.

ments with some 78 countries. Under these agreements, a country has the right to undertake measures to extradite persons accused, in that country, of serious crimes.

First of all, let me make clear at the outset that there is no question that, if Mr. Galvao is invited to appear before this Committee at UN headquarters, the United States will—as in the case of other petitioners—take the necessary steps to enable him to travel to the headquarters district, in accordance with Section 11 of the Headquarters Agreement. However, the members of this Committee will also be aware that Section 11, while entitling invited persons to travel to the headquarters district, and contemplating routine measures of protection while they are in transit, does not grant them immunity from legal process. Such immunity is granted by Section 15 of the Headquarters Agreement, whose benefits are limited by its own terms, to resident representatives of members of the Organization, and to certain members of their staffs. Accordingly, Mr. Galvao, while present in the United States, would not enjoy immunity from legal process.

May I note, in passing, that while the United States is not party to the General Convention on Privileges and Immunities of the United Nations, the situation would in no way be changed if we were party, since the General Convention does not confer any immunity on invitees.

As members of the Committee are aware, the Government of Portugal seeks custody over Mr. Galvao in connection with certain serious charges, alleging criminal acts. It may be that some of these charges, at least by name, might prove to come within terms of the Extradition Convention of May 7, 1908 between Portugal and the United States. Accordingly, it would appear very likely that the Government of Portugal will initiate proceedings in the courts of this country for Mr. Galvao's extradition.

The United States is prepared as I noted earlier to comply fully with its obligations under the Headquarters Agreement. At the same time, however, neither the Government nor the courts of this country have any choice but to comply with whatever legal obligations they may have under the Extradition Convention. In the light of these considerations, we think it incumbent upon the United States Delegation to set forth this situation unequivocally to the Committee in order that its decision regarding the issuance of an invitation or the granting of the request for a hearing to Mr. Galvao may proceed without any possible misunderstanding.

Mr. Chairman, in view of these considerations, we suggest that the Committee, rather than granting Mr. Galvao's request for a hearing, might wish to invite him to submit a statement in writing or make an audiotape recording which could be heard by the Committee. While we recognize that such a procedure is not as satisfactory as having a petitioner present in person, it would, nevertheless, permit Mr. Galvao to submit his views to the Committee and would at the same time eliminate the difficulties I have described.

[*"The Fourth Committee subsequently granted the request for a hearing. Mr. Galvão came to the United Nations from Brazil on December 9, gave his testimony on the same day, and returned to Brazil on December 10."* 58 American Journal of International Law *458 (1964).*]

TREATMENT OF ALIENS

It is universally agreed that the jurisdiction of states is limited to the extent that international law protects aliens and alien property situated within their territory.[1] Whenever treatment of an alien constitutes a violation of international customary or treaty law, the state of which the injured alien is a national has a legal *right* to make a diplomatic protest against, and submit a claim for damages to, the state responsible for the wrong, which in turn has a legal *duty* to make reparation. International law does not require a state to take up the claim of its national, and it does not allow a state to take up the claim unless the injured alien is its national.[2] A state incurs international responsibility for an injury suffered by an alien only if some fault of commission or omission can be attributed to its own officials; if, for example, state officials fail to exercise reasonable diligence to protect an alien from a harmful action by private persons or if they fail to take remedial steps after such an action, the state may be held responsible by the home state of the alien. A state may not press the claim of its national if the individual has not given the state charged with the wrong an opportunity to provide a remedy through its own processes. This rule does not apply, however, if there are no local remedies to exhaust or if the local courts are notoriously corrupt. International claims are always pressed against the central government of a state, even though a political subdivision may have been responsible for the wrong. As the only government having relations with other states, the central government is responsible under international law for all governmental acts or omissions that take place within the state, whether or not it has the authority under its own constitution to control its political subdivisions.

The most common method by which states press claims on behalf of their nationals is to proceed through "normal diplomatic channels." When, for example,

[1] An alien is a person who is not a national of the state in which he is present, whether or not he is there permanently or temporarily. Alien property is the property in a state that is owned by non-nationals.

[2] ". . . it is the bond of nationality between the state and the individual which alone confers upon the State the right of diplomatic protection. . . ." Panevezys-Soldertiskis Railway Case (1939), *Permanent Court of International Justice*, Series A/B 76, p. 16.

in 1891, eleven Italian nationals were lynched in New Orleans in consequence of a mob reaction against the Mafia, the Italian government recalled its minister from Washington in protest and insisted that the United States government give assurance that the guilty persons would be punished and that an indemnity would be paid. The basis of the Italian claim was that New Orleans authorities had not taken the necessary steps to protect the Italians, who were being held in jail for complicity in the murder of the local chief of police. Largely because of the nature of its federal system, the United States was unable to give assurance that the guilty persons would be punished, but Secretary of State James G. Blaine accepted responsibility for the wrong and an indemnity of $24,330 was paid to Italy.

In order to process the ever increasing number of international claims alleging mistreatment of aliens, states have sometimes by-passed the overcrowded and politically sensitive diplomatic channels by establishing a mixed claims commission and empowering it to settle outstanding claims between the two contracting parties. And sometimes a state awards a lump sum payment to another state to settle a group of outstanding claims.

What are the international rights of aliens, the deprivation of which constitutes a delict for which the alien's home state has a right to demand reparation? It is with regard to the content of these rights, not their existence or the processes by which they are protected, that international controversy has often erupted. It is agreed that each state may determine for itself whether or not to admit aliens into its territory and that, once admitted, aliens must obey local laws. It is also agreed that certain rights and privileges that are possessed by nationals, such as the franchise, may be denied to aliens. But international law requires that in matters of fundamental importance to the individual—such as the right to life and personal liberty—a state must treat aliens

at least as well as it treats its own nationals. If a state imprisons its own nationals only after a jury trial, for example, it must accord aliens the same right. Decision-makers in Communist states and in most of the underdeveloped world are of the opinion that this is all the law commands, that so long as aliens receive equality of treatment with nationals, international obligations are fulfilled. Most Western governments, on the other hand, claim that international law requires that states treat aliens in accordance with an "international minimum standard of justice," regardless of how they treat their own nationals.

Most governments and jurists in Europe and North America assert that a state has a right to expropriate alien property only if it is taken for "public purposes," if no discrimination is made between aliens and nationals, and if "prompt, adequate, and effective payment" is provided for.[3] "In principle, therefore, expropriation, as an exercise of territorial competence, is lawful, but the compensation rule makes the legality conditional."[4] These views, which are generally referred to as the "traditional norms," have lost much of their relevance in the wake of variations in state practice in recent years. There are apparently no limits now on the measures a state may consider to be necessary for the general welfare, or for "public purposes." Differences of opinion as to what constitutes prompt, adequate, and effective compensation indicate that there is no consensus on the matter. The acceptance by Western states of compromise lump sum payments that add up to less-than-full loaves has further eroded the full payment rule.

[3] Cordell Hull, United States Secretary of State, asserted in a letter to the Mexican Ambassador in 1938: "The government of the United States merely adverts to a self-evident fact when it notes that the applicable precedents and recognized authorities on international law support its declaration that, under every rule of law and equity, no government is entitled to expropriate private property, for whatever purpose, without provision for prompt, adequate, and effective payment therefore." 3 Hackworth, *Digest of International Law* 658–659.

[4] Brownlie, *Principles of Public International Law*, pp. 432–433.

Nevertheless, if only because almost all states continue to recognize the duty to pay some compensation,[5] expropriation without any compensation, and terms of compensation that are, in effect, disguised schemes of confiscation,[6] must still be regarded as forbidden by international law.[7]

The fact that almost all states continue to recognize an international duty to compensate for expropriated alien property, in a period when the developing states consider a strict application of the traditional norms to be an interference with their legal power to reform their political, economic, and social affairs, indicates an awareness that the requirements of a stable international economy include some legal protection of private property abroad. More

particularly, it suggests an awareness among decision-makers in the capital-importing states of the importance of foreign private capital to their economic development. But it is futile to insist upon a strict application of traditional norms; since the poorer states cannot raise the necessary capital to make full and prompt compensation, such an insistence would render any major social and economic programs impossible. Consequently, they are unwilling to accept the Western view. There is a need to start all over by developing rules to protect foreign investments that will receive the assent of all major groups of states. That a beginning has been made is illustrated by the increased use of lump sum payments that are based on capacity to pay rather than on the market value of the property seized.

The first selection that follows, the case of *Laura Janes* (*U.S.A.*) *v. United Mexican States*, illustrates a number of the traditional rules and processes of international law relating to state responsibility for the treatment of aliens, including the responsibility of the central government for the acts and omissions of its political subdivisions and the way damages are assessed in cases involving lack of diligence in apprehending and punishing a national who has harmed an alien. The remaining selections concern the controversial and politically sensitive matter of expropriation of alien property. Oliver J. Lissitzyn discusses the attitude of the new states toward the traditional norms. The procedure by which international claims are pressed by the home state of an alien is explained in a memorandum issued in 1961 by the United States Department of State. Finally, the decision of the United States Supreme Court in *Banco Nacional de Cuba v. Sabbatino* and the decision on remand by a United States District Court are included as a case study in the use of the "act of state" doctrine as a bar to recourse to national courts by an individual or a corporation whose property has been expropriated

---

[5] After much delay, Mexico finally agreed in 1938 to pay $24 million to compensate United States nationals whose oil and land holdings had been expropriated. Since the Suez Canal Company was nationalized in 1956, Egypt has paid over $80 million to former shareholders. Numerous states, including Bulgaria, Poland, Rumania, and Yugoslavia, have made lump sum payments to compensate for expropriated alien property.

[6] The terms of compensation by which Cuba offered to pay United States nationals for property expropriated in 1960 were labeled as "confiscatory" by the Department of State. The value of the expropriated property was to be determined solely by appraisers chosen by the Cuban President and Prime Minister. Payment was to be in bonds with terms of not less than 30 years and bearing 2 per cent interest. The interest, which was not to be cumulative from year to year, was to be paid only out of the yearly foreign exchange received by sales of sugar to the United States in excess of 3,000,000 Spanish long tons at a minimum price of 5.75 cents per English pound. Only in one of the ten years preceding 1960 was more than 3,000,000 Spanish long tons of sugar sold and the price of the sugar had never reached 5.75 cents.

[7] The Resolution on Permanent Sovereignty Over Natural Resources, adopted by an overwhelming majority (87–2–12) of the members of the General Assembly of the United Nations on December 14, 1962, clearly shows that there is a general consensus in support of the customary norm imposing a duty to pay some compensation to aliens for expropriated property: "Nationalization, expropriation or requisitioning shall be based on grounds or reasons of public utility, security or the national interest which are recognized as overriding purely individual or private interests, both domestic and foreign. In such cases the owner shall be paid appropriate compensation, in accordance with the rules in force in the State taking such measures in the exercise of its sovereignty and in accordance with international law. In any case where the question of compensation gives rise to a controversy, the national jurisdiction of the State taking such measures shall be exhausted. However, upon agreement by Sovereign States and other parties concerned, settlement of the dispute should be made through arbitration or international adjudication." Resolution 1803 (XVII), United Nations General Assembly, *Official Records*, Supp. No. 17 (A/5217), p. 15.

by a foreign state. The act of state doctrine, which is not required by international law but which is used with regularity by the courts of many states, precludes national courts from "inquiring into the validity of the public acts a recognized state committed within its own territory."[8] The Sabbatino case raised the question of whether or not United States courts could declare invalid the Cuban expropriation of the property of United States nationals on the ground that the seizure violated international law. In studying this case, one should keep in mind that national courts, regardless of their attitude toward the act of state doctrine, can do little to recover for nationals whose properties have been taken by foreign states. The jurisdiction of national courts is limited to the territory of their own states; unless the expropriated property comes within their jurisdiction, they are powerless to act. And almost all property that is the object of expropriation is either immovable or difficult to trace to its origin after it enters the flow of international commerce.

Laura Janes (U.S.A.) v. United Mexican States*

United States-Mexico, General Claims Commission, 1926

*   *   *

1. Claim is made by the United States of America in this case for losses and damages amounting to $25,000.00, which it is alleged in the Memorial were "suffered on account of the murder, on or about July 10, 1918, at a mine near El Tigre, Sonora, Mexico, of Byron Everett Janes," an American citizen. The claim is presented, as stated in the Memorial, "on behalf of

Laura May Buffington Janes, individually, and as guardian of her two minor children, Byron Everett Janes, Jr.; and Addison M. Janes; and Elizabeth Janes and Catherine Janes."

2. Briefly summarized, the allegations in the Memorial upon which the claim is based are as follows:

3. Byron Everett Janes, for some time prior to and until the time of his death on July 10, 1918, was Superintendent of Mines for the El Tigre Mining Company at El Tigre. On or about July 10, 1918, he was deliberately shot and killed at this place by Pedro Carbajal, a former employee of the Mining Company who had been discharged. The killing took place in the view of many persons resident in the vicinity of the company's office. The local police Comisario was informed of Janes' death within five minutes of the commission of the crime and arrived soon thereafter at the place where the shooting occurred. He delayed for half an hour in assembling his policemen and insisted that they should be mounted. The El Tigre Mining Company furnished the necessary animals and the posse, after the lapse of more than an hour from the time of the shooting, started in pursuit of Carbajal who had departed on foot. The posse failed to apprehend the fugitive. Carbajal remained at a ranch six miles south of El Tigre for a week following the shooting, and it was rumored at El Tigre that he came to that place on two occasions during his stay at the ranch. Subsequently information was received that Carbajal was at a mescal plant near Carrizal, about seventy-five miles south of El Tigre. This information was communicated to Mexican civil and military authorities, who failed to take any steps to apprehend Carbajal, until the El Tigre Mining Company offered a reward, whereupon a local military commander was induced to send a small detachment to Carrizal, which, upon its return, reported that Carbajal had been in this locality but had left before the arrival of the detachment, and that it was therefore impossible to apprehend him.

[8] Banco Nacional de Cuba v. Sabbatino 376 U.S. 398 (1964).
* Reprinted from 4 United Nations Reports of International Arbitral Awards 82.

4. It is alleged in the Memorial that the Mexican authorities took no proper steps to apprehend and punish Carbajal; that such efforts as were made were lax and inadequate; that if prompt and immediate action had been taken on one occasion there is reason to believe that the authorities would have been successful; that it was only after a money reward for the capture of Carbajal had been offered that some dilatory steps were taken to apprehend him in a nearby town where he was staying.

5. The Memorial contains allegations with respect to the earning capacity of Janes, the loss suffered by his wife and children because of his death, and their want of means of support.

6. To substantiate the allegations of fact in the Memorial of the United States and the charge that Mexican authorities failed to take effective steps to apprehend the man who shot Janes, there were filed with the Memorial certain affidavits, statements, and copies of reports of the American Consul at Tampico to the Department of State from which it appears that the consul addressed the Governor of Sonora, pointing out that the killing of other Americans in mining camps in Sonora in the past had gone unpunished and urging that the Mexican authorities take steps to apprehend Carbajal.

. 7. In the Answer filed by the Mexican Government it is denied, that the Mexican authorities failed to take appropriate steps to arrest and punish Carbajal. Accompanying the Answer is a certified copy of judicial proceedings showing the action taken to investigate the killing of Janes and the orders given with respect to his apprehension. Attention is also called to the use of an armed force to capture the fugitive concerning which information is given in evidence accompanying the Memorial of the United States.

* * *

9. An affidavit (Annex 12 to the Memorial) was furnished by L. R. Budrow, the General Manager of the Lucky Tiger Combination Gold Mining Company, an American corporation, owners of the stock of the Tigre Mining Company. In this affidavit Mr. Budrow states that on a visit he made to El Tigre shortly after Janes' death, he obtained the impression that very limited efforts had been made by the authorities at the time to capture Carbajal and that there was a general rumor in El Tigre that Carbajal was seen at that place a few nights after the murder. The affiant attached to his affidavit a report made by R. T. Mishler, Manager of the El Tigre Mining Company on April 11, 1925, with respect to the killing of Janes. The following extract from that report doubtless states in a substantially accurate way the facts with respect to the killing of Janes and the steps taken shortly thereafter by Mexican authorities to apprehend Carbajal:

"Mr. Janes had been Mine Superintendent of the Tigre Mine for six months preceding the tragedy.

"He had had trouble with a trammer named Pedro Carbajal and had given orders for his discharge.

"Mr. Janes and his Assistant, Mr. W. H. Williams, were accustomed to hire new men at the mine office, near the entrance to No. 4 Level which is situated about a hundred yards from the American quarters in the town of El Tigre. Carbajal had requested that he be reinstated in his work on two or three evenings before the tragedy and had been refused.

"On the evening of July 10 (1918) at about 3:30 P. M. he again requested work and was again refused.

"After Mr. Janes and Mr. Williams had left the office and were about half way up the path leading to their quarters, Carbajal started running after them brandishing a revolver. The Americans heard him when he had almost reached them. Mr. Janes dodged by him and started to run back toward the office. Mr. Williams stood still and said 'don't shoot'. Carbajal snapped his pistol, point blank at Mr. Williams, but it failed to go off. He then turned and fired at Mr. Janes as he was running down the path. The bullet entered the back near the spine causing Mr. Janes to fall. Carbajal ran up, placed his pistol at Mr. Janes' head and fired a second shot through the brain.

"Carbajal then went down the path, threatening with his pistol, a half dozen Mexicans gathered around the office, and disappeared up the canyon.

"The Comisario was advised within five minutes after the murder and was on the spot five minutes later. He lost a half hour in getting his policemen together and insisted that they should be mounted. The Company furnished the animals and the posse left Camp about 4:30 P.M. They returned about 7:00 P.M. and reported that they had not seen Carbajal. They were also out the following day, but without results.

"It is current talk that Carbajal stayed at a ranch 6 miles south of Tigre, for a week following the murder, and that he came into Tigre on two nights during the week, but it is most difficult to prove this story.

"Later word was received that Carbajal was at a mescal (native liquor) plant near Carrizal, 75 miles south of Tigre. Both the civil and military authorities were advised of this report. Finally the Major in charge of the District was persuaded to send a small detachment to Carrizal to investigate, with the promise by the Company of a substantial reward should Carbajal be captured. On their return the detachment reported that the man had left before they arrived."

10. Doubtless the evidence accompanying the Memorial of the United States furnishes accurate information with regard to the killing of Janes, and with regard to the preliminary steps taken looking to the apprehension of Carbajal. The evidence on this firstmentioned point is substantially the same as that given by witnesses whose statements are recorded in the record of judicial proceedings accompanying the Answer. With respect to these preliminary steps, we feel justified in reaching the conclusion that they were inefficient and dilatory. From an examination of the evidence on this point accompanying the Memorial, and more particularly from an examination of the records produced by the Mexican Government, we are constrained to reach the conclusion that there was clearly such a failure on the part of the Mexican authorities to take prompt and efficient action to apprehend the slayer as to warrant an award of indemnity. The grounds for such a conclusion can be shown by a brief statement of what those records reveal as to the action taken by the authorities.

11. It is shown that in the afternoon of July 10, 1918, the killing of Janes was brought to the notice of the local Judge, at El Tigre, and he appointed two men as experts to examine the body of the deceased. On the following day the Judge took the testimony of two persons employed by the El Tigre Mining Company. These men, who were not eyewitnesses of the murder, identified the corpse but gave no testimony concerning the facts of the killing. On July 12, the Judge took the statement of Guillermo A. Williams, an eyewitness of the killing. On July 13, the Judge took the statement of another eyewitness. On July 14, the statement of another eyewitness was taken.

12. On July 15, five days after the killing of Janes, when statements had been obtained from five men, the Judge, reciting that there had resulted from the proceedings up to that time sufficient merit for the prosecution of the person who killed Janes, issued an order to the *Comisario* to proceed to the capture of Carbajal.

13. On July 16, the Judge took the statement of another eyewitness to the murder. The *Comisario*, in reply to the order directing him to proceed to capture Carbajal, stated that, following immediate steps looking to the capture of Carbajal, which were unsuccessful, orders were given by means of warrants to different authorities where it was thought the accused might take refuge. On July 17, all papers in the case were forwarded by the local Judge to the Judge of First Instance of the District. The papers were received by the latter on July 22.

14. On July 30, the Judge of First Instance directed the arrest of Carbajal and on August 5, a communication in the nature of a circular was sent to the Judges of First Instance in the State of Sonora with the apparent purpose of enlisting their cooperation in the apprehension of the fugitive. This communication recited the

facts with regard to the killing of Janes and the preliminary investigations which had been conducted, and requested that the communication be returned to the Judge who transmitted it.

15. The circular was received by the Judge of First Instance at Arizpe on August 13, and by him brought to the notice of the Municipal President on August 14. On August 16, the Municipal President felt himself to be in a position to report that Carbajal was not found "in this section." The circular was evidently not received by the next Judge of First Instance on the route of transmission (the Judge at Sahuaripa) until October 14, about two months after it had reached the Judge of First Instance to whom it was originally transmitted. On October 15, it was sent to the Municipal President. On November 15, the communication was received by the Judge at Cananea and transmitted to the Municipal President on November 16. On December 3, the communication was forwarded to the Judge of First Instance at Nogales, Sonora. It thus is shown that from August 5, the date when the circular was first dispatched, until December 3, a period of about four months, the circular had reached but three judges.

16. In this manner, as shown by the record, the circular proceeded to Judges at Magdalena, Altar, Hermosillo, Ures, Guaymas, and Alamos, being received on February 12, 1919, seven months after the killing of Janes, by the Judge of First Instance at this last mentioned place. Thereupon it was returned to the Judge of First Instance at Moctezuma who had initiated its dispatch.

17. Carbajal, the person who killed Janes, was well known in the community where the killing took place. Numerous persons witnessed the deed. The slayer, after killing his victim, left on foot. There is evidence that a Mexican police magistrate was informed of the shooting within five minutes after it took place. The official records with regard to the action taken to apprehend and punish the slayer speak for themselves. Eight years have elapsed since

the murder, and it does not appear from the records that Carbajal has been apprehended at this time. Our conclusions to the effect that the Mexican authorities did not take proper steps to apprehend and punish the slayer of Janes is based on the record before us consisting of evidence produced by both Governments.

18. The respondent Government has not denied that, under the Convention of September 8, 1923, acts of authorities of Sonora may give rise to claims against the Government of Mexico. The Commission is of the opinion that claims may be predicated on such acts.

Measure of Damages for Failure of Apprehension and Punishment

19. The liability of the Mexican Government being stated there remains to be determined for what they are liable and to what amount. At times international awards have held that, if a State shows serious lack of diligence in apprehending and/or punishing culprits, its liability is a derivative liability, assuming the character of some kind of complicity with the perpetrator himself and rendering the State responsible for the very consequences of the individual's misdemeanor. . . .

20. A reasoning based on presumed complicity may have some sound foundation in cases of nonprevention where a Government knows of an *intended* injurious crime, might have averted it, but for some reason constituting its liability did not do so. The present case is different; it is one of nonrepression. Nobody contends either that the Mexican Government might have prevented the murder of Janes, or that it acted in any other form of connivance with the murderer. The international delinquency in this case is one of its own specific type, separate from the private delinquency of the culprit. The culprit is liable for having killed or murdered an American national; the Government is liable for not having measured up to its duty of diligently prosecuting and properly

punishing the offender. The culprit has transgressed the penal code of his country; the State, so far from having transgressed its own penal code (which perhaps not even is applicable to it), has transgressed a provision of international law as to State duties. The culprit can not be sentenced in criminal or civil procedure unless his guilt or intention in causing the victim's death is proven; the Government can be sentenced once the nonperformance of its judicial duty is proven to amount to an international delinquency, the theories on guilt or intention in criminal and civil law not being applicable here. The damage caused by the culprit is the damage caused to Janes' relatives by Janes' death; the damage caused by the Government's negligence is the damage resulting from the nonpunishment of the murderer. If the murderer had not committed his delinquency—if he had not slain Janes—Janes (but for other occurrences) would still be alive and earning the livelihood for his family; if the Government had not committed its delinquency—if it had apprehended and punished Carbajal—Janes' family would have been spared indignant neglect and would have had an opportunity of subjecting the murderer to a civil suit. Even if the nonpunishment were conceived as some kind of approval—which in the Commission's view is doubtful—still approving of a crime has never been deemed identical with being an accomplice to that crime; and even if nonpunishment of a murderer really amounted to complicity in the murder, still it is not permissible to treat this derivative and remote liability not as an attenuate form of responsibility, but as just as serious as if the Government had perpetrated the killing with its own hands. The results of the old conception are unsatisfactory in two directions. If the murdered man had been poor, or if, in a material sense, his death had meant little to his relatives, the satisfaction given these relatives should be confined to a small sum, though the grief and the indignity suffered may have been great. On the other hand; if the old theory is sustained and adhered to,

it would, in cases like the present one, be to the pecuniary benefit of a widow and her children if a Government did *not* measure up to its international duty of providing justice, because in such a case the Government would repair the pecuniary damage caused by the killing, whereas she practically never would have obtained such reparation if the State had succeeded in apprehending and punishing the culprit.

* * *

25. As to the measure of such a damage caused by the delinquency of a Government, the nonpunishment, it may be readily granted that its computation is more difficult and uncertain than that of the damage caused by the killing itself. The two delinquencies being different in their origin, character, and effect, the measure of damages for which the Government should be liable can not be computed by merely stating the damages caused by the private delinquency of Carbajal. But a computation of this character is not more difficult than computations in other cases of denial of justice such as illegal encroachment on one's liberty, harsh treatment in jail, insults and menaces of prisoners, or even nonpunishment of the perpetrator of a crime which is not an attack on one's property or one's earning capacity, for instance a dangerous assault or an attack on one's reputation and honor. Not only the individual grief of the claimants should be taken into account, but a reasonable and substantial redress should be made for the mistrust and lack of safety, resulting from the Government's attitude. If the nonprosecution and nonpunishment of crimes (or of specific crimes) in a certain period and place occurs with regularity such nonrepression may even assume the character of a nonprevention and be treated as such. One among the advantages of severing the Government's dereliction of duty from the individual's crime is in that it grants an opportunity to take into account several shades of denial of justice, more serious ones and lighter

ones (no prosecution at all; prosecution and release; prosecution and light punishment; prosecution, punishment and pardon), whereas the old system operates automatically and allows for the numerous forms of such a denial one amount only, that of full and total reparation.

26. Giving careful consideration to all elements involved, the Commission holds that an amount of $12,000, without interest, is not excessive as satisfaction for the personal damage caused the claimants by the nonapprehension and nonpunishment of the murderer of Janes.

* * *

Foreign Investments*

Oliver J. Lissitzyn

* * *

In traditional international law there has been a generally accepted "international standard" governing state responsibility for the treatment of aliens both as regards their person and their property. Thus, in case of expropriation or nationalization, the "international standard" has required the payment of what has often been described as "prompt, adequate and effective" compensation. "Adequate" compensation has been generally defined as payment of the full value of the property, which is normally determined by the market price. The institution of diplomatic protection of nationals abroad and the "international standard" were devices by which the more advanced states sought to assure—not always successfully—security of person and property for those of their citizens who wished to invest capital, utilize skills, or otherwise do business, in the less developed parts of the world. This rule was not seriously challenged until World War I.

* Reprinted from Oliver J. Lissitzyn, "International Law in a Divided World," *International Conciliation*, No. 542 (March 1963), by permission of the Carnegie Endowment for International Peace. Certain footnotes are omitted.

Subsequently, however, several seemingly coincidental historical events placed the traditional rule in jeopardy. In Russia, the new Soviet regime confiscated the private investments of foreigners as well as Russians on a vast scale and refused to pay any compensation. In Mexico, a socialist-inspired constitution adopted in 1917 paved the way for expropriation of foreign agrarian and oil properties, which gave rise to heated diplomatic controversies. In the course of the controversy concerning the expropriation of foreign-owned lands, Mexico declared that no rule of international law required payment of compensation for expropriations of "a general and impersonal" character that affected the property of citizens and aliens alike.[1] And many of the states carved out of the territory of the defeated Central Powers embarked on programs of agrarian reform that involved the redistribution of large tracts of land owned, in part, by Austrian, Hungarian, and German nationals.

There arose a lively debate between those who upheld the traditional "international standard" of compensation and those who sought to reduce the expropriating state's duty under international law to paying foreign nationals, including business firms, the same compensation as that granted to the state's citizens. At the 1930 Hague Conference for the Codification of International Law, the doctrine that aliens were entitled to an "international standard" of treatment—implying an international duty to pay compensation independent of national laws—was upheld by the narrow margin of 23 to 17 votes. The minority, which favored the "equality of treatment" doctrine, was composed of the seven Latin American nations which took part in the vote, four Asian and African nations, five successor states of central and eastern Europe, and Portugal.[2] Japan sided with the majority. Had all the Latin American states and the Soviet Union participated in the Conference, there probably would have been a majority against the "international standard." Because of the almost even split, the Conference adjourned without formulating any draft convention on the responsibility of states.

The norm of "prompt, adequate and effective" compensation has been further weakened since World War II by expropriations without payment of what was considered adequate compensation in countries of Eastern Europe, in Iran, Egypt, Cuba, and elsewhere. Attempts of the capital-exporting states to write the requirement of compensation into a widely accepted multilateral agreement have not been successful. The Asian African Legal Consultative Committee,[3] with Japan as the lone dissenter, has rejected the principle of an "international standard" of treatment of aliens, in favor, with some qualifications, of the "equality of treatment" doctrine, and has drafted a convention that provides for payment for expropriated foreign property "in accordance with local laws, regulations and orders."[4]

The view that the "international standard" of treatment of aliens, or at least the requirement of "prompt, adequate and effective" compensation, is not or should not be a generally binding norm of international law, has also been expressed by some jurists from the less developed nations in the International Law Commission and in the literature.[5] It is probable that if the formula were squarely put to a vote in the General Assembly, it would be rejected by a majority composed of most of the less developed nations and the Soviet bloc. It can no longer be counted on to protect the interests of foreign investors in all the less developed countries. In this matter, the attainment of independence by so many capital-importing nations has certainly contributed to the weakening of a norm of international law which once seemed firmly established.

It has been sometimes pointed out that the legal content of the "international standard" of treatment of aliens, as it was traditionally understood and enforced, coincided in large part with what are regarded today as basic human rights. But the less

developed nations, smarting under a sense of powerlessness and inferiority, regarded this institution as an imposition by the more powerful states. The resentment was intensified by the coercive measures—including military force—that the more advanced powers sometimes employed, not only to enforce their interpretation of the "standard," but also to exact concessions and other special privileges for their nationals and to intervene in the domestic affairs of the weaker states. In the strong words of a Mexican diplomat, "the doctrine of responsibility of states was merely the legal garb that served to cloak and protect the imperialistic interests of the international oligarchy during the nineteenth century and the first part of the twentieth."[6]

The understandable resentment that debtor nations feel against a rule of law established and enforced by their creditors has been only one of the factors that have weakened the force of international legal norms designed to protect foreign business interests. Another is the world-wide trend toward state intervention in economic life, manifested in an extreme form in the Communist countries, but evident also in the Western and less developed nations.

When states such as the United Kingdom and France nationalize industry, as they did after World War II, they generally have the means to assure payment of compensation acceptable to the private owners, including any foreign investors. The less developed countries, however, are usually unable to pay on terms approximating the "prompt, adequate and effective" compensation formula. When there is strong domestic pressure for social reform, it is likely to take precedence over the interests of foreign investors. Often there is also the fear that foreigners are depleting irreplaceable natural resources and that the nation is not getting a proper share of the proceeds of the exploitation.

Another factor of particular importance in newly independent nations, but not wholly confined to them, is that many foreign investments were made during the colonial period when the nation could not express its will. They are now felt to be a vestige of the colonial "bondage" that must be wiped out if the nation is to be really free to enjoy its resources. This factor may also be of importance in countries which, though formally "independent," were under strong foreign influence which they were too weak to resist. It probably contributed to the Communist seizure of power in China and is likely to play a significant role in the future policies of many countries not yet independent.

On the issue of protection of foreign investments, as on some others, the tendency of the less developed nations to challenge traditional international law has the encouragement of the Soviet bloc, although the motivation is not the same. The Communists are interested in weakening the economic and political power of the West and in undermining the private enterprise system throughout the world. The less developed nations are interested primarily in asserting their sovereignty and freedom in pursuing social reform.

An important factor contributing to the decline of the effectiveness of the traditional norms protecting foreign investments has been the growing reluctance of the capital-exporting states to enforce their claims by coercive means. Although the cold war and the fear that the use of coercion would play into the hands of the Communists have served to strengthen this reluctance, its origins may be traced back to the inter-war period. It is related to the revulsion against war, the mounting costs of coercion, and the wide acceptance of the belief—which finds strong support in the United Nations Charter and elsewhere—that as an instrument of policy the use of force by one state against another is no longer lawful.

It must be emphasized that we are speaking not of hard and fast policies pursued by the less developed nations as if they formed a solid bloc, but of tendencies. Had they formed a monolithic and determined bloc, the less developed nations, with Soviet support, could have pushed through the General Assembly—where the capital-exporting countries form a small minority—a resolution unequivocally declaring that there is no duty under international law to pay compensation for expropriated foreign property. Even though not formally binding, such a resolution would weaken the legal position of the capital-exporting states. In fact, the more extreme proposals, sponsored largely by Soviet-bloc states, have generally failed to get enough support from the less developed nations to be adopted. Thus, a Soviet amendment to the 1962 resolution on natural wealth and resources[7] which would have confirmed "the inalienable right of peoples and nations to the unobstructed execution of nationalization, expropriation and other measures," was rejected by 48 votes to 34, with 21 abstentions. Among the negative votes were those of ten African and Asian states (significantly including India) and sixteen Latin American nations (including Mexico and Brazil). Nineteen African and Asian and two Latin American states abstained. Only twenty-three African and Asian states—less than half the total number in the United Nations—cast their votes for this Soviet proposal.[8] Another Soviet amendment that would have "unreservedly" supported "measures taken by peoples and States to re-establish or strengthen their sovereignty over natural wealth and resources" and considered "inadmissible acts aimed at obstructing the creation, defence and strengthening of that sovereignty" had a larger measure of support. It was adopted in the Second Committee, but rejected in the plenary meeting by 41 votes to 38, with 15 abstentions. In the latter vote, it was supported by twenty-six African and Asian and two Latin American states. Again, the Soviets succeeded in attracting the votes of fewer than half of the African and Asian members of the United Nations.[9] Many of the spokesmen for the less developed nations in the course of the debate sought to reassure capital-exporting states by pointing to the clause on compensation and denying any intention to promote confiscation of foreign investments.[10]

The fear of offending states that extend economic and other assistance—as was frankly admitted in the debates—and the desire to obtain the largest possible majorities affirming permanent sovereignty over natural resources were largely responsible for this attitude rather than solicitude for the existing norms of international law. It suggests, however, an absence of doctrinaire and uncompromising hostility to the interests of the capital-exporting nations. Further, it suggests a recognition of the important role foreign private capital can play in economic development. Some of the spokesmen for the less developed countries seem to admit that there is a duty under international law to pay compensation for expropriated foreign property.[11] A further indication of the reluctance of the capital-importing states officially to repudiate this duty may be seen in the fact that acts of expropriation, such as those in Iran, Egypt, and Cuba, have been usually accompanied by provisions for compensation, although on terms not regarded as satisfactory by the investors.

Despite this pragmatic recognition of a common interest, many of the less developed nations have been reluctant to enter into general treaty commitments—even of a bilateral nature—not to expropriate foreign investments without the payment of just compensation. The United States, which is the prime source of private investment capital, has been able to conclude treaties containing such commitments with only eight less developed nations—the Republic of China (Taiwan), Ethiopia, Korea, Muscat, Nicaragua, Pakistan, and Vietnam —since World War II.[12] Many of these are heavily dependent on the United States for military and political support and cannot be regarded as representative of the attitudes of the less developed nations as a group. Even these treaties, furthermore, do not provide full security for the investors, if only because they are terminable on notice.

Schemes for general multilateral conventions guaranteeing foreign investments against confiscation are highly unlikely to attract the support of a significant number of less developed countries. The newly independent nations, in particular, would be loath in many cases to limit their freedom of action with respect to property acquired by foreigners during the colonial period. But unwillingness to enter into treaty commitments of a general nature does not preclude agreements to guarantee specific new investments on a selective basis.

Furthermore, experience indicates that the interest of the less developed nations in the maintenance of normal relations with the capital-exporting states and their business enterprises often leads to the settlement of foreign claims for expropriated investments and prematurely terminated concessions. Even the Communist governments of eastern Europe have entered into agreements with most of the capital-exporting states for the payment of lump-sum compensation on an installment basis for expropriations effected after World War II. Mexico and Iran reached agreements with the oil companies whose investments they nationalized, and Egypt settled the claim that arose from the premature cancellation of the Suez Canal concession. The compensation obtained by foreign investors pursuant to such settlements is generally not regarded in Western financial and legal circles as fully adequate. Nevertheless, it serves to alleviate the practical effects of the tendency of the less developed nations to disregard or challenge the traditional norms of international law designed for the protection of foreign property and business interests.

* * *

Notes

1. It should be noted however, that in this case and in others cited below some compensation

was actually paid. See p. 48. G. H. Hackworth, *Digest of International Law* (Washington, GPO, 1940–44), Vol. 3, p. 657; also, G. White, *Nationalisation of Foreign Property* (New York, Praeger, 1961), pp. 183–243.

2. G. H. Hackworth, "Responsibility of States for Damages Caused in Their Territory to the Person or Property of Foreigners," *AJIL*, Vol. 24, No. 3 (July 1930), p. 500.

3. The Committee was set up in November 1956 by Burma, Ceylon, India, Indonesia, Iraq, Japan, and Syria as the Asian Legal Consultative Committee. It was enlarged to include Morocco, Pakistan, Sudan, and the United Arab Republic. The word "African" was added to the title in 1958. The members are not regarded as official government representatives. See *Reports* of the Second (1958), Third (1960), and Fourth (1961) Sessions of the Committee, published by the Secretariat of the Committee in New Delhi; also, Kenzo Takayanagi, and Hideo Tanaka, "The First Session of the Asian Legal Consultative Committee," *The Japanese Annual of International Law*, No. 2 (1958), p. 110.

4. Asian African Legal Consultative Committee, *Reports,* 3rd Sess., 1960, pp. 83ff; 4th Sess., 1961, pp. 43, 46, 49, 141–142.

5. See, for example, *Yearbook of the International Law Commission, 1957* (New York, United Nations, 1958), Vol. I, pp. 155, 159–160; *ibid., 1959*, Vol. I, p. 151; *ibid., 1960*, Vol. I, p. 264; J. Castañeda, "The Underdeveloped Nations and the Development of International Law," *International Organization*, Vol. 15, No. I (Winter 1961), p. 38; S. N. Guha Roy, "Is the Law of Responsibility of States for Injuries to Aliens a Part of Universal International Law?," *AJIL*, Vol. 55, No. 4 (Oct. 1961), p. 863. Similar views have been voiced in the Sixth Committee.

6. Castañeda, *op. cit.,* p. 39.

7. General Assembly Res. 1803 (XVII), 14 Dec. 1962.

8. United Nations Doc. A/PV. 1193, 14 Dec. 1962, pp. 71–76.

9. United Nations Docs. A/5344/Add. 1, 12 Dec. 1962, and A/PV.1194, 14 Dec. 1962, pp. 2–5.

10. For the debates, see United Nations Docs. A/C.2/SRs. 834, 841–842, 845–846, 848, 850–859, 12 Nov.–7 Dec. 1962, and A/PVs. 1193–1194, 14 Dec. 1962.

11. See, for example, the remarks of Prime Minister Mossadegh of Iran, made at the height of the Anglo-Iranian oil crisis, SCOR, 6th Year, 563rd Mtg., 17 Oct. 1951, para. 125; and of the representative of Ceylon, United Nations Doc. A/C.2/SR.853, 30 Nov. 1962, p. 7.

12. Yet provisions for the protection of foreign property against expropriation without just compensation appear, curiously enough, in some bilateral treaties between less developed nations. See, for example, Art. 3 of the 1950 Treaty of Commerce between Afghanistan and India. *United Nations Treaty Series* (New York, United Nations, 1953), Vol. 167, p. 122.

United States Department of State Memorandum on International Claims, March 1, 1961 *

Since 1959, the Cuban Government and authorities have nationalized, intervened and otherwise taken millions of dollars' worth of property of American nationals. The United States Government has vigorously protested such takings and urged the Cuban Government either to return the property or pay prompt, adequate and effective compensation. Thus far, the Cuban Government has not returned properties or been willing to make an agreement for compensation.

The Department is unable to predict when and in what manner it will be possible to settle this problem. In the past the Department has settled similar problems (1) by submitting individual claims through the diplomatic channel to the foreign government concerned and obtaining restitution or compensation; (2) by obtaining a lump sum in settlement of all claims, with the amount paid distributed by an agency of the United States Government; or (3) by an agreement submitting all claims to an

* Reprinted from 56 *American Journal of International Law* 166 (1962) by permission of the American Society of International Law.

international arbitral tribunal for adjudication.

Since the United States Government has not obtained agreement with Cuba for restitution, payment of a lump sum or for international arbitration, the only possibility at present would be for the United States Government formally to espouse through the diplomatic channel individual claims of American nationals. While the Department can give no assurance that claims it espouses would be paid by the Cuban Government, it is ready to receive and consider for presentation any claim which is properly prepared and documented and is valid from an international legal standpoint.

The Department does not use forms for claims against foreign governments but has memoranda explaining how such claims should be prepared and documented. Its memorandum of March 1, 1961, on the preparation of claims for loss of or damage to property is attached.[1] In addition to the evidence which is mentioned in that memorandum, evidence should also be submitted showing that the American national exhausted such legal remedies as were available in Cuba and in the process sustained a denial of justice, as that term is understood in international law, or that the laws of Cuba do not provide a remedy or, if provided, that it would be futile to attempt to exhaust such remedy. The requirement for exhaustion of legal remedies is based upon the generally accepted rule of international law that international responsibility may not be invoked as regards reparation for losses or damages sustained by a foreigner until after exhaustion of the remedies available under local law. This, of course, does not mean that "legal remedies" must be exhausted if there are none to exhaust or if the procurement of justice would be impossible.

Each American national must decide whether to prepare a claim now, either with a view to its presentation through the diplomatic channel when ready, or in order that it will be ready in the event that a claims settlement with Cuba is effected at a later time. Each American national must also decide whether to "exhaust legal remedies" in Cuba, either with a view to obtaining restitution or adequate compensation or documentary evidence which could be used to show that justice could not be obtained by judicial proceedings. Generally, unsupported assertions to the effect that it would be useless to exhaust or attempt to exhaust legal remedies would, of course, have less evidentiary value than a court decree or other documentary evidence demonstrating the futility of exhausting or attempting to exhaust legal remedies.

An American national who does not wish to prepare a claim now may, if desired, submit a description of the claim to the Department for its records. The description should include, at least, the facts mentioned in paragraph "First" of the attached memorandum.[2]

Notes

1. Not printed here. It is furnished by the Department of State on request.
2. That paragraph reads: "Claim should be prepared in form of sworn statement, *in triplicate*. It should contain in narrative form a clear chronological statement of the essential facts relating to:
   "a. Citizenship of claimant or claimants.
   b. Full description of the property in question and its exact location when loss occurred.
   c. Time and manner of acquisition of claimant's ownership of the property or other interest therein.
   d. The action taken against the property which is considered as giving rise to a claim against a foreign government.
   e. Identification of persons, officials, agency, or forces taking such action and dates the action was taken.
   f. The nature and amount of damage resulting from action complained of."

Banco Nacional de Cuba v. Sabbatino*

Supreme Court of the United States, 1964

MR. JUSTICE HARLAN delivered the opinion of the Court.

The question which brought this case here, and is now found to be the dispositive issue, is whether the so-called act of state doctrine serves to sustain petitioner's claims in this litigation. Such claims are ultimately founded on a decree of the Government of Cuba expropriating certain property, the right to the proceeds of which is here in controversy. The act of state doctrine in its traditional formulation precludes the courts of this country from inquiring into the validity of the public acts a recognized foreign sovereign power committed within its own territory.

I

In February and July of 1960, respondent Farr, Whitlock & Co., an American commodity broker, contracted to purchase Cuban sugar, free alongside the steamer, from a wholly owned subsidiary of Compania Azucarera Vertientes-Camaguey de Cuba (C. A. V.), a corporation organized under Cuban law whose capital stock was owned principally by United States residents. Farr, Whitlock agreed to pay for the sugar in New York upon presentation of the shipping documents and a sight draft.

On July 6, 1960, the Congress of the United States amended the Sugar Act of 1948 to permit a presidentially directed reduction of the sugar quota for Cuba. On the succeeding day President Eisenhower exercised the granted power. The day of the congressional enactment, the Cuban Council of Ministers adopted "Law No. 851," which characterized this reduction in the Cuban sugar quota as an act of "aggression, for political purposes" on the part of the

* Reprinted from 376 U.S. 398 (1964).

United States, justifying the taking of counter measures by Cuba. The law gave the Cuban President and Prime Minister discretionary power to nationalize by forced expropriation property or enterprises in which American nationals had an interest. Although a system of compensation was formally provided, the possibility of payment under it may well be deemed illusory. Our State Department has described the Cuban law as "manifestly in violation of those principles of international law which have long been accepted by the free countries of the West. It is in its essence discriminatory, arbitrary, and confiscatory."

Between August 6 and August 9, 1960, the sugar covered by the contract between Farr, Whitlock and C. A. V. was loaded, destined for Morocco, onto the S. S. *Hornfels*, which was standing offshore at the Cuban port of Jucaro (Santa Maria). On the day loading commenced, the Cuban President and Prime Minister, acting pursuant to Law No. 851, issued Executive Power Resolution No. 1. It provided for the compulsory expropriation of all property and enterprises, and of rights and interests arising therefrom, of certain listed companies, including C. A. V., wholly or principally owned by American nationals. The preamble reiterated the alleged injustice of the American reduction of the Cuban sugar quota and emphasized the importance of Cuba serving as an example for other countries to follow "in the struggle to free themselves from the brutal claws of Imperialism." In consequence of the resolution, the consent of the Cuban Government was necessary before a ship carrying sugar of a named company could leave Cuban waters. In order to obtain this consent, Farr, Whitlock, on August 11, entered into contracts, identical to those it had made with C. A. V., with the Banco Para el Comercio Exterior de Cuba, an instrumentality of the Cuban Government. The S. S. *Hornfels* sailed for Morocco on August 12.

Banco Exterior assigned the bills of lading to petitioner, also an instrumentality of the Cuban Government, which instructed its agent in New York, Societe Generale, to deliver the bills and a sight draft in the sum of $175,250.69 to Farr, Whitlock in return for payment. Societe Generale's initial tender of the documents was refused by Farr, Whitlock, which on the same day was notified of C. A. V.'s claim that as rightful owner of the sugar it was entitled to the proceeds. In return for a promise not to turn the funds over to petitioner or its agent, C. A. V. agreed to indemnify Farr, Whitlock for any loss. Farr, Whitlock subsequently accepted the shipping documents, negotiated the bills of lading to its customer, and received payment for the sugar. It refused, however, to hand over the proceeds to Societe Generale. Shortly thereafter, Farr, Whitlock was served with an order of the New York Supreme Court, which had appointed Sabbatino as Temporary Receiver of C. A. V.'s New York assets, enjoining it from taking any action in regard to the money claimed by C. A. V. that might result in its removal from the State. Following this, Farr, Whitlock, pursuant to court order, transferred the funds to Sabbatino, to abide the event of a judicial determination as to their ownership.

Petitioner then instituted this action in the Federal District Court for the Southern District of New York. Alleging conversion of the bills of lading, it sought to recover the proceeds thereof from Farr, Whitlock and to enjoin the receiver from exercising any dominion over such proceeds. Upon motions to dismiss and for summary judgment, the District Court, 193 F. Supp. 375, sustained federal *in personam* jurisdiction despite state control of the funds. It found that the sugar was located within Cuban territory at the time of expropriation and determined that under merchant law common to civilized countries Farr, Whitlock could not have asserted ownership of the sugar against C. A. V. before making payment. It concluded that C. A. V. had a property interest in the sugar subject to the territorial jurisdiction of Cuba. The court

then dealt with the question of Cuba's title to the sugar, on which rested petitioner's claim of conversion. While acknowledging the continuing vitality of the act of state doctrine, the court believed it inapplicable when the questioned foreign act is in violation of international law. Proceeding on the basis that a taking invalid under international law does not convey good title, the District Court found the Cuban expropriation decree to violate such law in three separate respects: it was motivated by a retaliatory and not a public purpose; it discriminated against American nationals; and it failed to provide adequate compensation. Summary judgment against petitioner was accordingly granted.

The Court of Appeals, 307 F. 2d 845, affirming the decision on similar grounds, relied on two letters (not before the District Court) written by State Department officers which it took as evidence that the Executive Branch had no objection to a judicial testing of the Cuban decree's validity. The court was unwilling to declare that any one of the infirmities found by the District Court rendered the taking invalid under international law, but was satisfied that in combination they had that effect. We granted certiorari because the issues involved bear importantly on the conduct of the country's foreign relations and more particularly on the proper role of the Judicial Branch in this sensitive area. 372 U. S. 905. For reasons to follow we decide that the judgment below must be reversed.

*   *   *

Respondents, pointing to the severance of diplomatic relations, commercial embargo, and freezing of Cuban assets in this country, contend that relations between the United States and Cuba manifest such animosity that unfriendliness is clear, and that the courts should be closed to the Cuban Government. We do not agree. This Court would hardly be competent to undertake assessments of varying degrees of friendliness or its absence, and, lacking some definite touchstone for determination, we are constrained to consider any relationship, short of war, with a recognized sovereign power as embracing the privilege of resorting to United States courts. Although the severance of diplomatic relations is an overt act with objective significance in the dealings of sovereign states, we are unwilling to say that it should inevitably result in the withdrawal of the privilege of bringing suit. Severance may take place for any number of political reasons, its duration is unpredictable, and whatever expression of animosity it may imply does not approach that implicit in a declaration of war.

It is perhaps true that nonrecognition of a government in certain circumstances may reflect no greater unfriendliness than the severance of diplomatic relations with a recognized government, but the refusal to recognize has a unique legal aspect. It signifies this country's unwillingness to acknowledge that the government in question speaks as the sovereign authority for the territory it purports to control ... Political recognition is exclusively a function of the Executive. The possible incongruity of judicial "recognition," by permitting suit, of a government not recognized by the Executive is completely absent when merely diplomatic relations are broken.

The view that the existing situation between the United States and Cuba should not lead to a denial of status to sue is buttressed by the circumstance that none of the acts of our Government have been aimed at closing the courts of this country to Cuba, and more particularly by the fact that the Government has come to the support of Cuba's "act of state" claim in this very litigation.

* * *

IV

The classic American statement of the act of state doctrine, which appears to have taken root in England as early as 1674, *Blad* v. *Bamfield*, 3 Swans. 604, 36 Eng. Rep. 992, and began to emerge in the jurisprudence of this country in the late eighteenth and early nineteenth centuries, see, e. g., *Ware* v. *Hylton*, 3 Dall. 199, 230; *Hudson* v. *Guestier*, 4 Cranch 293, 294; *The Schooner Exchange* v. *M'Faddon*, 7 Cranch 116, 135, 136; *L'Invincible*, 1 Wheat. 238, 253; *The Santissima Trinidad*, 7 Wheat. 283, 336, is found in *Underhill* v. *Hernandez*, 168 U. S. 250, where Chief Justice Fuller said for a unanimous Court (p. 252):

"Every sovereign State is bound to respect the independence of every other sovereign State, and the courts of one country will not sit in judgment on the acts of the government of another done within its own territory. Redress of grievances by reason of such acts must be obtained through the means open to be availed of by sovereign powers as between themselves."

Following this precept the Court in that case refused to inquire into acts of Hernandez, a revolutionary Venezuelan military commander whose government had been later recognized by the United States, which were made the basis of a damage action in this country by Underhill, an American citizen, who claimed that he had been unlawfully assaulted, coerced, and detained in Venezuela by Hernandez.

None of this Court's subsequent cases in which the act of state doctrine was directly or peripherally involved manifest any retreat from *Underhill*. See *American Banana Co.* v. *United Fruit Co.*, 213 U. S. 347; *Oetjen* v. *Central Leather Co.*, 246 U. S. 297; *Ricaud* v. *American Metal Co.*, 246 U. S. 304; *Shapleigh* v. *Mier*, 299 U. S. 468; *United States* v. *Belmont*, 301 U. S. 324; *United States* v. *Pink*, 315 U. S. 203. On the contrary in two of these cases, *Oetjen* and *Ricaud*, the doctrine as announced in *Underhill* was reaffirmed in unequivocal terms.

Oetjen involved a seizure of hides from a Mexican citizen as a military levy by General Villa, acting for the forces of General Carranza, whose government was recognized by this country subsequent to the trial but prior to decision by this Court. The hides were sold to a Texas corporation which shipped them to the United States and assigned them to defendant. As assignee of the original owner, plantiff replevied the hides, claiming that they had been seized in violation of the Hague Conventions. In affirming a judgment for defendant, the Court suggested that the rules of the Conventions did not apply to civil war and that, even if they did, the relevant seizure was not in violation of them. 246 U. S., at 301–302. Nevertheless, it chose to rest its decision on other grounds. It described the designation of the sovereign as a political question to be determined by the legislative and executive departments rather than judicial, invoked the established rule that such recognition operates retroactively to validate past acts, and found the basic tenet of *Underhill* to be applicable to the case before it.

"The principle that the conduct of one independent government cannot be successfully questioned in the courts of another is as applicable to a case involving the title to property brought within the custody of a court, such as we have here, as it was held to be to the cases cited, in which claims for damages were based upon acts done in a foreign country, for it rests at last upon the highest considerations of international comity and expediency. To permit the validity of the acts of one sovereign State to be reëxamined and perhaps condemned by the courts of another would very certainly 'imperil the amicable relations between governments and vex the peace of nations.'" *Id.*, at 303–304.

In *Ricaud* the facts were similar—another general of the Carranza forces seized lead bullion as a military levy—except that the property taken belonged to an American citizen. The Court found *Underhill, American Banana,* and *Oetjen* controlling. Commenting on the nature of the principle established by those cases, the opinion stated that the rule

"does not deprive the courts of jurisdiction once acquired over a case. It requires only that, when it is made to appear that the foreign government has acted in a given way on the subject-matter of the litigation, the details of such action or the merit of the result cannot be questioned but must be accepted by our courts as a rule for their decision. To accept a ruling authority and to decide accordingly is not a surrender or abandonment of jurisdiction but is an exercise of it. It results that the title to the property in this case must be determined by the result of the action taken by the military authorities of Mexico. . . ." 246 U. S., at 309.

To the same effect is the language of Mr. Justice Cardozo in the *Shapleigh* case, *supra,* where, in commenting on the validity of a Mexican land expropriation, he said (299 U. S., at 471): "The question is not here whether the proceeding was so conducted as to be a wrong to our nationals under the doctrines of international law, though valid under the law of the situs of the land. For wrongs of that order the remedy to be followed is along the channels of diplomacy."

In deciding the present case the Court of Appeals relied in part upon an exception to the unqualified teachings of *Underhill, Oetjen,* and *Ricaud* which that court had earlier indicated. In *Bernstein* v. *Van Heyghen Freres Societe Anonyme,* 163 F. 2d 246, suit was brought to recover from an assignee property allegedly taken, in effect, by the Nazi Government because plaintiff was Jewish. Recognizing the odious nature of this act of state, the court, through Judge Learned Hand, nonetheless refused to consider it invalid on that ground. Rather, it looked to see if the Executive had acted in any manner that would indicate that United States Courts should refuse to give effect to such a foreign decree. Finding no such evidence, the court sustained dismissal of the complaint. In a later case involving similar facts the same court again assumed examination of the German acts improper, *Bernstein* v. *N. V. Nederlandsche-Amerikaansche Stoomvaart-Maatschappij,* 173 F. 2d 71, but, quite evidently following the implications of Judge Hand's opinion in the earlier case, amended its mandate to permit evidence of alleged invalidity, 210 F. 2d 375, subsequent to receipt by plaintiff's attorney of a letter from the Acting Legal Adviser to the State Department written for the purpose of relieving the court from any constraint upon the exercise of its jurisdiction to pass on that question.[1]

This Court has never had occasion to pass upon the so-called *Bernstein* exception, nor need it do so now. For whatever ambiguity may be thought to exist in the two letters from State Department officials on which the Court of Appeals relied,[2] 307 F. 2d, at 858, is now removed by the position which the Executive has taken in this Court on the act of state claim; respondents do not indeed contest the view that these letters were intended to reflect no more than the Department's then wish not to make any statement bearing on this litigation.

The outcome of this case, therefore, turns upon whether any of the contentions urged by respondents against the application of the act of state doctrine in the premises is acceptable: (1) that the doctrine does not apply to acts of state which violate international law, as is claimed to be the case here; (2) that the doctrine is inapplicable unless the Executive specifically interposes it in a particular case; and (3) that in any event, the doctrine may not be invoked by a foreign government plaintiff in our courts.

V

Preliminarily, we discuss the foundations on which we deem the act of state doctrine to rest, . . .

That international law does not require application of the doctrine is evidenced by the practice of nations. Most of the countries rendering decisions on the subject fail to follow the rule rigidly. No international arbitral or judicial decision discovered suggests that international law prescribes recognition of sovereign acts of foreign governments, see 1 Oppenheim's International Law §115aa (Lauterpacht, 8th ed. 1955), and apparently no claim has ever been raised before an international tribunal that failure to apply the act of state doctrine constitutes a breach of international obligation. If international law does not prescribe use of the doctrine, neither does it forbid application of the rule even if it is claimed that the act of state in question violated international law. The traditional view of international law is that it establishes substantive principles for determining whether one country has wronged another. Because of its peculiar nation-to-nation character the usual method for an individual to seek relief is to exhaust local remedies and then repair to the executive authorities of his own state to persuade them to champion his claim in diplomacy or before an international tribunal. See *United States* v. *Diekelman,* 92 U. S. 520, 524. Although it is, of course, true that United States courts apply international law as a part of our own in appropriate circumstances, *Ware* v. *Hylton,* 3 Dall. 199, 281; *The Nereide,* 9 Cranch, 388, 423; *The Paquete Habana,* 175 U. S. 677, 700, the public law of nations can hardly dictate to a country which is in theory wronged how to treat that wrong within its domestic borders.

Despite the broad statement in *Oetjen* that "The conduct of the foreign relations of our Government is committed by the Constitution to the Executive and Legislative . . . Departments," 246 U. S., at 302, it cannot of course be thought that "every case or controversy which touches foreign relations lies beyond judicial cognizance." *Baker* v. *Carr,* 369 U. S. 186, 211. The text of the Constitution does not require the act of state doctrine; it does not irrevocably remove from the judiciary the capacity to review the validity of foreign acts of state.

The act of state doctrine does, however, have "constitutional" underpinnings. It arises out of the basic relationships between branches of government in a system of separation of powers. It concerns the competency of dissimilar institutions to make and implement particular kinds of decisions in the area of international relations. The doctrine as formulated in past decisions expresses the strong sense of the Judicial Branch that its engagement in the task of passing on the validity of foreign acts of state may hinder rather than further this country's pursuit of goals both for itself and for the community of nations as a whole in the international sphere. Many commentators disagree with this view; they have striven by means of distinguishing and limiting past decisions and by advancing various considerations of policy to stimulate a narrowing of the apparent scope of the rule. Whatever considerations are thought to predominate, it is plain that the problems involved are uniquely federal in nature. If federal authority, in this instance this Court, orders the field of judicial competence in this area for the federal courts, and the state courts are left free to formulate their own rules, the purposes behind the doctrine could be as effectively undermined as if there had been no federal pronouncement on the subject.

We could perhaps in this diversity action avoid the question of deciding whether federal or state law is applicable to this aspect of the litigation. New York has enunciated the act of state doctrine in terms that echo those of federal decisions decided during the reign of *Swift* v. *Tyson*, 16 Pet. I. In *Hatch* v. *Baez*, 7 Hun. 596, 599 (N. Y. Sup. Ct.), *Underhill* was foreshadowed by the words, "the courts of one country are bound to abstain from sitting in judgment on the acts of another government done within its own territory." More recently, the Court of Appeals, *Salimoff & Co.* v. *Standard Oil Co.*, 262 N. Y. 220, 224, 186 N. E. 679, 681, has declared, "The courts of one independent government will not sit in judgment upon the validity of the acts of another done within its own territory even when such government seizes and sells the property of an American citizen within its boundaries." . . . Thus our conclusions

might well be the same whether we dealt with this problem as one of state law . . . or federal law.

However, we are constrained to make it clear that an issue concerned with a basic choice regarding the competence and function of the Judiciary and the National Executive in ordering our relationships with other members of the international community must be treated exclusively as an aspect of federal law. . . .

VI

If the act of state doctrine is a principle of decision binding on federal and state courts alike but compelled by neither international law nor the Constitution, its continuing vitality depends on its capacity to reflect the proper distribution of functions between the judicial and political branches of the Government on matters bearing upon foreign affairs. It should be apparent that the greater the degree of codification or consensus concerning a particular area of international law, the more appropriate it is for the judiciary to render decisions regarding it, since the courts can then focus on the application of an agreed principle to circumstances of fact rather than on the sensitive task of establishing a principle not inconsistent with the national interest or with international justice. It is also evident that some aspects of international law touch much more sharply on national nerves than do others; the less important the implications of an issue are for our foreign relations, the weaker the justification for exclusivity in the political branches. The balance of relevant considerations may also be shifted if the government which perpetrated the challenged act of state is no longer in existence, as in the *Bernstein* case, for the political interest of this country may, as a result, be measurably altered. Therefore, rather than laying down or reaffirming an inflexible and all-encompassing rule in this case, we decide only that the Judicial

Branch will not examine the validity of a taking of property within its own territory by a foreign sovereign government, extant and recognized by this country at the time of suit, in the absence of a treaty or other unambiguous agreement regarding controlling legal principles, even if the complaint alleges that the taking violates customary international law.

There are few if any issues in international law today on which opinion seems to be so divided as the limitations on a State's power to expropriate the property of aliens.[3] There is, of course, authority, in international judicial and arbitral decisions, in the expressions of national governments, and among commentators for the view that a taking is improper under international law if it is not for a public purpose, is discriminatory, or is without provision for prompt, adequate, and effective compensation. However, Communist countries, although they have in fact provided a degree of compensation after diplomatic efforts, commonly recognize no obligation on the part of the taking country. Certain representatives of the newly independent and underdeveloped countries have questioned whether rules of state responsibility toward aliens can bind nations that have not consented to them and it is argued that the traditionally articulated standards governing expropriation of property reflect "imperialist" interests and are inappropriate to the circumstances of emergent states.

The disagreement as to relevant international law standards reflects an even more basic divergence between the national interests of capital importing and capital exporting nations and between the social ideologies of those countries that favor state control of a considerable portion of the means of production and those that adhere to a free enterprise system. It is difficult to imagine the courts of this country embarking on adjudication in an area which touches more sensitively the practical and ideological goals of the various members of the community of nations.[4]

When we consider the prospect of the courts characterizing foreign expropriations, however justifiably, as invalid under international law and ineffective to pass title, the wisdom of the precedents is confirmed. While each of the leading cases in this Court may be argued to be distinguishable on its facts from this one—*Underhill* because sovereign immunity provided an independent ground and *Oetjen, Ricaud,* and *Shapleigh* because there was actually no violation of international law—the plain implication of all these opinions, and the import of express statements in *Oetjen* . . . and *Shapleigh* . . . is that the act of state doctrine is applicable even if international law has been violated. In *Ricaud,* the one case of the three most plausibly involving an international law violation, the possibility of an exception to the act of state doctrine was not discussed. Some commentators have concluded that it was not brought to the Court's attention, but Justice Clarke delivered both *Oetjen* and *Ricaud* opinions, on the same day, so we can assume principles stated in the former were applicable to the latter case.

The possible adverse consequences of a conclusion to the contrary of that implicit in these cases is highlighted by contrasting the practices of the political branch with the limitations of the judicial process in matters of this kind. Following an expropriation of any significance, the Executive engages in diplomacy aimed to assure that United States citizens who are harmed are compensated fairly. Representing all claimants of this country, it will often be able, either by bilateral or multilateral talks, by submission to the United Nations, or by the employment of economic and political sanctions, to achieve some degree of general redress. Judicial determinations of invalidity of title can, on the other hand, have only an occasional impact, since they depend on the fortuitous circumstance of the property in question being brought into this country. Such decisions would, if the acts involved were declared invalid, often be likely to give offense to the expropriating country; since the concept of territorial sovereignty is so deep seated, any state may resent the refusal of the courts of another sovereign to accord validity to acts within its territorial borders. Piecemeal dispositions of this sort involving the probability of affront to another state could seriously interfere with negotiations being carried on by the Executive Branch and might prevent or render less favorable the terms of an agreement that could otherwise be reached. Relations with third countries who have engaged in similar expropriations would not be immune from effect.

The dangers of such adjudication are present regardless of whether the State Department has, as it did in this case, asserted that the relevant act violated international law. If the Executive Branch has undertaken negotiations with an expropriating country, but has refrained from claims of violation of the law of nations, a determination to that effect by a court might be regarded as a serious insult, while a finding of compliance with international law would greatly strengthen the bargaining hand of the other state with consequent detriment to American interests.

Even if the State Department has proclaimed the impropriety of the expropriation, the stamp of approval of its view by a judicial tribunal, however impartial, might increase any affront and the judicial decision might occur at a time, almost always well after the taking, when such an impact would be contrary to our national interest. Considerably more serious and far-reaching consequences would flow from a judicial finding that international law standards had been met if that determination flew in the face of a State Department proclamation to the contrary. When articulating principles of international law in its relations with other states, the Executive Branch speaks not only as an interpreter of generally accepted and traditional rules, as

would the courts, but also as an advocate of standards it believes desirable for the community of nations and protective of national concerns. In short, whatever way the matter is cut, the possibility of conflict between the Judicial and Executive Branches could hardly be avoided.

Respondents contend that, even if there is not agreement regarding general standards for determining the validity of expropriations, the alleged combinations of retaliation, discrimination, and inadequate compensation makes it patently clear that this particular expropriation was in violation of international law. If this view is accurate, it would still be unwise for the courts so to determine. Such a decision now would require the drawing of more difficult lines in subsequent cases and these would involve the possibility of conflict with the Executive view. Even if the courts avoided this course, either by presuming the validity of an act of state whenever the international law standard was thought unclear or by following the State Department declaration in such a situation, the very expression of judicial uncertainty might provide embarrassment to the Executive Branch.

Another serious consequence of the exception pressed by respondents would be to render uncertain titles in foreign commerce, with the possible consequence of altering the flow of international trade. If the attitude of the United States courts were unclear, one buying expropriated goods would not know if he could safely import them into this country. Even were takings known to be invalid, one would have difficulty determining after goods had changed hands several times whether the particular articles in question were the product of an ineffective state act.

Against the force of such considerations, we find respondents' counteracting arguments quite unpersuasive. Their basic contention is that United States courts could make a significant contribution to the growth of international law, a contribution whose importance, it is said, would be magnified by the relative paucity of decisional law by international bodies. But given the fluidity of present world conditions, the effectiveness of such a patchwork approach toward the formulation of an acceptable body of law concerning state responsibility for expropriations is, to say the least, highly conjectural. Moreover, it rests upon the sanguine presupposition that the decisions of the courts of the world's major capital exporting country and principal exponent of the free enterprise system would be accepted as disinterested expressions of sound legal principle by those adhering to widely different ideologies.

*　*　*

Respondents claim that the economic pressure resulting from the proposed exception to the act of state doctrine will materially add to the protection of United States investors. We are not convinced, even assuming the relevance of this contention. Expropriations take place for a variety of reasons, political and ideological as well as economic. When one considers the variety of means possessed by this country to make secure foreign investment, the persuasive or coercive effect of judicial invalidation of acts of expropriation dwindles in comparison. The newly independent states are in need of continuing foreign investment; the creation of a climate unfavorable to such investment by wholesale confiscations may well work to their longrun economic disadvantage. Foreign aid given to many of these countries provides a powerful lever in the hands of the political branches to ensure fair treatment of United States nationals. Ultimately the sanctions of economic embargo and the freezing of assets in this country may be employed. Any country willing to brave any or all of these consequences is unlikely to be deterred by sporadic judicial decisions directly

affecting only property brought to our shores. If the political branches are unwilling to exercise their ample powers to effect compensation, this reflects a judgment of the national interest which the judiciary would be ill advised to undermine indirectly.

It is suggested that if the act of state doctrine is applicable to violations of international law, it should only be so when the Executive Branch expressly stipulates that it does not wish the courts to pass on the question of validity. See Association of the Bar of the City of New York, Committee on International Law, A Reconsideration of the Act of State Doctrine in United States Courts (1959). We should be slow to reject the representations of the Government that such a reversal of the *Bernstein* principle would work serious inroads on the maximum effectiveness of United States diplomacy. Often the State Department will wish to refrain from taking an official position, particularly at a moment that would be dictated by the development of private litigation but might be inopportune diplomatically. Adverse domestic consequences might flow from an official stand which could be assuaged, if at all, only by revealing matters best kept secret. Of course, a relevant consideration for the State Department would be the position contemplated in the court to hear the case. It is highly questionable whether the examination of validity by the judiciary should depend on an educated guess by the Executive as to probable result and, at any rate, should a prediction be wrong, the Executive might be embarrassed in its dealings with other countries. We do not now pass on the *Bernstein* exception, but even if it were deemed valid, its suggested extension is unwarranted.

However offensive to the public policy of this country and its constituent States an expropriation of this kind may be, we conclude that both the national interest and progress toward the goal of establishing the rule of law among nations are best served by maintaining intact the act of state doctrine in this realm of its application.

* * *

The judgment of the Court of Appeals is reversed and the case is remanded to the District Court for proceedings consistent with this opinion.

[*Seven Justices concurred.*]

MR. JUSTICE WHITE, dissenting.

I am dismayed that the Court has, with one broad stroke, declared the ascertainment and application of international law beyond the competence of the courts of the United States in a large and important category of cases. I am also disappointed in the Court's declaration that the acts of a sovereign state with regard to the property of aliens within its borders are beyond the reach of international law in the courts of this country. However clearly established that law may be, a sovereign may violate it with impunity, except insofar as the political branches of the government may provide a remedy. This backward looking doctrine, never before declared in this Court, is carried a disconcerting step further: not only are the courts powerless to question acts of state proscribed by international law but they are likewise powerless to refuse to adjudicate the claim founded upon a foreign law; they must render judgment and thereby validate the lawless act. Since the Court expressly extends its ruling to all acts of state expropriating property, however clearly inconsistent with the international community, all discriminatory expropriations of the property of aliens, as for example the taking of properties of persons belonging to certain races, religions or nationalities, are entitled to automatic validation in the courts of the United States. No other civilized country has found such a rigid rule necessary for the survival of the executive branch of its

government; the executive of no other government seems to require such insulation from international law adjudications in its courts; and no other judiciary is apparently so incompetent to ascertain and apply international law.

I do not believe that the act of state doctrine, as judicially fashioned in this Court, and the reasons underlying it, require American courts to decide cases in disregard of international law and of the rights of litigants to a full determination on the merits.

* * *

Of course, there are many unsettled areas of international law, as there are with domestic law, and these areas present sensitive problems of accommodating the interests of nations that subscribe to divergent economic and political systems. It may be that certain nationalizations of property for a public purpose fall within this area. Also, it may be that domestic courts, as compared to international tribunals, or arbitral commissions, have a different and less active role to play in formulating new rules of international law or in choosing between rules not yet adhered to by any substantial group of nations. Where a clear violation of international law is not demonstrated, I would agree that principles of comity underlying the act of state doctrine warrant recognition and enforcement of the foreign act. But none of these considerations relieve a court of the obligation to make an inquiry into the validity of the foreign act, none of them warrant a flat rule of no inquiry at all. The vice of the act of state doctrine, as formulated by the Court and applied in this case, where the decree is alleged not only to be confiscatory but also retaliatory and discriminatory and found by two courts to be a flagrant violation of international law, is that it precludes any such examination and proscribes any decision on whether Cuban

Law No. 851 contravenes an accepted principle of international law.

Notes

1. The letter stated:

"1. This government has consistently opposed the forcible acts of dispossession of a discriminatory and confiscatory nature practiced by the Germans on the countries or peoples subject to their controls.

* * *

3. "The policy of the Executive, with respect to claims asserted in the United States for the restitution of identifiable property (or compensation in lieu thereof) lost through force, coercion, or duress as a result of Nazi persecution in Germany, is to relieve American courts from any restraint upon the exercise of their jurisdiction to pass upon the validity of the acts of Nazi officials." State Department Press Release, April 27, 1949, 20 Dept. State Bull. 592.

2. Abram Chayes, the Legal Adviser to the State Department, wrote on October 18, 1961, in answer to an inquiry regarding the position of the Department by Mr. John Laylin, attorney for *amici:*

"The Department of State has not, in the *Bahia de Nipe* case or elsewhere, done anything inconsistent with the position taken on the Cuban nationalizations by Secretary Herter. Whether or not these nationalizations will in the future be given effect in the United States is, of course, for the courts to determine. Since the *Sabbatino* case and other similar cases are at present before the courts, any comments on this question by the Department of State would be out of place at this time. As you yourself point out, statements by the executive branch are highly susceptible of misconstruction."

A letter dated November 14, 1961, from George Ball, Under Secretary for Economic Affairs, responded to a similar inquiry by the same attorney:

"I have carefully considered your letter and have discussed it with the Legal Adviser. Our conclusion, in which the Secretary concurs, is that the Department should not comment on matters pending before the courts."

3. . . . We do not, of course, mean to say that there is no international standard in this area; we conclude only that the matter is not meet for adjudication by domestic tribunals.

4. There are, of course, areas of international law in which consensus as to standards is greater and which do not represent a battleground for conflicting ideologies. This decision in no way intimates that the courts of this country are broadly foreclosed from considering questions of international law.

Banco Nacional de Cuba v. Farr*

United States District Court, S.D. N. Y., 1965

FREDERICK VAN PELT BRYAN, D.J.

This case is before me on remand from the Supreme Court of the United States (*Banco Nacional de Cuba* v. *Sabbatino et al.,* 376 U. S. 398 (1964)), which reversed summary judgment in favor of defendants granted by the District Court (193 F. Supp. 375 (1961)) and affirmed by the Court of Appeals (2 Cir., 307 F.2d 845 (1962)). . . .

The claim of plaintiff Banco Nacional de Cuba (Banco), an instrumentality of the Cuban government, to the proceeds of the expropriated sugar is founded on the Cuban expropriation. Defendant Farr and defendant *Sabbatino,*[1] a State Court Receiver for C.A.V. who held the proceeds, took the position that the Cuban government was not entitled thereto but that the proceeds were the property of C.A.V. from whom the sugar was expropriated.

Judgment for the defendants below was granted on the ground that the expropriation of the sugar violated international law, was therefore invalid and unenforceable in our courts, and was ineffective to deprive

---

* Reprinted from 243 F. Supp. 957 (1965).

C.A.V. of its rights in the sugar and its proceeds.

The Supreme Court held that the "act of state doctrine" proscribed a challenge to the validity of the Cuban expropriation law in this case even if it violated international law. It reversed and remanded the case to the District Court for further proceedings.

On October 7, 1964, subsequent to the decision of the Supreme Court and before judgment was entered on remand, the President signed the Foreign Assistance Act of 1964 containing an amendment sponsored by Senators Hickenlooper and Sparkman, which precipitated the present phase of this litigation. (Section 301(d) (4) of Public Law 88-633, 78 Stat. 1009, 1013, hereafter referred to as the Hickenlooper Amendment.) The Amendment provided:

"Notwithstanding any other provision of law, no court in the United States shall decline on the ground of the federal act of state doctrine to make a determination on the merits giving effect to the principles of international law in a case in which a claim of title or other right is asserted by any party including a foreign state (or a party claiming through such state) based upon (or traced through) a confiscation or other taking after January 1, 1959, by an act of that state in violation of the principles of international law, including the principles of compensation and the other standards set out in this subsection: *Provided,* That this subparagraph shall not be applicable (1) in any case in which an act of a foreign state is not contrary to international law or with respect to a claim of title or other right acquired pursuant to an irrevocable letter of credit of not more than 180 days duration issued in good faith prior to the time of the confiscation or other taking, or (2) in any case with respect to which the President determines that application of the act of state doctrine is required in that particular case by the foreign policy interests of the United States and a suggestion to this effect is filed on his behalf in that case with the court, or (3) in any case in which the proceedings are commenced after January 1, 1966." [The Foreign Assistance Act of 1965 struck out provision (3). Public Law 89-171, 79 Stat. 653.]

* * *

The Hickenlooper Amendment by its terms applies "in a case in which a claim of title or other right is asserted by *** a foreign state (or a party claiming through such state) based upon *** a confiscation or other taking after January 1, 1959." It is quite plain that Congress meant the legislation to apply to confiscations occurring after January 1, 1959, the date on which Castro came to power. There can be no doubt that by its specific language the Amendment applied retroactively to past confiscations and transactions arising therefrom which had occurred between January 1, 1959 and the date of its enactment.

The Amendment does not deal with confiscations and transactions in the abstract. It deals with "cases" and the action which courts are to take upon such cases. It consistently uses the word "case" throughout its text. Nowhere does it distinguish between cases pending at the time of its enactment and cases which were commenced prior thereto. There is certainly no language which could be remotely said to exclude the case at bar.

The Amendment contains three exceptions, including that authorizing the President to determine that application of the act of state doctrine is required in a particular case by the foreign policy interests of the United States and to file a suggestion to this effect with the court. Another relates to the time by which law suits must be commenced in order for the Amendment to apply. Each of the exceptions applies "in any case." There is no doubt that when Congress intended to make exceptions it did so and it made no exceptions as to pending cases.

The direction to the courts is mandatory. It is provided that "no court in the United States *shall decline* on the ground of the federal act of state doctrine to make a determination" *in a case* which it describes. These words are not prospective as has been urged. They are mandatory in their intention and effect and require the courts to give retroactive effect to the directions of the Amendment.

* * *

The amendment was not a haphazard rider extraneous to the purposes of the bill to which it was added. It is part of a consistent pattern of legislation, the purpose of which was to protect private investment abroad and to discourage foreign expropriations. As carried over from previous years the Foreign Assistance Act already included provisions for the cut-off of foreign aid to countries which had expropriated property of American nationals. It also provided for cutting off all aid to Cuba and authorized an embargo on trade with that country. These provisions had been strengthened from year to year.

Congress was particularly concerned with the Cuban confiscations which had taken place on such a large scale. It was for this reason, as Senator Hickenlooper made clear, that the date of January 1, 1959 was used as the operative date. A prime concern was to prevent the Castro government from reaping the fruits of what Congress considered to be illegal and unconscionable acts in violation of international law. It can scarcely be assumed that Congress intended to exclude a substantial portion of the Cuban confiscations at which the statute was directed from the benefits of the statute in the absence of specific language to that effect.

It is true that the Amendment also had a broader purpose—to discourage illegal confiscations by foreign governments in violation of international law and thus to strengthen the flow of investment in commerce and protect American investments abroad under the aid program and otherwise. One of the ways in which it sought to do this was to insure that the United States did not become a "thieves' market."

* * *

I hold (1) that this is a case within the purview of the Hickenlooper Amendment; (2) that the Amendment is supervening law which must be applied here despite the opinion of the Supreme Court in *Sabbatino;* and (3) that I am therefore required to make a determination on the merits giving effect to the principles of international law as the Amendment provides.

* * *

While the act of state doctrine is not of constitutional dimensions, and there is no constitutional requirement that it be applied by the courts, this does not resolve the question of whether there is a constitutional impediment to a legislative direction that the courts abstain from applying it. Plaintiff urges that there is such an impediment, and that the legislative direction to the courts in the Amendment not to apply the doctrine is an unconstitutional interference with the judicial power. I do not agree.

There is no doubt that issues concerning international law as they may affect confiscations by foreign governments are within the constitutional jurisdiction and judicial competence of the courts, as *Sabbatino* makes clear. By applying the act of state doctrine the courts have merely declined as a matter of judicial policy to decide such issues where a decision may affect our foreign relations. The doctrine is a self-imposed discretionary rule of "judicial abnegation," 307 F.2d at 857, under which the court as a matter of policy declines to decide the issue of the validity of a foreign act of state.

The reasons why the courts determined on such a policy are significant. As *Sabbatino* also indicates, the conduct of foreign relations is particularly a concern of the political branches of the Government. It was because of apprehension that decisions on the merits concerning acts of confiscation by foreign governments might embarrass the political branches in conducting foreign relations and adversely affect the national interests in that area that the court adopted the policy of abstention.

When a determination is made by the political branches charged with the responsibility for foreign relations as to where the interests of the United States lie, it is not for the courts to say them nay. The basic reason for the application of the act of state doctrine disappears. To require that the doctrine be applied despite the express directions of the political branches on the subject would be to place the court in the position of having the last word in matters affecting foreign affairs, the determination of which is committed to other branches of the Government. This would be wholly inconsistent with the doctrine of separation of powers and with the very rationale of the act of state doctrine.

In any event Congress does not lack power to direct that the act of state doctrine be eliminated as an instrument of judicial decision.

* * *

Remaining is the disposition to be made of the case at bar in the light of what has thus far been held.

The moving defendants urge that judgment should be entered in their favor dismissing the complaint. Their position is that the Court of Appeals in this case has already held that

"Since the Cuban decree of expropriation not only failed to provide adequate compensation but also involved a retaliatory purpose and a discrimination against United States nationals, we hold that the decree was in violation of international law." 307 F.2d at 868.

And that court went on to conclude that

"[S]ince the Cuban decree violated international law, the appellant's title is invalid and the district court was correct in dismissing the complaint." 307 F.2d at 869.

Defendants contend that since I have held the act of state doctrine as enunciated

by the Supreme Court in *Sabbatino* to be inapplicable to this case under the Hickenlooper Amendment, this court is bound by the prior decision of the Court of Appeals, and without further inquiry on the merits, must give judgment for the defendants dismissing the complaint. Plainly I am bound by the decision of the Court of Appeals that the expropriation by the Cuban government violated international law. The opinion of the Supreme Court does not impair that holding. Its discussion of international law was limited to the question of compensation and did not relate to questions of discrimination and retaliation.

But defendants' position fails to take into account one vitally important factor. The Amendment provides that it shall not be applicable

"in any case with respect to which the President determines that application of the act of state doctrine is required in that particular case by the foreign policy interest of the United States and a suggestion to this effect is filed on his behalf in that case with the court."

That exception is an integral and essential part of the Amendment. It must be given effect.

* * *

Prior to the argument of the present motions counsel for the plaintiff formally requested that the President make a determination pursuant to the Amendment that the application of the act of state doctrine was required in this case by the foreign policy interests of the United States. Replying on the President's behalf the Acting Legal Adviser to the Secretary of State on November 27, 1964 said:

"We have been advised that in the opinion of the Department of Justice the cited provision is not applicable to the above case which, as you know, was decided by the Supreme Court under the name of *Banco Nacional de Cuba* v. *Sabbatino* prior to the passage of the amendment. Accordingly, the Department of State does not believe it is appropriate for the President to make any determination with respect to this case under section 620 (e) of the Foreign Assistance Act, as amended."

Thus, as far as the record in this case is concerned, the President has made no determination as to whether application of the act of state doctrine is required by the foreign policy interests of the United States. It appears that such a determination has been withheld upon the assumption, which I have now held to be erroneous, that the Hickenlooper Amendment did not apply to this case at all, and that the decision of the Supreme Court in *Sabbatino* remained applicable.

The United States on these motions urged that the Amendment did not apply to cases pending in the courts at the time of its enactment and thus would not apply to the case at bar. Its position is consistent with that taken by the Acting Legal Adviser of the Department of State in his letter of November 27, 1964.

It is plain to me that proper respect and consideration for the Executive Arm requires that the court give full opportunity to the President to make the determination provided for by the Amendment and, if in his wisdom he sees fit, to have a suggestion filed on his behalf that in this case application of the act of state doctrine is required by the foreign policy interests of the United States.

'This is not a situation where the court should make assumptions as to what the presidential position may or may not be on the basis of a confusing and somewhat incomplete record. On the contrary, it is a fundamental intendment and purpose of the Amendment that the Executive Branch be given full opportunity to express its views if it so desires. To fail to give it that opportunity would nullify the protections expressly given by the Amendment to the interests of United States foreign policy.

I would assume that the Executive Arm will be able to make such a determination and to file a suggestion with the court as the

Amendment provides if it so desires within sixty (60) days of the filing of this opinion. If more time is required the court should be so advised.

For these reasons determination of the question as to whether final judgment dismissing the complaint should be entered in this case will be withheld for a period of sixty (60) days for the purposes I have indicated.

It is so ordered.

Note

1. Subsequent to the decision of the Court of Appeals and before the decision of the Supreme Court, *Sabbatino* was discharged as receiver of C.A.V. and the funds in dispute were placed in escrow pending the outcome of this suit. After remand, pursuant to stipulation of the parties, the action was discontinued as against *Sabbatino* and the title was amended to name as defendants only the co-partners doing business as Farr, Whitlock & Co.

[*In Judge Bryan's Memorandum Opinion of November 15, 1965, he stated:**]

Up to the time when the opinion of July 30, 1965, was filed there had been no determination by the President that the application of the act of state doctrine to this case was required by the foreign policy interests of the United States, and no suggestion to that effect had been filed with the court. However, the record was incomplete and unclear as to the position which the President might desire to take on this question.

In order to afford the executive arm full opportunity to make such a determination and to express its view to the court if it so desired, I withheld decision for a period of sixty (60) days as to whether final judgment dismissing the complaint in this action should be entered. Prior to the expiration of that period the court received a letter from

* 5 *International Legal Materials: Current Documents* 1209 (1965). Reprinted by permission of the American Society of International Law.

the United States Attorney for the Southern District of New York dated September 29, 1965, reading as follows:

In its decision of July 30, 1965 this Court afforded the Executive Branch the opportunity to file a suggestion indicating whether the application of the act of state doctrine is required by the foreign policy interests of the United States, as provided for in Section 620 (e) (2) of the Foreign Assistance Act of 1961, as amended (22 U.S.C. 2370 [e] [2]). I am instructed to inform the Court that no determination has been made that application of the act of state doctrine is required in this case by the foreign policy interests of the United States.

So that there will be no ambiguity, the Court is advised that no such determination is contemplated.

This letter makes it clear that the President will make no suggestion to the court in this case as to the application of the act of state doctrine pursuant to the Hickenlooper Amendment. . . .

* * *

As I have held, application of the act of state doctrine to this case is now barred by the Hickenlooper Amendment since there will be no presidential suggestion to the contrary. The holding of the Supreme Court that the act of state doctrine bars determination on the merits no longer applies.

The Court of Appeals has already determined that absent the bar of the act of state doctrine the Cuban decree in this case on which plaintiff's claim is founded violated international law, that plaintiff's title, therefore, is invalid, and that defendants are entitled to judgment dismissing the complaint. I am plainly bound by that determination which is decisive of the issue now before me.

Defendants' motion to dismiss the complaint is therefore granted. . . .

Suggested Readings

Textbooks

Brierly. *The Law of Nations,* pp. 222–316.
Brownlie. *Principles of Public International Law,* pp. 250–444.
Fenwick. *International Law,* pp. 296–401, 552–584.
Gould. *An Introduction to International Law,* pp. 259–288, 370–410, 438–469, 507–533.
Jacobini. *International Law,* pp. 68–89, 116–144, 201–234.
Kaplan and Katzenbach. *The Political Foundations of International Law,* pp. 173–197.
Kelsen. *Principles of International Law,* pp. 343–380.
Sørensen. *Manual of Public International Law,* pp. 381–468, 531–604.
Svarlien. *An Introduction to the Law of Nations,* pp. 133–154, 229–260.
Tung. *International Law in an Organizing World,* pp. 134–143, 170–222, 230–279.
von Glahn. *Law Among Nations,* pp. 123–250, 333–412.

Territorial Jurisdiction

Baxter, Richard R., and Jan F. Triska. *The Law of International Waterways.* Cambridge, Mass.: Harvard University Press, 1964.
Bozcek, B. A. *Flags of Convenience.* Cambridge, Mass.: Harvard University Press, 1962.

Selak, Charles B. "A Consideration of the Legal Status of the Gulf of Aqaba," 52 *American Journal of International Law* 660 (1958).

Extradition

Green, L. C. "Political Offences, War Crimes and Extradition," 11 *International and Comparative Law Quarterly* 329 (1962).

Harvard Research in International Law. "Extradition," 29 *American Journal of International Law,* Special Supplement 16 (1935).

O'Higgins, Paul. "European Convention on Extradition," 9 *International and Comparative Law Quarterly* 491 (1960).

Immunities from Jurisdiction

Ahluwalia, Kuljit. *The Legal Status, Privileges and Immunities of the Specialized Agencies of the United Nations and Certain °Other International Organizations.* The Hague: Martinus Nijhoff, 1964.

Jenks, C. Wilfred. *International Immunities.* Dobbs Ferry, N.Y.: Oceana, 1961.

Sen, B. *A Diplomat's Handbook of International Law and Practice.* The Hague: Martinus Nijhoff, 1965.

Snee, Joseph M., and Kenneth A. Pye. *Status of Forces Agreements and Criminal Jurisdiction.* Dobbs Ferry, N.Y.: Oceana, 1957.

Sweeney, Joseph M. *The International Law of Sovereign Immunity.* Washington, D.C.: U.S. Government Printing Office, 1963.

Treatment of Aliens

Domke, Martin. "Indonesian Nationalization Measures Before Foreign Courts," 54 *American Journal of International Law* 305 (1960).

Dunn, Frederick S. *The Protection of Nationals.* Baltimore: Johns Hopkins Press, 1932.

Lillich, Richard B., and Gordon A. Christenson. *International Claims: Their Preparation and Presentation.* Syracuse, N.Y.: Syracuse University Press, 1962.

Tondel, Lyman M. (ed.). *The Aftermath of Sabbatino.* Dobbs Ferry, N.Y.: Oceana, 1965.

White, Gillian. *Nationalization of Foreign Property.* New York: Praeger, 1961.

Chapter V
The Law
of Treaties

Most of the specific rules that regulate the relations between states are contained in treaties, which are agreements between states, or organizations of states, that create legal rights and obligations between the parties. That treaties are frequently given some other designation, such as convention, agreement, pact, declaration, charter, or even exchange of notes, is of no fundamental significance in international law; their binding force depends not upon nomenclature but upon the intention of the parties to create legal rights and obligations.[1] Because of their importance, treaties are normally concluded in writing, but consent to be bound need not necessarily be so expressed, as is illustrated by the treaty of alliance concluded orally in 1697 between Peter the Great of Russia and Frederick III, Elector of Brandenberg.[2]

In the international legal system, which finds law in the consent of states, treaties are clearly superior to customary practice as a source of legal obligation. The treaty process is comparatively rapid and the norms it produces are more explicit and definite than are the norms of customary law; when properly drafted, a treaty leaves

[1] A "declaration," for example, may or may not be a legally binding international agreement. The Declaration of Paris of 1856 was clearly intended by the parties to create binding rules for the regulation of naval warfare, while statements by government officials prior to the adoption of the Universal Declaration of Human Rights indicate that its terms were not considered to be legally binding.

[2] In an opinion delivered in 1933, the Permanent Court of International Justice considered it to be beyond all dispute "that a reply orally given to the effect that the Norwegian Government would not make any difficulties in the settlement of the question of the recognition of Denmark's sovereignty over the whole of Greenland given by the Minister of Foreign Affairs, in response to a request by the diplomatic representative of a foreign Power, in regard to a question falling within his province, is binding upon the country to which the Minister belongs." *Eastern Greenland Case* (1933), Series A/B, No. 53, p. 71.

little or no question as to what the terms of the agreement are, although there may later be considerable controversy as to what the terms mean. It is true, of course, that the language of some treaties, particularly those of major political importance, is so general that the parties retain considerable latitude in interpretation. But this is not necessarily to be condemned; if all treaties were drafted in precise, unambiguous terms, decision-makers would be even more reluctant than they are to commit their states in matters that affect vital national interests. What might be called "calculated ambiguity" is sometimes a realistic precondition to the willingness of states to use the treaty device.

Most of the tens of thousands of treaties now in force are of a contractual nature, in that they concern matters of particular interest only to two or a few states— bilateral agreements that fix boundaries or provide for the return of fugitives from justice are illustrations. Although these contractual agreements create law, "inasmuch as they lay down rules of conduct which the parties are bound to observe as law,"[3] the designation "law-making treaties" is commonly used to refer to formal agreements that fasten upon a large number of parties an identical obligation. Included among these great multilateral treaties that have contributed so greatly to the modern law of nations are the Geneva Conventions on the Law of the Sea, the Vienna Convention on Diplomatic Relations, the General Convention on the Privileges and Immunities of the United Nations, and the Hague and Geneva Conventions on the Law of Warfare. Still other law-making treaties, such as the United Nations Charter and the Constitution of the International Labor Organization, have created important institutions of international life and accorded to them a certain legislative or quasi-

legislative capacity. As Brierly has stated, law-making treaties are "the substitute in the international system for legislation . . . their number is increasing so rapidly that the 'conventional law of nations' has taken its place beside the old customary law and already far surpasses it in volume."[4]

Although treaties form a more important source of international law than does customary practice, it must be emphasized that these formal agreements are made within the framework of customary norms that govern their *conclusion, validity, termination, revision,* and *interpretation.* States have, over a long period of time, concluded their agreements in a similar fashion, employed common clauses and standard forms, and used similar modes of interpretation. And in placid times, at least, they have exhibited a certain amount of consensus on the rules and principles that regulate revision and termination of treaties. It is the consensus contained in these practices that forms the basis of the "law of treaties," or, more descriptively, the law *about* treaties. Because of the importance of this area of law and the existence of considerable agreement as to its content, the International Law Commission of the United Nations decided as early as 1949 to attempt its codification in a Draft Convention on the Law of Treaties. The Commmission completed its work on July 18, 1966, when it adopted seventy-five articles which, with the exception of a few provisions that are presented as attempts to change or develop the law, are cogent evidence of customary law on the subject. On May 23, 1969, after making several drafting and substantive changes in the International Law Commission's work, the United Nations Conference on the Law of Treaties adopted the Vienna Convention on the Law of Treaties; the Convention will enter into

[3] L. Oppenheim, *International Law: A Treatise*, Vol. I, *Peace*, 8th ed. by Hersch Lauterpacht (London and New York: Longmans, Green and Co., 1955), p. 879.

[4] Brierly, *The Law of Nations*, p. 58

force when thirty-five states ratify or accede to it.[5]

Most of the rules governing the conclusion of treaties are widely, if not universally, accepted. A treaty is concluded, or brought into existence, when two or more states manifest consent to be bound by its terms. In the age of absolute monarchs and slow communications, a sovereign's agent was recognized as having "full power" both to negotiate and to bind his state. In modern practice, "full power" normally refers to authority to negotiate and to sign a treaty, which is then subject to ratification by the appropriate state organ.[6] However, if the parties so desire, a treaty does not require ratification, in which case signature alone is sufficient to bind states. The date on which a treaty comes into force is also determined by the intention of the parties, usually by specific reference in the text. In the case of some multilateral agreements, a minimum number of ratifications is necessary before the treaty has any binding force upon ratifying parties. A state that did not originally sign a treaty may become a party to it by "accession," but only with the consent of the other parties; such consent is often given in the treaty itself. According to Articles 102 and 103 of the United Nations Charter, treaties concluded by members of the organization shall be registered with the Secretariat; any treaty entered into after the establishment of the United Nations that is not so registered, although it retains its validity, may not be invoked before any organ of the United Nations, including the International Court of Justice.

In accepting a treaty, a state sometimes attaches a "reservation," which is defined in Article 2 (I) of the Vienna Convention as "a unilateral statement . . . made by a state, when signing, ratifying, accepting, approving or acceding to a treaty, whereby it purports to exclude or to modify the legal effect of certain provisions of the treaty in their application to that State." In the case of bilateral treaties, reservations present no particular difficulty; if the other party does not choose to accept the variation or exclusion the treaty will fall. But in the case of multilateral treaties, when some states are willing to accept reservations and others are not, they present one of the most complex and perplexing legal problems encountered in the rules governing conclusion of treaties. At one time, it was generally agreed that reservations were allowed only if the treaty concerned explicitly permitted them and if all parties were willing to accept them. In more recent times, however, the practice of permitting a reserving state to become a party vis à vis nonobjecting states has received wide acceptance. The advantage of this newer practice is that it promotes universality; its disadvantage, that it does so at the expense of depth of obligation. The International Court of Justice, in an advisory opinion given in 1951 on the admissibility of reservations to the Convention on the Prevention and Punishment of the Crime of Genocide, stressed the divergence of state practice and the intention of the General Assembly of the United Nations that the Convention should be made universal in scope; it then concluded that "a State which has made . . . a reservation which has been objected to by one or more parties to the Convention but not by others,

[5] The text of the International Law Commission's Draft Convention is reprinted in 61 *American Journal of International Law* 263 (1967). On December 5, 1966, the General Assembly adopted Resolution 2166 (XXI), which requested the Secretary General to convoke a diplomatic conference early in 1968 "to consider the law of treaties and to embody the results of its work in an international convention." At the first session of the United Nations Conference on the Law of Treaties, which took place in Vienna from March 26 to May 24, 1968, the Committee of the Whole adopted, with some changes, 65 of the articles in the International Law Commission Draft, deleted 1 article, and deferred the remaining 9 until the second session to be held in 1969. It also adopted 4 new articles and postponed consideration of 3 proposed new articles until the 1969 session. The text of the articles, as they emerged from the 1968 session, is reprinted in 7 *International Legal Materials: Current Documents* 770 (1968). The final text of the Vienna Convention on the Law of Treaties, henceforth referred to as the Vienna Convention, is reprinted on pp. 294–310.
[6] There is a wide variety of "appropriate state organs," ranging from the President in the United States and the Crown in the United Kingdom to the Standing Committee of the National People's Congress *and* the Chairman of the Government in Communist China.

can be regarded as being a party to the Convention if the reservation is compatible with the object and purpose of the Convention . . ."[7] The Vienna Convention adopts the view that the more modern practice, along with the "compatibility" doctrine expressed by the International Court, should be the general rule. Although the difficulty of defining "compatibility," among other problems, will cause the matter of reservations to multilateral treaties to remain a source of doctrinal controversy, it would seem that, on the whole, the Commission's approach serves the international community need for widespread acceptance of norms contained in the increasing number of law-making treaties.

Perhaps the most fundamental principle of international law, and surely the basic principle of the law of treaties, is that of *pacta sunt servanda*, which, according to the wording of Article 26 of the Vienna Convention, means that "every treaty in force is binding upon the parties to it and must be performed by them in good faith." Yet, as with contracts in municipal law, there are recognized requirements on which the *validity* of a treaty depends. It is generally agreed, for example, that a treaty entered into as a result of the personal coercion of a state's representative is voidable by that state. Similarly, if a state is induced to enter into a treaty by fraud, the particular clauses to which the fraud relates are voidable. These and a few other reasons for declaring a treaty to be invalid are universally recognized; but some purported grounds for invalidity, because of the danger they present to the sanctity of treaties, have led to considerable controversy.

One such ground was presented as *lex lata*, or law already in force, in Article 52 of the Vienna Convention, which declares that a treaty "is void if its conclusion has been procured by the threat or use of force

in violation of the principles of international law embodied in the Charter of the United Nations." Although this rule meets with general approval, some jurists hesitate to accept it because of the fear that it might open the door to a plethora of unfounded assertions of coercion and thus undermine treaty law in general.[8]

Another controversial view was adopted in Article 53 of the Vienna Convention, which asserts that a treaty "is void if, at the time of its conclusion, it conflicts with a peremptory norm of general international law." A "peremptory norm" is then loosely defined as "a norm accepted and recognized by the international community of States as a whole as a norm from which no derogation is permitted and which can be modified only by a subsequent norm of general international law having the same character." The problem of defining "peremptory norms," or rules having the character of *jus cogens*, is obviously the principal difficulty of this rule.[9] Although the Commission stopped short of compiling a list of such norms, ostensibly because to do so might lead to misunderstanding as to the position of norms not included, several of the members suggested that certain types of treaties, including agreements contemplating the unlawful use of force, or trade in slaves, or the commission of acts of piracy or genocide, would clearly conflict with peremptory norms.[10] But, in the absence of a general agreement on the precise content of *jus cogens*, the rule will

---

[7] *Reservations to the Convention on Genocide, International Court of Justice Reports* 15 (1951).

[8] See the International Law Commission's commentary to its Article 49, reprinted in 61 *American Journal of International Law* 407 (1967).

[9] According to Professor Verdross, a member of the International Law Commission, these norms are distinguished by the fact that "they do not exist to satisfy the needs of the individual states but the higher interests of the whole international community." Alfred Verdross, "*Jus Dispositivum* and *Jus Cogens* in International Law," 60 *American Journal of International Law* 58 (1966). Most of the norms of international law have the character of *jus dispositivum*, which means that they must be applied only if states have not agreed otherwise *inter se*. The rules relating to diplomatic immunities, for example, are binding only so long as states do not agree between themselves to alter them.

[10] See the International Law Commission's commentary to Article 50, reprinted in 61 *American Journal of International Law* 409 (1967).

surely be productive of considerable diplomatic controversy. Ian Brownlie, in referring to peremptory norms in general, not necessarily as they relate to the law of treaties, suggested the difficulty of employing the rule in the following thought-provoking question: "If a state uses force to implement the principle of self-determination, is it possible to assume that one aspect of *jus cogens* is more significant than another?"[11] The legal controversy that raged over the seizure of Goa by India in 1961 illustrates that this is not merely an academic question.[12]

Another controversial ground purported to serve as a justifiable basis for invalidating treaties is contained in the Communist doctrine of "unequal treaties," according to which an agreement that was not concluded on the basis of the sovereign equality of the parties is void *ab initio*.[13] A treaty between a powerful state and a weak state granting extensive economic privileges or military facilities to the former would be an obvious example. While Western writers and statesmen oppose this doctrine, ostensibly on the basis of its vagueness and the adverse effects it would have on the sanctity of treaties, it is increasingly regarded as just in the "unequal states." Oliver J. Lissitzyn has noted that:

In the attempt to provide justification for their efforts to change the *status quo*, the less developed nations increasingly rely on the argument that "unequal" or "inequitable" treaties, and treaties imposed by duress, are invalid *ab initio*. Attacking the treaty by which the United States obtained the Canal Zone, for example, the foreign minister of Panama called it "humiliating, injurious, unjust and inequitable," and said that it "does not conform to the principles, precepts and norms of international law, justice and international morality universally accepted today."[14]

[11] Brownlie, *Principles of Public International Law*, p. 418.
[12] See pp. 349–352.
[13] For a discussion of "unequal treaties" in Soviet theory and practice, see Jan F. Triska and Robert M. Slusser, *The Theory, Law, and Policy of Soviet Treaties* (Stanford: Stanford University Press, 1962), *passim*.
[14] Oliver J. Lissitzyn, "International Law in a Divided World," *International Conciliation*, No. 542 (March 1963), p. 56.

It is sometimes alleged that a state can declare a treaty void if it was concluded by an agent in violation of municipal law limitations on his treaty-making authority. This view is correct only within narrowly circumscribed limits. If, for example, the representative who purports to bind his state is a minor official and lacks authority from his government, his "agreement" is not valid. But when the contracting agent is properly authorized under international law, that is to say, when he is a high official who ordinarily represents his state in international relations, commitments he assumes on behalf of his state are normally binding. According to Article 46 (1) of the Vienna Convention, a state may not declare a treaty void on the ground that its consent was expressed in violation of a provision of municipal law "unless that violation was manifest and concerned a rule of its internal law of fundamental importance." Although the word "manifest" is exceedingly vague, section 2 of Article 46 seems to assert the view that this ground for invalidation applies only in cases where the other party is clearly aware of the failure of the contracting agent to comply with the municipal law of his state or where the lack of constitutional authority is so obvious that the other party must be deemed to be aware of it.

The political controversies that have raged over the authority of state agents to enter into binding agreements have centered not so much around the rules of international law as around the stipulations, real and alleged, of municipal law. It is possible that the greatest impact in international law that these controversies have had has been the increasing employment of alternatives to the term "treaty" as a designation for binding international agreements. While differences of mere nomenclature are immaterial to international law, they may have considerable significance in the municipal law of the parties. This is true of the United States, where a *treaty* may be ratified by the President only with the advice and consent of a two-thirds majority of the Senate, while the President acting alone may ratify *executive agreements*.

Executive agreements concluded by the President of the United States pledge the good faith of that country and, like other international agreements, continue to be binding until they are terminated in accordance with the rules of international law.[15] Although executive agreements are not mentioned in the written Constitution, executive practice and court decisions, over the frequent protests of senators and "states righters," have clearly incorporated them into municipal law on a level almost equal to that of treaties, which are declared by Article VI of the Constitution to be, along with the Constitution itself and national laws, the "supreme law of the land." Any law of one of the states within the federal system must yield when it is inconsistent with, or impairs the implementation of, an executive agreement.[16] While the authority of the President to enter into such agreements is clearly authorized by municipal law, the State Department has conceded, largely as a result of proddings by Senate committees, that there is a fundamental distinction in municipal law between an executive agreement and a treaty: an executive agreement "cannot alter the existing [federal] law and must conform to all statutory enactments [of Congress], whereas a treaty, if ratified by and with the advice and consent of the Senate . . . itself becomes the supreme law of the land and takes precedence over any prior statutory enactment."[17] The executive branch has also agreed that there are municipal law limits on the scope of the executive agreement-making power. According to Department of State Circular No. 175, issued on December 13, 1955, the executive agreement form "shall be used" only for international agreements that fall into one or more of the following categories:

a. Agreements which are made pursuant to or in accordance with existing legislation or a treaty;
b. Agreements which are made subject to Congressional approval or implementation; or
c. Agreements which are made under and in accordance with the President's Constitutional power.[18]

The inclusion of category (c) and the failure of Congress to adopt the often proposed "Bricker Amendment"[19] would seem to leave the President a wide scope of authority to conclude executive agreements without committing a "manifest" violation of municipal law provisions. Under international law, it would be difficult indeed for the United States to justify declaring an executive agreement void on the ground that a President should have used the treaty device.

Customary international law distinguishes between the *invalidity* of treaties, which suggests a legal "still-birth," and the *termination* and *revision* of treaties that are recognized as valid in their inception. The basic principle is that a valid treaty

---

[15] Assertions made by President Eisenhower and other members of his administration to the effect that a President could, through an executive agreement, bind the United States only for the term of his office are without foundation in either United States practice or international law. International obligations bind the subjects of international law, that is, states, not the temporary officeholders who represent states. For a discussion of the curious and inconsistent attitude of President Eisenhower on this matter, see Elmer Plishke, *Conduct of American Diplomacy* (Princeton, N.J.: Van Nostrand Co., 1967), pp. 467–468.

[16] United States v. Pink, 315 U.S. 203 (1942).

[17] United States Department of State Current Information Series No. 1, July 3, 1934, in 5 Hackworth, *Digest of International Law* 245; see also United States v. Guy W. Capps, Inc., 204 F. 2d 655 (1953).

[18] Reprinted in 50 *American Journal of International Law* 784 (1956).

[19] From 1952 through 1957, a number of proposals to amend the Constitution with respect to the making and effect of treaties and other international agreements was submitted to Congress. No proposal received the necessary two-thirds majority of either house of Congress, and interest in the effort has declined since 1957. The text of the so-called "Bricker Amendment," in the form approved by the Senate Committee on the Judiciary on June 4, 1953, read as follows:

"1. A provision of a treaty which conflicts with this Constitution shall not be of any force or effect.

2. A treaty shall become effective as internal law in the United States only through legislation which would be valid in the absence of treaty.

3. Congress shall have power to regulate all executive and other agreements with any foreign power or international organization. All such agreements shall be subject to the limitations imposed on treaties by this article.

4. The Congress shall have power to enforce this article by appropriate legislation."

may be either terminated or revised only with the consent of the parties. Many treaties stipulate the duration of the agreement and/or provide that a party may withdraw from the arrangement by giving advance notice to that effect. When the obligations assumed in a treaty are performed by the parties, the treaty is considered to have been "executed." The parties may terminate an "executory treaty" by express agreement or by entering into a new treaty relating to the same subject matter. A significant recent innovation in state practice relating to revision of treaties is the use of provisions in multilateral treaties that provide for amendment by specified majorities of the parties. According to Article 108 of the United Nations Charter, for example, the terms of the Charter can be amended by a two-thirds vote in the General Assembly and ratification by two-thirds of the members of the organization, if all the permanent members of the Security Council are among the ratifying states.

It is generally recognized that a material breach of a treaty by one of the parties entitles the other party, or other parties, either to consider that the agreement has been terminated or to continue to consider it as binding and seek its enforcement. These options are accepted as a means of securing the observance of treaty commitments. But, because of the risks inherent in this rule, Article 60 (3) of the Vienna Convention attempts to circumscribe the right of wronged parties so as not to permit a state to allege a trivial or fictitious breach as a pretext for denouncing a treaty that it no longer considers to serve its interests: the only type of breach that justifies termination is one that constitutes a violation of a provision "essential to the accomplishment of the object or purpose of the treaty."

It is also widely recognized that, if fundamental changes in the circumstances upon which a treaty rests take place, these changes may be invoked as a ground for terminating the treaty. This principle, known generally as the doctrine of *clausula rebus sic stantibus*, is based on the assumption that there is an "implied clause" in every treaty that provides that the agreement is binding only so long as the material circumstances on which it rests remain unchanged. The widespread acceptance of this doctrine results from an awareness that international law must, in addition to sanctifying the principle of *pacta sunt servanda*, make some allowance for the termination of obsolete or oppressive treaties that a party, or several parties, are unwilling either to revise or to terminate by agreement. But the doctrine is extremely dangerous to the security of treaties; unless it is carefully defined, it can serve to undermine international agreements by providing an excuse for breaches of treaty obligations that states find it inconvenient to fulfill. As Kaplan and Katzenbach have pointed out, more often than not "the only conditions which have changed are the political ones; one party has greatly increased its bargaining power."[20] Article 62 (1) of the Vienna Convention exhibits an awareness of this difficulty by allowing the invocation of the *clausula* only if "(a) the existence of those circumstances [which have changed] constituted an essential basis of the consent of the parties to be bound by the treaty; and (b) the effect of the change is radically to transform the extent of obligations still to be performed under the treaty." And Article 62 (2) expressly excludes treaties that fix boundaries from the operation of the doctrine in order to avoid an obvious source of threats to the peace.

A state of belligerency does not automatically terminate treaties between the parties in conflict. Indeed, treaties governing the rules of warfare are activated by the outbreak of hostilities. Whether or not treaties regulating the peaceful relations of states are terminated by war depends upon the compatibility of the provisions with

[20] Kaplan and Katzenbach, *The Political Foundations of International Law*, p. 24.

the state of hostilities.[21] Treaties of alliance are, of course, terminated, while treaties that were intended to be of a permanent nature, such as boundary settlements, are not. Some treaties, including those that regulate international postal services and extradition processes, are generally regarded as suspended in time of war and operative again at the conclusion of hostilities; to avoid any confusion, however, the modern practice is to make use of peace treaties to reactivate agreements that were suspended during conflicts.

Regarding *interpretation*, Article 31 (1) of the Vienna Convention asserts that the general rule is that a treaty "shall be interpreted in good faith in accordance with the ordinary meaning to be given to the terms of the treaty in their context and in the light of its object and purpose." The idea underlying this rule is that a treaty should be interpreted in accordance with the manifested common design of the parties and that the best way to ascertain their intention is to analyze the text itself, including its preamble and annexes. Other recognized aids employed in arriving at the true intentions of the parties include the records of the negotiations, supplementary interpretative agreements, and the subsequent conduct of the parties. Subsequent practice may even indicate an implied intention to revise a treaty; as Professor Lissitzyn has said, "when a treaty has been commonly applied by the parties in a manner different from that contemplated at the time of its conclusion, such subsequent practice and the new expectations connected with it may properly form the basis of interpretation."[22]

A fundamental difficulty in the law of treaties, as codified in the Vienna Convention, is the absence of a general disputes clause conferring compulsory jurisdiction on the International Court of Justice.[23] The limited procedural safeguards included in Articles 65 and 66 and the Annex do not adequately surround the various grounds for invalidity and termination with protection against their arbitrary use for the purpose of sloughing off inconvenient treaty obligations. This problem is compounded by the fact that the Vienna Convention is relatively barren as a source of argument for states seeking to secure compliance with treaty obligations, while it offers a diverse supply of arguments for states claiming that previously incurred obligations are invalid or terminated. In the final analysis, the rules and principles of the law of treaties will serve the international community's need for order and stability only if they are interpreted and executed in good faith. As Professor Verdross has noted, so long as the international community is composed of sovereign states, the classic words of Cornelius van Bynkershoek will continue to be true: "The civil law protects the contracts of individuals; good faith the contracts of princes. If you destroy good faith, you destroy the mutual intercourse of princes ... and you destroy even international law itself."[24]

The first selection to follow is the Vienna Convention on the Law of Treaties. This

---

[21] See Techt v. Hughes, Court of Appeals of New York, 229 N.Y. 222 (1920).
[22] Oliver J. Lissitzyn, *International Law Today and Tomorrow* (Dobbs Ferry, N.Y.: Oceana, 1965), p. 29.

[23] Professor Briggs, a former member of the International Law Commission, suggested that such a clause might be based on Article I of the Optional Protocols of Geneva and Vienna concerning the Compulsory Settlement of Disputes, which reads as follows: "Disputes arising out of the interpretation or application of the convention shall lie within the compulsory jurisdiction of the International Court of Justice and may accordingly be brought before the Court by an application made by any party to the dispute." Herbert W. Briggs, "Procedures for Establishing the Invalidity or Termination of Treaties Under the International Law Commission's 1966 Draft Articles on the Law of Treaties," 61 *American Journal of International Law* 988 (1967). It was agreed at the 1968 session of the Conference on the Law of Treaties that the Committee of the Whole would give consideration during its second session to the inclusion of a new article on procedures for settling disputes. The result was the modest addition of Article 66 and an Annex which, with the exception of claims of invalidity and termination based on *jus cogens*, do not confer jurisdiction on the International Court of Justice.
[24] Alfred Verdross, "*Jus Dispositivum* and *Jus Cogens* in International Law," 60 *American Journal of International Law* 63 (1966), n. 56.

is followed by a sociological appraisal by Richard B. Bilder of the attitude of foreign office officials toward treaties and issues of treaty breach; Professor Bilder contrasts the "treaty world of the International Law Commission" and the "treaty world of the foreign office." Selections from the Hearings on the Nuclear Test Ban Treaty before the United States Senate Committee on Foreign Relations are reprinted as illustrations of the thinking of national decision-makers on some fundamental aspects of the law of treaties, particularly the principle of *pacta sunt servanda* and the rules regarding response to treaty breach. The attitude of the Soviet Union toward the sanctity of treaties is discussed by V. M. Shurshalov in a selection from the *Soviet Yearbook of International Law*. Soviet treaty behavior is then discussed in a brief statement by United States Senator William J. Fulbright. A concrete application of the controversial *clausula rebus sic stantibus* is provided in an opinion issued in 1941 by Acting Attorney General Francis Biddle on the termination of United States treaty commitments under the International Load Line Convention. Finally, the effect of war on treaties is discussed in the case of *Argento v. Horn*.

Vienna Convention on the Law of Treaties*

Adopted by the United Nations Conference on the Law of Treaties, Vienna, May 23, 1969

Part I: Introduction

Article 1: Scope of the Present Convention

The present Convention applies to treaties between States.

* Reprinted from *United Nations Document* A/Conf. 39/27.

Article 2: Use of Terms

1. For the purposes of the present Convention:

a. "treaty" means an international agreement concluded between States in written form and governed by international law, whether embodied in a single instrument or in two or more related instruments and whatever its particular designation;

b. "ratification", "acceptance", "approval" and "accession" mean in each case the international act so named whereby a State establishes on the international plane its consent to be bound by a treaty;

c. "full powers" means a document emanating from the competent authority of a State designating a person or persons to represent the State for negotiating, adopting or authenticating the text of a treaty, for expressing the consent of the State to be bound by a treaty, or for accomplishing any other act with respect to a treaty;

d. "reservation" means a unilateral statement, however phrased or named, made by a State, when signing, ratifying, accepting, approving or acceding to a treaty, whereby it purports to exclude or to modify the legal effect of certain provisions of the treaty in their application to that State;

e. "negotiating State" means a State which took part in the drawing up and adoption of the text of the treaty;

f. "contracting State" means a State which has consented to be bound by the treaty, whether or not the treaty has entered into force;

g. "party" means a State which has consented to be bound by the treaty and for which the treaty is in force;

h. "third State" means a State not a party to the treaty;

i. "international organization" means an intergovernmental organization.

2. The provisions of paragraph 1 regarding the use of terms in the present Convention are without prejudice to the use of those terms or to the meanings which may be given to them in the internal law of any State.

Article 3: International Agreements Not Within the Scope of the Present Convention

The fact that the present Convention does not apply to international agreements concluded between States and other subjects of international law or between such other subjects of international law, or to international agreements not in written form, shall not affect:
a. the legal force of such agreements;
b. the application to them of any of the rules set forth in the present Convention to which they would be subject under international law independently of the Convention;
c. the application of the Convention to the relations of States as between themselves under international agreements to which other subjects of international law are also parties.

Article 4: Non-retroactivity of the Present Convention

Without prejudice to the application of any rules set forth in the present Convention to which treaties would be subject under international law independently of the Convention, the Convention applies only to treaties which are concluded by States after the entry into force of the present Convention with regard to such States.

Article 5: Treaties Constituting International Organizations and Treaties Adopted Within an International Organization

The present Convention applies to any treaty which is the constituent instrument of an international organization and to any treaty adopted within an international organization without prejudice to any relevant rules of the organization.

Part II: Conclusion and Entry into Force of Treaties

SECTION 1: CONCLUSION OF TREATIES

Article 6: Capacity of States to Conclude Treaties

Every State possesses capacity to conclude treaties.

Article 7: Full Powers

1. A person is considered as representing a State for the purpose of adopting or authenticating the text of a treaty or for the purpose of expressing the consent of the State to be bound by a treaty if:
a. he produces appropriate full powers; or
b. it appears from the practice of the States concerned or from other circumstances that their intention was to consider that person as representing the State for such purposes and to dispense with full powers.

2. In virtue of their functions and without having to produce full powers, the following are considered as representing their State:
a. Heads of State, Heads of Government and Ministers for Foreign Affairs, for the purpose of performing all acts relating to the conclusion of a treaty;
b. heads of diplomatic missions, for the purpose of adopting the text of a treaty between the accrediting State and the State to which they are accredited;
c. representatives accredited by States to an international conference or to an international organization or one of its organs, for the purpose of adopting the text of a treaty in that conference, organization or organ.

Article 8: Subsequent Confirmation of an Act Performed Without Authorization

An act relating to the conclusion of a treaty performed by a person who cannot be considered under article 7 as authorized to represent a State for that purpose is without legal effect unless afterwards confirmed by that State.

Article 9: Adoption of the Text

1. The adoption of the text of a treaty takes place by the consent of all the States participating in its drawing up except as provided in paragraph 2.

2. The adoption of the text of a treaty at an international conference takes place by the vote of two-thirds of the States present and voting, unless by the same majority they shall decide to apply a different rule.

Article 10: Authentication of the Text

The text of a treaty is established as authentic and definitive:
a. by such procedure as may be provided for in the text or agreed upon by the States participating in its drawing up; or
b. failing such procedure, by the signature, signature *ad referendum* or initialling by the representatives of those States of the text of the treaty or of the Final Act of a conference incorporating the text.

Article 11: Means of Expressing Consent to Be Bound by a Treaty

The consent of a State to be bound by a treaty may be expressed by signature, exchange of instruments constituting a treaty, ratification, acceptance, approval or accession, or by any other means if so agreed.

Article 12: Consent to Be Bound by a Treaty Expressed by Signature

1. The consent of a State to be bound by a treaty is expressed by the signature of its representative when:
a. the treaty provides that signature shall have that effect;
b. it is otherwise established that the negotiating States were agreed that signature should have that effect; or

c. the intention of the State to give that effect to the signature appears from the full powers of its representative or was expressed during the negotiation.

2. For the purposes of paragraph 1:
a. the initialling of a text constitutes a signature of the treaty when it is established that the negotiating States so agreed;
b. the signature *ad referendum* of a treaty by a representative, if confirmed by his State, constitutes a full signature of the treaty.

Article 13: Consent to Be Bound by a Treaty Expressed by an Exchange of Instruments Constituting a Treaty

The consent of States to be bound by a treaty constituted by instruments exchanged between them is expressed by that exchange when:
a. the instruments provide that their exchange shall have that effect; or
b. it is otherwise established that those States were agreed that the exchange of instruments should have that effect.

Article 14: Consent to Be Bound by a Treaty Expressed by Ratification, Acceptance or Approval

1. The consent of a State to be bound by a treaty is expressed by ratification when:
a. the treaty provides for such consent to be expressed by means of ratification;
b. it is otherwise established that the negotiating States were agreed that ratification should be required;
c. the representative of the State has signed the treaty subject to ratification; or
d. the intention of the State to sign the treaty subject to ratification appears from the full powers of its representatives or was expressed during the negotiation.

2. The consent of a State to be bound by a treaty is expressed by acceptance or approval under conditions similar to those which apply to ratification.

Article 15: Consent to Be Bound by a Treaty Expressed by Accession

The consent of a State to be bound by a treaty is expressed by accession when:
a. the treaty provides that such consent may be expressed by that State by means of accession;
b. it is otherwise established that the negotiating States were agreed that such consent may be expressed by that State by means of accession; or
c. all the parties have subsequently agreed that such consent may be expressed by that State by means of accession.

Article 16: Exchange or Deposit of Instruments of Ratification, Acceptance, Approval or Accession

Unless the treaty otherwise provides, instruments of ratification, acceptance, approval or accession establish the consent of a State to be bound by a treaty upon:
a. their exchange between the contracting States;
b. their deposit with the depositary; or
c. their notification to the contracting States or to the depositary, if so agreed.

Article 17: Consent to Be Bound by Part of a Treaty and Choice of Differing Provisions

1. Without prejudice to articles 19 to 23, the consent of a State to be bound by part of a treaty is effective only if the treaty so permits or the other contracting States so agree.
2. The consent of a State to be bound by a treaty which permits a choice between differing provisions is effective only if it is made clear to which of the provisions the consent relates.

Article 18: Obligation Not to Defeat the Object and Purpose of a Treaty Prior to Its Entry into Force

A State is obliged to refrain from acts which would defeat the object and purpose of a treaty when:
a. It has signed the treaty or has exchanged instruments constituting the treaty subject to ratification, acceptance or approval, until it shall have made its intention clear not to become a party to the treaty; or
b. it has expressed its consent to be bound by the treaty, pending the entry into force of the treaty and provided that such entry into force is not unduly delayed.

SECTION 2: RESERVATIONS

Article 19: Formulation of Reservations

A State may, when signing, ratifying, accepting, approving or acceding to a treaty, formulate a reservation unless:
a. the reservation is prohibited by the treaty;
b. the treaty provides that only specified reservations, which do not include the reservation in question, may be made; or
c. in cases not falling under sub-paragraphs a and b, the reservation is incompatible with the object and purpose of the treaty.

Article 20: Acceptance of and Objection to Reservations

1. A reservation expressly authorized by a treaty does not require any subsequent acceptance by the other contracting States unless the treaty so provides.
2. When it appears from the limited number of the negotiating States and the object and purpose of a treaty that the application of the treaty in its entirety between all the parties is an essential condition of the consent of each one to be bound by the treaty, a reservation requires acceptance by all the parties.

3. When a treaty is a constituent instrument of an international organization and unless it otherwise provides, a reservation requires the acceptance of the competent organ of that organization.

4. In cases not falling under the preceding paragraphs and unless the treaty otherwise provides:

a. acceptance by another contracting State of a reservation constitutes the reserving State a party to the treaty in relation to that other State if or when the treaty is in force for those States;

b. an objection by another contracting State to a reservation does not preclude the entry into force of the treaty as between the objecting and reserving States unless a contrary intention is definitely expressed by the objecting State;

c. an act expressing a State's consent to be bound by the treaty and containing a reservation is effective as soon as at least one other contracting State has accepted the reservation.

5. For the purposes of paragraphs 2 and 4 and unless the treaty otherwise provides, a reservation is considered to have been accepted by a State if it shall have raised no objection to the reservation by the end of a period of twelve months after it was notified of the reservation or by the date on which it expressed its consent to be bound by the treaty, whichever is later.

Article 21: Legal Effects of Reservations and of Objections to Reservations

1. A reservation established with regard to another party in accordance with articles 19, 20 and 23:

a. modifies for the reserving State in its relations with that other party the provisions of the treaty to which the reservation relates to the extent of the reservation; and

b. modifies those provisions to the same extent for that other party in its relations with the reserving State.

2. The reservation does not modify the provisions of the treaty for the other parties to the treaty *inter se*.

3. When a State objecting to a reservation has not opposed the entry into force of the treaty between itself and the reserving State, the provisions to which the reservation relates do not apply as between the two States to the extent of the reservation.

Article 22: Withdrawal of Reservations and of Objections to Reservations

1. Unless the treaty otherwise provides, a reservation may be withdrawn at any time and the consent of a State which has accepted the reservation is not required for its withdrawal.

2. Unless the treaty otherwise provides, an objection to a reservation may be withdrawn at any time.

3. Unless the treaty otherwise provides, or it is otherwise agreed:

a. the withdrawal of a reservation becomes operative in relation to another contracting State only when notice of it has been received by that State;

b. the withdrawal of an objection to a reservation becomes operative only when notice of it has been received by the State which formulated the reservation.

Article 23: Procedure Regarding Reservations

1. A reservation, an express acceptance of a reservation and an objection to a reservation must be formulated in writing and communicated to the contracting States and other States entitled to become parties to the treaty.

2. If formulated when signing the treaty subject to ratification, acceptance or approval, a reservation must be formally confirmed by the reserving State when expressing its consent to be bound by the treaty. In such a case the reservation shall be considered as having been made on the date of its confirmation.

3. An express acceptance of, or an objection to, a reservation made previously

to confirmation of the reservation does not itself require confirmation.

4. The withdrawal of a reservation or of an objection to a reservation must be formulated in writing.

Article 24: Entry into Force

1. A treaty enters into force in such manner and upon such date as it may provide or as the negotiating States may agree.

2. Failing any such provision or agreement, a treaty enters into force as soon as consent to be bound by the treaty has been established for all the negotiating States.

3. When the consent of a State to be bound by a treaty is established on a date after the treaty has come into force, the treaty enters into force for that State on that date, unless the treaty otherwise provides.

4. The provisions of a treaty regulating the authentication of its text, the establishment of the consent of States to be bound by the treaty, the manner or date of its entry into force, reservations, the functions of the depositary and other matters arising necessarily before the entry into force of the treaty apply from the time of the adoption of its text.

Article 25: Provisional Application

1. A treaty or a part of a treaty is applied provisionally pending its entry into force if:
a. the treaty itself so provides; or
b. the negotiating States have in some other manner so agreed.

2. Unless the treaty otherwise provides or the negotiating States have otherwise agreed, the provisional application of a treaty or a part of a treaty with respect to a State shall be terminated if that State notifies the other States between which the treaty is being applied provisionally of its intention not to become a party to the treaty.

Part III: Observance, Application and Interpretation of Treaties

Article 26: Pacta Sunt Servanda

Every treaty in force is binding upon the parties to it and must be performed by them in good faith.

Article 27: Internal Law and Observance of Treaties

A party may not invoke the provisions of its internal law as justification for its failure to perform a treaty. This rule is without prejudice to article 46.

Article 28: Non-retroactivity of Treaties

Unless a different intention appears from the treaty or is otherwise established, its provisions do not bind a party in relation to any act or fact which took place or any situation which ceased to exist before the date of the entry into force of the treaty with respect to that party.

Article 29: Territorial Scope of Treaties

Unless a different intention appears from the treaty or is otherwise established, a treaty is binding upon each party in respect of its entire territory.

Article 30: Application of Successive Treaties Relating to the Same Subject-matter

1. Subject to Article 103 of the Charter of the United Nations, the rights and obligations of States parties to successive treaties relating to the same subject-matter shall be determined in accordance with the following paragraphs.

2. When a treaty specifies that it is subject to, or that it is not to be considered as incompatible with, an earlier or later treaty, the provisions of that other treaty prevail.

3. When all the parties to the earlier treaty are parties also to the later treaty but the earlier treaty is not terminated or suspended in operation under article 59, the earlier treaty applies only to the extent that its provisions are compatible with those of the later treaty.

4. When the parties to the later treaty do not include all the parties to the earlier one:

a. as between States parties to both treaties the same rule applies as in paragraph 3;

b. as between a State party to both treaties and a State party to only one of the treaties, the treaty to which both States are parties governs their mutual rights and obligations.

5. Paragraph 4 is without prejudice to article 41, or to any question of the termination or suspension of the operation of a treaty under article 60 or to any question of responsibility which may arise for a State from the conclusion or application of a treaty the provisions of which are incompatible with its obligations towards another State under another treaty.

SECTION 3: INTERPRETATION OF TREATIES

Article 31: General Rule of Interpretation

1. A treaty shall be interpreted in good faith in accordance with the ordinary meaning to be given to the terms of the treaty in their context and in the light of its object and purpose.

2. The context for the purpose of the interpretation of a treaty shall comprise, in addition to the text, including its preamble and annexes:

a. any agreement relating to the treaty which was made between all the parties in connexion with the conclusion of the treaty;

b. any instrument which was made by one or more parties in connexion with the conclusion of the treaty and accepted by the other parties as an instrument related to the treaty.

3. There shall be taken into account, together with the context:

a. any subsequent agreement between the parties regarding the interpretation of the treaty or the application of its provisions;

b. any subsequent practice in the application of the treaty which establishes the agreement of the parties regarding its interpretation;

c. any relevant rules of international law applicable in the relations between the parties.

4. A special meaning shall be given to a term if it is established that the parties so intended.

Article 32: Supplementary Means of Interpretation

Recourse may be had to supplementary means of interpretation, including the preparatory work of the treaty and the circumstances of its conclusion, in order to confirm the meaning resulting from the application of article 31, or to determine the meaning when the interpretation according to article 31:

a. leaves the meaning ambiguous or obscure; or

b. leads to a result which is manifestly absurd or unreasonable.

Article 33: Interpretation of Treaties Authenticated in Two or More Languages

1. When a treaty has been authenticated in two or more languages, the text is equally authoritative in each language, unless the treaty provides or the parties agree that, in case of divergence, a particular text shall prevail.

2. A version of the treaty in a language other than one of those in which the text was authenticated shall be considered an authentic text only if the treaty so provides or the parties so agree.

3. The terms of the treaty are presumed to have the same meaning in each authentic text.

4. Except where a particular text prevails in accordance with paragraph 1, when a comparison of the authentic texts discloses a difference of meaning which the application of articles 31 and 32 does not remove, the meaning which best reconciles the texts, having regard to the object and purpose of the treaty, shall be adopted.

SECTION 4: TREATIES AND THIRD STATES

Article 34: General Rule Regarding Third States

A treaty does not create either obligations or rights for a third State without its consent.

Article 35: Treaties Providing for Obligations for Third States

An obligation arises for a third State from a provision of a treaty if the parties to the treaty intend the provision to be the means of establishing the obligation and the third State expressly accepts that obligation in writing.

Article 36: Treaties Providing for Rights for Third States

1. A right arises for a third State from a provision of a treaty if the parties to the treaty intend the provision to accord that right either to the third State, or to a group of States to which it belongs, or to all States, and the third State assents thereto. Its assent shall be presumed so long as the contrary is not indicated, unless the treaty otherwise provides.

2. A State exercising a right in accordance with paragraph 1 shall comply with the conditions for its exercise provided for in the treaty or established in conformity with the treaty.

Article 37: Revocation or Modification of Obligations or Rights of Third States

1. When an obligation has arisen for a third State in conformity with article 35, the obligation may be revoked or modified only with the consent of the parties to the treaty and of the third State, unless it is established that they had otherwise agreed.

2. When a right has arisen for a third State in conformity with article 36, the right may not be revoked or modified by the parties if it is established that the right was intended not to be revocable or subject to modification without the consent of the third State.

Article 38: Rules in a Treaty Becoming Binding on Third States Through International Custom

Nothing in articles 34 to 37 precludes a rule set forth in a treaty from becoming binding upon a third State as a customary rule of international law, recognized as such.

Part IV: Amendment and Modification of Treaties

Article 39: General Rule Regarding the Amendment of Treaties

A treaty may be amended by agreement between the parties. The rules laid down in Part II apply to such an agreement except in so far as the treaty may otherwise provide.

Article 40: Amendment of Multilateral Treaties

1. Unless the treaty otherwise provides, the amendment of multilateral treaties shall be governed by the following paragraphs.

2. Any proposal to amend a multilateral treaty as between all the parties must be notified to all the contracting States, each one of which shall have the right to take part in:

a. the decision as to the action to be taken in regard to such proposal;

b. the negotiation and conclusion of any agreement for the amendment of the treaty.

3. Every State entitled to become a party to the treaty shall also be entitled to become a party to the treaty as amended.

4. The amending agreement does not bind any State already a party to the treaty which does not become a party to the amending agreement; article 30, paragraph 4(b), applies in relation to such State.

5. Any State which becomes a party to the treaty after the entry into force of the amending agreement shall, failing an expression of a different intention by that State:

a. be considered as a party to the treaty as amended; and

b. be considered as a party to the unamended treaty in relation to any party to the treaty not bound by the amending agreement.

Article 41: Agreements to Modify Multilateral Treaties Between Certain of the Parties Only

1. Two or more of the parties to a multilateral treaty may conclude an agreement to modify the treaty as between themselves alone if:

a. the possibility of such a modification is provided for by the treaty; or

b. the modification in question is not prohibited by the treaty and:

  (i) does not affect the enjoyment by the other parties of their rights under the treaty or the performance of their obligations;

  (ii) does not relate to a provision, derogation from which is incompatible with the effective execution of the object and purpose of the treaty as a whole.

2. Unless in a case falling under paragraph 1(a) the treaty otherwise provides, the parties in question shall notify the other parties of their intention to conclude the agreement and the modification to the treaty for which it provides.

Part V: Invalidity, Termination and Suspension of the Operation of Treaties

SECTION I: GENERAL PROVISIONS

Article 42: Validity and Continuance in Force of Treaties

1. The validity of a treaty or of the consent of a State to be bound by a treaty may be impeached only through the application of the present Convention.

2. The termination of a treaty, its denunciation or the withdrawal of a party, may take place only as a result of the application of the provisions of the treaty or of the present Convention. The same rule applies to suspension of the operation of a treaty.

Article 43: Obligations Imposed by International Law Independently of a Treaty

The invalidity, termination or denunciation of a treaty, the withdrawal of a party from it, or the suspension of its operation, as a result of the application of the present Convention or of the provisions of the treaty, shall not in any way impair the duty of any State to fulfil any obligation embodied in the treaty to which it would be subject under international law independently of the treaty.

Article 44: Separability of Treaty Provisions

1. A right of a party, provided for in a treaty or arising under article 56, to denounce, withdraw from or suspend the operation of the treaty may be exercised only with respect to the whole treaty unless the treaty otherwise provides or the parties otherwise agree.

2. A ground for invalidating, terminating, withdrawing from or suspending

the operation of a treaty recognized in the present Convention may be invoked only with respect to the whole treaty except as provided in the following paragraphs or in article 60.

3. If the ground relates solely to particular clauses, it may be invoked only with respect to those clauses where:

a. the said clauses are separable from the remainder of the treaty with regard to their application;

b. it appears from the treaty or is otherwise established that acceptance of those clauses was not an essential basis of the consent of the other party or parties to be bound by the treaty as a whole; and

c. continued performance of the remainder of the treaty would not be unjust.

4. In cases falling under articles 49 and 50 the State entitled to invoke the fraud or corruption may do so with respect either to the whole treaty or, subject to paragraph 3, to the particular clauses alone.

5. In cases falling under articles 51, 52 and 53, no separation of the provisions of the treaty is permitted.

Article 45: Loss of a Right to Invoke a Ground for Invalidating, Terminating, Withdrawing from or Suspending the Operation of a Treaty

A State may no longer invoke a ground for invalidating, terminating, withdrawing from or suspending the operation of a treaty under articles 46 to 50 or articles 60 and 62 if, after becoming aware of the facts:

a. it shall have expressly agreed that the treaty is valid or remains in force or continues in operation, as the case may be; or

b. it must by reason of its conduct be considered as having acquiesced in the validity of the treaty or in its maintenance in force or in operation, as the case may be.

SECTION 2: INVALIDITY OF TREATIES

Article 46: Provisions of Internal Law Regarding Competence to Conclude Treaties

1. A State may not invoke the fact that its consent to be bound by a treaty has been expressed in violation of a provision of its internal law regarding competence to conclude treaties as invalidating its consent unless that violation was manifest and concerned a rule of its internal law of fundamental importance.

2. A violation is manifest if it would be objectively evident to any State conducting itself in the matter in accordance with normal practice and good faith.

Article 47: Specific Restrictions on Authority to Express the Consent of a State

If the authority of a representative to express the consent of a State to be bound by a particular treaty has been made subject to a specific restriction, his omission to observe that restriction may not be invoked as invalidating the consent expressed by him unless the restriction was notified to the other negotiating States prior to his expressing such consent.

Article 48: Error

1. A State may invoke an error in a treaty as invalidating its consent to be bound by the treaty if the error relates to a fact or situation which was assumed by that State to exist at the time when the treaty was concluded and formed an essential basis of its consent to be bound by the treaty.

2. Paragraph 1 shall not apply if the State in question contributed by its own conduct to the error or if the circumstances were such as to put that State on notice of a possible error.

3. An error relating only to the wording of the text of a treaty does not affect its validity; article 79 then applies.

Article 49: Fraud

If a State has been induced to conclude a treaty by the fraudulent conduct of another negotiating State, the State may invoke the fraud as invalidating its consent to be bound by the treaty.

Article 50: Corruption of a Representative of a State

If the expression of a State's consent to be bound by a treaty has been procured through the corruption of its representative directly or indirectly by another negotiating State, the State may invoke such corruption as invalidating its consent to be bound by the treaty.

Article 51: Coercion of a Representative of a State

The expression of a State's consent to be bound by a treaty which has been procured by the coercion of its representative through acts or threats directed against him shall be without any legal effect.

Article 52: Coercion of a State by the Threat or Use of Force

A treaty is void if its conclusion has been procured by the threat or use of force in violation of the principles of international law embodied in the Charter of the United Nations.

Article 53: Treaties Conflicting with a Peremptory Norm of General International Law (Jus Cogens)

A treaty is void if, at the time of its conclusion, it conflicts with a peremptory norm of general international law. For the purposes of the present Convention, a peremptory norm of general international law is a norm accepted and recognized by the international community of States as a whole as a norm from which no derogation is permitted and which can be modified only by a subsequent norm of general international law having the same character.

SECTION 2: TERMINATION AND SUSPENSION OF THE OPERATION OF TREATIES

Article 54: Termination of or Withdrawal from a Treaty Under Its Provisions or by Consent of the Parties

The termination of a treaty or the withdrawal of a party may take place:

a. in conformity with the provisions of the treaty; or
b. at any time by consent of all the parties after consultation with the other contracting States.

Article 55: Reduction of the Parties to a Multilateral Treaty Below the Number Necessary for Its Entry into Force

Unless the treaty otherwise provides, a multilateral treaty does not terminate by reason only of the fact that the number of the parties falls below the number necessary for its entry into force.

Article 56: Denunciation of or Withdrawal from a Treaty Containing No Provision Regarding Termination, Denunciation or Withdrawal

1. A treaty which contains no provision regarding its termination and which does not provide for denunciation or withdrawal is not subject to denunciation or withdrawal unless:

a. it is established that the parties intended to admit the possibility of denunciation or withdrawal; or
b. a right of denunciation or withdrawal may be implied by the nature of the treaty.

2. A party shall give not less than twelve months' notice of its intention to denounce or withdraw from a treaty under paragraph 1.

Article 57: Suspension of the Operation of a Treaty Under Its Provisions or by Consent of the Parties

The operation of a treaty in regard to all the parties or to a particular party may be suspended:

a. in conformity with the provisions of the treaty; or

b. at any time by consent of all the parties after consultation with the other contracting States.

Article 58: Suspension of the Operation of a Multilateral Treaty by Agreement Between Certain of the Parties Only

1. Two or more parties to a multilateral treaty may conclude an agreement to suspend the operation of provisions of the treaty, temporarily and as between themselves alone, if:

a. the possibility of such a suspension is provided for by the treaty; or

b. the suspension in question is not prohibited by the treaty and:
   i. does not affect the enjoyment by the other parties of their rights under the treaty or the performance of their obligations;
   ii. is not incompatible with the object and purpose of the treaty.

2. Unless in a case falling under paragraph 1(a) the treaty otherwise provides, the parties in question shall notify the other parties of their intention to conclude the agreement and of those provisions of the treaty the operation of which they intend to suspend.

Article 59: Termination or Suspension of the Operation of a Treaty Implied By Conclusion of a Later Treaty

1. A treaty shall be considered as terminated if all the parties to it conclude a later treaty relating to the same subject-matter and:

a. it appears from the later treaty or is otherwise established that the parties intended that the matter should be governed by that treaty; or

b. the provisions of the later treaty are so far incompatible with those of the earlier one that the two treaties are not capable of being applied at the same time.

2. The earlier treaty shall be considered as only suspended in operation if it appears from the later treaty or is otherwise established that such was the intention of the parties.

Article 60: Termination or Suspension of the Operation of a Treaty as a Consequence of Its Breach

1. A material breach of a bilateral treaty by one of the parties entitles the other to invoke the breach as a ground for terminating the treaty or suspending its operation in whole or in part.

2. A material breach of a multilateral treaty by one of the parties entitles:

a. the other parties by unanimous agreement to suspend the operation of the treaty in whole or in part or to terminate it either:
   i. in the relations between themselves and the defaulting State, or
   ii. as between all the parties;

b. a party specially affected by the breach to invoke it as a ground for suspending the operation of the treaty in whole or in part in the relations between itself and the defaulting State;

c. any party other than the defaulting State to invoke the breach as a ground for suspending the operation of the treaty in whole or in part with respect to itself if the treaty is of such a character that a material breach of its provisions by one party radically changes the position of every party with respect to the further performance of its obligations under the treaty.

3. A material breach of a treaty, for the purposes of this article, consists in:

a. a repudiation of the treaty not sanctioned by the present Convention; or

b. the violation of a provision essential to the accomplishment of the object or purpose of the treaty.

4. The foregoing paragraphs are without prejudice to any provision in the treaty applicable in the event of a breach.

5. Paragraphs 1 to 3 do not apply to provisions relating to the protection of the human person contained in treaties of a humanitarian character, in particular to provisions prohibiting any form of reprisals against persons protected by such treaties.

Article 61: Supervening Impossibility of Performance

1. A party may invoke the impossibility of performing a treaty as a ground for terminating or withdrawing from it if the impossibility results from the permanent disappearance or destruction of an object indispensable for the execution of the treaty. If the impossibility is temporary, it may be invoked only as a ground for suspending the operation of the treaty.

2. Impossibility of performance may not be invoked by a party as a ground for terminating, withdrawing from or suspending the operation of a treaty if the impossibility is the result of a breach by that party either of an obligation under the treaty or of any other international obligation owed to any other party to the treaty.

Article 62: Fundamental Change of Circumstances

1. A fundamental change of circumstances which has occurred with regard to those existing at the time of the conclusion of a treaty, and which was not foreseen by the parties, may not be invoked as a ground for terminating or withdrawing from the treaty unless:
a. the existence of those circumstances constituted an essential basis of the consent of the parties to be bound by the treaty; and
b. the effect of the change is radically to transform the extent of obligations still to be performed under the treaty.

2. A fundamental change of circumstances may not be invoked as a ground for terminating or withdrawing from a treaty:

a. if the treaty establishes a boundary; or
b. if the fundamental change is the result of a breach by the party invoking it either of an obligation under the treaty or of any other international obligation owed to any other party to the treaty.

3. If, under the foregoing paragraphs, a party may invoke a fundamental change of circumstances as a ground for terminating or withdrawing from a treaty it may also invoke the change as a ground for suspending the operation of the treaty.

Article 63: Severance of Diplomatic or Consular Relations

The severance of diplomatic or consular relations between parties to a treaty does not affect the legal relations established between them by the treaty except in so far as the existence of diplomatic or consular relations is indispensable for the application of the treaty.

Article 64: Emergence of a New Peremptory Norm of General International Law (Jus Cogens)

If a new peremptory norm of general international law emerges, any existing treaty which is in conflict with that norm becomes void and terminates.

SECTION 4: PROCEDURE

Article 65: Procedure to Be Followed with Respect to Invalidity, Termination, Withdrawal from or Suspension of the Operation of a Treaty

1. A party which, under the provisions of the present Convention, invokes either a defect in its consent to be bound by a treaty or a ground for impeaching the validity of a treaty, terminating it, withdrawing from it or suspending its operation, must notify the other parties of its claim. The notification shall indicate the measure proposed to be taken with respect to the treaty and the reasons therefor.

2. If, after the expiry of a period which, except in cases of special urgency, shall

not be less than three months after the receipt of the notification, no party has raised any objection, the party making the notification may carry out in the manner provided in article 67 the measure which it has proposed.

3. If, however, objection has been raised by any other party, the parties shall seek a solution through the means indicated in Article 33 of the Charter of the United Nations.

4. Nothing in the foregoing paragraphs shall affect the rights or obligations of the parties under any provisions in force binding the parties with regard to the settlement of disputes.

5. Without prejudice to Article 45, the fact that a State has not previously made the notification prescribed in paragraph 1 shall not prevent it from making such notification in answer to another party claiming performance of the treaty or alleging its violation.

Article 66: Procedures for Judicial Settlement, Arbitration and Conciliation

If, under paragraph 3 of article 65, no solution has been reached within a period of 12 months following the date on which the objection was raised, the following procedures shall be followed:

a. any one of the parties to a dispute concerning the application or the interpretation of article 53 or 64 may, by a written application, submit it to the International Court of Justice for a decision unless the parties by common consent agree to submit the dispute to arbitration;

b. any one of the parties to a dispute concerning the application or the interpretation of any of the other articles in Part V of the present Convention may set in motion the procedure specified in the Annex to the Convention by submitting a request to that effect to the Secretary-General of the United Nations.

Article 67: Instruments for Declaring Invalid, Terminating, Withdrawing from or Suspending the Operation of a Treaty

1. The notification provided for under article 65 paragraph 1 must be made in writing.

2. Any act declaring invalid, terminating, withdrawing from or suspending the operation of a treaty pursuant to the provisions of the treaty or of paragraphs 2 or 3 of article 65 shall be carried out through an instrument communicated to the other parties. If the instrument is not signed by the Head of State, Head of Government or Minister for Foreign Affairs, the representative of the State communicating it may be called upon to produce full powers.

Article 68: Revocation of Notifications and Instruments Provided for in Articles 65 and 67

A notification or instrument provided for in articles 65 or 67 may be revoked at any time before it takes effect.

SECTION 5: CONSEQUENCES OF THE INVALIDITY, TERMINATION OR SUSPENSION OF THE OPERATION OF A TREATY

Article 69: Consequences of the Invalidity of a Treaty

1. A treaty the invalidity of which is established under the present Convention is void. The provisions of a void treaty have no legal force.

2. If acts have nevertheless been performed in reliance on such a treaty:

a. each party may require any other party to establish as far as possible in their mutual relations the position that would have existed if the acts had not been performed;

b. acts performed in good faith before the invalidity was invoked are not rendered unlawful by reason only of the invalidity of the treaty.

3. In cases falling under articles 49, 50, 51 or 52, paragraph 2 does not apply with

respect to the party to which the fraud, the act of corruption or the coercion is imputable.

4. In the case of the invalidity of a particular State's consent to be bound by a multilateral treaty, the foregoing rules apply in the relations between that State and the parties to the treaty.

Article 70: Consequences of the Termination of a Treaty

1. Unless the treaty otherwise provides or the parties otherwise agree, the termination of a treaty under its provisions or in accordance with the present Convention:
a. releases the parties from any obligation further to perform the treaty;
b. does not affect any right, obligation or legal situation of the parties created through the execution of the treaty prior to its termination.

2. If a State denounces or withdraws from a multilateral treaty, paragraph 1 applies in the relations between that State and each of the other parties to the treaty from the date when such denunciation or withdrawal takes effect.

Article 71: Consequences of the Invalidity of a Treaty Which Conflicts with a Peremptory Norm of General International Law

1. In the case of a treaty which is void under article 53 the parties shall:
a. eliminate as far as possible the consequences of any act performed in reliance on any provision which conflicts with the peremptory norm of general international law; and
b. bring their mutual relations into conformity with the peremptory norm of general international law.

2. In the case of a treaty which becomes void and terminates under article 64, the termination of the treaty:
a. releases the parties from any obligation further to perform the treaty;
b. does not affect any right, obligation or legal situation of the parties created

through the execution of the treaty prior to its termination; provided that those rights, obligations or situations may thereafter be maintained only to the extent that their maintenance is not in itself in conflict with the new peremptory norm of general international law.

Article 72: Consequences of the Suspension of the Operation of a Treaty

1. Unless the treaty otherwise provides or the parties otherwise agree, the suspension of the operation of a treaty under its provisions or in accordance with the present Convention:
a. release the parties between which the operation of the treaty is suspended from the obligation to perform the treaty in their mutual relations during the period of the suspension;
b. does not otherwise affect the legal relations between the parties established by the treaty.

2. During the period of the suspension the parties shall refrain from acts tending to obstruct the resumption of the operation of the treaty.

Part VI: Miscellaneous Provisions

Article 73: Cases of State Succession, State Responsibility and Outbreak of Hostilities

The provisions of the present Convention shall not prejudge any question that may arise in regard to a treaty from a succession of States or from the international responsibility of a State or from the outbreak of hostilities between States.

Article 74: Diplomatic and Consular Relations and the Conclusion of Treaties

The severance or absence of diplomatic or consular relations between two or more States does not prevent the conclusion of treaties between those States. The conclusion of a treaty does not in itself affect the situation in regard to diplomatic or consular relations.

Article 75: Case of an Aggressor State

The provisions of the present Convention are without prejudice to any obligation in relation to a treaty which may arise for an aggressor State in consequence of measures taken in conformity with the Charter of the United Nations with reference to that State's aggression.

Part VII: Depositaries, Notifications, Corrections and Registration

Article 76: Depositaries of Treaties

1. The designation of the depositary of a treaty may be made by the negotiating States, either in the treaty itself or in some other manner. The depositary may be one or more States, an international organization or the chief administrative officer of the organization.

* * *

Article 80: Registration and Publication of Treaties

1. Treaties shall, after their entry into force, be transmitted to the Secretariat of the United Nations for registration or filing and recording, as the case may be, and for publication.

2. The designation of a depositary shall constitute authorization for it to perform the acts specified in the preceding paragraph.

Part VIII: Final Provisions

Article 81: Signature

The present Convention shall be open for signature by all States Members of the United Nations or of any of the specialized agencies or of the International Atomic Energy Agency or parties to the Statute of the International Court of Justice, and

by any other State invited by the General Assembly of the United Nations to become a party to the Convention, as follows: until 30 November 1969, at the Federal Ministry for Foreign Affairs of the Republic of Austria, and subsequently, until 30 April 1970, at United Nations Headquarters, New York.

Article 82: Ratification

The present Convention is subject to ratification. The instruments of ratification shall be deposited with the Secretary-General of the United Nations.

Article 83: Accession

The present Convention shall remain open for accession by any State belonging to any of the categories mentioned in article 81. The instruments of accession shall be deposited with the Secretary-General of the United Nations.

Article 84: Entry into Force

1. The present Convention shall enter into force on the thirtieth day following the date of deposit of the thirty-fifth instrument of ratification or accession.

2. For each State ratifying or acceding to the Convention after the deposit of the thirty-fifth instrument of ratification or accession, the Convention shall enter into force on the thirtieth day after deposit by such State of its instrument of ratification or accession.

* * *

Annex

1. A list of conciliators consisting of qualified jurists shall be drawn up and maintained by the Secretary-General of the United Nations. To this end, every State which is a Member of the United Nations or a party to the present Convention shall be invited to nominate two conciliators, and the names of the persons so nominated shall constitute the list. The

term of a conciliator, including that of any conciliator nominated to fill a casual vacancy, shall be five years and may be renewed. A conciliator whose term expires shall continue to fulfil any function for which he shall have been chosen under the following paragraph.

2. When a request has been made to the Secretary-General under article 66, the Secretary-General shall bring the dispute before a conciliation commission constituted as follows:

The State or States constituting one of the parties to the dispute shall appoint:

a. one conciliator of the nationality of that State or of one of those States, who may or may not be chosen from the list referred to in paragraph 1; and

b. one conciliator not of the nationality of that State or of any of those States, who shall be chosen from the list.

The State or States constituting the other party to the dispute shall appoint two conciliators in the same way. The four conciliators chosen by the parties shall be appointed within sixty days following the date on which the Secretary-General receives the request.

The four conciliators shall, within sixty days following the date of the last of their own appointments, appoint a fifth conciliator chosen from the list, who shall be chairman.

If the appointment of the chairman or of any of the other conciliators has not been made within the period prescribed above for such appointment, it shall be made by the Secretary-General within sixty days following the expiry of that period. The appointment of the chairman may be made by the Secretary-General either from the list or from the membership of the International Law Commission. Any of the periods within which appointments must be made may be extended by agreement between the parties to the dispute.

Any vacancy shall be filled in the manner prescribed for the initial appointment.

3. The Conciliation Commission shall decide its own procedure. The Commission, with the consent of the parties to the dispute, may invite any party to the treaty to submit to it its views orally or in writing. Decisions and recommendations of the Commission shall be made by a majority vote of the five members.

4. The Commission may draw the attention of the parties to the dispute to any measures which might facilitate an amicable settlement.

5. The Commission shall hear the parties, examine the claims and objections, and make proposals to the parties with a view to reaching an amicable settlement of the dispute.

6. The Commission shall report within twelve months of its constitution. Its report shall be deposited with the Secretary-General and transmitted to the parties to the dispute. The report of the Commission, including any conclusions stated therein regarding the facts or questions of law, shall not be binding upon the parties and it shall have no other character than that of recommendations submitted for the consideration of the parties in order to facilitate an amicable settlement of the dispute.

7. The Secretary-General shall provide the Commission with such assistance and facilities as it may require. The expenses of the Commission shall be borne by the United Nations.

Breach of Treaty and Response Thereto*

Richard B. Bilder

The concept of treaty breach plays an important rôle in both international law and foreign office practice. However, it is not clear that this rôle is the same in the two cases. If, as some of us suspect,

* Reprinted from Richard B. Bilder, "Breach of Treaty and Response Thereto," *Proceedings of the American Society of International Law* 193 (1967), by permission of the American Society of International Law.

foreign office officials look at treaties and issues of treaty breach differently from the way traditional international law assumes, we should ask whether this in any way affects the usefulness of our present treaty doctrine. Perhaps a first step is to see what any such differences in approach might be.

The Treaty World of the I.L.C. Draft

The International Law Commission's Draft Articles on the Law of Treaties reflect traditional international law in taking a predominantly formal approach to treaties and treaty breach.

Treaty is defined as an international agreement concluded between states in written form and governed by international law. The consent of parties to be bound by such an instrument is in general manifested by formal acts. Instruments meeting this test of form carry equally the consequence of *Pacta sunt servanda;* under the prime directive of Article 23, "Every treaty in force is binding upon the parties to it and must be performed by them in good faith." . . .

But the concept of obligation logically requires a concept of breach, and the system of the Draft Articles deals at least briefly with one aspect of this problem in Article 57. The Commentary to that article notes:

A violation of a treaty obligation, as of any other obligation, may give rise to a right of the other party to take non-forcible reprisals, and these reprisals may properly relate to the defaulting party's rights under the treaty.

However, Article 57 is concerned only with the exercise of reprisals affecting the treaty itself and limits such reprisals to cases of "material breach," which is defined as either a repudiation of the treaty not sanctioned by the articles of the draft convention or the violation of a provision essential to the accomplishment of the object or purpose of the treaty. Under

the provisions of the article, such a material breach of a bilateral treaty by one of the parties entitles the other to invoke the breach as a ground for terminating the treaty or suspending its operation in whole or in part. More complex rules apply to breach of multilateral treaties. Article 57 is the only place in the I.L.C. Draft in which breach is expressly mentioned.

Of course, the I.L.C. members are not unaware of the practical problems involved in defining what the obligations are that are "binding" and in determining what is "good faith." Should such problems arise, we are furnished the rules of Articles 27 to 29 as guides to interpretation, although the basic principle once again is that treaties are to be interpreted "in good faith." Should differences in interpretation as to the existence of material breach or other sorts of treaty disputes persist, and one party allege a ground for terminating, withdrawing from or suspending the operation of the treaty, Article 62 (3) enjoins the parties to seek a solution by the methods of peaceful settlement suggested in Article 33 of the U.N. Charter. However, compulsory judicial settlement is rejected since, as the Commentary notes, certain members "expressed the view that in the present state of international practice it would not be realistic for the Commission to put forward this solution to the procedural problem."

This I.L.C. world of treaties seems, outwardly at least, a fairly comfortable one for lawyers. Rule and no-rule, compliance and non-compliance are presumed to have at least reasonably definite boundaries which legal analysis, applied to the language of the instrument itself, or at most a narrow penumbra of associated facts can in principle determine. Form and language, at which we are experts govern, and from them flow obligation. Change in obligations normally occurs only by formal acts of the parties, or by practice where [sic] that clearly establishes agreement to the change, and are also ascertainable by legal techniques. Breach is clearly outside the game, a violation of its most basic rule—the sanctity of treaties.

Obviously, concessions must be made to the realities of international behavior, and recognition of the existence of at least some uncertainty and flexibility appears throughout the draft: in the several key references to an undefined "good faith," in the admission of practice as a treaty-modifying device, in the inherent vagueness of the rules of interpretation and the concept of "material breach," in the reluctant and limited acknowledgment of *rebus sic stantibus,* in the rejection of provisions for compulsory adjudication of treaty disputes, and in the frequent admissions in the commentary that all of this may in practice prove not quite so simple. Nevertheless, the articles in general define a behavioral world which our discipline can structure and our concepts can handle.

The question is how well the draft works; whether it furnishes reasonably useful guidance to foreign office officials in deciding the more important non-formal treaty issues with which they are actually faced. No doubt, the articles will be useful to treaty technicians in its treatment of various formal treaty questions, and it may satisfactorily describe substantive practice with respect to many types of treaties. But with respect to other treaties—perhaps the most significant in terms of foreign office problems and decisions—the Draft Articles may obscure rather than clarify the factors, processes and attitudes which really determine the issues and outcomes of treaty disputes.

The Treaty World of the Foreign Office

We all sense that the treaty world of the foreign office is a different world from that of the I.L.C. Draft, more murky, flexible and unruly. It is a world dominated not by form and logic but by function, process, and accommodation. It is a world in which obligation and no-obligation, compliance and breach may shade imperceptibly into one another and achieve operational definition only in the practical outcomes of the parties' interactions. It is a world in which issues of breach are frequently part of the treaty game rather than outside of it.

I doubt that at present anyone, even a foreign office official himself, has a clear picture of this treaty world. Few empirical attempts to fathom it have thus far been made and our knowledge rests largely on intuition, personal experience, and occasional anecdotal hints from officials concerned with such questions. However, let us speculate as to what this world might be like, as to the attitudes with which a hypothetical foreign office official—if I may use such an admittedly loose abstraction—approaches treaty problems.

First, most of us recognize that the official's primary concern in any treaty situation is not the integrity of the treaty itself but rather the integrity of the over-all pattern of his foreign policy position, domestically and externally, with respect both to his treaty partner and the world at large. To him the treaty is simply one element in a complex multitude of elements defining that over-all pattern, a pattern which is constantly changing as dynamic internal and external forces play upon it. In this larger context, any particular treaty issue may be of relatively little importance. Moreover, the official will be less concerned with the past balance of forces which formed the treaty than the present and future balance of forces in which it must be implemented. Thus, we can obviously only understand his approach to a treaty problem by seeing it in the total context in which he sees it.

Second, the official's world is one of continuing tension between his desire to maintain his own flexibility and freedom of maneuver to cope with changing circumstances and his desire for certainty and predictability of behavior on the part of foreign officials. Treaties frequently reflect an uneasy and uncertain compromise between these inconsistent objectives. Neither party intends to give up flexibility altogether but the price each pays is in less than guaranteed expectations.

Third, the official sees the treaty device not simply as a legal instrument for creating obligations but rather as a multi-purpose foreign policy tool. Of course, with many treaties or particular treaty provisions he may in fact be principally interested in the establishment of firm and clear expectations, upon which each party can rely and plan. The unique normative pressures inherent in the treaty device may greatly increase the probability that these expectations will be met. But in other cases, particular formal commitments of the treaty may be of relatively little importance to the official. For example, he may be using the treaty to communicate a foreign policy attitude, to encourage the growth of institutions or forms of international collaboration, to achieve propaganda objectives, to lay a basis for future bargaining, or to accomplish primarily domestic objectives. The SEATO Treaty or Human Rights Conventions might serve as examples of treaties where commitments are secondary. I suspect that some concept of what the treaty was really intended to do, why each party entered into it, has an important bearing on how seriously officials feel thay should take the formal obligations it appears to contain.

Fourth, to adapt some contracts' insights of my Wisconsin colleague, Stewart Macaulay, the official sees a treaty dispute not as an isolated transaction but rather as an incident in a continuing business relationship with his treaty partner. In our highly interdependent international system, he must inevitably conduct such relationships, whether it be by treaty or other means. As is often the case in business contract disputes, pressing his treaty partner unduly, "taking him to court," or "winning" the dispute may be seen as poor long-run business policy, and accommodation and compromise more sensible. Perhaps the recent handling of the Panama Canal dispute illustrates this point.

Finally, even where the official is deeply concerned with maintaining the integrity and reliability of the particular expectational framework set forth in a treaty, he recognizes that the treaty alone may constitute only one stone in the arch of that expectational framework. There are many alternative, overlapping or supplementary ways apart from formal treaty by which states recognize, define and enforce mutual expectations as to future conduct. In fact, perhaps a principal function of treaties is to reinforce and buttress already existing non-treaty pressures suggesting the mutual rationality of particular behavior; for example, by reducing the need for reciprocal competition, as in the Partial Nuclear Test-Ban Treaty or the no-claim provision of the Outer Space Treaty. Thus, an official assesses how he expects foreign officials to behave not on the basis of treaty commitments alone but on the basis of all the varied considerations and pressures which he sees as acting on those officials. Consequently, his expectations may remain reasonably stable, even though he permits a violation of an apparent obligation in a particular case, or they may be highly unstable, even though he is able to secure compliance in a particular case.

So much for some of our hypothetical official's attitudes towards treaties in general. How does he see treaty obligation and breach in particular?

Anyone who has worked in a foreign office knows that in general officials do take treaty obligations seriously and will not casually ignore them. If treaty restraints were not felt to have some effectiveness, states would not bother to enter into so many treaties or would enter into them with much less care than many show. The various factors which operate to reinforce this attitude have often been noted: the common interest in a system of stable expectations, a desire to maintain the usefulness of the treaty device, personal moral attitudes, fear of retaliation or adverse public response, bureaucratic pressures, and so forth.

Where foreign office practice may differ from traditional treaty doctrine, I suggest is thus not in a rejection of the basic principle of *Pacta sunt servanda* but in a broader and more permissive concept of what the "good faith" obligation really is. For I suspect that the official looks at his apparent treaty commitments not only in terms of the specific nature and scope of the conduct covered, but also in terms of what might be called the density of expectation of observance—how strongly he sees the parties as counting on it under different sets of conditions. Thus, he can think of treaty commitments as having greater or lesser weight under varying circumstances and as having shifting obligational force over time. His real commitment, as he sees it, is only to meet the fair and reasonable expectations of the officials of his treaty partner as those expectations now exist, measured in the light of their common attitudes towards the rôle of treaties in their dealings. Some treaty norms may be analogized to parking regulations, clear, yet with comparatively little sense of obligation. Others may be like homicide laws, with a high sense of obligation, yet an awareness by all that circumstances of necessity may arise in which they will be violated.

For example, even where flexibility is not, as it frequently is, explicit or implicit in the agreement itself, I wonder whether officials really think of any treaty commitments as totally foreclosing either of the treaty partners' power of policy choice. Both realize that in the present world the practical scope of commitment is limited by the possible emergence of strong internal or external pressures which may irresistibly compel one of the parties to eventual non-compliance. Both know that treaty commitments may perhaps temporarily stem such pressures but cannot indefinitely contain them, and that eventually something has to give.

Of course, the absence of compulsory adjudication or other effective implementation procedures may be enough to guarantee such "last-ditch flexibility," despite allegations of breach. That is, officials may be aware that one of them can always, as a last resort, simply disregard the agreement and often escape serious consequences. But we might even make an even more disturbing speculation—that officials may not think of non-compliance in such crisis cases as really breach at all, but rather as something tacitly understood by both parties, part of their joint expectations and bargain itself. Clearly, such an extremely broad *rebus sic stantibus* type of assumption threatens our ideals of treaty certainty and stability. Yet if officials did not believe they retained some flexibility when the heat was really on, they might be more reluctant than they are to enter into treaty commitments in our changeable and uncertain world. And treaties may be immensely valuable to officials in planning their interrelations, even though the commitments are not one hundred percent reliable.

What, then, will the official look at in making his sort of treaty interpretation? He will certainly look, as the I.L.C. Articles suggest, at the treaty language, its negotiating history, the then surrounding circumstances, and subsequent practice as furnishing at least some guide to the nature and density of his commitment. But he will also look at the kind of treaty it is and the kinds of reliance officials normally place in such treaties. And he will, in addition, look at everything that has happened since the treaty was entered into, the steps parties have taken in reliance on the treaty, and, in particular, the current situation: the current relations and bargaining strengths of the parties, the present fairness of the bargain, the practical internal and external pressures acting on various officials, the relative importance to each party of performance of the commitment, and the practical options in terms of both action and response with which each official is confronted. Finally, he will add a dash of awareness that officials may put less reliance in treaties than their rhetoric suggests and that they all recognize the need for some flexibility in changing circumstances. Out of all this the official will define a self-perceived "good faith" obligation—what he feels each of the treaty partners can honestly expect of the other under existing conditions. Of course, this may differ substantially from what the lawyer sees as the treaty obligation, and the parties' interpretations may differ between themselves. Yet each, by his own lights, may be acting in "good faith."

How does breach fit into the picture? Obviously, in this context both meaningful characterizations of breach and predictions of behavior in situations involving the possibility of breach many [sic] become highly uncertain. What is significant is, as so often in our field, not simply the potential legal postures of the parties, but also the more complex factors and processes which also contribute to their actual action and response.

The practical position is that in any situation involving potential allegations of breach, each of the treaty partners is faced with an array of options: to engage in or refrain from arguably violative conduct, to allege or not allege violation, to attempt to impose treaty or non-treaty sanctions in support of his position, to concede in the face of adverse response or press his position vigorously, to seek varied means of settlement including impartial adjudication, and so on. At each stage of the handling of the situation, each of the party's choices among these available options will be determined by his functional evaluation as to how helpful the exercise of any particular option will be in terms of his over-all policy objectives. This will necessarily involve an assessment of his treaty partner's reactions to any selected option.

Of course, in many cases, legal and political or other considerations may substantially overlap and the ostensible treaty norm may in fact strongly influence officials' treaty decisions. As suggested, the official is never indifferent to such norms. Moreover, where the treaty rule is precisely drafted and its applicability is reasonably clear to both parties, where the context indicates that both have relied on it and really mean it to be observed in existing circumstances, where the stakes are relatively small, and where pressures for compliance far outweigh those for non-compliance, reference to even narrowly conceived legal norms and adjustment of any disputes by law may be more convenient to all concerned. In many ways, it is easier to deal with problems in legal terms and perhaps most treaty provisons are of this relatively non-controversial type. In addition, in the comparatively rare situations where domestic or international adjudication is likely, technical legal positions will clearly be important to officials. Finally, the strength of a legal case may affect the general legitimacy of an official position as seen by the treaty partner, public, third states, or international organizations. The potential addressees of a position or the arena in which the dispute will be argued will, of course, bear on the importance of legal considerations. And obviously, where legal concerns are bureaucratically institutionalized in a powerful decision-making official such as a legal adviser, technical legal considerations will have greater weight.

But we all know that in many other cases the treaty norms themselves, at least as a lawyer might see them, may have much less impact on eventual official action or response. Conceivably, in light of all relevant factors, it may serve one party's interests to violate even a clear understanding. Or it may serve the other party's interests to ignore even the most flagrant breach, or to allege a violation where clearly none exists.

The various factors we've seen may contribute to such a result. In view of their permissive and flexible concept of obligation, officials, even in their own minds, may frequently find it hard to honestly label particular conduct as breach. Moreover, given the ambiguity both of many treaty provisions and of treaty doctrine itself, not to mention the resourcefulness of lawyers, respectable legal arguments may be developed by both sides and the persuasive value of a legal case in different arenas may be hard to gauge. Even where one party really believes that his own conduct is consistent with his treaty commitments or that his partner's conduct violates them, making a fuss may simply not be worthwhile in over-all policy terms, and he may prefer to compromise or let the matter drop. And, finally, as often pointed out, officials know that what appears as disputes over treaty interpretations are often really disputes over broader questions, such as the fairness and balance of the treaty itself. In such a case, both conduct arguably in breach and allegation of breach itself are frequently simple tools in a bargaining process to probe reactions, signal dissatisfaction with the existing deal, bring pressure for tacit or express amendment or renegotiation, or redefine or withdraw concessions to create bargaining pressures respecting issues external to the treaty. To deal with such cases as purely legal issues ignores the real problems involved.

The procedural context may reinforce this disinclination of officials to look at problems of treaty breach in technical legal terms. The likelihood of impartial legal determination of such issues is in most cases slight. Even where adjudication is possible, the reaction of a court or arbitral panel may be particularly hard to predict. Moreover, even the defensive party, whose immediate interest in the *status quo* might be best protected by a strictly legal interpretation, may not wish to commit himself to a principle of judicial settlement which may at a future time be invoked to limit his own flexibility. And especially where what is involved is essentially a demand for renegotiation, attempted reference by one party to impartial legal determination may be viewed by other parties as "not playing the game fairly."

The International Law Commission's refusal to provide in the Draft Articles for compulsory adjudication of treaty disputes seems to me to reflect the varied factors working against such purely legal solutions, and the parties' general reluctance to abdicate whatever bargaining control each has of the dispute situation. Once again, perhaps in our present world the flexibility inherent in the absence of such compulsory adjudication is a practical precondition to the willingness of states to use the treaty device as broadly as they have.

The interplay of official decisions in any such treaty dispute will of course eventually produce some outcome; for example, concession by one or the other party, continued disagreement with or without retaliation, submission to third-party settlement, compromise and amendment, or, possibly, even an attempt by one party to suspend or terminate the treaty. And technical arguments based on treaty norms will, as we have seen, play a more or less significant part in this bargaining process depending on the context. But the contributions of the norms themselves will be hard to disassociate from the other factors involved and it will consequently be difficult to predict outcome from the norms alone.

The important thing is that, after working out of each such breach-potential situation, the expectations of the parties may have a different shape and the treaty may mean a different thing. Since political as well as legal elements influence the decisions of the parties, what is going on is often not simply treaty interpretation but tacit or express renegotiation. In fact, modification achieved in this way may avoid the clumsiness, publicity and technical problems raised by formal amendment, a particularly useful consequence in the case of multilateral institutional agreements.

Of all this, the Draft Articles give us only a hint. . . .

Some Implications

If foreign office officials do in fact look at treaties and issues of breach somewhat in this way, what are the implications for international law? Let me briefly suggest some possibilities:

First, perhaps we should settle what we are trying to do with our Law of Treaties. It is the old law school question: Are we saying how we think states ought to behave or reflecting how they do behave or predicting how courts will decide disputes, or something of each of these? And is it possible to embrace all of the varied political factors which affect the action and response in any code of treaty law?

Second, as I believe Judge Jessup proposed some time ago, perhaps we need to think in terms not of a single monolithic Law of Treaties but rather of somewhat different rules for different kinds of treaties. An FCN treaty, the SEATO Treaty, the Geneva Accords, and the U.N. Charter may be simply too different in terms of their purposes, their obligational character, their political context, and the parties' attitudes towards them to be usefully encompassed by a single set of substantive rules. A zoologist may classify a cat and the tiger as morphologically alike, but the naturalist who seeks to understand behavior cannot ignore their differences. Our existing notions of obligation and breach may fit certain types of agreement very well, but on others they may hang like a sack.

Third, perhaps we should attempt to develop a better understanding of why states enter into treaties and what functions treaties serve in the international system. And we might ask whether, even in the case of treaty provisions whose norm-creating function is significant, our concept of

Pacta sunt servanda may not in many instances be much narrower and stricter than that actually held by the parties. Put another way, our doctrine of interpretation may not adequately reflect foreign office practice by failing to recognize the legitimacy of tentative or incomplete obligation, varying densities of commitment, ranges of permissible flexibility about a treaty norm, and the expectation-varying impact of events and pressures arising subsequent to the conclusion of the treaty. Thus, international law theory may frequently demand more of treaty partners than they actually demand of each other.

Fourth, perhaps we need to develop a more satisfying policy explanation of why and under what circumstances states *should* comply with treaty promises. To rest the explanation largely on the fact of formal solemnization and considerations of the so-called "stability of the international order" does not really seem to meet the pressing practical issues created for officials by such agreements as peace treaties, outdated or unequal "colonial" treaties, or treaties entered into by drastically different predecessor governments. If we are to expect governments to comply with burdensome and for them non-consensual agreements, we have to give a convincing reason why. Unfortunately, international courts have rarely had the freedom to evolve such meaningful treaty policy.

Fifth, the legal concept of breach may in many cases have only limited practical usefulness. In most cases there is procedurally no way in which an objective legal determination of breach or *a fortiori* "material breach" can be obtained. Often the parties may in any event not wish to obtain such a determination. And even where breach is clear, countries rarely consider it useful to resort to unilateral abrogation. In such a context, allegations of breach are frequently not really meant to be meaningful legal characterizations but are instead used as propaganda or bargaining counters in what may in actuality be a process of attempted renegotiation. The whole bias of the treaty system in practice seems to be towards accommodation rather than legal contention.

Sixth, the treaty device may in many respects be a more flexible and sensitive instrument than we have usually assumed, with a capacity for considerable informal responsiveness to changed circumstances. Far from creating once-and-for-all fixed expectations, variable only by formal act of the parties, it may be undergoing contsant tacit amendment as a result both of varying external circumstances and the parties' own action, inaction and response. ... Perhaps the distinction between the law-creating character of customary international law and treaties is in this sense less clear than we imagined, more formal than substantive.

Finally, the way in which treaty norms affect state behavior may be even more complex than we have thought. We have always realized that legal factors are only one of a variety of domestic and external pressures that act together on officials to produce a resultant decision. But, if treaty obligation is relative and changing, the legal input in this equation may often itself be shaped by such political factors. And perhaps this should not concern us unduly. Perhaps it is enough if treaties contribute to the working out of international relationships and problems, even if they prove a less than perfect and precisely definable instrument.

* * *

Pacta Sunt Servanda and National Interests*

Hearings on the Nuclear Test Ban Treaty Before the Senate Committee on Foreign Relations

Senator [Frank] Church. . . . You are a student of the diplomatic history of many

* Reprinted from "Hearings on the Nuclear Test Ban Treaty Before the Senate Committee on Foreign Relations," 88th Congress, 1st Session (1963), pp. 70–72.

countries over many generations. If we were to lift our sights beyond the immediate pattern of Russian perfidy, would it not be accurate to observe that nations usually comply with treaties that they enter into only so long as they find those treaties to conform to what they regard as their national interest? When their vital interests come in conflict with treaties they have previously entered into, hasn't it been rather habitual for sovereign nations to break them and then form new treaties that they believe will conform to their new interests as they see them?

Secretary [of State Dean] Rusk. Well, the path of history is littered with broken treaties, as you have observed, Senator Church. And in general, where vital interests are concerned, a nation by and large felt that it must take care of its vital interests and not give top priority to is [sic], shall we say, strictly legal commitments.

However, may I just add that "pacts are to be observed" is itself one of the vital interests of most countries. Therefore, particularly in those free countries that appreciate the importance of the steady growth of international law, it is a serious thing to break a treaty, and, therefore, you find countries that do observe their treaty obligations, even though that might be costly or inconvenient or troublesome or difficult, because *pacta sunt servanda* is still one of the great bases by which we can introduce some sort of law into the chaos of international relations.

Senator Church. With regard to the Russian record and the treaty that is now before us, we would want to look to the interests that we may have in common with the Soviet Union, rather than to any other consideration, in attempting to forecast whether or not the Russians will adhere to this particular treaty, is not that correct?

Secretary Rusk. I think we ought to consider whether or not this treaty seems to rest in a basic common interest of our two countries, not only as expressed by the leaders of our two countries, but their own best judgment as to what their own necessities are.

Senator Church. You already mentioned that we do have a rather dramatic and compelling common interest in the avoidance of nuclear war, in your response to the excellent questions put to you by Senator Gore. That would be one basis of common interest.

Secretary Rusk. I think that is correct.

Senator Church. Insofar as this treaty is concerned?

Secretary Rusk. I think that is right, sir.

Senator Church. Is it not also true that we both have a common interest in avoiding the poisoning of the air that even the Communists breathe with us?

Secretary Rusk. I agree. I think that is true.

Senator Church. That is a second common interest.

Secretary Rusk. That is correct, sir.

Senator Church. And is it not also true, as we stand upon our separate hydrogen bomb stockpiles and glower at one another, that we have a third common interest in doing what we can to retard the proliferation of these nuclear arsenals to other countries that do not now have them?

Secretary Rusk. There is no question about that, sir.

Senator Church. That is a third common interest?

Secretary Rusk. That is right, sir.

Senator Church. And though this treaty alone will not prevent such proliferation, its effect would be to retard it, would it not?

Secretary Rusk. That is our view. I believe that is right, sir.

Senator Church. So there is some rational basis, then, of considerable substance, for differentiating this treaty from the long list of treaties that have just been read to you which the Russians have broken.

Secretary Rusk. Senator, may I mention a fourth? Because I think these three elements you have mentioned are very important in combination. Since 1948, our own defense budget has multiplied by ap-

proximately five times. As a matter of our own economy, how many more times, if this uncontrolled and spiraling arms race goes on, how many more times do we multiply our defense budget by five? This is the problem we are facing here.

Senator Church. I would certainly accept that as a fourth possible common interest, Mr. Secretary.

Right of the United States to Withdraw from the Nuclear Test Ban Treaty in the Event of a Violation by Another Party*

Hearings on the Nuclear Test Ban Treaty Before the Senate Committee on Foreign Relations

Senator [Hubert] Humphrey. . . . Mr. Secretary, if the Soviets were to abrogate the treaty and were to have an explosion in one of the prohibited environments— let's say in the atmosphere or under water and we knew it—would we have to wait 90 days before we can respond with our answer either to test or to leave the obligations of the treaty?

Secretary [of State Dean] Rusk. It is our view that we would not have to wait 90 days, because the obligation of the Soviet Union not to test in the prohibited environment is central to the very purposes and existence of this agreement, and it is clearly established through precedents of American practice and international law over many decades that where the essential consideration in a treaty or agreement fails through violation on the other side that we ourselves are freed from those limitations.

Now, I would be very glad to make available to the committee a legal brief on this point, because where the gut of the

---

* Reprinted from "Hearings on the Nuclear Test Ban Treaty Before the Senate Committee on Foreign Relations," 88th Congress, 1st Session (1963), pp. 37–40.

treaty collapses, we are not limited just by the withdrawal clause.

* * *

AUGUST 12, 1963

Opinion of the Legal Adviser

Subject: Right of the United States to withdraw from the nuclear test ban treaty in the event of violation by another party.

Article IV of the Treaty Banning Nuclear Weapon Tests in the Atmosphere, in Outer Space and Underwater provides, inter alia:

"Each Party shall in exercising its national sovereignty have the right to withdraw from the Treaty if it decides that extraordinary events, related to the subject matter of this Treaty, have jeopardized the supreme interests of its country. It shall give notice of such withdrawal to all other Parties to the treaty three months in advance."

The question has been raised whether the United States would have to give 3 months notice prior to withdrawing if another party conducted nuclear weapon tests in the atmosphere, or committed some other act in plain violation of the treaty. The answer is "No."

A breach of treaty obligations by one party is considered in international law to give other parties the right to terminate their obligations under the treaty. Article IV is not intended as a restriction of that right. The three original parties recognized that events other than violations of the treaty might jeopardize a country's "supreme interests" and require that country to resume testing in the prohibited environments. Article IV permits withdrawal, upon 3 months' notice, in this case. If another party violated the treaty, the United States could treat the violation as an "extraordinary event" within the meaning of Article IV, or it could withdraw from the treaty immediately.

I. THE GENERAL RULE

In international law, violation of a treaty by one party makes the treaty voidable at the option of the other parties. I Lauterpacht, "Oppenheim's International Law" 947 (8th ed. 1955). . . . Whether there has been a violation, and whether it is serious enough to justify termination is for each party, acting in good faith, to decide. The right to void the treaty must be exercised within a reasonable time after the violation has become known, I Lauterpacht, 948.

The right of unilateral abrogation for cause has apparently never been adjudicated in an international court.[1] It has, however, been confirmed by publicists generally, and by United States, British, and Soviet authorities, among others.

The British view is "that, in general terms, such a right exists; [and] that the exercise of this right is optional at the discretion of the party wronged." McNair, "The Law of Treaties, British Practice and Opinions" 515 (1st ed. 1938).[2] Soviet authorities have taken the same position:

"The annulment of a treaty by one signatory in the event of the nonfulfillment by the other of key terms is held to be legal," Academy of Sciences of the U.S.S.R., Institute of State and Law, "International Law" 280.

The United States has consistently affirmed its unilateral right to terminate treaties in the event of violation by another party. Green Hackworth, then Legal Adviser of the Department of State and later a judge of the International Court of Justice, declared in 1935.

"The weight of opinion as expressed, at least in the United States, appears to incline to the view that a state may by its own unilateral act terminate a treaty as between itself and a state which it regards as having violated such treaty." Memorandum of the Legal Adviser of the Department of State, February 27, 1935, V Hackworth, "Digest of International Law" 346 (1943).

In 1791, James Madison wrote that a breach of a treaty by one party "discharges the other," which is then "at liberty to take advantage or not of the breach, as dissolving the treaty," V Moore, "Digest of International Law" 321 (1906).

At least four Secretaries of State and one President have expressed the same view. Secretary of State Frelinghuysen termed the Clayton-Bulwer treaty "voidable at the option of the United States" because Great Britain had "persistently violated her agreement not to colonize the Central American coast." Quoted in *Hooper* v. *U.S.*, 22 Ct. Cl. 408, 417 (1887). And in a memorandum for the President in 1896 concerning that treaty, Secretary of State Olney said Great Britain "undoubtedly did not fully comply with the provisions of the treaty" and that this "might well have been made the ground for an annulment of the treaty altogether,"[3] III Moore, 205. Secretary of State Lansing took the same position in a communication to the Swiss Minister in Washington concerning the effect of German violations of the treaty with Prussia of 1828, II Hyde, "International Law Chiefly as Interpreted and Applied by the United States" 1542 (2d rev. ed. 1945). The right of abrogation upon breach by another party was affirmed in a dictum by President Coolidge in his award as arbitrator in a dispute between Chile and Peru. Opinion and award of the arbitrator, 19 Am. J. Int'l L. 393, 398 (1925). Secretary of State Hughes also signed the award.

Finally, the Supreme Court has also declared the principle. Mr. Justice Iredell, in *Ware* v. *Hylton*, said it was "a part of the law of nations, that if a treaty be violated by one party, it is at the option of the other party, if innocent, to declare, in consequence of the breach, that the treaty is void" (3 Dallas 199, 261 (1796); see also *Charlton* v. *Kelly*, 229 U.S. 447 (1913)).

The most restrictive position on the right of unilateral abrogation for cause is taken by the Harvard Law Research Draft Convention on the Law of Treaties, which rejects the right and substitutes instead provisional suspension pending referral to an international tribunal, 29 Am. J. Int'l L., Supp. 1077, 1094 (1935). This position has been rejected by subsequent writers, and finds no support in international practice.

II. INTERNATIONAL PRACTICE

The right to abrogate or annul a treaty on the ground that another party has committed a breach has been exercised rarely. The United States appears to have invoked it only once. In 1798, when relations between France and the United States were strained, Congress passed an act, signed by the President, declaring that—

"Whereas the treaties concluded between the United States and France have been repeatedly violated on the part of the French Government; and the just claims of the United States for reparation of the injuries so committed have been refused, and their attempts to negotiate an amicable adjustment of all complaints between the two nations have been repelled with indignity: * * * the United States are of right freed and exonerated from the stipulations of the treaties and of the consular convention, heretofore concluded between the United States and France; * * *" 1 Stat. 578, V Moore, 356.[4]

France did not recognize the U.S. termination. For an account of subsequent negotiations see V Moore, "History and Digest of the International Arbitrations to Which the United States Has Been a Party" 4429 (1898).

In 1933, a Greek Court refused to extradite Samuel Insull, then under indictment in the United States for violation of the bankruptcy laws. The United States denounced the treaty but did not abrogate it. In a communication to the Greek Minister of Foreign Affairs, the American Minister to Greece, termed the decision "utterly untenable and a clear violation of the American-Hellenic Treaty of Extradition * * *" and stated:

"Accordingly I am instructed to give formal notice herewith of my Government's denunciation of the treaty with a view to its termination at the earliest date possible under its pertinent provisions," 28 Am. J. Int'l L. 307, 311 (1934).

The issue was later resolved by a protocol to the extradition treaty, IV Hackworth, "Digest of International Law" 118.

In 1870, Russia denounced the Black Sea clauses of the Treaty of Paris on the ground that the other parties had violated several of its essential clauses. For an account of British practice, see McNair, 540–570 (2d ed.).

Unilateral abrogation has normally been met by vigorous protests from the other parties. However, the protests have been the result of disagreement over the facts rather than over the principle of law. See II Hyde, 1543, McNair, 568 (2d ed.).

III. MATERIALITY OF THE BREACH

Most publicists limit the right of abrogation to cases of a substantial breach by the other party. Hyde says abrogation by one party is justified by the "failure of a contracting state to observe a *material stipulation* of its agreement * * *," although he also notes the futility of attempting "to enunciate rules pointing decisively to the circumstances when abrogation by one party is to be excused." II Hyde, 1541. [Italic supplied.] The rule is sometimes stated in terms of the nonfulfillment of "key terms" (U.S.S.R., "International Law" 280) or "breach of a stipulation which is material to the main object," Hall, "A Treatise on International Law" 409 (8th ed. Higgins 1924). Under the proposed draft restatement, termination of the entire agreement is justified only when the violation "has the effect of depriving the aggrieved party of an essential benefit of the agreement," "Re-

statement," section 162. The draft articles on the Law of Treaties of the International Law Commission, prepared by G. C. Fitzmaurice, require a "fundamental breach of the treaty in an essential respect, going to the root or foundation of the treaty relationship between the parties, * * *" II Yearbook of the International Law Commission 31 (1957), A/CN.4/SER. A/1957 (Add.1).

Hackworth, however, does not so limit the right of abrogation, and Lauterpacht states:[5]

"There is no unanimity on this point, since some make a distinction between essential and nonessential provisions of the treaty, and maintain that only violation of essential provisions creates a right for the other party to cancel the treaty. Others oppose this distinction, maintaining that it is not always possible to distinguish essential from nonessential provisions, that the binding force of a treaty protects nonessential as well as essential provisions, and that it is for the injured party to consider for itself whether violation of a treaty, even in its least essential parts, justifies its cancellation." I Lauterpacht, 947.

The primary undertakings of the nuclear test ban treaty are contained in articles I and IV. Article I obligates the parties not to conduct nuclear weapon tests or other nuclear explosions in the atmosphere, underwater, or in outer space. Underground explosions are permitted if they do not spread radioactive debris beyond the territory of the country in which they are conducted. Parties are also prohibited from "causing, encouraging, or in any way participating in" the carrying out of prohibited tests or explosions by others. Article IV requires 3 months' notice of withdrawal in the case of an "extraordinary event" jeopardizing "supreme interests." Breach of any of these obligations, all of which are fundamental, would justify withdrawal from the treaty under appropriate circumstances.

IV. MULTILATERAL TREATIES

The right of a party to terminate its obligations under a multilateral treaty because another party has breached it depends upon the nature of the treaty. A breach by one party obviously does not give any other party the right to bring the whole treaty to an end. At most, the aggrieved party may consider itself released from its obligations under the treaty.

In the case of multilateral treaties creating obligations necessarily dependent on the corresponding performance of other parties, a breach by one party justifies withdrawal by any other party. A disarmament treaty has been cited as an example of such a treaty in an analysis of unilateral withdrawal from multilateral treaties, II Yearbook of the International Law Commission 52–55 (1957). The nuclear test ban is of the same character. The undertaking of each party to refrain from testing nuclear weapons is given in return for a similar undertaking by each of the other parties.

However, in the case of a multilateral treaty consisting of a mutual and reciprocal interchange of benefits and concessions, such as a copyright or consular convention, a breach by one party does not justify general withdrawal by another party. Rather, it justifies only a reciprocal breach of obligations. For example, if state A refused to honor its obligations to state B under a copyright convention, state B could be released, if it chose, from its obligations to state A. It would not, however, be released from its obligations to other parties to the convention. Ibid.

Notes

1. It has, however, been alluded to in at least two cases before the Permanent Court of International Justice, "Diversion of Water From the River Meuse," P.C.I.J., ser. A/B, No. 70, 50 (1937); *Case concerning the Factory at Cherzow*, P.C.I.J., ser. A, No. 9, 31 (1927).

2. The second edition of McNair deals with the law of treaties generally, rather than with British practice. In the second edition, he limits the exercise of the right to cases of "fundamental breach." Id. at 571 (2d ed., 1961).

3. The United States alleged that Great Britain had violated the treaty by exercising sovereignty over British Honduras, and by treating that territory as a British colony. The British considered the allegation "wholly untenable," on the ground that the treaty was not intended to cover British Honduras. However, they also assumed that the United States would be entitled to abrogate the treaty if Great Britain had violated it, McNair, 567–568 (2d ed.).

4. The treaties with France were abrogated by act of Congress. However, the President may, acting alone, declare a treaty inoperative or suspended. See 40 Ops. Att'y Gen. 119, 123 (1941). See also "Restatement," sec. 167.

5. In the first edition of his "Law of Treaties," McNair said flatly, "* * * it is not possible to say that some stipulations are essential ones and some are not, and that only a breach of one of the former class gives rise to the right; it must be assumed that each stipulation forms part of the consideration which induced the other party to enter into the treaty," at 515.

Juridical Content of the Principal *Pacta Sunt Servanda* and Its Realization in International Relations*

V. M. Shurshalov

. . . pacta sunt servanda does not have an absolute importance and, for this reason, cannot be applied to every treaty. International practice, as we know, contains not a few examples of unequal treaties. It would be utterly reactionary to insist that treaties of this kind be observed. It follows, from what has been said, that pacta sunt servanda embraces only lawfully concluded treaties, and only in relation

* Reprinted from V. M. Shurshalov, "Juridical Content of the Principle *Pacta Sunt Servanda* and Its Realization in International Relations," *Soviet Yearbook of International Law* 166 (1958), by permission of the Soviet Association of International Law. (English summary)

to them can it play a progressive role.

It is particularly important to stress this just now when the imperialist powers, under cover of the principle pacta sunt servanda, seek to maintain the aggressive blocs, extortionate and unequal treaties, . . . In view of the foregoing, the content of the principle under discussion can be defined in the following way.

The state, in accordance with the principle pacta sunt servanda, is obliged scrupulously and in full measure to carry out international treaties lawfully concluded and which do not contradict existing international law. Rejection of treaty obligations can be justified only in the following exceptional cases: a) when a revolution or a national-liberation struggle gives rise to a new social structure and a new state authority, which is entitled to denounce the humiliating and unacceptable treaties of the deposed government; b) when one of the counter-agents is no longer an international law subject, as a result of merging of several states into a single state or the division of one state into two or more; c) when the obligations are associated with the territory over which the corresponding state has lost territorial supremacy.

It seems that enumeration of the exceptional circumstances justifying rejection of international obligations greatly facilitates the task of disclosing the principle pacta sunt servanda, since the need for enumerating the multifarious conditions when the state cannot refuse to carry out the agreement disappears. . . .

The international relations of recent years testify to the growing importance of pacta sunt servanda for treaty practice and the progressive development of international law.

And this is perfectly understandable, since international treaties can further co-operation between states and strengthen friendship between the peoples only when they are scrupulously and fully observed by the contracting parties.

The international treaty becomes a genuine instrument of peace, a means of settling the numerous and complex questions of international life, and the decisive condition for lessening international tension only through the principle pacta sunt servanda.

This explains why the peace-loving countries and above all the Soviet Union are vitally interested in strict and unswerving observance of this principle. And, conversely, the ruling circles of the imperialist countries, pursuing the "positions-of-strength" policy and seeking to accentuate international tension, systematically violate international treaties, though in words they hypocritically pose as champions of pacta sunt servanda.

What is more, they, contrary to the facts, frequently resort to utterly groundless charges against the Soviet Union, accusing it of violating international obligations, the aim being to blame it for the failure to achieve a settlement of vital international questions by way of negotiation and agreed decisions. For example, with this aim in view a group of scientists was formed under the auspices of Stanford University in the United States to study Soviet treaty practice. The group has already put out two books: "Soviet Russia and the East, 1920–27," "Soviet Russia and the West, 1920–27," which contain falsifications about the treaty practice of the USSR. The US State Department has circulated these books among American embassies in all countries with instructions to popularize them.

Yet the whole world knows that the historic Decree on Peace, published in 1917, contains the Leninist principles of the foreign policy of the world's first state of working people. As one of its basic foreign-policy principles the Soviet state has proclaimed the sovereign equality of nations, big and small, non-interference in the internal affairs of other states, non-aggression and peaceful co-existence. The treaty practice of the USSR has always been based, and is based now, upon these principles.

Consequently, both the conclusion of international agreements and their fulfilment have always been the practical realization of the Leninist principles. And the exceptional loyalty of the Soviet Union to its obligations is adequately proved by the 40-year treaty practice of the Soviet state. . . . The consistent loyalty of the USSR to its obligations has been pointed out many times by prominent statesmen in a number of countries. For instance, Sir Winston Churchill said that on the basis of his experience, the Union of Soviet Socialist Republics had never violated either its obligations or treaties.

On Soviet Treaty Violations*

Senator William J. Fulbright

Mr. Fulbright. Mr. President, as pointed out in the comprehensive work— sponsored by the Hoover Institution on War, Revolution, and Peace—on "The Theory, Law, and Policy of Soviet Treaties," covering all Soviet treaties through 1957, the U.S.S.R. had entered into more treaties with the United States than it had entered into with any other nation.

A list,† prepared by the Assistant Legal Adviser for Treaty Affairs, of the U.S. Department of State, includes 128 treaties and other international agreements now in force between the United States and the U.S.S.R.

Of this list, 70 are treaties—that is, formal instruments which have been entered into by the United States, with the advice and consent of the U.S. Senate.

The significant fact that emerges from an examination of the 70 treaties to which the United States and the Soviet Union

* Reprinted from *United States Congressional Record,* Vol. 109, Part 13 (September 24, 1964), p. 17827.
† See *Congressional Record,* Vol. 109, Part 13, September 24, 1964, pp. 17827–17830.

are parties is that only 6 of them are viewed as having been violated by the Soviet Union. And of the six violated by the Soviet Union, one is the Kellogg-Briand Pact of 1928, which was a renunciation of war as an instrument of national policy. Another is the Charter of the United Nations, which, according to the Department of State, the Soviet Union has violated in various of its terms. Three of the other treaties are treaties of peace with Hungary, Rumania, and Bulgaria. The final one is the Convention on Prisoners of War of 1949.

Fifty-eight other, less formal, international agreements to which the United States and the Soviet Union are parties are included in the list. Of these 58 other agreements, the Department of State views the Soviet Union as in violation of 21. Included among the other international agreements the Soviet has violated are the Roosevelt-Litvinov agreements establishing diplomatic relations with the Soviet Union, certain lend-lease agreements, the Yalta agreements relating to prisoners of war and civilians, the Atlantic Charter, a series of armistice agreements, the Potsdam agreements, and various others. It should be noted that none of the agreements in the latter category was a treaty, in the formal sense of having to be approved by the Senate. Perhaps they should have been, but they were not.

The Doctrine of *Rebus Sic Stantibus* and the International Load Line Convention*

Opinion of Acting United States Attorney General Francis Biddle

It is clear from its general nature that the convention was a peacetime agreement. As stated in its preamble the

* Reprinted from 40 *Opinions of Attorneys General* 119 (1941).

contracting governments entered into it "to promote safety of life and property at sea by establishing in common agreement uniform principles and rules with regard to the limits to which ships on international voyages may be loaded" (47 Stat. 2228). This general purpose, as the terms of the convention demonstrate, was to be achieved by limiting international competition in the loading of cargo vessels. That peacetime commerce and voyages were assumed as the basis of the convention is also demonstrated by the nature of its detailed provisions and regulations. A perusal of them leaves no doubt that peacetime commerce was a basic assumption of the treaty. The present situation with respect to shipping is a wholly different one. Conditions essential to the operation of the convention, and assumed as a basis for it, are in almost complete abeyance. Of the 36 governments which acceded to or ratified the convention prior to September 1, 1935, ten (Germany, Great Britain, Canada, China, Finland, India, Italy, Japan, New Zealand and the Soviet Union) are at war. Sixteen of the said 36 governments are under military occupation. Others, of which may be mentioned the Irish Free State, Portugal and Sweden, may be said to be striving with varying success to preserve a precarious neutrality in the widespread armed conflict now prevalent. International shipping is not being carried on under normal conditions subject to agreements arrived at for the purpose of regulating international voyages freely undertaken and completed. On the contrary, the actual destruction of vessels engaged in such commerce, however loaded, is one of the principal means by which the war is now being conducted among various of the contracting parties. Restraints imposed by the convention with respect to load lines are of small moment indeed in a war directed in large part toward the utter destruction of all shipping except that which is tolerated by self-interest. The German Government, which is a party to the convention, has not only invaded and conquered many governments that are likewise parties to the convention and removed their shipping from normal participation in international commerce, but carries on its own international shipping primarily in waters subject solely to its own military control. It is well known that the international sea lanes are the rendezvous for varied instrumentalities of war set loose for the destruction of shipping. It is equally well known that a serious shortage exists in shipping in the case of numerous, if not all, signatories to the convention, including those whose defenses the Congress has declared essential to the defense of the United States. The shortage referred to by the Secretary of the Interior, Petroleum Coordinator, is due to the conditions briefly referred to above. In short, the implicit assumption of normal peacetime international trade, which is at the foundation of the Load Line Convention, no longer exists.

Under these circumstances there is no doubt in my mind that the convention has ceased to be binding upon the United States. It is a well-established principle of international law, rebus sic stantibus, that a treaty ceases to be binding when the basic conditions upon which it was founded have essentially changed. Suspension of the convention in such circumstances is the unquestioned right of a state adversely affected by such essential change.

* * *

It is sometimes said that the change which brings the principles into operation must be essential or fundamental. But whether or not this is an integral part of the principle itself, there can be no doubt that the changed conditions affecting the Load Line Convention are most essential and most fundamental.

As to procedure to be adopted by the Government that relies on the principle of rebus sic stantibus, it may well be that ordinarily the procedure would call for the Government to inform the other parties to the treaty with respect to the matter and request agreement for termination or suspension of the treaty. The matter of procedure, however, does not affect the right of termination or suspension. Since a number of the contracting states have been overrun by military power, and normal international procedures, so far as here pertinent, are no longer available but are submerged in the swiftly changing conditions inherent in the world situation, the procedure by prior notification and consent preferred by some of the authorities need not be followed, though of course it may be pursued if desired in relation to those governments with respect to which it is still feasible. The fundamental character of the change in conditions underlying the treaty, however, leaves the Government of the United States entirely free to declare the treaty inoperative or to suspend it for the duration of the present emergency.

Argento v. Horn *

United States Court of Appeals, Sixth Circuit, 1957

Upon application of the Republic of Italy, certified by the Secretary of State of the United States, and upon complaint of the Italian Consul for Ohio and Kentucky, extradition proceedings were initiated against the appellant in the United States District Court for the Northern District of Ohio. After a hearing pursuant to 18 U.S.C.A. § 3184, the United States Commissioner concluded that the evidence was sufficient to sustain the charge that the appellant was the same Tommaso Argento who had been convicted *in absentia* and sentenced to life imprisonment in Italy in 1931 for a murder committed there in 1922.

* Reprinted from 241 F. 2d 258 (1957).

The Commissioner accordingly committed the appellant to custody pending surrender to the Republic of Italy. By writ of habeas corpus and action for declaratory judgment, the appellant attacked the legality of his arrest, commitment and detention. This appeal is from the judgment of the district court upholding the Commissioner's order.

Appellant's primary demand for freedom is based upon a most fundamental contention. It is his claim that there exists no valid extradition treaty between the United States of America and the Republic of Italy, and that in the absence of such a treaty, there is no legal authority for the surrender to Italy of a fugitive in the United States. . . .

Without question the appellant is on sound ground in asserting that he cannot be extradited to Italy in the absence of a valid treaty so providing. That the Executive is without inherent power to seize a fugitive criminal and surrender him to a foreign nation has long been settled. . . .

While Congress might conceivably have authorized extradition in the absence of a treaty, it has not done so. The law is clear. . . .

As to the existence of a valid extradition treaty between the United States and Italy, the parties are in agreement upon the underlying facts. They differ completely in the conclusions to be drawn from them.

A treaty of extradition was concluded between the two nations in 1868, 15 Stat. 629. Valid amendments were made to the treaty in 1869 and 1885, 16 Stat. 767 and 24 Stat. 1001. Murder was one of the crimes made extraditable by the treaty.

On December 11, 1941, 55 Stat. 797, the Congress of the United States declared that a state of war existed between the United States and Italy. At the conclusion of the war a treaty of peace was concluded, effective September 15, 1947. 61 Stat. 1245. This peace treaty, which was duly ratified by the United States Senate, provided in Article 44 as follows:

"1. Each Allied or Associated Power will notify Italy, within a period of six months from the coming into force of the present Treaty, which of its pre-war bilateral treaties with Italy it desires to keep in force or revive. Any provisions not in conformity with the present Treaty shall, however, be deleted from the above-mentioned treaties.

"2. All such treaties so notified shall be registered with the Secretariat of the United Nations in accordance with Article 102 of the Charter of the United Nations.

"3. All such treaties not so notified shall be regarded as abrogated." 61 Stat. 1386.

On February 6, 1948, the Secretary of State of the United States notified the Republic of Italy that the United States desired to keep in force or revive, among others, the Extradition Treaty of 1868, as amended.

It is the appellant's position that under established principles of international law the outbreak of war between Italy and the United States in 1941 operated to abrogate completely the extradition treaty previously existing between the two nations. That being so, the appellant argues that in order to revive the extradition treaty it was necessary to make a new treaty, and that a new treaty under the Constitution of the United States could have been made only by the President, with the explicit concurrence of the Senate by a two-thirds vote. U.S.Const. Article II, Section 2. The appellees concede in their brief, as they obviously must, "that it would * * * require the concurring action of the President and the Senate to re-enact a treaty once dead as distinguished from one which is dormant or held in abeyance. * * *"

Whether the war between Italy and the United States completely annulled the previous extradition treaty is thus the central question before us. If the war did have that effect, the appellant is correct in his position that there is now no treaty of extradition between the two nations, since it is conceded that the "notification" of February 6, 1948, was not submitted to the United States Senate for its advice and consent.

Early publicists adopted the view that war *ipso facto* abrogates all treaties between the belligerent nations. In more recent times, however, this theory has been rejected by the textwriters in international law, and it seems never to have been espoused by courts in the United States.

*   *   *

While it is therefore settled, at least in this country, that all treaties are not automatically abrogated by the outbreak of war between the parties, it is not easy to postulate an applicable standard to determine whether a particular treaty has survived a war. The difficulty was stated more definitively than was the solution in Karnuth v. United States, 1929, 279 U.S. 231, at page 236, 49 S.Ct. 274, at page 276, 73 L.Ed. 677:

"The effect of war upon treaties is a subject in respect of which there are widely divergent opinions. The doctrine sometimes asserted, especially by the older writers, that war *ipso facto* annuls treaties of every kind between the warring nations, is repudiated by the great weight of modern authority; and the view now commonly accepted is that 'whether the stipulations of a treaty are annulled by war depends upon their intrinsic character.' 5 Moore's Digest of International Law, § 779, p. 383. But as to precisely what treaties fall and what survive, under this designation, there is lack of accord. The authorities, as well as the practice of nations, present a great contrariety of views. The law of the subject is still in the making, and, in attempting to formulate principles at all approaching generality, courts must proceed with a good deal of caution. But there seems to be fairly common agreement that at least the following treaty obligations remain in force: Stipulations in respect of what shall be done in a state of war; treaties of cession, boundary, and the like; provisions giving the right to citizens or subjects of one of the high contracting powers to continue to hold and transmit land in the territory of the other; and, generally, provisions which represent completed acts. On the other hand, treaties of amity, of alliance, and the like, having a political character, the object of which 'is to promote relations of harmony between nation and nation,' are generally regarded as belonging to the class of treaty stipulations that are absolutely annulled by war. Id., p. 385, quoting Calvo, Droit Int. (4th Ed.) IV. 65, § 1931."

Counsel have cited us to no decision, and we have found none, specifically relating to the effect of war upon a treaty of extradition. Such a treaty does not conveniently fit into either of the alternative classifications set out in the Karnuth opinion quoted above. If the question were to be decided in a vacuum, the conclusion could only be that it is extremely doubtful that war *ipso facto* abrogates a treaty of extradition. Fortunately, however, the question need not be so decided, but can and must be decided against the background of the actual conduct of the two nations involved, acting through the political branches of their governments.

* * *

The consummation of the treaty of peace with Italy in 1947 containing Article 44 providing for "notification" by the United States of each pre-war bilateral treaty it desired to keep in force or revive, the ratification of that treaty by the United States Senate, the subsequent notification by our State Department with regard to the extradition treaty, and the conduct of the political departments of the two nations in the ensuing nine years, evidencing their unqualified understanding that the extradition treaty is in full force and effect, all make it obvious that the political departments of the two governments considered the extradition treaty not abrogated but merely suspended during hostilities. There is, to be sure, a certain circuity of reasoning in deciding that the parties did not need to make a new treaty of extradition for the reason that they did not in fact make one. Yet it is exactly that pragmatic and cautious approach that, if the question is doubtful, the authorities enjoin. Terlinden v. Ames, 184 U.S. 270, 22 S.Ct. 484, supra. "A construction of a treaty by the political department of the Government, while not conclusive upon a court called upon to construe such a treaty in a matter involving personal rights, is nevertheless of much weight." . . .

It is our conclusion that the treaty of extradition between the United States and Italy was not terminated but merely suspended during the war, and that it is now in effect.

* * *

Suggested Readings

Textbooks

Brierly. *The Law of Nations,* pp. 317–345.
Brownlie. *Principles of Public International Law,* pp. 487–509.
Fenwick. *International Law,* pp. 514–551.
Gould. *An Introduction to International Law,* pp. 289–346.
Jacobini. *International Law,* pp. 145–200.

Kaplan and Katzenbach. *The Political Foundations of International Law*, pp. 23–26, 236–246.

Kelsen. *Principles of International Law,* pp. 454–505.

Sørensen. *Manual of Public International Law*, pp. 175–246.

Svarlien. *An Introduction to the Law of Nations*, pp. 261–283.

Tung. *International Law in an Organizing World*, pp. 325–364.

von Glahn. *Law Among Nations*, pp. 413–450.

Specialized Works

Byrd, Elbert M. *Treaties and Executive Agreements in the United States.* The Hague: Martinus Nijhoff, 1960.

Hoyt, Edwin C. *The Unanimity Rule in the Revision of Treaties: A Re-examination.* The Hague: Martinus Nijhoff, 1959.

Lissitzyn, Oliver, J. "Treaties and Changed Circumstances (*Rebus Sic Stantibus*)," 61 *American Journal of International Law* 895 (1967).

McNair, Lord Arnold D. *The Law of Treaties.* Oxford: Clarendon Press, 1961.

Schwelb, Egon. "Some Aspects of International *Jus Cogens* as Formulated by the International Law Commission," 61 *American Journal of International Law* 946 (1967).

Chapter VI
Legal
Regulation
of Use
# of Force

RESORT TO FORCE

Hugo Grotius and other early publicists in international law sought to establish a distinction between lawful and unlawful resort to war, but, by 1800, such efforts were abandoned, and states were recognized as having the right to resort to war as an instrument of national policy. Resort to war in the nineteenth century was a question of fact, not of law. International law was concerned with defining the points at which war commenced and terminated —that is to say, with declarations of war, peace treaties, and the like—as points of reference to distinguish between the status of war and the status of peace. If war had commenced, the laws of warfare between belligerents and the laws of neutrality between belligerents and neutrals came into existence and conflicting laws of peace were set aside for the duration. W. E. Hall, writing in 1880, expressed the nineteenth-century view: "International law has no

alternative but to accept war, independently of the justice of its origin, as a relation which the parties to it may set up, if they choose, and to busy itself only in regulating the effects of the relation."[1]

Paradoxically, nineteenth-century norms, while silent on resort to war, purported to regulate resort to force in situations *short of war*. Armed reprisals were permitted as a means of self-help to compel a delinquent state to conform to the law and to make reparation for the injury caused by its illegal conduct, but such uses of force were lawful only if conducted in accordance with rather strict rules: they had to be preceded by a request for redress, and they could not be grossly out of proportion to the wrongful acts that provoked them. Use of force in self-

[1] W. E. Hall, *A Treatise on International Law*, 8th ed. by A. P. Higgins (Oxford: Clarendon Press, 1924), p. 82. (Various editions from 1880 to 1924)

defense was also strictly limited, in that the state seeking to justify a forceful action short of war on this ground was called upon to demonstrate that the action was *necessary* and was not *excessive*. The widely recognized right to use force to protect the lives and property of nationals abroad was permitted only if the action did not amount to intervention in the political affairs of an independent state.

In practice, these restrictions were often disregarded, and it was possible to evade them altogether by declaring war. In 1902, for example, Britain, Germany, and Italy established a pacific blockade off the coast of Venezuela to force that state to honor numerous claims against it by citizens of the three Powers. Under the distinctions of the day, a pacific blockade, which was a reprisal measure, differed from a hostile blockade in two significant respects: no formal state of war existed and blockading ships could take action only against the ships of the delinquent state. When the United States protested that the ships of third states were being stopped, the blockading powers solved their legal problem merely by asserting that a state of war existed.

World War I was the catalyst for a radical transformation of international law norms relating to resort to force. The outbreak of that war created widespread disillusionment with the balance of power system as *the* approach to peace, while its extreme destructiveness signaled the urgent need to construct other approaches. International law and international organization, both of which had demonstrated their usefulness in regulating the peaceful relations of states, were pressed into service by the adoption of the League of Nations Covenant. Much of the significant history of international relations since that time was centered around efforts to improve upon that beginning by closing "gaps" and eliminating "loopholes."

J. L. Brierly did not exaggerate when he stated that:

The Covenant changed the whole foundations of the law, (1) by creating express obligations to employ pacific means of settling disputes and not to resort to war without first exhausting those means, and (2) by establishing a central organization of states empowered to pass judgement on the observance of those obligations by individual states and to apply sanctions in the event of the obligations being violated.[2]

The legal prohibitions on resort to force by states were further strengthened by the Kellogg-Briand Pact of 1928, which was eventually signed or acceded to by some sixty-three states. While, under certain circumstances, the law of the Covenant permitted a state to resort to war after complying with the specified procedural steps of peaceful settlement,[3] the Pact prohibited war "as an instrument of national policy." Neither the Covenant nor the Pact prohibited resort to war in support of League decisions or in self-defense; and since both documents referred specifically to "war" rather than to "use of force," it was possible to conclude that use of force short of war, if exercised in accordance with traditional norms, was permitted.

It is significant that the disillusionment that resulted from the failure of the new norms and the League to keep the peace led not to the abandonment of the effort to use international law and international organization to eradicate the scourge of war but to an attempt to close the legal and organizational "gaps" in the League system. The United Nations Charter was the result. The Charter expressly obligates all members of the United Nations not only to refrain from resorting to war but to "refrain in their international relations from the threat or use of force against the territorial integrity or political independence of any State, or in any other manner inconsistent with the Purposes of the United Nations." The "inherent right of individual and collective self-defense" remains,

[2] Brierly, *The Law of Nations*, p. 408.
[3] See Articles 12, 13, 15, and 16 of the Covenant, reprinted in this section on pp. 340–342.

according to Article 51, "if an armed attack occurs against a Member of the United Nations, until the Security Council has taken the measures necessary to maintain international peace and security." Self-defense measures must be immediately reported to the Security Council, which is the linchpin of the United Nations peacekeeping system in that it is empowered to determine "the existence of any threat to the peace, breach of the peace, or act of aggression" and to "make recommendations or decide what measures shall be taken" to maintain or restore the peace. And, with the sole exception of forceful measures against a renewal of aggression by the ex-enemy states of World War II, enforcement action under regional arrangements, such as N.A.T.O., are made subject by Article 53 to the authorization of the Security Council. It is now generally agreed that, under the law of the Charter, the use of force in inter-state relations is permissible only in individual or collective self-defense or under the auspices of a competent international organ.

This significant development of norms, from the Covenant to the Charter, has not saved "succeeding generations from the scourge of war" nor has it brought "peace in our time." States have been more willing to agree to the creation of the norms than to the creation of adequate means for assuring their observance; in a sense, international law norms have outstripped international organizational means. And, apart from the fact that saying so does not make it so, ambiguities in the wording of the relevant Charter provisions permit varying interpretations of the norms. In the absence of authoritative interpretations by the "organized international community," each state remains free to interpret the provisions for itself. When is use of force in "self-defense" justified? Does inaction by the Security Council constitute tacit authorization of enforcement action by a regional organization? These and numerous similar questions go unanswered by author-

itative tribunals; national decision-makers use legal reasoning to answer them, but only after having made policy decisions on the basis of national interests.

This is not to say that the Charter prohibitions are wholly ineffective. Most, if not all, national decision-makers see in these prohibitions "an overriding community policy for preventing total disaster"[4] in our thermonuclear age. It is clearly understood that even minor breaches of the peace carry the risk of escalating into a nuclear holocaust. Consequently, appreciations of national interests support the general application of the norms, if they do not always support their particular application in specific instances where vital interests seem to require the use of force. And when force is resorted to, decision-makers feel a compulsion to justify its use under the law of the Charter.

The materials that follow are divided into two sections. The purpose of the first section is to provide the reader with a knowledge of the traditional and contemporary norms that purport to regulate resort to force by states. The judgment in the "Naulilaa Incident Arbitration" is a classic statement of the requirements of armed reprisals under traditional international law. The conditions for the lawful exercise of self-defense are stated in correspondence by United States Secretary of State Daniel Webster relating to the *Caroline* incident of 1837 and in excerpts from the judgment of the Nürnberg Tribunal. The development of twentieth-century norms regulating resort to force by states is provided by sections from the League of Nations Covenant, the Kellogg-Briand Pact, and the United Nations Charter. A brief selection from J. L. Brierly's *The Law of Nations* is included as a knowledgeable interpretation of the controversial right to use force in self-defense under Article 51 of the Charter. Finally, an excerpt from the Corfu Channel

[4] Kaplan and Katzenbach, *The Political Foundations of International Law*, p. 216.

case is reprinted as an interpretation by the International Court of Justice of the kinds of action to which it is permissible to react by forcible measures under the law of the Charter.

The selections included in the second section place the norms relating to resort to force in the context of political crises that do not "go to court." In case studies involving the seizure of Goa by India in 1961, the United States "quarantine" during the Cuban missile crisis, and the military activities of the United States in Vietnam, uses of force are defended and criticized, by partisans and scholars, in terms of the norms of international law.

I. The Norms—Traditional and Contemporary

Armed Reprisals: Naulilaa Incident Arbitration*

Portuguese-German Arbitral Tribunal, 1928

[*"On October 19, 1914 a German official and two German officers from German South-west Africa were killed at the Portuguese post of Naulilaa in Angola under the following circumstances. A party of Germans had crossed into Angola to discuss with the Portuguese authorities the importation of food supplies into German Southwest Africa. Due to difficulties in interpreting, misunderstandings arose between the parties. In the course of a discussion a Portuguese officer seized the bridle of a German official's horse and the official struck him. At that time a German officer drew his pistol. The Portuguese officer ordered his men to fire and the official and two officers were killed. Portuguese authorities subsequently interned the German interpreter and a German soldier. The authorities of German Southwest Africa did not communicate with the Portuguese authorities, but in alleged reprisal for the incident German troops attacked and destroyed certain forts and posts in Angola. These events took place prior to the entry of Portugal into the World War. After the* war, the Portuguese Government claimed damages on account of the incident. Alois de Meuron, a Swiss lawyer, was designated on August 15, 1920 as arbitrator to determine in conformance with paragraph 4 of the annex to articles 297–298 of the Treaty of Versailles the amount of the Portuguese claims. On February 9, 1928 two other arbitrators, both Swiss nationals, Robert Guex and Robert Fazy, were added to the tribunal. In an award rendered July 31, 1928 the arbitrators stated that the death of the German official and of two German officers was not the consequence of an act contrary to the law of nations on the part of the Portuguese authorities. . . ."* 6 Hackworth, Digest of International Law *154.*]

* * *

Reprisals are an act of self-help (*Selbsthilfehandlung*) on the part of the injured state, responding *after an unsatisfied demand* to an act contrary to international law on the part of the offending state. They have the effect of suspending momentarily in the relations of the two states the observance of this or that rule of international law. They are limited by the experience of humanity and the rules of good faith, applicable in the relations of state with state. *They would be illegal if a previous act contrary to international law had not furnished the reason for them.* They aim to

---

* Reprinted from 2 *United Nations Reports of International Arbitral Awards* 1012.

impose on the offending state reparation for the offense or the return to legality in avoidance of new offenses.

* * *

The first prerequisite, sine qua non, for the right to exercise reprisals is an occasion furnished by a previous act contrary to international law. This prerequisite—of which the German argument recognizes the necessity—is lacking, which would suffice to quash the defense invoked by the German government.

Even if the arbiters had found on the part of the Portuguese authorities an act contrary to international law, which could in principle give occasion for reprisals, the German argument would nevertheless fail for two other reasons, either of which is decisive.

Reprisals are only lawful when preceded by an unsatisfied demand. The use of force is only justified by its character of necessity. . . .

The necessity of a proportion between the reprisals and the offense would appear to be recognized in the German answer. Even if one admitted that international law does not require that the reprisal be approximately measured by the offense, one should certainly consider as excessive, and thus illegal, reprisals out of all proportion with the act which motivated them. Now in this case . . . there has been evident disproportion between the incident of Naulilaa and the six acts of reprisals which followed it.

The arbiters conclude that the German aggressions of October, November and December, 1914, on the Angola frontier, cannot be considered as lawful reprisals for the Naulilaa incident . . ., in view of the lack of sufficient occasion, of previous demand and of admissible proportion between the alleged offense and the reprisals taken. [Translation]

Self Defense—The Caroline Incident*

Note from Daniel Webster, United States Secretary of State, to Henry S. Fox, British Minister to Washington, April 24, 1841

[*During the Canadian insurrection of 1837, an American vessel, the* Caroline, *was used to transport men and materials across the Niagara River to the rebels. A body of Canadian militia, acting under orders of a British officer, crossed the river at night and, in an American port, seized the vessel, set fire to it, and sent it adrift over the falls. Several deaths resulted from the incident. During the diplomatic controversy that followed, Secretary of State Webster answered the British claim that the destruction of the* Caroline *was a lawful act of self-defense. His argument that self-defense is a strictly limited right and his statement of the conditions for its exercise have met with general approval.*]

. . . it will be for her Majesty's government to show upon what state of facts and what rules of national law the destruction of the "Caroline" is to be defended. It will be for that government to show a necessity of self-defence, instant, overwhelming, leaving no choice of means, and no moment for deliberation. It will be for it to show, also, that the local authorities of Canada, even supposing the necessity of the moment authorized them to enter the territories of the United States at all, did nothing unreasonable or excessive; since the act, justified by the necessity of self-defence, must be limited by that necessity, and kept clearly within it. It must be shown that admonition or remonstrance to the persons on board the "Caroline" was impracticable, or would have been unavailing. It must be shown that daylight could not be waited for; that there could be no attempt at discrimination between the innocent and

---

* Reprinted from *The Works of Daniel Webster* (Boston: Little, Brown, 1851), Vol. IV, p. 261.

the guilty; that it would not have been enough to seize and detain the vessel; but that there was a necessity, present and inevitable, for attacking her in the darkness of the night, while moored to the shore, and while unarmed men were asleep on board, killing some and wounding others, and then drawing her into the current above the cataract, setting her on fire, and careless to know whether there might not be in her the innocent with the guilty, or the living with the dead, committing her to a fate which fills the imagination with horror. A necessity for all this the government of the United States cannot believe to have existed.

* * *

Self-Defense Plea at Nürnberg*

Judgment of the Nürnberg Tribunal, September 30, 1946

* * *

On the 1st March, Hitler issued a directive regarding the Weser Exercise which contained the words:

"The development of the situation in Scandinavia requires the making of all preparations for the occupation of Denmark and Norway by a part of the German Armed Forces. This operation should prevent British encroachment on Scandinavia and the Baltic; further, it should guarantee our ore base in Sweden and give our Navy and Air Force a wider start line against Britain . . . The crossing of the Danish border and the landings in Norway must take place simultaneously . . . It is most important that the Scandinavian States as well as the Western opponents should be taken by surprise by our measures."

On the 24th March the naval operation orders for the Weser Exercise were issued, and on the 30th March the defendant

* Reprinted from *Nazi Conspiracy and Aggression— Opinion and Judgment* (1947).

Doenitz as Commander in Chief of U-boats issued his operational order for the occupation of Denmark and Norway. On the 9th April 1940, the German forces invaded Norway and Denmark.

. . . it is clear that as early as October 1939 the question of invading Norway was under consideration. The defense that has been made here is that Germany was compelled to attack Norway to forestall an Allied invasion, and her action was therefore preventive.

It must be remembered that preventive action in foreign territory is justified only in case of "an instant and overwhelming necessity for self-defense, leaving no choice of means and no moment of deliberation." (The Caroline Case, Moore's Digest of International Law, Vol. II, p. 412.) How widely the view was held in influential German circles that the Allies intended to occupy Norway cannot be determined with exactitude. Quisling asserted that the Allies would intervene in Norway with the tacit consent of the Norwegian Government. The German Legation at Oslo disagreed with this view, although the Naval Attaché at that Legation shared it.

* * *

. . . it is clear that when the plans for an attack on Norway were being made they were not made for the purpose of forestalling an imminent Allied landing, but, at the most, that they might prevent an Allied occupation at some future date.

When the final orders for the German invasion of Norway were given, the diary of the Naval Operations Staff for March 23, 1940, records:

"A mass encroachment by the English into Norwegian territorial waters . . . is not to be expected at the present time."

And Admiral Assmann's entry for March 26 says:

"British landing in Norway not considered serious."

* * *

It was further argued that Germany alone could decide, in accordance with the reservations made by many of the Signatory Powers at the time of the conclusion of the Kellogg-Briand Pact, whether preventive action was a necessity, and that in making her decision her judgment was conclusive. But whether action taken under the claim of self-defense was in fact aggressive or defensive must ultimately be subject to investigation and adjudication if international law is ever to be enforced.

* * *

In the light of all the available evidence it is impossible to accept the contention that the invasions of Denmark and Norway were defensive, and in the opinion of the Tribunal they were acts of aggressive war.

League of Nations Covenant, Articles 12, 13, 15, 16*

Article 12

1. The Members of the League agree that if there should arise between them any dispute likely to lead to a rupture they will submit the matter either to arbitration *or judicial settlement* or to enquiry by the Council, and they agree in no case to resort to war until three months after the award by the arbitrators *or the judicial decision* or the report by the Council.

2. In any case under this article the award of the arbitrators *or the judicial decision* shall be made within a reasonable time, and the report of the Council shall be made within six months after the submission of the dispute.

Article 13

1. The Members of the League agree that whenever any dispute shall arise be-

* The texts printed in italics indicate amendments adopted by the League.

tween them which they recognise to be suitable for submission to arbitration *or judicial settlement*, and which cannot be satisfactorily settled by diplomacy, they will submit the whole subject-matter to arbitration *or judicial settlement*.

2. Disputes as to the interpretation of a treaty, as to any question of international law, as to the existence of any fact which, if established, would constitute a breach of any international obligation, or as to the extent and nature of the reparation to be made for any such breach, are declared to be among those which are generally suitable for submission to arbitration *or judicial settlement*.

3. *For the consideration of any such dispute, the court to which the case is referred shall be the Permanent Court of International Justice, established in accordance with Article 14, or any tribunal agreed on by the parties to the dispute or stipulated in any Convention existing between them.*

4. The Members of the League agree that they will carry out in full good faith any award *or decision* that may be rendered, and that they will not resort to war against a Member of the League which complies therewith. In the event of any failure to carry out such an award *or decision*, the Council shall propose what steps should be taken to give effect thereto.

* * *

Article 15

1. If there should arise between Members of the League any dispute likely to lead to a rupture, which is not submitted to arbitration *or judicial settlement* in accordance with Article 13, the Members of the League agree that they will submit the matter to the Council. Any party to the dispute may effect such submission by giving notice of the existence of the dispute to the Secretary-General, who will make all necessary arrangements for a full investigation and consideration thereof.

2. For this purpose, the parties to the dispute will communicate to the Secretary-General, as promptly as possible, statements of their case with all the relevant facts and papers, and the Council may forthwith direct the publication thereof.

3. The Council shall endeavour to effect a settlement of the dispute, and if such efforts are successful, a statement shall be made public giving such facts and explanations regarding the dispute and the terms of settlement thereof as the Council may deem appropriate.

4. If the dispute is not thus settled, the Council either unanimously or by a majority vote shall make and publish a report containing a statement of the facts of the dispute and the recommendations which are deemed just and proper in regard thereto.

5. Any Member of the League represented on the Council may make public a statement of the facts of the dispute and of its conclusions regarding the same.

6. If a report by the Council is unanimously agreed to by the members thereof other than the Representatives of one or more of the parties to the dispute, the Members of the League agree that they will not go to war with any party to the dispute which complies with the recommendations of the report.

7. If the Council fails to reach a report which is unanimously agreed to by the members thereof, other than the Representatives of one or more of the parties to the dispute, the Members of the League reserve to themselves the right to take such action as they shall consider necessary for the maintenance of right and justice.

8. If the dispute between the parties is claimed by one of them, and is found by the Council, to arise out of a matter which by international law is solely within the domestic jurisdiction of that party, the Council shall so report, and shall make no recommendation as to its settlement.

9. The Council may in any case under this article refer the dispute to the Assembly. The dispute shall be so referred at the request of either party to the dispute provided that such request be made within fourteen days after the submission of the dispute to the Council.

10. In any case referred to the Assembly, all the provisions of this article and of Article 12 relating to the action and powers of the Council shall apply to the action and powers of the Assembly, provided that a report made by the Assembly, if concurred in by the Representatives of those Members of the League represented on the Council and of a majority of the other Members of the League, exclusive in each case of the Representatives of the parties to the dispute, shall have the same force as a report by the Council concurred in by all the members thereof other than the Representatives of one or more of the parties to the dispute.

Article 16

1. Should any Member of the League resort to war in disregard of its covenants under Articles 12, 13 or 15, it shall, *ipso facto*, be deemed to have committed an act of war against all other Members of the League, which hereby undertake immediately to subject it to the severance of all trade or financial relations, the prohibition of all intercourse between their nationals and the nationals of the Covenant-breaking State, and the prevention of all financial, commercial or personal intercourse between the nationals of the Covenant-breaking State and the nationals of any other State, whether a Member of the League or not.

2. It shall be the duty of the Council in such case to recommend to the several Governments concerned what effective military, naval or air force the Members of the League shall severally contribute to the armed forces to be used to protect the covenants of the League.

3. The Members of the League agree, further, that they will mutually support one another in the financial and economic

measures which are taken under this article, in order to minimise the loss and inconvenience resulting from the above measures, and that they will mutually support one another in resisting any special measures aimed at one of their number by the Covenant-breaking State, and that they will take the necessary steps to afford passage through their territory to the forces of any of the Members of the League which are co-operating to protect the covenants of the League.

4. Any Member of the League which has violated any covenant of the League may be declared to be no longer a Member of the League by a vote of the Council concurred in by the Representatives of all the other Members of the League represented thereon.

Treaty for the Renunciation of War, 1928 (Kellogg-Briand Pact) *

Persuaded that the time has come when a frank renunciation of war as an instrument of national policy should be made to the end that the peaceful and friendly relations now existing between their peoples may be perpetuated; . . .

Article I

The High Contracting Parties solemnly declare in the names of their respective peoples that they condemn recourse to war for the solution of international controversies, and renounce it as an instrument of national policy in their relations with one another.

Article II

The High Contracting Parties agree that the settlement or solution of all disputes or conflicts of whatever nature or of whatever origin they may be, which may arise among

* Reprinted from *United States Treaty Series* No. 796.

them, shall never be sought except by pacific means. . . .

United Nations Charter, Article 2, Paragraph 3 and 4, Chapters VI, VII, and VIII

Art. 2. . . . 3. All Members shall settle their international disputes by peaceful means in such a manner that international peace and security, and justice, are not endangered.

4. All Members shall refrain in their international relations from the threat or use of force against the territorial integrity or political independence of any state, or in any other manner inconsistent with the Purposes of the United Nations.

* * *

Chapter VI: Pacific Settlement of Disputes

Art. 33. 1. The parties to any dispute, the continuance of which is likely to endanger the maintenance of international peace and security, shall, first of all, seek a solution by negotiation, enquiry, mediation, conciliation, arbitration, judicial settlement, resort to regional agencies or arrangements, or other peaceful means of their own choice.

2. The Security Council shall, when it deems necessary, call upon the parties to settle their dispute by such means.

Art. 34. The Security Council may investigate any dispute, or any situation which might lead to international friction or give rise to a dispute, in order to determine whether the continuance of the dispute or situation is likely to endanger the maintenance of international peace and security.

Art. 35. 1. Any Member of the United Nations may bring any dispute, or any situation of the nature referred to in Article 34, to the attention of the Security Council or of the General Assembly.

2. A state which is not a Member of the United Nations may bring to the attention of the Security Council or of the General Assembly any dispute to which it is a party if it accepts in advance, for the purposes of the dispute, the obligations of pacific settlement provided in the present Charter. . . .

Art. 36. 1. The Security Council may, at any stage of a dispute of the nature referred to in Article 33 or of a situation of like nature, recommend appropriate procedures or methods of adjustment.

2. The Security Council should take into consideration any procedures for the settlement of the dispute which have already been adopted by the parties.

3. In making recommendations under this Article the Security Council should also take into consideration that legal disputes should as a general rule be referred by the parties to the International Court of Justice in accordance with the provisions of the Statute of the Court.

Art. 37. 1. Should the parties to a dispute of the nature referred to in Article 33 fail to settle it by the means indicated in that Article, they shall refer it to the Security Council.

2. If the Security Council deems that the continuance of the dispute is in fact likely to endanger the maintenance of international peace and security, it shall decide whether to take action under Article 36 or to recommend such terms of settlement as it may consider appropriate.

Art. 38. Without prejudice to the provisions of Articles 33 to 37, the Security Council may, if all the parties to any dispute so request, make recommendations to the parties with a view to a pacific settlement of the dispute.

Chapter VII: Action with Respect to Threats to the Peace, Breaches of the Peace, and Acts of Aggression

Art. 39. The Security Council shall determine the existence of any threat to the peace,

breach of the peace, or act of aggression and shall make recommendations, or decide what measures shall be taken in accordance with Articles 41 and 42, to maintain or restore international peace and security.

Art. 40. In order to prevent an aggravation of the situation, the Security Council may, before making the recommendations or deciding upon the measures provided for in Article 39, call upon the parties concerned to comply with such provisional measures as it deems necessary or desirable. Such provisional measures shall be without prejudice to the rights, claims, or position of the parties concerned. The Security Council shall duly take account of failure to comply with such provisional measures.

Art. 41. The Security Council may decide what measures not involving the use of armed force are to be employed to give effect to its decisions, and it may call upon the Members of the United Nations to apply such measures. These may include complete or partial interruption of economic relations and of rail, sea, air, postal, telegraphic, radio, and other means of communication, and the severance of diplomatic relations.

Art. 42. Should the Security Council consider that measures provided for in Article 41 would be inadequate or have proved to be inadequate, it may take such action by air, sea, or land forces as may be necessary to maintain or restore international peace and security. Such action may include demonstrations, blockade, and other operations by air, sea, or land forces of Members of the United Nations.

Art. 43. 1. All Members of the United Nations, in order to contribute to the maintenance of international peace and security, undertake to make available to the Security Council, on its call and in accordance with a special agreement or agreements, armed forces, assistance, and facilities, including rights of passage, necessary for the purpose of maintaining international peace and security.

2. Such agreement or agreements shall

govern the numbers and types of forces, their degree of readiness and general location, and the nature of the facilities and assistance to be provided.

* * *

Art. 51. Nothing in the present Charter shall impair the inherent right of individual or collective self-defense if an armed attack occurs against a Member of the United Nations, until the Security Council has taken the measures necessary to maintain international peace and security. Measures taken by Members in the exercise of this right of self-defense shall be immediately reported to the Security Council and shall not in any way affect the authority and responsibility of the Security Council under the present Charter to take at any time such action as it deems necessary in order to maintain or restore international peace and security.

Chapter VIII: Regional Arrangements

Art. 52. 1. Nothing in the present Charter precludes the existence of regional arrangements or agencies for dealing with such matters relating to the maintenance of international peace and security as are appropriate for regional action, provided that such arrangements or agencies and their activities are consistent with the Purposes and Principles of the United Nations.

2. The Members of the United Nations entering into such arrangements or constituting such agencies shall make every effort to achieve pacific settlement of local disputes through such regional arrangements or by such regional agencies before referring them to the Security Council.

3. The Security Council shall encourage the development of pacific settlement of local disputes through such regional arrangements or by such regional agencies either on the initiative of the states con-

cerned or by reference from the Security Council.

4. This Article in no way impairs the application of Articles 34 and 35.

Art. 53. The Security Council shall, where appropriate, utilize such regional arrangements or agencies for enforcement action under its authority. But no enforcement action shall be taken under regional arrangements or by regional agencies without the authorization of the Security Council, with the exception of measures against any enemy state, as defined in paragraph 2 of this Article, provided for pursuant to Article 107 or in regional arrangements directed against renewal of aggressive policy on the part of any such state, until such time as the Organization may, on request of the Governments concerned, be charged with the responsibility for preventing further aggression by such a state.

2. The term "enemy state" as used in paragraph 1 of this Article applies to any state which during the Second World War has been an enemy of any signatory of the present Charter.

Art. 54. The Security Council shall at all times be kept fully informed of activities undertaken or in contemplation under regional arrangements or by regional agencies for the maintenance of international peace and security.

"On Article 51 of the United Nations Charter"*

J. L. Brierly

The precise scope of the right of self-defence under the law of the Charter is the subject of controversy. Some writers contend that the combined effect of Article 2 (4) and Article 51 is to cut down the right of self-defence to cases falling

* Reprinted from J. L. Brierly, *The Law of Nations*, 6th ed. by Sir Humphrey Waldock (New York and Oxford: Oxford University Press, 1963), pp. 416–421, by permission of Clarendon Press, Oxford.

precisely within the words in Article 51 'if an armed attack occurs'; these writers, in short, take the view that today Article 51 is the exclusive source of the authority to have recourse to self-defence, so that any 'threat or use of force' not falling precisely within its terms—i.e. not amounting to self-defence with reference to an armed attack—is automatically a violation of Article 2 (4). The other view is that the opening words 'nothing in the present Charter shall impair the *inherent* right of individual or collective self-defence' show a clear intention not to impair the 'inherent', i.e. the existing, natural right of states to use force in self-defence; in other words, they show that the right of self-defence today does not have its source in the Charter but is an independent right rooted in general international law, and that the purpose of Article 51 was simply to remove possible doubts as to the impact of the Security Council's powers upon the right of states individually or collectively to have recourse to force in self-defence. This view derives some support from the *travaux préparatoires* of the Charter. Committee I at San Francisco, which dealt with Article 2 (4), said[1] outright that 'the use of arms in legitimate self-defence remains admitted and unimpaired'. Then the records show that Article 51 was introduced into the Charter in Committee III/4 primarily for the purpose of harmonizing regional organizations for defence with the powers and responsibilities given to the Security Council for maintaining peace; and they do not indicate any conscious intention upon the part of Committee III/4, in including the words 'if an armed attack occurs', to put outside the law forcible self-defence against unlawful acts of force not amounting to an armed attack. . . . the words have to be read in their context, and Article 51 has to be interpreted as a whole; and when this is done, the appropriateness of applying the principle of effectiveness to the words in question so as to produce a maximum

restriction on the right of self-defence becomes very doubtful. The question at issue is whether the words were intended to lay down an express restriction on that right or are merely descriptive of a particular category of self-defence with respect to which it was desired to underline that the right of individual, and more especially of collective, self-defence had not been taken away in the process of conferring power on the Security Council to take 'preventive' and 'enforcement' measures for the maintenance of peace. When the Article begins with the statement that nothing in the treaty shall *impair* an *inherent* ('imprescriptible' in the Russian, 'natural' in the French, texts) right, it is not easy to presume an intention in the following words drastically to impair that right; and there are too many uncertainties and contradictions in Article 51 to make it possible to solve the problem simply by giving maximum effect to the words 'if an armed attack occurs'.

First, the French text—*dans un cas où un Membre des Nations Unies est l'objet d'une agression armée*—is not expressed in the form of a condition and suggests that the English 'if' was used to express an hypothesis rather than a condition—which is, of course, one of the natural uses of 'if'. Secondly, if 'effective interpretation' is to be applied to the words 'if an armed attack occurs', so as to produce a restriction on the inherent right, is the same thing to be done to the very next words in the Article 'against a Member of the United Nations'? If these words are given their full effect, the right of collective self-defence cannot be invoked to justify recourse to armed force in defence of a non-member state which is the victim of a flagrant aggression; but we know that this interpretation of the words was completely rejected by the United Nations with respect to the invasion of South Korea. Another difficulty lies in the word 'occurs'. Those who treat the words 'if an armed attack occurs' as restricting the right of self-defence also insist that it limits the right to cases where the 'armed attack' has actually begun, thus excluding the legitimacy of any recourse to force in the face of even the most imminent invasion or attack. Here again, the French text is a little different and more equivocal: *est l'objet d'une agression armée.* But in any event, if anticipatory recourse to force in face of an actually impending attack is never to be permitted, the limitation of self-defence to action 'until the Security Council has taken the measures necessary to *maintain* international peace' is not very aptly worded, for if the peace must first have been broken, it can only be 'restored', not 'maintained'; nor is the unsuitability of the word 'maintain' made less by the fact that in the second sentence of Article 51 we find the Council expressly empowered to intervene to *maintain or restore* peace. Further queries can be raised, for example, as to what exactly is covered by the words 'armed attack', and as to whether measures of pure self-defence can ever constitute 'a use or threat of force against the territorial integrity or political independence' of a state or an act 'inconsistent with the purposes of the United Nations' which are the acts prohibited by Article 2 (4).

Accordingly, the drafting of the Charter leaves the scope of the right to resort to force in self-defence in some uncertainty— an uncertainty which is not removed by the inconclusive nature of the state practice and United Nations practice up to date. What can be said with confidence is that under the Charter, as under general international law, a minimum condition of resort to armed force in self-defence is 'an instant and overwhelming necessity for self-defence, leaving no choice of means, and no moment for deliberation', the criterion applied by the Nuremberg Tribunal and originally formulated by the United States Secretary of State in the *Caroline* incident. What is also clear—and was rightly emphasized in the *Caroline*—is

that acts of self-defence must be strictly limited to the needs of defence and may not be converted into reprisals or punitive sanctions. . . .

Note

1. *United Nations Conference on International Organisation* (U.N.C.I.O.), vol. 6, p. 334.

The Corfu Channel Case (United Kingdom-Albania)*

International Court of Justice, 1949

[*On October 22, 1946, two British warships were damaged by mines while passing through the Straits of Corfu, a channel situated within Albania's territorial waters. Three weeks later, on November 13, British minesweepers swept the channel and cut the cables of several moored mines. Albania protested against the violation of her sovereignty and Britain claimed compensation for the damage to her ships while exercising the right of innocent passage through an international strait. The International Court of Justice upheld the British right to innocent passage and held Albania responsible for the damages inflicted. Concerning the minesweeping operation, the court said:*]

In addition to the passage of the United Kingdom warships on October 22nd, 1946, the second question in the Special Agreement relates to the acts of the Royal Navy in Albanian waters on November 12th and 13th, 1946. This is the minesweeping operation called "Operation Retail" by the Parties during the proceedings. This name will be used in the present Judgment.

After the explosions of October 22nd,

---

* Reprinted from *International Court of Justice Reports* 4 (1949).

the United Kingdom Government sent a note to the Albanian Government, in which it announced its intention to sweep the Corfu Channel shortly. The Albanian reply, which was received in London on October 31st, stated that the Albanian Government would not give its consent to this unless the operation in question took place outside Albanian territorial waters. Meanwhile, at the United Kingdom Government's request, the International Central Mine Clearance Board decided, in a resolution of November 1st, 1946, that there should be a further sweep of the Channel, subject to Albania's consent. The United Kingdom Government having informed the Albanian Government, in a communication of November 10th, that the proposed sweep would take place on November 12th, the Albanian Government replied on the 11th, protesting against this "unilateral decision of His Majesty's Government". It said it did not consider it inconvenient that the British fleet should undertake the sweeping of the channel of navigation, but added that, before sweeping was carried out, it considered it indispensable to decide what area of the sea should be deemed to constitute this channel, and proposed the establishment of a Mixed Commission for the purpose. It ended by saying that any sweeping undertaken without the consent of the Albanian Government outside the channel thus constituted, i.e., inside Albanian territorial waters where foreign warships have no reason to sail, could only be considered as a deliberate violation of Albanian territory and sovereignty.

After this exchange of notes, "Operation Retail" took place on November 12th and 13th. Commander Mestre, of the French Navy, was asked to attend as observer, and was present at the sweep on November 13th. The operation was carried out under the protection of an important covering force composed of an aircraft carrier, cruisers and other war vessels. This covering force remained throughout the operation at a certain distance to the west of the Channel, except for the frigate *St. Bride's Bay*, which was stationed in the Channel south-east of Cape Kiephali. The sweep began in the morning of November 13th, at about 9 o'clock, and ended in the afternoon near nightfall. The area swept was in Albanian territorial waters, and within the limits of the channel previously swept.

The United Kingdom Government does not dispute that "Operation Retail" was carried out against the clearly expressed wish of the Albanian Government. It recognizes that the operation had not the consent of the international mine clearance organizations, that it could not be justified as the exercise of a right of innocent passage, and lastly that, in principle, international law does not allow a State to assemble a large number of warships in the territorial waters of another State and to carry out minesweeping in those waters. The United Kingdom Government states that the operation was one of extreme urgency, and that it considered itself entitled to carry it out without anybody's consent.

The United Kingdom Government put forward two reasons in justification. First, the Agreement of November 22nd, 1945, signed by the Governments of the United Kingdom, France, the Soviet Union and the United States of America, authorizing regional mine clearance organizations, such as the Mediterranean Zone Board, to divide the sectors in their respective zones amongst the States concerned for sweeping. Relying on the circumstance that the Corfu Channel was in the sector allotted to Greece by the Mediterranean Zone Board on November 5th, i.e., before the signing of the above-mentioned Agreement, the United Kingdom Government put forward a permission given by the Hellenic Government to resweep the navigable channel.

The Court does not consider this argument convincing.

It must be noted that, as the United

Kingdom Government admits, the need for resweeping the Channel was not under consideration in November 1945; for previous sweeps in 1944 and 1945 were considered as having effected complete safety. As a consequence, the allocation of the sector in question to Greece, and, therefore, the permission of the Hellenic Government which is relied on, were both of them merely nominal. It is also to be remarked that Albania was not consulted regarding the allocation to Greece of the sector in question, despite the fact that the Channel passed through Albanian territorial waters.

But, in fact, the explosions of October 22nd, 1946, in a channel declared safe for navigation, and one which the United Kingdom Government, more than any other government, had reason to consider safe, raised quite a different problem from that of a routine sweep carried out under the orders of the mine clearance organizations. These explosions were suspicious; they raised a question of responsibility.

Accordingly, this was the ground on which the United Kingdom Government chose to establish its main line of defence. According to that Government, the *corpora delicti* must be secured as quickly as possible, for fear they should be taken away, without leaving traces, by the authors of the minelaying or by the Albanian authorities. This justification took two distinct forms in the United Kingdom Government's arguments. It was presented first as a new and special application of the theory of intervention, by means of which the State intervening would secure possession of evidence in the territory of another State, in order to submit it to an international tribunal and thus facilitate its task.

The Court cannot accept such a line of defence. The Court can only regard the alleged right of intervention as the manifestation of a policy of force, such as has, in the past, given rise to most serious abuses and such as cannot, whatever be the present defects in international organization, find a place in international law. Intervention is perhaps still less admissible in the particular form it would take here; for, from the nature of things, it would be reserved for the most powerful States, and might easily lead to perverting the administration of international justice itself.

The United Kingdom Agent, in his speech in reply, has further classified "Operation Retail" among methods of self-protection or self-help. The Court cannot accept this defence either. Between independent States, respect for territorial sovereignty is an essential foundation of international relations. The Court recognizes that the Albanian Government's complete failure to carry out its duties after the explosions, and the dilatory nature of its diplomatic notes, are extenuating circumstances for the action of the United Kingdom Government. But to ensure respect for international law, of which it is the organ, the Court must declare that the action of the British Navy constituted a violation of Albanian sovereignty.

This declaration is in accordance with the request made by Albania through her Counsel, and is in itself appropriate satisfaction.

The method of carrying out "Operation Retail" has also been criticized by the Albanian Government, the main ground of complaint being that the United Kingdom, on that occasion, made use of an unnecessarily large display of force, out of proportion to the requirements of the sweep. The Court thinks that this criticism is not justified. It does not consider that the action of the British Navy was a demonstration of force for the purpose of exercising political pressure on Albania. The responsible naval commander, who kept his ships at a distance from the coast, cannot be reproached for having employed an important covering force in a region where twice within a few months his ships had been the object of serious outrages.

FOR THESE REASONS,
THE COURT,
. . . on the second question put by the Special Agreement of March 25th, 1948,
. . . unanimously,

Gives judgment that by reason of the acts of the British Navy in Albanian waters in the course of the Operation of November 12th and 13th, 1946, the United Kingdom violated the sovereignty of the People's Republic of Albania, and that this declaration by the Court constitutes in itself appropriate satisfaction.

II. Application of the Norms in Political Crises

A. The Conquest of Goa, 1961

The Question of Goa in the United Nations Security Council*

In his letter of December 18, 1961, to the President of the Security Council, the Permanent Representative of Portugal informed the President that the "Indian Government has followed up its build-up of armed forces and provocations . . . [some of which had been mentioned in the Portuguese Representative's letters to the President of December 8, 11, and 16, 1961] with a full-scale unprovoked armed attack on the territories of Goa, Damao and Diu, comprising the Portuguese State of India", and requested the President "to convene the Security Council *immediately* to put a stop to the condemnable act of aggression of the Indian Union, ordering an immediate cease-fire and the withdrawal forthwith from the Portuguese territories of Goa, Danão and Diu of the all invading forces of the Indian Union". In the debate that followed the Security Council's adoption of this agenda item and the seating of both the Portuguese and Indian Representatives by invitation for participation without voting rights, the Indian

* Reprinted from 2 Whiteman, *Digest of International Law* 1140 (Washington, D.C.: U.S. Government Printing Office, 1963).

Representative, Mr. Jha, presented his Government's position in part as follows:

"I have already said that this is a colonial question, in the sense that part of our country is illegally occupied—occupied by right of conquest by the Portuguese. The fact that they have occupied it for 450 years is of no consequence because, during nearly 425 or 430 years of that period we really had no chance to do anything because we were under colonial domination ourselves. But during the last 14 years, from the very day when we became independent, we have not ceased to demand the return of the peoples under illegal domination to their own countrymen, to share their independence, their march forward to their destiny. I would like to put this matter very clearly before the Council: that Portugal has no sovereign right over this territory. There is no legal frontier—there can be no legal frontier—between India and Goa. And since the whole occupation is illegal as an issue—it started in an illegal manner, it continues to be illegal today and it is even more illegal in the light of resolution 1514—there can be no question of aggression against your own frontier: there can be no question of aggression against your own people, whom you want to bring into freedom.[1]

"That is the situation that we have to face. If any narrowminded, legalistic considerations —considerations arising from international law as written by European law writers—should arise, these writers were, after all, brought up in the atmosphere of colonialism. I pay all respect due to Grotius, who is supposed to be the father of international law, and we accept many tenets of international law. They are certainly regulating international life today. But the tenet which says, and which is quoted in support of colonial Powers having sovereign rights over territories which they won by conquest in Asia and Africa is no longer acceptable. It is the European concept and it must die. It is time, in the twentieth century, that it died."

Speaking again at a later session of the Security Council on the same day, the Representative of India stated—

". . . I have said that we accept international law: we are governed by the tenets of international law, but that we cannot in the twentieth century accept that part of international law which was laid down by European jurists— though great men, great jurists whose contribution to law has been really remarkable— specifying that colonies in Asia and Africa which were acquired by conquest conferred sovereignty on the colonial Power. That is no longer acceptable. International law is not a static institution. It is developing constantly. International law would be static, it would be dead driftwood, if it did not respond to the public opinion of the world. And it is responding every day, whether we like it or not. Resolution 1514, which has been referred to here and elsewhere very frequently, is the embodiment of that great leap forward in the public opinion of the world on these matters. There can be no getting away from that. Just as the process of decolonization is irreversible and irresistible, the embodiment of the principles in resolution 1514, which has been accepted by virtually every member around this table, is irresistible. One cannot go behind that now. That is the new dictum of international law. That is how international law is made, because it is not a dead institution but something that is developing all the time. . . ."

The Representative of Portugal, Mr. Garin, in response to statements of the Indian Representative, stated in part as follows:

". . . Indian attempts to annex the territories of the other sovereignties in the neighbourhood cannot find any legal justification. Such attempts could be legitimized only by the other sovereignties concerned, if they agreed to a formal transfer of their territories, but only if the transfer could be voluntary—never compulsory, much less by means of an armed aggression. It matters little whether those other sovereignties are held by whites or coloured people or, as in the case of the Portuguese State of India, by both whites and coloured people together. It likewise matters little if the territories belonging to those other sovereignties are large or small in size. The principle of sovereignty ought to be respected. The Indian Union has not done this in respect of the Portuguese State of India and is, therefore, guilty of a base breach of international law.

"It has been said here that international law as it is was made by Europeans. I submit that, so long as it is not replaced, it must be accepted and followed by civilized nations, and I am not aware that international law relating to sovereignty has been changed so far.

"The Indian Union may not argue that it has any rights over the territories of neighbouring pre-existing sovereignties. If the principle of sovereignty is not respected, then there is no knowing what conflicts may arise in every part of the world, shen [sic] a nation decides to seize the territory of another nation under some pretext or another. In the present case all kinds of pretexts have been cited. None of those pretexts justify the annexation of the Portuguese territories in India by the Indian Union. . . ."

The United States Ambassador to the United Nations, Mr. Stevenson, expressed the views of the United States Government, in part as follows:

"Let us be perfectly clear what is at stake here; it is the question of the use of armed force by one State against another and against its will, an act clearly forbidden by the Charter. We have opposed such action in the past by our closest friends as well as by others. We opposed it in Korea in 1950, in Suez and in Hungary in 1956 and in the Congo in 1960. And we do so again in Goa in 1961.

"The facts in this case are, unfortunately, all too clear. These territories have been under Portuguese dominion for over four centuries. They have been invaded by Indian armed forces.

The Government of India regards these territories as having the same status as the territories of the United Kingdom and France on the sub-continent from which those countries have voluntarily withdrawn. The Government of India has insisted that Portugal likewise withdraw. Portugal has refused, maintaining that it has a legal and moral right to these territories.

"We have repeatedly urged both of the parties to this dispute to seek by peaceful processes the resolution of a problem which has its roots in the colonial past. I do not at this time propose to concern myself with the merits of the dispute. We are not meeting here today to decide on the merits of this case; we are meeting to decide what attitude should be taken in this body when one of the Members of the United Nations casts aside the principles of the Charter and seeks to resolve a dispute by force.

"But what is at stake today is not colonialism; it is a bold violation of one of the most basic principles in the United Nations Charter, stated in these words from Article 2, paragraph 4:

"'All Members shall refrain in their international relations from the threat or use of force against the territorial integrity or political independence of any State, or in any other manner inconsistent with the Purposes of the United Nations.'

"We realize fully the depths of the differences between India and Portugal concerning the future of Goa. We realize that India maintains that Goa by right should belong to India. Doubtless India would hold, therefore, that its action is aimed at a just end. But, if our Charter means anything, it means that States are obligated to renounce the use of force, are obligated to seek a solution of their differences by peaceful means, are obligated to utilize the procedures of the United Nations when other peaceful means have failed."

Ambassador Stevenson stated later on the same day at a later session of the Security Council—

"It is clear as crystal on the basis of the facts and the complaint that the issue before the Security Council is not the right or the wrong of Portugal's colonial policy; it is the right or the wrong of one nation seeking to change an existing political and legal situation by the use

of armed force. That is expressly forbidden in the Charter. . . ."

At the end of the debate in the Security Council on December 18, 1961, two draft resolutions were submitted, both failing of adoption. The first draft resolution, submitted by Ceylon, Liberia, and the United Arab Republic, recalling General Assembly Resolutions 1514 (XV) and 1542 (XV), would have rejected the Portuguese complaint of aggression against India and called upon Portugal to terminate hostile action and to cooperate with India in the liquidation of her colonial possessions in India. This resolution (S/5032) was defeated by a vote of 4 in favor and 7 against.

The second draft resolution, introduced by France, Turkey, the United Kingdom, and the United States, recalling that in article 2 of the Charter all members are obligated to settle their disputes by peaceful means and to refrain from the threat or use of force in a manner inconsistent with the purposes of the United Nations, would have called for an immediate cessation of hostilities, called upon the Government of India to withdraw its forces immediately to positions prevailing before December 17, 1961, urged the parties to work out a permanent solution of their differences by peaceful means in accordance with the principles embodied in the Charter, and requested the Secretary-General to provide such assistance as might be appropriate. This draft resolution (S/5033) received 7 votes in favor and 4 against, but was vetoed by the negative vote of the Soviet Union.

Note

1. By Resolution 1514 (XV) of December 14, 1960, entitled "Declaration on the Granting of Independence to Colonial Countries and

Peoples" to which the Indian Representative referred, the General Assembly declared that:

"1. The subjection of peoples to alien subjugation, domination and exploitation constitutes a denial of fundamental human rights, is contrary to the Charter of the United Nations and is an impediment to the promotion of world peace and co-operation;

"2. All peoples have the right to self-determination; by virtue of that right they freely determine their political status and freely pursue their economic, social and cultural development;

"3. Inadequacy of political, economic, social or educational preparedness should never serve as a pretext for delaying independence;

"4. All armed action or repressive measures of all kinds directed against dependent peoples shall cease in order to enable them to exercise peacefully and freely their right to complete independence, and the integrity of their national territory shall be respected;

"5. Immediate steps shall be taken, in Trust and Non-Self-Governing Territories or all other territories which have not yet attained independence, to transfer all powers to the peoples of those territories, without any conditions or reservations, in accordance with their freely expressed will and desire, without any distinction as to race, creed or colour, in order to enable them to enjoy complete independence and freedom;

"6. Any attempt aimed at the partial or total disruption of the national unity and the territorial integrity of a country is incompatible with the Purposes and Principles of the Charter of the United Nations;

"7. All States shall observe faithfully and strictly the provisions of the Charter of the United Nations, the Universal Declaration of Human Rights and the present Declaration on the basis of equality, non-interference in the internal affairs of all States, and respect for the sovereign rights of all peoples and their territorial integrity." U.N. Gen. Ass. Off. Rec. 15th Sess., Agenda item 87, Annexes, p. 8.

B. Resort to Force and the Cuban Missile Crisis

Inter-American Treaty of Reciprocal Assistance, 1947 (Rio Pact)*

Article 1. The High Contracting Parties formally condemn war and undertake in their international relations not to resort to the threat or the use of force in any manner inconsistent with the provisions of the Charter of the United Nations or of this Treaty.

Article 2. As a consequence of the principle set forth in the preceding Article, the High Contracting Parties undertake to submit every controversy which may arise between them to methods of peaceful settlement and to endeavor to settle any such controversy among themselves by means of the procedures in force in the Inter-American System before referring it to the General Assembly or the Security Council of the United Nations.

Article 3. 1. The High Contracting Parties agree that an armed attack by any State against an American State shall be considered as an attack against all the American States and, consequently, each one of the said Contracting Parties undertakes to assist in meeting the attack in the exercise of the inherent right of individual or collective self-defence recognized by Article 51 of the Charter of the United Nations.

* * *

Article 5. The High Contracting Parties shall immediately send to the Security Council of the United Nations, in conformity with Articles 51 and 54 of the Charter of the United Nations, complete information concerning the activities undertaken or in contemplation in the exercise

*Reprinted from 17 *United States Department of State Bulletin* 565 (1947).

of the right of self-defense or for the purpose of maintaining inter-American peace and security.

Article 6. If the inviolability or the integrity of the territory or the sovereignty or political independence of any American State should be affected by an aggression which is not an armed attack or by an extra-continental or intra-continental conflict, or by any other fact or situation that might endanger the peace of America, the Organ of Consultation shall meet immediately in order to agree on the measures which must be taken in case of aggression to assist the victim of the aggression or, in any case, the measures which should be taken for the common defense and for the maintenance of the peace and security of the Continent.

Article 7. In the case of a conflict between two or more American States, without prejudice to the right of self-defense in conformity with Article 51 of the Charter of the United Nations, the High Contracting Parties, meeting in consultation shall call upon the contending States to suspend hostilities and restore matters to the *status quo ante bellum*, and shall take in addition all other necessary measures to reestablish or maintain inter-American peace and security and for the solution of the conflict by peaceful means. The rejection of the pacifying action will be considered in the determination of the aggressor and in the application of the measures which the consultative meeting may agree upon.

Article 8. For the purposes of this Treaty, the measures on which the Organ of Consultation may agree will comprise one or more of the following: recall of chiefs of diplomatic missions; breaking of diplomatic relations; breaking of consular relations; partial or complete interruption of economic relations or of rail, sea, air, postal, telegraphic, telephonic, and radiotelephonic or radiotelegraphic communications; and use of armed force.

* * *

Article 20. Decisions which require the application of the measures specified in Article 8 shall be binding upon all the Signatory States which have ratified this Treaty with the sole exception that no State shall be required to use armed force without its consent.

* * *

Resolution Adopted by the Organization of American States, October 23, 1962 *

. . . The Eighth Meeting of Consultation of the Ministers of Foreign Affairs of the American Republics in Punta del Este in January, 1962, agreed in Resolution II "To urge the member states to take those steps that they may consider appropriate for their individual and collective self-defense, and to cooperate, as may be necessary or desirable, to strengthen their capacity to counteract threats or acts of aggression, subversion, or other dangers to peace and security resulting from the continued intervention in this hemisphere of Sino-Soviet powers, in accordance with the obligations established in treaties and agreements such as the Charter of the Organization of American States and the Inter-American Treaty of Reciprocal Assistance";

The Ministers of Foreign Affairs of the American Republics meeting informally in Washington, October 2 and 3, 1962, reasserted "the firm intention of the Governments represented and of the peoples of the American Republics to conduct themselves in accordance with the principles of the regional system, staunchly sustaining and consolidating the principles of the Charter of the Organization of

* Reprinted from 74 *United States Department of State Bulletin* 722 (1962). The Resolution was adopted by the Council on Oct. 23 by a vote of 19 to 0, with 1 abstention Uruguay abstained on Oct. 23 because its delegate had not received instructions from his Government; on Oct. 24 Uruguay cast an affirmative vote, making approval of the resolution unanimous.

American States, and affirmed the will to strengthen the security of the Hemisphere against all aggression from within or outside the Hemisphere and against all developments or situations capable of threatening the peace and security of the Hemisphere through the application of the Inter-American Treaty of Reciprocal Assistance of Rio de Janeiro. It was the view of the Ministers that the existing organizations and bodies of the inter-American system should intensify the carrying out of their respective duties with special and urgent attention to the situation created by the communist regime in Cuba and that they should stand in readiness to consider the matter promptly if the situation requires measures beyond those already authorized."

The same meeting "recalled that the Soviet Union's intervention in Cuba threatens the unity of the Americas and its democratic institutions, and that this intervention has special characteristics which, pursuant to paragraph 3 of Resolution II of the Eighth Meeting of Consultation of Ministers of Foreign Affairs, call for the adoption of special measures, both individual and collective";

Incontrovertible evidence has appeared that the Government of Cuba, despite repeated warnings, has secretly endangered the peace of the Continent by permitting the Sino-Soviet powers to have intermediate and middle-range missiles on its territory capable of carrying nuclear warheads;

THE COUNCIL OF THE ORGANIZATION OF AMERICAN STATES, MEETING AS THE PROVISIONAL ORGAN OF CONSULTATION, RESOLVES:

1. To call for the immediate dismantling and withdrawal from Cuba of all missiles and other weapons with any offensive capability;

2. To recommend that the member states, in accordance with Articles 6 and 8 of the Inter-American Treaty of Reciprocal Assistance, take all measures, individually and collectively, including the use of armed force, which they may deem necessary to ensure that the Government of Cuba cannot continue to receive from the Sino-Soviet powers military material and related supplies which may threaten the peace and security of the Continent and to prevent the missiles in Cuba with offensive capability from ever becoming an active threat to the peace and security of the Continent;

3. To inform the Security Council of the United Nations of this resolution in accordance with Article 54 of the Charter of the United Nations and to express the hope that the Security Council will, in accordance with the draft resolution introduced by the United States, dispatch United Nations observers to Cuba at the earliest moment;

4. To continue to serve provisionally as Organ of Consultation and to request the Member States to keep the Organ of Consultation duly informed of measures taken by them in accordance with paragraph two of this resolution.

The Cuban Quarantine*

Quincy Wright

* * *

The Soviet Threat

It is difficult to find that the Soviet Union violated any obligation of international law in shipping missiles to, and installing them in, Cuba, at the request of the Castro government. Under general international law, states are free to engage in trade in any articles whatever in time of peace. Treaties have been made restricting trade in arms, but no such treaty had been ratified by the Soviet Union, and the United States has refused to ratify such

* Reprinted from Quincy Wright, "The Cuban Quarantine," 57 *American Journal of International Law* 546 (1963) by permission of the American Society of International Law.

treaties on the ground, among others, that they might prevent countries without arms manufacture from providing for their defense.

It has been argued that the installation of "offensive missiles" was a "threat of force" or a "threat to peace," violating the Soviet obligations under Articles 2 (4) and 39 of the United Nations Charter. "Displays of force" by naval vessels off the coast or by the mobilization of land forces on a frontier have been utilized by many states, including the United States, as a means to induce a state to modify its policy or as a preparation to defend itself from anticipated attack. Mobilizations by European Powers for such purposes had much to do with the initiation of the first World War. Dangerous as they are, customary international law did not consider such "displays of force" illegal so long as they remained on the high seas or on the state's own territory, unless there was evidence of an immediate intention to use them for attack. Such displays, however, constitute "threats of force" and consequently would appear forbidden by the U.N. Charter unless justifiable as measures of individual or collective self-defense. Khrushchev and Castro claimed that the missiles were shipped to, and installed in, Cuba only for that purpose. Khrushchev had promised that he would assist in the defense of Cuba and it can hardly be doubted, in view of the Bay of Pigs affair, the President's somewhat ambiguous statement after that incident, the economic measures taken by the United States to embarrass the Castro regime, and the public demands for invasion of Cuba by many American politicians, particularly during the election campaign of 1962, that Castro was justified in believing he needed assistance in defense. Furthermore, he may well have considered that the deterrent influence of medium-range missiles, threatening American cities, was the only feasible defense against the overwhelming naval, military, air, and

missile power which the United States was capable of launching against Cuba. Khrushchev and Castro could defend this opinion by citing the American establishment of medium-range missile bases in Turkey and other countries near the Soviet Union to deter the latter from invading them.

In principle, a sovereign state is free to take, within its territory, measures which it deems necessary for its defense, unless some obligation of international law or treaty forbids, and other states are free to assist it in such defense. This is well recognized by the United States in making large contributions of money, material and personnel to its allies to assist in their defense.

It was said, however, that the inherently offensive character of the long-range missiles in Cuba, the secrecy with which they were sent, the deception practiced by Soviet officials in denying that offensive missiles were being sent, the traditional attitude of the United States under the Monroe Doctrine, and the attitude of the Organization of American States under the Rio and Bogotá treaties opposing foreign intervention in the Western Hemisphere, constituted circumstances which made the sending of missiles to Cuba illegal.

It may be that some weapons should be regarded as inherently offensive, but no agreement to this effect has been made, and general international law, following the opinion of most strategists, has regarded the offensive or defensive character of weapons as dependent on their intended use. Any weapon can be used either defensively or offensively.

There is no rule of international law that requires publicity for collective defense measures, though such a rule may be desirable and indeed necessary if the installations are to have deterrent influence. While Soviet deception, asserted by President Kennedy and Ambassador Stevenson, certainly could not improve relations and would render any agreement based on such deception voidable, it could not clearly demonstrate that the purpose of the missiles was not defensive. . . .

* * *

. . . neither the Monroe Doctrine nor inter-American treaties can impose obligations of international law on the Soviet Union, though politically they constitute a warning to non-American countries of attitudes likely to be taken by the American countries. The Soviet Union was certainly aware that a nuclear missile attack upon the United States or any other American country would bring about nuclear retaliation from the United States, whether the missiles were launched from Cuba or from Russia, and it also seems clear that neither Khrushchev nor the Soviet people wanted nuclear war.

No satisfactory evidence has been presented to indicate that Khrushchev's purpose in sending the missiles was other than to deter attack on Cuba, and his willingness to withdraw them when the United States made the conditional pledge not to invade Cuba would support this defensive intent on his part.

It is possible that Castro hoped to use the presence of missiles as a threat to expand his influence among the Caribbean republics. It can also be argued that Castro violated obligations under inter-American agreements and resolutions by his close relations with the Communist Powers, but such intentions or obligations of Castro could not impose obligations on the Soviet Union. It is difficult, therefore, to support the allegation that the Soviet Union violated international obligations in sending and installing missiles in Cuba.

The Quarantine

Efforts have been made to justify the United States quarantine, declared by President Kennedy in a radio broadcast on October 22, 1962, and put into effect the next evening, on the following grounds:

1. It was a "pacific blockade" traditionally recognized in international law as constituting a "peaceful method" for settling a dispute as called for by Article 2 (3) of the U.N. Charter.

2. It was not directed against the territorial integrity or political independence of any state and was not contrary to any purpose of the United Nations, and was therefore consistent with the obligations of the United States under Article 2 (4) of the Charter.

3. It was justified by the Rio Treaty and resolutions of the Consultative Organ of the O.A.S. in pursuance of that treaty, and could not be regarded as "enforcement action" requiring prior consent of the Security Council under Article 53 of the U.N. Charter.

4. It was initiated as a measure of individual and collective self-defense in response to a "threat of force" amounting, under present conditions, to "armed attack," and was, therefore, permissible under Article 51 of the Charter, prior to submission to the United Nations as normally required by Article 37 of the Charter.

Pacific Blockade

Pacific blockade was a procedure often used in the 19th and early 20th centuries, generally by one or several large Powers against a small state, and was generally considered acceptable in international law if it conformed to the rules of "reprisal." The legitimacy of reprisals was held to depend on three conditions: that the purpose was to obtain remedy for injury resulting from illegal action, that non-coercive methods to obtain such remedy had failed, and that the measures taken were not out of proportion to the injury suffered. Furthermore, with specific reference to pacific blockade, it was held, especially by the United States, that, differing from a war blockade, it did not permit interference with vessels of a third state, but only with vessels of the blockading and the blockaded states. Thus a Senate resolution of 1858 asserted that American vessels on the high seas are not subject to search in time of peace, and, in accord with this principle, the United States objected to stoppage of its vessels by the pacific blockade established by Germany, Italy, and Great Britain against Venezuela in 1902. Under these conditions a pacific blockade may prove ineffective, and consequently it may lead to a declaration of war, permitting a war blockade, as was indeed the case with the Venezuelan blockade of 1902.

An effort to justify the quarantine by the historic doctrine of pacific blockade, therefore, fails because the United States did not make it clear what illegal act of Cuba it was trying to remedy and, if it had been claimed that Castro's installation of the missiles manifested allegiance to Communism in violation of obligations of Cuba under O. A. S. resolutions, noncoercive means of settlement had not been exhausted. Indeed, negotiations to remedy the situation could not be utilized because the United States had broken diplomatic relations with Castro and induced his expulsion from the O. A. S. at the Punta del Este Conference of January, 1962.

Furthermore, if the quarantine was a pacific blockade directed against Cuba, only Cuban or American vessels could be stopped, but the quarantine was designed primarily to stop Soviet vessels. Under the American concept of freedom of the seas and pacific blockade, this would be illegal, unless conditions for reprisals against the Soviet Union existed. This was alleged, but, as noted, it is difficult to show that the Soviet Union, in its relations with Cuba, had violated any obligation of international law owed to the United States.

Finally, even if the quarantine had conformed to the traditional conception of pacific blockade, it could not, in spite of its name, be reconciled with the obligations of all Members of the United Nations to "settle their international disputes by peaceful means in such a manner that international peace and security, and justice, are not endangered," and to "refrain in their international relations from the threat or use of force against the territorial integrity or political independence of any state, or in any other manner inconsistent with the Purposes of the United Nations." The quarantine, as indicated by the President's Proclamation of 7:06 p.m., October 23, 1962, putting it into effect, implied use of land, sea and air forces to prevent delivery of the prohibited materials to Cuba by intercepting vessels within a designated zone around Cuba; directing stopping, visiting, and searching them; and using force to the extent necessary, if they tried to escape or resist. Such procedures are not "peaceful means" but "threats or uses of force," and they do endanger both international peace and justice, and have in the past sometimes resulted in war. Furthermore, the Charter seems to specify the "peaceful means" intended by Article 2 (3), by the terms of Article 33, which requires:

The parties to any dispute . . . likely to endanger the maintenance of international peace and security, shall, first of all, seek a solution by negotiation, enquiry, mediation, conciliation, arbitration, judicial settlement, resort to regional agencies or arrangements, or other peaceful means of their own choice.

Blockade, even if called "pacific," seems to be excluded, particularly by the phrase "of their own choice," unless applied with the constructive consent of the state against which it is directed, a condition possibly applicable to Cuba but not to the Soviet Union.

Territorial Integrity and Political Independence

It has been argued that the obligations imposed by Article 2 (4) of the Charter cannot be understood unless the paragraph is read as a whole, and that a threat or use of force is not directed "against the territorial integrity" of a state unless its purpose is permanent acquisition of the territory belonging to that state, and that it is not directed against the "political independence" of another state unless its purpose is permanent subjection of that state to domination. Common sense, however, suggests that invasion and occupation of a state's territory by armed force, whatever the purpose or whatever the intended duration, violates that state's "territorial integrity," and that use or threat of military force against a state's vessels on the high seas to induce its government to change its policy or to abandon its rights violates the state's "political independence." This common-sense interpretation is supported by the final clause of Article 2 (4), which forbids threat or use of force "in any other manner inconsistent with the Purposes of the United Nations." The first purpose of the United Nations is to "maintain international peace and security . . . and to bring about by peaceful means, and in conformity with the principles of justice and international law, adjustment or settlement of international disputes or situations which might lead to a breach of the peace." Clearly, territorial invasion and forcible reprisals are uses of force in "a manner inconsistent" with these purposes, and are therefore forbidden by Article 2 (4), as are declarations of war, stimulation of guerrilla activities abroad, or complicity in military expeditions departing from the state's territory. The quarantine, therefore, in addition to being a non-peaceful means forbidden by Article 2 (3), was a "threat of force" forbidden by Article 2 (4), unless coming within one of the special exceptions to be discussed in the next sections.

Authority of the Organization of American States

The main argument put forward by the United States to justify the quarantine was that it was permitted by Articles 6 and 8 of the Rio Treaty of 1947, implemented by the Consultative Organ of the Organization of American States in its resolution at Washington on October 23, 1962. This argument suffers from the fact that Article 3 of the Rio Treaty permits *unilateral* action of forcible character only in case of defense against armed attack. Article 6, however, provides:

If the inviolability or the integrity of the territory or the sovereignty or political independence of any American State should be affected by an aggression which is not an armed attack or by an extra-continental or an intra-continental conflict, or by any other fact or situation that might endanger the peace of America, the Organ of Consultation shall meet immediately in order to agree on the measures which must be taken in case of aggression to assist the victim of the aggression or, in any case, the measures which should be taken for the common defense and for the maintenance of the peace and security of the Continent.

Article 8 provides: "For the purposes of this Treaty, the measures on which the Organ of Consultation may agree will comprise . . .: [among others] use of armed force."

At a meeting on October 23, 1962, in Washington, the Organ of Consultation of the O. A. S. passed a resolution with 19 affirmative votes:

1. To call for the immediate dismantling and withdrawal from Cuba of all missiles and other weapons with any offensive capability;
2. To recommend that the member states, in accordance with Articles 6 and 8 of the Inter-American Treaty of Reciprocal Assistance [the Rio Treaty], take all measures, individually and

collectively, including the use of armed force, which they may deem necessary to ensure that the Government of Cuba cannot continue to receive from the Sino-Soviet powers military material and related supplies which may threaten the peace and security of the Continent and to prevent the missiles in Cuba with offensive capability from ever becoming an active threat to the peace and security of the Continent . . .

This resolution might justify action against Cuba on the ground that as a member of O. A. S. Cuba had constructively consented and so was legally bound by it. It was passed after the initial declaration of unilateral action by the President on October 22, but before the quarantine was formally proclaimed on the evening of October 23, to go into effect at 2:00 p.m. on October 24. The Consultative Organ of the O. A. S. was, it is true, hardly in a position to give a free judgment, as contemplated by the Rio Treaty. It was faced by a *fait accompli*, but formally the United States acted in conformity with the resolution. The resolution could not, however, in law affect the rights of the Soviet Union, against which the quarantine was primarily directed. A state's rights, under international law, cannot be reduced by a treaty to which it is not a party.

The question also arises whether the quarantine constitutes "enforcement action" which, under the United Nations Charter, cannot be instituted by a regional organization such as the O. A. S. without prior consent of the Security Council. It has been suggested that "enforcement action," as used in Article 53, includes only "enforcement measures under Chapter VII" referred to in Article 2 (7), and binding upon states by virtue of a Security Council decision, and that it does not include action taken by a state on the basis of a "recommendation" of a United Nations organ or an organ of a regional agency.

Diplomatic and economic measures recommended by the Consultative Organ

of the O. A. S. against the Dominican Republic in September, 1960, and against Cuba by the Punta del Este meeting in January, 1962, were considered by the United Nations, but it took no action, thus sustaining the competence of the O. A. S. Measures of this kind, it has been suggested, come within the "resort to regional agencies or arrangements" contemplated by Article 33 of the Charter. This article, however, characterizes such resort as "peaceful means of their own choice," and it seems difficult to consider the quarantine as a peaceful means of Cuba's choice, even though in accord with the Rio Treaty to which Cuba is a party, and with the recommendations of the Consultative Organ of the O. A. S. It seems rather to be enforcement action, and Article 53 says that "no enforcement action shall be taken under regional arrangements or by regional agencies without the authorization of the Security Council." Application of this article to the O. A. S. resolution is supported by the fact that Article 51 of the Charter, which permits "collective self-defense" without prior Security Council approval, was adopted at San Francisco on behalf of the American States because it was thought that Article 53, as provided at Dumbarton Oaks, would prevent forcible, autonomous measures by these states.

On the other hand, in order to justify the "Uniting for Peace" Resolution of 1950, "action" in Article 11, paragraph 2, of the Charter was held to refer only to "action" by the United Nations because of a Security Council "decision" and not to "action" by states because of a "recommendation" of the General Assembly or the Security Council. This construction has been supported by the International Court of Justice.[1] A similar interpretation may be given to "enforcement action" in Article 53. This interpretation makes it possible for the United States to justify the quarantine against Cuba by the O. A. S. resolution, but it certainly cannot justify its action against the Soviet Union by that resolution.

Necessary Defense

Finally it has been argued that the quarantine and the O. A. S. resolution were justified as measures of "individual or collective self-defense" permitted by Article 51 of the Charter. It is suggested that the term "armed attack," which alone justified such defense without prior United Nations authority, must be interpreted to include a serious threat of armed attack. Reference has been made to the statement by Secretary of State Webster in the *Caroline* case, generally accepted prior to the Charter, that military defensive action was permissible in case of "an instant and overwhelming necessity," thus creating a limited right of preventive action; that such a construction is necessary in the nuclear age because to delay defensive action until an actual nuclear attack would be suicidal, and that the Charter supports this construction by forbidding "threat" as well as "use" of force in Article 2, paragraph 4.

These arguments are not convincing. It appears that the Charter intended to limit the traditional right of defense by states to actual armed attack, even though it forbade "threat of force" and authorized the Security Council to intervene to stop "threats to the peace." Professor, now Judge, Philip Jessup wrote in 1948:

This restriction in Article 51 very definitely narrows the freedom of action which states had under international law. A case could be made out for self-defense in the traditional law where the injury was threatened but no attack had yet taken place. Under the Charter, alarming military preparations by a neighboring state would justify a resort to the Security Council, but would not justify resort to anticipatory force by the state which believed itself threatened.[2]

The obligation of states to refrain from threats to the peace under Article 2, paragraph 4, and the competence of the United Nations to take action in case of a threat to the peace under Article 39, were not intended to give a unilateral right of military self-defense in case of such threats. For that reason, self-defense against "threats" was excluded in Article 51, and states were explicitly obliged to submit disputes or situations which they think threaten peace, to the United Nations and to refrain from unilateral use of force. Article 33 requires "peaceful means" to settle disputes, "the continuance of which is likely to endanger the maintenance of international peace and security." This and the following articles specify such means, and Article 37 declares: "Should the parties to a dispute of the nature referred to in Article 33 fail to settle it by means indicated in that Article, they shall refer it to the Security Council. The United States did submit its quarantine measures to the Security Council, but only after it had decided to act unilaterally. It asked for a resolution noting the "serious threat" to the peace in the Caribbean and calling for the withdrawal of missiles in Cuba as a provisional measure under Article 40 of the Charter. The Soviet Union and Cuba asked for a resolution to consider the "threat to peace" or, according to Cuba, "act of war" by the U.S. "blockade." No resolution was passed, but the Secretary General, declaring that the issue involved "the very fate of mankind" and that "some of the measures which the Council is called upon to approve, are very unusual and I might say, even extraordinary, except in wartime," at the request of a large number of Member governments, assumed a mediatorial rôle and assisted in bringing about agreements which ended the quarantine.

*   *   *

The quarantine itself was a preventive measure to be enforced with conventional weapons, prior to an armed attack by Cuba or the Soviet Union upon the United

States or any other American country, and without authority of the United Nations or the consent of all the states which might be injured by its application. It could not, therefore, be justified under the terms of Article 2, paragraph 4, of the Charter and the recognized exceptions, such as that in Article 51, to this general prohibition against the threat or use of force in international relations. It should be noted in extenuation that, while a few vessels were boarded and others diverted, force was not actually used and, in spite of the incomplete fulfillment of the agreement, the quarantine was ended on November 21, 1962. On the principle of proportionality, defensive measures not involving military action are doubtless permissible against "threats of force" less than "armed attack."

* * *

Notes

1. Advisory Opinion on Certain Expenses of the United Nations, [1962] I. C. J. Rep. 151; 56 A.J.I.L. 1062 (1962).
2. Philip Jessup, A Modern Law of Nations 166 (New York, Macmillan, 1948). After an exhaustive discussion of "The Use of Force in Self-Defence," Ian Brownlie concludes that "the beginning of an armed attack is a condition precedent for resort to force in self-defence." 37 Brit. Yr. Bk. of Int. Law 266 (1962).

Defensive Quarantine and the Law *

Leonard C. Meeker, DEPUTY LEGAL ADVISER, UNITED STATES DEPARTMENT OF STATE

. . . Varying processes of analysis could be pursued and a number of theories could be relied on to attack or to sustain

* Reprinted from Leonard C. Meeker, "Defensive Quarantine and the Law," 57 *American Journal of International Law* 515 (1963), by permission of the American Society of International Law.

the legal validity of the defensive quarantine adopted by the United States in October, 1962. Rather than explore or seek to evaluate arguments in this wide range, the present report will confine itself to a description of the basis in international law upon which the United States Government has rested the measures which it took.

In the days after the missiles were discovered in Cuba and before the proclamation of defensive quarantine was issued, officials of the Government were well aware of the novelty and difficulty of the question presented. They were concerned that any actions to be taken by the United States should rest on the soundest foundation in law and should appear in that light to all the world, including the Government of the Soviet Union.

Traditional International Law

The quarantine was designed to prevent the further introduction of strategic missiles into Cuba. Because it had this purpose of interdiction and because naval vessels would be used to carry it out, the press and other commentators were quick to analogize the quarantine to the concept of "blockade" in international law. To the extent that traditional "blockade" implies and requires a state of belligerency or war, the United States did not seek to justify the quarantine as a blockade. There was no assertion of a state of war or belligerency.

Such conditions would not form the sole basis for measures such as the defensive quarantine. Another concept in traditional international law is that of "pacific blockade." Whatever the views that may be held as to the availability of such a doctrine, the United States did not rest its case on that ground.

The available and relevant sources of law applicable to the situation of Soviet strategic missiles in Cuba did not stop with the international law of the nineteenth century or that in existence at the beginning of World War II. New legal structures had been built in the aftermath of the war. Two are of special importance here: the Inter-American Treaty of Reciprocal Assistance and the Charter of the United Nations. Let us look first at the Rio Treaty of 1947.

The Rio Treaty

The Rio Treaty was concluded by all of the American Republics in order " to assure peace, through adequate means, to provide for effective reciprocal assistance to meet armed attacks against any American State, and . . . to deal with threats of aggression against any of them." The treaty provides for collective action, not only in the case of armed attack, which is covered by Article 3, but also:

If the inviolability or the integrity of the territory or the sovereignty or political independence of any American State should be affected by an aggression which is not an armed attack . . . or by any other fact or situation that might endanger the peace of America . . . (Article 6.)

In such cases, the Organ of Consultation, consisting of the Foreign Ministers of the Member States, or representatives specifically designated for the purpose, is to

meet immediately in order to agree on the measures which must be taken in case of agression to assist the victim of the aggression or, in any case, the measures which should be taken for the common defense and for the maintenance of the peace and security of the Continent. (Article 6.)

The Organ of Consultation acts " by a vote of two-thirds of the Signatory States which have ratified the Treaty." (Article 17.)

The treaty is equally explicit as to the measures which may be taken by the Organ of Consultation in any situation covered by Article 6. These measures are listed in Article 8 and specifically include " use of armed force." Article 20 further specifies that decisions to take any of the measures listed in Article 8 shall be binding, except that " no State shall be required to use armed force without its consent."

As early as 1960, the Seventh Meeting of Foreign Ministers of the Organization of American States condemned " the intervention or the threat of intervention . . . by an extracontinental power in the affairs of the American republics. . . ." At the Eighth Meeting, in 1962, the Foreign Ministers declared that " the continental unity and the democratic institutions of the hemisphere are now in danger." The source of that danger was identified as " the subversive offensive of communist governments." Among the " outstanding facts in this intensified offensive " was " the existence of a Marxist-Leninist government in Cuba which is publicly aligned with the doctrine and foreign policy of the communist powers."

At the Eighth Meeting, at Punta del Este, the Foreign Ministers, acting as Organ of Consultation under the Rio Treaty, took the first collective measures designed to deal with the threat. It prohibited all trade in arms with Cuba, and excluded the present government of that country from participation in the organs and organizations of the inter-American system. On October 2 and 3, 1962, the Foreign Ministers of the American States met again, this time informally. They reiterated that "the Soviet Union's intervention in Cuba threatens the unity of the Americas and of its democratic institutions," and that this called "for the adoption of special measures, both individual and collective."

Against this background, the Council of the Organization of American States met on October 23 and constituted itself as the Provisional Organ of Consultation in accordance with Article 12 of the Rio Treaty. The Organ considered the evidence before it of the secret introduction of Soviet strategic missiles into Cuba. The Organ concluded that it was confronted with a situation that might endanger the peace of America within the meaning of Article 6. Having made this judgment, the Organ invoked its authority to take one or more of the measures listed in Article 8 of the Rio Treaty.

The resolution which the Organ adopted recommended

that the member states, in accordance with Articles 6 and 8 of the Inter-American Treaty of Reciprocal Assistance, take all measures, individually and collectively, including the use of armed force, which they may deem necessary to ensure that the Government of Cuba cannot continue to receive from the Sino-Soviet powers military material and related supplies which may threaten the peace and security of the Continent and to prevent the missiles in Cuba with offensive capability from ever becoming an active threat to the peace and security of the Continent.

The United States Proclamation of a defensive quarantine was based on the action of the O. A. S. under the Rio Treaty. It was the conclusion of the United States Government that this treaty and the resolution of October 23, 1962, clearly authorized the defensive quarantine of Cuba. Here it is relevant to note that the Rio Treaty bound all of the American Republics, including Cuba. Indeed, it continues to do so today. There was thus a consensual basis in treaty, as between the United States and Cuba, for the defensive quarantine.

The contention has sometimes been made that, while the quarantine of Cuba may have been lawful as between the United States and Cuba, it could not be legally effective as regards countries outside the American Republics, such as the U.S.S.R. To begin with, this contention involves an anomaly not readily to be accepted. It would have us conclude that the quarantine —an application of least force to the situation of clandestine strategic missiles in Cuba—was illegal in its application to Soviet shipping on the high seas (because the U.S.S.R. was not bound by the Rio Treaty), while an air strike or invasion confined to the territory of Cuba would have been legally sanctioned.

But is such an assertion of illegality really sustainable as a proposition of inter-national law? The Rio Treaty created a regional organization to maintain regional peace and security. If its purposes and activities are in conformity with the relevant provisions of the United Nations Charter, extra-hemispheric countries such as the U.S.S.R. are not in a position to attack the organization's activities within the region.

The Charter of the United Nations

The United Nations Charter specifically recognizes regional organizations and assigns to them an important place in carrying out the purposes of the United Nations. Article 52(1) states that

Nothing in the present Charter precludes the existence of regional arrangements or agencies for dealing with such matters relating to the maintenance of international peace and security as are appropriate for regional action, provided that such arrangements or agencies and their activities are consistent with the Purposes and Principles of the United Nations.

Article 54 provides that "The Security Council shall at all times be kept fully informed of activities undertaken or in contemplation under regional arrangements or by regional agencies for the maintenance of international peace and security." In accordance with this provision, the Organ of Consultation directed that the Security Council should be informed of the contents of the resolution of October 23.

The framers of the Charter met in San Francisco in 1945 after the basic outlines of the most significant regional arrangement, the inter-American system, were already established. The meeting was held subsequent to the Conference of the American Republics at which the Act of Chapultepec was approved. This Act recommended the execution of a treaty to establish a regional arrangement, and specifically provided that the "use of armed force to prevent or repel aggression" constituted "regional action which might appropriately be taken by the regional arrangements."

The debates at the San Francisco Conference concerning regional organizations were held against this background, and the inter-American system provided the principal context for the discussions.

When Article 52 was debated at the San Francisco Conference, the Chairman of the committee charged with considering regional arrangements, speaking as the delegate of Colombia, made the following statement concerning the relationship between the inter-American system and Chapter VIII of the Charter:

The Act of Chapultepec provides for the collective defense of the hemisphere and establishes that if an American nation is attacked all the rest consider themselves attacked. Consequently, such action as they may take to repel aggression, authorized by the article which was discussed in the subcommittee yesterday, is legitimate for all of them. Such action would be in accord with the Charter, by the approval of the article, and a regional arrangement may take action, provided it does not have improper purposes as, for example, joint aggression against another state. From this, it may be deduced that the approval of this article implies that the Act of Chapultepec is not in contravention of the Charter.

No delegate disputed this statement.

When the Rio Treaty was concluded in 1947, not only the purposes but even the very language of the Act of Chapultepec was incorporated into the new treaty. Thus the purposes and activities of the regional arrangement which the treaty created are properly considered in the light of the San Francisco discussion of the inter-American system. Measured by the standards set forth in Chapter VIII of the United Nations Charter, the defensive quarantine of Cuba should be considered valid and lawful.

Relationship of the Quarantine to Security Council Action

In considering the lawfulness of the defensive quarantine of Cuba under the United Nations Charter, it is necessary also to consider some other provisions. One of these is Article 53, paragraph 1, which reads in part:

The Security Council shall, where appropriate, utilize such regional arrangements or agencies for enforcement action under its authority. But no enforcement action shall be taken under regional arrangements or by regional agencies without the authorization of the Security Council . . .

It is evident with this, as with other Charter provisions dealing with the rôle of the Security Council, that it rested on the premise of a Council effectively exercising on behalf of the Members of the United Nations "primary responsibility for the maintenance of international peace and security."

The unfolding of history has shown a lack of agreement among the Council's permanent Members such that the Council has been disabled from performing its functions as originally intended. This has, of necessity, thrown an unexpected responsibility onto other mechanisms provided in the Charter. A dozen years ago the General Assembly's adoption of the Uniting for Peace Resolution signaled a stage in the constitutional development of the United Nations. The Cuban quarantine of 1962 marked an assumption of increased responsibility by a regional organization. Accompanying a decline in the affirmative authority of the Security Council, it should not be surprising to find also some contraction in the Council's negative authority to preclude action by other bodies.

When the Rio Treaty Organ of Consultation met last October, was there a requirement that the Security Council must expressly authorize the measures recommended by the regional organ before American Republics could lawfully carry them out? This question has several elements: (a) Was *prior* authorization by the Council necessary? (b) Did the Organ of Consultation recommendation constitute "enforcement action" within the meaning of Article 53? (c) Must "authorization" be *express*?

Prior authorization. It should not be assumed that "authorization of the Security Council" automatically and necessarily means *prior* authorization. On this point it is illuminating to recall a 1960 precedent. In September of that year the Security Council had met, on Soviet request, to consider diplomatic and economic measures voted against the Dominican Republic by the Foreign Ministers of the American Republics meeting at San José the preceding month. The U.S.S.R. asked the Council to approve these measures after they had been taken. The Soviet theory quite evidently was that the Council could appropriately give its "authorization" after the fact.

Meaning of "enforcement action." The 1960 precedent is interesting from another point of view. The upshot of the Security Council debate then was that the Council rejected the Soviet contention that the measures in question constituted "enforcement action" requiring "authorization." Similarly, early in 1962, the Council rejected contentions that the measures decided on at Punta del Este regarding Cuba required any authorization by the Council.

In addition to the earlier Council precedents, there was also to be considered the usage of the term elsewhere in the Charter, and a recent advisory opinion of the International Court of Justice. The term "enforcement action" appears at several places in the Charter. In addition to Article 53, there is, for example, Article 2, paragraph 5, which obligates Members of the United Nations to "refrain from giving assistance to any state against which the United Nations is taking preventive or enforcement action." And Article 5 provides that

A Member of the United Nations against which preventive or enforcement action has been taken by the Security Council may be suspended from the exercise of the rights and privileges of membership by the General Assembly upon the recommendation of the Security Council.

The "preventive" and "enforcement" action mentioned in these articles refers to action which the Council is authorized to take under Articles 40, 41, and 42. Article 40 provides for taking of "preventive action" in the form of provisional measures. Such measures are orders of the Council with which Member States are bound to comply. Articles 41 and 42 empower the Council to enforce its decisions by calling upon United Nations Members to apply certain measures or by taking action directly through air, sea, or land forces which are at the disposal of the Security Council. Again, in acting under Articles 41 and 42, the Security Council does more than recommend to Members steps which they might take to meet a threat to peace and security. Rather it decides upon measures and issues orders of enforcement which Members States are obligated under the Charter to carry out.

Council actions under Articles 40, 41, and 42 are to be distinguished from recommendations made by the Council under Article 39 or by the General Assembly in the discharge of its responsibilities as set forth in Chapter IV of the Charter. This distinction between a Security Council measure which is obligatory and constitutes "action," on the one hand, and a measure which is recommended either by the Council or by the General Assembly, on the other, has been supported by the Advisory Opinion of the International Court of Justice on Certain Expenses of the United Nations (July 20, 1962).[1] The Court held that the measures taken by the General Assembly and the Security Council in Suez and the Congo were not enforcement action, in part, because they were only recommendatory as to participating states.[2]

Thus, in the context of the United Nations bodies, it may be persuasively argued that "enforcement action" does not include action by a United Nations body which is not obligatory on all the Members. As used in Article 53(1), "enforcement action" refers to action by a regional organization rather than to action by an organ of the United Nations, but the words are properly given the same meaning in this context. As understood by the United States, "enforcement action" means obligatory action involving the use of armed force. Thus, "enforcement action," as the phrase appears in Article 53(1), should not be taken to comprehend action of a regional organization which is only recommendatory to the members of the organization.

As was pointed out earlier, the O. A. S. resolution authorizing the quarantine was agreed upon pursuant to Article 6 of the Rio Treaty. As a recommendation of the "use of armed force" it was specifically authorized by Article 8 of that treaty. And it is, by the express terms of Article 20, the one measure which, when agreed upon by the Organ of Consultation, Member States are not obligated to carry out. Since states signatories of the Rio Treaty were not obligated to carry out the resolution recommending quarantine, it should not be held to constitute "enforcement action" under Article 53(1) requiring Security Council authorization.

Must "authorization" be express? Just as some commentators have readily assumed that the Security Council must give prior authorization, some have also assumed that the authorization must be express. In the light of the paralysis of the Council through abuse of the veto and in the light of the consequent constitutional evolution of the United Nations, this assumption cannot be made with assurance.

The United States, immediately following President Kennedy's address of October 22, placed the Cuban situation before the Security Council and asked for an urgent meeting of the Council. The Council met even before the Organ of Consultation under the Rio Treaty adopted its resolution of October 23 and before the proclamation of defensive quarantine was issued or carried into effect. The Council did not see fit to take any action in derogation of the quarantine. Although a resolution condemning the quarantine was laid before the Council by the Soviet Union, the Council subsequently, by general consent, refrained from acting upon it and instead chose to promote the course of a negotiated settlement, with the assistance of the Secretary General.

If in the past the abstention or even the absence of a permanent Member from the Council has been held sufficient to supply "the concurring votes of the permanent Members" for the purpose of adopting a Security Council resolution, might it not equally be thought that the Council's course of action last October, when confronted by the quarantine of Cuba, could constitute such authorization as the Charter might require if Article 53 should be considered applicable? The Council let the quarantine continue, rather than supplant it. While the quarantine continued, and with knowledge of it, the Council encouraged the parties to pursue the course of negotiation between the United States and the Soviet Union. Thus, if it were thought that authorization was necessary (which was not the view of the United States), such authorization may be said to have been granted by the course which the Council adopted.

Charter Limitation on the "Threat or Use of Force"

Before leaving the Charter of the United Nations it is relevant also to consider Article 2, paragraph 4, which provides:

All Members shall refrain in their international relations from the threat or use of force against the territorial integrity or political independence of any state, or in any other manner inconsistent with the Purposes of the United Nations.

It was recognized that the defensive quarantine was dependent, ultimately, upon the use of naval forces for its effectiveness. Accordingly, there was acknowledged to be a threat, and potentially a use, of armed force. However, it did not follow that this must contravene Article 2, paragraph 4.

In considering the obligations imposed on Members by that article, it should be noted that not all threats or uses of force are prohibited; only those which are inconsistent with the purposes of the United Nations are covered by Article 2, paragraph 4. The presence of the word "other" in the concluding clause of the paragraph makes this clear. Even assuming that the measures taken could be considered to impinge upon the territorial integrity or political independence of some state or states, they would not be contrary to Article 2, paragraph 4, as long as they were not inconsistent with the purposes of the United Nations. The defensive quarantine, as indicated earlier, was considered to be in accordance with Chapter VIII of the Charter.

It is clear that collective action for peace and security which the Security Council may take under Chapter VII does not contravene Article 2, paragraph 4. It is also clear that individual or collective self-defense against armed attack, in accordance with Article 51, does not violate the Charter. Here it may be noted that the United States, in adopting the defensive quarantine of Cuba, did not seek to justify it as a measure required to meet an "armed attack" within the meaning of Article 51. Nor did the United States seek to sustain its action on the ground that Article 51 is not an all-inclusive statement of the right of self-defense and that the quarantine was a measure of self-defense open to any country to take individually for its own defense in a case other than "armed attack." Indeed, as shown by President Kennedy's television address of October 22 and by other statements of the Government, reliance was not placed on either contention, and the United States took no position on either of these issues.

The quarantine was based on a collective judgment and recommendation of the American Republics made under the Rio Treaty. It was considered not to contravene Article 2, paragraph 4, because it was a measure adopted by a regional organization in conformity with the provisions of Chapter VIII of the Charter. The purposes of the Organization and its activities were considered to be consistent with the purposes and principles of the United Nations as provided in Article 52. This being the case, the quarantine would no more violate Article 2, paragraph 4, than measures voted by the Council under Chapter VII, by the General Assembly under Articles 10 and 11, or taken by United Nations Members in conformity with Article 51.

Finally, in relation to the Charter limitation on threat or use of force, it should be noted that the quarantine itself was a carefully limited measure proportionate to the threat and designed solely to prevent any further build-up of strategic missile bases in Cuba.

Conclusion

From the point of view of the lawyer, one may conclude from this history that the steps taken by the United States in instituting the quarantine were in the tradition of the common law. No new doctrines of wide application were enunciated. One single situation was considered on its individual facts, and the limited action decided upon rested on the narrowest and clearest grounds. It is by such a process of accretion that the law of nations, like the common law, is built.

Notes

1. [1962] I.C.J. Rep. 151; digested in 56 A.J.I.L. 1053 (1962).

2. Specifically, the Court stated:

"The word 'action' must mean such action as is solely within the province of the Security Council. It cannot refer to recommendations which the Security Council might make, as for instance under Article 38, because the General Assembly under Article 11 has a comparable power. The 'action' which is solely within the province of the Security Council is that which is indicated by the title of Chapter VII of the Charter, namely 'Action with respect to threats to the peace, breaches of the peace, and acts of aggression'. If the word 'action' in Article 11, paragraph 2, were interpreted to mean that the General Assembly could make recommendations only of a general character affecting peace and security in the abstract, and not in relation to specific cases, the paragraph would not have provided that the General Assembly may make recommendations on questions brought before it by States or by the Security Council. Accordingly, the last sentence of Article 11, paragraph 2, has no application where the necessary action is not enforcement action."

C. Resort to Force and the Vietnam Hostilities

Final Declaration of the Geneva Conference on the Problem of Restoring Peace in Indo-China, July 21, 1954*

1. The Conference takes note of the Agreements ending hostilities in Cambodia, Laos and Viet Nam and organising international control and the supervision of the execution of the provisions of these Agreements.

2. The Conference expresses satisfaction

* Reprinted from 60 *American Journal of International Law* 643 (1966) by permission of the American Society of International Law.

at the ending of hostilities in Cambodia, Laos and Viet Nam; the Conference expresses its conviction that the execution of the provisions set out in the present declaration and in the Agreements on the cessation of hostilities will permit Cambodia, Laos and Viet Nam henceforth to play their part, in full independence and sovereignty, in the peaceful community of nations.

3. The Conference takes note of the declarations made by the Governments of Cambodia and of Laos of their intention to adopt measures permitting all citizens to take their place in the national community, in particular by participating in the next general elections, which, in conformity with the constitution of each of these countries, shall take place in the course of the year 1955, by secret ballot and in conditions of respect for fundamental freedoms.

4. The Conference takes note of the clauses in the Agreement on the cessation of hostilities in Viet Nam prohibiting the introduction into Viet Nam of foreign troops and military personnel as well as of all kinds of arms and munitions. The Conference also takes note of the declarations made by the Governments of Cambodia and Laos of their resolution not to request foreign aid, whether in war material, in personnel or in instructors except for the purpose of the effective defence of their territory and, in the case of Laos, to the extent defined by the agreements on the cessation of hostilities in Laos.

5. The Conference takes note of the clauses in the Agreement on the cessation of hostilities in Viet Nam to the effect that no military base under the control of a foreign state may be established in the regrouping zones of the two parties, the latter having the obligation to see that the zones allotted to them shall not constitute part of any military alliance and shall not be utilised for the resumption of hostilities or in the service of an aggressive policy. The Conference also takes note of

the declarations of the Governments of Cambodia and Laos to the effect that they will not join in any agreement with other states if this agreement includes the obligation to participate in a military alliance not in conformity with the principles of the Charter of the United Nations or, in the case of Laos, with the principles of the Agreement on the cessation of hostilities in Laos or, so long as their security is not threatened, the obligation to establish bases on Cambodian or Laotian territory for the military forces of foreign Powers.

6. The Conference recognises that the essential purposes of the Agreement relating to Viet Nam is to settle military questions with a view to ending hostilities and that the military demarcation line is provisional and should not in any way be interpreted as constituting a political or territorial boundary. The Conference expresses its conviction that the execution of the provisions set out in the present declaration and in the Agreement on the cessation of hostilities creates the necessary basis for the achievement in the near future of a political settlement in Viet Nam.

7. The Conference declares that, so far as Viet Nam is concerned, the settlement of political problems, effected on the basis of respect for the principles of independence, unity and territorial integrity, shall permit the Vietnamese people to enjoy the fundamental freedoms, guaranteed by democratic institutions established as a result of free general elections by secret ballot. In order to ensure that sufficient progress in the restoration of peace has been made, and that all the necessary conditions obtain for free expression of the national will, general elections shall be held in July 1956, under the supervision of an international commission composed of representatives of the member states of the International Supervisory Commission, referred to in the Agreement on the cessation of hostilities. Consulations will be held on this subject between the competent representative authorities of the two zones from 20th July, 1955, onwards.

8. The provisions of the Agreement on the cessation of hostilities intended to ensure the protection of individuals and of property must be most strictly applied and must, in particular, allow everyone in Viet Nam to decide freely in which zone he wishes to live.

9. The competent representative authorities of the Northern and Southern zones of Viet Nam, as well as the authorities of Laos and Cambodia, must not permit any individual or collective reprisals against persons who have collaborated in any way with one of the parties during the war, or against members of such persons' families.

10. The Conference takes note of the declaration of the Government of the French Republic to the effect that it is ready to withdraw its troops from the territory of Cambodia, Laos and Viet Nam, at the request of the governments concerned and within periods which shall be fixed by agreement between the parties except in the cases where, by agreement between the two parties, a certain number of French troops shall remain at specified points and for a specified time.

11. The Conference takes note of the declaration of the French Government to the effect that for the settlement of all the problems connected with the re-establishment and consolidation of peace in Cambodia, Laos and Viet Nam, the French Government will proceed from the principle of respect for the independence and sovereignty, unity and territorial integrity of Cambodia, Laos and Viet Nam.

12. In their relations with Cambodia, Laos and Viet Nam, each member of the Geneva Conference undertakes to respect the sovereignty, the independence, the unity and the territorial integrity of the above-mentioned states, and to refrain from any interference in their internal affairs.

* * *

United States Declaration on Indo-China*

Statement Made by Under Secretary of State Walter B. Smith at the Concluding Indo-China Plenary Session at Geneva, July 21, 1954

As I stated on July 18, my Government is not prepared to join in a declaration by the Conference such as is submitted. However, the United States makes this unilateral declaration of its position in these matters:

Declaration

The Government of the United States being resolved to devote its effort to the strengthening of peace in accordance with the principles and purposes of the United Nations takes note of the agreements concluded at Geneva on July 20 and 21, 1954 between (a) the Franco-Laotian Command and the Command of the Peoples Army of Viet-Nam; (b) the Royal Khmer Army Command and the Command of the Peoples Army of Viet-Nam; (c) Franco-Vietnamese Command and the Command of the Peoples Army of Viet-Nam and of paragraphs 1 to 12 inclusive of the declaration presented to the Geneva Conference on July 21, 1954 declares with regard to the aforesaid agreements and paragraphs that (i) it will refrain from the threat or the use of force to disturb them, in accordance with Article 2 (4) of the Charter of the United Nations dealing with the obligation of members to refrain in their international relations from the threat or use of force; and (ii) it would view any renewal of the aggression in violation of the aforesaid agreements with grave concern and as seriously threatening international peace and security.

Reprinted from 60 *American Journal of International Law* 645 (1966) by permission of the American Society of International Law.

In connection with the statement in the declaration concerning free elections in Viet-Nam my Government wishes to make clear its position which it has expressed in a declaration made in Washington on June 29, 1954, as follows:

In the case of nations now divided against their will, we shall continue to seek to achieve unity through free elections supervised by the United Nations to insure that they are conducted fairly.

With respect to the statement made by the representative of the State of Viet-Nam, the United States reiterates its traditional position that peoples are entitled to determine their own future and that it will not join in an arrangement which would hinder this. Nothing in its declaration just made is intended to or does indicate any departure from this traditional position.

We share the hope that the agreements will permit Cambodia, Laos and Viet-Nam to play their part, in full independence and sovereignty, in the peaceful community of nations, and will enable the peoples of that area to determine their own future.

Southeast Asia Collective Defense Treaty, 1954*

Article I

The parties undertake, as set forth in the Charter of the United Nations, to settle any international disputes in which they may be involved by peaceful means in such a manner that international peace and security and justice are not endangered, and to refrain in their international relations from the threat or use of force in any manner inconsistent with the purposes of the United Nations.

* * *

* Reprinted from 60 *American Journal of International Law* 646 (1966) by permission of the American Society of International Law.

Article IV

1. Each party recognizes that aggression by means of armed attack in the treaty area against any of the parties or against any state or territory which the parties by unanimous agreement may hereafter designate, would endanger its own peace and safety, and agrees that it will in that event act to meet the common danger in accordance with its constitutional processes. Measures taken under this paragraph shall be immediately reported to the Security Council of the United Nations.

2. If, in the opinion of any of the parties, the inviolability or the integrity of the territory or the sovereignty or political independence of any party in the treaty area or of any other state or territory to which the provisions of paragraph 1 of this article from time to time apply is threatened in any way other than by armed attack or is affected or threatened by any fact or situation which might endanger the peace of the area, the Parties shall consult immediately in order to agree on the measures which should be taken for the common defense.

3. It is understood that no action on the territory of any state designated by unanimous agreement under paragraph 1 of this article or on any territory so designated shall be taken except at the invitation or with the consent of the government concerned.

Article V

The parties hereby establish a Council, on which each of them shall be represented, to consider matters concerning the implementation of this Treaty. The Council shall provide for consultation with regard to military and any other planning as the situation obtaining in the treaty area may from time to time require. The Council shall be so organized as to be able to meet at any time.

Article VI

This Treaty does not affect and shall not be interpreted as affecting in any way the rights and obligations of any of the parties under the Charter of the United Nations or the responsibility of the United Nations for the maintenance of international peace and security. . . .

* * *

Article VIII

As used in this Treaty, the "treaty area" is the general area of Southeast Asia, including also the entire territories of the Asian parties, and the general area of the Southwest Pacific not including the Pacific area north of 21 degrees 30 minutes north latitude. The parties may, by unanimous agreement, amend this article to include within the treaty area the territory of any state acceding to this Treaty in accordance with Article VII or otherwise to change the treaty area.

* * *

Understanding of the United States of America

The United States of America in executing the present Treaty does so with the understanding that its recognition of the effect of aggression and armed attack and its agreement with reference thereto in Article IV, paragraph 1 apply only to communist aggression but affirms that in the event of other aggression or armed attack it will consult under the provisions of Article IV, paragraph 2.

Protocol to the Southeast Asia Collective Defense Treaty, 1954

The parties to the Southeast Asia Collective Defense Treaty unanimously designate for the purposes of Article IV of the Treaty the states of Cambodia and Laos and the free territory under the jurisdiction of the state of Vietnam. . . .

The Legality of United States Participation in the Defense of Viet-Nam*

Legal Memorandum Prepared by Leonard C. Meeker, Legal Adviser of the United States Department of State, Submitted to the Senate Committee on Foreign Relations on March 8, 1966

I. The United States and South Viet-Nam Have the Right Under International Law to Participate in the Collective Defense of South Viet-Nam Against Armed Attack

In response to requests from the Government of South Viet-Nam, the United States has been assisting that country in defending itself against armed attack from the Communist North. This attack has taken the forms of externally supported subversion, clandestine supply of arms, infiltration of armed personnel, and most recently the sending of regular units of the North Vietnamese army into the South.

International law has long recognized the right of individual and collective self-defense against armed attack. South Viet-Nam and the United States are engaging in such collective defense consistently with international law and with United States obligations under the United Nations Charter.

A. SOUTH VIET-NAM IS BEING SUBJECTED TO ARMED ATTACK BY COMMUNIST NORTH VIET-NAM

The Geneva accords of 1954 established a demarcation line between North Viet-Nam and South Viet-Nam. They provided

*Reprinted from 54 *United States Department of State Bulletin* 474 (1966).

for withdrawals of military forces into the respective zones north and south of this line. The accords prohibited the use of either zone for the resumption of hostilities or to "further an aggressive policy."

During the 5 years following the Geneva conference of 1954, the Hanoi regime developed a covert political-military organization in South Viet-Nam based on Communist cadres it had ordered to stay in the South, contrary to the provisions of the Geneva accords. The activities of this covert organization were directed toward the kidnaping and assassination of civilian officials—acts of terrorism that were perpetrated in increasing numbers.

In the 3-year period from 1959 to 1961, the North Viet-Nam regime infiltrated an estimated 10,000 men into the South. It is estimated that 13,000 additional personnel were infiltrated in 1962, and, by the end of 1964, North Viet-Nam may well have moved over 40,000 armed and unarmed guerrillas into South Viet-Nam.

The International Control Commission reported in 1962 the findings of its Legal Committee:

. . . there is evidence to show that arms, armed and unarmed personnel, munitions and other supplies have been sent from the Zone in the North to the Zone in the South with the objective of supporting, organizing and carrying out hostile activities, including armed attacks, directed against the Armed Forces and Administration of the Zone in the South.

. . . there is evidence that the PAVN [People's Army of Viet Nam] has allowed the Zone in the North to be used for inciting, encouraging and supporting hostile activities in the Zone in the South, aimed at the overthrow of the Administration in the South.

Beginning in 1964, the Communists apparently exhausted their reservoir of Southerners who had gone North. Since then the greater number of men infiltrated into the South have been native-born North Vietnamese. Most recently, Hanoi has begun to infiltrate elements of the North Vietnamese army in increasingly larger numbers. Today, there is evidence that nine regiments of regular North Vietnamese forces are fighting in organized units in the South.

In the guerrilla war in Viet-Nam, the external aggression from the North is the critical military element of the insurgency, although it is unacknowledged by North Viet-Nam. In these circumstances, an "armed attack" is not as easily fixed by date and hour as in the case of traditional warfare. However, the infiltration of thousands of armed men clearly constitutes an "armed attack" under any reasonable definition. There may be some question as to the exact date at which North Viet-Nam's aggression grew into an "armed attack," but there can be no doubt that it had occurred before February 1965.

B. INTERNATIONAL LAW RECOGNIZES THE RIGHT OF INDIVIDUAL AND COLLECTIVE SELF-DEFENSE AGAINST ARMED ATTACK

International law has traditionally recognized the right of self-defense against armed attack. This proposition has been asserted by writers on international law through the several centuries in which the modern law of nations has developed. The proposition has been acted on numerous times by governments throughout modern history. Today the principle of self-defense against armed attack is universally recognized and accepted.

The Charter of the United Nations, concluded at the end of World War II, imposed an important limitation on the use of force by United Nations members. Article 2, paragraph 4, provides:

All Members shall refrain in their international relations from the threat or use of force against the territorial integrity or political independence of any state, or in any other manner inconsistent with the Purposes of the United Nations.

In addition, the sharter embodied a system of international peacekeeping through the organs of the United Nations. Article 24 summarizes these structural arrangements in stating that the United Nations members:

. . . confer on the Security Council primary responsibility for the maintenance of international peace and security, and agree that in carrying out its duties under this responsibility the Security Council acts on their behalf.

However, the charter expressly states in article 51 that the remaining provisions of the charter—including the limitation of article 2, paragraph 4, and the creation of United Nations machinery to keep the peace—in no way diminish the inherent right of self-defense against armed attack. Article 51 provides:

Nothing in the present Charter shall impair the inherent right of individual or collective self-defense if an armed attack occurs against a Member of the United Nations, until the Security Council has taken the measures necessary to maintain international peace and security. Measures taken by Members in the exercise of this right of self-defense shall be immediately reported to the Security Council and shall not in any way affect the authority and responsibility of the Security Council under the present Charter to take at any time such action as it deems necessary in order to maintain or restore international peace and security.

Thus, article 51 restates and preserves, for member states in the situations covered by the article, a long-recognized principle of international law. The article is a "saving clause" designed to make clear that no other provision in the charter shall be interpreted to impair the inherent right of self-defense referred to in article 51.

Three principal objections have been raised against the availability of the right of individual and collective self-defense in the case of Viet-Nam: (1) that this right applies only in the case of an armed attack on a United Nations member; (2) that it does not apply in the case of South Viet-Nam because the latter is not an independent sovereign state; and (3) that collective self-defense may be undertaken only by a regional organization operating under chapter VIII of the United Nations Charter. These objections will now be considered in turn.

C. THE RIGHT OF INDIVIDUAL AND COLLECTIVE SELF-DEFENSE APPLIES IN THE CASE OF SOUTH VIET-NAM WHETHER OR NOT THAT COUNTRY IS A MEMBER OF THE UNITED NATIONS

1. South Viet-Nam enjoys the right of self-defense. The argument that the right of self-defense is available only to members of the United Nations mistakes the nature of the right of self-defense and the relationship of the United Nations Charter to international law in this respect. As already shown, the right of self-defense against armed attack is an inherent right under international law. The right is not conferred by the charter, and, indeed, article 51 expressly recognizes that the right is inherent.

The charter nowhere contains any provision designed to deprive nonmembers of the right of self-defense against armed attack. Article 2, paragraph 6, does charge the United Nations with responsibility for insuring that nonmember states act in accordance with United Nations "Principles so far as may be necessary for the maintenance of international peace and security." Protection against aggression and self-defense against armed attack are important elements in the whole charter scheme for the maintenance of international peace and security. To deprive nonmembers of their inherent right of self-defense would not accord with the principles of the organization, but would instead be prejudicial to the maintenance of peace. Thus article 2, paragraph 6—and, indeed, the rest of the charter—should certainly not be construed to nullify or diminish the inherent defensive rights of nonmembers.

2. The United States has the right to assist in the defense of South Viet-Nam although the latter is not a United Nations member. The cooperation of two or more international entities in the defense of one or both against armed attack is generally referred to as collective self-defense. United States participation in the defense of South Viet-Nam at the latter's request is an example of collective self-defense.

The United States is entitled to exercise the right of individual or collective self-defense against armed attack, as that right exists in international law, subject only to treaty limitations and obligations undertaken by this country.

It has been urged that the United States has no right to participate in the collective defense of South Viet-Nam because article 51 of the United Nations Charter speaks only of the situation "if an armed attack occurs *against a Member of the United Nations.*" This argument is without substance.

In the first place, article 51 does not impose restrictions or cut down the otherwise available rights of United Nations members. By its own terms, the article preserves an inherent right. It is, therefore, necessary to look elsewhere in the charter for any obligation of members restricting their participation in collective defense of an entity that is not a United Nations member.

Article 2, paragraph 4, is the principal provision of the charter imposing limitations on the use of force by members. It states that they:

. . . shall refrain in their international relations from the threat or use of force against the territorial integrity or political independence of any state, or in any other manner inconsistent with the Purposes of the United Nations.

Action taken in defense against armed attack cannot be characterized as falling within this proscription. The record of the San Francisco conference makes clear that article 2, paragraph 4, was not intended to restrict the right of self-defense against armed attack.

One will search in vain for any other provision in the charter that would preclude United States participation in the collective defense of a nonmember. . . .

D. THE RIGHT OF INDIVIDUAL AND COLLECTIVE SELF-DEFENSE APPLIES WHETHER OR NOT SOUTH VIET-NAM IS REGARDED AS AN INDEPENDENT SOVEREIGN STATE

1. South Viet-Nam enjoys the right of self-defense. It has been asserted that the conflict in Viet-Nam is "civil strife" in which foreign intervention is forbidden. Those who make this assertion have gone so far as to compare Ho Chi Minh's actions in Viet-Nam with the efforts of President Lincoln to preserve the Union during the American Civil War. Any such characterization is an entire fiction disregarding the actual situation in Viet-Nam. The Hanoi regime is anything but the legitimate government of a unified country in which the South is rebelling against lawful national authority.

The Geneva accords of 1954 provided for a division of Viet-Nam into two zones at the 17th parallel. Although this line of demarcation was intended to be temporary, it was established by international agreement, which specifically forbade aggression by one zone against the other.

The Republic of Viet-Nam in the South has been recognized as a separate international entity by approximately 60 governments the world over. It has been admitted as a member of a number of the specialized agencies of the United Nations. The United Nations General Assembly in 1957 voted to recommend South Viet-Nam for membership in the organization, and its admission was frustrated only by the veto of the Soviet Union in the Security Council.

In any event there is no warrant for the suggestion that one zone of a temporarily divided state—whether it be Germany, Korea, or Viet-Nam—can be legally overrun by armed forces from the other zone, crossing the internationally recognized line of demarcation between the two. Any such doctrine would subvert the international agreement establishing the line of demarcation, and would pose grave dangers to international peace.

The action of the United Nations in the Korean conflict of 1950 clearly established the principle that there is no greater license for one zone of a temporarily divided state to attack the other zone than there is for one state to attack another state. South Viet-Nam has the right that South Korea had to defend itself and to organize collective defense against an armed attack from the North. A resolution of the Security Council dated June 25, 1950, noted "with grave concern the armed attack upon the Republic of Korea by forces from North Korea," and determined "that this action constitutes a breach of the peace."

2. The United States is entitled to participate in the collective defense of South Viet-Nam whether or not the latter is regarded as an independent sovereign state.

* * *

There is nothing in the charter to suggest that United Nations members are precluded from participating in the defense of a recognized international entity against armed attack merely because the entity may lack some of the attributes of an independent sovereign state. Any such result would have a destructive effect on the stability of international engagements such as the Geneva accords of 1954 and on internationally agreed lines of demarcation. Such a result, far from being in accord with the charter and the purposes of the United Nations, would undermine them and would create new dangers to international peace and security.

* * *

F. THE UNITED STATES HAS FULFILLED ITS
OBLIGATIONS TO THE UNITED NATIONS

A further argument has been made that the members of the United Nations have conferred on United Nations organs—and, in particular, on the Security Council—exclusive power to act against aggression. Again, the express language of article 51 contradicts that assertion. A victim of armed attack is not required to forgo individual or collective defense of its territory until such time as the United Nations organizes collective action and takes appropriate measures. To the contrary, article 51 clearly states that the right of self-defense may be exercised "*until* the Security Council has taken the measures necessary to maintain international peace and security."[1]

As indicated earlier, article 51 is not literally applicable to the Viet-Nam situation since South Viet-Nam is not a member. However, reasoning by analogy from article 51 and adopting its provisions as an appropriate guide for the conduct of members in a case like Viet-Nam, one can only conclude that United States actions are fully in accord with this country's obligations as a member of the United Nations.

Article 51 requires that:

Measures taken by Members in the exercise of this right of self-defense shall be immediately reported to the Security Council and shall not in any way affect the authority and responsibility of the Security Council under the present Charter to take at any time such action as it deems necessary in order to maintain or restore international peace and security.

The United States has reported to the Security Council on measures it has taken in countering the Communist aggression in Viet-Nam. In August 1964 the United States asked the Council to consider the situation created by North Vietnamese attacks on United States destroyers in the Tonkin Gulf. The Council thereafter met to debate the question, but adopted no resolutions. Twice in February 1965 the United States sent additional reports to the Security Council on the conflict in Viet-Nam and on the additional measures taken by the United States in the collective defense of South Viet-Nam. In January 1966 the United States formally submitted the Viet-Nam question to the Security Council for its consideration and introduced a draft resolution calling for discussions looking toward a peaceful settlement on the basis of the Geneva accords.

At no time has the Council taken any action to restore peace and security in Southeast Asia. The Council has not expressed criticism of United States actions. Indeed, since the United States submission of January 1966, members of the Council have been notably reluctant to proceed with any consideration of the Viet-Nam question.

The conclusion is clear that the United States has in no way acted to interfere with United Nations consideration of the conflict in Viet-Nam. On the contrary, the United States has requested United Nations consideration, and the Council has not seen fit to act.

* * *

II. The United States Has Undertaken Commitments to assist South Viet-Nam in Defending Itself Against Communist Aggression from the North

* * *

B. THE UNITED STATES UNDERTOOK AN
INTERNATIONAL OBLIGATION TO DEFEND
SOUTH VIET-NAM IN THE SEATO TREATY

Later in 1954 the United States negotiated with a number of other countries and signed the Southeast Asia Collective Defense Treaty. The treaty contains in the first paragraph of article IV the following provision:

Each Party recognizes that aggression by means of armed attack in the treaty area against any of the Parties or against any State or territory which the Parties by unanimous agreement may hereafter designate, would endanger its own peace and safety, and agrees that it will in that event act to meet the common danger in accordance with its constitutional processes. Measures taken under this paragraph shall be immediately reported to the Security Council of the United Nations.

Annexed to the treaty was a protocol stating that:

The Parties to the Southeast Asia Collective Defense Treaty unanimously designate for the purposes of Article IV of the Treaty the States Cambodia and Laos and the free territory under the jurisdiction of the State of Vietnam.

Thus, the obligations of article IV, paragraph 1, dealing with the eventuality of armed attack, have from the outset covered the territory of South Viet-Nam. The facts as to the North Vietnamese armed attack against the South have been summarized earlier, in the discussion of the right of self-defense under international law and the Charter of the United Nations. The term "armed attack" has the same meaning in the SEATO treaty as in the United Nations Charter.

Article IV, paragraph 1, places an obligation on each party to the SEATO treaty to "act to meet the common danger in accordance with its constitutional processes" in the event of an armed attack. The treaty does not require a collective determination that an armed attack has occurred in order that the obligation of article IV, paragraph 1, become operative. Nor does the provision require collective decision on actions to be taken to meet the common danger. As Secretary Dulles pointed out when transmitting the treaty to the President, the commitment in article IV, paragraph 1, "leaves to the judgment of each country the type of action to be taken in the event an armed attack occurs."

The treaty was intended to deter armed aggression in Southeast Asia. To that end it created not only a multilateral alliance but also a series of bilateral relationships. The obligations are placed squarely on "each Party" in the event of armed attack in the treaty area— not upon "the Parties," a wording that might have implied a necessity for collective decision. The treaty was intended to give the assurance of United States assistance to any party or protocol state that might suffer a Communist armed attack, regardless of the views or actions of other parties. The fact that the obligations are individual, and may even to some extent differ among the parties to the treaty, is demonstrated by the United States understanding, expressed at the time of signature, that its obligations under article IV, paragraph 1, apply only in the event of *Communist* aggression, whereas the other parties to the treaty were unwilling so to limit their obligations to each other.

Thus, the United States has a commitment under article IV, paragraph 1, in the event of armed attack, independent of the decision or action of other treaty parties. A joint statement issued by Secretary Rusk and Foreign Minister Thanat Khoman of Thailand on March 6, 1962, reflected this understanding:

The Secretary of State assured the Foreign Minister that in the event of such aggression, the United States intends to give full effect to its obligations under the Treaty to act to meet the common danger in accordance with its constitutional processes. The Secretary of State reaffirmed that this obligation of the United States does not depend upon the prior agreement of all other parties to the Treaty, since this Treaty obligation is individual as well as collective.

Most of the SEATO countries have stated that they agreed with this interpretation. None has registered objection to it.

When the Senate Committee on Foreign Relations reported on the Southeast Asia Collective Defense Treaty, it noted that the treaty area was further defined so that the "Free Territory of Vietnam" was an area "which, if attacked, would fall under the protection of the instrument." In its conclusion the committee stated:

The committee is not impervious to the risks which this treaty entails. It fully appreciates that acceptance of these additional obligations commits the United States to a course of action over a vast expanse of the Pacific. Yet these risks are consistent with our own highest interests.

The Senate gave its advice and consent to the treaty by a vote of 82 to 1.

* * *

III. Actions by the United States and South Viet-Nam Are Justified Under the Geneva Accords of 1954

A. DESCRIPTION OF THE ACCORDS

The Geneva accords of 1954[2] established the date and hour for a cease-fire in Viet-Nam, drew a "provisional military demarcation line" with a demilitarized zone on both sides, and required an exchange of prisoners and the phased regroupment of Viet Minh forces from the south to the north and of French Union forces from the north to the south. The introduction into Viet-Nam of troop reinforcements and new military equipment (except for replacement and repair) was prohibited. The armed forces of each party were required to respect the demilitarized zone and the territory of the other zone. The adherence of either zone to any military alliance, and the use of either zone for the resumption of hostilities or to "further an aggressive policy," were prohibited. The International Control Commission was established, composed of India, Canada and Poland, with India as chairman. The task of the Commission was to supervise the proper execution of the provisions of the cease-fire agreement. General elections that would result in reunification were required to be held in July 1956 under the supervision of the ICC.

B. NORTH VIET-NAM VIOLATED THE ACCORDS FROM THE BEGINNING

From the very beginning, the North Vietnamese violated the 1954 Geneva accords. Communist military forces and supplies were left in the South in violation of the accords. Other Communist guerrillas were moved north for further training and then were infiltrated into the South in violation of the accords.

C. THE INTRODUCTION OF UNITED STATES MILITARY PERSONNEL AND EQUIPMENT WAS JUSTIFIED

The accords prohibited the reinforcement of foreign military forces in Viet-Nam and the introduction of new military equipment, but they allowed replacement of existing military personnel and equipment. Prior to late 1961 South Viet-Nam had received considerable military equipment and supplies from the United States, and the United States had gradually enlarged its Military Assistance Advisory Group to slightly less than 900 men. These actions were reported to the ICC and were justified as replacements for equipment in Viet-Nam in 1954 and for French training and advisory personnel who had been withdrawn after 1954.

As the Communist aggression intensified during 1961, with increased infiltration and a marked stepping up of Communist terrorism in the South, the United States found it necessary in late 1961 to increase substantially the numbers of our military personnel and the amounts and types of equipment introduced by this country into South Viet-Nam. These increases were justified by the international law principle that a material breach of an agreement by one party entitles the other at least to withhold compliance with an equivalent, corresponding, or related provision until the defaulting party is prepared to honor its obligations.[3]

In accordance with this principle, the systematic violation of the Geneva accords by North Viet-Nam justified South Viet-Nam in suspending compliance with the provision controlling entry of foreign military personnel and military equipment.

D. SOUTH VIET-NAM WAS JUSTIFIED IN REFUSING TO IMPLEMENT THE ELECTION PROVISIONS OF THE GENEVA ACCORDS

The Geneva accords contemplated the reunification of the two parts of Viet-Nam. They contained a provision for general elections to be held in July 1956 in order to obtain a "free expression of the national will." The accords stated that "consultations will be held on this subject between the competent representative authorities of the two zones from 20 July 1955 onwards."

There may be some question whether South Viet-Nam was bound by these election provisions. As indicated earlier, South Viet-Nam did not sign the cease-fire agreement of 1954, nor did it adhere to the Final Declaration of the Geneva conference. The South Vietnamese Government at that time gave notice of its objection in particular to the election provisions of the accords.

However, even on the premise that these provisions were binding on South Viet-Nam, the South Vietnamese Government's failure to engage in consultations in 1955, with a view to holding elections in 1956, involved no breach of obligation. The conditions in North Viet-Nam during that period were such as to make impossible any free and meaningful expression of popular will.

Some of the facts about conditions in the North were admitted even by the Communist leadership in Hanoi. General Giap, currently Defense Minister of North Viet-Nam, in addressing the Tenth Congress of the North Vietnamese Communist Party in October 1956, publicly acknowledged that the Communist leaders were running a police state where executions, terror, and torture were commonplace. A nationwide election in these circumstances would have been a travesty· No one in the North would have dared to vote except as directed. With a substantial majority of the Vietnamese people living north of the 17th parallel, such an election would have meant turning the country over to the Communists without regard to the will of the people. The South Vietnamese Government realized these facts and quite properly took the position that consultations for elections in 1956 as contemplated by the accords would be a useful formality.[4]

IV. The President Has Full Authority to Commit United States Forces in the Collective Defense of South Viet-Nam

There can be no question in present circumstances of the President's authority to commit United States forces to the defense of South Viet-Nam. The grant of authority to the President in article II of the Constitution extends to the actions of the United States currently undertaken in Viet-Nam. In fact, however, it is unnecessary to determine whether this grant standing alone is sufficient to authorize the actions taken in Viet-Nam. These actions rest not only on the exercise of Presidential powers under article II but on the SEATO treaty—a treaty advised and consented to by the Senate—and on actions of the Congress, particularly the joint resolution of August 10, 1964. When these sources of authority are taken together—article II of the Constitution, the SEATO treaty, and actions by the Congress—there can be no question of the legality under domestic law of United States actions in Viet-Nam.

* * *

Notes

1. An argument has been made by some that the United States, by joining in the collective

defense of South Viet-Nam, has violated the peaceful settlement obligation of article 33 in the charter. This argument overlooks the obvious proposition that a victim of armed aggression is not required to sustain the attack undefended while efforts are made to find a political solution with the aggressor. Article 51 of the charter illustrates this by making perfectly clear that the inherent right of self-defense is impaired by "Nothing in the present Charter," including the provisions of article 33.

2. These accords were composed of a bilateral cease-fire agreement between the "Commander-in-Chief of the People's Army of Viet Nam" and the "Commander-in-Chief of the French Union forces in Indo-China," together with a Final Declaration of the Conference, to which France adhered. However, it is to be noted that the South Vietnamese Government was not a signatory of the cease-fire agreement and did not adhere to the Final Declaration. South Viet-Nam entered a series of reservations in a statement to the conference. This statement was noted by the conference, but by decision of the conference chairman it was not included or referred to in the Final Declaration.

3. This principle of law and the circumstances in which it may be invoked are most fully discussed in the Fourth Report on the Law of Treaties by Sir Gerald Fitzmaurice, articles 18, 20 (U.N. doc. A/CN.4/120(1959)) II Yearbook of the International Law Commission 37 (U.N. doc. A/CN.4/SER.A/1959/Add.1) and in the later report by Sir Humphrey Waldock, article 20 (U.N. doc. A/CN.4/156 and Add. 1–3 (1963)) II Yearbook of the International Law Commission 36 (U.N. doc. A/CN.4/SER.A/1963/Add.1). Among the authorities cited by the fourth report for this proposition are: II Oppenheim, International Law, 136, 137 (7th ed. Lauterpacht 1955); I Rousseau, Principes généraux du droit international public 365 (1944); II Hyde, International Law 1660 et seq. (2d ed. 1947); II Guggenheim, Traité de droit international public 84, 85 (1935); Spiropoulos, Traité théorique et pratique de droit international public 289 (1933); Verdross, Völkerrecht, 328 (1950); Hall, Treatise 21 (8th ed. Higgins 1924); 3 Accioly, Tratado de Direito Internacional Publico 82 (1956–57). See also draft articles 42 and 46 of the Law of Treaties by the International Law Commission, contained in the report on the work of its 15th session (General Assembly, Official Records, 18th Session, Supplement No. 9 (A/5809)).

4. In any event, if North Viet-Nam considered there had been a breach of obligation by the South, its remedies lay in discussion with Saigon, perhaps in an appeal to the co-chairmen of the Geneva conference, or in a reconvening of the conference to consider the situation. Under international law, North Viet-Nam had no right to use force outside its own zone in order to secure its political objectives.

United States Intervention in Vietnam is Illegal*

Lawyers Committee on American Policy Towards Vietnam

Point 1

The Unilateral Military Intervention of the United States in Vietnam Violates the Charter of the United Nations. The Charter's Exceptional Authorization of individual and collective Self-Defense "if an Armed Attack Occurs Against a Member of the United Nations" does Not Apply in the Case of Vietnam.

The Charter of the United Nations is a treaty that specifically obligates the United States (1) to refrain from the unilateral use or threat of force in international relations (Article 2 (4)) and (2) to settle international disputes by peaceful means.

The Charter creates a very narrow exception to the broad prohibition of unilateral force. This exception (Article 51) affirms the "inherent right of individual or collective self-defense if an *armed attack* occurs against *a Member of the United Nations. . . .*"

The Department [of State] Brief seizes upon the word "inherent" to argue that prior to the adoption of the United Nations Charter, states possessed a broad right of self-defense; that this right is not dimin-

* Reprinted from *The New York Times* (January 15, 1967), p. E9, by permission of the Lawyers Committee on American Policy Towards Vietnam.

ished by Article 51. Hence, it argues, the exercise of this right of "collective self-defense" by the United States on behalf of South Vietnam is not inconsistent with the Charter.

This contention is fallacious for several reasons:

I. THERE HAS BEEN NO "ARMED ATTACK" UPON SOUTH VIETNAM WITHIN THE MEANING OF ARTICLE 51 OF THE CHARTER

The question crucial for world order is— What kind of grievance permits a state to act in "self-defense"?

The right of self-defense under the Charter exists only if an "armed attack" has occurred. The language of Article 51 is unequivocal. The concrete term "armed attack" was deliberately introduced into the Charter to eliminate the discretion of states to determine for themselves the scope of permissible self-defense—that is, to wage war without *prior* U.N. authorization. A claim for self-defense is permissible only "when the necessity for action is instant, overwhelming, and leaving no choice of means, and no moment for deliberation." This definition of self-defense was stated in classic form by Secretary of State Daniel Webster in the *Caroline Case*, (VII Moore's Digest of International Law, 919) and was affirmed in the Nuremberg judgment and by un-animous vote of the U.N. General Assembly at its First Session. Res. 95 (1).

The State Department Memorandum acknowledges that a *specific* form of aggression, namely, an "*armed attack*" is an essential condition precedent to the use of force in self-defense, and that a mere allegation of indirect aggression does not entitle a state to wage war by unilateral discretion. However, the Memorandum blurs the essential distinction between the broad and vague *general* concept of aggression and the narrow one of armed attack. Evidently endeavoring to justify the U.S.'s open combat actions against North Vietnam and in South

Vietnam which started on February 7, 1965, the State Department merely alleges the occurrence of an armed attack by North Vietnam "before February 1965," without providing a convincing demonstration of why its allegations about the gradual infiltration of North Vietnamese guerrillas over a period of ten years in support of the Vietcong insurgency should be regarded as an armed attack.

The Department Brief quotes selectively from the reports of the International Control Commission to support its claims of subversion and infiltration over the "years." It fails, however, to acknowledge passages in the reports of the ICC that criticize the forbidden, and progressively increasing, military build-up of South Vietnam by the United States that commenced almost immediately after the Geneva Accords of 1954. It is in the context of this gradually increasing American military build-up of South Vietnam and American military presence in South Vietnam that one must assess the contention that the infiltration of 40,000 North Vietnamese between 1954 and 1965 should be viewed as an armed attack.

The Department Brief itself provides the reasoning with which to reject its charge of "armed attack" by North Vietnam. The long-smoldering conditions of unrest, subversion and infiltration in South Vietnam that it describes is an example of the very opposite of an emergency demanding immediate response "leaving no choice of means, and no moment for deliberation" and justifying a claim of self-defense. The State Department's argument, if accepted, would broaden Article 51 far beyond either its intended or desirable meaning. Whereas the Charter limits the use of force by unilateral decision to specific emergencies where there is no time to seek authorization from the Security Council, the State Department's doctrine would grant all states—and even "entities" which are not sovereign states— a dangerous and virtually unlimited discretion to decide when force shall be used. This is in clear contrast to the letter and spirit of the Charter.

The Department Brief does not even sustain its charge of indirect aggression. It indicates that prior to 1964 the "infiltrators" were South Vietnamese that had previously moved North after July 1954. Moreover, the lumping together of "40,000 armed and unarmed guerillas" is not meaningful. How can an unarmed Vietnamese who moves from one zone of his own country to another be classified as a "guerilla" and "infiltrator", contributing to "armed attack"? Above all, the implication that by 1964 the Southern insurgents had been reinforced by 40,000 guerillas from the North is altogether misleading; for this figure, even if correct, fails to deduct all those who during a whole decade died, became incapacitated, were taken prisoners, deserted, or simply withdrew from or never participated in the insurgency.

The Mansfield Report shows that before 1965 infiltration from the North "was confined primarily to political cadres and military leadership." On the other hand it notes that by 1962, "United States military advisers and service forces in South Vietnam totaled approximately 10,000 men." The Report makes plain that significant armed personnel were introduced from the North only *after* the United States had intervened when "total collapse of the Saigon government's authority appeared imminent in the early months of 1965." It states (at p. 1):

"United States combat troops in strength arrived at that point in response to the appeal of the Saigon authorities. The Vietcong *counter-response* was to increase their military activity with forces strengthened by intensified *local* recruitment and infiltration of regular North Vietnamese troops. With the change in the composition of the opposing forces the character of the war also changed sharply." The Report (p. 3) underscores that sig-

nificant forces from the North followed and did not precede the direct involvement of the United States.

To summarize this crucial point—self-defense is legally permissible only in response to a particularly grave, immediate emergency—described in international law and the Charter as "armed attack." The kind of force allegedly employed by North Vietnam in South Vietnam cannot appropriately be regarded as an "armed attack" within the meaning of Article 51. Therefore a claim to act in self-defense is unavailable to South Vietnam; and, *a fortiori*, unavailable to the United States as an ally acting in collective self-defense.

2. THE UNITED STATES FAILED TO FULFILL ITS CHARTER OBLIGATION TO SEEK A PEACEFUL SOLUTION IN VIETNAM

The State Department also ignores the obligation under the Charter to seek *first of all* a peaceful solution by any method of the disputant's own choice, within or outside the machinery of the United Nations. This legal requirement is elaborated in Article 33 (1): "The parties to any dispute, the continuance of which is likely to endanger the maintenance of international peace and security, shall *first of all*, seek a solution by negotiation, enquiry, mediation, conciliation, arbitration, judicial settlement, resort to regional agencies or arrangements, or other peaceful means of their own choice."

The United States has had many years within which to seek a peaceful solution of the Vietnam situation. Indeed, a report prepared for the American Friends Service Committee—"Peace in Vietnam"—discussing "The Negotiation Puzzle", points out that "a careful reading of the *New York Times* shows that the United States has rejected no fewer than seven efforts to negotiate an end to the war" (p. 51), citing efforts by U Thant, President de Gaulle, Hanoi and others, made long before the United States embarked upon an active combat role in February, 1965.

Ever since the mid-1950's the reports of the International Control Commission contain many complaints about South Vietnam's deliberate and systematic sabotage of the machinery created by the Geneva Accords to prevent dangerous developments. The United States has done little to dispel the belief that it has favored a "military solution" to the conflict in Vietnam.

3. THE DOCTRINE OF "COLLECTIVE SELF-DEFENSE" CANNOT JUSTIFY THE UNITED STATES MILITARY INTERVENTION IN THE CIVIL WAR IN SOUTH VIETNAM

If the conflict in South Vietnam is a civil war the intervention of the United States is a violation of the undertaking, fundamental in international law, that one state has no right to intervene in the internal affair of other countries.

It seems most correct to regard the present conflict in South Vietnam as essentially a civil war among, what James Reston has described a "tangle of competing individuals, regions, religions and sects . . . [among] a people who have been torn apart by war and dominated and exploited by Saigon for generations." (*New York Times*, April 3, 1966.)

The Charter of the United Nations is silent on the subject of civil war. It has been generally assumed, however, that a civil war is a matter essentially within the domestic jurisdiction of a state (Article 2(7)), and that therefore even the United Nations is obliged to refrain from intervening unless the civil war is identified by a competent organ of the U.N. as a threat to international peace. Certainly if the United Nations must stay aloof from civil wars, then it is even clearer that individual states are likewise obliged to refrain from interfering in civil wars. The weight of opinion among international lawyers lays stress upon a duty of non-intervention in ongoing civil wars.

Even if North Vietnam and South Vietnam are accorded the status of separate entities in international law, approximating the status of independent countries, rather than being "temporary zones" of a single country as decreed by the Geneva Accords, the United States may not respond to the intervention of North Vietnam in the civil war in the South by bombing the North. There is no legal basis for an outside state to respond to an intervention by another state in a civil war with a military attack on the territory of the intervening state. Neither Germany under Hitler nor Italy under Mussolini claimed that their intervention in behalf of Franco during the Spanish Civil War would have vindicated their use of military force upon the territory of the Soviet Union, a state intervening in behalf of the Loyalists. Correspondingly, the Soviet Union, intervening in behalf of Spain's legitimate government, did not claim any right to use military force against Germany or Italy. It is sobering to realize that if the United States was lawfully entitled to bomb North Vietnam in response to North Vietnam's intervention in the Southern civil war, then North Vietnam or any of its allies would have been lawfully entitled to bomb the United States in response to the United States' much more massive intervention in that civil war.

4. THE "REQUEST" OF THE "GOVERNMENT" OF SOUTH VIETNAM DOES NOT PROVIDE A LEGAL BASIS FOR "COLLECTIVE SELF-DEFENSE"

The evidence shows that in many respects the present Saigon regime, just as its predecessors since 1954, is a client government of the United States. These governments seem to have been incapable of independent action, as regards either inviting American assistance or requesting modification or termination of American assistance. Furthermore, these regimes have been unable to act on behalf of their people or even to rule effectively the territory under their control. The present government has no constitutional basis, and is incapable even of achieving stability on its own side in the face of the emergency represented by the ongoing civil war, a factor that normally postpones protest movement until the civil war is settled. The recurring protests of Buddhists, Catholics, business leaders, students, intellectuals, and other civilian groups in South Vietnam are dramatic evidence of the tenuous existence and the repressive quality of Premier Ky's regime.

If the United States were to withdraw from South Vietnam the Ky government would collapse. In what sense, then, is such a regime sufficiently constituted as a government to authorize military intervention of the United States on its own behalf? It is hardly comforting to rely upon the Soviet suppression of the Nagy uprising of 1956 in Hungary as a useful precedent to support what the United States is doing in Vietnam on a far larger and sustained scale.

5. THE KOREAN PRECEDENT DOES NOT JUSTIFY THE UNILATERAL INTERVENTION OF THE UNITED STATES IN VIETNAM

The State Department's reliance upon the Korean precedent to sustain "the right to organize collective defense," is inadequate to establish a legal basis for the unilateral U. S. military intervention in Vietnam. General Ridgway, among others, has pointed to some of the important differences between Korea and Vietnam (*Look Magazine*, April 5, 1966, p. 82):

"In South Korea, we had a workable government. . . . We acted in concert with many nations and had been *deputized* by the *United Nations* to repel the aggressor in its name."

In Korea, a massive invasion (armed attack) from the North had occurred, as attested to by United Nations observers; nevertheless, the United States did not claim a right of "collective self-defense" on behalf of the South but brought the case before the United Nations Security Council, and thereafter acted in the name of the United Nations.

Point II

The Military Presence of the United States in Vietnam Violates the Geneva Accords of 1954

The State Department claims that the U. S. military intervention in Vietnam is compatible with the Geneva Accords of 1954 and, in fact, is based on U. S. assurances made at the time of their signing.

The Geneva Conference dealt with the situation created by the defeat of the French in their 8-year war against the Viet Minh for control over the whole of Vietnam. After the battle at Dien Bien Phu in June 1954, the Viet Minh occupied the major part of the country north of the thirteenth parallel. However, Ho Chi Minh agreed to withdraw his forces to the north of the seventeenth parallel in exchange for two central commitments: (1) the unconditional promise that all foreign military forces in Vietnam would be removed, and (2) that within two years elections would be held under international supervision to unify the country, so that the temporary division of Vietnam into a northern and southern zone would end by July 1956.

The United States pledged on July 21, 1954 not "to disturb" the Geneva Accords. Article 6 of the Final Declaration of the Geneva Conference explicity stated that "the military demarcation line is provisional and shall not in any way be interpreted as constituting a political or territorial boundary."

It is generally acknowledged that Hanoi initially carried out the central provisions of the Accords and eschewed violence south of the seventeenth parallel because it expected to win the elections and did not wish to alienate those whose electoral support it sought. (See, e.g., Fourth Interim Report of the International Control Commission, Vietnam No. 3, Command Paper 9654 [1954]). Nevertheless, on July 16, 1955, the Diem regime, with United States backing, announced that it would not participate in the prescribed nation-wide elections and would not even negotiate with Hanoi, as also prescribed in the Accords, about their modalities. The fact that the Accords granted Diem a full year (July 1955-July 1956) to demand any safeguards for fair elections refutes the State Department's assertion that Diem's obstruction of the central provision of the Geneva Settlement—reunification—was justified because the elections would not have been fair in the North.

As late as September 18, 1961, the International Control Commission (ICC) insisted upon compliance with the obligation to hold elections for reunification. In a Special Report of June 2, 1962, the ICC declared that the United States "increased military aid" to South Vietnam and that the United States' "factual military alliance" with South Vietnam violated the Geneva Agreement.

Point III

The United States Is Not Committed by the SEATO Treaty or Otherwise to Intervene in Vietnam

The State Department's claim that the United States military involvement in Vietnam is in fulfillment of its obligation under the Southeast Asia Collective Defense Treaty is untenable. The argument is a late discovery. SEATO was not mentioned in the official U.S. announcements in February 1965, when the bombing of North Vietnam commenced. In March 1965, the State Department, in a Memorandum entitled "Legal Basis for the United States Actions Against North Vietnam," did not refer to SEATO. Neither Secretary of State Rusk, in an address on Vietnam before the American Society of International Law in April 1965, nor President Johnson, in a statement on July 28, 1965 explaining "Why We Are in Vietnam," made any reference to SEATO.

In fact, the SEATO Treaty does not enlarge the legal basis for the use of force contained in the U.N. Charter. The State Department misleadingly asserts that the Treaty's Article 4 (1) creates an "*obligation* . . . to meet the common danger in the event of *armed aggression*". The term "*armed aggression*" is not contained in the Treaty. Repeating the language of the U.N. Charter, Article 4 (1), speaks of "aggression by means of *armed attack*." Since an armed attack has not occurred, SEATO does not authorize defensive action; if an armed attack *had* occurred, SEATO would be redundant, as the use of force would be permissible under Article 51 of the Charter.

In the event of an "armed attack" the United States would have had, at most, the legal *right*, but certainly not an *obligation*, to assist South Vietnam. None of the other SEATO parties regard military intervention in Vietnam as legally required by SEATO. On the contrary, two leading members of SEATO—Pakistan and France —have publicly denounced the United States' role in the Vietnam war.

Article 4 (2) of the SEATO Treaty makes clear that if South Vietnam were threatened "in any way *other* than by armed attack," the (SEATO) parties "shall consult immediately in order to agree on the measures which should be taken for the common defense." And Article 2 of the Treaty makes clear that "subversive activities directed from without" does *not* constitute "an armed attack," but call for consultation by the treaty members. *Consultation* is not unilateral military assistance. Indeed, the Treaty presupposes unanimous *agreement* among the other seven partners before any SEATO power would be authorized to offer military support. In 1964, the unanimity requirement was reinterpreted by the United States to mean that "measures" could be taken in the absence of a dissenting vote among the SEATO partners.

* * *

Point IV

The Intensity and Destructiveness of United States Warfare in Vietnam is Contrary to International Law

The intensity, indiscriminateness, and destructiveness of United States war actions in Vietnam violate basic rules of warfare that have been part of international law at least since the formulation of the Hague Conventions in 1907.

These actions are particularly reprehensible so far as North Vietnam is concerned. It has never been denied that the United States military presence vastly exceeds that of the North in South Vietnam. Under the Geneva Accords, the United States is not entitled to introduce military personnel and equipment anywhere in Vietnam (except man-for-man and piece-for-piece replacements as of the status of July 1954) and much less to participate in active fighting in that country. Even if, as the Department Brief contends, reprisal or response to violations of the Geneva Accords by North Vietnam were justified, the United States would be entitled to disregard these Accords only in proportion to their disregard by North Vietnam.

Long before the advent of the United Nations, it was a basic rule of international law that force used in reprisal must be proportional to the illegal provocation. In the leading case of the pre-United Nations era on the subject (the *Naulilaa Incident*, involving the shelling of Portuguese forts by Germany in 1914), a German-Portuguese Mixed Tribunal emphasized that reprisals "are limited by considerations of humanity and good faith"; and more generally, that, "One should certainly consider as excessive, and therefore illegal, reprisals out of all proportion with the act which motivated them." Bombing North Vietnam, as of February, 1965, in alleged reprisal for Vietcong attacks on two American airbases in South Vietnam, certainly seems to flaunt this rule of proportionality.

* * *

NEUTRALITY AND THE LAW OF WARFARE

A vast body of customary and treaty norms is designed, on the one hand, to regulate the relations of states formally at war or engaged in hostilities in an undeclared war (the law of warfare) and, on the other hand, to regulate the relations between the belligerents and neutral states (the law of neutrality). These norms, in their present form, are largely the product of the events and experience of the nineteenth century, that is to say, they are the product of a period when resort to war as an instrument of national policy was not prohibited by law and when it was generally thought that law could best serve the needs of the international community by confining the locale and minimizing the destructiveness of violence.

The law of neutrality, much of which was codified at the Second Hague Peace Conference of 1907,[1] lent support to the effectiveness of the nineteenth-century "balance of power" system. By encouraging and facilitating nonparticipation in war, the norms tended to prevent conflicts from spreading; and with powerful

[1] Sections of the Hague Conventions on the Rights and Duties of Neutral Powers and Persons in War on Land and on the Rights and Duties of Neutral Powers in Naval War are reprinted in this section on pp. 391–395.

neutrals able to enter conflicts to redress the "balance," belligerents were inclined to adopt limited objectives. Conversely, the political system of the nineteenth century lent support to the effectiveness of the norms, in that neutrals were generally powerful enough to assert their neutral rights effectively.[2]

In general, the law of neutrality required that neutral states refrain from giving assistance to either side in a conflict, and that belligerents respect the territory of neutrals and permit normal private intercourse between nationals of neutral and belligerent states. Belligerents were allowed to take extraordinary measures in order to wage war successfully, but they were required to refrain from disrupting any more than was necessary the normal activities of neutral states and their nationals. A brief reference to some of the particular rules will illustrate the principles. As an aspect of the neutral duty of impartiality, governments of neutral states were forbidden to supply belligerents with arms, ammunition, vessels, or military provisions. But, in deference to the idea of "business as usual," the supply of war materials to belligerents by neutral nationals was not unlawful; and, with the exception of the fitting out or arming of vessels by their nationals, neutral governments were not obligated to prevent it. On the other hand, in order to prosecute the war, belligerents could, in disregard of the peacetime right of freedom of the seas, "visit and search" neutral merchant ships suspected of carrying war materials, or "contraband," to the enemy. But this belligerent right was circumscribed by duties: before the cargo of a neutral ship could be confiscated, the vessel had to be taken to a belligerent port for a determination by a prize court of the propriety of the seizure, the destination of the ship,

and the nature of the cargo. A belligerent could establish a blockade off the coast of the enemy and then seize the cargo of any neutral ship that sought to "break through"; the cargo of a blockade runner, regardless of whether or not it consisted of war materials, was considered to be contraband and hence subject to seizure. But a blockade was not legally established unless it was announced in advance and was "effective."

These rules, because of disagreement as to what was meant by "contraband," "effectiveness" of blockade, and the like, have always been a source of controversy between belligerents and neutrals. During the two world wars of the twentieth century, they were practically abandoned. The principal reasons for this breakdown would seem to be, as Kaplan and Katzenbach have said, "technological developments, particularly submarines, expanding concepts of economic warfare, and the absence of a number of strong neutrals capable of asserting their rights effectively."[3] Both sides in both wars violated the traditional norms with almost total abandon. For example, the British government expanded the definition of contraband to include any commodity destined for Germany and established the "long-distance blockade." The rules requiring that merchant vessels be escorted to port for a hearing before a prize court gave way to the German policy of unrestricted submarine warfare. Early in both wars, the rights of neutrals were practically obliterated.

Of equal importance was the fact that the leading neutral, the United States, sloughed off its neutral duties during the months before it entered World War II. In September 1940, President Roosevelt announced that the United States had supplied Britain with fifty overage destroyers in return for ninety-nine year leases on eight naval bases in the Caribbean.

[2] For a discussion of the relationship of the "balance of power" system and the law of neutrality, see Kaplan and Katzenbach, *The Political Foundations of International Law,* pp. 217–225.

[3] *Ibid.,* pp. 220–221.

And in March 1941, the United States adopted the so-called "Lend-Lease Bill," which authorized the President, *inter alia*, to sell, transfer title to, exchange, lend, lease, or otherwise dispose of any materials that would assist any state "whose defense the President deems vital to the defense of the United States."[4] These and similar unneutral acts of other states that had not formally entered the war led to the widespread use of the term "nonbelligerency" to describe an intermediate stage between belligerency and neutrality.

In addition to the obvious disinclination of states to continue to exhibit their consent to the particulars of the traditional law of neutrality, it is now widely believed that the fundamental principle of neutral impartiality has been eliminated by the provisions of the United Nations Charter that permit, if not actually require, nonbelligerents to discriminate against aggressors and in favor of their victims. If and when the Security Council begins to function as originally intended by regularly determining which party in a conflict is the aggressor and by calling for collective measures against it, the right to remain neutral, at least for members of the United Nations, will unquestionably be restricted. Even in the absence of such action by the Security Council, states now claim the right to determine for themselves which side in a conflict has resorted to force "in violation of its covenants" and to discriminate against it. Indeed, the United States made use of the legal prohibitions on the right to resort to war that were established in the League of Nations Covenant and the Kellogg-Briand Pact to justify its unneutral behavior prior to its entry into World War II.[5] A Soviet jurist expressed the idea with characteristic frankness: "With aggression an international crime, neutrality becomes a form of connivance at this crime."[6]

In an age characterized by the politics of cold war and anticolonialism, national decision-makers have evinced little interest in reviving the nineteenth-century norms that purported to regulate the relations between belligerents and neutrals. Both the states committed to one side or the other in the cold war and those that are not have demonstrated by their behavior that unneutral activities are thought to be in their best interests. In the inter-state and the internal hostilities[7] that have erupted since World War II, nonbelligerents have regularly supplied their friends and allies with the sinews of war. The law of neutrality is in drastic need of revision if it is once again to receive the consent of states that is necessary to make it reasonably effective. And it is possible, as Kaplan and Katzenbach have suggested, that the present international system cannot sustain "a definite body of international law governing the rights and obligations of neutrals that applies to all armed conflicts, regardless of how they originate or regardless of who participates in them."[8]

The law of warfare, which governs the conduct of belligerents in battle, was, like the law of neutrality, placed under heavy strain by widespread violations during the two world wars. New techniques of warfare tended to undermine the effectiveness of this set of norms no less than they did the traditional law of neutrality. But, unlike in the case of the norms regulating neutrality, the general principles and many of the specific rules of the law of warfare continue to be recognized by states as serving important

---

[4] For the text of the law, see 35 *American Journal of International Law*, Supplement (1941) 76.
[5] "No longer can it be argued that the civilized world must behave with rigid impartiality toward both an aggressor . . . and the victims of unprovoked attack. We need not now . . . deal with the just and the unjust alike." Address of Attorney General Robert H. Jackson before the Inter-American Bar Association, March 27, 1941, reprinted in 35 *American Journal of International Law* 348 (1941).
[6] Eugene A. Korovin, "The Second World War and International Law," 40 *American Journal of International Law* 754 (1946).
[7] For a discussion of international law and internal war, see the selection by Richard A. Falk that is reprinted in this section on pp. 395–401.
[8] Kaplan and Katzenbach, *The Political Foundations of International Law*, p. 225.

national and international needs. And because it is generally agreed that these norms cover the activities of all belligerents, whether they are fighting lawful or unlawful wars, the law of warfare is unaffected by recent developments in the norms regarding resort to force.

The consent of states to the rules and principles of the law of warfare has been expressed through customary practice and through several multilateral agreements, particularly the Hague and Geneva Conventions.[9] It is clear that the interests of states are served by these norms. By agreeing to, and abiding by, rules regarding prisoners of war, for example, national decision-makers attempt to ensure a certain amount of decent treatment of their own troops captured in battle; and by establishing a reputation for norm compliance, enemy troops may be induced to surrender rather than fight to the death. By agreeing to norms that prohibit activities that are generally considered to be brutal or inhumane, such as the use of poison gas or the bombardment of defenseless cities, decision-makers attempt to assure that their own nationals do not fall victim to these practices; and failure to comply with these norms may stimulate hatred in the enemy and, consequently, reinforce his will to fight on. Rules that limit destruction and thereby make postwar reconstruction less burdensome have an obvious utility. And although cynics may not agree, it would seem that more than self-interest underlies the law of warfare. As Wesley L. Gould has said, "some people take pride in having attained a state of civilization at which they can behave with some decency even toward enemies."[10]

While it is true that the rules regulating warfare are not always well observed, it must be emphasized that violations are much better publicized than are instances of compliance. By doing even a pedestrian job of mitigating some of the horrors of war, they serve a useful purpose.

In order to improve the effectiveness of the law of warfare, there is a particular need to update the prohibitions and to strengthen the sanctions that support norm compliance. In the thermonuclear age, law that expressly prohibits the use of "dum-dum bullets" and the poisoning of wells, while remaining silent on the use of hydrogen bombs, seems grossly out of date. Although it is possible to "reason by analogy" and conclude, as a Tokyo District Court did in 1963,[11] that the use of nuclear weapons is proscribed, it is equally possible to conclude that their use is permitted.[12] In 1961, the General Assembly of the United Nations adopted a resolution that stated that the use of such weapons was in violation of the United Nations Charter and "the laws of humanity," but the negative vote of twenty states, including the United States, casts in doubt its legal significance.[13] Consequently, the vitally important question of the legality of the use of nuclear weapons remains a matter of doctrinal controversy.

The traditional means by which belligerents sought to enforce compliance with the rules of warfare consisted, first, of complaints transmitted to enemy and neutral states, with the particular purpose of influencing opinion in neutral states, possibly to the extent of turning neutrals into participants; and, secondly, of reprisals, which are acts otherwise prohibited

---

[9] Sections of Hague Convention IV of 1907 on Law and Customs of War on Land and the Geneva Convention Relative to Treatment of Prisoners of War, 1949, are reprinted in this section on pp. 402–408.

[10] Gould, *An Introduction to International Law,* pp. 626–627.

[11] See *Shimoda and Others v. The State*, reprinted in this section on pp. 408–415.

[12] According to the *United States Army Basic Field Manual 27–10* (1956), "The use of explosive atomic weapons, whether by air, sea, or land forces, cannot as such be regarded as violative of international law in the absence of any customary rule of international law or international convention restricting their employment."

[13] "Declaration on the Prohibition of the Use of Nuclear and Thermonuclear Weapons," General Assembly, *Official Records*, 16th Session, Supplement No. 17 (A/5100), pp. 4–5.

by the law of warfare but which may be taken exceptionally in order to compel the enemy to discontinue illegal acts of warfare.[14] Following World War II, an essentially new means of enforcing compliance came into existence with the widespread use of war crimes trials. Although these trials were not without precedent, never before had those accused of violations of the law of warfare been tried in such large numbers.

The International Military Tribunal, sitting at Nürnberg and composed of members from the United States, the Soviet Union, Britain, and France, began the trial of twenty-two German leaders accused of crimes against peace, war crimes, and crimes against humanity on November 14, 1945. In its judgment of October 1, 1946, 19 convictions were returned, including 12 death sentences.[15] The International Military Tribunal for the Far East, sitting in Tokyo, handed down its judgment on November 12, 1947. All of the 25 Japanese leaders who were accused were found guilty and, of these, 7 received death sentences. In addition to these international tribunals, American, British, French, Soviet, and other military tribunals conducted trials of war criminals. A good statistical summary is provided by Gerhard von Glahn:

By late November, 1948, a total of 7,109 defendants had been arrested for war crimes, including the "major cases" at Nuremberg and Tokyo. Of these, 3,686 had been convicted and 924 trials had resulted in acquittals. Of those convicted, death sentences were received by 1,019, and 33 defendants had committed suicide. Prison sentences were received by 2,667 and 2,499 cases were still pending. Numerous files remained open, however, where war crimes had been committed, but the cul-

prits had disappeared. In the intervening years' many of these, particularly in France and in Germany, have been discovered by their own governments and have been tried. . . . Thus by early 1964 some 5,500 individuals had been tried in West Germany, with about 1,000 cases still pending.[16]

Whether or not these trials, which did not extend to "war criminals" among the victorious allies, can be regarded as "a salutary object lesson for future prospective offenders against the law of war"[17] is debatable, but it is certain that they helped to clarify the international community consensus on the illegality of certain types of belligerent behavior.

The first two selections that follow, Hague Conventions V and XIII on the Rights and Duties of Neutral Powers in Land and Naval War, are generally regarded as expressing a significant portion of the customary law of neutrality in inter-state conflicts. These documents are followed by a discussion by Richard A. Falk of the traditional norms that apply to the behavior of states toward internal conflicts. In this selection from a larger essay by Professor Falk, emphasis is placed on traditional norms and distinctions and on the need to reformulate the law to bring it more into accord with the needs of an age characterized by conflicts *within* states. The next four selections relate to the law of warfare. The first, a brief portion of *Basic Field Manual 27–10* (1940), United States War Department, succinctly states the commonly recognized basic principles of the law of warfare. More extensive sections of Hague Convention IV of 1907 on the Laws and Customs of War on Land and of the 1949 Geneva Convention Relative to the Treatment of Prisoners of War provide a significant portion of the modern rules of warfare. Extensive excerpts from a 1963 decision of a Japanese court, *Shimoda and*

[14] Experience has demonstrated that reprisals are dangerous means of securing norm compliance. More often than not, it seems, the original violator of the law, instead of reforming his behavior, counters with still more reprisal measures; before long, the conflict tends to degenerate to the point where no quarter is shown.
[15] Herman Goering escaped execution by committing suicide after he was sentenced; Martin Bormann, who was tried in absentia and sentenced to death, has never been found.

[16] von Glahn, *Law Among Nations*, pp. 709–710.
[17] *Ibid.*, p. 708.

Others v. The State, are included as a well-reasoned and challenging analysis of the legality of the use of nuclear weapons against cities and civilian populations. Finally, two selections that relate to war crimes trials are reprinted. The first, "Principles of International Law Recognized in the Charter and Judgment of the Nürnberg Tribunal," was prepared by the International Law Commission at the request of the United Nations General Assembly, which by a unanimous vote on December 11, 1946, affirmed "the principles of international law recognized by the Charter of the Nürnberg Tribunal and the Judgment of that Tribunal." Excerpts from *United States v. Wilhelm List, et al.* (the Hostages case), one of the many judgments handed down by the United States Military Tribunal subsequent to the major trials by the International Military Tribunal at Nürnberg, illustrate the reasoning used in trials of persons charged with violations of the law of warfare.

Hague Convention V of 1907 on Rights and Duties of Neutral Powers and Persons in War on Land*

Chapter I. The Rights and Duties of Neutral Powers

Article 1. The territory of neutral Powers is inviolable.

Article 2. Belligerents are forbidden to move troops or convoys of either munitions of war or supplies across the territory of a neutral Power.

Article 3. Belligerents are likewise forbidden to—

a. Erect on the territory of a neutral Power a wireless telegraphy station or other apparatus for the purpose of communicating with belligerent forces on land or sea;

b. Use any installation of this kind established by them before the war on the territory of a neutral Power for purely military purposes, and which has not been opened for the service of public messages.

Article 4. Corps of combatants can not be formed nor recruiting agencies opened on the territory of a neutral Power to assist the belligerents.

Article 5. A neutral Power must not allow any of the acts referred to in articles 2 to 4 to occur on its territory.

It is not called upon to punish acts in violation of its neutrality unless the said acts have been committed on its own territory.

Article 6. The responsibility of a neutral Power is not engaged by the fact of persons crossing the frontier separately to offer their services to one of the belligerents.

Article 7. A neutral Power is not called upon to prevent the export or transport, on behalf of one or other of the belligerents, of arms, munitions of war, or, in general, of anything which can be of use to any army or a fleet.

Article 8. A neutral Power is not called upon to forbid or restrict the use on behalf of the belligerents of telegraph or telephone cables or of wireless telegraphy apparatus belonging to it or to companies or private individuals.

Article 9. Every measure of restriction or prohibition taken by a neutral Power in regard to the matters referred to in articles 7 and 8 must be impartially applied by it to both belligerents.

A neutral Power must see to the same obligation being observed by companies or private individuals owning telegraph or telephone cables or wireless telegraphy apparatus.

Article 10. The fact of a neutral Power resisting, even by force, attempts to violate its neutrality can not be regarded as a hostile act.

* Reprinted from 36 *United States Statutes at Large* 2310.

Chapter II. Belligerents Interned and Wounded Tended in Neutral Territory

Article 11. A neutral Power which receives on its territory troops belonging to the belligerent armies shall intern them, as far as possible, at a distance from the theatre of war.

It may keep them in camps and even confine them in fortresses or in places set apart for this purpose.

It shall decide whether officers can be left at liberty on giving their parole not to leave the neutral territory without permission.

Article 12. In the absence of a special convention to the contrary, the neutral Power shall supply the interned with the food, clothing, and relief required by humanity.

At the conclusion of peace the expenses caused by the internment shall be made good.

Article 13. A neutral Power which receives escaped prisoners of war shall leave them at liberty. If it allows them to remain in its territory it may assign them a place of residence.

The same rule applies to prisoners of war brought by troops taking refuge in the territory of a neutral Power.

Article 14. A neutral Power may authorize the passage over its territory of the sick and wounded belonging to the belligerent armies, on condition that the trains bringing them shall carry neither personnel nor war material. In such a case, the neutral Power is bound to take whatever measures of safety and control are necessary for the purpose.

The sick or wounded brought under these conditions into neutral territory by one of the belligerents, and belonging to the hostile party, must be guarded by the neutral Power so as to ensure their not taking part again in the military operations. The same duty shall devolve on the neutral State with regard to wounded or sick of the other army who may be committed to its care.

Article 15. The Geneva Convention applies to sick and wounded interned in neutral territory.

Chapter III. Neutral Persons

Article 16. The nationals of a State which is not taking part in the war are considered as neutrals.

Article 17. A neutral can not avail himself of his neutrality—

a. If he commits hostile acts against a belligerent;

b. If he commits acts in favor of a belligerent, particularly if he voluntarily enlists in the ranks of the armed force of one of the parties.

In such a case, the neutral shall not be more severely treated by the belligerent as against whom he has abandoned his neutrality than a national of the other belligerent State could be for the same act.

Article 18. The following acts shall not be considered as committed in favor of one belligerent in the sense of article 17, letter (b):

a. Supplies furnished or loans made to one of the belligerents, provided that the person who furnishes the supplies or who makes the loans lives neither in the territory of the other party nor in the territory occupied by him, and that the supplies do not come from these territories;

b. Services rendered in matters of police or civil administration. . . .

* * *

Chapter V. Final Provisions

Article 20. The provisions of the present Convention do not apply except between contracting Powers, and then only if all the belligerents are parties to the Convention. . . .

Hague Convention XIII of 1907 on Rights and Duties of Neutral Powers in Naval War*

Article 1. Belligerents are bound to respect the sovereign rights of neutral Powers and to abstain, in neutral territory or neutral waters, from any act which would, if knowingly permitted by any Power, constitute a violation of neutrality.

Article 2. Any act of hostility, including capture and the exercise of the right of search, committed by belligerent war-ships in the territorial waters of a neutral Power, constitutes a violation of neutrality and is strictly forbidden.

Article 3. When a ship has been captured in the territorial waters of a neutral Power, this Power must employ, if the prize is still within its jurisdiction, the means at its disposal to release the prize with its officers and crew, and to intern the prize crew.

If the prize is not in the jurisdiction of the neutral Power, the captor Government, on the demand of that Power, must liberate the prize with its officers and crew.

Article 4. A prize court can not be set up by a belligerent on neutral territory or on a vessel in neutral waters.

Article 5. Belligerents are forbidden to use neutral ports and waters as a base of naval operations against their adversaries, and in particular to erect wireless telegraphy stations or any apparatus for the purpose of communicating with the belligerent forces on land or sea.

Article 6. The supply, in any manner, directly or indirectly, by a neutral Power to a belligerent Power, of war-ships, ammunition, or war material of any kind whatever, is forbidden.

Article 7. A neutral Power is not bound to prevent the export or transit, for the use of either belligerent, of arms, ammunition, or, in general, of anything which could be of use to an army or fleet.

Article 8. A neutral Government is

*Reprinted from 36 *United States Statutes at Large* 2415.

bound to employ the means at its disposal to prevent the fitting out or arming of any vessel within its jurisdiction which it has reason to believe is intended to cruise, or engage in hostile operations, against a Power with which that Government is at peace. It is also bound to display the same vigilance to prevent the departure from its jurisdiction of any vessel intended to cruise, or engage in hostile operations, which had been adapted entirely or partly within the said jurisdiction for use in war.

Article 9. A neutral Power must apply impartially to the two belligerents the conditions, restrictions, or prohibitions made by it in regard to the admission into its ports, roadsteads, or territorial waters, of belligerent war-ships or of their prizes.

Nevertheless, a neutral Power may forbid a belligerent vessel which has failed to conform to the orders and regulations made by it, or which has violated neutrality, to enter its ports or roadsteads.

Article 10. The neutrality of a Power is not affected by the mere passage through its territorial waters of war-ships or prizes belonging to belligerents.

Article 11. A neutral Power may allow belligerent war-ships to employ its licensed pilots.

Article 12. In the absence of special provisions to the contrary in the legislation of a neutral Power, belligerent war-ships are not permitted to remain in the ports, roadsteads, or territorial waters of the said Power for more than twenty-four hours, except in the cases covered by the present Convention.

Article 13. If a Power which has been informed of the outbreak of hostilities learns that a belligerent war-ship is in one of its ports or roadsteads, or in its territorial waters, it must notify the said ship to depart within twenty-four hours or within the time prescribed by local regulations.

Article 14. A belligerent war-ship may not prolong its stay in a neutral port beyond the permissible time except on account of damage or stress of weather. It must depart as soon as the cause of the delay is at an end.

The regulations as to the question of the length of time which these vessels may remain in neutral ports, roadsteads, or waters, do not apply to war-ships devoted exclusively to religious, scientific, or philanthropic purposes.

Article 15. In the absence of special provisions to the contrary in the legislation of a neutral Power, the maximum number of war-ships belonging to a belligerent which may be in one of the ports or roadsteads of that Power simultaneously shall be three.

Article 16. When war-ships belonging to both belligerents are present simultaneously in a neutral port or roadstead, a period of not less than twenty-four hours must elapse between the departure of the ship belonging to one belligerent and the departure of the ship belonging to the other.

The order of departure is determined by the order of arrival, unless the ship which arrived first is so circumstanced that an extension of its stay is permissible.

A belligerent war-ship may not leave a neutral port or roadstead until twenty-four hours after the departure of a merchant ship flying the flag of its adversary.

Article 17. In neutral ports and roadsteads belligerent war-ships may only carry out such repairs as are absolutely necessary to render them seaworthy, and may not add in any manner whatsoever to their fighting force. The local authorites of the neutral Power shall decide what repairs are necessary, and these must be carried out with the least possible delay.

Article 18. Belligerent war-ships may not make use of neutral ports, roadsteads, or territorial waters for replenishing or increasing their supplies of war material or their armament, or for completing their crews.

Article 19. Belligerent war-ships may only revictual in neutral ports or roadsteads to bring up their supplies to the peace standard.

Similarly these vessels may only ship sufficient fuel to enable them to reach the nearest port in their own country. They may, on the other hand, fill up their bunkers built to carry fuel, when in neutral countries which have adopted this method of determining the amount of fuel to be supplied.

If, in accordance with the law of the neutral Power, the ships are not supplied with coal within twenty-four hours of their arrival, the permissible duration of their stay is extended by twenty-four hours.

Article 20. Belligerent war-ships which have shipped fuel in a port belonging to a neutral Power may not within the succeeding three months replenish their supply in a port of the same Power.

Article 21. A prize may only be brought into a neutral port on account of unseaworthiness, stress of weather, or want of fuel or provisions.

It must leave as soon as the circumstances which justified its entry are at an end. If it does not, the neutral Power must order it to leave at once; should it fail to obey, the neutral Power must employ the means at its disposal to release it with its officers and crew and to intern the prize crew.

Article 22. A neutral Power, must, similarly, release a prize brought into one of its ports under circumstances other than those referred to in article 21.

Article 23. A neutral Power may allow prizes to enter its ports and roadsteads, whether under convoy or not, when they are brought there to be sequestrated pending the decisions of a Prize Court. It may have the prize taken to another of its ports.

If the prize is convoyed by a war-ship, the prize crew may go on board the convoying ship.

If the prize is not under convoy, the prize crew are left at liberty.

Article 24. If, notwithstanding the notification of the neutral Power, a belligerent ship of war does not leave a port where it is not entitled to remain, the neutral Power is entitled to take such measures as it considers necessary to render the ship incapable of taking the sea during the war, and the commanding officer of the ship must facilitate the execution of such measures.

When a belligerent ship is detained by a neutral Power, the officers and crew are likewise detained.

The officers and crew thus detained may be left in the ship or kept either on another vessel or on land, and may be subjected to the measures of restriction which it may appear necessary to impose upon them. A sufficient number of men for looking after the vessel must, however, be always left on board.

The officers may be left at liberty on giving their word not to quit the neutral territory without permission.

Article 25. A neutral Power is bound to exercise such surveillance as the means at its disposal allow to prevent any violation of the provisions of the above articles occurring in its ports or roadsteads or in its waters.

Article 26. The exercise by a neutral Power of the rights laid down in the present Convention can under no circumstances be considered as an unfriendly act by one or other belligerent who has accepted the articles relating thereto.

Article 27. The contracting Powers shall communicate to each other in due course all laws, proclamations, and other enactments regulating in their respective countries the status of belligerent war-ships in their ports and waters, by means of a communication addressed to the Government of the Netherlands, and forwarded immediately by that Government to the other contracting Powers.

Article 28. The provisions of the present Convention do not apply except between contracting Powers, and then only if all the belligerents are parties to the Convention. . . .

The Old International Law of Internal War*

Richard A. Falk

The rights and duties of nations are governed, first of all, by the status accorded to the factions in conflict. Traditional international law provides three relevant statuses: (1) rebellion, (2) insurgency, (3) belligerency. These characterizations of a challenge to the authority of an incumbent regime are designed to distinguish among conflicts along a continuum of ascending intensity.[1] Rebellion is supposed to be invoked in response to a sporadic challenge to the legitimate government, whereas insurgency and belligerency are intended to apply to situations of sustained conflict, a serious challenge carried on through a considerable period of time over a wide space and involving large numbers of people within the society.

If the faction seeking to seize the power of the state seems susceptible to rapid suppression by normal procedures of internal security, then it is supposed to be treated as a "rebellion." For instance, Kotzsch indicates that "domestic violence is called rebellion or upheaval so long as there is sufficient evidence that the police force of the parent state will reduce [*sic;* induce] the seditious party to respect the municipal legal order."[2] If the status of rebellion is given to an occasion of "internal war," then external help to the rebels constitutes illegal intervention. Furthermore, the incumbent government can demand that foreign states accept the inconvenience of domestic regulations designed to suppress the rebellion, such as the closing of ports or interference with normal commerce. Foreign states have no duty to remain aloof (as nonparticipants) or neutral, and therefore are free to render affirmative

* Reprinted from Richard A. Falk, "Janus Tormented: The International Law of Internal War," in James N. Rosenau (ed.), *International Aspects of Civil Strife* (Princeton, N.J.: Princeton University Press, 1964), pp. 197–209, by permission of the publisher. Certain footnotes are omitted.

assistance to the incumbent as requested. There is also the duty to prevent domestic territory from being used as an organizing base for hostile activities overseas. This duty is imposed upon foreign states regardless of the scope of the internal war, but it seems to be especially applicable in a situation that precedes recourse by rebels to the instruments of violence. Thus if an internal war is a "rebellion," foreign states are forbidden to help the rebels and are permitted to help the incumbent, whereas the incumbent is entitled to impose domestic restrictions upon commerce and normal alien activity in order to suppress the rebellion.

International law thus purports to give no protection to participants in a rebellion. Rebellion usefully covers minor instances of internal war of a wide variety: violent protest involving a single issue (Indian language riots, Soviet food riots) or an uprising that is so rapidly suppressed as to warrant no acknowledgment of its existence on an extranational level (East European rebellions against Soviet dominion in 1953 and 1956). These norms of identification are, however, vague and seldom serve *expressis verbis* to adjust the relation between the rebellion as a state of affairs and international actors affected in various ways by its existence.

It is even more significant, however, to suggest the separation between the *facts* of strife and the *decisional process* by which national officials invoke norms to explain and justify a national response. The self-determination of norms identifying the legal status of civil strife severely restricts any role of law connected with the establishment of an objective status binding on all actors uniformly through the system. A decree of marriage or divorce usually generates a status for the parties that is given universal respect. International law is not generally able to fulfill this role of status creation for internal strife on a system level, although it does so bilaterally, and occasionally on a regional or bloc basis. The existence of international institutions provides a structural basis for further centralization of procedures of status creation in this sensitive area.

"Insurgency" is a catch-all designation provided by international law to allow states to determine the quantum of legal relations to be established with the insurgents. It is an international acknowledgment of the existence of an internal war but it leaves each state substantially free to control the consequences of this acknowledgment. This contrasts with "belligerency," which establishes a common regime of rights and duties that exist independent of the will of a particular state. On a factual level, almost all that can be said about insurgency is that it is supposed to constitute more sustained and substantial intrastate violence than is encountered if the internal war is treated as a "rebellion." It also serves as a partial internationalization of the conflict, without bringing the state of belligerency into being. This permits third states to participate in an internal war without finding themselves "at war," which would be the consequence of intervention on either side once the internal war had been identified as a state of belligerency. Interventionary participation in an insurgency may arouse protest and hostile response, but it does not involve the hazards and inconveniences that arise if a state of war is established with one or the other factions.

Hersh Lauterpacht suggests the relative vagueness of the legal concept of insurgency by observing that "[t]he difference between the status of belligerency and that of insurgency in relation to foreign States may best be expressed in the form of the proposition that belligerency is a relation giving rise to definite rights and obligations, while insurgency is not."[3] The unreliability of the factual test becomes evident if one realizes that such major internal wars as the Cuban independence wars in the late nineteenth century and the Spanish Civil War of 1936–1939 were both treated by many principal nations as instances of insurgency. The insurgent is often given extensive rights by foreign states and is usually assumed to have the duty to conform to applicable rules of international law. Thus, for instance, British courts respected, as valid, Falangist legislation enacted to apply to territory under the control of the insurgency and accepted an insurgent claim of immunity for a public vessel under insurgent control.[4] These decisions had the consequence of treating the Franco faction as equivalent to a foreign sovereign state with respect to activity carried on within its orbit of effective administration. Such deferential treatment is a flagrant disregard of the incumbent government's normal claim to be the exclusive agent of the state for all matters within *national* jurisdiction. However, it represents a characteristic attempt by international law and national actors to use law to reconcile the claims of formal right with the facts of effective control; to maintain trade with a port under insurgent control it is essential to heed the administration of it by insurgent institutions even if this requires a disregard of the regime of law created by the government acknowledged in world affairs as the sole and legitimate seat of national authority. Actually, foreign states are rather free, given limitations of capability, to determine their own relations with insurgent and incumbent. Ordinarily insurgents are permitted to use the high seas for naval and air operations against the incumbent, provided that there is no interference with the shipping of third states. Thus, although third states have no duty to respect insurgent rights and no duty to subject themselves to the obligations of neutrality, there is a characteristic tendency to regard insurgent operations on the high seas as non-piratical and to give some domestic deference to the governmental nature of an insurgent regime for territory under its control (for example, insurgent legislation and official acts are often validated to the extent relevant to the outcome of a domestic legal controversy).

For humanitarian reasons, there is an increasing willingness to regard the laws of war as applicable to protracted conflict if it is carried on in a form that entitles it to the status of an insurgency. The acceptance of this viewpoint by the incumbent is conclusive. Third states cannot treat an internal war as a "rebellion" once it has been identified as an "insurgency" by the parent government.

In general, the status of insurgency is a flexible instrument for the formulation of claims and tolerances by third states. If it is used to protect the economic and private interests of nationals and to acknowledge political facts arising from partial successes by the insurgents in an internal war, then it can adjust relative rights and duties without amounting to a mode of illegal intervention in internal affairs. Trouble arises, however, when third states use the status of insurgency to influence the outcome of an internal war. Political objectives distort the connection between the status of insurgency and the existence of the facts warranting it; such a distortion is often disguised, however, by the decentralized grant of competence that authorizes the third state to characterize an internal war and to proceed as it sees fit.

A special application of insurgent status involves the occasional claim of third states to treat certain actions on the high seas as piratical. Thus, for instance, the Nyon Agreement concluded by several states during the Spanish Civil War provided for collective measures to destroy submarines that attacked third-power shipping on the high seas if they attacked in a manner forbidden by Part IV of the London Treaty of 1930, governing submarine attacks on merchant shipping. The characterization of insurgents as "pirates" by the incumbent is not binding on third states. Nevertheless, it is generally conceded that unrecognized insurgent operations on the high seas can be treated by third parties as piratical, provided that the factual conditions of belligerency do not exist. Even when this is done, it is, as Lauterpacht observes, infrequent that the notion of piracy is extended to the officers and crews of insurgent ships seized for piratical operations.[5]

Belligerency, as distinct from insurgency, is a formalization of the relative rights and duties of all actors vis-à-vis an internal war. Kotzsch puts it simply: ". . . the recognition of belligerency gives rise to definite rights and obligations under international law, insurgency does not."[6] Usually the conferral of belligerent status is achieved by indirect means rather than by explicit statement. Commonly, acknowledgment of belligerent rights on the high seas to either faction establishes a state of belligerency. International law treats an internal war with the status of belligerency as essentially identical to a war between sovereign states. This also means that an interventionary participation on behalf of either the incumbent or the insurgent is an act of war against the other. That is, as with a truly international war, a state is given the formal option of joining with one of the belligerents against the other or of remaining impartial.[7] Of course, the sharpness of the choice is belied by the history of international relations, which abounds in instances of partiality and participation that are treated as fully compatible with neutral status.

Belligerent status, if objectively determined by the community, would enable supranational actors to have a technique to justify treatment of serious internal wars as international wars. That is, rebellions and insurgencies could be treated as remaining within the scope of domestic jurisdiction, subject to the traditional distribution of claims and duties between internal factions and external actors. But belligerencies should be internationalized, thereby vindicating the claims of regional or global institutions to restore internal peace either by reference to constitutional (incumbent) or normative (insurgent; human rights) legitimacy. This new notion of belligerency requires an explicit assumption of competence by the relevant institu-

tions first to confer the status, then to act in view of it. Traditions of sovereignty and the split associated with the cold war are formidable obstacles to this recommended centralization of supranational authority over *serious* internal wars. The status of belligerency would be equivalent to determination of the seriousness of the internal war; that is, it would be a flexible and formal way for the regional or global organization to convey its claim of competence to the actors in the community. Criteria of seriousness could be formulated to restrict somewhat the judgment of belligerency by the organization, or at least to give the judgment a greater appearance of restriction.

The degree to which incumbent and third states have discretion over the decision to recognize belligerent status is virtually unrestricted; diplomatic practice also seems to waver between the duty of third states to allow insurgents to claim belligerent rights if certain factual conditions are present and the discretionary nature of the insurgent claim. If the incumbent claims belligerent rights on the high seas, then it operates to confer the status of belligerency upon the entire conflict. Third states are expected thereafter to regulate their relations in a way that accords each faction formal parity; partiality shown to either faction is regarded as an act of war, or at least as a violation of neutral rights. The insurgent faction, for instance, must then also be able to assert belligerent rights on the high seas. The humanitarian laws of warfare become fully applicable to all hostilities.[8] Among the specific claims authorized by acquiring belligerent status, the following are quite prominent: the right to obtain credit abroad, to enter foreign ports, to maintain blockades, to engage in visit and search procedures, and to confiscate contraband.

The incumbent government cannot oblige third states to accept its claim to exercise belligerent rights unless certain factual conditions are satisfied. Hersh Lauterpacht summarizes these conditions in the following way: ". . . first, there must exist within the State an armed conflict of a general (as distinguished from a purely local) character; second, the insurgents must occupy and administer a substantial portion of national territory; third, they must conduct the hostilities in accordance with the rules of war and through organized armed forces acting under a responsible authority; fourthly, there must exist circumstances which make it necessary for outside States to define their attitude by means of recognition of belligerency."[9] These conditions are supposed to govern the propriety of attaching the status of belligerency. If these conditions are not satisfied, then it is premature to grant belligerent rights to either warring faction. Once they are met, however, then it is arguable that it is intervention to refuse recognition of the insurgency as belligerency. As there is no objective way to meet the test of belligerency, attention is often given to the conduct of the incumbent that discloses a willingness to negotiate with the insurgent elite on the level of equality. Such a demonstration often forms part of an argument that there can arise a duty for third nations to treat a given internal war as an instance of belligerency.[10]

The status accorded to an internal war is designed primarily to reconcile its character as violent conflict with the orderly maintenance of the interests of third states. A presumption in favor of stability in the world allows foreign states to intervene on behalf of the incumbent in the situation of mere rebellion. However, if the intrastate conflict is sustained in time and place, it becomes interventionary, according to the traditional theory, to help either faction. Therefore, the notions of insurgency and belligerency are designed to allow third states to remain neutral and yet to have some control over interferences with their normal activities that result from strife between internal factions.

There are several difficulties with this form of response by international law to the phenomenon of internal war. First, the tendency of nations to avoid express bestowals of status makes it hard to establish the precise nature of claims by third states; the functional role attributed to the distinctions between rebellion, insurgency, and belligerency is more an invention of commentators than a description of state behavior. Second, the decentralized assertion of claims to treat an internal war as rebellion, insurgency, or belligerency makes it impossible to standardize what is permitted and what is forbidden with sufficient clarity to enable a protesting party to identify a violation; thus international law cannot do much to promote community policies favoring nonintervention, self-determination, and the rights of peoples to resort to revolution by distinguishing among various types of internal wars.[11] The basic duty of third states to maintain impartiality is difficult to implement. Third, the goals of noninterference are incompatible with the revolutionary ideology of China and the Soviet bloc and the anti-colonial commitments of the Afro-Asian nations. Notions of support for wars of national liberation and anti-colonial wars are direct repudiations of the duty to refrain from evaluating the contending claims of the factions in an internal war. The old international law based its regime upon the factual character of the conflict and not upon the justice of certain insurgent causes. If major national actors reject in practice and doctrine the policies of impartiality in the traditional system, then adherence to the rules becomes self-destructive for the remainder of the community.[12] Although it sounds paradoxical, offsetting participation by nations in internal wars may often be more compatible with the notions of nonintervention than is an asymmetrical refusal to participate. Therefore, the decline of mutuality makes the idea of nonintervention obsolete, even dangerous, if mechanically applied by the non-Communist and nonmodernizing nations in the world.

As a consequence, several desiderata

exist. First, objective tests and centralized interpretations of the factual character of an internal war are necessary. Second, a rule of mutuality is needed to act as a basis for applying policies of nonparticipation in sustained instances of civil conflict. Third, it would be helpful to have procedures to enable an expression of community approval, most probably through the agency of supranational institutions, for certain instances of insurgency; approval would thereby serve to authorize some forms of outside participation. The Congo Operation suggests the growth of a community willingness to remove internal wars from the sanctuary of "domestic jurisdiction," especially if the magnitude of the conflict is considerable and if the alternative is likely to be interventionary participation by the big powers.

Traditional international law bases its response to civil war upon the factual characteristics of the conflict and its material effect upon externally situated international actors. Thus a third state with shipping interests subject to harassment on the high seas was regarded as more entitled to accord recognition of rights to an insurgent faction than was a state unaffected by the internal war. Today, however, the interdependence of domestic and international conflict, the special attitude of Communists and newly independent states toward the outcome of internal wars fought for political objectives, and the dangers of nuclear war escalating from internal war create new requirements of minimum order.[13] The rules and processes of law must be revised to take appropriate account of these extralegal developments. We need, first of all, to discriminate between internal wars that it is safe to treat as domestic so as to proscribe participation by nations or supranational institutions, and those that it is not because the internal arena of conflict is the scene of indirect aggression or because it represents a struggle for certain minimum domestic rights that the world as an emerging and limited community is

coming to recognize as mandatory.[14] Once this discrimination seems to have been made, then, as has been indicated, it is important to develop processes for regional and universal management of internal wars with an important strategic impact on patterns of international conflict or upon firm and overwhelming crystallizations of international morality. If community institutions fail to perform in a situation where an internal war is an arena within which third powers seek to extend their national domain of political influence, then it is essential to authorize neutralizing participation by others. The rules of nonparticipation would thus be made subject to suspension whenever any major international actor violates them; this premise of mutuality must be introduced into the legal process so as to reconcile interests of collective self-defense with notions of respect for applicable legal rules.

Notes

1. This standard view is expressed in relation to grants of recognition: ". . . it is believed to be the nature and extent of the insurrectionary achievement, rather than any other consideration, that afford the test of the propriety of recognition." Charles Cheney Hyde, *International Law Chiefly as Interpreted and Applied by the United States I*, 2nd rev. edn., (Boston: Little, Brown and Company, 1945), p. 202.
2. Lothar Kotzsch, *The Concept of War in Contemporary History and International Law* (Geneva: Librairie E. Droz, 1956), p. 230.
3. Hersh Lauterpacht, *Recognition in International Law* (Cambridge: Cambridge University Press, 1947), p. 270; hereinafter cited as *Recognition*.
4. The leading case came before the House of Lords in Great Britain: The Arantzazu Mendi, [1939] A.C. 256; cf. also Banco de Bilbao v. Rey, [1938] 2 K.B. 176.
5. Lauterpacht, *Recognition*, p. 304.
6. Kotzsch, *op. cit.*, p. 233.
7. The compatibility of this option with the United Nations system is open to serious question [even for non-Members; see Article

2(6)]. Certainly, once a determination of aggression has been made authoritatively by a principal organ of the Organization, then other states are not "at liberty" to help the state or states characterized as the aggressor nor are states free to remain neutral [see Article 2(5)]. The formal claims of the Charter must, however, be regarded as no more than *potential* norms of restraint in view of *actual* patterns of practice. Practice continues to affirm the option of states to decide for themselves, and so the textual statement possesses a continuing validity, despite the presence of a formal agreement (Charter) pledging Members of the United Nations to renounce discretion in this area of national behavior.

8. It is significant that Article 3 of the Geneva Conventions of 1949, regulating aspects of the conduct of international war, makes the humanitarian norms applicable "in the case of armed conflict not of an international character occurring in the territory of one of the High Contracting Parties." Also Article 4 of the Prisoners of War Convention and Article 13 of the Wounded and Sick Convention extend coverage to "members of regular armed forces who profess allegiance to a Government or an authority not recognized by the Detaining Power"; this presumably applied to any factual *or* legal state of prolonged insurgency. However, if the insurgency is conducted by unconventional military techniques, then it is unclear under what conditions the personnel qualify as members of "regular armed forces." For a discussion of when various rules of the law of war (especially the Geneva Conventions of 1949) apply to guerrilla warfare, see Morris Greenspan, "International Law and Its Protection for Participants in Unconventional Warfare," *The Annals*, Vol. 341 (May 1962), pp. 30–41.

9. Lauterpacht, *Recognition*, p. 176.

10. This argument is urged with respect to the Algerian War of Independence by Mohammed Bedjaoui, *Law and the Algerian Revolution* (Brussels: Publications of the International Association of Democratic Lawyers, 1961).

11. At best, *norms of relationship* are established by the *specific* responses of individual states. The status distinctions may help to clarify and identify the character of a specific response, thereby fulfilling the role of international law to provide national actors with a medium of communication. There are no norms generated that set system-wide standards of response.

Participation by the United Nations or a regional organization may qualify this assertion somewhat.

12. And yet the violation of clear norms by law-oriented societies leads to confused behavior that disappoints the conscience of the community, both within the society of the actor and without. The United States' response to Castro's Marxism-Leninism illustrates the difficulties of either ignoring or adhering to applicable legal restraints.

13. For an exciting exposition of the relations between legal order and the maintenance of peace in the contemporary world, see Myres S. McDougal and Florentino P. Feliciano, *Law and Minimum World Public Order: The Legal Regulation of International Coercion* (New Haven: Yale University Press 1961,), especially chaps. 1–4.

14. For a fuller development of this theme, see Richard A. Falk, *Law, Morality, and War in the Contemporary World* (New York: Frederick A. Praeger, 1963).

United States War Department, Rules of Land Warfare*

1. *General.* Among civilized nations the conduct of war is regulated by certain well-established rules known as the rules or laws of war. These rules cover and regulate warfare both on land and sea. . . .

* * *

4. *Basic Principles.* Among the so-called unwritten rules or laws of war are three interdependent basic principles that underlie all of the other rules or laws of civilized warfare, both written and unwritten, and form the general guide for conduct where no more specific rule applies, to wit:

a. The *principle of military necessity*, under which, subject to the principles of humanity and chivalry, a belligerent is justified in applying any amount and any kind of force to compel the complete

* Reprinted from *Basic Field Manual* 27–10 (1940).

submission of the enemy with the least possible expenditure of time, life, and money;

b. The *principle of humanity*, prohibiting employment of any such kind or degree of violence as is not actually necessary for the purpose of the war; and

c. The *principle of chivalry*, which denounces and forbids resort to dishonorable means, expedients, or conduct.

5. *Force of rules*. a. The unwritten rules are binding upon all civilized nations. They will be strictly observed by our forces, subject only to such exceptions as shall have been directed by competent authority by way of legitimate reprisals for illegal conduct of the enemy.

Hague Convention IV of 1907 on the Laws and Customs of War on Land*

* * *

According to the views of the High Contracting Parties, these provisions, the wording of which has been inspired by the desire to diminish the evils of war, as far as military requirements permit, are intended to serve as a general rule of conduct for the belligerents in their mutual relations and in their relations with the inhabitants.

It has not, however, been found possible at present to concert Regulations covering all the circumstances which arise in practice;

On the other hand, the High Contracting Parties clearly do not intend that unforeseen cases should, in the absence of a written undertaking, be left to the arbitrary judgment of military commanders.

Until a more complete code of the laws of war has been issued, the High Contracting Parties deem it expedient to declare that, in cases not included in the Regulations adopted by them, the inhabitants and the belligerents remain under the protec-

* Reprinted from 36 *United States Statutes at Large* 2277.

tion and the rule of the principles of the law of nations, as they result from the usages established among civilized peoples, from the laws of humanity, and the dictates of the public conscience.

* * *

Art. 1. The Contracting Powers shall issue instructions to their armed land forces which shall be in conformity with the Regulations respecting the Laws and Customs of War on Land, annexed to the present Convention.

* * *

Annex to the Convention: Regulations Respecting the Laws and Customs of War on Land

SECTION I.—ON BELLIGERENTS

Chapter I.—The Qualifications of Belligerents

Art. 1. The laws, rights, and duties of war apply not only to armies, but also to militia and volunteer corps fulfilling the following conditions;

1. To be commanded by a person responsible for his subordinates;
2. To have a fixed distinctive emblem recognizable at a distance;
3. To carry arms openly; and
4. To conduct their operations in accordance with the laws and customs of war.

In countries where militia or volunteer corps constitute the army, or form part of it, they are included under the denomination "army."

Art. 2. The inhabitants of a territory which has not been occupied, who, on the approach of the enemy, spontaneously take up arms to resist the invading troops without having had time to organize themselves in accordance with article 1, shall be regarded as belligerents if they carry arms openly and if they respect the laws and customs of war.

Art. 3. The armed forces of the belligerent parties may consist of combatants and non-combatants. In the case of capture by the enemy, both have a right to be treated as prisoners of war.

*   *   *

SECTION II.—HOSTILITIES

Chapter I.—Means of Injuring the Enemy, Sieges, and Bombardments

Art. 22. The right of belligerents to adopt means of injuring the enemy is not unlimited.

Art. 23. In addition to the prohibitions provided by special Conventions, it is especially forbidden—

a. To employ poison or poisoned weapons;
b. To kill or wound treacherously individuals belonging to the hostile nation or army;
c. To kill or wound any enemy who, having laid down his arms, or having no longer means of defence, has surrendered at discretion;
d. To declare that no quarter will be given;
e. To employ arms, projectiles, or material calculated to cause unnecessary suffering;
f. To make improper use of a flag of truce, of the national flag or of the military insignia and uniform of the enemy, as well as the distinctive badges of the Geneva Convention;
g. To destroy or seize the enemy's property, unless such destruction or seizure be imperatively demanded by the necessities of war;
h. To declare abolished, suspended, or inadmissible in a court of law the rights and actions of the nationals of the hostile party.

A belligerent is likewise forbidden to compel the nationals of the hostile party to take part in the operations of war directed against their own country, even if they were in the belligerent's service before the commencement of the war.

Art. 24. Ruses of war and the employment of measures necessary for obtaining information about the enemy and the country are considered permissible.

Art. 25. The attack or bombardment, *by whatever means,* of towns, villages, dwellings, or buildings which are undefended is prohibited.

Art. 26. The officer in command of an attacking force must, before commencing a bombardment, except in cases of assault, do all in his power to warn the authorities.

Art. 27. In sieges and bombardments all necessary steps must be taken to spare, as far as possible, buildings dedicated to religion, art, science, or charitable purposes, historic monuments, hospitals, and places where the sick and wounded are collected, provided they are not being used at the time for military purposes.

It is the duty of the besieged to indicate the presence of such buildings or places by distinctive and visible signs, which shall be notified to the enemy beforehand.

Art. 28. The pillage of a town or place, even when taken by assault, is prohibited.

Chapter II.—Spies

Art. 29. A person can only be considered a spy when, acting clandestinely or on false pretences, he obtains or endeavors to obtain information in the zone of operations of a belligerent, with the intention of communicating it to the hostile party.

Thus, soldiers not wearing a disguise who have penetrated into the zone of operations of the hostile army, for the purpose of obtaining information, are not considered spies. Similarly, the following are not considered spies: Soldiers and civilians, carrying out their mission openly, intrusted with the delivery of despatches intended either for their own army or for the enemy's army. To this class belong likewise persons sent in balloons for the purpose of carrying despatches and, generally, of maintaining communications between the different parts of an army or a territory.

Art. 30. A spy taken in the act shall not be punished without previous trial.

Art. 31. A spy who, after rejoining the army to which he belongs, is subsequently captured by the enemy, is treated as a prisoner of war, and incurs no responsibility for his previous acts of espionage.

* * *

SECTION III.—MILITARY AUTHORITY OVER THE TERRITORY OF THE HOSTILE STATE

Art. 42. Territory is considered occupied when it is actually placed under the authority of the hostile army.

The occupation extends only to the territory where such authority has been established and can be exercised.

Art. 43. The authority of the legitimate power having in fact passed into the hands of the occupant, the latter shall take all the measures in his power to restore, and ensure, as far as possible, public order and safety, while respecting, unless absolutely prevented, the laws in force in the country.

Art. 44. A belligerent is forbidden to force the inhabitants of territory occupied by it to furnish information about the army of the other belligerent, or about its means of defense.

Art. 45. It is forbidden to compel the inhabitants of occupied territory to swear allegiance to the hostile Power.

Art. 46. Family honor and rights, the lives of persons, and private property, as well as religious convictions and practice, must be respected.

Private property can not be confiscated.

Art. 47. Pillage is formally forbidden.

Art. 48. If, in the territory occupied, the occupant collects the taxes, dues, and tolls imposed for the benefit of the State, he shall do so, as far as is possible, in accordance with the rules of assessment and incidence in force, and shall in consequence be bound to defray the expenses of the administration of the occupied territory to the same extent as the legitimate Government was so bound.

Art. 49. If, in addition to the taxes mentioned in the above article, the occupant levies other money contributions in the occupied territory, this shall only be for the needs of the army or of the administration of the territory in question.

Art. 50. No general penalty, pecuniary or otherwise, shall be inflicted upon the population on account of the acts of individuals for which they can not be regarded as jointly and severally responsible.

Art. 51. No contribution shall be collected except under a written order, and on the responsibility of a commander-in-chief.

The collection of the said contribution shall only be effected as far as possible in accordance with the rules of assessment and incidence of the taxes in force.

For every contribution a receipt shall be given to the contributors.

Art. 52. Requisitions in kind and services shall not be demanded from municipalities or inhabitants except for the needs of the army of occupation. They shall be in proportion to the resources of the country, and of such nature as not to involve the inhabitants in the obligation of taking part in military operations against their own country.

Such requisitions and services shall only be demanded on the authority of the commander in the locality occupied.

Contributions in kind shall as far as possible be paid for in cash; if not, a receipt shall be given and the payment of the amount due shall be made as soon as possible.

Art. 53. An army of occupation can only take possession of cash, funds, and realizable securities which are strictly the property of the State, depots of arms, means of transport, stores and supplies, and, generally, all movable property belonging to the State which may be used for military operations.

All appliances, whether on land, at sea, or in the air, adapted for the transmission of news, or for the transport of persons or things, exclusive of cases governed by naval law, depots of arms, and, generally, all kinds of munitions of war, may be seized, even if they belong to private individuals, but must be restored and compensation fixed when peace is made.

Art. 54. Submarine cables connecting an occupied territory with a neutral territory shall not be seized or destroyed except in the case of absolute necessity. They must likewise be restored and compensation fixed when peace is made.

Art. 55. The occupying State shall be regarded only as administrator and usufructuary of public buildings, real estate, forests, and agricultural estates belonging to the hostile State, and situated in the occupied country. It must safeguard the capital of these properties, and administer them in accordance with the rules of usufruct.

Art. 56. The property of municipalities, that of institutions dedicated to religion, charity and education, the arts and sciences, even when State property, shall be treated as private property.

All seizure of, destruction or willful damage done to institutions of this character, historic monuments, works of art and science, is forbidden, and should be made the subject of legal proceedings.

Geneva Convention Relative to the Treatment of Prisoners of War of August 12, 1949*

The undersigned Plenipotentiaries of the Governments represented at the Diplomatic Conference held at Geneva from April 21 to August 12, 1949, for the purpose of revising the Convention concluded at Geneva on July 27, 1929, relative to the Treatment of Prisoners of War, have agreed as follows:

* United States Department of State, *General Foreign Policy Series* 34, p. 84.

Article 1. The High Contracting Parties undertake to respect and to ensure respect for the present Convention in all circumstances.

Article 2. In addition to the provisions which shall be implemented in peace time, the present Convention shall apply to all cases of declared war or of any other armed conflict which may arise between two or more of the High Contracting Parties, even if the state of war is not recognized by one of them.

The Convention shall also apply to all cases of partial or total occupation of the territory of a High Contracting Party, even if the said occupation meets with no armed resistance.

Although one of the Powers in conflict may not be a party to the present Convention, the Powers who are parties thereto shall remain bound by it in their mutual relations. They shall furthermore be bound by the Convention in relation to the said Power, if the latter accepts and applies the provisions thereof.

Article 3. In the case of armed conflict not of an international character occurring in the territory of one of the High Contracting Parties, each Party to the conflict shall be bound to apply, as a minimum, the following provisions:

1. Persons taking no active part in the hostilities, including members of armed forces who have laid down their arms and those placed *hors de combat* by sickness, wounds, detention, or any other cause, shall in all circumstances be treated humanely, without any adverse distinction founded on race, colour, religion or faith, sex, birth or wealth, or any other similar criteria.

To this end the following acts are and shall remain prohibited at any time and in any place whatsoever with respect to the above-mentioned persons:

a. violence to life and person, in particular murder of all kinds, mutilation, cruel treatment and torture;

b. taking of hostages;

c. outrages upon personal dignity, in particular, humiliating and degrading treatment;

d. the passing of sentences and the carrying out of executions without previous judgment pronounced by a regularly constituted court affording all the judicial guarantees which are recognized as indispensable by civilized peoples.

2. The wounded and sick shall be collected and cared for.

An impartial humanitarian body, such as the International Committee of the Red Cross, may offer its services to the Parties to the conflict.

The Parties to the conflict should further endeavour to bring into force, by means of special agreements, all or part of the other provisions of the present Convention.

The application of the preceding provisions shall not affect the legal status of the Parties to the conflict.

Article 4. A. Prisoners of war, in the sense of the present Convention, are persons belonging to one of the following categories, who have fallen into the power of the enemy:

1. Members of the armed forces of a Party to the conflict, as well as members of militias or volunteer corps forming part of such armed forces.

.2 Members of other militias and members of other volunteer corps, including those of organized resistance movements, belonging to a Party to the conflict and operating in or outside their own territory, even if this territory is occupied, provided that such militias or volunteer corps, including such organized resistance movements, fulfil the following conditions:

a. that of being commanded by a person responsible for his subordinates;

b. that of having a fixed distinctive sign recognizable at a distance;

c. that of carrying arms openly;

d. that of conducting their operations in accordance with the laws and customs of war.

3. Members of regular armed forces who profess allegiance to a government or an authority not recognized by the Detaining Power.

4. Persons who accompany the armed forces without actually being members thereof, such as civilian members of military aircraft crews, war correspondents, supply contractors, members of labour units or of services responsible for the welfare of the armed forces, provided that they have received authorization from the armed forces which they accompany, who shall provide them for that purpose with an identity card similar to the annexed model.

5. Members of crews, including masters, pilots and apprentices, of the merchant marine and the crews of civil aircraft of the Parties to the conflict, who do not benefit by more favourable treatment under any other provisions of international law.

6. Inhabitants of a non-occupied territory, who on the approach of the enemy spontaneously take up arms to resist the invading forces, without having had time to form themselves into regular armed units, provided they carry arms openly and respect the laws and customs of war.

B. The following shall likewise be treated as prisoners of war under the present Convention:

1. Persons belonging, or having belonged, to the armed forces of the occupied country, if the occupying Power considers it necessary by reason of such allegiance to intern them, even though it has originally liberated them while hostilities were going on outside the territory it occupies, in particular where such persons have made an unsuccessful attempt to rejoin the armed forces to which they belong and which are engaged in combat, or where they fail to comply with a summons made to them with a view to internment.

2. The persons belonging to one of the categories enumerated in the present Article, who have been received by neutral or non-belligerent Powers on their territory and whom these Powers are required to intern under international law, without pre-

judice to any more favourable treatment which these powers may choose to give and with the exception of Articles 8, 10, 15, 30, fifth paragraph, 58–67, 92, 126 and, where diplomatic relations exist between the Parties to the conflict and the neutral or non-belligerent Power concerned, those Articles concerning the Protecting Power. Where such diplomatic relations exist, the Parties to a conflict on whom these persons depend shall be allowed to perform towards them the functions of a Protecting Power as provided in the present Convention, without prejudice to the functions which these Parties normally exercise in conformity with diplomatic and consular usage and treaties.

C. This Article shall in no way affect the status of medical personnel and chaplains as provided for in Article 33 of the present Convention.

Article 5. The present Convention shall apply to persons referred to in Article 4 from the time they fall into the power of the enemy and until their final release and repatriation.

Should any doubt arise as to whether persons, having committed a belligerent act and having fallen into the hands of the enemy, belong to any of the categories enumerated in Article 4, such persons shall enjoy the protection of the present Convention until such time as their status has been determined by a competent tribunal.

* * *

Article 12. Prisoners of war are in the hands of the enemy Power, but not of the individuals or military units who have captured them. Irrespective of the individual responsibilities that may exist, the Detaining Power is responsible for the treatment given them.

Prisoners of war may only be transferred by the Detaining Power to a Power which is a party to the Convention and after the Detaining Power has satisfied itself of the willingness and ability of such transferee

Power to apply the Convention. When prisoners of war are transferred under such circumstances, responsibility for the application of the Convention rests on the Power accepting them while they are in its custody.

Nevertheless, if that Power fails to carry out the provisions of the Convention in any important respect, the Power by whom the prisoners of war were transferred shall, upon being notified by the Protecting Power, take effective measures to correct the situation or shall request the return of the prisoners of war. Such requests must be complied with.

Article 13. Prisoners of war must at all times be humanely treated. Any unlawful act or omission by the Detaining Power causing death or seriously endangering the health of a prisoner of war in its custody is prohibited, and will be regarded as a serious breach of the present Convention. In particular, no prisoner of war may be subjected to physical mutilation or to medical or scientific experiments of any kind which are not justified by the medical, dental or hospital treatment of the prisoner concerned and carried out in his interest.

Likewise, prisoners of war must at all times be protected, particularly against acts of violence or intimidation and against insults and public curiosity.

Measures of reprisal against prisoners of war are prohibited.

Article 14. Prisoners of war are entitled in all circumstances to respect for their persons and their honour.

Women shall be treated with all the regard due to their sex and shall in all cases benefit by treatment as favourable as that granted to men.

Prisoners of war shall retain the full civil capacity which they enjoyed at the time of their capture. The Detaining Power may not restrict the exercise, either within or without its own territory, of the rights such capacity confers except in so far as the captivity requires.

Article 15. The Power detaining prisoners of war shall be bound to provide free of charge for their maintenance and for the medical attention required by their state of health.

Article 16. Taking into consideration the provisions of the present Convention relating to rank and sex, and subject to any privileged treatment which may be accorded to them by reason of their state of health, age or professional qualifications, all prisoners of war shall be treated alike by the Detaining Power, without any adverse distinction based on race, nationality, religious belief or political opinions, or any other distinction founded on similar criteria.

Article 17. Every prisoner of war, when questioned on the subject, is bound to give only his surname, first names and rank, date of birth, and army, regimental, personal or serial number, or failing this, equivalent information.

If he wilfully infringes this rule, he may render himself liable to a restriction of the privileges accorded to his rank or status....

No physical or mental torture, nor any other form of coercion, may be inflicted on prisoners of war to secure from them information of any kind whatever. Prisoners of war who refuse to answer may not be threatened, insulted, or exposed to unpleasant or disadvantageous treatment of any kind. . . .

Article 18. All effects and articles of personal use, except arms, horses, military equipment and military documents, shall remain in the possession of prisoners of war, likewise their metal helmets and gas masks and like articles issued for personal protection. Effects and articles used for their clothing or feeding shall likewise remain in their possession, even if such effects and articles belong to their regulation military equipment.

At no time should prisoners of war be without identity documents. The Detaining Power shall supply such documents to prisoners of war who possess none.

Badges of rank and nationality, decorations and articles having above all a personal or sentimental value may not be taken from prisoners of war.

Sums of money carried by prisoners of war may not be taken away from them except by order of an officer, and after the amount and particulars of the owner have been recorded in a special register and an itemized receipt has been given, legibly inscribed with the name, rank and unit of the person issuing the said receipt. Sums in the currency of the Detaining Power, or which are changed into such currency at the prisoner's request, shall be placed to the credit of the prisoner's account as provided in Article 64.

The Detaining Power may withdraw articles of value from prisoners of war only for reasons of security; when such articles are withdrawn, the procedure laid down for sums of money impounded shall apply.

Such objects, likewise sums taken away in any currency other than that of the Detaining Power and the conversion of which has not been asked for by the owners, shall be kept in the custody of the Detaining Power and shall be returned in their initial shape to prisoners of war at the end of their captivity.

Article 19. Prisoners of war shall be evacuated, as soon as possible after their capture, to camps situated in an area far enough from the combat zone for them to be out of danger.

* * *

Shimoda and Others v. The State (Japanese Government)*

Tokyo District Court, December 7, 1963

[*The claimants in this case, five residents of Hiroshima and Nagasaki who sought compensation from the Japanese Government for*

* Reprinted from *Japanese Annual of International Law* 212 (1964) by permission of the Japan Branch of the International Law Association.

damages sustained by the atomic attacks on those cities, were denied a remedy, largely on procedural grounds. The decision is especially important because it is the sole attempt by a legal tribunal to assess the legality of the use of nuclear weapons.]

* * *

III. Cause of the plaintiffs' claims.

1. Atomic bombing and its effect.

(1) Around 8:15 a.m. on August 6, 1945, a B-29 bomber piloted by Colonel Tibbetts, U.S. Army Air Forces, dropped a bomb called a uranium bomb on the City of Hiroshima under the orders of U.S. President H. S. Truman. The uranium bomb exploded in the air. A furious bomb-shell blast with a streak of strong flash followed, and buildings in Hiroshima collapsed with a crash. The city was blacked out by a cloud of dust caused by the blast, and was everywhere enveloped in raging flames. All mortals including pregnant women and babies at the breasts of their mothers who were within a radius of some four kilometers of the epicenter, were killed in an instant. Also, in other areas people were horribly wounded on their bodies, owing to the special power of injury of the explosion; or they were flooded with radial rays and suffered from atomic bomb injuries, although they were not scarred on their bodies. And there is still no end to consequential deaths even today, ten and several years after.

(2) Around 11:02 a.m. on August 9, 1945, three days after the aerial bombardment of Hiroshima, another B-29 bomber piloted by Major Sweeney, U.S. Army Air Forces, dropped a bomb called plutonium bomb on the City of Nagasaki. The plutonium bomb exploded in the air into a fire-ball of some 70 meters in diameter. The next instant, the fire-ball expanded quickly, struck the earth, and turned into white smoke while changing all things on the earth into radioactive things. Consequently, also in Nagasaki, the same destruction and extremely cruel casualty to innocent people occurred as in Hiroshima.

* * *

2. International law aspects.

The dropping of the atomic bomb was a hostile act taken by the United States, which was then in a state of war with Japan, and was an illegal act of hostility contrary to the positive international law of that day (treaties and customary laws).

(1) a. By the St. Petersburg Declaration (December 11, 1868), the parties agreed upon the following matters: The crisis of war must be limited as much as possible with the advance of civilization. The one just objective of war is to weaken the enemy's military force, and in order to accomplish this objective, as many people as possible must be placed out of battle. The use of a weapon designed to increase the pain of people placed out of battle, or to bring about their death, is beyond the limits of the above objective of war and contrary to humanity. Therefore, in case of war, the contracting parties promise to renounce the freedom of use by land forces or sea forces of explosives and combustive projectiles under 400 grammes.

b. The Hague Regulations respecting the Laws and Customs of War on Land, 1899, which are a code pertaining to the general law of war on land, mention in article 22 the use of poison or poisonous weapons, and the use of such weapons, projectiles, and other materials causing unnecessary pain as matters especially prohibited. The same Regulations prohibit in article 25 attack and bombardment on undefended cities, and provide for the necessity of previous notice in case of bombardment (article 26) and the limitation of the objective of attack to military objectives (article 27).

c. The same conclusion is also drawn from the interpretation of the Declaration (1907) prohibiting the use of special projectiles (dum-dum bullets by popular name), which was adopted at the Second Hague Conference, and the Protocol (1925) respecting the prohibition of poison gas, etc., which was adopted in Geneva.

d. Article 22 of the Draft Rules of Air Warfare, 1923, prohibits aerial bombardment for the purpose of terrorizing the civilian population, destroying private property not of military character, or injuring non-combatants. The same Draft Rules provide in article 24 that aerial bombardment is legitimate only when directed at a military objective (paragraphs 1 and 2); that the bombardment of cities, towns, villages, dwellings, or buildings not in the immediate neighborhood of operations of land forces is prohibited (paragraph 3); that in cases where bombardment cannot be made without the indiscriminate bombardment of the civilian population, bombardment must be abstained (paragraph 3); that in the immediate neighborhood of the operations of land forces, bombardment is legitimate only where the military concentration is sufficiently important to justify such bombardment, having regard to the danger caused to the civilian population (paragraph 4); and that a belligerent State is liable to pay compensation for injuries to person and property caused by violation of the provisions of this article (paragraph 5). The Draft Rules of Air Warfare are not positive law, but we can recognize the effect of their contents as a logical international law or a customary international law. The Convention on the Prevention and Punishment of Genocide was adopted by the United Nations General Assembly in 1948. The contents of this convention, which was adopted after the atomic bombing in question, existed as a logical international law of mankind before the dropping of the atomic bomb; and they were nothing but what was later stipulated.

e. The above international laws respecting acts of hostility naturally apply to atomic bombing as positive international law of that day. Although the atomic bomb is a new weapon, and it is difficult contextually to apply the above international laws directly or mutatis mutandis to the atomic bomb, we should apply the proper clauses directly or mutatis mutandis to the atomic bomb true to the spirit of legislation of the whole text, including the clauses concerned; and we should not take the view that each of the above international laws does not apply or has become invalid by reason of change of circumstances by the appearance of the atomic bomb. Even if the above positive international laws do not apply directly or mutatis mutandis, their spirit must be said to have the effect of natural law or logical international law.

(2) a. It was previously stated that the tremendous power of destruction of the atomic bombs dropped on Hiroshima and Nagasaki resulted in indiscriminate casualties without distinguishing between combatant and non-combatant within a radius of some four kilometers of the epicenter. This effect of the atomic bomb was a well-known fact among persons who had hands in the research and production of the atomic bomb in the United States, including President Truman. Further, the Hiroshima and Nagasaki of that day were not centers of war potential of Japan; and they were neither important military bases nor so-called defended places against occupation. Therefore, the acts of atomic bombing Hiroshima and Nagasaki were so-called indiscriminate bombardments. The acts were clearly contrary to the express provisions of articles 25, 26 and 27 of the Hague Regulations respecting the Laws and Customs of War on Land, and to articles 22 and 24 of the Draft Rules of Air Warfare.

b. The severity and cruelty of the pain caused to the human body by the power of injury of the atomic bomb, is more tremendous than that of poison or poisonous weapons which are prohibited by article 26 of the Hague Regulations respecting the Laws and Customs of War on Land; and the act of use of the atomic bomb is necessarily illegal from the interpretation of the Declaration prohibiting dum-dum bullets and the Protocol respecting the prohibition of poison gas, etc.

c. Japan of that day had no atomic bomb, of course. It is a matter of general anticipation that the defeat of Japan was inevitable, and the defeat was regarded as a matter of time. Therefore, the atomic bombs were not dropped for the purpose of crushing the war potential of Japan, but as a terrorizing measure intended to make officials and people of Japan lose their fighting spirit. Nor were they dropped as a measure of defense of the United States, or for retaliation. Such is clear from the fact that a committee on the social and political meaning of atomic power, which was composed of seven scientists including Professor James Frank as chairman, recommended against the atomic bombing of Japan and so informed the Secretary of the Army. At the same time, 64 scientists who participated in the research and production of the atomic bomb presented a petition to the President to the same effect as the report of the above committee. The report and the petition, however, were disregarded; and the atomic bomb was dropped without notice on Hiroshima and Nagasaki.

(3) The defendant State alleges that it is difficult to form an immediate conclusion on the question whether the atomic bombing was contrary to international law, and as a reason alleges that no positive international law existed on the use of the atomic bomb, and that the illegality of the atomic bomb cannot be deduced from the interpretation of treaties like the Hague Regulations respecting the Laws and Customs of War on Land. However, since logical interpretation is admitted as a general principle of interpretation of international law, the allegation of the defendant State is without reason.

. . . the defendant State seems to have the view that any measure except those definitely prohibited can be used in war until the enemy surrenders. This view is,

however, that of a Merchant of Death, or a Politician of Death, and it is highly regrettable.

* * *

[The Court] . . . (2) As a premise for judging how the above acts of atomic bombing are treated by positive international law, we will begin by considering what international law has existed with regard to war, especially to hostile acts among modern countries since the latter half of 19th Century.

The following are the chronological enumeration of international laws concerning this case:

1886. St. Petersburg Declaration respecting the prohibition of the explosives and incendiaries under 400 grammes.

1899. Convention respecting the Laws and Customs of War on Land . . . concluded at the First Hague Peace Conference; and its annex, Regulations respecting the Laws and Customs of War on Land . . . (the so-called Regulations respecting War on Land).

1899. Declaration concerning expanding bullets (the so-called Declaration prohibiting dum-dum bullets).

1899. Declaration concerning projectiles launched from balloons in the air (the so-called Declaration prohibiting aerial bombardment).

1899. Declaration concerning projectiles diffusing asphyxiating or deleterious gases (the so-called Declaration prohibiting poison gases).

1907. Convention respecting the Laws and Customs of War on Land . . . which was concluded in the Second Hague Peace Conference (the revision of the Convention of the same name in the First Hague Peace Conference).

1907. Declaration prohibiting aerial bombardment.

1922. Treaty of Five Countries concerning submarines and poisonous gases.

1923. Draft Rules concerning Air Warfare (Draft Rules of Air Warfare).

1925. Protocol prohibiting the use in war of asphyxiating, deleterious or other gases and bacteriological methods of warfare (Protocol respecting the prohibition of poison gases, etc.).

(3) In the above-mentioned laws and regulations, there is no direct provision with regard to the atomic bomb, a new weapon which appeared during World War II.

On the ground of this fact, the defendant State alleges that the question of violation of positive international law does not arise, since there was neither international customary law nor treaty law prohibiting the use of atomic bombs at that time, and the use is not prohibited clearly by positive international law.

Of course, it is right that the use of a new weapon is legal, as long as international law does not prohibit it. However, the prohibition in this case is understood to include not only the case where there is an express provision of direct prohibition but also the case where it is necessarily regarded that the use of a new weapon is prohibited, from the interpretation and analogical application of existing international laws and regulations (international customary laws and treaties). Further, we must understand that the prohibition includes also the case where, in the light of principles of international law which are the basis of the above-mentioned positive international laws and regulations, the use of a new weapon is admitted to be contrary to the principles. For there is no reason why the interpretation of international law must be limited to grammatical interpretation, any more than in the interpretation of municipal law.

(4) There is also an argument that a new weapon is not an object of regulation of international law at all, but such argument has not a sufficient ground as mentioned above. It is right and proper that any weapon contrary to the custom of civilized countries and to the principles of international law, should be prohibited even if there is no express provision in the laws and regulations. Only where there is no provision in the statutory [international] law, and as long as a new weapon is not contrary to the principles of international law, can the new weapon be used as a legal means of hostility.

. . . we cannot regard a weapon as legal only because it is a new weapon, and it is still right that a new weapon must be exposed to the examination of positive international law.

(5) Next, we will examine the international laws and regulations concerned at that time, with regard to the act of atomic bombing.

First of all, there arises the question whether the act of atomic bombing is admitted by the laws and regulations respecting air raids, since the act is an aerial bombardment as a hostile act by military plane.

No general treaty respecting air raids has been concluded. However, according to customary law recognized generally in international law with regard to a hostile act, a defended city and an undefended city are distinguished with regard to bombardment by land forces, and a defended place and an undefended place are distinguished with regard to bombardment by naval forces. Against the defended city and place, indiscriminate bombardment is permitted, while in the case of an undefended city and place, bombardment is permitted only against combatant and military installations (military objectives) and bombardment is not permitted against non-combatant and non-military installations (non-military objectives). Any contrary bombardment is necessarily regarded as an illegal act of hostility. . . . This principle is clear from the following provisions: Article 25 of the Hague Regulations respecting War on Land provides that "the attack or bombardment, by any means whatever, of towns, villages, habitations, or buildings, which are not defended, is prohibited." "The Convention concerning bombardment by naval forces in time of war" . . . *adopted at the Hague Peace Conference of* 1907, *provides in article* 1 *that "the bombardment of undefended ports, towns, villages, dwellings, or other buildings by naval forces is prohibited . . . ,"* and in article 2 that "among the above-mentioned objects against which bombard-ment is prohibited are not included military works, military or naval establishments, depots of arms or war material, workshops or plants which could be utilized for the needs of a hostile fleet or army, and men-of-war in the harbor. . . ."

(6) With regard to air warfare, there are "Draft Rules of Air Warfare." Article 24 of the Draft Rules provides that: "(1) Aer-ial bombardment is legitimate only when directed at a military objective, that is to say, an object of which the destruction or injury would constitute a distinct military advantage to the belligerent. (2) Such bom-bardment is legitimate only when directed exclusively at the following objectives: military forces; military works; military establishments or depots; factories con-stituting important and well-known centers engaged in the manufacture of arms, am-munition, or distinctively military supplies; lines of communication or transportation used for military purposes. (3) The bom-bardment of cities, towns, villages, dwell-ings, or buildings not in the immediate neighborhood of the operations of land forces is prohibited. In cases where the objectives specified in paragraph (2) are so situated that they cannot be bombarded without the indiscriminate bombardment of the civilian population, the aircraft must abstain from bombardment. (4) In the immediate neighbourhood of the operations of land forces, the bombardment of cities, towns, villages, dwellings, or buildings is legitimate, provided there exists a reason-able presumption that the military con-centration is sufficiently important to justify such bombardment, having regard to the danger thus caused to the civilian popula-tion . . . ." Further, article 22 provides . . . that "aerial bombardment for the purpose

of terrorizing the civilian population, of destroying or damaging private property not of military character, or of injuring non-combatants, is prohibited." In other words, this Draft Rules of Air Warfare prohibit useless aerial bombardment. . . .

In these provisions, stricter expressions are used than in the case of bombardment by land and naval forces, but what they mean is understood to be the same as the distinction between the defended city (place) and undefended city (place). The Draft Rules of Air Warfare cannot directly be called positive law, since they have not yet become effective as a treaty. However, international jurists regard the Draft Rules as authoritative with regard to air warfare. Some countries regard the substance of the Rules as a standard of action by armed forces, and the fundamental provisions of the Draft Rules are consistently in confor-mity with international laws and regula-tions, and customs at that time. Therefore, we can safely say that the prohibition of indiscriminate aerial bombardment on an undefended city and the principle of mili-tary objective, which are provided for by the Draft Rules, are international custom-ary law, also from the point that they are in common with the principle in land and sea warfare. Further, since the distinction of land, sea, and air warfare is made by the place and purpose of warfare, *we think that there is also sufficient reason for existence of the argument that, regarding the aerial bom-bardment of a city on land, the laws and regulations respecting land warfare analogi-cally apply since the aerial bombardment is made on land.*

(7) Then, what is the distinction between a defended city and an undefended city? Generally speaking, a defended city is a city resisting any possible occupation at-tempt by land forces. A city which is far distant from the battlefield, and is not in pressing danger of the enemy's occupation, even if there exist defensive installations or armed forces, cannot be said to be a defended city, since there is no military

necessity of indiscriminate bombardment; and in this case the bombardment and aerial bombardment only against military objectives is admitted. On the contrary, against a city resisting a possible occupation attempt by the enemy, indiscriminate bombardment is permitted out of military necessity, since an attack made upon the distinction between military objective and non-military objective has little military effect and cannot accomplish the expected purposes. *Thus, we can say that it is a long-standing, generally recognized principle in international law respecting air raids, that indiscriminate aerial bombardment is not permitted on an undefended city and that only aerial bombardment on military objective is permitted.*

Of course, it is naturally anticipated that the aerial bombardment of a military objective is attended with the destruction of non-military objectives or casualty of non-combatants; and this is not illegal if it is an inevitable result accompanying the aerial bombardment of a military objective. However, it necessarily follows that in an undefended city, an aerial bombardment directed at a non-military objective, and an aerial bombardment without distinction between military objectives and non-military objectives (the so-called blind aerial bombardment) is not permitted in the light of the above-mentioned principle.

The power of injury and destruction of the atomic bomb is tremendous . . . and even such small-scale atomic bombs as those dropped on Hiroshima and Nagasaki discharge energy equivalent to a 20,000-ton TNT bomb in the past. If an atomic bomb of such power of destruction once explodes, it is clear that it brings almost the same result as complete destruction of a middle-size city, to say nothing of indiscrimination of military objective and non-military objective. *Therefore, the act of atomic bombing on an undefended city, setting aside that on a defended city, should be regarded in the same light as a blind aerial bombardment; and it must be said to be a hostile act contrary to international law of the day.*

* * *

(9) Against the above conclusion, there is a counter-argument that the war of the day was the so-called total war, in which it was difficult to distinguish between combatant and non-combatant, and between military objective and non-military objective, and that the principle of military objective was not necessarily carried through during World War II.

The concept of military objective is prescribed in various expressions by the above-mentioned treaties, but the content is not always fixed and changes with time. It is difficult to deny that the scope is gradually spreading under the form of total war. For all the above reasons, however, we cannot say that the distinction between military objective and non-military objective has gone out of existence. For example, schools, churches, temples, shrines, hospitals and private houses cannot be military objectives, however total the war may be. If we understand the concept of total war to mean that all people who belong to a belligerent are more or less combatant, and all production means production injuring the enemy, there arises the necessity to destroy the whole people and all the property of the enemy; and it becomes nonsensical to distinguish between military objective and non-military objective. However, the advocacy of the concept of total war in recent times has the intent of pointing out the fact that the issue of a war is not decided only by armed forces and weapons, but that the other factors, that is to say, chiefly economic factors like source of energy, materials, productive capacity of industry, food, trade, etc., or human factors like population, man-power, etc., have a far-reaching control on the war method and war potential. The concept of total war is not advocated in such a vague meaning as stated above, and there was no actual example of such situation. *Accordingly, it is wrong to say that the distinction between military objective and non-military objective has gone out of existence because of total war.*

* * *

(11) Besides, the atomic bombing . . . of Hiroshima and Nagasaki is regarded as contrary to the principle of international law [in that] means which give unnecessary pain in war . . . are prohibited. . . .

* * *

The issues in this sense are whether atomic bombing comes within the purview of "the employment of poison or poisonous weapons" prohibited by article 23 (a) of the Hague Regulations respecting war on land, and of each forbidden provision of the "Declaration prohibiting each the use of projectiles the sole object of which is the diffusion of asphyxiating or deleterious gases" . . . of 1899, and the "Protocol prohibiting the use in war of asphyxiating, poisonous and other gases, and bacteriological methods of warfare" of 1925. With regard to this point, there is not an established theory among international jurists in connection with the difference of poison, poison-gas, bacterium, etc. from atomic bombs. However, judging from the fact that the St. Petersburg Declaration declares that ". . . . considering that the use of a weapon which increases uselessly the pain of people who are already placed out of battle and causes their death necessarily is beyond the scope of this purpose, and considering that the use of such a weapon is thus contrary to humanity . . ." and that article 23 (e) of the Hague Regulations respecting War on Land prohibits "the employment of such arms, projectiles, and material as cause unnecessary injury," we can safely see that besides poison, poison-gas and bacterium the use of the means of injuring the enemy which causes at least the same or more

injury is prohibited by international law. The destructive power of the atomic bomb is tremendous, but it is doubtful whether atomic bombing really had an appropriate military effect at that time and whether it was necessary. It is a deeply sorrowful reality that the atomic bombing on both cities of Hiroshima and Nagasaki took the lives of many civilians, and that among the survivors there are people whose lives are still imperilled owing to the radial rays, even today 18 years later. In this sense, *it is not too much to say that the pain brought by the atomic bombs is severer than that from poison and poison-gas, and we can say that the act of dropping such a cruel bomb is contrary to the fundamental principle of the laws of war that unnecessary pain must not be given.*

* * *

Principles of International Law Recognized in the Charter and Judgment of the Nürnberg Tribunal*

Report of the International Law Commission, Second Session, 1950

Principle I. Any person who commits an act which constitutes a crime under international law is responsible therefor and liable to punishment.

Principle II. The fact that internal law does not impose a penalty for an act which constitutes a crime under international law does not relieve the person who committed the act from responsibility under international law.

Principle III. The fact that a person who committed an act which constitutes a crime under international law acted as

* Reprinted from United Nations General Assembly, *Official Records,* 5th Session, Supp. No. 12 (A/1316), p. 11.

Head of State or responsible Government official does not relieve him from responsibility under international law.

Principle IV. The fact that a person acted pursuant to order of his Government or of a superior does not relieve him from responsibility under international law, provided a moral choice was in fact possible to him.

Principle V. Any person charged with a crime under international law has the right to a fair trial on the facts and law.

Principle VI. The crimes hereinafter set out are punishable as crimes under international law:

a. Crimes against peace:

i. Planning, preparation, initiation or waging of a war of aggression or a war in violation of international treaties, agreements or assurances;

ii. Participation in a common plan or conspiracy for the accomplishment of any of the acts mentioned under (i).

b. War crimes:

Violations of the laws or customs of war which include, but are not limited to, murder, ill-treatment or deportation to slave-labour or for any other purpose of civilian population of or in occupied territory, murder or ill-treatment of prisoners of war or persons on the seas, killing of hostages, plunder of public or private property, wanton destruction of cities, towns, or villages, or devastation not justified by military necessity.

c. Crimes against humanity:

Murder, extermination, enslavement, deportation and other inhuman acts done against any civilian population, or persecutions on political, racial or religious grounds, when such acts are done or such persecutions are carried on in execution of or in connexion with any crime against peace or any war crime.

Principle VII. Complicity in the commission of a crime against peace, a war crime, or a crime against humanity as set forth in Principle VI is a crime under international law.

United States v. Wilhelm List, et al. (The Hostages Case)*

United States Military Tribunal at Nürnberg, 1948

[*The defendants in this case, ten German military officers, were charged with the commission of war crimes and crimes against humanity, including the murder of thousands of civilians in Greece, Yugoslavia, and Albania in connection with alleged hostage or reprisal actions; the plundering, looting, or wanton destruction of property in Norway, Greece, Yugoslavia, and Albania; and the torture, persecution, imprisonment in concentration camps, and deportation to slave labor of thousands of civilians in occupied territory. Eight of the defendants were found guilty under one or more counts and two not guilty under any count.*]

* * *

The defendants invoke the defensive plea that the acts charged as crimes were carried out pursuant to orders of superior officers whom they were obliged to obey. . . . The rule that superior order is not a defense to a criminal act is a rule of fundamental criminal justice that has been adopted by civilized nations extensively. It is not disputed that the municipal law of civilized nations generally sustained the principle at the time the alleged criminal acts were committed. This being true, it properly may be declared as an applicable rule of international law.

It cannot be questioned that acts done in time of war under the military authority of an enemy cannot involve any criminal liability on the part of officers or soldiers if the acts are not prohibited by the conventional or customary rules of war. Implicit obedience to orders of superior officers is almost indispensable to every military system. But this implies obedience to lawful

* Reprinted from 11 *Trials of War Criminals Before the Nürnberg Military Tribunals* 757.

orders only. If the act done pursuant to a superior's orders be murder, the production of the order will not make it any less so. It may mitigate but it cannot justify the crime. We are of the view, however, that if the illegality of the order was not known to the inferior, and he could not reasonably have been expected to know of its illegality, no wrongful intent necessary to the commission of a crime exists and the interior [sic] will be protected. But the general rule is that members of the armed forces are bound to obey only the lawful orders of their commanding officers and they cannot escape criminal liability by obeying a command which violates international law and outrages fundamental concepts of justice. In the German War Trials (1921), the German Supreme Court of Leipzig in The Llandovery Castle case said:

"Patzig's order does not free the accused from guilt. It is true that, according to paragraph 47 of the Military Penal Code, if the execution of an order in the ordinary course of duty involves such a violation of the law as is punishable, the superior officer issuing such an order is alone responsible. According to No. 2, however, the subordinate obeying such an order is liable to punishment, if it was known to him that the order of the superior involved the infringement of civil or military law."

It is true that the foregoing rule compels a commander to make a choice between possible punishment by his lawless government for the disobedience of the illegal order of his superior officer, or that of lawful punishment for the crime under the law of nations. To choose the former in the hope that victory will cleanse the act of its criminal characteristics manifests only weakness of character and adds nothing to the defense.

We concede the serious consequences of the choice especially by an officer in the army of a dictator. But the rule becomes one of necessity, for otherwise the opposing army would in many cases have no protection at all against criminal excesses ordered by superiors.

The defense relies heavily upon the writings of Professor L. Oppenheim to sustain their position. It is true that he advocated this principle throughout his writings. As a co-author of the British "Manual of Military Law," he incorporated the principle there. It seems also to have found its way into the United States "Rules of Land Warfare" (1940). We think Professor Oppenheim espoused a decidedly minority view. It is based upon the following rationale: "The law cannot require an individual to be punished for an act which he was compelled by law to commit." The statement completely overlooks the fact that an illegal order is in no sense of the word a valid law which one is obliged to obey. The fact that the British and American Armies may have adopted it for the regulations of its own armies as a matter of policy does not have the effect of enthroning it as a rule of international law. We point out that army regulations are not a competent source of international law. They are neither legislative nor judicial pronouncements. They are not competent for any purpose in determining whether a fundamental principle of justice has been accepted by civilized nations generally. It is possible, however, that such regulations, as they bear upon a question of custom and practice in the conduct of war, might have evidentiary value, particularly if the applicable portions had been put into general practice. It will be observed that the determination, whether a custom or practice exists, is a question of fact. Whether a fundamental principle of justice has been accepted, is a question of judicial or legislative declaration. In determining the former, military regulations may play an important role but in the latter they do not constitute an authoritative precedent.

* * *

International law has never approved the defensive plea of superior order as a mandatory bar to the prosecution of war criminals. This defensive plea is not available to the defendants in the present case, although, if the circumstances warrant, it may be considered in mitigation of punishment. . . .

It is urged that Control Council Law No. 10* is an *ex post facto* act and retroactive in nature as to the crime charged in the indictment. The act was adopted on 20 December 1945, a date subsequent to the dates of the acts charged to be crimes. It is a fundamental principle of criminal jurisprudence that one may not be charged with crime for the doing of an act which was not a crime at the time of its commission. We think it could be said with justification that Article 23h of the Hague Regulations of 1907 operates as a bar to retroactive action in criminal matters. In any event, we are of the opinion that a victorious nation may not lawfully enact legislation defining a new crime and make it effective as to acts previously occurring which were not at the time unlawful. It therefore becomes the duty of a tribunal trying a case charging a crime under the provisions of Control Council Law No. 10 to determine if the acts charged were crimes at the time of their commission and that Control Council Law No. 10 is in fact declaratory of then existing international law.

This very question was passed upon by the International Military Tribunal in the case of the United States *vs.* Hermann Wilhelm Goering in its judgment entered on 1 October 1946. Similar provisions appearing in the Charter creating the International Military Tribunal and defining the crimes over which it had jurisdiction were held to be devoid of retroactive features in the following language:

"The Charter is not an arbitrary exercise of power on the part of the victorious nations, but

* Entitled "Punishment of Persons Guilty of War Crimes, Crimes Against Peace and Against Humanity," this law was enacted by British, French, Soviet, and United States commanders in Germany "in order to establish a uniform legal basis . . . for the prosecution of war criminals and other similar offenders, other than those dealt with by the International Military Tribunal . . . ."

in view of the Tribunal, as will be shown, it is the expression of international law existing at the time of its creation; and to that extent is itself a contribution to international law."

We adopt this conclusion. Any doubts in our mind concerning the rule thus announced go to its application rather than to the correctness of its statement. The crimes defined in Control Council Law No. 10 . . . were crimes under pre-existing rules of international law, some by conventional law such as that exemplified by the Hague Regulations of 1907 clearly make the war crimes herein quoted crimes under the proceedings of that convention. In any event, the practices and usages of war which gradually ripened into recognized customs with which belligerents were bound to comply recognized the crimes specified herein as crimes subject to punishment. It is not essential that a crime be specifically defined and charged in accordance with a particular ordinance, statute, or treaty if it is made a crime by international convention, recognized customs and usages of war, or the general principles of criminal justice common to civilized nations generally. If the acts charged were in fact crimes under international law when committed, they cannot be said to be *ex post facto* acts or retroactive pronouncements.

* * *

The major issues involved in the present case gravitate around the claimed right of the German armed forces to take hostages from the innocent civilian population to guarantee the peaceful conduct of the whole of the civilian population and its claimed right to execute hostages, members of the civil population, and captured members of the resistance forces in reprisal for armed attacks by resistance forces, acts of sabotage and injuries committed by unknown persons.

. . . We limit our discussion to the right to take hostages from the innocent civilian population of occupied territory as a guaranty against attacks by unlawful resistance forces, acts of sabotage and the unlawful acts of unknown persons, and the further right to execute them if the unilateral guaranty is violated.

Neither the Hague Convention of 1907, nor any other conventional law for that matter, says a word about hostages in the sense that we are to use the term in the following discussion. But certain rules of customary law and certain inferences legitimately to be drawn from existing conventional law lay down the rules applicable to the subject of hostages. In former times prominent persons were accepted as hostages as a means of insuring observance of treaties, armistices, and other agreements, the performance of which depended on good faith. This practice is now obsolete. Hostages under the alleged modern practice of nations are taken (*a*) to protect individuals held by the enemy, (*b*) to force the payment of requisitions, contributions, and the like, and (*c*) to insure against unlawful acts by enemy forces or people. We are concerned here only with the last provision. That hostages may be taken for this purpose cannot be denied.

The question of hostages is closely integrated with that of reprisals. A reprisal is a response to an enemy's violation of the laws of war which would otherwise be a violation on one's own side. It is a fundamental rule that a reprisal may not exceed the degree of the criminal act it is designed to correct. Where an excess is knowingly indulged, it in turn is criminal and may be punished. Where innocent individuals are seized and punished for a violation of the laws of war which has already occurred, no question of hostages is involved. It is nothing more than the infliction of a reprisal. Throughout the evidence in the present case, we find the term hostage applied where a reprisal only was involved.

Under the ancient practice of taking hostages they were held responsible for the good faith of the persons who delivered them, even at the price of their lives. This barbarous practice was wholly abandoned by a more enlightened civilization. The idea that an innocent person may be killed for the criminal act of another is abhorrent to every natural law. We condemn the injustice of any such rule as a barbarous relic of ancient times. But it is not our province to write international law as we would have it; we must apply it as we find it.

For the purposes of this opinion the term "hostages" will be considered as those persons of the civilian population who are taken into custody for the purpose of guaranteeing with their lives the future good conduct of the population of the community from which they were taken. The term "reprisal prisoners" will be considered as those individuals who are taken from the civilian population to be killed in retaliation for offenses committed by unknown persons within the occupied area.

An examination of the available evidence on the subject convinces us that hostages may be taken in order to guarantee the peaceful conduct of the populations of occupied territories and, when certain conditions exist and the necessary preliminaries have been taken, they may, as a last resort, be shot. The taking of hostages is based fundamentally on a theory of collective responsibility. The effect of an occupation is to confer upon the invading force the right of control for the period of the occupation within the limitations and prohibitions of international law. The inhabitants owe a duty to carry on their ordinary peaceful pursuits and to refrain from all injurious acts toward the troops or in respect to their military operations. The occupant may properly insist upon compliance with regulations necessary to the security of the occupying forces and for the maintenance of law and order. In the accomplishment of this objective, the occupant may only, as a last resort, take and execute hostages.

Hostages may not be taken or executed as a matter of military expediency. The occupant is required to use every available method to secure order and tranquility before resort may be had to the taking and execution of hostages. Regulations of all kinds must be imposed to secure peace and tranquility before the shooting of hostages may be indulged. These regulations may include one or more of the following measures: (1) the registration of the inhabitants, (2) the possession of passes or identification certificates, (3) the establishment of restricted areas, (4) limitations of movement, (5) the adoption of curfew regulations, (6) the prohibition of assembly, (7) the detention of suspected persons, (8) restrictions on communication, (9) the imposition of restrictions on food supplies, (10) the evacuation of troublesome areas, (11) the levying of monetary contributions, (12) compulsory labor to repair damage from sabotage, (13) the destruction of property in proximity to the place of the crime, and any other regulation not prohibited by international law that would in all likelihood contribute to the desired result.

If attacks upon troops and military installations occur regardless of the foregoing precautionary measures and the perpetrators cannot be apprehended, hostages may be taken from the population to deter similar acts in the future provided it can be shown that the population generally is a party to the offense, either actively or passively. Nationality or geographic proximity may under certain circumstances afford a basis for hostage selection, depending upon the circumstances of the situation. This arbitrary basis of selection may be deplored but it cannot be condemned as a violation of international law, but there must be some connection between the population from whom the hostages are taken and the crime committed. If the act was committed by isolated persons or bands from distant localities without the knowledge or approval of the population or public authorities, and which, therefore, neither the authorities nor the population could have prevented, the basis for the taking of hostages, or the shooting of hostages already taken, does not exist.

It is essential to a lawful taking of hostages under customary law that proclamation be made, giving the names and addresses of hostages taken, notifying the population that upon the recurrence of stated acts of war treason the hostages will be shot. The number of hostages shot must not exceed in severity the offenses the shooting is designed to deter. Unless the foregoing requirements are met, the shooting of hostages is in contravention of international law and is a war crime in itself. Whether such fundamental requirements have been met is a question determinable by court martial proceedings. A military commander may not arbitrarily determine such facts. An order of a military commander for the killing of hostages must be based upon the finding of a competent court martial that necessary conditions exist and all preliminary steps have been taken which are essential to the issuance of a valid order. The taking of the lives of innocent persons arrested as hostages is a very serious step. The right to kill hostages may be lawfully exercised only after a meticulous compliance with the foregoing safeguards against vindictive or whimsical orders of military commanders.

We are also concerned with the subject of reprisals and the detention of members of the civilian population for the purpose of using them as the victims of subsequent reprisal measures. The most common reason for holding them is for the general purpose of securing the good behavior and obedience of the civil population in occupied territory. The taking of reprisals against the civilian population by killing members thereof in retaliation for hostile acts against the armed forces or military operations of the occupant seems to have been originated by Germany in modern times. It has been invoked by Germany in the Franco-Prussian War, World War I, and in World War II. No other nation has resorted to the killing of members of the civilian population to secure peace and order insofar as our investigation has revealed. . . . While American, British, and French manuals for armies in the field seem to permit the taking of such reprisals as a last resort, the provisions do not appear to have been given effect. The American manual provides in part—

"The offending forces or populations generally may lawfully be subjected to appropriate reprisals. Hostages taken and held for the declared purpose of insuring against unlawful acts by the enemy forces or people may be punished or put to death if the unlawful acts are nevertheless committed."

The British field manual provides in part—

"Although collective punishment of the population is forbidden for the acts of individuals for which it cannot be regarded as collectively responsible, it may be necessary to resort to reprisals against a locality or community, for same act committed by its inhabitants, or members who cannot be identified."

In two major wars within the last 30 years, Germany has made extensive use of the practice of killing innocent members of the population as a deterrent to attacks upon its troops and acts of sabotage against installations essential to its military operations. The right to so do has been recognized by many nations including the United States, Great Britain, France, and the Soviet Union. There has been complete failure on the part of the nations of the world to limit or mitigate the practice by conventional rule. This requires us to apply customary law. That international agreement is badly needed in this field is self-evident.

International law is prohibitive law and no conventional prohibitions have been invoked to outlaw this barbarous practice. The extent to which the practice has been employed by the Germans exceeds the most elementary notions of humanity and justice. They invoke the plea of military necessity, a term which they confuse with convenience and strategical interests. Where legality and expediency have coincided, no fault can be found insofar as international law is concerned. But where legality of action is absent, the shooting of innocent members of the population as a measure of reprisal is not only criminal but it has the effect of destroying the basic relationship between the occupant and the population. Such a condition can progressively degenerate into a reign of terror. Unlawful reprisals may bring on counter reprisals and create an endless cycle productive of chaos and crime. To prevent a distortion of the right into a barbarous method of repression, international law provides a protective mantle against the abuse of the right.

* * *

Military necessity has been invoked by the defendants as justifying the killing of innocent members of the population and the destruction of villages and towns in the occupied territory. Military necessity permits a belligerent, subject to the laws of war, to apply any amount and kind of force to compel the complete submission of the enemy with the least possible expenditure of time, life, and money. In general, it sanctions measures by an occupant necessary to protect the safety of his forces and to facilitate the success of his operations. It permits the destruction of life of armed enemies and other persons whose destruction is incidentally unavoidable by the armed conflicts of the war; it allows the capturing of armed enemies and others of peculiar danger, but it does not permit the killing of innocent inhabitants for purposes of revenge or the satisfaction of a lust to kill. The destruction of property to be lawful must be imperatively demanded by the necessities of war. Destruction as an end in itself is a violation of international law. There must be some reasonable connection between the destruction of property and the overcoming of the enemy forces. It is lawful to destroy railways, lines of communication, or any other property that might be utilized by the enemy. Private homes and churches even may be destroyed if necessary for military operations. It does not admit the wanton devastation of a district or the willful infliction of suffering upon its inhabitants for the sake of suffering alone.

The issues in the present case raise grave questions of international law. Military men the world over debate both the law and the policy involved in the prosecution for war crimes of the high ranking commanders of defeated armies. This is partially brought about by the possibility of future wars and the further possibility that the victors of the present may be the vanquished of the future. This only serves to impress the Tribunal with the absolute necessity of affording the defendants a fair and impartial trial under the rules of international law as they were at the time the alleged offenses were committed. Unless this be done, the hand of injustice may fall upon those who so vindictively contend for more far reaching pronouncements, sustained by precedents which we would hereby establish.

Strict discipline is necessary in the organization of an army, and it becomes hard for many to believe that a violation of the orders of a superior may bring about criminal liability. Love of country and adherence to duty intervene to palliate unlawful conduct. The passage of time and the thankfulness for a return to peaceful pursuits tend to lessen the demand that war criminals answer for their crimes. In addition thereto, there is a general feeling that excesses occur in all armies, no matter how well disciplined, and that military trials are held to convict the war criminals of the vanquished while those of the victor are cleansed by victory. Unless civilization is to give way to barbarism in the conduct of war, crime must be punished. If international law as it applies to a given case is hopelessly inadequate, such inadequacy should be pointed out. If customary international law has become outmoded, it should be so stated. If conventional international law sets forth an unjust rule, its enforcement will secure its correction. If all

war criminals are not brought to the bar of justice under present procedures, such procedures should be made more inclusive and more effective. If the laws of war are to have any beneficent effect, they must be enforced.

The evidence in this case recites a record of killing and destruction seldom exceeded in modern history. Thousands of innocent inhabitants lost their lives by means of a firing squad or hangman's noose, people who had the same inherent desire to live as do these defendants. Wherever the German armed forces were found, there also were the SS (Die Schutzstaffeln der Nationalsozialistischen Deutschen Arbeiterpartei), the SD (Der Sicherheitsdienst des Reichsfuehrer SS), the Gestapo (Die Geheime Staatspolizei), the SA (Die Sturmabteilungen der Nationalsozialistischen Deutschen Arbeiterpartei), the administrators of Goering's Four Year Plan, and the Einsatzstab Rosenberg, all participating in the administration of the occupied territories in varying degrees. Mass shootings of the innocent population, deportations for slave labor, and the indiscriminate destruction of public and private property, not only in Yugoslavia and Greece but in many other countries as well, lend credit to the assertion that terrorism and intimidation was the accepted solution to any and all opposition to the German will. It is clear, also, that this had become a general practice and a major weapon of warfare by the German Wehrmacht. The German attitude seems to be reflected in the introduction to the German War Book, as translated by J. H. Morgan [John Murray, London, 1915] on pages 53–55 wherein it is stated:

"If therefore, in the following work the expression 'the law of war' is used, it must be understood that by it is meant not a *lex scripta* introduced by international agreements, but only a reciprocity of mutual agreement; a limitation of arbitrary behaviour, which custom and conventionality, human friendliness and a calculating egotism have erected, but for the observance of which there exists no express sanction, but only 'the fear of reprisals' decides. * * * Moreover the officer is a child of his time. He is subject to the intellectual tendencies which influence his own nation; the more educated he is the more will this be the case. The danger that, in this way, he will arrive at false views about the essential character of war must not be lost sight of. The danger can only be met by a thorough study of war itself. By steeping himself in military history an officer will be able to guard himself against excessive humanitarian notions, it will teach him that certain severities are indispensable to war, nay more, that the only true humanity very often lies in a ruthless application of them. It will also teach him how the rules of belligerent intercourse in war have developed, how in the course of time they have solidified into general usages of war, and finally it will teach him whether the governing usages of war are justified or not, whether they are to be modified or whether they are to be observed."

It is apparent from the evidence of these defendants that they considered military necessity, a matter to be determined by them, a complete justification of their acts. We do not concur in the view that the rules of warfare are anything less than they purport to be. Military necessity or expediency do not justify a violation of positive rules. International law is prohibitive law. Articles 46, 47, and 50 of the Hague Regulations of 1907 make no such exceptions to its enforcement. The rights of the innocent population therein set forth must be respected even if military necessity or expediency decree otherwise. . . .

* * *

It has been suggested in the course of the trial that an element of unfairness exists from the inherent nature of the organizational character of the Tribunal. It is true, of course, that the defendants are required to submit their case to a panel of judges from a victor nation. It is unfortunate that the nations of the world have taken no steps to remove the basis of this criticism. The lethargy of the world's statesmen in dealing with this matter, and many other problems of international relations, is well known. It is a reproach upon the initiative and intelligence of the civilized nations of the world that international law remains in many respects primitive in character. But it is a matter with which this Tribunal cannot deal, other than in justifying the confidence reposed in its members by insuring to the defendants a fair, dispassionate, and impartial determination of the law and the facts. A tribunal of this character should through its deliberations and judgment disclose that it represents all mankind in an effort to make contribution to a system of international law and procedure, devoid of nationalist prejudices. This we have endeavored to do. To some this may not appear to be sufficient protection against bias and prejudice. Any improvement, however, is dependent upon affirmative action by the nations of the world. It does not rest within the scope of the functions of this Tribunal.

* * *

Suggested Readings

Textbooks

Brierly. *The Law of Nations,* pp. 387–432.
Fenwick. *International Law,* pp. 634–768.
Gould. *An Introduction to International Law,* pp. 576–674.
Jacobini. *International Law,* pp. 235–358.

Kaplan and Katzenbach. *The Political Foundations of International Law*, pp. 198–230.
Kelsen. *Principles of International Law*, pp. 16–173.
Sørensen. *Manual of Public International Law*, pp. 739–854.
Svarlien. *An Introduction to the Law of Nations*, pp. 333–415.
Tung. *International Law in an Organizing World*, pp. 382–479.
von Glahn. *Law Among Nations*, pp. 498–725.

Resort to Force

Bowett, D. W. *Self-Defense in International Law*. Manchester: Manchester University Press, 1958.
Brownlie, Ian. *International Law and the Use of Force by States*. London: Oxford University Press, 1963.
Christol, Carl O. "Maritime Quarantine: The Naval Interdiction of Offensive Weapons and Associated Matériel to Cuba, 1962," 57 *American Journal of International Law* 524 (1963).
Falk, Richard A. (ed.). *The Vietnam War and International Law*. Princeton, N.J.: Princeton University Press, 1968.
Larson, David L. (ed.). *The "Cuban Crisis" of 1962: Selected Documents and Chronology*. Boston: Houghton Mifflin Co., 1963.
Raskin, Marcus G., and Bernard B. Fall (eds.). *The Viet-Nam Reader: Articles and Documents on American Foreign Policy and the Viet-Nam Crisis*. New York: Vintage, 1965.
Wright, Quincy. "The Goa Incident," 56 *American Journal of International Law* 617 (1962).

Neutrality and the Law of Warfare

Castren, Eric. *The Present Law of War and Neutrality*. Helsinki: Finnish Academy of Science and Letters, 1954.
Greenspan, Morris. *The Modern Law of Land Warfare*. Berkeley and Los Angeles: University of California Press, 1959.
Horwitz, Solis. "The Tokyo Trial," *International Conciliation*, No. 465 (November 1950).
Kotzsch, Lothar. *The Concept of War in Contemporary History and International Law*. Geneva: Droz, 1956.
Kunz, Josef L. "The Chaotic Status of the Laws of War and the Urgent Necessity for Their Revision," 45 *American Journal of International Law* 36 (1951).
Schwartzengerger, Georg. *The Legality of Nuclear Weapons*. London: Stevens, 1958.
Woetzel, Robert K. *The Nuremberg Trials in International Law*. New York: Praeger, 1960.

Chapter VII
The Development of International Law

It is clear that J. L. Brierly was correct when he wrote that international law is "neither a myth on the one hand, nor a panacea on the other, but just one institution among others which we can use for the building of a better international order."[1] It is equally clear that if international law is to serve this purpose effectively, it must be continuously developed by *revision in content, expansion of scope,* and *improvement of the means of securing compliance,* so that it is kept in accord with the changing needs of the international community. In times of rapid political, economic, and technological change, the development of law, both within and among states, tends to lag behind; its content becomes unstable and uncertain, and its effectiveness is minimized. If the development processes of a legal system are inadequate, a "crisis" of

[1] Brierly, *The Law of Nations,* p. v.

law emerges. The rapidly changing world of the twentieth century is going through such a crisis. Whether or not the developmental processes it has created, and is creating, will prove adequate is one of the fundamental questions of contemporary international law.

The generally recognized rules and principles of international law that were inherited by the twentieth-century international community were created by the major Western powers during the preceding three centuries, when international relations revolved around *their* mutual relations and *their* relations with the overseas world. It was the major Western powers who made the law of the seas because it was their ships that encompassed the waters of the world; it was these powers who made the laws of warfare because it was their armed forces that waged the major wars; it was these powers who formulated the rules designed to protect aliens because it was their nationals who traveled abroad for business and pleasure. By their practice and their treaties, they legislated the standards of official conduct that were recognized as legally binding on governments. Furthermore, their legal doctrine asserted that the norms they had created were automatically binding on new states that entered the international community; and another of their doctrines authorized them to use "self-help" measures, including armed reprisals, to coerce compliance with the norms.

The international law of the nineteenth century, when contrasted with that of the twentieth century, appears to have been stable and reasonably effective. There are several reasons for this, including the fact that the major "lawmakers" and "law enforcers" shared similar value systems; and since the great powers of the West had a preponderant influence in the creation of the law, its content was fairly well adjusted to the realities of power. Another reason for its effectiveness was the limited scope of its content. As Professor Lissitzyn has noted, since international law "did not purport to regulate the means by which a state could protect its major interests, it was generally not subjected to great strains."[2] Governments retained legal freedom to go to war whenever they chose; and significant categories of state conduct, including numerous activities that might adversely affect the interests of other states, were considered to fall under what was called the "domestic jurisdiction" of a single state. These matters, which included immigration policies and practically the entire scope of economic relations, were not, in the absence of treaties that arranged mutual concessions, regulated or controlled by international law. The treatment by a state of its own nationals was considered to be a matter exclusively within the jurisdiction of each state.

Viewed in this way, the stability and effectiveness of international law in the nineteenth century can be seen as both an expression of its strength and of its weakness. The international community of the twentieth century is going through a crisis in international law largely because it is attempting to correct the weaknesses of nineteenth-century law at a time when it has lost the major elements of its strength.

Of particular importance is the fact that power is no longer concentrated in the capitals of the major Western states. Decision-makers in Communist and in many of the less-developed states are unwilling to accept the proposition that the customary law of the West is automatically binding on them. Instead, they accept as law only those rules and principles that are considered to serve their interests—an attitude that is not unlike that of the major Western powers in the nineteenth century. And with the current world power distribution, the fear of nuclear holocaust, and the politics of influence in a cold war setting, the former "law enforcers" are unwilling or unable to coerce compliance with traditional norms.[3] The realistic international community response to this challenge of an eroding consensus on significant portions of customary law is clear: large bodies of that law, including norms relating to such matters as title to territory, succession, and treatment of aliens, must be reformulated if the law is to receive the widespread consent of states that is necessary to make it effective.[4]

[3] As a reflection of this change in the international political environment, the doctrine that condoned armed reprisals has been abandoned.
[4] The attitude of the new states toward the traditional norms of international law has been expressed time and again in the Sixth Committee of the General Assembly of the United Nations. Judge Radhabinod Pal, an Indian jurist and former Chairman of the International Law Commission, summarized the views expressed during the 1962 session as follows: "As to the 30 or 40 new states which had arisen since the end of the First World War, it was questioned to what extent they ought to be bound by rules of international law which they had not helped to create and which very often ran counter to their interests. The formal answer, it was suggested, was very simple: when a state acceded to the international community it automatically was understood to conform to its rules and institutions. The substance of the problem was, however, declared much more complex and difficult. If numerous

[2] Oliver J. Lissitzyn, "International Law in a Divided World," *International Conciliation*, No. 542 (March 1963), p7.

Equally important is the need, in an increasingly volatile and interdependent world, to expand the scope of law so as to cut more deeply into the "reserved domain" of unregulated state behavior. That the international community is already moving in this direction is clear: the modern law of nations strictly circumscribes the right of states to resort to force; multilateral treaties cover significant aspects of the entire range of international economic and technological relations, including financial transactions, monetary policy, sanitary regulations, telecommunications, and aviation. Even the ideal of international guarantees protecting the fundamental rights of individuals against their own governments has found a place, albeit an uncertain one, in modern international law. These advances are largely the result of the conclusion of law-making treaties. When a state accepts a treaty obligation relating to a particular subject, that subject is removed from the purely domestic domain.[5]

Since the establishment of the League of Nations, the development of international law has been accomplished primarily through the creation of international organizations *by* law-making treaties and the conclusion of law-making treaties *through* international organizations. The constituent instruments of international

organizations, such as the Charter of the United Nations and the Articles of Agreement of the International Bank for Reconstruction and Development, are law-making treaties of the first importance, in that they create obligations for member states which, in many instances, were hitherto not within the general scope of law. These instruments have also brought into existence an entirely new branch of international law, the internal law of international institutions, which establishes the competence of organizations and regulates the functioning of their organs. Furthermore, the practice of an organization may give rise to customary rules that supplement its constituent instrument.

An acceleration of the law-making process through the conclusion of multilateral treaties followed the creation of the League of Nations. The Assembly of the League was, in a sense, a continuous international conference; it drew up and opened for signature a large number of treaties, such as the Convention on Traffic in Women and Children of 1921 and the Slavery Convention of 1926. The Assembly also initiated the holding of a number of special conferences at which a wide variety of additional conventions was adopted. The result of these activities was that "multipartite law-making conventions doubled and tripled in extent, until the new conventional law exceeded many times in bulk the older customary law."[6]

The founders of the United Nations clearly perceived that the future of international law was linked to the future of international organization. One of the reasons for creating the United Nations, states the preamble, was "to establish conditions under which justice and respect for the obligations arising from treaties and other sources of international law can be maintained." And Article 13 instructs the General Assembly to "initiate studies and make recommendations for the purpose

---

rules of international law did not have the active support of a large sector of the international community, the entire machinery for the peaceful solution of disputes would, it was felt, be without foundation." Radhabinod Pal, "Future Role of the International Law Commission in the Changing World," 9 *United Nations Review* 31 (1962).

[5] This doctrine was clearly stated by the Permanent Court of International Justice in its advisory opinion on *Nationality Decrees in Tunis and Morocco* (1923): "The question whether a certain matter is or is not solely within the jurisdiction of a state is an essentially relative question; it depends upon the development of international relations. Thus, in the present state of international law, questions of nationality are, in the opinion of the Court, in principle within the reserved domain.

"For the purpose of the present opinion, it is enough to observe that it may well happen that, in a matter which, like that of nationality, is not, in principle, regulated by international law, the right of a state to use its discretion is nevertheless restricted by obligations which it may have undertaken towards other states. In such a case, jurisdiction which, in principle, belongs solely to the state, is limited by rules of international law." Series A/B No. 4.

[6] Fenwick, *International Law*, p. 39.

of . . . encouraging the progressive development of international law and its codification." At its second session, in 1947, the General Assembly established the International Law Commission to assist it in this task.[7] Because its membership reflects a wide variety of political viewpoints and combines technical expertise with experience in government, the Commission is peculiarly well adapted to serve as an instrument for promoting agreement upon rules and principles of international law. Its work on various topics, including the law of the sea, has provided the basis not only for codifying customary law but for revising its content so as to bring it more nearly into accord with the felt needs of an expanding international community. As J. L. Brierly has noted, "it is primarily through the Commission, if at all, that we may hope to see the divergencies [in attitudes toward customary norms] in some measure harmonized and more stable foundations laid for the law of the new international society now emerging."[8]

The General Assembly has also encouraged other organs of the United Nations, including the specialized agencies, to initiate studies and prepare draft conventions that contribute to the development of international law. The Secretariat, for example, drafted the Convention on the Privileges and Immunities of the United Nations. The Commission on Human Rights, a functional commission of ECOSOC, prepared, in addition to the Universal Declaration of Human Rights, the Convention on Genocide, the Covenant on Civil and Political Rights, the Covenant on Economic, Social, and Cultural Rights, and numerous other treaties intended to provide some international protection of fundamental human rights. The Legal Committee of the International Civil Aviation Organization initiated work that led to the signature of several conventions, including the Convention on Offenses and Certain Other Acts Committed on Board Aircraft.[9]

The contribution of international organizations to the development of international law goes beyond that of initiating law-making treaties. Certain specialized agencies of the United Nations and several regional organizations, especially the European Communities, have been given the authority in their constituent instruments not only to propose conventions but, in regard to some matters, to make binding rules by qualified majority vote. The International Civil Aviation Organization, for example, can adopt by majority action rules on flight paths and safety standards; the High Authority of the European Coal and Steel Community can create rules and apply regulations directly on the internal affairs of member states—in most cases without a particular member having a veto. There has been little difficulty in getting states to comply with these rules, largely because national decision-makers are aware that they cannot afford to forgo the many benefits that accrue to their states from membership in these organizations.

International organizations also contribute to the development of customary international law by providing a clear, concentrated forum for state practice. Particularly in the General Assembly of the United Nations, where more than 120 states are represented, the statements and the votes of representatives on legal matters provide evidence of existing customary law, as is illustrated by the discussion on, and the adoption of, the resolution affirming the principles of the Nürnberg Charter and Judgment. Still other resolutions amount to "an interpretation of the rules and principles which the Charter already contains and which are in consequence binding upon member states, authoritative by reason of

---

[7] The Statute of the International Law Commission is reprinted in this section on pp. 433–437.
[8] Brierly, *The Law of Nations*, p. 86.

[9] For the text of the Convention, signed by sixteen states in Tokyo in September 1963, see 2 *International Legal Materials: Current Documents* 1042 (1963).

the standing of the United Nations."[10] And, although the General Assembly has no general legislative power, resolutions incorporating declarations of rights and duties that are not expressly declaratory of existing law, when adopted by a majority verging on unanimity, or without significant opposition, contribute to the formation of customary rules. "Collective acts of states, repeated by and acquiesced in by sufficient numbers with sufficient frequency, eventually attain the status of law."[11]

These improvements in the processes by which international law is developed have not been devoid of problems and difficulties. Of particular importance is the fact that no means have been devised within the United Nations family of organizations to resolve differences in interpretation placed on provisions of the constituent instrument by the organization concerned and by member states.[12] The General Assembly and certain other organs have the right to request an advisory opinion from the International Court of Justice, but the opinion has no binding force and cannot put an end to the dispute if the states concerned do not accept it. For example, the advisory opinion on *Certain Expenses of the United Nations* (1962),[13] which confirmed the assertion by the General Assembly that it could assess member states to pay for extraordinary peace-keeping activities, has not induced France, the Soviet Union, and several other states to reverse their position that the General Assembly's claim of authority was *ultra vires* under the terms of the Charter. Similarly, the repeated adoption by the General Assembly of resolutions that condemn the *apartheid* policy of the

government of South Africa, although they purport to declare the law of the Charter and are regularly approved by majorities verging on unanimity, has not induced that state either to concede their legal effect or to alter its practice.

The selections that follow clarify and illustrate the progress and the problems of the international community effort to develop international law in a divided and rapidly changing world. The first selection, the Statute of the International Law Commission, outlines the organization and the functions of that important instrument for the development of law. The second selection, a case study by Robert L. Friedheim of the two United Nations Conferences on the Law of the Sea, illustrates the problems and the prospects of negotiating agreements on international law in a world divided into "satisfied" and "dissatisfied" states. The next two selections, articles by George A. Codding, Jr., and Rosalyn Higgins, discuss the contributions of the World Health Organization, the International Civil Aviation Organization, and the political organs of the United Nations to the development of international law. Next, the advisory opinion of the International Court of Justice on "Certain Expenses of the United Nations" is reprinted as an illustration of the application of legal techniques to the difficult problem of Charter interpretation; a brief excerpt from the dissenting opinion by the Soviet member of the Court suggests the extent to which political disagreements are translated into legal disagreements. Finally, the difficulty of interpreting the Charter and, additionally, of bringing the law of the Charter to bear on governments is illustrated by selections from the debate in the General Assembly on the continuing issue of *apartheid* in South Africa. The principal issue posed in the debate is the extent to which Article 2, paragraph 7, of the Charter, which prohibits the United Nations from intervening "in matters which are essenti-

---

[10] Michel Virally, "The Sources of International Law," in Sørensen, *Manual of Public International Law,* p. 162.
[11] Rosalyn Higgins, *The Development of International Law Through the Political Organs of the United Nations* (London: Oxford University Press, 1963), p. 2.
[12] For an excellent analysis of the problems of Charter interpretation and development, see Inis L. Claude, Jr., *Swords into Plowshares: The Problems and Progress of International Organization,* 3rd ed. (New York: Random House, 1964), pp. 148–173.
[13] The text of the opinion is reprinted in this section on pp. 454–465.

ally within the domestic jurisdiction of any State," as interpreted by individual members, can vitiate much of the remainder of the Charter, as interpreted by the organization. The inability of the United Nations to enforce its interpretation of the Charter against South Africa also illustrates the increasingly obvious fact that, while revision of the content of law improves the prospects for general compliance, expansion of the scope of law can make for more difficult problems of enforcement.

Statute of the International Law Commission*

Article 1

1. The International Law Commission shall have for its object the promotion of the progressive development of international law and its codification.

2. The Commission shall concern itself primarily with public international law, but is not precluded from entering the field of private international law.

Chapter I. Organization of the International Law Commission

Article 2

1. The Commission shall consist of twenty-five members who shall be persons of recognized competence in international law.

2. No two members of the Commission shall be nationals of the same State.

3. In case of dual nationality a candidate shall be deemed to be a national of the State in which he ordinarily exercises civil and political rights.

Article 3

The members of the Commission shall be elected by the General Assembly from a

* Reprinted from *United Nations Document* A/CN. 4/4/Rev. 1 (1962).

list of candidates nominated by the Governments of States Members of the United Nations.

Article 4

Each Member may nominate for election not more than four candidates, of whom two may be nationals of the nominating State and two nationals of other States.

Article 5

The names of the candidates shall be submitted in writing by the Governments to the Secretary-General by the first of June of the year in which an election is held, provided that a Government may in exceptional circumstances substitute for a candidate whom it has nominated before the first of June another candidate whom it shall name not later than thirty days before the opening of the General Assembly.

Article 6

The Secretary-General shall as soon as possible communicate to the Governments of States Members the names submitted, as well as any statements of qualifications of candidates that may have been submitted by the nominating Governments.

Article 7

The Secretary-General shall prepare the list referred to in article 3 above, comprising in alphabetical order the names of all the candidates duly nominated, and shall submit this list to the General Assembly for the purposes of the election.

Article 8

At the election the electors shall bear in mind that the persons to be elected to the Commission should individually possess the qualifications required and that in the Commission as a whole representation of the main forms of civilization and of the principal legal systems of the world should be assured.

Article 9

1. The twenty-five candidates who obtain the greatest number of votes and not less than a majority of the votes of the Members present and voting shall be elected.

2. In the event of more than one national of the same State obtaining a sufficient number of votes for election the one who obtains the greatest number of votes shall be elected and if the votes are equally divided the elder or eldest candidate shall be elected.

Article 10

The members of the Commission shall be elected for five years. They shall be eligible for re-election.

Article 11

In the case of a casual vacancy, the Commission itself shall fill the vacancy having due regard to the provisions contained in articles 2 and 8 of this Statute.

Article 12

The Commission shall sit at the European Office of the United Nations at Geneva. The Commission shall, however, have the right to hold meetings at other places after consultation with the Secretary-General.

Article 13

Members of the Commission shall be paid travel expenses, and shall also receive a special allowance, the amount of which shall be determined by the General Assembly.

Article 14

The Secretary-General shall, so far as he is able, make available staff and facilities required by the Commission to fulfil its task.

Chapter II. Functions of the International Law Commission

Article 15

In the following articles the expression "progressive development of international law" is used for convenience as meaning the preparation of draft conventions on subjects which have not yet been regulated by international law or in regard to which the law has not yet been sufficiently developed in the practice of States. Similarly, the expression "codification of international law" is used for convenience as meaning the more precise formulation and systematization of rules of international law in fields where there already has been extensive State practice, precedent and doctrine.

A. PROGRESSIVE DEVELOPMENT OF
INTERNATIONAL LAW

Article 16

When the General Assembly refers to the Commission a proposal for the progressive development of international law, the Commission shall follow in general a procedure on the following lines:

a. It shall appoint one of its members to be Rapporteur;

b. It shall formulate a plan of work;

c. It shall circulate a questionnaire to the Governments, and shall invite them to supply within a fixed period of time data and information relevant to items included in the plan of work;

d. It may appoint some of its members to work with the Rapporteur on the preparation of drafts pending receipt of replies to this questionnaire;

e. It may consult with scientific institutions and individual experts; these experts need not necessarily be nationals of Members of the United Nations. The Secretary-General will provide, when necessary and within the limits of the budget, for the expenses of these consultations of experts;

f. It shall consider the drafts proposed by the Rapporteur;

g. When the Commission considers a draft to be satisfactory, it shall request the Secretary-General to issue it as a Commission document. The Secretariat shall give all necessary publicity to this document which shall be accompanied by such explanations and supporting material as the Commission considers appropriate. The publication shall include any information supplied to the Commission in reply to the questionnaire referred to in subparagraph (c) above;

h. The Commission shall invite the Governments to submit their comments on this document within a reasonable time;

i. The Rapporteur and the members appointed for that purpose shall reconsider the draft taking into consideration these comments and shall prepare a final draft and explanatory report which they shall submit for consideration and adoption by the Commission;

j. The Commission shall submit the draft so adopted with its recommendations through the Secretary-General to the General Assembly.

Article 17

1. The Commission shall also consider proposals and draft multilateral conventions submitted by Members of the United Nations, the principal organs of the United Nations other than the General Assembly, specialized agencies, or official bodies established by inter-governmental agreement to encourage the progressive development of international law and its codification, and transmitted to it for that purpose by the Secretary-General.

2. If in such cases the Commission deems it appropriate to proceed with the study of such proposals or drafts, it shall follow in general a procedure on the following lines:

a. The Commission shall formulate a plan of work, and study such proposals or drafts, and compare them with any other proposals and drafts on the same subjects;

b. The Commission shall circulate a questionnaire to all Members of the United Nations and to the organs, specialized agencies and official bodies mentioned above which are concerned with the question, and shall invite them to transmit their comments within a reasonable time;

c. The Commission shall submit a report and its recommendations to the General Assembly. Before doing so, it may also, if it deems it desirable, make an interim report to the organ or agency which has submitted the proposal or draft;

d. If the General Assembly should invite the Commission to proceed with its work in accordance with a suggested plan, the procedure outlined in article 16 above shall apply. The questionnaire referred to in paragraph (c) of that article may not, however, be necessary.

B. CODIFICATION OF INTERNATIONAL LAW

Article 18

1. The Commission shall survey the whole field of international law with a view to selecting topics for codification, having in mind existing drafts whether governmental or not.

2. When the Commission considers that the codification of a particular topic is necessary or desirable, it shall submit its recommendations to the General Assembly.

3. The Commission shall give priority to requests of the General Assembly to deal with any question.

Article 19

1. The Commission shall adopt a plan of work appropriate to each case.

2. The Commission shall, through the Secretary-General, address to Governments a detailed request to furnish the texts of laws, decrees, judicial decisions, treaties, diplomatic correspondence and other documents relevant to the topic being studied and which the Commission deems necessary.

Article 20

The Commission shall prepare its drafts in the form of articles and shall submit them to the General Assembly together with a commentary containing:

a. Adequate presentation of precedents and other relevant data, including treaties, judicial decisions and doctrine;
b. Conclusions relevant to:
i. The extent of agreement on each point in the practice of States and in doctrine;
ii. Divergencies and disagreements which exist, as well as arguments invoked in favour of one or another solution.

Article 21

1. When the Commission considers a draft to be satisfactory, it shall request the Secretary-General to issue it as a Commission document. The Secretariat shall give all necessary publicity to the document including such explanations and supporting material as the Commission may consider appropriate. The publication shall include any information supplied to the Commission by Governments in accordance with article 19. The Commission shall decide whether the opinions of any scientific institution or individual experts consulted by the Commission shall be included in the publication.

2. The Commission shall request Governments to submit comments on this document within a reasonable time.

Article 22

Taking such comments into consideration, the Commission shall prepare a final draft and explanatory report which it shall submit with its recommendations through the Secretary-General to the General Assembly.

Article 23

1. The Commission may recommend to the General Assembly:
a. To take no action, the report having already been published;
b. To take note of or adopt the report by resolution;

c. To recommend the draft to Members with a view to the conclusion of a convention;
d. To convoke a conference to conclude a convention.

2. Whenever it deems it desirable, the General Assembly may refer drafts back to the Commission for reconsideration or redrafting.

Article 24

The Commission shall consider ways and means for making the evidence of customary international law more readily available, such as the collection and publication of documents concerning State practice and of the decisions of national and international courts on questions of international law, and shall make a report to the General Assembly on this matter.

Chapter III. Co-operation with Other Bodies

Article 25

1. The Commission may consult, if it considers necessary, with any of the organs of the United Nations on any subject which is within the competence of that organ.

2. All documents of the Commission which are circulated to Governments by the Secretary-General shall also be circulated to such organs of the United Nations as are concerned. Such organs may furnish any information or make any suggestions to the Commission.

Article 26

1. The Commission may consult with any international or national organizations, official or non-official, on any subject entrusted to it if it believes that such a procedure might aid it in the performance of its functions.

2. For the purpose of distribution of documents of the Commission, the Secretary-General, after consultation with the

Commission, shall draw up a list of national and international organizations concerned with questions of international law. The Secretary-General shall endeavour to include on this list at least one national organization of each Member of the United Nations.

* * *

The "Satisfied" and "Dissatisfied" States Negotiate International Law: A Case Study*

Robert L. Friedheim

* * *

An examination of the two United Nations Conferences on the Law of the Sea held in Geneva in 1958 and 1960 will help illuminate some of the difficulties in creating a law to which there is common consent—and therefore in employing law as the road to peace.

This article will address itself—by an analysis of the content of the debates at Geneva—to the different attitudes that representatives of states and bloc groups brought to the negotiating table. Because the difference in attitudes was so sharp, the conferences proved to be less successful than hoped for by advocates of world law. Not only were participants split on the question of the substantive content of the law, but they also differed on the nature of the international system, present and future, and on the proper means of negotiating law in a United Nations-sponsored conference, which is itself a special political area with distinctive characteristics.

* Reprinted from Robert L. Friedheim, "The Satisfied and Dissatisfied States Negotiate International Law: A Case Study," *World Politics* (October 1965), by permission of the publisher.

I

The first set of attitudes to be considered is that of those states at the law of the sea conferences who were dissatisfied with the legal status quo. They cannot all be labeled "new states," although most were. Although many were, not all were "revolutionary states" who felt compelled to "export their ideological impetus."[1] Nor can they be described as lacking an international-law tradition, because the Latin American states, which are included in this category, are very much in that tradition. Rather, the common factor was that these states were "have-not" states, most of whom were located in the southern half of the world, and most of whom believed that their interests were not served by present concepts of international law. . . .

The "dissatisfied" were heavily represented at the law of the sea conferences. The core of this category was composed of states that in the United Nations General Assembly are associated with the Asian-African, Arab, and Latin American caucusing groups and the anti-colonial common-interest group.[2] These constituted fifty-four of the eighty-six states represented at the first conference, and fifty-six of the eighty-eight at the second. In addition, some of the members of the underdeveloped common-interest group who were not also members of the regional and anti-colonial groups felt discriminated against under present concepts of international law.[3]

The key attitude expressed by the dissatisfied states was a strong, conscious, and often expressed belief that the conference process was a *political* process. They clearly understood that their operations were to be guided by practices usually known collectively as parliamentary diplomacy. This meant bloc organization, bloc voting, bloc-sponsored proposals, bloc-sponsored candidates for the elective offices of the conferences, and bloc attempts to manipulate the rules of procedure. The groups of the dissatisfied were the most organized,

evident, and self-conscious at the conferences. Mr. Ahmed Shukairi, chairman of
the Saudi Arabian delegation, was very outspoken in referring to the Arab states
"attending the conference . . . as a voting
group."[4] Other instances of frank references
to blocs are too numerous to list. The
dissatisfied took advantage of their
numbers by frequently sponsoring multinational proposals.[5]

Probably the major reason why the
dissatisfied considered the conference process as political and why a considerable
number of representatives reflecting this
position demonstrated great parliamentary
skill was the large proportion of dissatisfied
delegations which had as representatives
men with recent General Assembly experience. Twenty of the dissatisfied states
had at least one representative (five states
had several) who was not only a "professional diplomat" but also—in Philip
Jessup's phrase—a "professional parlia-
mentarian."[6] Three other delegations had
senior advisors who learned the art of
parliamentary maneuver in the General
Assembly.[7]

This is not to say that the dissatisfied controlled the conferences either by dominating
a majority of the votes taken or by getting a
majority of their proposals accepted. While
the incidence of bloc voting was relatively
high among the dissatisfied groups, so were
the absence rates of members, which reduced the number of total votes the group
cast. None of the dissatisfied except the
underdeveloped group was among the
groups that most frequently voted with
the majority. But their evident, organized
efforts constantly harassed their opponents,
and frequently forced them either to water
down or to withdraw proposals opposed by
the dissatisfied bloc. Even more important
was the ability of the dissatisfied groups to
mobilize their numbers to dominate voting
on key proposals. While their general
record for effectiveness was not good, they
could point with satisfaction to several
successful attempts to block passage of the

various United States proposals for a six-
mile territorial sea and a twelve-mile
contiguous fishing zone, and to force
elimination from a British proposal of a
fifteen-mile limit on the use of straight
baselines. They could also point to more
positive victories such as enlarging to
twenty-four miles the baseline to be
drawn from headland to headland in
delimiting bays, forcing through an Indian
proposal which gave the coastal state
"sovereign" rather than exclusive rights
over the continental shelf, and gaining
majorities for several proposals sponsored
jointly by Asian-African and Latin American states which increased the authority of
the coastal states over fishing in waters off
their coasts.

The satisfied states were annoyed by the
political strategy used by the dissatisfied.
But they were profoundly shocked by the
dissatisfied's analogous assumption—that
the *subject matter* to be dealt with in
the conferences should also be political. The
dissatisfied made frequent reference to the
General Assembly resolution that allowed
political factors to be considered in formulating the law of the sea: "[The conferences]
should take into account not only the legal
but also the technical, biological, economic,
and political aspects of the problem."[8]
These states early in the first conference
made it evident that they understood this to
mean carte blanche to fight for furthering
what they conceived of as their own interests. While this motive was not uncharacter-
istic of most participating states and groups,
the dissatisfied seemed more conscious of
their interests and more outspoken in
defending them.

A statement by the Vietnamese delegate,
Mr. Buu-kinh, in a debate on the continental shelf, can scarcely be plainer: "His
delegation would prefer to see the criterion
of depth alone retained, particularly as the
waters off its own shores were relatively
shallow and did not reach a depth of 200
metres for more than 200 miles."[9] The
Mexican delegate, Mr. Gomez Robledo, in

discussing a Canadian proposal on reservations to any convention signed as a result of the conference, was equally candid: "Representatives wishing to permit reservations had been reproached for defending national interests; but they were attending the conference for that very purpose."[10] Or, as Mr. Caabasi of Libya flatly remarked about a United States proposal on the breadth of the territorial sea: ". . . His delegation had voted against the United States proposal because it contained provisions which were contrary to his country's interests."[11]

Since these dissatisfied states were so insistent and outspoken in asserting that the conference process was a political means of attaining their own national interest, they were no less definite in assigning to the states opposing them the same self-interested motives. For example, Dr. Alfonso Garcia Robles of Mexico, advocating a broad belt of territorial sea, ascribed to the narrow-seas advocates the motive of sheer self-interest. He ignored entirely any reference to traditional historic and legal doctrines of freedom of the seas: "It had been suggested that the States whose fleets carried almost all the world's maritime transport should be asked why they opposed the extension of the breadth of the territorial sea to twelve miles. He could not see what would be the point in putting such a question. Gidel had given the answer when he had stated that a dominant factor in the dispute was the inequality of sea power; the greater a State's sea power, the more it would tend to limit the breadth of its territorial sea, for it had no need to look to international law for means to exercise special powers over a broad zone of sea adjacent to its coasts. Unfortunately, the maritime powers, which were usually also fishing powers, were not confining themselves to exercising special powers in the areas of sea adjacent to their coasts, but were only too often attempting to exercise them in the territorial sea of other countries, too."[12]

Just as these states saw the conference process in terms of politics and their own interests, so they regarded international law. They saw it as a cloak, a set of ideas used to camouflage self-interest, the domination by the few of the many. Nothing could be more candid than these remarks by Dr. Jorge Castaneda of Mexico: "Rigid adherence to the traditional rules of international law could prove disastrous to all concerned, for the traditional rules on the regime of the sea had been created by the great Powers for their own purposes before many major problems had arisen and before the birth of the new states which now formed the majority."[13]

The same theme was repeated again and again by delegates of many of the dissatisfied states. For example, Mr. Ba Han, of Burma: ". . . In the past international law had been a body of rules and usages adopted by powerful states. However, the international situation had changed and new sovereign independent states had emerged, keenly conscious of their liberty."[14] Mr. Ulloa Sotomayor, of Peru: "Rules of international law had sometimes been unilaterally created in the interests of great powers; it was therefore reasonable for certain rules of law to be initiated by small States in their legitimate interests. . . . It was inadmissible that a sort of colonialism of the high seas should be allowed in the name of freedom of the seas."[15] Mr. Diallo, of Guinea: "With regard to 'historic rights,' . . . the concept was nothing other than a manifestation of the right of the strongest and a vestige of colonialism, which [Guinea] would oppose in all its forms. To perpetuate those rights would be a grave injustice to the young States that were struggling not only for political but also for economic independence."[16]

* * *

These views of the dissatisfied are, in effect, a denial of the entire history and body of international law. Several Latin American delegates did in fact deny that the great international-law writers of the past had ever had anything more in mind than protecting the interests of the states or organizations to which they owed allegiance. As Mr. Melo Lecaros of Chile put it, ". . . The rise and development of the law of the sea had been prompted by one single factor: interest. Political or economic interest had always prevailed in defining the law of the sea through the centuries. Grotius had not argued for the freedom of the seas simply as an intellectual concept, but to defend the interests of the Dutch East India Company. Selden's sole aim in refuting Grotius had been to defend England's interests. Things had changed very greatly since that time. The rule of law had been extended, but it was impossible to overlook the fact that the reason for the existence of law was interest. Law had been created by man for the use of man."[17] Mr. Llosa of Peru also felt it necessary to tilt against Hugo Grotius, the very "father of international law," who, he said, ". . . did not write a work on international law but a treatise to vindicate the claims of the Dutch East India Company, by whom he had been retained, to freedom of navigation and trade."[18] So international law had moved in the wrong direction from the outset!

The dissatisfied states were acutely aware of the factor of time in regard to international law. The new states among the group, those who often set its tone and behavioral pattern, were quite naturally very conscious of their own recent independence and separate national existence. They demanded that international law take them into account, and consider their interests and desires; they demanded participation and the right of consultation in formation of international law. . . .

A close and perhaps necessary corollary of this extreme self-consciousness is that the new states and their allies did not recognize, and would not consider binding upon themselves, that law which was created before they became independent states. Expressions of this attitude at the conferences abound. Mr. Bocobo of the Philippines: ". . . The newer countries valued their freedom above all else and refused to accept certain rules of international law evolved before they had attained statehood."[19] Mr. Loutfi of the United Arab Republic: ". . . The majority of the new countries that had gained their independence since [the Hague Conference of 1930] had adopted a limit in excess of three miles. Their argument that the three-mile rule constituted a principle of international law was thus devoid of substance."[20] Mr. Ba Han of Burma ". . . could not accept the suggestion that abandonment of the three-mile rule was a concession. That alleged rule had been established by others at a time when his own country, for one, was completely helpless under foreign rule."[21]

There was an impatience with, rather than a reverence for, age and tradition, a feeling that the old laws should be swept away or remolded so that the newer states could help create new laws for new conditions. In stating Afghanistan's position on the access of landlocked states to the sea, Mr. Tabibi remarked: "Besides, many of [the international instruments in question] were very old and an historic conference such as the present should replace them by others which would contribute to the development of international law, particularly since the signatories of the instruments relating to the rights of landlocked countries were mainly European countries".[22] . . .

The keynote, the driving force, of this attitude was the need for change. Change for these states replaced history and tradition as a commander of respect. Symbolic were the remarks of the Korean delegate, Mr. Kim: "Several representatives had stressed how useful the three-mile limit had been in the past—at a time when it had been consistent with prevailing conditions. But those conditions had changed, and the three-mile limit was no longer adequate. Korea . . . earnestly hoped the Conference would adopt a principle better adapted to the varying conditions obtaining in the different parts of the world."[23] Consistent with their enthusiasm for change, the dissatisfied states were fond of calling those who were satisfied with the main aspects of international law "conservatives," while their own group was labeled "progressive."

* * *

II

Those states with an international-law tradition manifested a behavioral pattern very different from that of the dissatisfied states. This group included all states represented that had a Western European political tradition—some twenty-three states in all. The core of the category was composed of the Western European, Benelux, European Community, and Scandinavian caucusing groups, and the NATO common-interest group. Usually voting with these groups were the "White Commonwealth" states, five European states not represented in the General Assembly, and Israel. In addition, the votes of five United States cold-war allies—Japan, Pakistan, and the Republics of China, Korea, and Vietnam—could frequently be counted upon by the satisfied.

Although heavily outnumbered, the states in this category can be said statistically to have dominated the conferences. All the satisfied groups were able to command the votes of their members approximately eighty percent of the time on substantive issues. They also had an outstanding record of voting with the majority on both substantive and procedural issues. With additional votes coming from the five non-UN-member European states and the five United States cold-war allies, the satisfied voted with the majority on forty-three of sixty-six roll-call votes on substantive issues, and on ten of twelve votes on procedural issues. Another significant index of the "success" of the satisfied was the high percentage of proposals made by its members that were adopted by the conferences. Eighteen states each proposed more than

two percent of the total number of amendments adopted. Of these states, fourteen were either in the satisfied category or were states such as Japan and Pakistan that ordinarily voted with the satisfied.

It should be noted, however, that statistics on the law of the sea conferences do not tell the whole story of the successes and failures of the satisfied. Although they controlled a majority of the votes taken, and proposed most of the amendments accepted, the satisfied failed to gain majorities for their proposals on *key issues* such as the breadth of the territorial sea and fishing rights in areas beyond the territorial sea. They failed here because they were unable to persuade the dissatisfied that the measures desired also guarded the interests of the dissatisfied. The failure can be laid in large part to the fact that the satisfied couched their arguments in terms of traditional law—which the dissatisfied did not recognize and would not accept—instead of in terms of more realistic political-economic bargaining. Although their political positions at the conferences were not uniform—ranging from flexibility on the part of the United States and the United Kingdom to extreme conservatism and legalism on the part of continental powers such as France and the Federal Republic of Germany—still they shared a common belief that international law exists, that it is fundamentally just, that it provides a hope for adjustment of interests as well as protection of interests. They showed clear agreement with the broad background of sea-law doctrine and its cornerstone, freedom of the seas. Many states showed great pride in their past roles as formulators of international law: the Dutch continually invoked Grotius and Bynkershoek; the Spanish, Vitoria; the French, their great international lawyers.

* * *

Unfortunately the satisfied states' concept of law interfered with their understanding the process by which law must be negotiated in a contemporary international setting. They did not act as if they understood that the political process by which substantive questions are negotiated will itself help shape the results. In particular, many of the satisfied refused to admit that conferences with legal subjects on the agendas are political—that they provide forums in which agreements are forged by states when they believe that such agreements protect their mutual interests. Moreover, United Nations-sponsored conferences are legislative in nature. That is, they operate under the rules of parliamentary diplomacy, and decisions depend upon forming majorities. In such an arena, it is extremely difficult, and perhaps impossible, to create a majority that will vote for and be willing to be bound by what it believes to be an abstractly perfect legal or administrative formula. The satisfied tended to view the conferences as an opportunity to promulgate a legal code consistent with their international-law doctrine. They viewed apprehensively the possibility that past law and the international-law tradition were only two factors among many that would be considered in creating conventions to which a majority of states could agree politically. Such conventions would add to mere codification an element of progressive development—that is, the creation of new rules of international law—which the satisfied delegates deplored.

The remarks of Swedish delegate, Mr. Sture Petren, illustrate precisely the reluctance of the satisfied to accept the notion of progressive development: "Mr. Petren . . . emphasized the difference between the 'progressive development' of international law and its 'codification.' In practice, the development of law and its codification could not easily be separated. . . . Any conventions which might be drafted by the Conference, whether they related to the codification or the development of law, would therefore be of a mixed nature, containing both old rules of law and new ones.

These two kinds of law had not at all the same legal effect. The old rules, if they were based on customary law, bound all mankind independently of the new conventions to be concluded, whereas the new rules, which would come into being only through the conventions, would bind only those states which signed and ratified those conventions. Other states would not be bound to recognize or observe them. The Swedish delegation therefore felt that the Conference should proceed with caution, and should not depart too radically from existing law."[24]

The satisfied delegates were not averse to using political tactics at the conference; in fact they were quite skilled at forming voting groups, making bloc proposals, lobbying, and manipulating the rules of procedure. All the while they were publicly deploring the very use of such tactics by others and implicitly apologizing for finding it necessary to use them themselves. One after another satisfied delegate took the floor to excoriate blocs and bloc voting. They felt issues should be handled as ideas "on their merits." Typical was a British appeal to de-emphasize national and bloc interests for "wider considerations."[25]

Another major blunder of the satisfied states was their failure to answer the charge of the dissatisfied that the former were interested in preserving the present law because it protected their own interests. It is true that their interests did coincide with their doctrinal views. Their key doctrine, freedom of the seas, while theoretically opening the seas to all, in practice can only be exploited by those who have existent navies and merchant fleets. The satisfied states are the biggest shippers, have the biggest surface fleets, have large, important trade and fishing interests. But the satisfied states could have answered this accusation in political and economic terms, and have declared that freedom of the seas is open-ended and in fact generous to small powers, since without it the powerful could physically control large areas of the sea.

Dumbfounded by the attack of the dissatisfied on what the satisfied regarded as a liberal concept, the latter fell back on rigid, legalistic defenses. At times this tactic was used politically simply to discourage change. But the evident dismay of many satisfied delegates indicated that they could not understand the need to answer this attack by different tactics and different language. All they could do was deplore the attack on the law of the sea. For example, Dr. Max Sorensen of Denmark felt that ". . . a trend which, over the past few decades, had weakened rather than strengthened the authority of the international law of the sea should be halted, and Denmark would cooperate wholeheartedly with other nations in restoring the authority of the law."[26]

* * *

Submission of competing amendments to the same article, differing only in detail, was characteristic of the satisfied states at the conferences. Only infrequently would a legal specialist from one Western state agree that another's handling of details was technically correct and sufficiently comprehensive to cover all contingencies. This often meant that states of similar outlook which submitted proposals differing only in detail would maintain their competing proposals into the voting stage, instead of uniting to back one of the texts. As a result, it became difficult to get a detailed proposal adopted. When no agreement on details could be reached among these states, the committee or the conference adopted the most general proposal or the original International Law Commission text. While the desire of the legally sophisticated to write comprehensive codes is understandable, it would have been much more to the point to put greater effort into forming a consensus on basic issues. Without such a consensus, it is impossible to negotiate on details.

* * *

III

From this article it may be concluded that the results achieved by the Conferences on the Law of the Sea, like those of any United Nations-sponsored international conference, were dictated by the willingness of the participating states to create essentially political agreements. States or groups of states which assume that a specialized subject matter such as international law should not be subject to the political rough-and-tumble associated with parliamentary diplomacy, but dealt with logically within the broad lines of its past development, are bound to be disappointed by results achieved in a conference.

Indeed, one conclusion that might be drawn from the study of attitudes of dissatisfied states at the law of the sea conferences is that future conferences would be useless for codifying and developing law because of the hostility of dissatisfied states toward international law, a remnant of their European and imperialist past. Their concern with sovereignty, their suspicion of legal details, their wholly political attitude —all make it unlikely that they will be willing to agree to universal norms. By characterizing international law as an institutionalization of the values of the "top dogs" of the European-centered past, the dissatisfied seemed to demonstrate that they could not conceive that states might value law for its normative quality. They could not acknowledge that states have in the past compromised in negotiating legal subjects in order to create a pattern of orderly relationships even though their interests might not be fully served by such norms, or even that order itself may be to the interest of a state.

This attitude of the dissatisfied bodes ill for the possibility of creating universality in the law in our time. If, however, this is to be an end actively sought, international conferences, or some other United Nations-sponsored device, will probably be necessary to gain consent of the dissatisfied. And if conferences are to be used for this purpose it must be recognized, and not merely ruefully as Mr. Petren of Sweden did, that "progressive development" is guided by political considerations and that the results of a conference will be an undifferentiated mixture of "progressive development" and "codification." No purpose is served by deploring a "diplomacy of the sea" and distinguishing it from a true "law of the sea."

The course of attempting to achieve universality by means of conferences presents the satisfied with knotty problems. To avoid utter failure, the satisfied must alter their outlook on international law and on negotiating it.

The burden of responsibility for bringing conferences dealing with international law to successful conclusions rests with the states most devoted to international law. This does not mean that these states should make drastic changes in the law or sacrifice vital interests merely to foster agreement for agreement's sake. What is necessary is a recognition on the part of satisfied states that an international conference is a forum in which political negotiations must not be looked upon with distaste, and a determination on their part to find common interests, and to make real attempts to talk to other participants in terms which all understand. Such changes in attitude—if forthcoming—are no guarantee of success; indeed, they may only hasten failure by more clearly demonstrating the real reasons for disagreement. But a realistic appraisal of the conference process as a political process is the only approach which will make success even remotely possible.

Notes

1. Richard A. Falk, "Revolutionary Nations and the Quality of International Legal Order," in Morton A. Kaplan, ed., *The Revolution in World Politics* (New York 1962), 323.
2. Although the Soviet-bloc states are members of the anticolonialist group, a full discussion of their conduct must be omitted for reasons of space. However, it should be pointed out that the Soviet-bloc states should not be classified as "dissatisfied." Although often allied with the dissatisfied, the Soviet bloc did not participate in the all-out assault on law *per se* so characteristic of the dissatisfied states. The positions adopted by the Soviet Union (and her satellites) at the conferences were typical of a conservative revolutionary state ambivalently trying to accomplish two ends—on the one hand, export of revolutionary principles and harassment of cold-war enemies; on the other, a genuine attempt to negotiate commonly accepted legal principles in areas where important material interests would be protected if normative behavior could be enforced. For a discussion of conservative revolutionary states, see Falk, 315.
3. The reader should not assume that the characteristics ascribed to a category of states created for purposes of analysis are wholly applicable to all states that generally fall into that category.
4. United Nations Conference on the Law of the Sea, *Official Records,* Vol. III, First Committee (A/CONF. 13/39), 4th meeting, par. 30. Hereafter all citations from the records, documents, or reports of both UN Conferences on the Law of the Sea will be made with the official UN document number.
5. See, for example, A/CONF. 13/C.5/L.6 (19 "dissatisfied" sponsors), A/CONF. 13/C.3/L.65, 66, 66/Rev. 1 (12 sponsors), A/CONF. 19/C.1/L.2/Rev. 1 (18 sponsors), A/CONF. 19/C.1/L.6 (16 sponsors), A/CONF. 19/L. 9 (10 sponsors), among many others.
6. "International Negotiations Under Parliamentary Procedure," *Lectures on International Law and the United Nations* (Ann Arbor, University of Michigan Law School, 1957), 419.
7. These figures were compiled from the list of delegations to the Conferences on the Law of the Sea and to Sessions XII, XIII, XIV, and XV of the General Assembly.
8. General Assembly Resolution 1105, XI Session, par. 2. For example, see A/CONF. 13/42, 19th meeting, par. 33.
9. A/CONF. 13/42, 11th meeting, par. 14.
10. A/CONF. 13/38, 9th plenary meeting, par. 34.
11. *Ibid.,* 14th plenary meeting, par. 66.
12. A/CONF. 19/8, 10th meeting, par. 12.
13. A/CONF. 13/41, 13th meeting, par. 22.
14. A/CONF. 13/39, 4th meeting, par. 6.

15. *Ibid.*, 5th meeting, par. 13.
16. A/CONF. 19/8, 18th meeting, par. 6.
17. A/CONF. 19/8, 14th meeting, par. 13–14.
18. A/CONF. 13/41, 23rd meeting, par. 11.
19. A/CONF. 13/39, 50th meeting, par. 1.
20. *Ibid.*, 21st meeting, par. 4.
21. A/CONF. 13/38, 14th plenary meeting, par. 51.
22. A/CONF. 13/43, 8th meeting, par. 32.
23. A/CONF. 13/39, 15th meeting, par. 14.
24. A/CONF. 13/39, 6th meeting, par. 1–2; see also par. 24–25; 18th meeting, par. 10.
25. A/CONF. 13/39, 53rd meeting, par. 10.
26. *Ibid.*, 4th meeting, par. 10.

Contributions of the World Health Organization and the International Civil Aviation Organization to the Development of International Law*

George A. Codding, Jr.

Both the World Health Organization and the International Civil Aviation Organization carry out a wide range of activities which may be interpreted as contributing to the development of international law. . . . I will confine my remarks only to those procedural aspects of the work of these two agencies which give the impression of being a significant attack on some of the more important problems involved in the international legislative process. While many of the specific defects of the international legislative process outlined 45 years ago by Professor Manley O. Hudson have been eliminated by the inclusion of procedural articles in treaties and by other similar expedients, there still remain a great many problems that must be overcome if international law is ever to approach the flexibility of the domestic legislative process.[1]

* Reprinted from George A. Codding, Jr., "Contributions of the World Health Organization and the International Civil Aviation Organization to the Development of International Law," *Proceedings of the American Society of International Law* 147 (1965), by permission of the American Society of International Law.

Of special importance are: (1) the slow and often uncertain ratification procedure which makes it extremely difficult to determine the extent of the application of a multilateral treaty; (2) the ever-present possibility of a multitude of reservations to a multilateral treaty which would make it difficult to know its substance in any particular relationship; and (3) the difficulty of providing a method which will permit frequent and expert revision of multilateral treaties. There is an additional problem, that of the rising cost to governments in money and personnel, resulting from the steadily increasing number and complexity of international conferences and meetings. At the moment, the strain on resources and talent that this produces is hardest on the smaller and the underdeveloped nations, but it is rapidly becoming difficult for all. WHO and ICAO have procedures designed to deal with all four problems.

WHO's approach is contained in Articles 19, 20, and 21 of its Constitution. The first two of these articles give the Health Assembly, WHO's plenary body, the authority to adopt conventions or agreements with respect to any matter within the competence of the organization. In brief, all such instruments which receive at least a two-thirds vote of the Health Assembly come into force for each Member "when accepted by it in accordance with its constitutional process."[2] Rather than leaving this "acceptance" to the normal, sometimes very slow, process in each Member State, under Article 21 each Member undertakes the obligation to "take action relative to the acceptance of such convention or agreement" within a period of eighteen months after its adoption by the Health Assembly.[3]

Another approach is provided for in the adoption of Health Regulations. First, Article 21 of the Constitution of WHO authorizes the World Health Assembly to adopt regulations concerning: (1) sanitary and quarantine requirements; (2) medical nomenclature; (3) standards with respect to diagnostic procedure; (4) standards with respect to the safety, purity, and potency of biological, pharmaceutical and similar products; and (5) advertising and labeling of such products. Second, it provides that all regulations so adopted shall come into force for all Members after due notice has been given of their adoption by the Health Assembly, except for such Members as notify the Director General of rejection or of reservations within the period stated in the notice.[4]

This power was used to create the Nomenclature Regulations in 1948 and the International Sanitary Regulations in 1951. The latter, dealing with measures to stop the spread of the pestilential diseases—cholera, plague, relapsing fever, typhus fever, and yellow fever—superseded and brought up to date a series of twelve international sanitary conventions dating back to 1903. Both of these documents have been the subject of numerous amendments.[5]

The World Health Organization also used an interesting procedure as regards reservations to the International Sanitary Regulations. During the process of drafting the Regulations it was decided that reservations should not be allowed to emasculate this important document. If the prescriptions contained therein were to accomplish the purpose for which they were adopted, all states should follow them. Accordingly, the Health Assembly was given the power to screen all reservations to the Regulations for acceptability and to refuse any reservation which was considered to detract substantially from the character and purpose of the Regulations. The Regulations were not to come into force for the state concerned until the offensive reservation was withdrawn.[6]

Twenty-five states submitted some 73 reservations to the Sanitary Regulations. These were examined by the Health Assembly and 38 were rejected as incompatible with the purpose of the Regulations. By 1958, the Director General of WHO was able to report that: "Most of the rejected reservations have now been withdrawn and the States concerned are therefore bound by the Regulations."[7]

The mandate of the International Civil Aviation Organization to attack problems of multilateral treaty-making is contained in Articles 37, 54, and 90 of the ICAO convention. Article 37 authorizes the ICAO to adopt international standards and recommend practices dealing with a wide variety of technical matters essential to the safe and swift operation of international civil aviation.[8] Briefly, a recommended practice is one the uniform application of which is regarded as desirable in the interests of safety, regularity, and efficiency of international air navigation; but there is no legal obligation on the Member States to obey. The international standard, on the other hand, is recognized as necessary for the safety or regularity of international air navigation and is binding on all Members of ICAO.[9] Regulations are a combination of the two and are designated as Annexes to the ICAO Convention.

ICAO uses an interesting variation on the WHO procedure in the adoption of these Annexes and in their application. The task of adopting them is given not to a plenary body but to the 27-member Council. The Council is a permanent body, the members of which serve 3-year terms and are eligible for re-election. The Council is also a representative body in that when the ICAO Assembly elects states to send individuals to serve on the Council it must give adequate representation to: (1) the states of chief importance in air transport, (2) the states which make the largest contribution to the provision of facilities for international civil air navigation, and (3) other states as necessary to insure that all the major geographical areas of the world are represented.[10]

To "be adopted" (to use the terms of the Convention) an annex must receive a two-thirds majority vote of the members of the Council at a meeting called especially for that purpose. Any regulation thus adopted "becomes effective" (again to use the terms of the Convention) three months after its submission to the contracting states or within some other time limit established by the Council, *unless the majority of contracting states register their disapproval with the Council.*[11] Silence, therefore, means approval.

In order to make certain that Member States will be willing to accept the results of such a radical procedure, ICAO has created a fairly long and complicated drafting process.[12] This process begins with the preparation of a working draft by specialists within ICAO's own secretariat. It is transmitted to the Air Navigation Commission, a body of twelve experts in the science and practice of aeronautics chosen by the Council, for examination. If the draft is approved by this body, a Technical Division meeting is called. An ICAO Technical Division meeting is actually a conference open to the technical experts of any Member State which cares to participate and to observers from international organizations and non-member states invited by the Council. All observations and suggestions from the Technical Division meeting are forwarded to the Air Navigation Commission. The commission then has the task of drafting the final version of the international standards and recommended procedures, which is submitted to the Council for its adoption.

The ICAO Convention provides that any state which finds it impracticable to comply with any of the international standards and procedures adopted by the Council is under the obligation to notify ICAO immediately of the differences between its own practices and those established by the Annex. This information is at once transmitted to all Member States.[13]

The ICAO has used this process to create fifteen separate regulations. These regulations deal with such important matters in air navigation as: personnel licensing, rules of the air, meteorology, aeronautical charts, units of measurement to be used in air-ground communications, airworthiness of aircraft, facilitation of arrivals and departures, aircraft nationality and registration marks, operation of aircraft, aeronautical communication, search and rescue, aircraft accident inquiry, and aerodromes. Six of the regulations came into effect in 1948, three in 1949, three in 1950, two in 1951, and one in 1954.

That the procedures adopted by ICAO are effective is evident from the fact that none of the annexes offered by the Council have been turned down by a majority of Member States; and as a general rule the derogations to the standards and procedures notified by Member States have not been overly numerous, nor have they dealt with important considerations.[14]

While amendments to these documents must also receive a two-thirds majority vote of the Council and must be submitted to Member States for approval, as was the case in the original adoption, the rest of the process is much more streamlined. The Air Navigation Commission keeps all fifteen annexes under constant scrutiny. If this body comes to the conclusion that an amendment is needed, that information is transmitted directly to the Council which, if it agrees as it usually does, moves directly to the adoption procedure.[15] While the more general regulations, such as Annex 2 dealing with the Rules of the Air, have been amended only a few times, the more detailed and technical regulations have been subjected to frequent change.[16] Annex 1, dealing with Personnel Licensing, for instance, has undergone 155 amendments from September, 1948, to January, 1965; and Annex 6, on the Operation of Aircraft, was amended 149 times from July, 1948, to January, 1965.[17]

Precedents can be found for most of the special procedures adopted by WHO and ICAO. WHO's method of creating conventions and agreements, for instance, is but a variation on I.L.O.'s procedure for creating Labor Conventions. ICAO, in its turn, borrowed much of its special procedure for making technical regulations from the Paris Convention of 1919 which created ICAO's immediate predecessor, the International Commission for Air Navigation (ICAN). The main difference is that the Paris Convention provided that changes in technical regulations were to be made by the entire Commission, on which each member of ICAN had the right to be represented, rather than the limited membership Council under ICAO's Convention.[18]

The procedures of both the WHO and ICAO derive something from the practices of the two oldest international organizations, the International Telecommunication Union and the Universal Postal Union. The whole process of "contracting out" (to use the term employed by Professor Skubiszewski in a recent article),[19] which involves an agreement in a treaty to permit someone other than plenipotentiaries to process technical matters, was pioneered by the I.T.U. in the last century. To be more specific, at its St. Petersburg Conference in 1875, the I.T.U. divorced the transitory details subject to periodic modification from the more permanent and basic principles in its Telegraph Convention. These details were put into "Regulations" which could be revised periodically by administrative experts rather than plenipotentiary delegates and "accepted" by the telegraph administrations of the contracting states rather than ratified by the usual diplomatic process.[20]

The contribution of the Universal Postal Union lies in pioneering the idea that regulations can be made applicable to national authorities without any positive act of national acceptance. In its first convention, that created by the congress of 1874, the members of the U.P.U. included a provision stating that those postal administrations which fail to respond to a proposal put to them by the International Bureau within a period of three months were considered to be in agreement with the proposal.[21] Later, the words "in agreement" were changed to "abstention."[22] This has not been an idle provision for the U.P.U. From 1874 to 1963 it has been used some 122 times.[23]

The modifications of the usual international legislative procedure adopted by the World Health Organization and the International Civil Aviation Organization have permitted these two organizations to make valuable contributions to international law. In the case of WHO the most important contribution is without doubt the International Sanitary Regulations. This document, so basic to the prevention of the spread of pestilential diseases and one of the few multilateral treaties of its scope without serious loopholes due to incompatible reservations, has been described by Professor Jenks as "one of the major achievements of the international legislative process."[24]

In the case of the ICAO, the major contribution is in the international standards and recommended practices and procedures which permit international air navigation to be carried on with safety, regularity, and efficiency. ICAO's enlightened procedures for modification permit the ICAO to keep up with the rapid changes that are taking place in civil aviation and at the same time to avoid being bogged down in many of the ordinary time-consuming activities of other international organizations.

The special procedures adopted by these two bodies should not, however, be considered a panacea for the difficulties encountered by all organizations in the international legislative process. In the first place, these two agencies are engaged in highly specialized work. States seem to be more willing to accept flexibility in method in their work—because it is both specialized and largely non-political—while insisting upon rigidity in other agencies. In the second place, the constant innovations in the techniques of air transportation demand a very flexible process for ICAO. (WHO's Health Regulations must also keep up with rapid changes in methods of transportation.) These two elements are not necessarily present in the operations of other international organizations.

These procedures have limited application even in the two organizations under discussion. The WHO process has been used in only two specific areas. The ICAO innovations, on the other hand, have been used much more widely with regard to subject matter, but probably have a more limited application because of the fact that the Soviet Union is not a Member.

Nevertheless, the experiences of WHO and ICAO have a high potential value. Other international agencies could possibly adapt them profitably to their own use, particularly those agencies whose activities are of a technical nature. A combination of all the special procedures of ILO, WHO, ICAO, ITU and UPU in one international organization provides exciting speculation. In any case, it is becoming increasingly obvious that some major changes are needed in the international legislative process if the international community is to be able to keep up with the amount of work that is being delegated by states to international organizations. The WHO and ICAO have, at least, made a start.

Notes

1. For a fuller discussion of the problems involved in the international legislative process, see 1 Hudson, International Legislation xiii–lx (Washington, D. C.: Carnegie Endowment for International Peace, 1931); Clyde Eagleton, International Government 183–186 (3rd ed., N. Y.: Ronald Press, 1957); and C. Wilfred Jenks, The Common Law of Mankind 173–200 (London: Stevens and Sons, 1958).
2. See Constitution of the World Health Organization, Art. 19. This document is found in WHO, Basic Documents 1–18 (14th ed.) (Geneva, December, 1963).
3. If a Member does not accept the convention or agreement within the specified time limit, it must furnish the Director General with a statement of the reasons for non-acceptance. WHO has not yet used Arts. 19 and 20.
4. Art. 22.

5. See, for instance, International Sanitary Regulations (2nd annotated ed., Geneva, 1961).
6. States would remain bound, however, to the earlier sanitary conventions to which they were a party. See "The International Sanitary Regulations (WHO Regulations, No. 2)," 10 Chronicle of the World Health Organization, 315 (Nos. 9–10, Spec. No.).
7. WHO, The First Ten Years of the World Health Organization 260 (Geneva, 1958).
8. The following areas are included: (1) communications systems and air navigation aids, including ground marking; (2) characteristics of airports and landing areas; (3) rules of the air and air traffic control practices; (4) licensing of operating and mechanical personnel; (5) airworthiness of aircraft; (6) registration and identification of aircraft; (7) collection and exchange of meteorological information; (8) log books; (9) aeronautical maps and charts; (10) customs and immigration procedures; (11) aircraft in distress and investigation of accidents; and (12) such other matters concerned with the safety, regularity, and efficiency of air navigation as may from time to time appear appropriate. See ICAO, Convention on International Civil Aviation 20–21 (3rd ed., Montreal, 1963).
9. See ICAO, International Standards and Recommended Practices, Personnel Licensing, Annex 1, p. 3 (5th ed., Montreal, November, 1962).
10. In 1963 the Council was made up of the following countries: Argentina, Australia, Belgium, Brazil, Canada, Colombia, Congo (Brazzaville), West Germany, France, India, Indonesia, Italy, Japan, Lebanon, Malagasy Republic, Mexico, Netherlands, Nicaragua, Nigeria, Norway, Philippines, South Africa, Spain, Tunisia, United Arab Republic, United Kingdom, and United States.
11. Art. 90.
12. The manner in which each annex was created is summarized at the beginning of the official text. See, for instance, Annex 1, *op. cit.*, p. 3. One of the best over-all discussions of the method by which the ICAO creates its annexes is to be found in R. H. Mankiewicz, "L'adoption des annexes à la convention de Chicago par le Conseil de l'Organisation de l'Aviation Civile Internationale," Beiträge zum internationalen Luftrecht. Festschrift zu Ehren von Prof. Dr. Jur. Alex Meyer 82–94 (Dusseldorf, 1954).

13. Art. 38. Further, aircraft or personnel not in compliance with international standards must have the particulars of such shortcomings endorsed on their respective certificates of airworthiness or licenses. Aircraft whose certificates are so endorsed, and personnel whose licenses are so endorsed, are permitted to participate in international air navigation only with the express permission of the states whose territory is entered. Arts. 39 and 40.

14. Mankiewicz, *loc. cit.* 87, especially note 22.

15. Art. 54 (m).

16. ICAO, International Standards, Rules of the Air, Annex 2, p. 5 (4th ed., Montreal, May, 1960).

17. See Personnel Licensing, Annex 1, *op cit.,* p. 3; and ICAO, International Standards and Recommended Practices, Operation of Aircraft, Annex 6, p. 3 (5th ed., Montreal, October, 1957).

18. Modifications of the provisions of ICAN's Technical Regulations demanded a three-fourths approving vote of all states represented at the Commission's meeting and two-thirds of the total possible vote which could be cast if all the state-members were represented. See U. S. State Department, International Convention Relating to the Regulation of Aerial Navigation Dated October 13, 1919, with the Annexes to the Convention and Protocols of Proposed Amendments, pp. 9–10 (State Department Pub. 2143. Washington, D. C.: U. S. Government Printing Office, 1944).

19. See Krzysztof Skubiszewski, "Forms of Participation of International Organizations in the Lawmaking Process," 18 International Organization 800 (1964).

20. See George A. Codding, Jr., International Telecommunication Union 28 (Leiden: E. J. Brill, 1952).

21. See Traité concernant la création d'une Union générale des postes (1874), Règlement de détail et d'ordre pour l'exécution du traité, Art. XXVII. This document can be found in UPU, Documents du Congrès postal international, réuni à Berne du 15 Septembre au 9 Octobre 1874, pp. 155–164 (Bern, 1875).

22. See UPU, Documents de Congrès postal universel de Paris, 1878, p. 664 (Bern, 1879).

23. See George A. Codding, Jr., Universal Postal Union 107 (New York: New York University Press, 1964).

24. Jenks, *op. cit.* 187.

The Development of International Law by the Political Organs of the United Nations*

Rosalyn Higgins

* * *

International treaties and international custom have long been recognized as sources of international law. Yet only comparatively recently has it been admitted that international organizations are a significant forum in which to search for such sources of law. And the acknowledgment of the contribution of *political* organs to the development of international law has been even longer in coming. The political organs of the United Nations provide a clear forum for the practice of states, whether this practice comprises the total of their individual acts or the performance of collective acts. Further, the organs themselves have tasks to perform which also contribute to the clarification and development of law. Why, then, has there been a certain reluctance to concede a law-creating rôle to the political organs of the United Nations? Partly it has been due to continuing emphasis on state sovereignty, with a concomitant reluctance to attribute indirect law-developing rôles to international bodies; partly because the contractual theories of law development have ostensibly been reinforced by the Charter distinctions between "decisions" and "recommendations" as well as by stipulated voting majorities; and partly because of the intellectual problems presented by the necessity of distinguishing state practice from the practice of organs *qua* organs.

Before we turn to an analysis of the actual methods by which political organs of the

* Reprinted from Rosalyn Higgins, "The Development of International Law by the Political Organs of the United Nations," *Proceedings of the American Society of International Law* 116 (1965), by permission of the American Society of International Law.

United Nations can develop law, there are some basic objections which must be met.

First, insofar as the attitudes taken by states in international organizations largely reflect their self-interest and political motivations, how can they be said to be participating in a law-creating process? The answer, very briefly, is that so far as custom is concerned, politically motivated state practice in non-institutionalized bilateral and multilateral diplomacy is accepted as evidence. There is no logical reason why it should not also be within the framework of international organization. What matters is that *opinio juris* should be brought to bear here also: state practice becomes evidence of law only when the vast majority of states believe themselves to be legally bound.

It is notoriously difficult both to ascertain the *moment* at which usage becomes custom and the *number* of states which have to feel bound before a custom emerges. On the former point some marginal help is provided by the practice of international organizations, because of the frequent presentation of resolutions incorporating rules of law, on which there is an open and ascertainable vote. On the latter point— the *number* of states which have to feel bound by a rule of law—the U.N. system seems to me to present a complication, because it provides for certain voting majorities for the passing of decisions which do not necessarily correspond with the quantification which we seek to identify in the realm of custom.

Second, insofar as the organs under consideration are, by definition, political, it may be argued that they pay no attention to law or at most only give lip service to it. I think it can be shown, however . . . that in fact these organs find it helpful politically to invoke legal principles in order to reach normative decisions. The collective processes in a United Nations organ help to focus attention upon the need for mutual observance of the rules. Indeed, in some cases reference to a widely accepted rule of law can serve as a bridge between differing ideologies.

* * *

A. Methods by Which International Law Is Clarified and Developed in the Political Organs of the United Nations

When one talks of the development of a norm, one means really two things: first, the process by which the content of the norm emerges; and second, the means by which states come, or are introduced, to feel that it is binding upon them. In other words, the legal development of a rule comprises both the material source and the formal source. I therefore propose to look at these separately.

I. *The process by which the content of norms is clarified or developed:*

a. Decisions which U.N. organs take concerning their own jurisdiction and competence, when acquiesced in by sufficient numbers over a period of time, form "Charter Law" if they fall into some recognizable pattern. A customary practice of internal Charter practice thus becomes established. The degree and length of acquiescence need here perhaps to be less marked than elsewhere, because the U.N. organs undoubtedly have initial authority to make such decisions. The aspects of treaty interpretations and customary practice in this field merge very closely.

Even decisions on the internal workings of the United Nations may ultimately come to establish not only a special "Charter constitutional law," but may in time evidence a special new branch of the customary law on the interpretation of treaties.

b. On occasions United Nations organs may seek to pass resolutions deliberately declaratory of existing law. One may cite for example General Assembly Resolution 375 (IV), the Declaration on the Rights and Duties of States, though in the event this particular Declaration was not in fact adopted. It covers certain traditional rights and duties in 14 basic articles, ranging from jurisdiction to intervention to sovereign equality. Although the General Assembly is not a legislative body, the adoption of such a type of resolution by an overwhelming majority or by unanimous vote would surely provide probative evidence of the belief of states concerning certain rules of law.

c. United Nations political organs may also pass resolutions which may be described as confirmatory of existing law, where perhaps areas of doubt have existed. The unanimous General Assembly approval of the Nuremberg principles in Resolution 95 (1) served this function.

d. Similarly, there may exist competing claims within an area of law where the rules are generally agreed upon. A political organ of the United Nations may decide to draw up a declaratory resolution on the law. This outcome may involve debates, the examination of the issues in particular committees, invitations to governments to extend their opinions, and the request for guiding memoranda from the Secretariat. All these processes were in evidence in the history of General Assembly Resolution 1803 (XVII) on Permanent Sovereignty over Natural Resources. These events and the final votes and resolutions are also surely part of the law-developing process of the United Nations, though I am well aware that this very sort of process sets up its own counter-tendencies of arriving at declarations of a low level of specificity. The recognition of "appropriate compensation" in Resolution 1803 allows room both for certain states to feel that they have triumphed in the death throes of the "adequate, effective and prompt" requirement; and for advocates in the capital-exporting countries to argue that "appropriate" in this context must be read to mean "adequate, effective and prompt"! No matter. The Soviet doctrine of "no compensation" has been clearly removed from the scene, and useful confirmation in other areas has occurred.

e. The political organs of the United Nations may pass resolutions which recommend the adoption of new rules of law. This may be done either by the drawing up of draft conventions for states to accept—General Assembly Resolutions 96 (I) and 180 (II) on Genocide and 369 (IV) on the Declaration of Death of Missing Persons being cases in point; or by merely adopting resolutions.

No clearer example of the latter method exists than General Assembly Resolution 1962 (XVIII)—the Declaration of Legal Principles Governing the Activities of States in the Exploration and Use of Outer Space. Significantly, this last resolution was adopted upon the recommendation of the First, and not the Sixth, Committee. It does not "bind" states, but estoppels may arise in relation to votes in favor of it, the doctrine of acquiescence will operate in relation to it, and it has an undoubted place in the law-creating process.

f. The political organs of the United Nations—and this is especially true of the Security Council—have to make decisions which in fact apply specific rules to particular situations. Although these organs may frequently seek to avoid attributing "guilt" or even "illegality" to one side or the other in a particular dispute, the resolutions passed at the culmination of a debate are often based upon a legal requirement to be found in the Charter. Further, to arrive at a resolution the Security Council may find it necessary to go beyond pointing out the relevance of certain Charter articles to this particular situation, and indicate specific rules of general international law which govern the case in question. Dr. Schachter has aptly classified this law-creating rôle as the conversion of "soft law" into harder, more precise law. If the decision of the organ is widely supported, it has probative value as evidence by the parties of their legal obligations; and the repetition of a stream of similar decisions provides the foundation for custom. Once again, the interpretative and developing functions are closely interwoven. This is true, whether the dispute concerns, for example, the relevance of Article 2 (7) to the placing of a matter on the agenda or the classification of certain retaliatory incursions into adjoining territory as impermissible.

g. Rules internal to the Organization, or concerning the status and rights of the Organization, frequently emerge as the result of functional necessity. The pragmatism of the Congo operation is typical of functionalism at work.

It seems to me that there is an interesting relationship which could usefully be explored—though not within the confines of this short paper—between functionalism and implied powers. In the *Reparation for Injuries* case the Court found that the United Nations had capacity to bring international claims. Although it is in a sense the Court that is "law-creating" here, it is in another sense merely declaring what the law *is*. Whereas it is arguable that the seeds of international personality are in the Charter itself, the authority to use it to bring claims was given to the United Nations not by the Charter but *by the Members, subsequently.* "The Court concludes that the Members have endowed the Organization with capacity to bring international claims when necessitated by the discharge of its functions." (I.C.J. Rep. 1949, pp. 179–180.) The relationship between implied powers and functionalism is apparent here: but the point I wish to make is that U.N. political organs have at least an initial discretion to decide what actions are necessary to carry out their functions— whether it be an Interim Committee, a Peace Observation Committee, the right to hold prisoners of war, or whatever—and upon that practice its implied powers will be built.

Functionalism does not always rest on implied powers, however. The need for the United Nations to represent the interests of universality, for example, has had direct results in terms of legal development. Thus the very fact that international treaties are concluded under United Nations auspices tends to lead to developments in the law in favor of a flexible approach to treaty questions. This has been true in the matter of reservations, where the universal character of the United Nations was a telling factor in reducing the old rule (that no reservation may be effective against a state without its express consent) to a mere guiding principle. Again, we may cite the interrelated activities of the General Assembly, the Sixth Committee and the International Law Commission on the extension of participation in conventions concluded under League of Nations auspices. In spite of the careful formulas selected, certain inroads are undoubtedly being made upon the old norm of unanimity in treaty revision.

h. United Nations treaty functions must be mentioned as a fertile area for legal developments. The very ability of the United Nations to make treaties with other organizations and states has led to a whole new field of treaty law. Moreover, the requirement, affecting states, of registration under Article 102, as well as the depositary functions of the Secretary General, has seen the emergence of a rich practice gradually forming a customary law.

B. Methods by Which States Come to Be Bound by Developing Norms

This interesting area—a mixture of constitutional technique, public opinion and psychology—can only be touched on briefly here. Both Dr. Skubiszewski and Professor Tammes have shown that the constitutional provisions and the practical realities of international organizations have a significant rôle to play in securing behavioral compliance. "Behavioural compliance is not, of course, the same as *opinio juris*: but there is, quite obviously, a very close relationship between them." Emphasis on the general duty of states to co-operate in carrying out Charter obligations, the specific pressures to submit reports and information on certain matters, the intermingling in resolutions of developing norms with well established rules, are all techniques relevant to this point. There is a psychological pressure upon a government not to vote against a law-creating resolution if virtually all other states are likely to vote for it. Indeed, states are further encouraged not to cast contrary votes by allowing them the right to have their objections or conditions fully recorded in the minutes. One could continue the list. Above all, most states have a long-term interest in supporting U.N. norm-based procedures, for these are tangible evidence of the common interest, and thoughts of reciprocity and a shared desire to avoid nuclear war hold good here as elsewhere.

Certain Expenses of the United Nations*

International Court of Justice, Advisory Opinion of July 20, 1962

* * *

The Court finds no "compelling reason" why it should not give the advisory opinion which the General Assembly requested by its resolution 1731 (XVI). It has been argued that the question put to the Court is intertwined with political questions, and that for this reason the Court should refuse to give an opinion. It is true that most interpretations of the Charter of the United Nations will have political significance, great or small. In the nature of things it could not be otherwise. The Court, however, cannot attribute a political character to a request which invites it to undertake an essentially judicial task, namely, the interpretation of a treaty provision.

In the preamble to the resolution requesting this opinion, the General Assembly expressed its recognition of "its need for

* Reprinted from *International Court of Justice Reports* 151 (1962).

authoritative legal guidance." In its search for such guidance it has put to the Court a legal question—a question of the interpretation of Article 17, paragraph 2, of the Charter of the United Nations. . . .

The question on which the Court is asked to give its opinions is whether certain expenditures which were authorized by the General Assembly to cover the costs of the United Nations operations in the Congo (hereinafter referred to as ONUC) and of the operations of the United Nations Emergency Force in the Middle East (hereinafter referred to as UNEF), "constitute 'expenses of the Organization' within the meaning of Article 17, paragraph 2, of the Charter of the United Nations."

* * *

The text of Article 17 is in part as follows:
1. The General Assembly shall consider and approve the budget of the Organization.
2. The expenses of the Organization shall be borne by the Members as apportioned by the General Assembly.

Although the Court will examine Article 17 in itself and in its relation to the rest of the Charter, it should be noted that at least three separate questions might arise in the interpretation of paragraph 2 of this Article. One question is that of identifying what are "the expenses of the Organization;" a second question might concern apportionment by the General Assembly; while a third question might involve the interpretation of the phrase "shall be borne by the Members." It is the second and third questions which directly involve "the financial obligations of the Members," but it is only the first question which is posed by the request for the advisory opinion. The question put to the Court has to do with a moment logically anterior to apportionment, just as a question of apportionment would be anterior to a question of Members' obligation to pay.

* * *

The text of Article 17, paragraph 2, refers to "the expenses of the Organization" without any further explicit definition of such expenses. It would be possible to begin with a general proposition to the effect that the "expenses" of any organization are the amounts paid out to defray the costs of carrying out its purposes, in this case, the political, economic, social, humanitarian and other purposes of the United Nations. The next step would be to examine, as the Court will, whether the resolutions authorizing the operations here in question were intended to carry out the purposes of the United Nations and whether the expenditures were incurred in furthering these operations. Or, it might simply be said that the "expenses" of an organization are those which are provided for in its budget. But the Court has not been asked to give an abstract definition of the words "expenses of the Organization." It has been asked to answer a specific question related to certain identified expenditures which have actually been made, but the Court would not adequately discharge the obligation incumbent on it unless it examined in some detail various problems raised by the question which the General Assembly has asked.

It is perhaps the simple identification of "expenses" with the items included in a budget, which has led certain arguments to link the interpretation of the word "expenses" in paragraph 2 of Article 17, with the word "budget" in paragraph 1 of that Article; in both cases, it is contended, the qualifying adjective "regular" or "administrative" should be understood to be implied. Since no such qualification is expressed in the text of the Charter, it could be read in, only if such qualification must necessarily be implied from the provisions of the Charter considered as a whole, or from some particular provision thereof which makes it unavoidable to do so in order to give effect to the Charter.

It is a consistent practice of the General Assembly to include in the annual budget resolutions, provision for expenses relating to the maintenance of international peace and security. Annually, since 1947, the General Assembly has made anticipatory provision for "unforeseen and extraordinary expenses" arising in relation to the "maintenance of peace and security." In a Note submitted to the Court by the Controller on the budgetary and financial practices of the United Nations, "extraordinary expenses" are defined as "obligations and expenditures arising as a result of the approval by a council, commission or other competent United Nations body of new programmes and activities not contemplated when the budget appropriations were approved."

The annual resolution designed to provide for extraordinary expenses authorizes the Secretary-General to enter into commitments to meet such expenses with the prior concurrence of the Advisory Committee on Administrative and Budgetary Questions, except that such concurrence is not necessary if the Secretary-General certifies that such commitments relate to the subjects mentioned and the amount does not exceed $2 million. At its fifteenth and sixteenth sessions, the General Assembly resolved "that if, as a result of a decision of the Security Council, commitments relating to the maintenance of peace and security should arise in an estimated total exceeding $10 million" before the General Assembly was due to meet again, a special session should be convened by the Secretary-General to consider the matter. The Secretary-General is regularly authorized to draw on the Working Capital Fund for such expenses but is required to submit supplementary budget estimates to cover amounts so advanced. These annual resolutions on unforeseen and extraordinary expenses were adopted without a dissenting vote in every year from 1947 through 1959, except for 1952, 1953, and 1954, when the adverse votes are attributable to the fact that the resolution included the specification of a controversial item—United Nations Korean War decorations.

Turning to paragraph 2 of Article 17, the Court observes that, on its face, the term "expenses of the Organization" means all the expenses and not just certain types of expenses which might be referred to as "regular expenses." An examination of other parts of the Charter shows the variety of expenses which must inevitably be included with the "expenses of the Organization" just as much as the salaries of staff or the maintenance of buildings.

For example, the text of Chapters IX and X of the Charter with reference to international economic and social cooperation, especially the wording of those articles which specify the functions and powers of the Economic and Social Council, anticipated the numerous and varied circumstances under which expenses of the Organization could be incurred and which have indeed eventuated in practice.

Furthermore, by Article 98 of the Charter, the Secretary-General is obligated to perform such functions as are entrusted to him by the General Assembly, the Security Council, the Economic and Social Council, and the Trusteeship Council. Whether or not expenses incurred in his discharge of this obligation become "expenses of the Organization" cannot depend on whether they be administrative or some other kind of expenses.

The Court does not perceive any basis for challenging the legality of the settled practice of including such expenses as these in the budgetary amounts which the General Assembly apportions among the Members in accordance with the authority which is given to it by Article 17, paragraph 2.

* * *

Article 17 is the only article in the Charter which refers to budgetary authority or to the power to apportion expenses, or otherwise to raise revenue, except for Articles 33 and 35, paragraph 3, of the Statute of the Court which have no bearing on the point here under discussion. Nevertheless, it has been argued before the Court that one type of expenses, namely those resulting from operations for the maintenance of international peace and security, are not "expenses of the Organization" within the meaning of Article 17, paragraph 2, of the Charter, inasmuch as they fall to be dealt with exclusively by the Security Council, and more especially through agreements negotiated in accordance with Article 43 of the Charter.

The argument rests in part upon the view that when the maintenance of international peace and security is involved, it is only the Security Council which is authorized to decide on any action relative thereto. It is argued further that since the General Assembly's power is limited to discussing, considering, studying and recommending, it cannot impose an obligation to pay the expenses which result from the implementation of its recommendations. This argument leads to an examination of the respective functions of the General Assembly and of the Security Council under the Charter, particularly with respect to the maintenance of international peace and security.

Article 24 of the Charter provides:

In order to ensure prompt and effective action by the United Nations, its Members confer on the Security Council primary responsibility for the maintenance of international peace and security. . . .

The responsibility conferred is "primary," not exclusive. This primary responsibility is conferred upon the Security Council, as stated in Article 24, "in order to ensure prompt and effective action." To this end, it is the Security Council which is given a power to impose an explicit obligation of compliance if for example it issues an order or command to an aggressor under Chapter VII. It is only the Security Council which can require enforcement by coercive action against an aggressor.

The Charter makes it abundantly clear, however, that the General Assembly is also to be concerned with international peace and security. Article 14 authorizes the General Assembly to "recommend measures for the peaceful adjustment of any situation, regardless of origin, which it deems likely to impair the general welfare or friendly relations among nations including situations resulting from a violation of the provisions of the present Charter setting forth the purposes and principles of the United Nations." The word "measures" implies some kind of action, and the only limitation which Article 14 imposes on the General Assembly is the restriction found in Article 12, namely, that the Assembly should not recommend measures while the Security Council is dealing with the same matter unless the Council requests it to do so. . . .

By Article 17, paragraph 1, the General Assembly is given the power not only to "consider" the budget of the Organization, but also to "approve" it. The decision to "approve" the budget has a close connection with paragraph 2 of Article 17, since thereunder the General Assembly is also given the power to apportion the expenses among the Members and the exercise of the power of apportionment creates the obligation, specifically stated in Article 17, paragraph 2, of each Member to bear that part of the expenses which is apportioned to it by the General Assembly. When those expenses include expenditures for the maintenance of peace and security, which are not otherwise provided for, it is the General Assembly which has the authority to apportion the latter amounts among the Members. The provisions of the Charter which distribute functions and powers to the Security Council and to the General Assembly give no support to the view that such distribution excludes from the powers of the General Assembly the power to provide for the financing of measures designed to maintain peace and security.

The practice of the Organization throughout its history bears out the foregoing elucidation of the term "action" in the last sentence of Article 11, paragraph 2. Whether the General Assembly proceeds under Article 11 or under Article 14, the implementation of its recommendations for setting up commissions or other bodies involves organizational activity—action—in connection with the maintenance of international peace and security. Such implementation is a normal feature of the functioning of the United Nations. Such committees, commissions or other bodies or individuals, constitute, in some cases, subsidiary organs established under the authority of Article 22 of the Charter. The functions of the General Assembly for which it may establish such subsidiary organs include, for example, investigation, observation and supervision, but the way in which such subsidiary organs are utilized depends on the consent of the State or States concerned. The Court accordingly finds that the argument which seeks, by reference to Article 11, paragraph 2, to limit the budgetary authority of the General Assembly in respect of the maintenance of international peace and security, is unfounded.

The Court has considered the general problem of the interpretation of Article 17, paragraph 2, in the light of the general structure of the Charter and of the respective functions assigned by the Charter to the General Assembly and to the Security Council, with a view to determining the meaning of the phrase "the expenses of the Organization." The Court does not find it necessary to go further in giving a more detailed definition of such expenses. The Court will, therefore, proceed to examine the expenditures enumerated in the request for the advisory opinion. In determining whether the actual expenditures authorized constitute "expenses of the Organization within the meaning of Article 17, paragraph 2, of the Charter," the Court agrees that such expenditures must be tested by their relationship to the purposes of the United Nations in the sense that if an expenditure were made for a purpose which is not one of the purposes of the United Nations, it could not be considered an "expense of the Organization."

The purposes of the United Nations are set forth in Article 1 of the Charter. The first two purposes as stated in paragraphs 1 and 2, may be summarily described as pointing to the goal of international peace and security and friendly relations. The third purpose is the achievement of economic, social, cultural and humanitarian goals and respect for human rights. The fourth and last purpose is: "To be a center for harmonizing the actions of nations in the attainment of these common ends."

The primary place ascribed to international peace and security is natural, since the fulfillment of the other purposes will be dependent upon the attainment of that basic condition. These purposes are broad indeed, but neither they nor the powers conferred to effectuate them are unlimited. Save as they have entrusted the Organization with the attainment of these common ends, the Member States retain their freedom of action. But when the Organization takes action which warrants the assertion that it was appropriate for the fulfillment of one of the stated purposes of the United Nations, the presumption is that such action is not *ultra vires* [of] the Organization.

In the legal systems of States, there is often some procedure for determining the validity of even a legislative or governmental act, but no analogous procedure is to be found in the structure of the United Nations. Proposals made during the drafting of the Charter to place the ultimate authority to interpret the Charter in the International Court of Justice were not accepted; the opinion which the Court is in course of rendering is an *advisory* opinion.

As anticipated in 1945, therefore, each organ must, in the first place at least, determine its own jurisdiction. If the Security Council, for example, adopts a resolution purportedly for the maintenance of international peace and security and if, in accordance with a mandate or authorization in such resolution, the Secretary-General incurs financial obligations, these amounts must be presumed to constitute "expenses of the Organization."

Similarly, obligations of the Organization may be incurred by the Secretary-General, acting on the authority of the Security Council or of the General Assembly, and the General Assembly "has no alternative but to honour these engagements."

The obligation is one thing: the way in which the obligation is met—that is from what source the funds are secured—is another. The General Assembly may follow any one of several alternatives: it may apportion the cost of the item according to the ordinary scale of assessment; it may apportion the cost according to some special scale of assessment; it may utilize funds which are voluntarily contributed to the Organization; or it may find some other method or combination of methods for providing the necessary funds. In this context, it is of no legal significance whether, as a matter of book-keeping or accounting, the General Assembly, chooses to have the item in question included under one of the standard established sections of the "regular" budget or whether it is separately listed in some special account or fund. The significant fact is that the item is an expense of the Organization and under Article 17, paragraph 2, the General Assembly therefore has authority to apportion it.

The expenditures enumerated in the request for an advisory opinion may conveniently be examined first with reference to UNEF and then to ONUC. In each case, attention will be paid first to the operations and then to the financing of the operations.

In considering the operations in the Middle East, the Court must analyze the functions of UNEF as set forth in resolutions of the General Assembly. Resolution 998 (ES–I) of 4 November 1956 requested the Secretary-General to submit a plan "for the setting up, with the consent of the nations concerned, of an emergency international United Nations Force to secure and supervise the cessation of hostilities in accordance with all the terms of" the General Assembly's previous resolution 997 (ES–I) of 2 November 1956. The verb "secure" as applied to such matters as halting the movement of military forces and arms into the area and the conclusion of a cease-fire, might suggest measures of enforcement, were it not that the Force was to be set up "with the consent of the nations concerned".

In his first report on the plan for an emergency international Force the Secretary-General used the language of resolution 998 (ES–I) in submitting his proposals. The same terms are used in General Assembly resolution 1000 (ES–I) of 5 November in which operative paragraph 1 reads:

Establishes a United Nations Command for an emergency international force to secure and supervise the cessation of hostilities in accordance with all the terms of General Assembly resolution 997 (ES–I) of 2 November 1956.

This resolution was adopted without a dissenting vote. In his second and final report on the plan for an emergency international Force of 6 November, the Secretary-General, in paragraphs 9 and 10, stated:

While the General Assembly is enabled to *establish* the Force with the consent of those parties which contribute units to the Force, it could not request the Force to be *stationed* or *operate* on the territory of a given country without the consent of the Government of that country. This does not exclude the possibility that the Security Council could use such a Force within the wider margins provided under Chapter VII of the United Nations Charter. I would not for the present consider it necessary to elaborate this point further, since no use of

the Force under Chapter VII, with the rights in relation to Member States that this would entail, has been envisaged.

The point just made permits the conclusion that the setting up of the Force should not be guided by the needs which would have existed had the measure been considered as part of an enforcement action directed against a Member country. There is an obvious difference between establishing the Force in order to secure the cessation of hostilities, with a withdrawal of forces, and establishing such a Force with a view to enforcing a withdrawal of forces.

Paragraph 12 of the Report is particularly important because in resolution 1001 (ES–I) the General Assembly, again without a dissenting vote, "*Concurs* in the definition of the functions of the Force as stated in paragraph 12 of the Secretary-General's report." Paragraph 12 reads in part as follows:

. . . the functions of the United Nations Force would be, when a cease-fire is being established, to enter Egyptian territory with the consent of the Egyptian Government, in order to help maintain quiet during and after the withdrawal of non-Egyptian troops, and to secure compliance with the other terms established in the resolution of 2 November 1956. The Force obviously should have no rights other than those necessary for the execution of its functions, in cooperation with local authorities. It would be more than an observers' corps, but in no way a military force temporarily controlling the territory in which it is stationed; nor, moreover, should the Force have military functions exceeding those necessary to secure peaceful conditions on the assumption that the parties to the conflict take all necessary steps for compliance with the recommendations of the General Assembly.

It is not possible to find in this description of the functions of UNEF, as outlined by the Secretary-General and concurred in by the General Assembly without a dissenting vote, any evidence that the Force was to be used for purposes of enforcement. Nor can such evidence be found in the subsequent operations of the Force, operations which did not exceed the scope of the functions ascribed to it.

The financing of UNEF presented perplexing problems and the debates on these problems have even led to the view that the General Assembly never, either directly or indirectly, regarded the expenses of UNEF as "expenses of the Organization within the meaning of Article 17, paragraph 2, of the Charter." With this interpretation the Court cannot agree. In paragraph 15 of his second and final report on the plan for an emergency international Force of 6 November 1956, the Secretary-General said that this problem required further study. Provisionally, certain costs might be absorbed by a nation providing a unit, "while all other costs should be financed outside the normal budget of the United Nations." Since it was "obviously impossible to make any estimate of the costs without a knowledge of the size of the corps and the length of its assignment," the "only practical course . . . would be for the General Assembly to vote a general authorization for the cost of the Force on the basis of general principles such as those here suggested."

Paragraph 5 of resolution 1001 (ES–I) of 7 November 1956 states that the General Assembly "*Approves provisionally* the basic rule concerning the financing of the Force laid down in paragraph 15 of the Secretary-General's report."

In an oral statement to the plenary meeting of the General Assembly on 26 November 1956, the Secretary-General said:

. . . I wish to make it equally clear that while funds received and payments made with respect to the Force are to be considered as coming outside the regular budget of the Organization, the operation is essentially a United Nations responsibility, and the Special Account to be established must, therefore, be constructed as coming within the meaning of Article 17 of the Charter.

At this same meeting, after hearing this statement, the General Assembly in resolution 1122 (XI) noted that it had "*provision-*

ally approved the recommendations made by the Secretary-General concerning the financing of the Force." It then authorized the Secretary-General "to establish a United Nations Emergency Force Special Account to which funds received by the United Nations, outside the regular budget, for the purpose of meeting the expenses of the Force shall be credited and from which payments for this purpose shall be made." The resolution then provided that the initial amount in the Special Account should be $10 million and authorized the Secretary-General "pending the receipt of funds for the Special Account, to advance from the Working Capital Fund such sums as the Special Account may require to meet any expenses chargeable to it." The establishment of a Special Account does not necessarily mean that the funds in it are not to be derived from contributions of Members as apportioned by the General Assembly.

The next of the resolutions of the General Assembly to be considered is 1089 (XI) of 21 December 1956, which reflects the uncertainties and the conflicting views about financing UNEF. The divergencies are duly noted and there is ample reservation concerning possible future action, but operative paragraph 1 follows the recommendation of the Secretary-General "that the expenses relating to the Force should be apportioned in the same manner as the expenses of the Organization." The language of this paragraph is clearly drawn from Article 17:

1. *Decides* that the expenses of the United Nations Emergency Force, other than for such pay, equipment, supplies and services as may be furnished without charge by Governments of Member States, shall be borne by the United Nations and shall be apportioned among the Member States, to the extent of $10 million, in accordance with the scale of assessments adopted by the General Assembly for contributions to the annual budget of the Organization for the financial year 1957.

This resolution, which was adopted by the requisite two-thirds majority, must have rested upon the conclusion that the expenses of UNEF were "expenses of the Organization" since otherwise the General Assembly would have had no authority to decide that they "shall be borne by the United Nations" or to apportion them among the Members. It is further significant that paragraph 3 of this resolution, which established a study committee, charges this committee with the task of examining "the question of the *apportionment* of the expenses of the Force in excess of $10 million . . . and the principle or the formulation of *scales of contributions different from the scale of contributions* by Member States to the ordinary budget for 1957." The italicized words show that it was not contemplated that the Committee would consider any method of meeting these expenses except through some form of apportionment although it was understood that a different *scale* might be suggested.

Resolution 1151 (XII) of 22 November 1957, while contemplating the receipt of more voluntary contributions, decided in paragraph 4 that the expenses authorized "shall be borne by the Members of the United Nations in accordance with the scales of assessments adopted by the General Assembly for the financial years 1957 and 1958, respectively."

Almost a year later, on 14 November 1958, in resolution 1263 (XIII) the General Assembly, while "*Noting with satisfaction* the effective way in which the Force continues to carry out its function," requested the Fifth Committee "to recommend such action as may be necessary to finance this continuing operation of the United Nations Emergency Force."

The Court concludes that, from year to year, the expenses of UNEF have been treated by the General Assembly as expenses of the Organization within the meaning of Article 17, paragraph 2, of the Charter.

The operations in the Congo were initially authorized by the Security Council in the resolution of 14 July 1960 which was adopted without a dissenting vote. The resolution, in the light of the appeal from the Government of the Congo, the report of the Secretary-General and the debate in the Security Council, was clearly adopted with a view to maintaining international peace and security. However, it is argued that the resolution has been implemented in violation of provisions of the Charter inasmuch as under the Charter it is the Security Council that determines which States are to participate in carrying out decisions involving the maintenance of international peace and security, whereas in the case of the Congo the Secretary-General himself determined which States were to participate with their armed forces or otherwise.

By paragraph 2, of the resolution of 14 July 1960 the Security Council "*Decides* to authorize the Secretary-General to take the necessary steps, in consultation with the Government of the Republic of the Congo, to provide the Government with such military assistance as may be necessary." Paragraph 3 requested the Secretary-General "to report to the Security Council as appropriate." The Secretary-General made his first report on 18 July and in it informed the Security Council which States he had asked to contribute forces or material, which ones had complied, the size of the units which had already arrived in the Congo (a total of some 3,500 troops), and some detail about further units expected.

On 22 July the Security Council by unanimous vote adopted a further resolution in which the preamble states that it had considered this report of the Secretary-General and appreciated "the work of the Secretary-General and the support so readily and so speedily given to him by all Member States invited by him to give assistance." In operative paragraph 3, the Security Council "*Commends* the Secretary-General for the prompt action he has taken to carry out resolution S/4387 of the Security Council, and for his first report."

On 9 August the Security Council adopted a further resolution without a dissenting vote in which it took note of the second report and of an oral statement of the Secretary-General and in operative paragraph 1: "*Confirms* the authority given to the Secretary-General by the Security Council resolutions of 14 July and 22 July 1960 and requests him to continue to carry out the responsibility placed on him thereby." This emphatic ratification is further supported by operative paragraphs 5 and 6 by which all Member States were called upon "to afford mutual assistance" and the Secretary-General was requested to "implement this resolution and to report further to the Council as appropriate."

The Security Council resolutions of 14 July, 22 July and 9 August, 1960 were noted by the General Assembly in its resolution 1474 (ES–IV) of 20 September adopted without a dissenting vote, in which it "fully supports" these resolutions. Again without a dissenting vote, on 21 February 1961 the Security Council reaffirmed its three previous resolutions and the General Assembly Resolution 1474 (ES–IV) of 20 September 1960 and reminded "all States of their obligations under these resolutions."

Again without a dissenting vote on 24 November 1961, the Security Council, once more recalling the previous resolutions, reaffirmed "the policies and purposes of the United Nations with respect to the Congo (Leopoldville) as set out" in those resolutions. Operative paragraphs 4 and 5 of this resolution renew the authority to the Secretary-General to continue the activities in the Congo.

In the light of such a record of reiterated consideration, confirmation, approval and ratification by the Security Council and by the General Assembly of the actions of the Secretary-General in implementing the resolution of 14 July 1960, it is impossible to reach the conclusion that the operations in question usurped or impinged upon the prerogatives conferred by the Charter on the Security Council. . . .

For the reasons stated, financial obligations which, in accordance with the clear and reiterated authority of both the Security Council and the General Assembly, the Secretary-General incurred on behalf of the United Nations, constitute obligations of the Organization for which the General Assembly was entitled to make provision under the authority of Article 17.

In relation to ONUC, the first action concerning the financing of the operation was taken by the General Assembly on 20 December 1960, after the Security Council had adopted its resolutions of 14 July, 22 July and 9 August, and the General Assembly had adopted its supporting resolution of 20 September. This resolution 1583 (XV) of 20 December referred to the report of the Secretary-General on the estimated cost of the Congo operations from 14 July to 31 December 1960, and to the recommendations. It decided to establish an *ad hoc* account for the expenses of the United Nations in the Congo. It also took note of certain waivers of cost claims and then decided to apportion the sum of $48.5 million among the Member States "on the basis of the regular scale of assessment" subject to certain exceptions. It made this decision because in the preamble it had already recognized:

. . . that the expenses involved in the United Nations operations in the Congo for 1960 constitute 'expenses of the Organization' within the meaning of Article 17, paragraph 2, of the Charter of the United Nations and that the assessment thereof against Member States creates binding legal obligations on such States to pay their assessed shares.

By its further resolution 1590 (XV) of the same day, the General Assembly authorized the Secretary-General "to incur commitments in 1961 for the United Nations operations in the Congo up to the total of $24 million for the period from 1 January to 31 March 1961." On 3 April 1961, the General Assembly authorized the Secretary-General to continue until 21 April "to incur commitments for the United Nations operations in the Congo at a level not to exceed $8 million per month."

Importance has been attached to the statement included in the preamble of General Assembly resolution 1619 (XV) of 21 April 1961 which reads:

Bearing in mind that the extraordinary expenses for the United Nations operations in the Congo are essentially different in nature from the expenses of the Organization under the regular budget and that therefore a procedure different from that applied in the case of the regular budget is required for meeting these extraordinary expenses,

However, the same resolution in operative paragraph 4:

Decides further to apportion as expenses of the Organization the amount of $100 million among the Member States in accordance with the scale of assessment for the regular budget subject to the provisions of paragraph 8 below [paragraph 8 makes certain adjustments for Member States assessed at the lowest rates or who receive certain designated technical assistance] pending the establishment of a different scale of assessment to defray the extraordinary expenses of the Organization resulting from these operations.

The conclusion to be drawn from these paragraphs is that the General Assembly has twice decided that even though certain expenses are "extraordinary" and "essentially different" from those under the "regular budget," they are none the less "expenses of the Organization" to be apportioned in accordance with the power granted to the General Assembly by Article 17, paragraph 2. This conclusion is strengthened by the concluding clause of paragraph 4 of the two resolutions just cited which states that the decision therein to use the scale of assessment already adopted for the regular budget is made "pending the establishment of a *different scale of assessment* to defray the extraordinary expenses." The only alternative—and that means the "different procedure"—contemplated was another *scale* of assessment and not some method other than assessment. "Apportionment" and "assessment" are terms which relate only to the General Assembly's authority under Article 17.

For these reasons,

THE COURT IS OF OPINION,

by nine votes to five,

that the expenditures authorized in General Assembly resolutions 1583 (XV) and 1590 (XV) of 20 December 1960, 1595 (XV) of 3 April 1961, 1619 (XV) of 21 April 1961 and 1633 (XVI) of 30 October 1961 relating to the United Nations operations in the Congo undertaken in pursuance of the Security Council resolutions of 14 July, 22 July and 9 August 1960 and 21 February and 24 November 1961, and General Assembly resolutions 1474 (ES-IV) of 20 September 1960 and 1599 (XV), 1600 (XV) and 1601 (XV) of 15 April 1961, and the expenditures authorized in General Assembly resolutions 1122 (XI) of 26 November 1956, 1089 (XI) of 21 December 1956, 1090 (XI) of 27 February 1957, 1151 (XII) of 22 November 1957, 1204 (XII) of 13 December 1957, 1337 (XIII) of 13 December 1958, 1441 (XIV) of 5 December 1959 and 1575 (XV) of 20 December 1960 relating to the operations of the United Nations Emergency Force undertaken in pursuance of General Assembly resolutions 997 (ES-I) of 2 November 1956, 998 (ES-I) and 999 (ES-I) of 4 November 1956, 1000 (ES-I) of 5 November 1956, 1001 (ES-I) of 7 November 1956, 1121 (XI) of 24 November 1956 and 1263 (XIII) of 14 November 1958, constitute "expenses of the Organization" within the meaning of Article 17, paragraph 2, of the Charter of the United Nations.

* * *

[*Dissenting opinion by Judge Koretsky:*]

* * *

People say that you cannot have two coachmen in the driver's seat. In the cause of the struggle for international peace and security, in the question of their maintenance or restoration, in questions of "action with respect to threats to the peace, breaches of the peace, and acts of aggression", the organizational confusion would only have been harmful. Therefore the Charter clearly enough delimits the functions of the Security Council and those of the General Assembly.

To place the Security Council, as the Opinion does, beside the General Assembly, considering them as interchangeable in solving and implementing the tasks of maintaining international peace and security, would be objectively to replace the Security Council by the General Assembly, to put the Council aside and thereby undermine the very foundations of the Organization. It does not befit the Court to follow this line. It has been said that you cannot leave one word out of a song. The Charter represents one of the most important international multilateral treaties, from which it is impossible to leave out any of its provisions either directly or through an interpretation that is more artificial than skilful.

The Court's Opinion thus limits the powers of the Security Council and enlarges the sphere of the General Assembly. The Opinion achieves this by *(a)* converting the recommendations that the General Assembly may make into some kind of "action", and *(b)* reducing this action, for which the Security Council has the authority, to "enforcement or coercive action", particularly against aggression.

* * *

The budget of the Organization provides for all the expenses necessary for its maintenance (in the narrow sense of this word). These are usually called common expenses, running expenses, and the budget itself is called a regular budget, budget proper,

etc. What kind of expenses are these? In each of the annual budgets of the United Nations, the expenses are enumerated. They are expenses for the sessions of the General Assembly, the councils, commissions and committees, for special conferences, investigations and inquiries, for Headquarters, the European Office, Information Centres, hospitality, advisory social welfare functions, etc. These expenses are contrasted with the so-called operational expenses for the various kinds of economic, social and technical assistance programmes. Determined by the various interests of different countries they are usually financed through voluntary contributions, in any case outside the regular budget. In the document submitted by the Secretariat (Dossier No. 195) on the "Budgetary and Financial Practice of the United Nations" there is a division into two parts: (1) *Regular budget* (General Fund and Working Capital Fund), and (2) Trust Funds, Reserve Accounts and Special Accounts *outside the regular budget.* The document enumerates thirteen such Special Accounts among which it names: Special Account for UNEF and *ad hoc* Account for the United Nations operations in the Congo.

* * *

One cannot consider that decisions of the Security Council regarding the participation of any Member State in concrete peace-keeping operations are not obligatory for a given Member. Its obligation to participate in a decided operation was based on Articles 25 and 48 of the Charter. Agreements envisaged in Article 43 proceed from this general obligation. Article 43 says that all Members undertake to make available to the Security Council *on its call* armed forces, etc. Agreements must (not may) specify the terms of participation, the size of armed forces to be made available, the character of assistance, etc., envisaging all the ensuing financial consequences as well.

The General Assembly may only *recommend* measures. Expenses which might arise from such recommendations should not lead to an obligatory apportionment of them among all Members of the United Nations. That would mean to convert a non-mandatory recommendation of the General Assembly into a mandatory decision; this would be to proceed against the Charter, against logic and even against common sense.

* * *

The Law of the Charter and *Apartheid* in South Africa*

Discussion in the General Assembly of the United Nations on the Question of the Adoption of the Agenda for the Seventh Session, October 17, 1952

[*On September 12, 1952, thirteen states proposed the inclusion in the provisional agenda of the General Assembly of "the question of race conflict resulting from the policies of* apartheid *of the Government of the Union of South Africa." These policies, the proposal alleged, were "creating a dangerous and explosive situation, which constitutes both a threat to international peace and a flagrant violation of the basic principles of human rights and fundamental freedoms which are enshrined in the Charter of the United Nations." In opposing the proposal, the representative of South Africa claimed that, since the item dealt with a matter which was essentially within the domestic jurisdiction of his state, the General Assembly was not authorized by the Charter either to include it on the agenda or to discuss it. His argument, which has been repeated time and again in the Assembly, is*

based on Article 2, paragraph 7, of the Charter, which reads: "Nothing contained in the present Charter shall authorize the United Nations to intervene in matters which are essentially within the domestic jurisdiction of any State or shall require the Members to submit such matters to settlement under the present Charter; but this principle shall not prejudice the application of enforcement measures under Chapter VII." Following the debate, the Assembly placed the item on the agenda by 45 votes to 6 with 8 abstentions. Later in the session, the Assembly adopted a resolution which,* inter alia, *declared that "in a multiracial society harmony and respect for human rights and freedoms and the peaceful development of a unified community are best assured when patterns of legislation and practice are directed towards ensuring equality before the law of all persons regardless of race, creed or colour, and when economic, social, cultural and political participation of all racial groups is on a basis of equality;" affirmed that "governmental policies of Member States which are not directed toward these goals, but which are designed to perpetuate or increase discrimination, are inconsistent with the pledges of Members under Article 56 of the Charter"; and called upon "all Member States to bring their policies into conformity with their obligations under the Charter to promote the observance of human rights and fundamental freedoms."**]

Mr. JOOSTE (Union of South Africa): In the General Committee, I placed on record my Government's protest against the inclusion in the agenda of the item entitled, "The question of race conflict in South Africa resulting from the policies of *apartheid* of the Government of the Union of South Africa". In doing so, I made it clear that final decisions on the inclusion of

* Reprinted from United Nations General Assembly *Official Records*, 7th Session, Plenary Meetings (1952), pp. 53–69.

* Resolution 616 (VII) A and B, General Assembly *Official Records*, 7th Session, Supplement 20 (A/2361), pp. 8–9. For a more complete account of General Assembly action on this question, see Louis B. Sohn (ed.), *Cases on United Nations Law* (Brooklyn: The Foundation Press, 1956), pp. 627–670.

items in the agenda rested with the Assembly, where all delegations were represented.
. . .

* * *

The question of whether this Organization has the right, under the terms of the Charter, to interfere in the matter before us, is one of great importance to my country. I feel, therefore, that the matter of competence is one which should be dealt with in this Assembly at this stage, before it is thrown open for a debate which, if our experience serves as an indication, will inevitably be acrimonious and will only confuse the issue which I am raising.

Therefore, under the terms of rule 80 of our rules of procedure, I ask that the question of competence should be decided upon by the Assembly before voting on the recommendation of the General Committee that the item should be placed on the agenda of this session. I move that the Assembly should pass the following motion:

"Having regard to the provisions of Article 2, paragraph 7, of the Charter, the General Assembly decides that it is not competent to consider the item entitled, 'The question of race conflict in South Africa resulting from the policies of *apartheid* of the Government of the Union of South Africa' ". . . .

Permit me to examine the phraseology of Article 2, paragraph 7. The initial phrase reads: "Nothing contained in the present Charter shall authorize the United Nations to intervene. . . ." The word "nothing" is clear and unequivocal. It means simply that nothing in the Charter, no provision therein, be it interpreted as it may, shall authorize intervention by the United Nations in the domestic affairs of a Member State. No possible interpretation of any provision of the Charter can serve to alter the meaning of the word "nothing". After all, an interpretation of a provision is merely the provision itself as interpreted. And as the

United Nations has no greater competence than that conferred upon it by the Charter, it is perfectly clear that the United Nations is not competent to interpret any article of the Charter in such a way as to authorize intervention when the Charter itself categorically states that nothing contained in it shall authorize intervention.

It is true that there is an exception to the principle of non-intervention laid down in Article 2, paragraph 7. That exception is in respect of the application of enforcement measures under Chapter VII. The exception is expressly stated in Article 2, paragraph 7, itself. No other exceptions are mentioned in the rest of the Charter, nor can they be inferred from any of its provisions. The universally accepted maxim that *expressio unius est exclusio alterius* must, therefore, necessarily be of application. In plain language, had there been any intention to allow exceptions other than that relating to the application of enforcement measures under Chapter VII, that intention would have been clearly expressed or would have been readily ascertainable as a necessary inference from the terms of the Charter. The provisions of Article 2, paragraph 7, were therefore clearly intended to have an overriding effect in relation to the other provisions of the Charter, subject only to the exception relating to enforcement measures.

* * *

In 1948, the representative of India suggested that the word "intervention" was used in a specialized international sense, namely, in the sense of dictatorial interference, and that the passing of resolutions would not constitute the type of intervention envisaged by Article 2, paragraph 7.

This argument was ingenious, but entirely misleading. Dictatorial interference is, under general international law, an illegal intervention by a State in the affairs of another State affecting the latter's political independence or territorial integrity. This is the sort of intervention which is prohibited by paragraph 4 of Article 2. The word "intervention" is not specifically used in that paragraph, but by necessary implication the obligation contained therein is the obligation not to intervene, that is to say, to refrain from dictatorial interference or intervention in the technical sense. In paragraph 7 of Article 2, however, the word "intervene" bears its ordinary dictionary meaning and includes interference. There is no indication that it must be understood in the narrow sense.

Bearing in mind the different functions and powers of the General Assembly and the Security Council, it is clear that the latter is empowered to interfere dictatorially in certain circumstances, and the exception made in the second part of paragraph 7 admits quite clearly that the Security Council may so intervene. But the General Assembly has no power to intervene in the technical sense, that is to say, to interfere dictatorially. It may only make recommendations and discuss questions or matters within the scope of the Charter. The word "intervene", in relation to the General Assembly, can, therefore, only have the wider meaning of "interference".

It must be noted that the prohibition in paragraph 7 of Article 2 does not apply only in respect of the activities of the Security Council, but in respect of the activities of the United Nations, including, therefore, the General Assembly. All activities of the General Assembly in relation to matters which are essentially within the domestic jurisdiction of a Member State are, therefore, forbidden. Activities of the General Assembly are confined to the making of recommendations, the passing of resolutions and the discussion of matters falling within the scope of the Charter. They are all provided for in the Charter as competent activities of the General Assembly. But nothing in the Charter shall authorize the General Assembly, as an organ of the United Nations, to engage in activities amounting to intervention in matters of essentially domestic concern. Intervention must, therefore, be understood to apply to all activities of the General Assembly, clearly including the making of recommendations, the passing of resolutions and the discussion of matters within the scope of the Charter. If any of these activities is of such a nature as to amount to an interference in the essentially domestic affairs of a Member State, it is forbidden by Article 2, paragraph 7, of the Charter. Discussion is one of those activities, but if discussion amounts to interference in matters of essentially domestic concern, it is forbidden, and the same applies to all other activities of the General Assembly. . . .

Let us now return to the word "essentially" in the phrase "intervene in matters which are essentially within the domestic jurisdiction of any State". It has been suggested that the use of the word "essentially" was intended to have the effect of limiting the safeguard only to certain matters and also that its use, instead of the word "solely", which appeared in Article 15, paragraph 8, of the Covenant of the League of Nations and in chapter VIII, section A, paragraph 7, of the original Dumbarton Oaks draft, justifies a narrower meaning of intervention and shows an intent to increase the jurisdiction of the United Nations.

Evidence emerging from the San Francisco records proves that the word "essentially" was used in order to widen the scope of domestic jurisdiction and not to narrow it. When it was suggested that the word "solely", which was used in the Dumbarton Oaks draft, should be retained instead of the word "essentially", which appeared in the San Francisco draft, Mr. Dulles pointed out the inadvisability of the proposed amendment. He said:

"That would again destroy the whole effect of the limitation, because what is there in the world today that is solely domestic?" . . .

Let us now look a little closer at the

meaning of the words "domestic jurisdiction". We have on previous occasions argued that, according to international law, the relationship between a State and its nationals, including the treatment of these nationals, is a matter of exclusive domestic jurisdiction which allows no interference either by another State or by any organization, subject only to any treaty obligations under the terms of which a State may have waived its inherent rights of sovereignty. This argument was advanced by us in reply to the contention that a matter which might be regarded as domestic by a particular State is nevertheless a matter to which the rules of international law apply, by virtue of the fact that matters of international concern transcend matters of national concern. . . .

It has been argued that Article 2, paragraph 7, does not apply when there is an alleged question of human rights. In reply to this argument I would say that if the founders of the United Nations had wished to exclude human rights from the sphere of domestic jurisdiction, they would have done so specifically, as they did in the case of enforcement measures under Chapter VII of the Charter. . . .

If the United Nations were to be permitted to intervene in regard to sub-paragraph (c) of Article 55—which concerns the promotion of human rights—on the ground that matters contained therein are not excluded by the provisions of Article 2, paragraph 7, then the General Assembly would be equally permitted to intervene in regard to matters set out in sub-paragraphs (a) and (b), that is, economic and social matters, higher standards of living, full employment, health legislation, etc. Is there any Member State in the United Nations which would be prepared to submit to such intervention? Almost the whole field of internal administration of the State is covered by social, economic, cultural and health activities. To state that the United Nations would have the right to intervene is to state

a conclusion so far-reaching that it has merely to be stated to be rejected. . . .

Mr. SANTA CRUZ (Chile): . . . We have no text defining what is meant by a question falling exclusively within the jurisdiction of States, but of one thing I am convinced: the State concerned cannot itself be the sole judge of whether a given situation is within its exclusive jurisdiction, for that would enable any State to evade the fulfilment of its international obligations. We therefore have to try to find other methods of deciding which questions are exclusively within the national competence of States and which are not.

Jurists have tried unsuccessfully to define these matters. At one time, lists were compiled of the questions that were to be regarded as being within the exclusive jurisdiction of States, but events have rendered those lists obsolete, and many of the matters contained in them have come to form part of international agreements, of treaties, and are therefore a matter of international law. It is not possible, therefore, to say precisely what matters are within the exclusive jurisdiction of States. On the other hand, it is possible to know when a matter is not within the exclusive jurisdiction of States; it is when the matter in question is the subject of an international agreement, whether bilateral or multilateral. The international law created by conventions and agreements among countries removes a number of questions from the exclusive competence of States. In the past, the slave trade, the white slave traffic and the traffic in narcotic drugs were regarded as questions falling exclusively within the domestic jurisdiction of States, but agreements of an international character have brought these matters within the competence of international law.

Now, since the adoption of the Charter, all fundamental human rights have formed part of international law, since they are included in that multilateral treaty, the Charter. For the idea of respect for funda-

mental rights and freedoms and the idea of non-discrimination on grounds of race, sex or religion, are to be found in the Charter more than any other; they are to be found in six separate places beginning with the Preamble and Article 1, which lays down the purposes and principles of the Charter. Article 55, in turn, provides that "the United Nations shall promote . . . universal respect for, and observance of, human rights and fundamental freedoms for all without distinction as to race, sex, language or religion". Article 56 adds that "all Members pledge themselves to take joint and separate action in co-operation with the Organization for the achievement of the purposes set forth in Article 55". . . .

This interpretation, furthermore, is the one which the General Assembly and the other organs of the United Nations have consistently accepted. The General Assembly and the Economic and Social Council have on many occasions discussed infringements of fundamental human rights affecting countries in all geographical areas and in all political sectors, including the Union of South Africa. They have dealt with the infringements resulting from the existence of slavery in some countries, with charges of forced labour, with racial discrimination, with infringement of trade union rights. And they have made recommendations to Member States addressed, it is true, not to individual countries but to groups of countries—which is the same thing—regarding the national measures which might be adopted to ensure full employment or raise the standard of living of the people of those countries or throughout the world.

Suggested Readings

Textbooks

Brierly. *The Law of Nations*, pp. 94–125.
Brownlie. *Principles of Public International Law*, pp. 254–260, 518–541.
Fenwick. *International Law*, pp. 37–40, 97–106, 585–602, 769–773.
Gould. *An Introduction to International Law*, pp. 101–131, 470–506.
Jacobini. *International Law: A Text*, pp. 359–374.
Kaplan and Katzenbach. *The Political Foundations of International Law*, pp. 265–340.
Kelsen. *Principles of International Law*, pp. 294–306, 506–507.
Sørensen. *Manual of Public International Law*, pp. 55–115, 157–164, 605–672.
Svarlien. *An Introduction to the Law of Nations*, pp. 40–61.
Tung. *International Law in an Organizing World*, pp. 26–38.
von Glahn. *Law Among Nations*, pp. 36–53, 729–734.

Specialized Works

Bowett, D. W. *The Law of International Institutions*. London: Stevens, 1963.
Briggs, Herbert W. *The International Law Commission*. Ithaca, N.Y.: Cornell University Press, 1965.
Higgins, Rosalyn. *The Development of International Law Through the Political Organs of the United Nations*. London: Oxford University Press, 1963.

Jenks, C. W. *The Common Law of Mankind.* London: Stevens, 1958.

Lauterpacht, Sir Hersch. *The Development of International Law by the International Court.* New York: Praeger, 1958.

Syatauw, J. J. G. *Some Newly Established Asian States and the Development of International Law.* The Hague: Martinus Nijhoff, 1961.

Wright, Quincy. *Contemporary International Law: A Balance Sheet*, rev. ed. New York: Random House, 1961.

Appendix

STATUTE OF THE INTERNATIONAL COURT OF JUSTICE

Art. 1. *The International Court of Justice* established by the Charter of the United Nations as the principal judicial organ of the United Nations shall be constituted and shall function in accordance with the provisions of the present Statute.

Chapter I: Organization of the Court

Art. 2. The Court shall be composed of a body of independent judges, elected regardless of their nationality from among persons of high moral character, who possess the qualifications required in their respective countries for appointment to the highest judicial offices, or are jurisconsults of recognized competence in international law.

Art. 3. 1. The Court shall consist of fifteen members, no two of whom may be nationals of the same state.

2. A person who for the purposes of membership in the Court could be regarded as a national of more than one state shall be deemed to be a national of the one in which he ordinarily exercises civil and political rights.

Art. 4. 1. The members of the Court shall be elected by the General Assembly and by the Security Council from a list of persons nominated by the national groups in the Permanent Court of Arbitration, in accordance with the following provisions.

2. In the case of Members of the United Nations not represented in the Permanent Court of Arbitration, candidates shall be nominated by national groups appointed for this purpose by their governments under the same conditions as those prescribed for members of the Permanent Court of Arbitration by Article 44 of the Convention of The Hague of 1907 for the pacific settlement of international disputes.

3. The conditions under which a state which is a party to the present Statute but is not a Member of the United Nations may participate in electing the members of the Court shall, in the absence of a special agreement, be laid down by the General Assembly upon recommendation of the Security Council.

Art. 5. 1. At least three months before the date of the election, the Secretary-General of the United Nations shall address a written request to the members of the Permanent Court of Arbitration belonging to the states which are parties to the present Statute, and to the members of the national groups appointed under Article 4, paragraph 2, inviting them to undertake, within a given time, by national groups, the nomination of persons in a position to accept the duties of a member of the Court.

2. No group may nominate more than four persons, not more than two of whom shall be of their own nationality. In no case may the number of candidates nominated by a group be more than double the number of seats to be filled.

Art. 6. Before making these nominations, each national group is recommended to consult its highest court of justice, its legal faculties and schools of law, and its national academies and national sections of international academies devoted to the study of law.

Art. 7. 1. The Secretary-General shall prepare a list in alphabetical order of all the persons thus nominated. Save as provided in Article 12, paragraph 2, these shall be the only persons eligible.

2. The Secretary-General shall submit this list to the General Assembly and to the Security Council.

Art. 8. The General Assembly and the Security Council shall proceed independently of one another to elect the members of the Court.

Art. 9. At every election, the electors shall bear in mind not only that the persons to be elected should individually possess the qualifications required, but also that in the body as a whole the representation of the main forms of civilization and of the principal legal systems of the world should be assured.

Art. 10. 1. Those candidates who obtain an absolute majority of votes in the General Assembly and in the Security Council shall be considered as elected.

2. Any vote of the Security Council, whether for the election of judges or for the appointment of members of the conference envisaged in Article 12, shall be taken without any distinction between permanent and non-permanent members of the Security Council.

3. In the event of more than one national of the same state obtaining an absolute

majority of the votes both of the General Assembly and of the Security Council, the eldest of these only shall be considered as elected.

Art. 11. If, after the first meeting held for the purpose of the election, one or more seats remain to be filled, a second and, if necessary, a third meeting shall take place.

Art. 12. 1. If, after the third meeting, one or more seats still remain unfilled, a joint conference consisting of six members, three appointed by the General Assembly and three by the Security Council, may be formed at any time at the request of either the General Assembly or the Security Council, for the purpose of choosing by the vote of an absolute majority one name for each seat still vacant, to submit to the General Assembly and the Security Council for their respective acceptance.

2. If the joint conference is unanimously agreed upon any person who fulfils the required conditions, he may be included in its list, even though he was not included in the list of nominations referred to in Article 7.

3. If the joint conference is satisfied that it will not be successful in procuring an election, those members of the Court who have already been elected shall, within a period to be fixed by the Security Council, proceed to fill the vacant seats by selection from among those candidates who have obtained votes either in the General Assembly or in the Security Council.

4. In the event of an equality of votes among the judges, the eldest judge shall have a casting vote.

Art. 13. 1. The members of the Court shall be elected for nine years and may be re-elected; provided, however, that of the judges elected at the first election, the terms of five judges shall expire at the end of three years and the terms of five more judges shall expire at the end of six years.

2. The judges whose terms are to expire at the end of the above-mentioned initial periods of three and six years shall be chosen by lot to be drawn by the Secretary-

General immediately after the first election has been completed.

3. The members of the Court shall continue to discharge their duties until their places have been filled. Though replaced, they shall finish any cases which they may have begun.

4. In the case of the resignation of a member of the Court, the resignation shall be addressed to the President of the Court for transmission to the Secretary-General. This last notification makes the place vacant.

Art. 14. Vacancies shall be filled by the same method as that laid down for the first election, subject to the following provision: the Secretary-General shall, within one month of the occurrence of the vacancy, proceed to issue the invitations provided for in Article 5, and the date of the election shall be fixed by the Security Council.

Art. 15. A member of the Court elected to replace a member whose term of office has not expired shall hold office for the remainder of his predecessor's term.

Art. 16. 1. No member of the Court may exercise any political or administrative function, or engage in any other occupation of a professional nature.

2. Any doubt on this point shall be settled by the decision of the Court.

Art. 17. 1. No member of the Court may act as agent, counsel, or advocate in any case.

2. No member may participate in the decision of any case in which he has previously taken part as agent, counsel, or advocate for one of the parties, or as a member of a national or international court, or of a commission of enquiry, or in any other capacity.

3. Any doubt on this point shall be settled by the decision of the Court.

Art. 18. 1. No member of the Court can be dismissed unless, in the unanimous opinion of the other members, he has ceased to fulfil the required conditions.

2. Formal notification thereof shall be made to the Secretary-General by the Registrar.

3. This notification makes the place vacant.

Art. 19. The members of the Court, when engaged on the business of the Court, shall enjoy diplomatic privileges and immunities.

Art. 20. Every member of the Court shall, before taking up his duties, make a solemn declaration in open court that he will exercise his powers impartially and conscientiously.

Art. 21. 1. The Court shall elect its President and Vice-President for three years; they may be re-elected.

2. The Court shall appoint its Registrar and may provide for the appointment of such other officers as may be necessary.

Art. 22. 1. The seat of the Court shall be established at The Hague. This, however, shall not prevent the Court from sitting and exercising its functions elsewhere whenever the Court considers it desirable.

2. The President and the Registrar shall reside at the seat of the Court.

Art. 23. 1. The Court shall remain permanently in session, except during the judicial vacations, the dates and duration of which shall be fixed by the Court.

2. Members of the Court are entitled to periodic leave, the dates and duration of which shall be fixed by the Court, having in mind the distance between The Hague and the home of each judge.

3. Members of the Court shall be bound, unless they are on leave or prevented from attending by illness or other serious reasons duly explained to the President, to hold themselves permanently at the disposal of the Court.

Art. 24. 1. If, for some special reason, a member of the Court considers that he should not take part in the decision of a particular case, he shall so inform the President.

2. If the President considers that for some special reason one of the members of the Court should not sit in a particular case, he shall give him notice accordingly.

3. If in any such case the member of the Court and the President disagree, the matter

shall be settled by the decision of the Court.

Art. 25. 1. The full Court shall sit except when it is expressly provided otherwise in the present Statute.

2. Subject to the condition that the number of judges available to constitute the Court is not thereby reduced below eleven, the Rules of the Court may provide for allowing one or more judges, according to circumstances and in rotation, to be dispensed from sitting.

3. A quorum of nine judges shall suffice to constitute the Court.

Art. 26. 1. The Court may from time to time form one or more chambers, composed of three or more judges as the Court may determine, for dealing with particular categories of cases; for example, labor cases and cases relating to transit and communications.

2. The Court may at any time form a chamber for dealing with a particular case. The number of judges to constitute such a chamber shall be determined by the Court with the approval of the parties.

3. Cases shall be heard and determined by the chambers provided for in this Article if the parties so request.

Art. 27. A judgment given by any of the chambers provided for in Articles 26 and 29 shall be considered as rendered by the Court.

Art. 28. The chambers provided for in Articles 26 and 29 may, with the consent of the parties, sit and exercise their functions elsewhere than at The Hague.

Art. 29. With a view to the speedy despatch of business, the Court shall form annually a chamber composed of five judges which, at the request of the parties, may hear and determine cases by summary procedure. In addition, two judges shall be selected for the purpose of replacing judges who find it impossible to sit.

Art. 30. 1. The Court shall frame rules for carrying out its functions. In particular, it shall lay down rules of procedure.

2. The Rules of the Court may provide for assessors to sit with the Court or with any of its chambers, without the right to vote.

Art. 31. 1. Judges of the nationality of each of the parties shall retain their right to sit in the case before the Court.

2. If the Court includes upon the Bench a judge of the nationality of one of the parties, any other party may choose a person to sit as judge. Such person shall be chosen preferably from among those persons who have been nominated as candidates as provided in Articles 4 and 5.

3. If the Court includes upon the Bench no judge of the nationality of the parties, each of these parties may proceed to choose a judge as provided in paragraph 2 of this Article.

4. The provisions of this Article shall apply to the case of Articles 26 and 29. In such cases, the President shall request one or, if necessary, two of the members of the Court forming the chamber to give place to the members of the Court of the nationality of the parties concerned, and, failing such, or if they are unable to be present, to the judges specially chosen by the parties.

5. Should there be several parties in the same interest, they shall, for the purpose of the preceding provisions, be reckoned as one party only. Any doubt upon this point shall be settled by the decision of the Court.

6. Judges chosen as laid down in paragraphs 2, 3, and 4 of this Article shall fulfil the conditions required by Articles 2, 17 (paragraph 2), 20, and 24 of the present Statute. They shall take part in the decision on terms of complete equality with their colleagues.

Art. 32. 1. Each member of the Court shall receive an annual salary.

2. The President shall receive a special annual allowance.

3. The Vice-President shall receive a special allowance for every day on which he acts as President.

4. The judges chosen under Article 31, other than members of the Court, shall

receive compensation for each day on which they exercise their functions.

5. These salaries, allowances, and compensation shall be fixed by the General Assembly. They may not be decreased during the term of office.

6. The salary of the Registrar shall be fixed by the General Assembly on the proposal of the Court.

7. Regulations made by the General Assembly shall fix the conditions under which retirement pensions may be given to members of the Court and to the Registrar, and the conditions under which members of the Court and the Registrar shall have their traveling expenses refunded.

8. The above salaries, allowances, and compensations shall be free of all taxation.

Art. 33. The expenses of the Court shall be borne by the United Nations in such a manner as shall be decided by the General Assembly.

Chapter II: Competence of the Court

Art. 34. 1. Only states may be parties in cases before the Court.

2. The Court, subject to and in conformity with its Rules, may request of public international organizations information relevant to cases before it, and shall receive such information presented by such organizations on their own initiative.

3. Whenever the construction of the constituent instrument of a public international organization or of an international convention adopted thereunder is in question in a case before the Court, the Registrar shall so notify the public international organization concerned and shall communicate to it copies of all the written proceedings.

Art. 35. 1. The Court shall be open to the states parties to the present Statute.

2. The conditions under which the Court shall be open to other states shall, subject to the special provisions contained in treaties in force, be laid down by the Security Council, but in no case shall such conditions place the parties in a position of inequality before the Court.

3. When a state which is not a Member of the United Nations is a party to a case, the Court shall fix the amount which that party is to contribute towards the expenses of the Court. This provision shall not apply if such state is bearing a share of the expenses of the Court.

Art. 36. 1. The jurisdiction of the Court comprises all cases which the parties refer to it and all matters specially provided for in the Charter of the United Nations or in treaties and conventions in force.

2. The states parties to the present Statute may at any time declare that they recognize as compulsory *ipso facto* and without special agreement, in relation to any other state accepting the same obligation, the jurisdiction of the Court in all legal disputes concerning:

a. the interpretation of a treaty;

b. any question of international law;

c. the existence of any fact which, if established, would constitute a breach of an international obligation;

d. the nature or extent of the reparation to be made for the breach of an international obligation.

3. The declarations referred to above may be made unconditionally or on condition of reciprocity on the part of several or certain states, or for a certain time.

4. Such declarations shall be deposited with the Secretary-General of the United Nations, who shall transmit copies thereof to the parties to the Statute and to the Registrar of the Court.

5. Declarations made under Article 36 of the Statute of the Permanent Court of International Justice and which are still in force shall be deemed, as between the parties to the present Statute, to be acceptances of the compulsory jurisdiction of the International Court of Justice for the period which they still have to run and in accordance with their terms.

6. In the event of a dispute as to whether

the Court has jurisdiction, the matter shall be settled by the decision of the Court.

Art. 37. Whenever a treaty or convention in force provides for references of a matter to a tribunal to have been instituted by the League of Nations, or to the Permanent Court of International Justice, the matter shall, as between the parties to the present Statute, be referred to the International Court of Justice.

Art. 38. 1. The Court, whose function is to decide in accordance with international law such disputes as are submitted to it, shall apply:

a. international conventions, whether general or particular, establishing rules expressly recognized by the contesting states;

b. international custom, as evidence of a general practice accepted as law;

c. the general principles of law recognized by civilized nations;

d. subject to the provisions of Article 59, judicial decisions and the teachings of the most highly qualified publicists of the various nations, as subsidiary means for the determination of rules of law.

2. This provision shall not prejudice the power of the Court to decide a case *ex aequo et bono,* if the parties agree thereto.

Chapter III: Procedure

Art. 39. 1. The official languages of the Court shall be French and English. If the parties agree that the case shall be concluded in French, the judgment shall be delivered in French. If the parties agree that the case shall be conducted in English, the judgment shall be delivered in English.

2. In the absence of an agreement as to which language shall be employed, each party may, in the pleadings, use the language which it prefers; the decision of the Court shall be given in French and English. In this case the Court shall at the same time, determine which of the two texts shall be considered as authoritative.

3. The Court shall, at the request of any party, authorize a language other than French or English to be used by that party.

Art. 40. 1. Cases are brought before the Court, as the case may be, either by the notification of the special agreement or by a written application addressed to the Registrar. In either case the subject of the dispute and the parties shall be indicated.

2. The Registrar shall forthwith communicate the application to all concerned.

3. He shall also notify the Members of the United Nations through the Secretary-General, and also any other states entitled to appear before the Court.

Art. 41. 1. The Court shall have the power to indicate, if it considers that circumstances so require, any provisional measures which ought to be taken to preserve the respective rights of either party.

2. Pending the final decision, notice of the measures suggested shall forthwith be given to the parties and to the Security Council.

Art. 42. 1. The parties shall be represented by agents.

2. They may have the assistance of counsel or advocates before the Court.

3. The agents, counsel, and advocates of parties before the Court shall enjoy the privileges and immunities necessary to the independent exercise of their duties.

Art. 43. 1. The procedure shall consist of two parts: written and oral.

2. The written proceedings shall consist of the communication to the Court and to the parties of memorials, counter-memorials and, if necessary, replies; also all papers and documents in support.

3. These communications shall be made through the Registrar, in the order and within the time fixed by the Court.

4. A certified copy of every document produced by one party shall be communicated to the other party.

5. The oral proceedings shall consist of the hearing by the Court of witnesses, experts, agents, counsel, and advocates.

Art. 44. 1. For the service of all notices upon persons other than the agents, counsel, and advocates, the Court shall apply direct to the government of the state upon whose territory the notice has to be served.

2. The same provision shall apply whenever steps are to be taken to procure evidence on the spot.

Art. 45. The hearing shall be under the control of the President or, if he is unable to preside, of the Vice-President; if neither is able to preside, the senior judge present shall preside.

Art. 46. The hearing in Court shall be public, unless the Court shall decide otherwise, or unless the parties demand that the public be not admitted.

Art. 47. 1. Minutes shall be made at each hearing and signed by the Registrar and the President.

2. These minutes alone shall be authentic.

Art. 48. The Court shall make orders for the conduct of the case, shall decide the form and time in which each party must conclude its arguments, and make all arrangements connected with the taking of evidence.

Art. 49. The Court may, even before the hearing begins, call upon the agents to produce any document or to supply any explanations. Formal note shall be taken of any refusal.

Art. 50. The Court may, at any time, entrust any individual, body, bureau, commission, or other organization that it may select, with the task of carrying out an enquiry or giving an expert opinion.

Art. 51. During the hearing any relevant questions are to be put to the witnesses and experts under the conditions laid down by the Court in the rules of procedure referred to in Article 30.

Art. 52. After the Court has received the proofs and evidence within the time specified for the purpose, it may refuse to accept any further oral or written evidence that one party may desire to present unless the other side consents.

Art. 53. 1. Whenever one of the parties does not appear before the Court, or fails to defend its case, the other party may call upon the Court to decide in favor of its claim.

2. The Court must, before doing so, satisfy itself, not only that it has jurisdiction in accordance with Articles 36 and 37, but also that the claim is well founded in fact and law.

Art. 54. 1. When, subject to the control of the Court, the agents, counsel, and advocates have completed their presentation of the case, the President shall declare the hearing closed.

2. The Court shall withdraw to consider the judgment.

3. The deliberations of the Court shall take place in private and remain secret.

Art. 55. 1. All questions shall be decided by a majority of the judges present.

2. In the event of an equality of votes, the President or the judge who acts in his place shall have a casting vote.

Art. 56. 1. The judgment shall state the reasons on which it is based.

2. It shall contain the names of the judges who have taken part in the decision.

Art. 57. If the judgment does not represent in whole or in part the unanimous opinion of the judges, any judge shall be entitled to deliver a separate opinion.

Art. 58. The judgment shall be signed by the President and by the Registrar. It shall be read in open court, due notice having been given to the agents.

Art. 59. The decision of the Court has no binding force except between the parties in respect of that particular case.

Art. 60. The judgment is final and without appeal. In the event of dispute as to the meaning or scope of the judgment, the Court shall construct it upon the request of any party.

Art. 61. An application for revision of a judgment may be made only when it is based upon the discovery of some fact of such a nature as to be a decisive factor, which fact was, when the judgment was given, unknown to the Court and also to the party claiming revision, always provided that such ignorance was not due to negligence.

2. The proceedings for revision shall be opened by a judgment of the Court expressly recording the existence of the new fact, recognizing that it has such a character as to lay the case open to revision and declaring the application admissible on this ground.

3. The Court may require previous compliance with the terms of the judgment before its admits proceedings in revision.

4. The application for revision must be made at latest within six months of the discovery of the new fact.

5. No application for revision may be made after the lapse of ten years from the date of the judgment.

Art. 62. 1. Should a state consider that it has an interest of a legal nature which may be affected by the decision in the case, it may submit a request to the Court to be permitted to intervene.

2. It shall be for the Court to decide upon this request.

Art. 63. 1. Whenever the construction of a convention to which states other than those concerned in the case are parties is in question, the Registrar shall notify all such states forthwith.

2. Every state so notified has the right to intervene in the proceedings; but if it uses this right, the construction given by the judgment will be equally binding upon it.

Art. 64. Unless otherwise decided by the Court, each party shall bear its own costs.

Chapter IV: Advisory Opinions

Art. 65. 1. The Court may give an advisory opinion on any legal question at the request of whatever body may be authorized by or in accordance with the Charter of the United Nations to make such a request.

2. Questions upon which the advisory opinion of the Court is asked shall be laid before the Court by means of a written request containing an exact statement of the question upon which an opinion is required, and accompanied by all documents likely to throw light upon the question.

Art. 66. 1. The Registrar shall forthwith give notice of the request for an advisory opinion to all states entitled to appear before the Court.

2. The Registrar shall also, by means of a special and direct communication, notify any state entitled to appear before the Court or international organization considered by the Court, or, should it not be sitting, by the President, as likely to be able to furnish information on the question, that the Court will be prepared to receive, within a time limit to be fixed by the President, written statements, or to hear, at a public sitting to be held for the purpose, oral statements relating to the question.

3. Should any such state entitled to appear before the Court have failed to receive the special communication referred to in paragraph 2 of this Article, such state may express a desire to submit a written statement or to be heard; and the Court will decide.

4. States and organizations having presented written or oral statements or both shall be permitted to comment on the statements made by other states or organizations in the form, to the extent, and within the time limits which the Court, or, should it not be sitting, the President, shall decide in each particular case. Accordingly, the Registrar shall in due time communicate any such written statements to states and organizations having submitted similar statements.

Art. 67. The Court shall deliver its advisory opinions in open court, notice having been given to the Secretary-General and to the representatives of Members of the United Nations, of other states and of international organizations immediately concerned.

Art. 68. In the exercise of its advisory functions the Court shall further be guided by the provisions of the present Statute which apply in contentious cases to the extent to which it recognizes them to be applicable.

Chapter V: Amendment

Art. 69. Amendments to the present Statute shall be effected by the same procedure as is provided by the Charter of the United Nations for amendments to that Charter, subject however to any provisions which the General Assembly upon recommendation of the Security Council may adopt concerning the participation of states which are parties to the present Statute but are not Members of the United Nations.

Art. 70. The Court shall have power to propose such amendments to the present Statute as it may deem necessary, through written communications to the Secretary-General, for consideration in conformity with the provisions of Article 69.

Guide to Latin Terms

a fortiori	by the stronger reason; all the more	*ex aequo et bono*	in justice and fairness; equitable settlement of a dispute
ab initio	from the beginning	*ex hypothesi*	upon the hypothesis or supposition
ad hoc	respecting this; for a particular purpose	*ex parte*	from one side or party only
ad interim	in the meantime	*ex post facto*	after the event
ad referendum	to be referred; to be deferred for subsequent attention	*expressis verbis*	in clear language
animus belligerandi	the intention to make war	*fons et origo*	the source or origin—usually of a doctrine
casus belli	a cause of war	*generalia specialibus non derogant*	general terms do not control special terms
casus foederis	a case falling within the provisions of a treaty	*hors de combat*	out of the combat; worsted
cessante ratione legis cessat, et ipsa lex	where the reason for the existence of a law ceases, the law itself should also cease	*hostes humani generis*	enemies of the human race
clausula rebus sic stantibus	the controversial doctrine that a treaty is binding only so long as there is no fundamental change in the circumstances which existed at the time the treaty was concluded	*in fiere*	in the making; incomplete
		in personum	against a specific person, as opposed to *in rem*
		in rem	against a thing and not against a person
		inter alia	among other things
delicta juris gentium	offenses against the law of nations	*inter partes*	between the parties

inter se — among themselves

intra fauces terrae — between the headlands of a bay

ipso jure — by the law itself

jure gestionis — activities of a state in a nonsovereign capacity

jure imperii — activities of a state in a sovereign capacity

jus ad rem — the right to a thing that has its foundation in an obligation incurred by another person

jus cogens — law that is binding, irrespective of the will of the parties

jus dispositivum — law that can be modified by contrary agreement

lex ferenda — law which it is desired to establish

lex lata — law already in force

locus — a place; location

modus vivendi — a temporary agreement

mutatis mutandis — the necessary changes being made

non bis in idem — no one shall be tried twice for the same offense

pacta sunt servanda — agreements are binding

persona non grata — a diplomatic agent who is unwelcome in the country to which he is accredited

prima facie — at first sight; from the appearance

proprio vigore — by its own force and vigor

ratione temporis — by the reason of time

res inter alios acta — acts or matters that, in law, exclusively concern others

res inter alios acta alteri nocere non debet — transactions between certain parties ought not to prejudice third parties

res judicata — a decided issue

status quo — the existing state of affairs

terra firma — firm land; dry land

terra communis — territory that belongs to everyone; commonly owned

terra nullius — territory that belongs to no one and is subject to occupation

ubi societas, ibi ius — where there is society, there is law

ultra vires — beyond a person's authority and jurisdiction

uti possidetis — as you possess

vel non — or not

Table of Cases

The principal cases reproduced in this book are in italics and
the page numbers on which they begin in boldface. The cases
that are cited in the essays, discussed in courts' opinions, or
contained in footnotes are in ordinary type.

Index

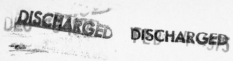